THE SELECTED

CANTERBURY TALES

Seeking the Woman in Late Medieval and Renaissance Writings:
Essays in Feminist Contextual Criticism
(ed., with Janet E. Halley)

Chaucer's Poetic Alchemy:
A Study of Value and Its Transformation in The Canterbury Tales

W. W. NORTON & COMPANY

New York * *London*

GEOFFREY CHAUCER

THE SELECTED

CANTERBURY
TALES

A
NEW
VERSE
TRANSLATION

Translated and with an Introduction by

SHEILA FISHER

Middle English text from *The Canterbury Tales: Fifteen Tales and General Prologue, 2nd Edition*
by Geoffrey Chaucer, edited by V. A. Kolve and Glending Olson. Copyright © 2005, 1989 by
W. W. Norton & Company, Inc. Used by permission of W. W. Norton & Company, Inc.

Middle English interstitial materials are taken primarily from the text of W. W. Skeat, *The Com-
plete Works of Geoffrey Chaucer* (Oxford: Clarendon Press, 1972), which Kolve and Olson use as
the major source for their Middle English text in the Norton Critical Edition of *The Canterbury
Tales*. The spellings in the insertions are changed only slightly in places in order to bring them
into conformity with standard editorial practices in more recent Middle English editions of *The
Tales*. In these instances, choices for spelling of the Middle English insertions have been based
on the Riverside edition of Chaucer (ed. Larry Benson) and on John H. Fisher's edition (see Sug-
gestions for Further Reading for full citations of these editions).

For information about permission to reproduce selections from this book,
write to Permissions, W. W. Norton & Company, Inc.,
500 Fifth Avenue, New York, NY 10110

For information about special discounts for bulk purchases, please contact
W. W. Norton Special Sales at specialsales@wwnorton.com or 800-233-4830

Manufacturing by RR Donnelley, Harrisonburg
Book design by Chris Welch
Production manager: Anna Oler

Library of Congress Cataloging-in-Publication Data

Chaucer, Geoffrey, d. 1400.
[Canterbury tales. Selections]
The selected Canterbury tales : a new verse translation / Geoffrey Chaucer ;
translated and with an introduction by Sheila Fisher. — 1st ed.
p. cm.
Text in English with Middle English original on facing page.
Includes bibliographical references.
ISBN 978-0-393-07945-6 (hardcover)
1. Christian pilgrims and pilgrimages—Poetry. 2. Storytelling—Poetry.
3. Tales, Medieval. I. Fisher, Sheila. II. Title.
PR1867.F57 2011
821'.1—dc22
2010053552

W. W. Norton & Company, Inc.
500 Fifth Avenue, New York, N.Y. 10110
www.wwnorton.com

W. W. Norton & Company Ltd.
Castle House, 75/76 Wells Street, London W1T 3QT

1 2 3 4 5 6 7 8 9 0

FOR MY FAMILY

for Sonia and Dana, my daughter and husband,

AND

for Shirley, Charlie, and Sally, my mother, father, and sister,

WITH ALL LOVE AND GRATITUDE

FOR MAKING "THILKE PARFIT GLORIOUS PILGRIMAGE" WITH ME

Contents

Acknowledgments   xi

Introduction and Background   xv

A Chaucerian Lexicon   xlvii

The General Prologue   3

The Knight's Tale   61

The Miller's Prologue and Tale   195

The Reeve's Prologue and Tale   243

The Cook's Prologue and Tale   275

The Wife of Bath's Prologue and Tale   285

The Clerk's Prologue and Tale   367

The Merchant's Prologue and Tale   457

The Franklin's Prologue and Tale   535

The Pardoner's Prologue and Tale   591

The Prioress's Prologue and Tale   637

The Prologue and Tale of Sir Thopas
and The Prologue to the Tale of Melibee   657

The Nun's Priest's Prologue and Tale   681

The Parson's Prologue and Chaucer's Retraction   727

Suggestions for Further Reading   737

Acknowledgments

Any project in the works for ten years will have gathered behind it a number of people whose wisdom, support, and kindness were crucial to getting the job done. In my case, these "sondry folk" are bookended by two groups, one stretching back into the past and one stretching out into the future: my teachers and my students. The late Vernon Judson Harward of the English Department at Smith College, my first medieval professor, is the reason I became a Chaucerian. He did nothing to make *The Tales* easier than they should be, and thus made it clear that their very complexity is the source of their ongoing appeal. My students continue to teach me how richly textured and new Chaucer is and always will be.

Among the medievalists who have been my mentors, I would like particularly to thank Marie Borroff and R. A. Shoaf, the co-advisers of my dissertation on Chaucer at Yale. Their inspiration runs throughout this work. Marie Borroff's brilliant and beautiful translations of *Sir Gawain and the Green Knight* and *Pearl* strike a pitch-perfect balance between capturing the meaning and replicating the intricate poetic structures of these poems. The artistry of her translations has been my guide. Over the years, R. A. Shoaf's innovative scholarship has taught me new ways of gauging Chaucer's continued presence in our collective literary consciousness. I would like to thank Al and also J. Stephen Russell for their willingness to provide endorsements of this translation for inclusion in my prospectus. And my thanks to Bonnie Krueger, with whom I've shared the ins and outs of doing this project for many years. Bonnie's invitation, years back, to contribute a piece on women and gender for her *Cambridge Companion to Medieval Romance* made me want to do in my writing what I do in my teaching: render medieval literature in general, and Chaucer in particular, accessible and comprehensible to as wide an audience as I can.

My colleagues in the English Department at Trinity College have been wonderful throughout this process. Their advice when I presented portions of this translation in the context of our department's monthly *Salon* was astute and encouraging. I am especially grateful to Lucy Ferriss for organizing the *Salon,* to David Rosen for comments about how to translate the northern dialect of the students in *The Reeve's Tale,* and to Paul Lauter, then-chair of the English Department, for his ongoing advice and encouragement. Without the support and wisdom of Margaret Grasso and Roberta Rogers-Bednarek, my work in the English Department, as teacher and former chair, would have been much more onerous and much less pleasant. I'd also like to thank Dean of Faculty Rena Fraden for her persistent encouragement of this work.

David Laurence, Director of the MLA Office of Research and ADE, provided me with important information about enrollments in Chaucer courses; and Patricia Bunker, reference librarian at Trinity College, quickly and expertly assembled data about enrollments nationwide in graduate and undergraduate programs as I was preparing the prospectus for the book.

Central to my work on this translation is the extraordinary scholarship of all the editors whom Larry Benson brought together in *The Riverside Chaucer* and of John H. Fisher (no relation!) in his *Complete Poetry and Prose of Geoffrey Chaucer.* These are the two editions of Chaucer's Middle English text upon which I've based my translation. The erudition of their notes and commentary has been invaluable to me in framing my own annotations.

You would not be reading this book without the unflagging efforts of my literary agent, Anne Marie O'Farrell of the Marcil-O'Farrell Literary Agency. My heartfelt thanks are due to Anne Marie and to Denise Marcil, as well as to Christine Morehouse. Chris's expert advice on the prospectus gave focus and coherence to my plans for the project. I would also like to thank Suzanne Conklin Akbari and Alfred David for their insightful and helpful comments on the text. It has been a privilege to work with my editor at W. W. Norton & Company, Vice President Alane Salierno Mason, whose commitment to my book has made its publication possible, and with her assistant, Denise Scarfi, who has provided patient guidance on the last phases of the project.

I can only say, with Chaucer in his Retraction, that, if, after all this generous advice and support, there are still flaws, as there will be, in this text, that you "arrette it to the defaute of myn unkonnynge and nat to my wyl."

Finally, more gratitude than I can ever express goes to my family, to whom this work is dedicated:

To my sister Sally Fisher, who, when I couldn't find data I needed, sent me straight to my reference librarian and saved me much stress and time. And to Sally, too, for long cell-phone conversations on the way home from work, for a constant willingness to hash over our dreams and aspirations, and for the faith that we will both get to where we want to be going.

To my father, Charlie Fisher, who has been helping me realize my goals and ambitions for my entire life; who pushed this project along by wondering out loud whether it would ever get done; and who has shared with me illuminating conversations about the ways in which his polishing of his paintings and my revisings of my translation become significant acts of creation as we remake our work to try to get it right.

To my mother, Shirley Carpowits Fisher, who passed away before this book was done, but who, more than anyone, is its source and inspiration. My mother taught me how much fun it is to write iambic pentameter couplets. She could whip off rhymed stanzas more quickly than she could tie hair ribbons, and she won a significant number of jingle contests when she was young. Throughout our lives, we exchanged rhyming poems on greeting cards. How I wish she were here to see where her knack for rhyming ended up.

And to my daughter and my husband, Sonia Brand-Fisher and Dana Brand, both of whom put up with all this for years with unfailing good humor.

To Sonia, who was willing to listen to expurgated versions of *The Tales* even before she knew what the Middle Ages were. She has been considerably entertained, since then, to learn what they really say. In the summer of 2007, Sonia served as research assistant for this project, editing, typing, and tracking down references. More recently, she read large portions of the translation aloud to me so that I could tell whether what made sense to the eye meant the same to the ear. Sonia has also offered many well-honed variants on lines that were causing me trouble. In the process, she improved whole passages of the text and showed that she has inherited the family affinity for couplets.

And to Dana, who just never stops letting me know that he believes in what I'm doing more than I do. Dana put me in touch with his agents, Anne Marie

O'Farrell and Christine Morehouse, and, as a result, made sure that my project was in the same capable hands as his own recent books on baseball fandom and travel. He has read and commented on versions of this work over the years and has in the process helped significantly. He has listened to me vent. Without his patience, his love, and his confidence in me, I would never have made it out of Southwark.

Introduction and Background

The Reasons for This Translation

My desire to do a translation of Chaucer's *Canterbury Tales* began with frustration I felt at the turn of the millennium as I watched, with sincere enjoyment, the many excellent movie versions of Shakespeare's plays and Austen's novels that were appearing back then. Every time I turned around, here was a new, beautifully costumed, limpidly lit movie of *Hamlet* or *Much Ado About Nothing*, of *Sense and Sensibility* or *Mansfield Park*.[1] I admired them and applauded the ways in which they were presenting really respectable popularizations of masterworks of the English literary tradition. Still, for a Chaucerian, all of these fine films got to be maddening, and I began to feel like the kind of jealous poor relative you might encounter in either of these authors' works. Why them, and not Chaucer? And why right at that moment leading up to the millennium? Obviously, for these privileged authors, there was something in the stories, in the themes, even in the rich, difficult, and poetic language that appeared in the well-crafted screenplays, capable of grabbing modern audiences and making them aware of history at just the moment when we as a culture were collectively obsessed both with time passing and time to come.

But, disgruntled, I saw no one rushing to make movies of Chaucer's stories, and in the process, to make Chaucer accessible and popular, and as loved and revered as Shakespeare and Austen.[2] Why not? After all, Chaucer wrote very fine

---

1 For example, *Romeo and Juliet* (dir. Baz Luhrmann, 1996), *Hamlet* (dir. Kenneth Branagh, 1996), *Shakespeare in Love* (dir. John Madden, 1998), *A Midsummer Night's Dream* (dir. Michael Hoffman, 1999), *Pride and Prejudice* (major BBC miniseries, 1995), *Sense and Sensibility* (dir. Ang Lee, 1995), *Emma* (dir. Douglas McGrath, 1996), and *Mansfield Park* (BBC, 1999), to name a few.

2 There was a British miniseries of *The Canterbury Tales* in 1996. *A Knight's Tale*—which bears no resemblance to Chaucer's tale of the same name, features Chaucer as a character, and is hardly in the same league as the works listed in note 1—appeared in 2001. And a BBC miniseries in 2003 presented adaptations of selected *Canterbury Tales* meant to update and place them in a contemporary setting.

stories too, stories with themes that could resonate with contemporary viewers/ readers. The question that really bothered me was this: If Chaucer is dubbed, however inaccurately, "the Father of English poetry," why was he, at the millennium, relatively ignored? Why wasn't he being considered for the kinds of adaptations that would make him as current, viable, and available as Shakespeare and Austen? The answer might well lie in the language in which Chaucer originally wrote: his Middle English. Because of its different grammatical forms and odd spellings of otherwise familiar words, it's a more difficult version of English for us to read than Shakespeare's, which is essentially our own.

It seemed, then, at least in the United States, that Chaucer risked becoming erased from our popular consciousness, if he had ever really been there, in ways that other great English authors were not. Unlike Shakespeare and many other earlier American and English writers (let alone classical writers like Homer), Chaucer was not regularly taught in American high schools, even in Advanced Placement courses. Students' lack of familiarity with his writing before they came to college didn't go far toward increasing their interest in him when they did. I began to wonder if it might be possible to make Chaucer more visible in high school and college curricula as well as more present in a popular consciousness if there were a new translation of him—one that communicated his vividness and variety, and sounded like him and his language, even (especially) for those readers who would probably never read him in the original. Maybe there needed to be a new translation of his most famous and approachable work, *The Canterbury Tales*, one that paid close attention to and tried to provide a faithful rendering of his poetry in Modern English. And that is what I hope I have done.

But Chaucer, of course, is more than poetic forms, meter, and rhyme. He is also his period's most sophisticated voice for the kinds of intricately varied topics, themes, and content that make their way, often to the surprise of contemporary readers, into medieval poetry. He tackled subjects, beings, and doings that other poets may have used before him, but that no other poets had probed so deeply, and with such nuance, irony, and ambiguity, as the tumultuous fourteenth century was coming to an end. He was the only English poet until Shakespeare to explore and represent with such complexity, insight, and detail the workings of character and personality. That is reason enough for making him vividly present to a contemporary audience as the new millennium moves forward on its way.

Chaucer's Life

It is not always easy to make the distant past as present as we might like. When we approach the biography of a medieval writer, we need to do so with caution. Often, evidence is fragmentary or scant, or in the instances of all those anonymous authors from the Middle Ages, nonexistent. In Chaucer's case, we are lucky that there is a decent amount of evidence about his life in the records left from his career as a civil servant in royal service. And yet there is also the peculiar fact that none of these records makes a single mention of him as a poet, even though they may list how much wine or cloth a year he received as compensation for his services.[3]

Geoffrey Chaucer's father, John, was a vintner—a major wine merchant involved in importing wines to England from France. This was, then as now, a lucrative trade. His mother, Agnes Copton, was also a member of a prosperous London family. Chaucer, therefore, would have belonged securely to the wealthy upper middle class, a class that throughout the fourteenth century was becoming increasingly prominent economically and politically.[4] Interestingly enough, Chaucer explores and often satirizes its values in a number of his *Canterbury Tales*.

Born in London sometime in the early 1340s (the exact date isn't known), Chaucer most likely had the standard education, perhaps at a local cathedral school, provided to most boys of his social class, who would have studied Latin and both ecclesiastical and secular texts. In his late teens, he became a page to Elizabeth, Countess of Ulster, the wife of Prince Lionel (the third son of Edward III); he also fought in the Hundred Years' War. In fact, there are records of his capture and subsequent ransom in 1360. It's a nice bit of Chaucerian trivia that Geoffrey the soldier was ransomed for less than a nobleman's horse captured at the same time. Chaucer, it seems, did not go to university. But absent any records about his higher education, it is not unreasonable to conjecture that, instead, he attended the Inns of Chancery and the Inns of Court. The former would have provided career training in clerical functions, including the preparation of offi-

---

3   These records were edited by M. M. Crow and C. C. Olson in *Chaucer's Life-Records* (Oxford: Oxford University Press, 1966).

4   It is important to keep in mind that the fourteenth century did not have our precise labels for social classes. When I apply contemporary designations to medieval society, I am suggesting a rough equivalency between a given medieval social class and our own.

cial documents, for a man of his class with upwardly mobile aspirations. The latter was roughly the medieval equivalent of law school.

Whatever his higher education might have been, as Chaucer's poetry shows, his learning was broad and, in some instances, deep. He knew Latin, of course, and English, but also French and Italian. He knew major religious, philosophical, and theological texts, along with political writings. He was well versed in contemporary literature and in many secular classical texts, insofar as they would have been available to him. (He would not, for example, have read Homer in the original, not only because he did not read Greek but because these texts would not have been accessible in the late fourteenth century.) And he had deeper pockets of knowledge in specific fields such as astronomy and astrology and also alchemy. In Chaucer's time, astrology, like astronomy, was considered a legitimate science; indeed, the two were linked in their study of the stars and planets and their influences on human life. Alchemy was a more ambiguous undertaking, involving for some practitioners considerable learning and research that provided the basis for chemistry, while for others, it was a chance to swindle and con.[5]

It was, then, Chaucer's diverse and diversified education—as page, soldier, and (most likely) student at the Inns of Chancery and the Inns of Court—that would have provided him the kind of training appropriate to someone who was fashioning himself to be a civil servant. This is precisely the course that Chaucer's career followed: early on, he became a courtier and esquire in the royal household and later in the household of John of Gaunt, second son of Edward III. The fourteenth century in Europe saw a burgeoning need and appreciation for the talents of the "new men," courtiers of the upper middle class. While they didn't possess the bloodlines of the aristocracy, in most instances they possessed a far superior education (remember that the current Prince Charles is the first English heir to the throne ever to go to university) and a set of valuable skills, many of them involving the dexterous use of language. During the late 1360s and the 1370s, Chaucer traveled widely to France, Spain, and Italy on one or another diplomatic mission. Such deputations involved him in journeys associated with the second marriage of Prince Lionel to an heiress of the powerful Visconti family in Milan, and later, with the difficult negotiations for the marriage of King Rich-

---

5   Nonetheless, a vast body of scientific as well as ecclesiastical writing was associated with alchemy, as Chaucer makes clear in *The Canon's Yeoman's Tale*.

ard II. These travels, as I will discuss later, were central to his literary education. Chaucer's role as civil servant also brought him literary patronage. It was for his employer, John of Gaunt, that he wrote the first of his major poems, *The Book of the Duchess* (c. 1369), a dream vision elegy to mark the anniversary of the death from plague of John of Gaunt's first wife, Blanche of Lancaster.

Chaucer was also beginning to establish his personal life in the late 1360s. Sometime toward the end of 1366, he married Philippa de Roet, a lady-in-waiting to Queen Philippa, wife of Edward III. Philippa de Roet is listed throughout her life as receiving remunerations and grants from her service as a lady-in-waiting: first in the household of the Countess of Ulster (where she may have met Chaucer); then for Queen Philippa; and later, for Constance of Castile, second wife of John of Gaunt. It may well be that her own social status was somewhat higher than Chaucer's. Certainly, she was well connected. Her father was Gilles de Roet, who had come to England from Hainault with Queen Philippa and her company. Her sister, Katherine Swynford, was for decades the mistress of Chaucer's patron, John of Gaunt. Indeed, toward the end of their lives, in 1396, Gaunt finally married Katherine, so that Chaucer, in effect, became the brother-in-law of a prince.

Geoffrey Chaucer and Philippa de Roet had two sons, Thomas and Lewis, and possibly two daughters, Elizabeth and Agnes (the records are vague about the girls' parentage). There has, however, been some scholarly conjecture that Thomas Chaucer may have been the illegitimate son of John of Gaunt. There is also some conjecture that Lewis Chaucer, born sometime around 1380, could have been the child of Cecily Champain, a woman who released Chaucer from charges of "raptus" in 1380. What exactly these charges meant is the source of much scholarly research, deliberation, and debate. In the legal language of the fourteenth century, *raptus* could signify either rape or abduction (it was not uncommon to abduct wards and heirs because of custody issues and legal suits). Because it's not clear which of these charges had been brought against Chaucer and then dropped, it is unclear whether Lewis was the product of this "raptus." And it is equally unclear exactly what type of marriage Geoffrey and Philippa shared. We do know, given the record of annuities in her name, that Philippa would have been a wealthy woman in her own right. As was common for such medieval "two-career couples" whose positions attached them to different royal households, it is likely they would have spent a number of years of their marriage not living together in the same place. Philippa died in 1387.

Once Chaucer returned to England in the 1370s from his various trips abroad, his résumé begins to bear some resemblance to that of one of his Canterbury characters, the Franklin. Chaucer spent nearly a dozen years, beginning in 1374, as the Controller of Customs and Subsidy of Wools, Skins and Hides. This would have been a position of considerable importance in the English economy because England's wool was valued internationally and was one of its primary exports. As Controller of Customs for the Port of London, Chaucer would have worked with groups of people as widely ranging in class and profession as the pilgrims he assembles in *The Canterbury Tales*. In this position, he would have been at the center of London's commercial life and of the intricacies and complexities involved with activities in the busy port. Scholars have long pointed out that if Chaucer got his literary education during the 1360s and 1370s in France and Italy, it may well have been this "real world" education amid the diverse and varied aspects of London life that gave him the material (and the insights into human nature) to create *The Canterbury Tales*. In the 1380s, he moved from London to Kent, where he was elected a member of Parliament and held the office of Justice of the Peace. The end of the decade saw Richard II appointing him to the important and demanding post of Clerk of the King's Works, in charge of overseeing construction and maintenance on a diverse set of projects and buildings, from the Tower of London to Westminster Palace. One of his last official appointments in his long and varied career as a civil servant came in the early 1390s, when he was appointed Forester to the king.

Annual gifts like a pitcher of wine a day from Edward III and Richard II as well as monetary annuities from John of Gaunt meant that Chaucer was quite prosperous during most of his "working years." But as the political turmoil of the eighties and nineties unfolded, and as Chaucer moved into the last decade of his life, he sometimes had trouble collecting his annuities, and there is evidence that he was at times in debt. With the death of Gaunt in 1399 and the exile of his son Henry Bolingbroke, Chaucer may have felt his own sense of the never-ending spinning of Fortune's wheel. But even with the deposition and death of Richard II in 1399 and the ascension of Bolingbroke to become Henry IV, Chaucer's fortunes were not entirely secure because he also had trouble collecting promised payments from the new king. Chaucer might not have actually fallen on hard times so much as he experienced leaner ones as he moved toward the end of his life.

It may well have been in a period of relative quiet in 1387 that Chaucer began writing *The Canterbury Tales*, his last great work, which he died without finishing. But, looking back over Chaucer's career as civil servant and as poet, it doesn't seem that he needed respites in employment in order to produce poetry. Not only did he complete what some scholars consider his masterwork, *Troilus and Criseyde*, while he was in his last years as Controller of Customs (among other duties), but he continued work on *The Tales* even when he was Clerk of the King's Works. Nonetheless, Chaucer had fewer official duties as the century and his life drew to a close. On Christmas Eve 1399, Chaucer took a fifty-three-year lease on a house on the grounds of Westminster Abbey (leases of such length were not uncommon). He died, according to the inscription on his sixteenth-century tomb, on October 25, 1400, at the venerable old age of sixty or so. As a resident of Westminster Close, he was buried in the Abbey. His burial initiated what was to become the Poets' Corner in the Abbey, and thus, in England's literary landscape, a famed pilgrimage site in its own right.

Chaucer's Times

Change did not happen as quickly in the fourteenth century as it does today; various fundamental institutions, values, and assumptions inherited from the past would remain constant throughout the fourteenth century and well beyond. Yet a number of dramatic events and changes set in motion profound shifts in the ways people lived their lives and imagined themselves and their places in the world. Indeed, it's this contradiction between stability and change, between entrenched ideas and new circumstances, between old assumptions and new practices, between the ideal and the real that may well be one of the defining characteristics of the late Middle Ages. Set within a detailed and recognizable historical setting, in a deliberately rendered representation of immediate reality, *The Canterbury Tales* registers and engages many of these assumptions and changes, and the aspects of fourteenth-century life that were in flux.

While medieval people, like people of all times, could hold opinions and attitudes that differed considerably, most people living in England during the fourteenth century would have shared a number of central assumptions about their world, and first, that everyone around them was Christian. This was not far from the truth. While the countries of continental Europe showed, to greater or lesser extents, some modicum of toleration toward the Jews and Muslims living within their borders, by Chaucer's time there were, essentially, no Jews left in England.

They had been expelled in 1290 by decree of Edward I, for a number of reasons, not least that increased restrictions on the ability of Jews to lend money made them far less significant to the financial health of the monarchy. Chaucer undoubtedly encountered Jews and Muslims during his travels on the Continent, especially in Italy and Spain. But residents of fourteenth-century England who, like Chaucer's fictional Prioress, had never left the island would not have met a Jew during the course of their lifetimes. For them, their immediate world was entirely Christian.

The hegemony of Christianity throughout Europe showed itself in many ways. Christian theology, doctrine, and ideology, it is fair to say, influenced virtually every aspect of human existence. For Christianity was not only the only religion; it was also a particularly powerful presence in people's everyday lives, regardless of their social class and education. (Those who chose flagrantly to flout Christian ideals knew what awaited them if they didn't mend their ways.) The Church was the central intellectual as well as spiritual force in medieval culture; it was the heart and lifeblood of the medieval university. The writings of ecclesiastical authorities in fields that might not seem to us at first glance to be linked to religion—political philosophy, economics, astronomy, aesthetics, and rhetoric, to name a few—articulated theories about the secular as well as the religious realms. While there was certainly secular art, as the writings of Jean de Meun, Dante, Petrarch, Boccaccio, and Chaucer make clear, the Church was the inspiration for and the patron of some of the richest and most complex artworks of the period, from monumental Gothic cathedrals to increasingly realistic and emotionally expressive paintings and sculptures to the tiniest of illuminated prayer books.

Yet commentaries from within the Church itself and also from secular critics and satirists make its failings abundantly clear. The Church's corruption and materialism were lampooned in both high and popular culture. In the fourteenth century, such corruption was reaching a new peak. Disputes between the papacy, secular powers, and secular states caused the migration of the papal court from Rome to Avignon, where it remained throughout most of the century. This period, called by some "The Babylonian Captivity," lasted from 1309 to 1377; it was widely perceived as a period of extravagant materialism among the French popes who were elected during the papacy's stay in Avignon. When, in 1377, the papacy returned to Rome, any hope for stability became short lived; conflicting interests soon seated an alternate pope, who retreated back to Avignon. The resulting Western Schism lasted till 1417. During the last decades of Chaucer's life, English allegiance swung to the pope in Rome because of ongoing English animosity against the French during the Hundred Years' War. The Christian Church was the closest the Middle Ages had to a multinational corporation as it spread its power—secular and material as well as religious, theological, and ideological—throughout the known world. No wonder, then, that medieval writers energetically satirized every level of delinquent clergy in the Church hierarchy; indeed, these satires produced a series of recognizable anticlerical stereotypes and clichés as common as cartoon caricatures of corrupt politicians in our own day. And they were meant for the same purpose. They could provide the basis for efforts to rehabilitate the Church as well as for movements to curb its various forms of corruption.

If the centrality of Christianity was one of the foundation stones of medieval life, another key assumption was that society was rightly arranged in a "natural" hierarchy—"natural" insofar as it was ordained by God and reflected in the natural world that God had created. Within this structure, there was a place for everyone, and everyone had a place: the social class into which he or she was born. It was the hallmark of a pious person, if one accepted and lived in accordance with the responsibilities, duties, and dictates of one's own social class.

According to medieval social theory, the Christian flock was divided into three main classes, or estates ("estate" in this context shares an etymological root with the word "status"): the Clergy; the Aristocracy; and the Commons. As the earthly shepherds tending the Christian flock, the Clergy were at the top of this essentially pyramidal structure. Next came the Aristocracy, those members of "the blood" who inherited large landholdings by virtue of their birth, an important distinction in an age that considered land the major form of wealth. It was the duty of the nobility and Aristocracy to rule, to conduct the secular affairs of state, and to provide military protection for the rest of society. At the bottom, constituting by far the largest class, was the Commons, those who were not members of the Clergy and who did not have the blood of the Aristocracy running through their veins. It was their duty to provide sustenance for the other two classes. As the base of the pyramid, the Commons was both the largest and the most diverse class; in it belonged not only well-educated and wealthy professional men like Chaucer himself or his fictional Canterbury pilgrims, the Franklin and the Doctor, but also illiterate peasants who were indentured to their lord's land. In between were the craftspeople, the guilds members, the artisans, and the merchants who kept society running, fed, clothed.

But while society was hierarchical and would remain this way for centuries to come, in the fourteenth century, it was becoming less rigidly stratified than it had been before. This increasing social fluidity did not necessarily indicate real ideological or political change, Rather, it came in response to dramatic demographic changes precipitated by a variety of natural forces, beginning with an extended period of bad weather, bad harvests, and subsequent famines during the first quarter of the century. What the famines started, the Black Death sustained. It arrived in England after its journey across Europe from the Middle East in 1348. When it left in 1349, it took, conservatively, around a third of England's population with it, and perhaps more than half by the time subsequent assaults of the bubonic plague in 1368 and 1372 had subsided. In some locales, the Black Death literally devastated the population, killing 90 percent of inhabitants before it was through.

The Black Death's rampage produced a wide spectrum of social reactions and repercussions, ranging from blatant hedonism and materialism, the result of a carpe diem mentality, to severe asceticism, the result of a conviction that the Black Death was God's punishment for human sin. (The ascetic reaction has been made famous by its parody in *Monty Python and the Holy Grail* as a parade of self-flagellants hit themselves in the head with books.) Such social, personal, and psychological confusion was to be expected in the wake of a disaster of this magnitude. Still another significant result was an economic upheaval that brought increased fluidity to the hierarchical structures of medieval society. For one thing, with such dramatic and precipitous death rates, many people inherited much sooner. In a time when laws of primogeniture gave the lion's share of a family's legacy to firstborn sons and the largest dowry to firstborn daughters, sons and daughters further behind in the birth order might now find themselves inheriting more than they would ever have expected. Across all social classes, there were fewer people to inherit more: more goods, more gold, more land.

Because the Black Death was more democratic in its effects than most forces in medieval society, aristocrats were as likely to die as peasants. England was primarily an agrarian society in which land was the most important and enduring form of wealth. Farming that land was crucial not only to sustaining the population with food but also to providing the aristocracy with revenues from food production. Fewer peasants to farm the land meant fewer revenues for members of the aristocracy, some of whom became impoverished to the point of selling off family landholdings. Rich members of the commons, like Chaucer's Franklin, could acquire social ascendancy by buying lands and often set out to imitate the aristocracy. The social fluidity that this practice produced could even result in intermarriage between members of the aristocracy and what we might now call the haute bourgeoisie or nouveaux riches. What is more, with a shortage of agricultural labor, peasants were able to bargain for greater pay, and, in some instances, to leave one demesne (sometimes legally, sometimes not) in order to seek higher wages on another.

In England, both of these consequences of demographic change produced in response their own kinds of sometimes futile legislation meant to reassert the social status quo and protect the social hierarchy. Sumptuary laws sought to restrict the wearing of certain fabrics, furs, and colors to members of the aristocracy, thus preventing "lesser" people from adopting opulent clothing styles and materials in imitation of their "betters"—a feeble attempt to keep upwardly mobile members of the commons from masquerading as their social superiors. New labor laws attempted to keep peasants on their own demesnes and to limit wages in order to prevent them from gaining too much economic power and exercising what amounted to a quite literal form of social mobility. Sumptuary laws were virtually impossible to enforce, as the history of such laws in many times and places consistently shows. Labor laws were somewhat easier to enforce but stirred such outrage that, in 1381, a group of peasants, mostly from the south of London, marched on the city in England's first agrarian uprising, the Peasants' Revolt. The protesters demanded the repeal of new taxes and protection against repressive labor laws and foreign competition in specific crafts and guilds. The violent revolt was brutally quashed by Richard II—an act that would later figure in his own undoing. Bolstered by the popular support he could rally in defiance of Richard, Henry Bolingbroke marched back to England from exile on his way to becoming the last king of Chaucer's lifetime and the one to see this turbulent century to its close.

The Status of Women

If late fourteenth-century England experienced some degree of social fluidity and upheaval, women would certainly have participated in it. Yet that upheaval was not directly related to, caused by, or responsive to women. In the fourteenth

century, women occupied a separate class and status.[6] Many laws regulated the
lives of women simply because they were women, regardless of their place in
the social hierarchy. It is virtually impossible to generalize about the condition
of all women across the whole of Europe and England in the late Middle Ages.
Some regions, for example, were more lenient about women inheriting than oth-
ers; some were more tolerant about granting women the rights of property own-
ership. But distinctly dualistic theorizations about women pervaded Europe,
originating in classical writings that, in turn, were adopted and inflected by
Christian thinkers. From the classical period through the Middle Ages and
beyond, these views tended to define women as "either/or"—either remarkably
good or remarkably bad, Virgin or Whore. In the Christian tradition, this meant
that women could be either as evil as Eve or as marvelous as Mary, the embodi-
ment of the flesh and its appetites or the radiant example of the heights and
holiness to which human nature should aspire.

The actual laws, strictures, and statutes regulating real women's lives often
seemed designed more with Eve in mind than Mary. In general, women were not
the major inheritors of property if there were male heirs in a family, although
they were not without some inheritance rights of their own. When they mar-
ried, their property, in the form of a dower, went directly to their husbands; the
law guaranteed, however, that this property would return to them on their hus-
bands' death. They could inherit a third of their husbands' estate (the other two
thirds to be divided equally between their children, on the one hand, and the
Church, on the other), but they would not have control over any property, with
the possible exception of personal effects, while their husbands were living. Still,
women did have certain ownership rights. They could operate businesses as
femmes seules (the legal status of single women), even if they were married. And
regardless of their marital status, they could be sued and taxed as free agents.
Yet, in a court of law, women's testimony was seen, in general, as no more reliable
and credible than a child's. Often, it was simply not admissible. It did, however,
have its place in cases of rape and sexual assault if a woman had another female
witness to confirm her story. Women were, not surprisingly, less well educated
than men, and in an age in which the vast majority of human beings were illiter-
ate, illiteracy rates were markedly higher among women than among men.

---

6   The title of Shulamith Shahar's book *The Fourth Estate* (New York: Routledge, 1983) makes this
separateness clear.

But even while women across classes may have confronted similar attitudes and curtailments of legal rights and opportunities, it would be misleading to suggest that the life of an aristocratic woman was more limited than the life of a peasant man. In a traditional and hierarchical society, upper-class women enjoyed significant privileges through birth and marriage. In some circumstances, when an aristocratic husband was away at war, his wife would take over all of his functions and responsibilities. These duties demanded a wide array of skills and knowledge—from supervising the agricultural activities on her land to defending her demesne to adjudicating at manorial courts. Of course, a woman's ability to exercise this kind of privilege and power depended solely on the will of her husband. If a husband was not disposed to hand authority over to his wife, he could appoint a man in his household to assume these functions and pack his wife and other female relatives and attendants off to a convent for safekeeping while he was away.

Given the centrality of Christianity to medieval life, the Church was an area in which women might be expected to exercise some power and authority. For both aristocratic men and women, if birth order prevented inheriting the estate or receiving a sufficiently large dowry to make a good marriage, the Church provided the chance to enter a prestigious profession. In some instances, though, this was not an unmixed blessing. For one thing, because of family circumstances and pressures, people temperamentally and spiritually unsuited to the Church could wind up there: hence, some of the corruption, worldliness, and materialism demonstrated by both male and female clergy. For another, although a clerical profession was open mostly to members of the upper classes (one needed the equivalent of a wedding fee in order to enter), some monastic institutions, and especially those populated by women, were actually beset by severe poverty and want. (The feminization of poverty has a long social history.) As the Middle Ages progressed, there were fewer convents in England, and those remaining were poorer. What is more, the level of education among nuns was decreasing, as the university, from which women were barred, came to replace the monastery as the center of learning. By the end of Chaucer's lifetime, it was not really expected that nuns would know Latin other than by rote in order to participate in Church services. Still, the vast majority of the writing and intellectual and creative work produced by women in the Middle Ages originated in convents. One need think only of the works of Hildegard von Bingen and of Héloïse, and, closer to Chaucer's home and time, of the great fourteenth-century English mystic Julian of Norwich, to realize the intellectual scope that, at its best, monastic life could afford women.

Needless to say, most medieval women became wives and mothers. And it is probably also needless to say that, by marital laws, men had power over the material reality and the general conduct of women's lives, including the right to exercise physical control over their wives. The law condoned domestic violence against women in the same way it condoned physical abuse as a necessary corrective for unruly children. While murder, of course, was not sanctioned, a husband who killed his wife because he caught her in the act of adultery would not be prosecuted to the full extent of the law.

Both law and social custom shaped medieval marriages. Throughout this period, and especially (though not exclusively) among the upper classes, marriage was an arranged affair. Economics, and in the case of the aristocracy and nobility, politics dictated the formation of marital alliances. The long- and short-term interests of the family took precedence over the wishes of the partners in the newly formed couple. This is not to say that some couples did not grow to love each other. And perhaps some had the luck to fall in love early on. But love, or at least romantic love, was not viewed as essential to a good marriage. Divorce was not legal, and, as the Wife of Bath demonstrates, in certain circles and from certain perspectives, remarriage was not condoned. Nonetheless, husbands, primarily in the upper classes, found "legal" ways of disposing of wives, especially if they failed to produce male heirs. Marriages, as we see in *The Clerk's Tale*, could be annulled on the basis of consanguinity, nonconsummation, or other retrospectively trumped-up charges in order to free the husband to make a new, more advantageous, and more fertile match.

As Eileen Power suggested many decades ago,[7] peasant and bourgeois women may well have made the greatest contributions through their labor to their families' lives and livelihoods. But it would be impossible for us, from our own historical vantage, to gauge exactly what the ability to make such a contribution might mean to working women in terms of their sense of autonomy, power, or control over their lives. Did they take pride in their economic contributions to their families, or were they too beset by material necessity to feel more than oppressed by the burden of work?

---

7 See her *Medieval Women* (reissued Cambridge: Cambridge University Press, 2008).

We may never be able accurately to assess how powerful medieval women of various social classes really were, or really felt. But we may sell them short by underestimating the widely ranging strengths and capabilities of women in the Middle Ages. Their influence might well be shadowed by the fear of their power that seems to emerge in many of the medieval texts written by men. And it might also be shadowed by that particular and well-known influence exerted by the courtly lady and her position in medieval literature.

Courtly Love and Chivalry

Of all aspects of the late medieval world with which modern audiences are familiar, none may be more famous than courtly love and chivalry. Together, they create many of our notions, both stereotyped and accurate (sometimes both at the same time), of how the Middle Ages conducted romantic relationships. For all the social changes that have occurred over the centuries, a number of these ideas and ideals are still interestingly at play in some of our own notions about what romance should be. Chaucer, along with his culture and its literature, was deeply interested in love and in the ways in which men and women related to each other, although not all relationships, of course, were particularly courtly.

In order to understand these two medieval cultural forces within their own social context, it's important to remember that chivalry and courtly love are not actually the same thing (regardless of the way in which we hear the terms used interchangeably). Although chivalry eventually became associated with courtly love in literature, art, and culture, it was, historically, an earlier code of conduct more concerned with a knight's relationship as vassal to his liege lord than with his relationships to women. Chivalry expressed the knight's vassalage in terms of masculine integrity and the obligations the knight owed his lord (as well as the other way around). It defined modes of honorable behavior in and out of battle. Only part of that code of conduct involved protecting women, because women were not the only ones who merited protection. The true knight protected the weak and the oppressed from the injustices that threatened them, whether those suffering were women, children, old people, or knights brought unjustly to disgrace and dishonor by unchivalric foes.

Courtly love, on the other hand, was an ethos and a set of values focused on defining the right conduct of romantic relationships between men and women. Sometime during the twelfth century in the South of France, courtly love entered medieval Europe from Spain, where it existed as part of Islamic culture. From there, it spread rapidly throughout Europe until, in the thirteenth century, it was influencing cultural traditions across the Continent and bringing with it a set of ideas about romantic relationships between men and women that had not previously been present in medieval European art. There are a number of important points to keep in mind about courtly love, the most important of which is this: the minute one articulates a rule or tenet of courtly love, one can find a text, situation, story, tapestry, or painting that seems to articulate exactly the opposite.

In essence, courtly love was heterosexual romantic love as it was associated with and located in the court (hence the name). It was by, for, and about nobles and aristocrats. (If it was associated with members of the lower classes, as we see in *The Miller's Tale,* this was very often done so satirically by writers who, after all, came from the upper classes.) What is more, courtly love was primarily an artistic phenomenon, the creation of poets and storytellers—a fiction that first found its way into troubadours' lyrics and then into the longer narratives that became the genre of medieval romance. As time passed, some of the values and behaviors associated with courtly love "trickled down," as it were, into actual medieval actions and attitudes; life *can* at times imitate art. But courtly love was not so much an historical expression of real behavior between men and women as it was a way of articulating an idealized form of love in literature and in art. It wasn't called *fin'amor*—refined love—for nothing.

Courtly love most often involves the worship of the lady, who is seen as the repository of all that is ideal. She possesses a physical beauty that mirrors her virtue and goodness, and a poise and graciousness demanding that obeisance be paid her. It is she whom the knight strives to win. But, because she is the paragon of all that's beautiful and good, not surprisingly, the knight is unworthy of her until he has proven his honor, his loyalty, and his love. Doing so can require not only feats of derring-do (the typical cliché of the knight slaying the dragon comes immediately to mind) but also a refinement of the self, of the inner man, a growth in his own nobility and virtue. Hence courtly love becomes associated, if not conflated, with chivalry: the virtues of chivalry are those that would make a knight worthy of his lady. The actual structure of allegiances found in the chivalric code can be transposed onto the courtly love relationship so that the knight becomes, in essence, the lady's vassal, and she exists in relation to him in the same position of superiority that his own lord would occupy. The lady becomes his ruler; he becomes her servant in love. She is above him, the proto-typical lady on the pedestal, honored and coveted, until, after much emotional (and sometimes physical) turmoil, she can be won.

In medieval art, we find two distinct but related kinds of courtly love, the Platonic and the sensual. The Platonic is most famously embodied in the rela-tionship between Dante and Beatrice. Dante worshipped Beatrice from afar to such an extent that she became his ideal of goodness, womanhood, and virtue, someone whom he deeply loved with no desire for physical contact; indeed, the very intensity and purity of his love would have defied mere sexual passion. After her early death, she also became the inspiration for his *Divine Comedy*. He would struggle through his art to be worthy of her and to write of her in a way that would immortalize her and connect her with all that is central to the medieval Christian ethos. Her influence brings him to birth as a poet, and in the *Paradiso*, at the end of the epic through which she has been his muse and guide, we find her enshrined in heaven in the divine rose.

At the other end of the spectrum was sensual courtly love. It involved the same idealization, the same worship, the same effort on the man's part to make himself worthy of the woman. But this time, he exerts his efforts with the hope of being with his lady physically as well as emotionally. The lady is to be wooed—and won. In this case, love finds its highest expression in the physical consum-mation of the relationship and in sexual fulfillment. This kind of courtly love is the stuff of many of the plots of medieval romance. Its most famous exam-ple comes from the Arthurian tradition in the tale of the ill-fated relationship between Guenevere and Lancelot. Of course, Guenevere and Lancelot also raise another aspect of courtly love: often, whether it was Platonic or sensual, courtly love was love that existed—that specifically needed to exist—outside of mar-riage. Dante, after all, was married to Gemma Donati.

In an era when most aristocratic marriages were arranged, courtly love, this most exalted kind of earthly love between a man and a woman, could achieve its status and perfection only by being freely chosen, and thus by existing outside the confines of marriage. It most often involved love at first sight. The rapidity with which the man (and sometimes the woman) fell in love was proof of its worth, its truth, its inevitability. And of its uncontrollability. This, of course, cre-ated a number of intriguing problems and tensions in medieval romances. The tragedy of Camelot is only one example of the irresolvable conflicts of loyalty and obligation that courtly love could cause. Chaucer's *Knight's Tale* is another. It shows how courtly love pits men of the same blood, sworn to brotherhood and imprisoned together in hostile territory, against each other as they become rivals for the same woman.

This aspect of courtly love raises the important question of how the Church could have tolerated an idealized form of secular romantic love that essentially (at least in many of its appearances) advocated adultery. Certainly, the Church would not look kindly on this, and certainly, the Church would rail against such immoral frivolity in literary and artistic works. And it did. But the Church was not beyond seeing some things metaphorically. In one of the most interesting, potentially ironic, and yet totally predictable shifts of the Middle Ages, by the late thirteenth and fourteenth centuries, the language of courtly love and its worship of the woman was becoming applied to the veneration of the Virgin Mary. She became "our Lady," *Notre Dame, Madonna,* the most exquisite courtly lady of all. And, in the writings of both male and female mystics that began to proliferate in the thirteenth century, we can find applied to Christ the language of courtly love worship infused with a kind of eroticism meant to betoken the ecstastic desire for spiritual union with the Godhead.

The influence of Catholicism notwithstanding, in many respects, the Middle Ages was significantly less prudish about representations of sensuality and sexuality in art than Victorian England (or some decades of twentieth-century America). It should not therefore be surprising, though it often is, that when we come to the descriptions of sex and love in comic medieval literature depicting the lower classes, we often get bawdy body humor and some pretty outrageous acts. In such representations of nonaristocratic characters and their liaisons, the typical courtly love triangle becomes the scene of farcical cuckolding through the medieval genre of fabliaux—raunchy short stories in which the plotlines invariably involve having the trickster tricked amid many sexual shenanigans. Chaucer was as much a master of this genre as he was of the romance. He produced some of the most artistically dexterous and complex as well as funniest fabliaux in the medieval literary tradition. The range of lovers and love situations in *The Canterbury Tales* can leave no doubt that relationships between men and women were among Chaucer's major themes, explored with a breadth of tones and forms that quite literally stretch from the sublime to the ridiculous.

"Global" Literature in the Middle Ages

Long before our current explorations of global and cross-cultural literature, medieval European writers grounded their very sense of what literature was and how it operated in what they understood as a global context. Even though, given their perspective and knowledge, the world was much smaller for them than it is for us today, medieval writers produced literature with a keen sense of its active relationship to texts from other times and other places. This whole period, it is true, wrestled with the dualistic and polarizing differentiations between secular and ecclesiastical writings, between holy and earthly texts, with a zeal that would be almost incomprehensible to us without some of the political and religious events of our own lifetimes. Still, it is also true that for a writer like Chaucer, who was both self-consciously English and recognizably European, to write involved a process of encountering, studying, ingesting, digesting, and often revising the major ecclesiastical and secular texts of his culture. For medieval poets in general and for Chaucer in particular, to make literature was specifically to write within and sometimes against a tradition of European and Latin/classical texts. No one in his age would have written otherwise. Originality was not then at the premium it is today; medieval writers would have understood and valued that concept much differently than we do. Making literature in the Middle Ages meant adopting and adapting previous written authorities. The Wife of Bath makes her culture's awareness of this practice clear as she begins her *Prologue* by taking on the ecclesiastical authorities whose writings have defined her society's concepts of women and marriage.

In Chaucer's time, the transmission and dissemination of literary texts would have been viewed largely in terms of translation. Indeed, translation was seen as a form of literary creation, of "original" poetic making, of giving texts new life within another cultural context. It is in relationship to this understanding of medieval artistic creation and translation that we can view Chaucer's work, in its own time, as a form of self-consciously global literature. This perspective underlines both a common trans-European cultural heritage and the ways in which the same text, in a different social and regional context, attains a different meaning. Interestingly, in his Retraction at the end of *The Canterbury Tales*, Chaucer places his translations among the works he decides *not* to retract, both because they involve conspicuously moral writings, like Boethius's *Consolation of*

Philosophy, and because, one presumes, he finds an artistic and poetic usefulness and legitimacy in the act of translation.

Almost every literary work, then, had its own sources, its pedigree, its lineage. And that lineage grew and developed as subsequent writers took up earlier works (whether famous or obscure) and made them their own. The sources for Chaucer's texts would have been written in Latin, Italian, French, and sometimes even English. In the fourteenth century, Latin was the lingua franca, comprehensible to the educated classes throughout Europe, the language of ecclesiastical texts, of state documents, and of some secular literature. Yet, for many reasons, some literary, some religious, some political, some social, the late twelfth and thirteenth centuries saw an increasing emphasis on a region's own distinct language or dialect and on the importance of producing writing in that region's vernacular, instead of the authorized Latin.[8] Thus, Dante became one of the preeminent new voices for using the "vulgar," that is, the "common" tongue, not only to express the emotional anguish of courtly love in his *Vita Nuova* but also to articulate much more ambitious artistic projects as he undertook to write an epic in the vernacular in his *Divine Comedy.*

The importance of using the vernacular in creating poetry was not only to glorify the local language and to respond to the demands of regional pride but also to make poetry more accessible to a greater number of people. While the vast majority remained illiterate throughout Europe in the thirteenth and fourteenth centuries, literacy rates were slowly increasing, and a growing audience was emerging for vernacular texts, both sacred and profane. In the second half of the fourteenth century, John Wycliffe, the Oxford theologian with supposed connections to the heretical Lollards, was at work on the first translation of the Bible into English. Fiercely critical of Church corruption, Wycliffe hoped his translation would allow more people to encounter God's word directly, unmediated by priestly intervention. The accessibility of and demand for texts in the vernacular would begin to increase dramatically with the invention of printing in the fifteenth century. Later in that century, when William Caxton introduced printing to England, he immediately turned to Chaucer. And thus *The Canterbury Tales* became the first literary text to be printed in English.

---

8   For further reading, see Ernst Robert Curtius's classic study *European Literature and the Latin Middle Ages,* trans. Willard R. Trask (Princeton: Princeton University Press, 1991), and Marcia L. Colish, *Medieval Foundations of the Western Intellectual Tradition* (New Haven: Yale University Press, 1999).

The Literary Background of The Canterbury Tales

The fictional late fourteenth-century setting of Chaucer's *Canterbury Tales* can bear striking resemblances to his own world. In this "reality," twenty-nine pilgrims from diverse social and geographical locations in England (plus the Host of the Tabard Inn, their gathering place, and the narrator) set out from Southwark, on the South Bank of the Thames, which was then a suburb of London, to make the trip of approximately three days and fifty-four miles to Canterbury. There they will visit the shrine of Saint Thomas Becket, who was killed in Canterbury Cathedral by the henchmen of Henry II on December 29, 1170. Becket's shrine provided the English with their own homegrown pilgrimage destination, one whose popularity rose throughout the Middle Ages. It was, after all, a more convenient site for making religious pilgrimage than Rome or Jerusalem for men and women who didn't have the time, resources, or inclination to travel farther afield. Chaucer's fictional pilgrimage, like its historical counterparts, brings with it overtones of penance and remorse, and the hope for purification, absolution, and redemption. But by the end of the fourteenth century, pilgrimages had begun to attract to themselves rather different kinds of undertones. They were falling into disrepute to the extent that the Church itself was starting to discourage the practice of pilgrimage except for the most sincerely devout. In an age well before package tours and ocean cruises, pilgrimages could provide people with an opportunity for organized travel, guaranteed socializing, and readily available camaraderie. They gave people the chance to get out and get moving. Going on pilgrimage for some could have as little connection to religion or spirituality as going on spring break for college students has a connection to a passion for cultural anthropology. It is against this backdrop that Chaucer sets the scene for his *Canterbury Tales*.

Along their way to Canterbury, Chaucer's pilgrims will tell stories to each other, as doubtless many historical pilgrims did in order to while away the time both on the road and in the inns and hostelries where they rested. We know of important medieval literary works that originated on pilgrimage routes; the *Song of Roland* most likely grew and developed as it was told and retold along the trail to St. James's shrine at Santiago de Compostela. But Chaucer's pilgrims have an additional incentive to inspire their storytelling: his pilgrims will be organized into a competition, formed at the suggestion of the innkeeper, Harry Bailey, their Host at the Tabard Inn. The Host makes them swear to tell two stories on the way to Canterbury and two on the way back. He will be the judge of the storytelling competition; its prize will be a dinner for the winner, paid for by the rest of the pilgrims, back at the Tabard Inn when the pilgrimage is over. But by the time we get to the end of *The Tales* and the Prologue to *The Parson's Tale,* it is clear that somewhere along the way the plans have changed. The Host distinctly suggests that the Parson's performance, delivered at the gates of Canterbury, is the last tale to be told. Since Chaucer died without finishing *The Canterbury Tales*, this intriguing inconsistency between the initial plans and the final statement about them remains a literary mystery. It may well be that Harry Bailley's ambitious plans for four tales per pilgrim and a round trip journey were always only that: a fictional character's plans to get them all back to the Tabard Inn for a large, expensive feast. This may not really have been Chaucer's own plan at all.

There is historical precedent, then, for pilgrimages like the one in *The Tales* and historical evidence that stories got told on them. But in an age when literary art was made by adopting and adapting prior literary sources, what literary precedent is there for *The Canterbury Tales* as a whole? If the central idea is the pilgrimage, Chaucer's work has behind it all those stories, reaching back in the European tradition to epics like Homer's *Odyssey* and Virgil's *Aeneid,* which took the journey as their organizing principle. Along with this motif, Chaucer would inherit all the themes and issues that went with it: the movement through the obstacles and challenges that constitute a testing of the self; the encounters with forces that can bring forth self-knowledge; and the journey outward from the home space that ultimately brings the protagonist back home (or sometimes to a new homeland) with a renewed or expanded sense of self in relation to society, history, culture, and individual moral responsibility. Starting in the twelfth century, the Middle Ages gave its own particular narrative shape to this motif of the journey: the medieval romance. In the romance, a literary grandchild of the epic, the knight as hero journeys out on his quest from his home court, encounters obstacles meant to test him, achieves (or not) the goal of his quest, and returns, if he is lucky, to his court, changed somehow and needing to integrate his new knowledge into his life and character.

All of the themes associated with the motif of the journey in epic and romance can pertain to the pilgrimage. But the pilgrimage is a particular kind of journey, one that is specific in time, space, and purpose. For these reasons, it brings with it themes and issues unique to itself. The pilgrimage, whether historical or fictional, is always, from the start, self-consciously metaphorical because it always has a twofold resonance: in both this world and the next, or, more specifically, through this world *into* the next. In the Middle Ages, the pilgrimage was a journey through physical space that could bring its own very literal forms of testing, given some of the hardships encountered by the traveler. It was not uncommon for pilgrimage trains to be beset by bandits, outlaws, ruffians, and con artists. The journey could be arduous, exposing pilgrims to extreme weather and rugged terrain. But, since the pilgrimage was a journey of atonement that had as its destination a sacred space, its hardships allowed pilgrims to practice repentance and demonstrate worthiness for the absolution waiting at the journey's end. If Christ suffered for them, they should and could suffer for him on the pilgrimage trail. Reaching the pilgrimage site, meditating on one's soul there, and praying for absolution would bring spiritual fulfillment and return one to life renewed and advanced along the journey toward salvation. The pilgrimage was a metaphor for life and for how to conduct the journey through it in such a way that one would reach one's ultimate destination: out of this life and the space of physical, earthly pilgrimage and into the next, the ultimate goal. Or, as Chaucer's Parson says, pilgrimage leads to the New Jerusalem.

Chaucer, then, structures his collection of tales according to the overarching literary motif of the journey. But he also has literary precedent for assembling individual stories into a collection, what we might today call an anthology, of tales more or less unified around a central purpose. Taken as a whole, Chaucer's work participates in the genre known as the frame-tale collection, which had been around at least since the classical period. A frame-tale collection brings together a group of disparate stories, sometimes linked thematically, within a frame that provides the motivating reason for gathering them all in one place. One of the most important classical examples of the frame-tale collection was Ovid's *Metamorphoses*, a group of stories that retold classical myths about shape-shifting, such as the legend of Narcissus's transformation. Interestingly, Ovid's collection happened to be one of Chaucer's favorite works; he often alludes to the *Metamorphoses* and adapts and adopts stories from this source throughout *The Canterbury Tales*. Closer to home (at least temporally) among Chaucer's frame-tale sources was not only Giovanni Sercambi's *Novelle*, but also, and especially, Giovanni Boccaccio's *Decameron*. While the scholarly jury is still out about whether Chaucer knew the *Decameron*, there is good reason to believe that he did. Arguably, no other medieval writer influenced Chaucer more than Boccaccio. Boccaccio's *Il Filostrato* (*The One Prostrate in Love*) is so close in some passages to Chaucer's *Troilus and Criseyde* that it would seem Chaucer had it right alongside him when he was writing. And yet his work is so radically altered from Boccaccio's at key points that these differences give us a glimpse into the patterns of deliberate change that Chaucer made as he was adopting and adapting this source. In the same way, if Chaucer considerably lengthened Boccaccio's *Il Filostrato* when he wrote *Troilus and Criseyde*, he dramatically shortened Boccaccio's long epic of Thebes, *Il Teseide*, when he wrote his *Knight's Tale*. Given some of the similarities between the *Decameron* and *The Canterbury Tales*, it seems hard to imagine that, during one of his trips to Italy, Chaucer had not been able to read through Boccaccio's frame-tale collection at least once, even if he himself never owned a copy.

Boccaccio's *Decameron*, like Chaucer's *Canterbury Tales*, is set in a contemporary milieu and takes as its raison d'être a contemporary historical event. For Boccaccio, this event is a journey out of Florence to the seemingly safer site of the hill town of Fiesole during an onslaught of the plague. Ten aristocratic Florentines (seven women and three men) travel to a villa up in the hills, and, while they are there for ten days until the plague passes, they tell stories to amuse themselves. Ten tellers; ten stories; ten days; a hundred stories—some of them clearly sources (or at least analogues) for *Canterbury Tales* such as *The Reeve's Tale* and *The Clerk's Tale*. Boccaccio's stories range widely from the sublime to the ridiculous, as do Chaucer's. But there is one important element that Boccaccio's frame-tale collection lacks and that is central to Chaucer's, a psychological element that goes beyond the fact that Chaucer's pilgrims are competing against one another in a way that brings the profit motive squarely into the center of this spiritual undertaking. Chaucer has adopted and adapted the genre of previous frame-tale collections so that he can underline the psychology or psychologies of storytelling. The focus on this interior psychological element may be one of the main reasons that Chaucer's *Canterbury Tales* has remained so compelling and appealing.

Unlike other composers of frame-tale collections, unlike even Boccaccio who assigns individual tales to individual tellers, Chaucer does not simply match tales to tellers in some predictable, easy, or transparent way. Instead, his pairings of tellers and tales show us how the stories to which we're drawn and which we tell reveal a significant amount about ourselves. Certainly, they can confirm others' ideas about who or what we are, but they can also challenge preconceived notions that others have about us. The stories we tell, in many ways, tell us. In the end, as each of his pilgrims takes his or her turn at telling tales, each becomes, for that moment, an artist. Self-consciousness about making art and what it means to be an artist run as central themes throughout *The Canterbury Tales*.

The General Prologue to *The Tales* gives us portraits of each of the pilgrims going to Canterbury. Interestingly, there is no direct literary model or precedent for *The General Prologue* taken as a whole, although there are literary sources for the character types found in each of the portraits. These portraits can't help but set up expectations for the kinds of tales the individual pilgrims will tell, expectations that Chaucer will sometimes gratify, sometimes defy, and sometimes tease. What is more, in a way that emphasizes Chaucer's focus on character and characterization in *The Canterbury Tales*, he expands the scope of the frame-tale collection by often filling the space between the tales with prologues and epilogues that express the dramatic interactions among the pilgrims. In this linking material, he moves away from the tales themselves to emphasize our awareness of the frame and of the pilgrimage. More particularly, he makes us see that this is a diverse group of individuals, who, even if they're joined together only for a brief time, will interact with each other in significant and sometimes very intense ways. As they converse, squabble, grovel, preen, and even insult one another, at times brutally, they reveal a good deal about themselves. We learn about their characters as they move into and through their own stories and as they react to the stories they hear. One of Chaucer's major contributions to the genre of the frame-tale collection and one of his major contributions to the history of world literatures is his examination of the intricacies of human character in *The Canterbury Tales*. The confessions of some of his pilgrims show his complex grasp of the contradictions, depths, nuances, joy, and pain of life, and of the compensatory gestures, including storytelling, that humans make to ease pain, to fill voids. Not until Shakespeare will English literature produce another such artist of the human character. Chaucer's *Canterbury Tales* explore how storytelling is one of the resources human beings have for creating themselves, and how stories themselves can ease or cause pain, can fill or create voids. As his characters throw themselves into the storytelling competition, it is clear that stories matter, that literature counts. It is one truly worthwhile, yet always problematic way to pass the time till the pilgrimage is over.

Some Words on Chaucer's Language and This Translation

What I have tried to provide here is the kind of translation I would find most useful if I were a reader interested in coming to know Chaucer, perhaps for the first time, or if I were a student in a class that didn't have time to learn to read Chaucer in the original Middle English. To that end, I've offered a wide selection of fourteen *Canterbury Tales* in order to give a sense of their range, scope, and diversity. This book includes all the tales of Part I (or what is often called the A-Fragment), which introduces the pilgrims, initiates the storytelling, and demonstrates how the pilgrims quickly reveal their competitive edge (these texts include *The General Prologue* and the tales of the Knight, Miller, Reeve, and Cook). It also offers all the interlinked tales of what, almost a century ago, George Lyman Kittredge dubbed the "Marriage Group": the tales of the Wife of Bath, the Clerk, the Merchant, and the Franklin, which explore how men and women interact with each other and how power gets distributed in marriage. There is the confessional prologue and exemplum of Chaucer's sexually ambiguous Pardoner, who, like the Wife of Bath, explores the interconnections between sex and money, as well as the virulently anti-Semitic miracle tale of his pretty Prioress, which gives insight into social and religious attitudes of later medieval England. And there is both the self-parodying, totally inept *Tale of Sir Thopas* told by Chaucer's own pilgrim-surrogate who, as we see in *The General Prologue*, narrates *The Tales* as a whole, and the masterfully arch beast fable told by the Nun's Priest. Finally, we are brought to the gates of Canterbury with *The Parson's Prologue* and to the end of Chaucer's poetic career with his prose Retraction of his writings.

We need a translation in the first place, of course, because Chaucer wrote in Middle English, the form of the language that would have existed from roughly 1066 (the date of the Norman Conquest) through around 1500. Middle English is the direct ancestor of our own Modern English, the phase of the language that would have begun to develop during the Renaissance when English was becoming standardized in its grammar and orthography, largely through the advent and influence of printing. With time, patience, and a little training, we can all read Middle English, once we get used to odd spellings and grammatical forms and some vocabulary that has fallen out of currency. (The same cannot be said for Old English, a more distant ancestor, that requires much more time and training to master.) But many readers, for many understandable reasons, don't have that much time (or patience). As I worked on moving Chaucer's verse from Middle into Modern English, I particularly tried to shape a translation that reproduces as "authentically" and faithfully as it can the sound, the rhythm, the poetry, and the poetic devices of Chaucer's writing.

My translation has made every effort to address the complexities of Chaucer's work as a piece—or rather, as many different pieces—of poetry. (He also wrote two long tales in prose, not included here: *The Tale of Melibee* and *The Parson's Tale*.) Throughout, I have tried to offer an effective and accurate translation of the poetic forms that Chaucer has chosen for his individual tales. Most often, that form is the iambic pentameter couplet, which Chaucer introduced into English literature. He may well have imagined that such couplets provide the greatest degree of flexibility for representing, in rhyming poetry, large expanses of narrative as well as many different voices and many different kinds of conversation. But there are places in *The Canterbury Tales,* such as in the stories of the Clerk and the Prioress, where Chaucer needs a more complex and more formal kind of verse. In these instances, he uses another of his poetic inventions, the seven-line rhyme royal stanza (a stanza composed of iambic pentameter lines arranged in an *ababbcc* rhyme), the form he uses in his *Troilus and Criseyde.* When Chaucer uses rhyme royal, I have tried my best to re-create it.

Any attempt to be faithful to Chaucer's poetic forms involves, of course, attention not only to rhyme, but also to meter. As often as possible, I have maintained the iambic pentameter that characterizes Chaucer's line. Like Shakespeare, Chaucer himself was not totally consistent in his use of this meter. All his lines don't contain ten syllables, or five feet, or five consistent iambs in a row. At times, one finds hypermetric lines. At other times, one finds lines that lack some syllables; the opening line of *The General Prologue* is not only one of the most famous in all of Chaucer's works, but it is also "headless," that is, lacking the initial unstressed syllable. Thus, since Chaucer allowed himself some latitude with the number of syllables in a line, I have taken similar liberties, but not always in the exact spots where Chaucer does. (My translation of his opening line of *The General Prologue* is not headless.) And I have done my level best to make the lines scan.

In a similar way, I have tried to maintain Chaucer's rhyme scheme throughout. This is not to say that I make my rhyme on exactly the same words that Chaucer does. That would be impossible since one of the biggest differences between Chaucer's Middle English and our Modern English is the sounds of the two languages. Words that rhyme in Middle English ("melodye" and "eye") do not necessarily rhyme in Modern English ("melody" and "eye").[9] Rhyme in Chaucer's *Tales* can be tremendously important in linking sound and meaning. Like Shakespeare in the closing couplets of his sonnets, Chaucer was a master at working end rhyme for all it's worth, joining words through rhyme in order to reinforce or make meaning—sometimes through sound, sometimes through sense, sometimes through both. I have made every effort to capture in this translation those instances when rhyme really matters (as, for example, in the couplet that concludes the Miller's portrait of beautiful Alison, the sexy young wife of a doting old farmer/carpenter).[10]

But rhyme is an important element in Chaucer's writings for another reason, one that might not be readily apparent to a contemporary *reader*. I am italicizing the word "reader" here in order to emphasize the fact that a large number of people in Chaucer's own audience would have encountered his work for the first time by hearing the work read out loud (maybe even by Chaucer himself, in a court setting), rather than by reading the text silently to themselves; it was probably the case that, in the Middle Ages, when one read privately, one still read out loud. Because Chaucer's literature would have initially been intended for court entertainment and for oral performance—in other words, to be *heard*—its sound and its rhymes are of particular importance as part of its essence and meaning. For this reason, I have tried to resort to "eye rhyme" as little as possible, though doing so is unavoidable. And if, in some instances, the eye rhyme allows a linkage of words in the rhyming position in a way that underlines theme, meaning, and sense, I have opted for that choice.

In keeping with my goal of letting Chaucer sound like Chaucer, I have deliberately not tried to update the language, vocabulary, diction, and tone of his writing in order to make it, in that way, more accessible or "modern sounding" for a contemporary audience. This work was, after all, written in the fourteenth century, and I have tried to maintain its tone and its flavor. But neither have I tried to create an artificial sense of the archaic in this translation. For example,

9 In order to get an easy approximation of the way Chaucer's Middle English sounded, when reading a passage of Middle English, pronounce every single consonant (there are no silent *k*'s, for example, in Middle English) and then pronounce all the vowels as you would say them if you were speaking a modern Romance language.

10 It will probably be immediately obvious to readers that my rhymes are based on vowel sounds as they are pronounced in American English.

where Chaucer would have consistently made a distinction between "ye" (you plural) and "thou" (you singular), I simply translate second-person pronouns in the "you" forms because doing so sounds more natural to us and avoids unnecessarily archaic or cutesy-sounding "Olde English" kinds of formulations. In some rare instances, though, and for effect, I deliberately maintain this distinction and use "thou," "thee," and "thine" (as in the case of *The Prioress's Tale*) in order to underline the various pretensions, affectations, and artifices of a given speaker.

If Chaucer can with any accuracy be viewed as "the father of English poetry," it is because he was molding and modeling the English language into an idiom capable of sophisticated poetic expression. By any lights, he was remarkably successful at doing so. Yet, since he was one of the first to begin this long and arduous process, I'm going to have the temerity to say that all of his lines aren't flawless. He gives himself the license to use throw-away words to pad the meter and to use not-such-inspired tag phrases to end lines and create easy rhymes. This, of course, shouldn't open the door for a translator to run wild with such liberties. But I've given myself license to use some of these devices since Chaucer did, especially where he did, and even in some places where he didn't.

For example, in order to accommodate meter as well as for rhetorical effect, Chaucer seems to be a great lover of asyndeton and polysyndeton. He will also often use a coordinating conjunction at the beginning of a poetic line. Since these are devices that the poet himself employs, often to fill out a line's meter, I have used them as I needed, even when, in a given spot, Chaucer didn't do the same. (In another spot, however, he may have used one of these devices and, for metrical reasons, I couldn't.) In the same way, Chaucer often resorts, as do many narrative poets who write long expanses of rhymed verse, to line fillers and tags to complete a line and its meter. I have thus felt free to do so, inserting filler syllables like "then" and "thus," "here" and "there," as needed and in ways that, I hope, don't alter meaning.

In Chaucer's time, verbs did not come in contracted forms as they do today. Since the ability to use contractions is important in composing a poetic translation both in order to fit the exigencies of meter and, for some characters, in order to create an informality of tone, I have used contractions where I thought appropriate. My justification for this choice is that Chaucer himself used his own form of contraction: he would have relied on elision, the process of collapsing syllables in reading lines of poetry aloud, in order to make lines scan. This elision mirrors the ways in which we hear, and sometimes, depending upon the writer, we even see "evening" collapsed to "ev'ning" or "heaven" to "heav'n" in English poetry. Middle English poetry was familiar with elision. Thus, for example, where Chaucer might write "Canterbury," he would count on the word's ability to elide some vowels as necessary in order to produce the sound more metrically suitable for some lines: "Cant'rb'ry." Following Chaucer's lead, then, I have felt free to use contractions where they are appropriate and necessary.

While it is difficult to re-create the sound of Chaucer's English in a Modern English translation, I have tried to draw attention to the importance of sound when it seems to me that Chaucer places a particular emphasis on it in order to create meaning. I try to maintain alliteration where Chaucer chooses it as a poetic device, and I try to avoid it where Chaucer did not see fit, despite a temptation to do so in order to dress up a line. If a particular line gains some of its impact and meaning from sibilance or percussiveness or onomatopoeia, I try my best to capture those devices. We don't know exactly how Chaucer's own language sounded, of course. But coming as close as we can to reconstructing its sounds lets us know where in his text Chaucer was playing, as does any poet, with the importance of sound in its contribution to sense. This contribution would have had a special significance in Chaucer's day because, as noted earlier, poetry was an oral performance as much as it was a text written to be read and experienced in private. Chaucer may have been particularly aware of the importance of sound to his poetry in *The Tales* because they create the fiction of a multitude of voices heard aloud as the pilgrims tell their stories on the road to Canterbury.

Finally, there are lines, groups of lines, whole passages of some of Chaucer's writing that might not strike the modern reader as the world's most scintillating poetry. Some passages aren't meant to do too much more than the basic narrative work of getting us from point A to point B in the plot. Sometimes, even if those lines and passages have their own thematic purposes (as does the long catalogue of trees in the description of the funeral pyre in *The Knight's Tale*), they may not be particularly appealing to contemporary tastes. Sometimes the syntax of Chaucer's lines can be rather tortured. If I have tried to capture to the best of my ability the beauty, the wit, the humor, the lyricism, the satire, and the descriptive vividness that make Chaucer's poetry masterful, moving, and memorable, I have also tried to be faithful to his poetry in those instances when it might not be any of those wonderful things. Even as I have tried to make the poetry readable and enjoyable for a contemporary audience, I have not streamlined him, modernized him, prettified him, or smoothed off the rough edges. They are there in Chaucer's writing, and they are there in my translation.

But such passages are precious, too, and poignant. They remind us that, even if *The Canterbury Tales* contains the writing of Chaucer with which most contemporary readers are familiar, it remains, nonetheless, an unfinished masterpiece. It will always be a work in progress, and in this way, will always share that kinship with our persistently provisional understanding of these tales. Whether Chaucer would have edited and revised any of what we might call the rough patches if he had lived to complete *The Canterbury Tales,* who can say? But I have left them there, as they are, as a reminder. For even if this translation tries both to be faithful to Chaucer's text and to make his work accessible to a twenty-first-century reader, nothing, finally, can erase his distance from us. In the end, would we have it any other way?

A Chaucerian Lexicon

Chaucer's vocabulary falls into three basic categories: (1) words that mean the same and can sometimes be virtually spelled the same in Middle and Modern English; (2) words that mean something different in Middle and Modern English or that have disappeared entirely from Modern English usage; and (3) words that look the same in Middle and Modern English, but that have come, over time, to take on somewhat different meanings. The first two categories are fairly easy to translate. The third category, however, contains many false cognates (they look as if they should mean one thing when, in fact, they mean another), or words that imply a number of different meanings all at the same time.

Often in this translation, in order to maintain sound, rhyme, or the multiple meanings inherent in a Middle English word, I have transliterated (as opposed to translated) a Middle English word into its current Modern English form, even though the meaning of the word has changed, or was in the process of changing in the Middle Ages. Below is a lexicon of the words in this category that occur with some frequency in *The Canterbury Tales*. They are listed first in boldface, in their Modern English spelling, and then in italics, in their Middle English spelling, followed by the definition or range of meanings that the word had in Middle English and that I wish to suggest in my translation. Included in this list are Cato and Solomon, whose names recur with such frequency in *The Canterbury Tales* that they can be viewed as terms or catchphrases, in the same way that the names "Freud" and "Darwin" have become associated with specific concepts in our own Modern English lexicon.

astrology (*astrologie/astrologye*): in the Middle Ages, astrology included what we today call astronomy as well as astrology. The two were combined into one area of inquiry involving the study of the stars and the zodiac as well as the study of horoscopes. The medieval imagination believed that one's horoscope influenced one's body and thus determined appropriate medical treatments based on one's temperament, date of birth, and star signs.

bachelor (*bachelor/bachiler*): an unmarried man, but also a man who has completed a beginning level of training in a specific field. The term can refer to a university student who has earned a specific degree (as we today refer to a Bachelor of Arts degree) or to a young knight who is in the early stages of his training.

Cato (*Cato/Caton/Catoun*): not to be confused with Cato, the Roman statesman. Most often in Chaucer, the reference is to Dionysius Cato, the presumed author of a work named *The Distichs of Cato* (third to fourth century c.e.), a popular elementary schoolbook that was a collection of adages and maxims. "Cato" became a shorthand for proverbial wisdom.

cheer (*chere/cheere*): look, expression, face, or manner

child (*childe/chylde*): a baby or child, but also a young aristocratic male or a young knight

clerk (*clerke*): a member of the clergy or a university student either in training to take religious orders or in preparation for clerical (ecclesiastical) employment. The term can also be used loosely at times to refer to any intellectual authority.

complexion (*complexioun/compleccioun*): one's temperament or characteristics as they are established according to the medieval medical theory of the four humors, or else the color of one's skin, as it is based on the balance of the humors—see **humors**

counterfeit (*countrefete/contrefete*): vb., to counterfeit (to fake), but also, more neutrally, to imitate

courage (*corage/courage*): not only in the Modern English sense of bravery, but more frequently, in Middle English, meaning heart, or emotions. It also often carries the overtone of sexual energy, desire, or potency.

coverchief (*coverchief/coverchef*): a woman's headdress, headscarf, or kerchief, often made of linen, but in some instances elaborately styled and embellished

craft (*craft*): cleverness, skillfulness, or deceptiveness, but also a field of learning or study or an art or occupation

dalliance (*daliaunce/dalliance*): small talk, chitchat, gossip, but also flirtation or sexual relations

dame (*dame*): literally, "lady." An honorific usually applied as a mode of address to women of the upper classes. It can also mean mother or the mistress of a household.

degree (*degre/degree*): rank, social class or standing, status, reputation

disparage (*disparage*): n. or vb., as, in Modern English, dishonor; but in Middle English the word often carries the specific connotation of undergoing a degradation of social class, often through marital or sexual affiliation

don (*Don*): Sir, honorific form of address, often used ironically in *The Tales*

estate (*estat/estaat*): rank, social class, status, state, condition

florin (*floryn*): gold coin; the English florin was worth around six shillings

free (*fre*): in addition to the Modern English sense of the word, it can, in Middle English, mean gracious, generous, magnanimous, or not servile or in bondage

gentle (*gentil/gentile*): along with the Modern English meaning, the word most often in Middle English means noble in character and/or in social class (as in "gentle man"), well mannered, gracious, and genteel

gentleness (*gentillesse*): along with the Modern English meaning, the word most often in Middle English means gentility or nobility of rank and/or character

ghost (*ghoste*): spirit

gloss (*glose*): n.—interpretation or explanation; vb.—to interpret and explain; also to beguile, flatter, cajole, sweet-talk, or deceive

groat (*grote*): silver coin worth around fourpence

humors (*humors*): medieval medicine believed that the body was composed of four humors or bodily fluids that were associated with the four physical elements. Water was cold and moist and air was hot and moist, whereas earth was cold and dry and fire was hot and dry. The humors or bodily fluids were melancholy (black bile; cold and dry), choler (yellow bile; hot and dry), phlegm (cold and moist), and blood (hot and moist). The relationship and balance of the humors controlled one's physical health and one's temperament, because they produced personality types that were melancholic, choleric, phlegmatic, or sanguine depending on which humor was dominant.

kind (*kind; kinde; kynd; kynde*): n.—in Middle English, nature (as in the natural world), kind (as in species or type), or disposition; adj.—kind in the Modern English sense, but also natural or innate, intrinsic

knave (*knave*): servant, peasant, villain, or boy child

lay (*lay*): the Breton *lai* (French) or lay was a courtly literary narrative, much shorter than a romance, presented in rhymed verse and often performed to musical accompaniment

lists (*listes/lystes*): Modern English lists or enclosures for tournament grounds, or the confrontation/battle that would take place within those grounds

lust (*lust/lest*): in Middle English, the word can mean desire or pleasure of any kind, not just sexual; by the fourteenth century, however, it was beginning to acquire distinctly sexual undertones and overtones in certain contexts

lusty (*lusty*): merry, jolly, cheerful, desirous, or vigorous, but, by Chaucer's time, also beginning to acquire the sexual meaning it has in Modern English

page (*page*): little boy, young servant, or pageboy

physic (*phisik*): medicine, remedy

prick (*prikke/pricke*): n.—point of a weapon, a jab or stab; vb.—to jab, stab, pierce, or spur. In Middle English, as in Modern English slang, it can often carry a double entendre meaning penis or sexual intercourse.

pricking (*prikinge*): hard riding or spurring, often with the same double entendre as **prick**

prime (*prime*): the first part of the day, stretching from 6 to 9 a.m., named after one of the Canonical Hours, the divisions of the day for prayer services in monasteries and convents. The Canonical Hours were Matins (around 2 a.m.), Lauds (before dawn), Prime (6 a.m.), Terce (9 a.m.), Sext (noon), None (3 p.m.), Vespers (sunset or early evening), and Compline (before bed).

privacy (*privetee*): secrecy, privacy, secret or confidential affairs

private (*privee*): secret, hidden, private, confidential

quaint (*queynte*): adj.—strange, curious, clever, ingenious, elegant, or highly contrived; n.—female genitalia (as in cunt). Chaucer frequently puns on the word *queynte* in *The Tales*.

science (*science*): field of learning, expertise, or art, or learning itself, knowledge, or wisdom

silly (*sely*): blessed, innocent, happy, but also pitiful, wretched, unfortunate, or hapless. In the fourteenth century, the word was also attaining a meaning closer to its Modern English equivalent of foolish or silly.

smart (*smerte*): n.—pain or hurt; adj.—painful; adv.—painfully; vb.—to hurt or be hurting, to cause pain or be in pain

solace (*solas/solaas*): comfort, solace, satisfaction, pleasure, often with a sexual undertone

Solomon (*Salomon/Salamon*): King of Israel (see I Kings). Chaucer refers to Solomon often, and in a variety of contexts. On the one hand, his name in the Middle Ages is almost synonymous with wisdom, and to him are often attributed maxims, proverbs, and adages that actually come from other sources. On the other hand, he is also often cited in association with marriage because of the Song of Songs and with women because of his many wives and concubines. Frequently, when linked with women, the emphasis is on Solomon's folly, not his wisdom.

squire (*squyer/squire*): unlike a full-fledged knight, a squire was generally a younger man, a knight-in-training who accompanied and served an older knight

tail (*tayl*): tail, with the double entendre on genitalia, both male and female

wanton (*wantoun*): jovial or amorous, but also beginning to have the Modern English sense of promiscuous or unchaste

wife (*wyf/wife*): in Middle English, the word could mean either wife or woman, with no particular implication about her marital status

THE SELECTED

CANTERBURY
TALES

THE GENERAL PROLOGUE

Here bigynneth the Book of the Tales of Caunterbury.

Whan that Aprill with his shoures sote
The droghte of Marche hath perced to the rote,
And bathed every veyne in swich licour,
Of which vertu engendred is the flour;
Whan Zephirus eek with his swete breeth   5
Inspired hath in every holt and heeth
The tendre croppes, and the yonge sonne
Hath in the Ram his halfe cours y-ronne;
And smale fowles maken melodye,
That slepen al the night with open yë—   10
So priketh hem Nature in hir corages—
Than longen folk to goon on pilgrimages,
And palmeres for to seken straunge strondes,
To ferne halwes, couthe in sondry londes;
And specially, from every shires ende   15
Of Engelond to Caunterbury they wende,
The holy blisful martir for to seke,
That hem hath holpen, whan that they were seke.
        Bifel that, in that seson on a day,

THE GENERAL PROLOGUE

Here begins the Book of the Tales of Canterbury.

When April comes and with its showers sweet
Has, to the root, pierced March's drought complete,
And then bathed every vein in such elixir
That, by its strength, engendered is the flower;
When Zephirus[1] with his sweet breath   5
Inspires life anew, through grove and heath,
In tender shoots, and when the spring's young sun
Has, in the Ram,[2] full half its course now run,
And when small birds begin to harmonize
That sleep throughout the night with open eyes   10
(So nature, stirring them, pricks up their courage),
Then folks, too, long to go on pilgrimage,
And palmers hope to seek there, on strange strands,
Those far-off shrines well known in many lands;
And especially, from every shire's end   15
Of England, to Canterbury they wend;
The holy, blessed martyr[3] they all seek,
Who has helped them when they were sick and weak.
It happened, in that season, on a day

1 **Zephirus:** Zephyr, or the West Wind.
2 **the Ram:** The zodiacal sign of Aries.
3 **The holy, blessed martyr:** Saint Thomas Becket was killed by Henry II's henchmen of on December 29, 1170, in Canterbury Cathedral. The setting of his martyrdom became England's premier pilgrimage site in the Middle Ages.

In Southwerk at the Tabard as I lay   20
Redy to wenden on my pilgrimage
To Caunterbury with ful devout corage,
At night was come into that hostelrye
Wel nyne and twenty in a companye
Of sondry folk, by aventure y-falle   25
In felawshipe, and pilgrims were they alle,
That toward Caunterbury wolden ryde.
The chambres and the stables weren wyde,
And wel we weren esed atte beste.
And shortly, whan the sonne was to reste,   30
So hadde I spoken with hem everichon
That I was of hir felawshipe anon,
And made forward erly for to ryse,
To take oure wey, ther as I yow devyse.
      But natheles, whyl I have tyme and space,   35
Er that I ferther in this tale pace,
Me thinketh it acordaunt to resoun
To telle yow al the condicioun
Of ech of hem, so as it semed me,
And whiche they weren, and of what degree,   40
And eek in what array that they were inne;
And at a knight than wol I first beginne.
      A KNIGHT ther was, and that a worthy man,
That fro the tyme that he first bigan
To ryden out, he loved chivalrye,   45
Trouthe and honour, fredom and curteisye.
Ful worthy was he in his lordes werre,
And therto hadde he riden, no man ferre,
As wel in Cristendom as in hethenesse,
And evere honoured for his worthinesse.   50

In Southwark, at the Tabard[4] as I lay   20
Ready to start out on my pilgrimage
To Canterbury, with true, devoted courage,
At night, there came into that hostelry,
Fully nine-and-twenty in a company
Of sundry folks, as chance would have them fall   25
In fellowship, and pilgrims were they all,
Who, toward Canterbury, wished to ride.
The chambers and the stables were all wide,
And we were put at ease with all the best.
And, shortly, when the sun went to its rest,   30
I had so spoken with them, every one,
That I was in their fellowship anon,
And to rise early I gave them my vow,
To make our way, as I will tell you now.
But, nonetheless, while I have time and space,   35
Before much further in this tale I pace,
It seems quite right and proper to relate
To you the full condition and the state
Of each of them, just as they seemed to me,
And what they were, and of what degree,   40
And also of the clothes they were dressed in,
And with a knight, then, I will first begin.
A KNIGHT there was, and that, a worthy man,
Who, from the time when he first began
To ride to war, he loved most chivalry,   45
Truth and honor, largesse and courtesy.
Full worthy he, to fight in his lord's war,
No other man had ridden half so far,
As much in Christian as in heathen lands,
And all honor his worthiness commands;   50

---

4   **Southwark**: A suburb of London south of the Thames; **the Tabard**: name of the inn. In Middle English, a *tabard* is a loosely fitting coat; this was probably used as the motif on the inn's sign.

At Alisaundre he was whan it was wonne;
Ful ofte tyme he hadde the bord bigonne
Aboven alle naciouns in Pruce.
In Lettow hadde he reysed and in Ruce,
No Cristen man so ofte of his degree.   55
In Gernade at the sege eek hadde he be
Of Algezir, and riden in Belmarye.
At Lyeys was he and at Satalye,
Whan they were wonne; and in the Grete See
At many a noble armee hadde he be.   60
At mortal batailles hadde he been fiftene,
And foughten for oure feith at Tramissene
In listes thryes, and ay slayn his foo.
This ilke worthy knight hadde been also
Somtyme with the lord of Palatye,   65
Ageyn another hethen in Turkye;
And everemore he hadde a sovereyn prys.
And though that he were worthy, he was wys,
And of his port as meke as is a mayde.
He nevere yet no vileinye ne sayde   70
In al his lyf, unto no maner wight.
He was a verray, parfit, gentil knight.
But for to tellen yow of his array,
His hors were gode, but he was nat gay.
Of fustian he wered a gipoun   75
Al bismotered with his habergeoun,
For he was late y-come from his viage,
And wente for to doon his pilgrimage.
  With him ther was his sone, a young SQUYER,
A lovyere, and a lusty bacheler,   80
With lokkes crulle, as they were leyd in presse.

At Alexandria he was, when it was won.[5]
At banquets, he was many times the one
Seated with honor above all knights in Prussia;
In Lithuania, he'd raided, and in Russia,
Unrivalled among knightly Christian men.   55
In Granada, at the siege, he'd also been
Of Algeciras; he rode at Belmarin.
At Ayas and at Adalia he had been
When they fell; and then in the Great Sea[6]
At fine armed conquests, he fought worthily.   60
In fifteen mortal battles had he been,
And thrice he fought for God at Tlemcen
Alone in lists, and always slew his foe.
And this same worthy knight had been also
At one time fighting alongside Balat's lord   65
Against another Turkish heathen horde;
And always was his fame a sovereign prize.
Not only was he worthy, he was wise,
And in his bearing, meek as is a maid.
In all his life, no rude word had he said   70
To any man, however much his might.
He was a true and perfect gentle knight.
But now to tell you about his array,
His horse was good, but his dress was not gay.
His tunic was of fustian, coarse and plain,   75
Which by his rusty mailcoat was all stained,
For just lately he'd come from his voyage,
And now he went to make his pilgrimage.
      With him there was his son, a young SQUIRE,
A lover and in arms, a bachelor,   80
His locks waved like they'd seen a curling press.

5 **At Alexandria**, etc.: The Knight's many widely ranging campaigns represent both places where English knights were known to have fought in Chaucer's lifetime and battles against non-Christians. Insofar as is possible, the places here are given their modern names. The Knight's battles cover a vast portion of the known world in the fourteenth century.

6 **Great Sea**: The Mediterannean.

Of twenty yeer of age he was, I gesse.
Of his stature he was of evene lengthe,
And wonderly delivere, and of greet strengthe.
And he hadde been somtyme in chivachye   85
In Flaundres, in Artoys, and Picardye,
And born him wel, as of so litel space,
In hope to stonden in his lady grace.
Embrouded was he, as it were a mede
Al ful of fresshe floures, whyte and rede.   90
Singinge he was, or floytinge, al the day;
He was as fresh as is the month of May.
Short was his gowne, with sleves longe and wyde.
Wel coude he sitte on hors, and faire ryde.
He coude songes make and wel endyte,   95
Juste and eek daunce, and wel purtreye and wryte.
So hote he lovede that by nightertale
He sleep namore than dooth a nightingale.
Curteys he was, lowly, and servisable,
And carf biforn his fader at the table.   100
    A YEMAN hadde he, and servaunts namo
At that tyme, for him, liste ryde so;
And he was clad in cote and hood of grene.
A sheef of pecok arwes brighte and kene
Under his belt he bar ful thriftily.   105
Wel coude he dresse his takel yemanly:
His arwes drouped noght with fetheres lowe,
And in his hand he bar a mighty bowe.
A not-heed hadde he, with a broun visage.
Of wodecraft wel coude he al the usage.   110
Upon his arm he bar a gay bracer,
And by his syde a swerd and a bokeler,

About twenty years of age he was, I guess.
In his stature, he was of average length,
And wonderfully deft, and of great strength.
He'd ridden sometimes with the cavalry   85
In Flanders, in Artois, and Picardy,[7]
And fared quite well, within small time and space,
In hope of standing in his lady's grace.
Embroidered was he, as if he were a bed
All full of fresh spring flowers, white and red.   90
Singing he was, or fluting, all the day;
He was as fresh as is the month of May.
Short was his gown, its sleeves hung long and wide.
Well could he sit his horse, and nicely ride.
And also he wrote songs, both verse and note,   95
He jousted and he danced, he drew and wrote.
So hotly loved he that when nighttime came,
The nightingale and he slept both the same.
Courteous and meek, to serve, quite able,
He carved before his father at the table.[8]   100

    A YEOMAN had he—no servants beside,
For at this time, that's how he chose to ride,
And he was clad in coat and hood of green.
A sheaf of peacock arrows, bright and keen,
Under his belt, he bore quite properly   105
(For he could tend his gear quite yeomanly;
His arrows did not droop with feathers low),
And in his hand he bore a mighty bow.
A close-cropped head had he, a face well browned.
No man more skilled in woodcraft might be found.   110
Upon his arm he wore a gay wrist guard,
And by his side a small shield and a sword,

---

   7 **In Flanders,** etc.: These were battles fought in Northern Europe as part of England's Hundred Years' War with France (1337–1453), during which England attempted to regain control over significant territories to which it claimed rights in France.

   8 **carved before his father**: One of the tasks of a squire was to carve meats and game at the table for the knight whom the squire attended; here, it is also a sign of filial obedience and loyalty.

And on that other syde a gay daggere,
Harneised wel, and sharp as point of spere;
A Cristofre on his brest of silver shene.   115
An horn he bar, the bawdrik was of grene;
A forster was he, soothly, as I gesse.

      Ther was also a Nonne, a PRIORESSE,
That of hir smyling was ful simple and coy—
Hir gretteste ooth was but by Seynte Loy—   120
And she was cleped madame Eglentyne.
Ful wel she song the service divyne,
Entuned in hir nose ful semely;
And Frensh she spak ful faire and fetisly,
After the scole of Stratford atte Bowe,   125
For Frensh of Paris was to hire unknowe.
At mete wel y-taught was she with alle:
She leet no morsel from hir lippes falle,
Ne wette hir fingres in hir sauce depe.
Wel coude she carie a morsel, and wel kepe   130
That no drope ne fille upon hire brest.
In curteisye was set ful muchel hir lest.
Hir over-lippe wyped she so clene,
That in hir coppe was no ferthing sene
Of grece, whan she dronken hadde hir draughte.   135
Ful semely after hir mete she raughte,
And sikerly she was of greet disport,
And ful plesaunt, and amiable of port,
And peyned hire to countrefete chere
Of court, and to been estatlich of manere,   140

By his other side, a bright, gay dagger fell,
As sharp as a spear's point, and sheathed up well;
On his breast, a silver Christopher[9] was seen.   115
He bore a horn, its baldric was of green;
A forester, he was, truly, as I guess.
      There was also a Nun, a PRIORESS,[10]
Who in her smiling was simple and gracious;
Her greatest oath was "by Saint Eligius";[11]   120
And she was known as Madame Eglentine.[12]
Quite well she sang the liturgy divine,
Intoning it in her nose quite properly;
And French she spoke quite well and elegantly,
After the school[13] of Stratford-at-the-Bow,   125
Because Parisian French she did not know.
In dining, she was well taught overall;
She let no morsel down from her lips fall,
Nor wet her fingers in her sauce so deep;
Deftly she could lift up a bite, and keep   130
A single drop from falling on her breast.
In courtesy, she found what pleased her best.
Her upper lip she wiped so nice and clean
That in her cup no single speck was seen
Of grease, because she drank her drink so neat.   135
Quite daintily, she reached out for her meat.
And truthfully, she was so very pleasant,
And amiable, her manners excellent;
She pained herself to imitate the ways
Of court, and to be stately all her days,   140

---

9 **Christopher:** Medal of Saint Christopher, patron saint of travelers.

10 PRIORESS: Head of her convent, in charge of the spiritual health and material well-being of the nuns in her community.

11 **by Saint Eligius:** Reputed to be a particularly attractive French saint.

12 **Eglentine:** The name means "Briar Rose," and as many scholars have noted, is more appropriate to a courtly lady in a romance than a nun.

13 **After the school:** Meaning she spoke a provincial dialect rather than the more sophisticated French of the London court.

And to ben holden digne of reverence.
But, for to speken of hire conscience,
She was so charitable and so pitous,
She wolde wepe, if that she sawe a mous
Caught in a trappe, if it were deed or bledde.   145
Of smale houndes hadde she, that she fedde
With rosted flesh, or milk and wastel-breed.
But sore wepte she if oon of hem were deed,
Or if men smoot it with a yerde smerte;
And al was conscience and tendre herte.   150
Ful semely hir wimpel pinched was,
Hir nose tretys, hir eyen greye as glas,
Hir mouth ful smal, and therto softe and reed.
But sikerly she hadde a fair forheed—
It was almost a spanne brood, I trowe—   155
For hardily she was nat undergrowe.
Ful fetis was hir cloke, as I was war.
Of smal coral aboute hire arm she bar
A peire of bedes, gauded al with grene;
And theron heng a broche of gold ful shene,   160
On which ther was first write a crowned A,
And after, *Amor vincit omnia.*

    Another NONNE with hire hadde she,
That was hir chapeleyne, and PREESTES three.

    A MONK ther was, a fair for the maistrye,   165
An outrydere that lovede venerye:
A manly man, to been an abbot able.
Ful many a deyntee hors hadde he in stable,

And to be held worthy of reverence.
But, now, to speak about her conscience,
She was so full of pity and charity,
That she'd cry for a mouse that she might see
Caught in a trap, if it bled or was dead.   145
With her, she had her small hounds, which she fed
With roasted flesh, or milk and pure white bread.[14]
Sorely she wept if one of them were dead,
Or if men smote it so hard it would smart;
With her, all was conscience and tender heart.   150
Quite properly, her pleated wimple draped,
Her eyes blue gray as glass, her nose well shaped,
Her mouth quite small, and also soft and red.
But, certainly, she had a fair forehead;
It was almost a span in breadth,[15] I own;   155
For, truth to tell, she was not undergrown.
Quite elegant, her cloak, I was aware.
Made of small corals on her arm she'd bear
A rosary, set off with beads of green,
And thereon hung a broach of golden sheen,   160
On which the letter "A," inscribed and crowned
With "Amor vincit omnia"[16] was found.
        Another NUN riding with her had she,
Who was her secretary, and PRIESTS three.
        A MONK there was, the handsomest to see,   165
An outrider,[17] who most loved venery,[18]
A manly man, to be an abbot able.
Many a striking horse had he in stable,

14 **roasted flesh**, etc.: It is common to point out that the Prioress's dogs had a better diet than
that of the average late medieval peasant.
15 **a span in breadth**: The blue gray eyes, the red lips, and the broad forehead (a handspan broad)
of the Prioress were conventional traits assigned to courtly ladies in medieval romances.
16 **"Amor vincit omnia"**: Love conquers all.
17 **outrider**: A monk who was permitted to ride outside the monastery in order to conduct its
business.
18 **venery**: Hunting, but with an obvious pun on sexual pleasure.

And whan he rood, men mighte his brydel here
Ginglen in a whistling wind als clere   170
And eek as loude as dooth the chapel belle,
Ther as this lord was kepere of the celle.
The reule of Seint Maure or of Seint Beneit,
By cause that it was old and somdel streit,
This ilke monk leet olde thinges pace,   175
And held after the newe world the space.
He yaf nat of that text a pulled hen,
That seith that hunters ben nat holy men,
Ne that a monk, whan he is reccheless,
Is lykned til a fish that is waterlees   180
(This is to seyn, a monk out of his cloistre);
But thilke text held he nat worth an oistre.
And I seyde his opinioun was good:
What sholde he studie, and make himselven wood,
Upon a book in cloistre alwey to poure,   185
Or swinken with his handes and laboure
As Austin bit? How shal the world be served?
Lat Austin have his swink to him reserved!
Therfore he was a pricasour aright:
Grehoundes he hadde, as swifte as fowel in flight;   190
Of priking and of hunting for the hare
Was al his lust, for no cost wolde he spare.
I seigh his sleves purfiled at the hond
With grys, and that the fyneste of a lond;
And, for to festne his hood under his chin,   195
He hadde of gold y-wroght a ful curious pin:
A love-knotte in the gretter ende ther was.

And when he rode, men might his bridle hear
Jingling in a whistling wind as clear   170
And just as loud as tolls the chapel bell
Of the house where he was keeper of the cell.[19]
The rule of Saints Maurus and Benedict,[20]
Because it was so old and somewhat strict—
This same Monk let the old things pass away   175
And chose the new ways of the present day.
For that text he'd not give you one plucked hen
That said that hunters are not holy men,
Or that a monk who disobeys his order
Is likened to a fish out of the water—   180
That is to say, a monk out of the cloister.
But that text, he held not worth an oyster.
And I said his opinion was good.
What! Should he study, and make himself mad should
He, always poring over books in cloister,   185
Or should he work with his hands and labor
As Augustine bids?[21] How shall the world be served?
For Augustine, let this work be reserved!
A fine hard-pricking spursman he, all right;
He had greyhounds as swift as birds in flight;   190
In pricking and in hunting for the hare,
Lay all his lust; for no cost would he spare.
I saw his sleeves were fur lined at the hand
With rich, gray squirrel, the finest in the land;
And to fasten his hood beneath his chin,   195
He had, all wrought from gold, a fancy pin;
A love knot on the larger end was cast.

19 **keeper of the cell**: It is implied that the monk has the duty of supervising a smaller, dependent monastery, a duty to which he doesn't attend.

20 **Saints Maurus and Benedict**: Saint Benedict (fifth to sixth century), author of *The Rule of Saint Benedict*, which established principles for monastic living, and founder of the Benedictine order of monks; his follower Maurus introduced the rule to France.

21 **Augustine**: Bishop of Hippo (fourth to fifth century) and, as an early Church Father, one of the most significant voices in the establishment of Christian theology.

His heed was balled, that shoon as any glas,
And eek his face, as he had been anoint.
He was a lord ful fat and in good point: 200
His eyen stepe, and rollinge in his heed,
That stemed as a forneys of a leed;
His bootes souple, his hors in greet estat—
Now certeinly he was a fair prelat.
He was nat pale as a forpyned goost;   205
A fat swan loved he best of any roost.
His palfrey was as broun as is a berye.
        A FRERE ther was, a wantowne and a merye,
A limitour, a ful solempne man.
In alle the ordres foure is noon that can   210
So muchel of daliaunce and fair langage.
He hadde maad ful many a mariage
Of yonge wommen, at his owne cost.
Unto his ordre he was a noble post.
Ful wel biloved and famulier was he   215
With frankeleyns over al in his contree,
And eek with worthy wommen of the toun;
For he hadde power of confessioun,
As seyde himself, more than a curat,
For of his ordre he was licentiat.   220
Ful swetely herde he confessioun,
And plesaunt was his absolucioun;
He was an esy man to yeve penaunce
Ther as he wiste to have a good pitaunce.
For unto a povre ordre for to yive   225
Is signe that a man is wel y-shrive—
For if he yaf, he dorste make avaunt,

His head was bald, and it shone just like glass,
His face shone, too, as though he'd been anointed.
He was a lord full fat and well appointed;   200
His eyes rolled in his head and shone as bright
As fires under furnace pots cast light;
His boots were supple, his horses strong and fit;
Now, certainly, he was a fair prelate;
He was not pale like a tormented ghost.   205
A fat swan loved he best of any roast.
His palfrey was as brown as is a berry.
        A FRIAR there was, a wanton one, and merry,
A limitor,²² quite an important man.
In all four orders²³ is no one who can   210
Talk quite so smoothly, with such winning speech.
Many marriages made he in the breach
For young women and at his own expense.
In him, his order found a fine defense.
Quite well beloved and on close terms was he   215
With the franklins²⁴ all throughout his country,
And with all the town's most worthy women,
For he had the right to hear confession,
As he said, more than a curate surely,
For, by his order, he was licensed fully.   220
So, quite sweetly, would he hear confession,
And quite pleasant was his absolution:
He was an easy man in giving penance,
Where he knew he'd get more than a pittance.
If to a poor order one has given,   225
It's a sure sign that one's been well shriven;
If a man gave, he knew well what it meant:

22 **Limitor**: A friar who paid for rights to beg in a specific territory.

23 **four orders**: In the fourteenth century, there were four orders, or distinct groups, of friars: Franciscans, Augustinians, Carmelites, and Dominicans. Unlike monks who lived cloistered, friars were mendicants who lived primarily in urban areas, where, in light of their vows of poverty, they made their living by preaching and begging.

24 **franklins**: Wealthy upper-middle-class landowners; see Chaucer's pilgrim-franklin below.

He wiste that a man was repentaunt.
For many a man so hard is of his herte,
He may nat wepe althogh hym sore smerte: 230
Therfore, in stede of wepinge and preyeres,
Men moot yeve silver to the povre freres.
His tipet was ay farsed ful of knyves
And pinnes, for to yeven faire wyves.
And certeinly he hadde a murye note;   235
Wel coude he singe and pleyen on a rote;
Of yeddinges he bar outrely the prys.
His nekke whyt was as the flour-de-lys;
Therto he strong was as a champioun.
He knew the tavernes wel in every toun,   240
And everich hostiler and tappestere
Bet than a lazar or a beggestere,
For unto swich a worthy man as he
Acorded nat, as by his facultee,
To have with seke lazars aqueyntaunce: 245
It is nat honest, it may nat avaunce
For to delen with no swich poraille,
But al with riche and selleres of vitaille.
And over al, ther as profit sholde aryse,
Curteys he was, and lowely of servyse.   250
Ther nas no man nowher so vertuous.
He was the beste beggere in his hous,
[And yaf a certeyn ferme for the graunt: 252a
Noon of his bretheren cam ther in his haunt.]   252b
For thogh a widwe hadde noght a sho,
So plesaunt was his *In principio*,
Yet wolde he have a ferthing, er he wente.   255
His purchas was wel bettre than his rente.
And rage he coude, as it were right a whelpe;

He dared to boast that this man would repent.
For many a man is just so hard of heart,
He may not weep, though he may sorely smart.   230
Therefore, instead of giving tears and prayers,
Men must yield up their silver to poor friars.
His hood's tip always was stuffed full of knives
And pins, for him to give out to fair wives.
Certainly his merry voice was pleasing: 235
And he could play the fiddle well and sing;
For ballads, he took first prize utterly.
His neck was white as is the fleur-de-lis.
A strong champion was he in a brawl.
The taverns in each town, he knew them all;   240
Each inkeeper and every barmaid, too,
More than lepers or beggar girls, he knew,
Because, for such a worthy man as he,
It would not do, with his ability,
With sick lepers to have an acquaintance.   245
It is not right; it hardly can advance
Him if he has to spend time with the poor,
Just with the rich and victualers, for sure.
And over all, where profit should arise,
Polite was he, and served in humble guise.   250
No man was so effective anywhere:
He was, in his house, the best beggar there.
For private begging turf, he laid out rent;   252a
None of his brothers came there where he went;   252b
And although one were a shoeless widow,
So charming was his "In principio,"[25]
A farthing he would get before he went.   255
His income was much higher than his rent.
And he could rage just like a little whelp.

25 **"In principio"**: In the beginning, the opening lines of the Gospel of Saint John, often used by
friars in their preaching, greetings, or salutations.

In love-dayes ther coude he muchel helpe,
For there he was nat lyk a cloisterer,
With a thredbare cope, as is a povre scoler. 260
But he was lyk a maister or a pope:
Of double worsted was his semi-cope,
That rounded as a belle out of the presse.
Somwhat he lipsed, for his wantownesse,
To make his English swete upon his tonge; 265
And in his harping, whan that he hadde songe,
His eyen twinkled in his heed aright
As doon the sterres in the frosty night.
This worthy limitour was cleped Huberd.
      A MARCHANT was ther with a forked berd, 270
In mottelee, and hye on horse he sat;
Upon his heed a Flaundrish bever hat,
His bootes clasped faire and fetisly.
His resons he spak ful solempnely,
Souninge alway th'encrees of his winning. 275
He wolde the see were kept for any thing
Bitwixe Middleburgh and Orewelle.
Wel coude he in eschaunge sheeldes selle.
This worthy man ful wel his wit bisette:
Ther wiste no wight that he was in dette, 280
So estatly was he of his governaunce,
With his bargaynes and with his chevisaunce.
For sothe he was a worthy man with alle,
But sooth to seyn, I noot how men him calle.
      A CLERK ther was of Oxenford also, 285
That unto logik hadde longe y-go.
As leene was his hors as is a rake,
And he nas nat right fat, I undertake,

On love-days,²⁶ like a judge, well could he help,
For there, he was not like a cloisterer
In a threadbare cloak, like a poor scholar,   260
But like a master or the pope as well.
Of double worsted, rounded as a bell
Fresh from the casting, was his short, rich cloak.
With affectation, he lisped when he spoke,
To make his English sweet upon his tongue;   265
In his harping, whenever he had sung,
His eyes would twinkle in his head as bright
As do the stars upon a frosty night.
This worthy limitor was named Huberd.

    A MERCHANT was there, too, with a forked beard,   270
In mixed-hued clothes; high on his horse he sat;
Upon his head, a Flemish beaver hat,
And his fair boots were fastened stylishly.
He uttered his ideas quite solemnly,
Sounding always increase in his winning.   275
He wished the sea safe, more than anything,
Between the ports of Middleburgh and Orwell.²⁷
Well could he in exchange²⁸ his florins sell.
This worthy man quite deftly used his wit:
Were he in debt, no one would know of it,   280
So stately was he in his management
Of borrowing, buying, selling where he went.
Surely, he was a worthy man, in all,
But, truth to say, I don't know what he's called.

    A CLERK from Oxford was with us also,   285
Whose work in logic started long ago.
As skinny was his horse as is a rake,
And he was not so fat, I undertake;

---

26 **love-days**: Special days devoted to adjudicating disputes; often, clergy could serve as adjudicators.

27 **Middleburgh and Orwell**: Dutch and English ports, respectively.

28 **exchange**: Foreign exchange or currency sales.

But loked holwe, and therto soberly.
Ful thredbar was his overest courtepy,   290
For he hadde geten him yet no benefyce,
Ne was so worldly for to have offyce;
For him was levere have at his beddes heed
Twenty bokes, clad in blak or reed,
Of Aristotle and his philosophye,   295
Than robes riche, or fithele, or gay sautrye.
But al be that he was a philosophre,
Yet hadde he but litel gold in cofre;
But al that he mighte of his freendes hente,
On bokes and on lerninge he it spente,   300
And bisily gan for the soules preye
Of hem that yaf him wherwith to scoleye.
Of studie took he most cure and most hede.
Noght o word spak he more than was nede,
And that was seyd in forme and reverence,   305
And short and quik, and ful of hy sentence.
Souninge in moral vertu was his speche,
And gladly wolde he lerne, and gladly teche.
        A SERGEANT OF THE LAWE, war and wys,
That often hadde been at the Parvys,   310
Ther was also, ful riche of excellence.
Discreet he was and of greet reverence:
He semed swich, his wordes weren so wyse.
Justyce he was ful often in assyse,
By patente and by pleyn commissioun;   315
For his science and for his heigh renoun,

He looked hollow, and thus, grave and remote.
Quite threadbare was his outermost short coat;   290
He had as yet no clerical appointment,
And wasn't made for secular employment.
For he would rather have, at his bed's head,
Twenty books,[29] all well bound in black or red,
Of Aristotle and his philosophy   295
Than rich robes, or fiddle, or gay psaltery.[30]
But, for all that he was a philosopher,[31]
He had little gold piled in his coffer;
For anything that his friends to him lent,
On books and on his learning, it got spent.   300
Busily, for the souls of them he prayed
Who, so that he could go to school, had paid.
Of his studies, he took most care and heed.
Not one word spoke he more than he had need,
And that was said with dignity and respect,   305
And short, and quick, and full of intellect;
Resounding in moral virtue was his speech,
And gladly would he learn, and gladly teach.
    A SERGEANT OF THE LAW,[32] wary and wise,
Who often in Saint Paul's court did advise,   310
There was also, quite rich in excellence.
Dignified and judicious in each sense—
Or he seemed such, his words were all so wise.
He was often a judge at the assize,
With full commission—and through royal consent.   315
For all his learning and his fame's extent,

29 **Twenty books**, etc.: Given the expensiveness of handmade manuscripts, such a library would
have been quite costly.

30 **psaltery**: A small harp.

31 **a philosopher**: Alchemists, who sought to turn base metal into gold, were also called philoso-
phers. While some alchemists were frauds and con artists, others were not so much interested in mate-
rial wealth as the intellectual pursuit associated with alchemical research. Many alchemical findings
became the basis of the science of chemistry.

32 SERGEANT OF THE LAW: Judge serving under royal appointment.

Of fees and robes hadde he many oon.
So greet a purchasour was nowher noon:
Al was fee simple to him in effect;
His purchasing mighte nat been infect.   320
Nowher so bisy a man as he ther nas;
And yet he semed bisier than he was.
In termes hadde he caas and domes alle,
That from the tyme of King William were falle.
Therto he coude endyte, and make a thing;   325
Ther coude no wight pinche at his wryting,
And every statut coude he pleyn by rote.
He rood but hoomly in a medlee cote,
Girt with a ceint of silk, with barres smale;
Of his array telle I no lenger tale.   330
      A FRANKELEYN was in his companye.
Whyt was his berd as is the dayesye;
Of his complexioun he was sangwyn.
Wel loved he by the morwe a sop in wyn.
To liven in delyt was evere his wone,   335
For he was Epicurus owene sone,
That heeld opinioun that pleyn delyt
Was verray felicitee parfyt.
An housholdere, and that a greet, was he;
Seint Julian he was in his contree.   340
His breed, his ale, was alweys after oon;
A bettre envyned man was nowher noon.
Withoute bake mete was nevere his hous,
Of fish and flesh, and that so plentevous
It snewed in his hous of mete and drinke.   345

Fees and robes, he did have, many a one.
So great a land buyer elsewhere was none:
He would directly buy up the estate;
His purchase, no one could invalidate.   320
Nowhere was such a busy man as he;
He seemed busier than he was, actually.
He knew the precedents for everything
The law had done since William[33] was the king.
Fine legal texts, thus could he draft and draw   325
In which no one could find a single flaw;
Every statute, he could recite by rote.
He rode there in a simple mixed-hued coat.
A striped silk belt around his waist he wore;
About his dress, I won't tell any more.   330
    A FRANKLIN[34] rode there in his company,
And his beard was white as is the daisy;
His mood was sanguine, his face rosy red.
Well loved he, in the morning, wine-soaked bread;
To live in sheer delight was his one care,   335
For he was Epicurus's[35] own heir,
Who thought that to lead life in all its pleasure
Was true perfect bliss beyond all measure.
A householder, and a full great one, was he;
A Saint Julian[36] he was, in his country.   340
His bread, his ale, were always very fine;
No other man had better stocks of wine.
His house was never lacking in baked meat,
Or fish or flesh, in plenty so complete
That it snowed, in his house, with food and drink,   345

33 **William**: William the Conqueror, who came from France to conquer England at the Battle of Hastings in 1066.

34 A **FRANKLIN**: Wealthy landowner.

35 **Epicurus**: Greek philosopher (fourth to third century B.C.E.), whose school of thought argued for the essential goodness in life of happiness and pleasure; in the Middle Ages his ideas became linked with hedonism.

36 **Saint Julian**: Patron saint of hospitality.

Of alle deyntees that men coude thinke,
After the sondry sesons of the yeer,
So chaunged he his mete and his soper.
Ful many a fat partrich hadde he in mewe,
And many a breem and many a luce in stewe.   350
Wo was his cook, but if his sauce were
Poynaunt and sharp, and redy al his gere.
His table dormant in his halle alway
Stood redy covered al the longe day.
At sessiouns ther was he lord and sire;   355
Ful ofte tyme he was knight of the shire.
An anlas and a gipser al of silk
Heng at his girdel, whyt as morne milk.
A shirreve hadde he been, and a countour;
Was nowher such a worthy vavasour.   360
        An HABERDASSHER and a CARPENTER,
A WEBBE, a DYERE, and a TAPICER,
Were with us eek, clothed in o liveree
Of a solempne and greet fraternitee.
Ful fresh and newe hir gere apyked was;   365
Hir knyves were chaped noght with bras,
But al with silver; wroght ful clene and weel
Hire girdles and hire pouches everydeel.
Wel semed ech of hem a fair burgeys
To sitten in a yeldhalle on a deys.   370
Everich, for the wisdom that he can,
Was shaply for to been an alderman.
For catel hadde they ynogh and rente,
And eek hir wyves wolde it wel assente;
And elles certein were they to blame.   375
It is ful fair to been y-clept "*Madame,*"

With any dainties of which men could think,
According to the seasons of the year,
New dishes on his table would appear.
Fat partridges in coops, when he did like;
He kept his fish pond stocked with bream and pike. 350
And woe unto his cook if he'd not got
His gear set and the sauce, spicy and hot.
Covered and ready did his table stay
Set up for meals within the hall all day.
At county courts,[37] he was the lord and sire; 355
And went to Parliament to serve his shire.
A two-edged dagger and a purse of silk
Hung from his girdle, white as morning's milk.
A sheriff had he been, an auditor,[38]
And nowhere such a worthy landholder. 360
    A HABERDASHER and a CARPENTER,
A WEAVER, DYER, and a TAPESTRY MAKER—
They were all clothed in the same livery
Of one great parish guild fraternity.
All fresh and newly furbished was their gear; 365
On their knives no brass mountings were found here,
But only silver; fashioned just as fit,
Their girdles and their purses, every bit.
Each of them seemed such a worthy burgess[39]
He might sit in the guildhall on the dais. 370
And each, with all the wisdom that he can,
Was suited to be made an alderman.[40]
Income had they enough, and property,
To this their wives would certainly agree;
Or else, quite surely, they would all be blamed. 375
It is quite nice "My Lady" to be named,

37 **At county courts:** It was customary for the lord of the manor to adjudicate at sessions of the county court.
38 **an auditor:** Tax collector.
39 **burgess:** Wealthy citizen-tradesman.
40 **alderman:** Elected official of the city.

And goon to vigilyës al bifore,
And have a mantel royalliche y-bore.
    A Cook they hadde with hem for the nones,
To boille the chiknes with the mary-bones   380
And poudre-marchant tart and galingale.
Wel coude he knowe a draughte of London ale.
He coude roste, and sethe, and broille, and frye,
Maken mortreux, and wel bake a pye.
But greet harm was it, as it thoughte me,   385
That on his shine a mormal hadde he.
For blankmanger, that made he with the beste.
    A Shipman was ther, woninge fer by weste:
For aught I woot, he was of Dertemouthe.
He rood upon a rouncy, as he couthe,   390
In a gowne of falding to the knee.
A daggere hanginge on a laas hadde he
Aboute his nekke, under his arm adoun.
The hote somer hadde maad his hewe al broun;
And certeinly he was a good felawe.   395
Ful many a draughte of wyn had he y-drawe
Fro Burdeux-ward, whyl that the chapman sleep.
Of nyce conscience took he no keep:
If that he faught, and hadde the hyer hond,
By water he sente hem hoom to every lond.   400
But of his craft, to rekene wel his tydes,
His stremes and his daungers him bisydes,
His herberwe and his mone, his lodemenage,
Ther nas noon swich from Hulle to Cartage.
Hardy he was, and wys to undertake;   405
With many a tempest hadde his berd been shake.
He knew wel alle the havenes, as they were,

At feasts and vigils, to march first in line,
And have, borne royally, a mantel fine.

    For this trip, a COOK rode with them then
To boil the marrowbones up with the hens,   380
Along with spices tart and galingale.[41]
Well did he know a draught of London ale.
He could both roast and simmer, boil and fry,
Make stews and hash and also bake a pie.
But it was a real shame, it seemed to me,   385
That on his shin, a pus-filled sore had he.
A milky pudding made he with the best.

    A SHIPMAN was there, who lived in the west;
He came from Dartmouth, for all that I guessed.
To ride a packhorse he did try his best,   390
In a gown of coarse wool cloth cut to the knee.
A dagger hanging on a strap had he
Around his neck, under his arm coming down.
The hot summer had turned his skin all brown.
And certainly, he was a good fellow.   395
So many draughts of fine wine from Bordeaux
Had he drawn, while the merchants were asleep.
In a good conscience, small stock did he keep.
If, when he fought, he had the upper hand,
He sent them all, by water, back to land.[42]   400
But in the art of reckoning the tides,
The currents and all perils near, besides,
The moon and piloting and anchorage,
No one was so skilled from Hull to Carthage.[43]
Hardy and wise in what was undertaken,   405
With many tempests had his beard been shaken.
He knew well all the harbors that there were,

41 **galingale**: A sweet, powdered spice.
42 **by water, back to land**: The implication is that he threw them overboard.
43 **from Hull to Carthage**: From England either to Carthage in North Africa, or to Spain (Cartagena).

From Gootlond to the cape of Finistere,
And every cryke in Britayne and in Spayne;
His barge y-cleped was the Maudelayne.   410
      With us ther was a DOCTOUR OF PHISYK;
In al this world ne was ther noon him lyk
To speke of phisik and of surgerye,
For he was grounded in astronomye.
He kepte his pacient a ful greet deel   415
In houres, by his magik naturel.
Wel coude he fortunen the ascendent
Of his images for his pacient.
He knew the cause of everich maladye,
Were it of hoot or cold, or moiste, or drye,   420
And where engendred, and of what humour;
He was a verrey parfit practisour.
The cause y-knowe, and of his harm the roote,
Anon he yaf the seke man his boote.
Ful redy hadde he his apothecaries   425
To sende him drogges and his letuaries,
For ech of hem made other for to winne;
Hir frendschipe nas nat newe to biginne.
Wel knew he the olde Esculapius,
And Deiscorides, and eek Rufus,   430
Old Ypocras, Haly, and Galien,
Serapion, Razis, and Avicen,
Averrois, Damascien, and Constantyn,
Bernard, and Gatesden, and Gilbertyn.
Of his diete mesurable was he,   435
For it was of no superfluitee
But of greet norissing and digestible.

Stretching from Gotland to Cape Finisterre,[44]

And each inlet from Brittany to Spain;

His sailing ship was called the "Magdalene." 410

    With us was a DOCTOR OF MEDICINE;

No one was like him, all the world within,

To speak of medicine and surgery,

For he was schooled well in astrology.

Through natural magic,[45] he gave patients hope 415

By keeping close watch on their horoscope.

He could divine when planets were ascendant

To aid the star signs governing his patient.

Of every malady, he knew the source

In humors hot, cold, moist, or dry, of course, 420

And where they were engendered, from which humor.

He was a perfect, true practitioner.

The cause and root known of the malady,

At once he gave the sick their remedy.

Quite ready had he his apothecaries 425

To send him their drugs and electuaries,[46]

For each made profit for the other one—

Their friendship had not recently begun.

Well knew he his old Aesculapius,[47]

Dioscorides, and also Rufus, 430

Old Hippocrates, Hali, and Galen,

Rhazes, Avicenna, Serapion,

Averroes, Damascien, Constantinus,

Bernard, Gaddesden, Gilbertus Anglicus.

Of his own diet, moderate was he, 435

For it contained no superfluity,

But was nourishing and digestible.

---

44 **from Gotland to Cape Finisterre**: From Sweden to Spain.

45 **natural magic**: Science associated with medicine and its treatments.

46 **electuaries**: Medicinal compounds.

47 **Aesculapius**: The list of names of medical authorities that follows ranges from the ancient Greeks to the Persians and Arabs, down through the early Christians to recent medieval English authorities.

His studie was but litel on the Bible.
In sangwin and in pers he clad was al,
Lyned with taffata and with sendal;   440
And yet he was but esy of dispence.
He kepte that he wan in pestilence,
For gold in phisik is a cordial;
Therefore he lovede gold in special.

      A good WYF was ther of bisyde BATHE,   445
But she was somdel deef, and that was scathe.
Of clooth-making she hadde swiche an haunt,
She passed hem of Ypres and of Gaunt.
In al the parisshe wyf ne was ther noon
That to the offringe bifore hir sholde goon;   450
And if ther dide, certeyn so wrooth was she,
That she was out of alle charitee.
Hir coverchiefs ful fyne were of ground;
I dorste swere they weyeden ten pound
That on a Sonday weren upon hir heed.   455
Hir hosen weren of fyn scarlet reed,
Ful streite y-teyd, and shoos ful moiste and newe.
Bold was hir face, and fair, and reed of hewe.
She was a worthy womman al hir lyve:
Housbondes at chirche dore she hadde fyve,   460
Withouten other companye in youthe—
But therof nedeth nat to speke as nouthe—
And thryes hadde she been at Jerusalem.
She hadde passed many a straunge streem:
At Rome she hadde been, and at Boloigne,   465
In Galice at Seint Jame, and at Coloigne;
She coude muchel of wandringe by the weye.

His study was but little on the Bible.

In blood red and in blue he was all clad,

A lining of two kinds of silk he had.   440

Yet he was quite cautious with expenses;

He saved what he earned in pestilences.

In medicine, gold[48] works well for the heart,

Therefore, he'd loved gold from the very start.

     A good WIFE was there from nearby to BATH;   445

It was a pity she was deaf by half.

In cloth-making she had such a talent

She far passed those from Ypres and from Ghent.[49]

And throughout all her parish, there was no

Wife who might first to the offering go   450

Before her; if one did, so mad was she

That she lost any sense of charity.

Her coverchiefs of fine linen were found;

I dare swear that they weighed a full ten pounds,

The ones that, Sundays, sat upon her head.   455

Her stockings were all fine and scarlet red,

Quite tightly laced, her shoes quite soft and new.

Bold was her face, and fair, and red of hue.

All her life, she was a worthy woman,

Husbands at the church door, she'd had five then,   460

Not counting other company in youth—

No need to speak of that now, to tell the truth.

And thrice she had been to Jerusalem;[50]

Many a foreign sea, she'd covered them;

At Rome she'd been, and also at Boulogne,   465

At Saint James in Galicia and Cologne.

She knew much of wandering by the way.

---

48 **gold**: Gold was considered a medicine in the Middle Ages.

49 **from Ypres, and from Ghent**: The Low Countries were famous for making particularly fine cloth. Rivalries between English and Flemish clothmakers were especially intense in the late fourteenth century.

50 **Jerusalem**: The Wife had traveled to all the famous pilgrimage sites in Christendom, ranging from the most important in Jersusalem and Italy to those in Germany, France, and Spain.

Gat-tothed was she, soothly for to seye.
Upon an amblere esily she sat,
Y-wimpled wel, and on hir heed an hat   470
As brood as is a bokeler or a targe;
A foot-mantel aboute hir hipes large,
And on hir feet a paire of spores sharpe.
In felawschipe wel coude she laughe and carpe.
Of remedyes of love she knew per chaunce,   475
For she coude of that art the olde daunce.
          A good man was ther of religioun,
And was a povre PERSOUN of a toun,
But riche he was of holy thoght and werk.
He was also a lerned man, a clerk,   480
That Cristes gospel trewely wolde preche;
His parisshens devoutly wolde he teche.
Benigne he was, and wonder diligent,
And in adversitee ful pacient,
And swich he was y-preved ofte sythes.   485
Ful looth were him to cursen for his tithes,
But rather wolde he yeven, out of doute,
Unto his povre parisshens aboute
Of his offring, and eek of his substaunce.
He coude in litel thing han suffisaunce.   490
Wyd was his parisshe, and houses fer asonder,
But he ne lafte nat, for reyn ne thonder,
In siknes nor in meschief, to visyte
The ferreste in his parisshe, muche and lyte,
Upon his feet, and in his hand a staf.   495
This noble ensample to his sheep he yaf,
That first he wroghte, and afterward he taughte.
Out of the gospel he tho wordes caughte,
And this figure he added eek therto,
That if gold ruste, what shal iren do?   500
For if a preest be foul, on whom we truste,

Gap toothed[51] she was, it is the truth to say.
Quite easily on her ambling horse she sat,
Wearing a wimpled headdress and a hat   470
Like a buckler or a shield as broad and round;
A foot-mantle about her large hips wound,
And on her feet a pair of sharp spurs poked.
In fellowship, quite well she laughed and joked.
The remedies of love she knew by heart,   475
For of that old dance, she knew all the art.
      A good man was there of religion,
Of a town, he served as the poor PARSON.
But he was rich in holy thought and work.
He was also a learned man, a clerk,   480
And Christ's gospel truthfully he would preach;
His parishioners devoutly he would teach.
Gracious he was, a wonder of diligence,
And in adversity, he had such patience,
And in this, he had often tested been.   485
For tithes, he found it loathsome to curse men,
But he would rather give, there is no doubt,
To his poor parishioners, round about,
From Mass offerings and his own pay, too.
With little, he could easily make do.   490
Wide was his parish, the houses far asunder,
But he would not leave them, for rain or thunder,
If sickness or if trouble should befall
The farthest in his parish, great or small,
He'd go on foot; his staff in hand he'd keep.   495
This noble example he gave to his sheep:
That first he wrought, and afterward, he taught.
Out of the Gospels, those words he had caught,
And his own metaphor he added, too:
If gold should rust, then what will iron do?   500
For if a priest is foul, in whom we trust,

51 **Gap toothed**: This was considered a sign of being highly sexed.

No wonder is a lewed man to ruste;
And shame it is, if a preest take keep,
A shiten shepherde and a clene sheep.
Wel oghte a preest ensample for to yive,   505
By his clennesse, how that his sheep sholde live.
He sette nat his benefice to hyre,
And leet his sheep encombred in the myre,
And ran to London unto Seynte Poules
To seken him a chaunterie for soules,   510
Or with a bretherhed to been withholde,
But dwelte at hoom, and kepte wel his folde,
So that the wolf ne made it nat miscarie;
He was a shepherde and noght a mercenarie.
And though he holy were, and vertuous,   515
He was to sinful men nat despitous,
Ne of his speche daungerous ne digne,
But in his teching discreet and benigne.
To drawen folk to heven by fairnesse,
By good ensample, this was his bisinesse;   520
But it were any persone obstinat,
What so he were, of heigh or lough estat,
Him wolde he snibben sharply for the nones.
A bettre preest I trowe that nowher noon is.
He wayted after no pompe and reverence,   525
Ne maked him a spyced conscience,
But Cristes lore, and his apostles twelve,
He taughte, and first he folwed it himselve.
        With him ther was a PLOWMAN, was his brother,
That hadde y-lad of dong ful many a fother.   530
A trewe swinkere and a good was he,
Livinge in pees and parfit charitee.

No wonder that a foolish man should rust;
And it's a shame, if care he does not keep—
A shepherd to be shitty with clean sheep.
Well should a priest a good example give,   505
By his own cleanness, how his sheep should live.
His parish, he would not put out for hire
And leave his sheep encumbered in the mire
To run to London to Saint Paul's to switch
And be a chantry priest[52] just for the rich,   510
Nor by guild brothers[53] would he be detained;
But he stayed home and with his flock remained,
So that the wolf would not make it miscarry;
He was a shepherd, not a mercenary.
And though he holy was, and virtuous,   515
To sinners, he was not contemptuous,
Not haughty nor aloof was he in speech,
With courtesy and kindness would he teach.
To draw folks up to heaven with his fairness,
By good example: this was all his business.   520
But if there were a person who was stubborn,
Whoever he was, high or low rank born,
Then he would scold him sharply, at the least.
There is nowhere, I know, a better priest.
He waited for no pomp or reverence;   525
For him, no finicky, affected conscience,
But the words of Christ and his apostles twelve
He taught: but first, he followed them himself.
        With him, his brother who was a PLOWMAN rode;
Of dung, this man had hauled out many a load;   530
A true laborer, and a good one was he,
Living in peace and perfect charity.

52 chantry priest: A priest officiating in a chapel endowed by the wealthy so that he could pray
for the souls of those patrons.
53 guild brothers: The guilds often had their own churches and priests. Like chantry priests,
those officiating for guild brothers would earn considerably more income than a parish priest in a
poor, rural location.

God loved he best with al his hole herte
At alle tymes, thogh him gamed or smerte,
And thanne his neighebour right as himselve.   535
He wolde thresshe, and therto dyke and delve,
For Cristes sake, for every povre wight,
Withouten hyre, if it lay in his might.
His tythes payed he ful faire and wel,
Bothe of his propre swink and his catel.   540
In a tabard he rood upon a mere.

      Ther was also a Reve and a Millere,
A Somnour and a Pardoner also,
A Maunciple, and myself—ther were namo.

      The MILLERE was a stout carl for the nones;   545
Ful big he was of brawn, and eek of bones—
That proved wel, for over al ther he cam,
At wrastling he wolde have alwey the ram.
He was short-sholdred, brood, a thikke knarre:
Ther nas no dore that he nolde heve of harre,   550
Or breke it at a renning with his heed.
His berd as any sowe or fox was reed,
And therto brood, as though it were a spade.
Upon the cop right of his nose he hade
A werte, and theron stood a tuft of herys,   555
Reed as the bristles of a sowes erys;
His nosethirles blake were and wyde.
A swerd and a bokeler bar he by his syde.
His mouth as greet was as a greet forneys;
He was a janglere and a goliardeys,   560
And that was most of sinne and harlotryes.
Wel coude he stelen corn, and tollen thryes,
And yet he hadde a thombe of gold, pardee.
A whyt cote and a blew hood wered he.

God loved he best with all of his whole heart
At all times, though it caused him joy or smart,
And next, his neighbor, just as he loved himself.   535
He would thresh, dig ditches, and also delve,
For Christ's sake and the sake of each poor man,
And without pay, he'd do all that he can.
His tithes, with all due fairness, he'd not shirk,
But paid from what he owned and with his work.   540
In a workman's smock, he rode on a mare.

    A REEVE and a MILLER were also there,
A SUMMONER and then a PARDONER,
A MANCIPLE and myself—that's all there were.

    The MILLER was a stout churl, it is true;   545
Quite big he was in brawn, and in bones, too.
That stood him in good stead; for where he came,
He'd win the ram[54] in every wrestling game.
He was short necked and broad, a thick-thewed thug;
There was no door around he couldn't lug   550
Right off its hinges, or break with his head.
His beard, just like a sow or fox, was red,
And also broad, as though it was a spade.
Right up atop his nose's ridge was laid
A wart; on it, a tuft of hairs grew now,   555
Red as the bristles in ears of a sow;
His nostrils were quite black, and also wide.
A sword and buckler bore he by his side.
His mouth was as great as a great cauldron.
A jangling goliard, he was quite the one—   560
Of sin and harlotries, he most would tell.
He made three times his pay and stole corn well;
And yet, he had a thumb of gold,[55] all right.
A blue hood wore he, and a coat of white.

54 **the ram**: Prize for the winner of a wrestling game.

55 **a thumb of gold**: Ironic statement based on the old adage: "An honest Miller has a golden thumb." Millers were stereotyped as thieving.

A baggepype wel coude he blowe and sowne,   565
And therwithal he broghte us out of towne.
     A gentil MAUNCIPLE was ther of a temple,
Of which achatours mighte take exemple
For to be wyse in bying of vitaille,
For whether that he payde, or took by taille,   570
Algate he wayted so in his achat
That he was ay biforn and in good stat.
Now is nat that of God a ful fair grace,
That swich a lewed mannes wit shal pace
The wisdom of an heep of lerned men?   575
Of maistres hadde he mo than thryes ten
That weren of lawe expert and curious,
Of which ther were a doseyn in that hous
Worthy to been stiwardes of rente and lond
Of any lord that is in Engelond,   580
To make him live by his propre good
In honour, dettelees, but he were wood,
Or live as scarsly as him list desire,
And able for to helpen al a shire
In any cas that mighte falle or happe;   585
And yit this maunciple sette hir aller cappe.
     The REVE was a sclendre colerik man.
His berd was shave as ny as ever he can;
His heer was by his eres ful round y-shorn,
His top was dokked lyk a preest biforn.   590
Ful longe were his legges, and ful lene,
Ylyk a staf; ther was no calf y-sene.
Wel coude he kepe a gerner and a binne—
Ther was noon auditour coude on him winne.
Wel wiste he by the droghte and by the reyn   595
The yeldinge of his seed and of his greyn.

A bagpipe he knew how to blow and play. 565
And sounding it, he led us on our way.
    A good MANCIPLE[56] did business for a law school;
All food buyers could follow well his rule
For prudent buying; it would earn them merit;
For, whether he paid straight or took on credit, 570
In buying, he watched carefully and waited,
So he was in good shape and well ahead.
Now, is it not from God a sign of grace
That this unlearned man's wit can outpace
The wisdom of a heap of learned men? 575
Of his masters, he had more than thrice ten,
Who were quite skilled and expert in the law,
And in that house, a full dozen one saw
Worthy to be stewards of rents and land
For any lord who dwells now in England, 580
To make him live within the means he had
In debtless honor (unless he were mad),
Or as frugally as he could desire,
And able thus to help out all the shire
In any circumstance that may befall: 585
And yet this Manciple hoodwinked them all.
    The REEVE[57] was a slender, choleric man.
He shaved his beard as closely as one can;
His hair, short and up by his ears, he'd crop,
And, like a priest's, he'd dock it on the top. 590
Quite long his legs were; they were also lean,
And just like sticks; no calf was to be seen.
He could well guard the granary and bin;
No auditor around could with him win.
He knew well, by the drought and by the rain, 595
The yieldings of his seed and of his grain.

---

56 MANCIPLE: Business agent for a university, who purchased food and provisions for the institution. Chaucer's Manciple specifically works for a law school.
    57 The REEVE: Farm or estate manager.

His lordes sheep, his neet, his dayerye,
His swyn, his hors, his stoor, and his pultrye,
Was hoolly in this reves governinge,
And by his covenaunt yaf the rekeninge,   600
Sin that his lord was twenty yeer of age.
Ther coude no man bringe him in arrerage.
Ther nas baillif, ne herde, ne other hyne,
That he ne knew his sleighte and his covyne;
They were adrad of him as of the deeth.   605
His woning was ful fair upon an heeth;
With grene trees shadwed was his place.
He coude bettre than his lord purchace.
Ful riche he was astored prively;
His lord wel coude he plesen subtilly,   610
To yeve and lene him of his owne good,
And have a thank, and yet a cote and hood.
In youthe he hadde lerned a good mister:
He was a wel good wrighte, a carpenter.
This reve sat upon a ful good stot   615
That was al pomely grey and highte Scot.
A long surcote of pers upon he hade,
And by his syde he bar a rusty blade.
Of Northfolk was this reve of which I tell,
Bisyde a toun men clepen Baldeswelle.   620
Tukked he was as is a frere aboute;
And evere he rood the hindreste of oure route.

  A SOMONOUR was ther with us in that place,
That hadde a fyr-reed cherubinnes face,
For sawcefleem he was, with eyen narwe.   625
As hoot he was and lecherous as a sparwe,
With scalled browes blake, and piled berd;

His lord's sheep, his cattle, and his dairy,
His swine and horses, his livestock and poultry
Were wholly under this Reeve's governing,
And by his contract, he gave reckoning,   600
Because his lord, in age, was twenty years.
No man alive could bring him in arrears.
No bailiff, herdsman, worker there might be
But he knew all their tricks and treachery;
As they feared death, of him they were all scared.   605
His dwelling place upon a heath was fair;
All shaded with green trees on every hand.
He could, much better than his lord, buy land.
Quite richly had he stocked up, privately.
And he could please his lord so cleverly   610
That he'd lend to him from his lord's own goods,
And have his thanks, then, plus a coat and hood.
When he was young, he had learned a fine trade,
A good wright, a skilled carpenter he made.
The Reeve on his stout farm horse sat that day,   615
Which was called Scot and was a dapple gray.
His overcoat was long, of darkish blue,
And by his side, a rusty blade hung, too.
From Norfolk was this Reeve, of whom I tell,
From near a town that men call Baldeswell.   620
Like a friar's, he tucked his coat up fast.
In our company, he always rode the last.
        A SUMMONER[58] was with us in that place,
Who had a fiery-red cherubic face,[59]
Pimply was he, with eyes swollen and narrow.   625
Hot he was and lecherous as a sparrow,
With scabbed black brows; his beard had lost some hair.

58 A SUMMONER: Someone who served summonses to appear before the ecclesiastical court. Ecclesiastical courts in the Middle Ages adjudicated issues involving domestic and moral disputes.

59 fiery-red cherubic face: It's clear that the Summoner suffers from a skin condition. Often in medieval paintings, angels are depicted with bright red faces, but their faces glow from love of God.

Of his visage children were aferd.

Ther nas quiksilver, litarge, ne brimstoon,

Boras, ceruce, ne oille of tartre noon,   630

Ne oynement that wolde clense and byte,

That him mighte helpen of his whelkes whyte,

Nor of the knobbes sittinge on his chekes.

Wel loved he garleek, oynons, and eek lekes,

And for to drinken strong wyn, reed as blood.   635

Thanne wolde he speke, and crye as he were wood;

And whan that he wel dronken hadde the wyn,

Thanne wolde he speke no word but Latyn.

A fewe termes hadde he, two or three,

That he had lerned out of som decree—   640

No wonder is, he herde it al the day;

And eek ye knowen wel how that a jay

Can clepen "Watte" as well as can the Pope.

But whoso coude in other thing him grope,

Thanne hadde he spent al his philosophye;   645

Ay *"Questio quid iuris"* wolde he crye.

He was a gentil harlot and a kinde;

A bettre felawe sholde men noght finde:

He wolde suffre, for a quart of wyn,

A good felawe to have his concubyn   650

A twelf-month, and excuse him atte fulle;

Ful prively a finch eek coude he pulle.

And if he fond owher a good felawe,

He wolde techen him to have non awe

And of his visage, children were quite scared.
Not lead monoxide, mercury, or sulphur,
Not borax, white lead, or cream of tartar—   630
No single ointment that would cleanse or bite—
Could help him to remove those pustules white,
Nor cure the pimples sitting on his cheeks.
Well loved he garlic, onions, also leeks,[60]
And drinking blood red wine, strongly fermented;   635
Then he would speak and cry as though demented.
And when of this good wine he'd drunk his fill,
No words but Latin from his mouth would spill.
A few such terms he knew, like two or three,
That he had learned by hearing some decree—   640
It's no wonder, for he heard it all day;
And thus you know full well how any jay
Can call out "Walter" as well as the pope.[61]
But whoever might on other matters grope,
Then his philosophy was spent thereby;   645
Always, "Questio quid iuris,"[62] he would cry.
He was a noble rascal in his kind;
A better fellow men would never find.
And he would suffer, for a quart of wine,
A good fellow to have his concubine   650
A full year, and excuse him thus completely;
For he himself could pluck a finch[63] discreetly.
If he found a good fellow anywhere,
Then he would quickly teach to him that there

---

60 **garlic, onions, also leeks:** These foods in the Middle Ages were thought to arouse lust.

61 **any jay . . . pope:** Any talking bird that can imitate speech can say "Walter" as well as the pope can, and thus the Summoner can speak Latin, just as the jay can speak, purely from the force of imitation, not from any learnedness or awareness of what he's saying.

62 **"Questio quid iuris":** "The question is, what point of law applies." The Summoner would have learned this phrase from the ecclesiastical courts.

63 **pluck a finch:** To trick or blackmail, but the phrase could also have sexual and perhaps homosexual undertones.

In swich cas of the erchedeknes curs,   655
But-if a mannes soule were in his purs,
For in his purs he sholde y-punisshed be.
"Purs is the erchedeknes helle," seyde he.
But wel I woot he lyed right in dede:
Of cursing oghte ech gilty man him drede—   660
For curs wol slee, right as assoilling saveth—
And also war him of a *significavit*.
In daunger hadde he at his owene gyse
The yonge girles of the diocyse,
And knew hir counseil, and was al hir reed.   665
A gerland hadde he set upon his heed,
As greet as it were for an ale-stake;
A bokeler hadde he maad him of a cake.

      With him ther rood a gentil PARDONER
Of Rouncival, his freend and his compeer,   670
That streight was comen fro the court of Rome.
Ful loude he song, "Com hider, love, to me."
This somnour bar to him a stif burdoun,
Was nevere trompe of half so greet a soun.
This pardoner hadde heer as yelow as wex,   675
But smothe it heng, as dooth a strike of flex;
By ounces henge his lokkes that he hadde,
And therwith he his shuldres overspradde;
But thinne it lay, by colpons oon and oon;
But hood, for jolitee, wered he noon,   680
For it was trussed up in his walet.
Him thoughte he rood al of the newe jet;

Was no need to fear archdeacons' curses,[64]   655
Unless men's souls were found in their purses;
For in their purses, they will punished be.
"The purse is the archdeacon's hell," said he.
He downright lied, I know, in what he said;
Excommunication guilty men should dread.   660
Absolving saves, but cursing slays indeed;
Of *Significavit*,[65] men should well take heed.
Under his thumb, he had, as it did please
Him, the young girls[66] there of the diocese;
He counseled all who told him things in secret.   665
A garland he had fashioned and then set,
Big as an ale-house sign, upon his head.
He'd made a buckler from a loaf of bread.

　　With him, there rode a gentle PARDONER[67]
Of Roncevalles,[68] and good, close friends they were.   670
He'd come straight from the papal court at Rome,
And loudly sang, "Come hither, love, to me!"
With a stiff bass, the Summoner sang along;
No trumpet's sound was ever half so strong.
This Pardoner had hair yellow as wax,   675
But smooth it hung as does a hank of flax;
In skinny strands, the locks hung from his head,
And with them, he his shoulders overspread;
But thin it lay; its strands hung one by one.
For stylishness, a hood he would wear none,   680
Since it was trussed up within his wallet.
He thought he wore the latest fashions yet;

　　64 **archdeacons' curses**: Excommunication as punishment in the ecclesiastical courts over which archdeacons presided.

　　65 *Significavit*: Be it known. This was the first word of a decree of excommunication.

　　66 **young girls**: Chaucer's Middle English here is "girles," which can mean either girls or young people of both sexes.

　　67 A PARDONER: Employed by religious institutions to sell pardons and indulgences for sins. Such pardons and indulgences were believed to remit time off one's term spent in purgatory.

　　68 **Roncevalles**: A hospital in medieval London. Pardoners sold indulgences and pardons in order to fund such charitable institutions operated by the Church.

Dischevele, save his cappe, he rood al bare.
Swiche glaringe eyen hadde he as an hare.
A vernicle hadde he sowed on his cappe.   685
His walet lay biforn him in his lappe,
Bretful of pardoun comen from Rome al hoot.
A voys he hadde as smal as hath a goot.
No berd hadde he, ne nevere sholde have,
As smothe it was as it were late shave: 690
I trowe he were a gelding or a mare.
But of his craft, fro Berwik into Ware,
Ne was ther swich another pardoner.
For in his male he hadde a pilwe-beer,
Which that he seyde was Oure Lady veyl.   695
He seyde he hadde a gobet of the seyl
That seynt Peter hadde, whan that he wente
Upon the see, til Jesu Christ him hente.
He hadde a croys of latoun, ful of stones,
And in a glas he hadde pigges bones.   700
But with thise relikes, whan that he fond
A povre person dwellinge upon lond,
Upon a day he gat him more moneye
Than that the person gat in monthes tweye.
And thus, with feyned flaterye and japes,   705
He made the person and the peple his apes.
But trewely to tellen, atte laste,
He was in chirche a noble ecclesiaste.
Wel coude he rede a lessoun or a storie,
But alderbest he song an offertorie;   710
For wel he wiste, whan that song was songe,
He moste preche, and wel affyle his tonge

With loose hair, his head save for his cap was bare.
Such staring eyes he had, just like a hare.
A veronica[69] he'd sewn on his cap. 685
His wallet lay before him in his lap,
With pardons hot from Rome stuffed to the brim.
A voice high as a goat's came out of him.
No beard had he, nor should he wait for one;
His face smooth like his shaving'd just been done. 690
I think he was a gelding or a mare.
But, in his craft, from Berwick down to Ware,[70]
No pardoner like him in all the land.
In his bag was a pillowcase on hand,
And he declared it was Our Lady's veil; 695
He said he had a big piece of the sail
Saint Peter used upon his boat when he,
Before Christ took him, had gone out to sea.
He had a fake gold cross bedecked with stones,
A glass he had that carried some pig bones.[71] 700
But with these relics, whenever he spied
A poor parson out in the countryside,
On that day, much more money would he make
Than, in two months, the poor parson might take;
And thus, with his feigned flattery and japes, 705
He made the parson and people his apes.
But to tell the whole truth, now, finally,
In church, a noble ecclesiastic was he.
Well could he read a lesson or a story,
But best of all, he sang the offertory; 710
For well he knew, when that song had been sung,
Then he must preach and smoothly file his tongue

69 **A veronica**: A small medal meant to represent Saint Veronica's veil, which bore the image of Christ left on it when she gave him her veil to wipe his face on his way up Calvary.

70 **from Berwick . . . Ware**: From the Scottish Border down to Hertfordshire, i.e., from north to south.

71 **pig bones**: There was an active medieval trade in saints' relics, or body parts, usually bones, that were thought to carry special grace within them.

To winne silver, as he ful wel coude—
Therefore he song the murierly and loude.

      Now have I told you soothly, in a clause,   715
Th'estaat, th'array, the nombre, and eek the cause
Why that assembled was this compaignye
In Southwerk, at this gentil hostelrye,
That highte the Tabard, faste by the Belle.
But now is tyme to yow for to telle   720
How that we baren us that ilke night,
Whan we were in that hostelrye alight;
And after wol I telle of our viage,
And al the remenaunt of oure pilgrimage.
But first I pray yow, of youre curteisye,   725
That ye n'arette it nat my vileinye,
Thogh that I pleynly speke in this matere,
To tell yow hir wordes and hir chere,
Ne thogh I speke hir wordes properly.
For this ye knowen al so wel as I: 730
Whoso shal telle a tale after a man,
He moot reherce as ny as evere he can
Everich a word, if it be in his charge,
Al speke he never so rudeliche and large;
Or elles he moot telle his tale untrewe,   735
Or feyne thing, or finde wordes newe.
He may nat spare, althogh he were his brother;
He moot as wel seye o word as another.
Crist spak himself ful brode in Holy Writ,
And wel ye woot, no vileinye is it.   740
Eek Plato seith, whoso can him rede,
The wordes mote be cosin to the dede.
Also I prey yow to foryeve it me,
Al have I nat set folk in hir degree
Here in this tale, as that they sholde stonde;   745
My wit is short, ye may wel understonde.

      Greet chere made oure Hoste us everichon,
And to the soper sette he us anon;

To win his silver, as quite well could he;
Therefore, he sang quite loud and merrily.

      Now, I have told you truly, in a clause,   715
The rank, the dress, the number, and the cause
That brought together all this company
In Southwark, at this noble hostelry
That's called the Tabard, next door to the Bell.
But now it's time that to you I should tell   720
How that we all behaved on that same night
When we should in that hostelry alight;
Afterward, I will tell of our voyage
And all the rest about our pilgrimage.
But first I pray you, by your courtesy,   725
That you not blame my own vulgarity,
Although I might speak plainly in this matter,
When I tell you their words and their demeanor,
Or if I speak their words, exact and true.
For this you all know just as well as I do: 730
Whoever tells a tale after a man,
He must repeat, as closely as he can,
Every last word, if that is his duty,
Even if he has to speak quite rudely,
Or otherwise, he makes his tale untrue,   735
Or makes things up, or finds words that are new.
He may not spare, though that man were his brother;
He might as well say one word as another.
Christ himself plainly spoke in Holy Writ;
You know no vulgarity is in it.   740
And Plato says, whoever can him read,
That words must be the cousin to the deed.
Also, I pray you that you will forgive me
Although I've not ranked folks by their degree
Here in this tale, the way that they should stand.   745
My wit is short, you may well understand.

      Our Host put us at ease with his great cheer;
At once, he set up supper for us here.

He served us with vitaille at the beste.
Strong was the wyn, and wel to drinke us leste.   750
A semely man oure HOSTE was withalle
For to been a marshal in an halle;
A large man he was with eyen stepe—
A fairer burgeys was ther noon in Chepe.
Bold of his speche, and wys, and wel y-taught,   755
And of manhod him lakkede right naught.
Eek therto he was right a mery man,
And after soper pleyen he bigan,
And spak of mirthe amonges othere thinges—
Whan that we hadde maad oure rekeninges—   760
And seyde thus: "Now, lordinges, trewely,
Ye been to me right welcome hertely.
For by my trouthe, if that I shal nat lye,
I saugh nat this yeer so mery a compaignye
Atones in this herberwe as is now.   765
Fayn wolde I doon yow mirthe, wiste I how,
And of a mirthe I am right now bithoght,
To doon yow ese, and it shal coste noght.
        Ye goon to Caunterbury—God yow spede;
The blisful martir quyte yow your mede.   770
And wel I woot, as ye goon by the weye,
Ye shapen yow to talen and to pleye;
For trewely, confort ne mirthe is noon
To ryde by the weye doumb as a stoon;
And therfore wol I maken yow disport,   775
As I seyde erst, and doon yow som confort.
And if yow lyketh alle, by oon assent,
Now for to stonden at my jugement,
And for to werken as I shal yow seye,
To-morwe, whan ye ryden by the weye—   780
Now by my fader soule that is deed—
But ye be merye, I wol yeve yow myn heed.

He served us all with victuals that were fine;
It pleased us well to drink his good, strong wine.   750
An impressive man our HOST was, all in all;
He could have been a marshal in a hall.
A large man he, with eyes both bright and wide—
No fairer burgess anywhere in Cheapside—[72]
Bold in his speech, and wise, and quite well taught.   755
And in his manhood, he did lack for naught.
Moreover, he was quite a merry man;
After supper, to amuse us, he began,
And spoke of pleasure, among other things,
When we had settled up our reckonings.   760
He then said thus: "Now, my good lords, truly,
To me, you are quite welcome, heartily;
For, by my word, if that I shall not lie,
So merry a company, this whole year, I
Have not seen in this inn, as I see now.   765
I'd gladly make you happy, knew I how.
I've just thought what would be entertaining;
It'd please you, and it wouldn't cost a thing.
         You go to Canterbury—bless the Lord,
May the blissful martyr pay you your reward!   770
I know well, as you travel by the way,
You all intend to tell tales and to play;
For truly, comfort and mirth both have flown
If you ride on the way dumb as a stone;
Now, I know a way I can divert you,   775
As I have said, and give you comfort, too.
And if it pleases you to give assent
So you all agree to trust my judgment,
And to do according to what I say,
Tomorrow, when you all ride by the way,   780
Now, by the soul of my father who is dead,
Unless you're merry, I'll give you my head!

72 **Cheapside**: A major business area in the City of London.

Hold up youre hondes, withouten more speche."
     Oure counseil was nat longe for to seche;
Us thoughte it was noght worth to make it wys,   785
And graunted him withouten more avys,
And bad him seye his voirdit as him leste.
"Lordinges," quod he, "now herkneth for the beste,
But tak it nought, I prey yow, in desdeyn.
This is the poynt, to speken short and pleyn: 790
That ech of yow, to shorte with oure weye,
In this viage shal telle tales tweye,
To Caunterbury-ward, I mene it so,
And homward he shal tellen othere two,
Of aventures that whylom han bifalle.   795
And which of yow that bereth him best of alle,
That is to seyn, that telleth in this cas
Tales of best sentence and most solas,
Shal have a soper at oure aller cost
Here in this place, sitting by this post,   800
Whan that we come agayn fro Caunterbury.
And for to make yow the more mery,
I wol myselven goodly with yow ryde,
Right at myn owne cost, and be youre gyde.
And whoso wole my jugement withseye   805
Shal paye al that we spenden by the weye.
And if ye vouchesauf that it be so,
Tel me anon, withouten wordes mo,
And I wol erly shape me therfore."
     This thing was graunted, and oure othes swore   810
With ful glad herte, and preyden him also
That he wolde vouchesauf for to do so,
And that he wolde been oure governour
And of oure tales juge and reportour,
And sette a soper at a certeyn prys;   815
And we wol reuled been at his devys
In heigh and lowe; and thus, by oon assent,
We been acorded to his jugement.

Hold up your hands, now, without further speech."
     All our assent took not long to beseech.
It did not seem worthwhile to make a fuss,   785
For we did not need more time to discuss,
And we told him to give his verdict then.
"My lords," said he, "this plan is best. Now, listen.
But take it not, I pray you, with disdain.
This is the point, to speak now, short and plain: 790
Each one of you, to help shorten our way,
Along this journey, two tales you will say,
Toward Canterbury, as I mean you to,
And homeward, you'll tell us another two,
Of adventures that in old times did befall.   795
The one who bears himself the best of all—
That is to say, the one of you who might
Tell tales that have most meaning and delight—
Shall have a supper paid for by us all,
Sitting right near this post here in this hall,   800
When we all come again from Canterbury.
And to make you all even more merry,
I will myself quite gladly with you ride,
Right at my own expense, and be your guide.
Whoever will my judgment now gainsay   805
Shall pay for all we spend along the way.
If it be so, and all of you agree,
Without more words, at once, now you tell me,
And I'll make myself ready long before."
     This thing was granted, and our oaths we swore   810
With quite glad hearts, and we prayed him also
That he fully would agree to do so,
And that he would become our governor,
And of our tales, the judge and record keeper,
And set the supper at a certain price,   815
And we would all be ruled by his advice
In all respects; and thus, with one assent
We were all accorded with his judgment.

And therupon the wyn was fet anon;
We dronken, and to reste wente echon,   820
Withouten any lenger taryinge.
        Amorwe, whan that day bigan to springe,
Up roos oure Host and was oure aller cok,
And gadrede us togidre, alle in a flok;
And forth we riden, a litel more than pas,   825
Unto the watering of Seint Thomas,
And there oure Host bigan his hors areste,
And seyde, "Lordinges, herkneth, if yow leste.
Ye woot youre forward, and I it yow recorde.
If even-song and morwe-song acorde,   830
Lat se now who shal telle the firste tale.
As evere mote I drinke wyn or ale,
Whoso be rebel to my jugement
Shal paye for al that by the weye is spent.
Now draweth cut, er that we ferrer twinne;   835
He which that hath the shortest shal biginne.
Sire Knight," quod he, "my maister and my lord,
Now draweth cut for that is myn acord.
Cometh neer," quod he, "my lady Prioresse;
And ye, sire Clerk, lat be youre shamfastnesse,   840
Ne studieth noght. Ley hond to, every man!"
Anon to drawen every wight bigan,
And shortly for to tellen as it was,
Were it by aventure, or sort, or cas,
The sothe is this, the cut fil to the Knight,   845
Of which ful blythe and glad was every wight;
And telle he moste his tale, as was resoun,
By forward and by composicioun,
As ye han herd. What nedeth wordes mo?
And whan this gode man saugh it was so,   850

And thereupon, the wine was fetched in fast;
We drank, and to our rest we went at last,   820
Without us any longer tarrying.

      In the morning, as day began to spring,
Up rose our Host, and was, for us, the cock,
And gathered us together in a flock;
With slow gait, we started on our riding,   825
Till we came to Saint Thomas's Watering;[73]
And there, our Host began to stop his horse
And said, "Lords, listen—if you please, of course.
Let me remind you that you gave your word.
If evening-song and morning-song accord,[74]   830
Let see now who shall tell us the first tale.
As ever may I drink of wine or ale,
Whoso now rebels against my judgment
Shall pay for all that by the way is spent.
Now let's draw straws, and then we shall depart;   835
Whoever has the shortest straw will start.
Sir Knight, my master and my lord," he said,
"Now you draw first, for thus I have decided.
Come near," said he, "my lady Prioress.
And you, sir Clerk, leave off your bashfulness.   840
Don't study now. Lay hands to, every man!"
At once, to draw straws, everyone began;
To quickly tell the way it did advance,
Were it by fortune or by luck or chance,
The truth is this: the draw fell to the Knight,   845
For which we were quite glad, as it was right;
By agreement and arrangement, now he must
Tell us his tale, as it was only just,
As you have heard; what more words need be spent?
And when this good man saw the way it went,   850

73 **Saint Thomas's Watering**: Watering place for horses at a brook less than two miles from
Southwark.

74 **evening-song**, etc.: Your intention at night matches your intention the next morning.

As he that wys was and obedient
To kepe his forward by his free assent,
He seyde: "Sin I shal biginne the game,
What, welcome be the cut, a Goddes name!
Now lat us ryde, and herkneth what I seye."   855
And with that word we riden forth oure weye;
And he bigan with right a mery chere
His tale anon, and seyde as ye may heere.

Because he wise was, and obedient
To keep the word he gave by free assent,
He said, "Now, since I shall begin the game,
What, welcome is this straw, in the Lord's name!
Now, let us ride, and hearken what I say."   855
And with that word, we rode forth on our way,
And he began with then a merry cheer
His tale at once, and said as you may hear.

THE KNIGHT'S TALE

Here bigynneth the Knyghtes Tale.

Iamque domos patrias, Scithice post aspera gentis
Prelia, laurigero, & c.

Whylom, as olde stories tellen us,
Ther was a duk that highte Theseus;   860
Of Athenes he was lord and governour,
And in his tyme swich a conquerour,
That gretter was ther noon under the sonne.
Ful many a riche contree hadde he wonne;
What with his wisdom and his chivalrye,   865
He conquered al the regne of Femenye,
That whylom was y-cleped Scithia,
And weddede the quene Ipolita,
And broghte hire hoom with him in his contree
With muchel glorie and greet solempnitee,   870
And eek hire yonge suster Emelye.
And thus with victorie and with melodye
Lete I this noble duk to Athenes ryde,

THE KNIGHT'S TALE

Here begins the Knight's Tale.

Iamque domos patrias, Scithice post aspera gentis

Prelia, laurigero, & c.

[And now to the father lands, after the fierce battle with the Scithian people, in a laurel draped chariot, & c. —Statius, Thebaid][1]

Long ago, as the old stories tell us,
There was a duke who was called Theseus;   860
Of Athens, he was lord and governor,
And in his time, such a conqueror
That greater was there none beneath the sun.   5
So many a rich country had he won,
With his great wisdom and his chivalry;
He conquered all the land of Feminy,[2]
That formerly had been called Scithia,
And he had wed their queen Hippolyta,   10
And brought her home with him to his country
With much glory and great solemnity,   870
And also her young sister Emily.
And thus with melody and victory
Let I this noble duke to Athens ride,   15

1   The epigraph to *The Knight's Tale* comes from Statius's *Thebaid* (12.19–20), a Latin epic (first century C.E.) about the siege and fall of Thebes. *The Knight's Tale* is actually a shortened version of Boccaccio's fourteenth-century poem on the same topic, *Il Teseida*.

2   **Feminy**: Homeland of the Amazons.

And al his hoost, in armes, him bisyde.
  And certes, if it nere to long to here,   875
I wolde have told yow fully the manere
How wonnen was the regne of Femenye
By Theseus, and by his chivalrye;
And of the grete bataille for the nones
Bitwixen Athenës and Amazones;   880
And how asseged was Ipolita,
The faire hardy quene of Scithia;
And of the feste that was at hir weddinge,
And of the tempest at hir hoomcominge;
But al that thing I moot as now forbere.   885
I have, God woot, a large feeld to ere,
And wayke been the oxen in my plough.
The remenant of the tale is long ynough.
I wol nat letten eek noon of this route;
Lat every felawe telle his tale aboute,   890
And lat see now who shall the soper winne;
And ther I lefte, I wol ageyn biginne.
  This duk, of whom I make mencioun,
When he was come almost unto the toun,
In al his wele and in his moste pryde,   895
He was war, as he caste his eye asyde,
Where that ther kneled in the hye weye
A companye of ladies, tweye and tweye,
Ech after other clad in clothes blake;
But swich a cry and swich a wo they make,   900
That in this world nis creature livinge,
That herde swich another weymentinge;
And of this cry they nolde nevere stenten,
Til they the reynes of his brydel henten.
  "What folk ben ye, that at myn hoomcominge   905
Perturben so my feste with cryinge?"
Quod Theseus. "Have ye so greet envye
Of myn honour, that thus compleyne and crye?
Or who hath yow misboden or offended?

And all his host in arms there by his side.
      If it would not take too long, then truly
I would now tell you the story fully
Of how they won the land of Feminy,
This Theseus and all his cavalry; 20
And of the great battle that then went on
Between Athenians and Amazons; 880
And how besieged then was Hippolyta,
The fair and hardy queen of Scithia,
And of the feast then held at their wedding, 25
And of the tempest at their homecoming;
But all those things I must forbear for now.
I have, God knows, quite a large field to plow,
And in my plow, the oxen are too weak.
And this whole tale is long enough to speak. 30
No one in all this band will I delay;
Let everyone tell his tale in his way, 890
And let's see now who will the supper win;
Where I left off, I will again begin.
      This good duke, whom I have mentioned here, 35
When to his town he'd ridden very near
In his prosperity and in his pride,
He was aware, as he looked to the side,
That, on the highway, as he was passing through,
A band of ladies knelt there two by two, 40
One near the other, in black clothing clad;
Such was their woe and such their crying sad 900
That, in this world, there is no creature living
Who had ever heard such great lamenting;
And in their crying, they would never cease 45
Till by the reins they did his bridle seize.
      "What folk are you, who at my homecoming
Disturb my celebration with your crying?"
Said Theseus. "Have you such great envy,
You who lament, of my honor and me? 50
Or who has injured you, or you offended?

And telleth me if it may been amended,   910
And why that ye ben clothed thus in blak."
   The eldeste lady of hem alle spak,
When she hadde swowned with a deedly chere
That it was routhe for to seen and here.
She seyde: "Lord, to whom Fortune hath yiven   915
Victorie, and as a conquerour to liven,
Noght greveth us youre glorie and youre honour;
But we biseken mercy and socour.
Have mercy on oure wo and oure distresse.
Som drope of pitee, thurgh thy gentillesse,   920
Upon us wrecched wommen lat thou falle.
For certes, lord, ther nis noon of us alle,
That she ne hath been a duchesse or a quene;
Now be we caitifs, as it is wel sene,
Thanked be Fortune and hire false wheel,   925
That noon estat assureth to be weel.
And certes, lord, to abyden your presence,
Here in this temple of the goddesse Clemence
We han ben waytinge al this fourtenight;
Now help us, lord, sith it is in thy might.   930
   I, wrecche, which that wepe and waille thus,
Was whylom wyf to king Capaneus,
That starf at Thebes—cursed be that day!
And alle we that been in this array
And maken al this lamentacioun,   935
We losten alle oure housbondes at that toun,
Whyl that the sege theraboute lay.
And yet now the olde Creon, weylaway,
That lord is now of Thebes the citee,
Fulfild of ire and of iniquitee,   940
He, for despyt and for his tirannye,
To do the dede bodyes vileinye,
Of alle oure lordes whiche that ben y-slawe,
Hath alle the bodyes on an heep y-drawe,
And wol nat suffren hem, by noon assent,   945

And tell me now if it can be amended,   910
And why thus all of you are clothed in black."
     The eldest lady in their band spoke back,
Although she first swooned with a deathly cheer,   55
Which was a pity both to see and hear;
She said, "Lord, you to whom Fortune does give
Victory, as a conqueror to live,
Your glory doesn't grieve us, or your honor,
But we beseech your mercy and your succor.   60
Have mercy on our woe and our distress!
Some drop of pity, through your gentleness,   920
Upon us wretched women, pray let fall,
For, truly, lord, there's not one of us all
Who hasn't been a duchess or a queen.   65
Now, we are woeful wretches, as is seen;
To Fortune and her false wheel, thanks should be,
Who lets no rank enjoy prosperity.
Truly, lord, to await your presence we,
In this temple of the Goddess Clemency,   70
Have been staying an entire fortnight.
Now help us, lord, since it lies in your might.   930
     I, wretched one, weeping and wailing thus,
Have been the wife of King Cappaneus,
Who died at Thebes—cursèd be the day!—   75
And all of us who are in this array
And who make here the mourning that you see,
All our husbands within that town lost we,
While there all of the siege around it lay.   80
And yet, alas, old Creon—wey-la-way!—
Who, of Thebes, is now lord of that city,
All full of anger and iniquity,   940
He, out of spite and in his tyranny,
To the dead bodies does such villainy
Of all our lords and husbands, whom he slew,   85
That their bodies into a heap he drew;
He will not give assent, nor will allow

Neither to been y-buried nor y-brent,
But maketh houndes ete hem in despyt."
And with that word, withouten more respyt,
They fillen gruf and cryden pitously,
"Have on us wrecched wommen som mercy,   950
And lat oure sorwe sinken in thyn herte."
        This gentil duk doun from his courser sterte
With herte pitous, whan he herde hem speke.
Him thoughte that his herte wolde breke,
Whan he saugh hem so pitous and so mat,   955
That whylom weren of so greet estat.
And in his armes he hem alle up hente,
And hem conforteth in ful good entente;
And swoor his ooth, as he was trewe knight,
He wolde doon so ferforthly his might   960
Upon the tyraunt Creon hem to wreke,
That al the peple of Grece sholde speke
How Creon was of Theseus y-served,
As he that hadde his deeth ful wel deserved.
And right anoon, withouten more abood,   965
His baner he desplayeth, and forth rood
To Thebes-ward, and al his host bisyde.
No neer Athenës wolde he go ne ryde,
Ne take his ese fully half a day,
But onward on his wey that night he lay,   970
And sente anoon Ipolita the quene
And Emelye, hir yonge suster shene,
Unto the toun of Athenës to dwelle;
And forth he rit; ther is namore to telle.
        The rede statue of Mars, with spere and targe,   975
So shyneth in his whyte baner large,
That alle the feeldes gliteren up and doun;
And by his baner born is his penoun
Of gold ful riche, in which ther was y-bete

Their bodies to be burned or buried now,
But he makes hounds go eat them, out of hate."
    And with that word, their grief took added weight, 90
They fell facedown and they cried piteously,
"On us wretched women, have some mercy, 950
And let our sorrow sink into your heart."
    Down from his horse, this noble duke did start
With pitying heart, when this speech she did make. 95
It seemed to him that now his heart would break,
When he saw them piteous and prostrate,
Who, formerly, were of such high estate.
He gathered all of them up in his arms, 100
With good intent and comforted their harms,
And swore his oath, as he was a true knight,
That he would exercise then all his might 960
Against the tyrant to avenge them well,
So that soon people throughout Greece would tell 105
How Creon had by Theseus been served,
As one who had his death full well deserved.
And thus at once, without further delays,
He rides forth, and his banner, he displays.
He goes toward Thebes, his whole host at his side. 110
No nearer Athens would he go or ride,
Or take his ease completely half a day,
But on the road to Thebes, that night he lay. 970
At once, his queen Hippolyta he sent—
Emily, her bright young sister, also went— 115
Straight to the town of Athens, there to dwell,
And he rides forth; there is no more to tell.
    The red statue of Mars,[3] with spear and shield
Shone on his large white banner so the field
Would glitter up and down there where he went; 120
By his banner borne here is his pennant
Of rich gold, with embroidery worked through

---

3 **Mars**: Roman god of war.

The Minotaur, which that he slough in Crete.   980
Thus rit this duk, thus rit this conquerour,
And in his host of chivalrye the flour,
Til that he cam to Thebes, and alighte
Faire in a feeld, ther as he thoghte to fighte.
But shortly for to speken of this thing,   985
With Creon, which that was of Thebes king,
He faught, and slough him manly as a knight
In pleyn bataille, and putte the folk to flight;
And by assaut he wan the citee after,
And rente adoun bothe wal and sparre and rafter;   990
And to the ladyes he restored agayn
The bones of hir housbondes that were slayn,
To doon obsequies, as was tho the gyse.
But it were al to longe for to devyse
The grete clamour and the waymentinge   995
That the ladyes made at the brenninge
Of the bodyes, and the grete honour
That Theseus, the noble conquerour,
Doth to the ladyes, whan they from him wente;
But shortly for to telle is myn entente.   1000
Whan that this worthy duk, this Theseus,
Hath Creon slayn and wonne Thebes thus,
Stille in that feeld he took al night his reste,
And dide with al the contree as him leste.
        To ransake in the tas of bodyes dede,   1005
Hem for to strepe of harneys and of wede,
The pilours diden bisinesse and cure
After the bataille and disconfiture.
And so bifel, that in the tas they founde,
Thurgh-girt with many a grevous blody wounde,   1010
Two yonge knightes ligginge by and by,
Bothe in oon armes, wroght ful richely,
Of whiche two, Arcita highte that oon,

Of the Minotaur,[4] which in Crete he slew.   980
Thus rides this duke, thus rides this conqueror,
And in his host, of chivalry the flower,   125
Until he came to Thebes and did alight
On a fair field, where it seemed good to fight.
But, to speak shortly now about this thing,
Against Creon, who was of Thebes the king,
He fought, and slew him, manly, like a knight   130
In open battle, and put his folks to flight;
And by assault, he won the city after,
And tore down every wall and beam and rafter;   990
And he gave to the ladies, in their pain,
The bones of all their husbands who were slain,   135
To do their obsequies in their own way.
But it would now be far too long to say
How great was all the clamor and lamenting
That the ladies made there at the burning
Of the bodies, and then the great honor   140
That Theseus, the noble conqueror,
Made to the ladies, when from him they went;
To tell it shortly, that is my intent.   1000
So when this worthy duke, this Theseus,
Has Creon slain, and when he's won Thebes thus,   145
Still in that field, all night he took his ease,
And did with all the country what he pleased.

    Ransacking through dead bodies in a heap,
To see what clothes and armor they could keep,
The pillagers did business with great care,   150
After the battle and defeat made there.
And in that heap, they found—it happened thus—
Pierced with many wounds, bloody and grievous,   1010
Two young knights who, side by side, were lying,
Clad in armor of the same rich making,   155
Of which two, Arcite was called the one,

---

4 **the Minotaur**: Monster, half man and half bull, whom Theseus slew in the labyrinth in Crete.

And that other knight highte Palamon.
Nat fully quike ne fully dede they were,   1015
But by hir cote-armures and by hir gere
The heraudes knew hem best in special
As they that weren of the blood royal
Of Thebes, and of sustren two y-born.
Out of the tas the pilours han hem torn,   1020
And han hem caried softe unto the tente
Of Theseus, and he ful sone hem sente
To Athenës, to dwellen in prisoun
Perpetuelly: he nolde no raunsoun.
And whan this worthy duk hath thus y-don,   1025
He took his host, and hoom he rit anon
With laurer crowned as a conquerour;
And there he liveth in joye and in honour
Terme of his lyf; what nedeth wordes mo?
And in a tour, in angwish and in wo,   1030
Dwellen this Palamoun and eek Arcite
For everemore; ther may no gold hem quyte.
        This passeth yeer by yeer and day by day,
Til it fil ones, in a morwe of May,
That Emelye, that fairer was to sene   1035
Than is the lilie upon his stalke grene,
And fressher than the May with floures newe—
For with the rose colour stroof hire hewe,
I noot which was the fairer of hem two—
Er it were day, as was hir wone to do,   1040
She was arisen and al redy dight;
For May wole have no slogardye a-night.
The sesoun priketh every gentil herte,
And maketh him out of his sleep to sterte,
And seith "Arys, and do thyn observaunce."   1045
This maked Emelye have remembraunce
To doon honour to May, and for to ryse.
Y-clothed was she fresh, for to devyse:
Hir yelow heer was broyded in a tresse

And the other knight, he was called Palamon.
Not fully live, nor fully dead they were,
But by their coat of arms and by their armor
The heralds in particular well knew   160
That from the royal blood of Thebes, these two
Had come, and of two sisters they were born.
From the heap, the pillagers had them torn,   1020
And had them carried gently to the tent
Of Theseus, and he to Athens sent   165
Them, to dwell in prison perpetually—
No interest in their ransoming took he.
And when this worthy duke was finished then,
He took his host, and home he rode again
With laurel, crowned as is a conqueror;   170
And there he lives long in joy and honor
For all his life; what more is there to tell?
And in a tower, in woe and anguish dwell   1030
This Palamon and his friend Arcite nearby
For evermore; and no gold can them buy.   175
        This went on year by year, and day by day,
Until there came one fine morning in May,
When Emily, much fairer to be seen
Than is the lily on its stalk of green,
And fresher than May with its flowers new—   180
For with the rose's color vied her hue,
I don't know which was finer of the two—
Before the dawn, as was her wont to do,   1040
She woke and dressed as quickly as she might,
For May will have no sluggishness at night.   185
The season so pricks every gentle heart,
And makes it quickly out of its sleep start,
And says, "Arise, and do your service early."
This made Emily remember clearly
To wake and do all honor now to May.   190
And she was clothed quite freshly, for that day:
Her yellow hair was braided in a tress

Bihinde hir bak, a yerde long, I gesse.   1050
And in the gardin, at the sonne upriste,
She walketh up and doun, and as hire liste
She gadereth floures, party whyte and rede,
To make a sotil gerland for hire hede,
And as an aungel hevenysshly she song.   1055
          The grete tour, that was so thikke and strong,
Which of the castel was the chief dongeoun
(Theras the knightes weren in prisoun,
Of whiche I tolde yow and tellen shal),
Was evene joynant to the gardin wal   1060
Ther as this Emelye hadde hir pleyinge.
Bright was the sonne and cleer that morweninge,
And Palamon, this woful prisoner,
As was his wone, by leve of his gayler,
Was risen and romed in a chambre on heigh,   1065
In which he al the noble citee seigh,
And eek the gardin, ful of braunches grene,
Theras this fresshe Emelye the shene
Was in hire walk, and romed up and doun.
This sorweful prisoner, this Palamoun,   1070
Goth in the chambre rominge to and fro,
And to himself compleyninge of his wo.
That he was born, ful ofte he seyde, "Alas!"
And so bifel, by aventure or cas,
That thurgh a window, thikke of many a barre   1075
Of yren greet and square as any sparre,
He caste his eye upon Emelya,
And therwithal he bleynte and cryde "A!"
As though he stongen were unto the herte.
And with that cry Arcite anon up sterte   1080
And seyde, "Cosin myn, what eyleth thee,
That art so pale and deedly on to see?
Why crydestow? Who hath thee doon offence?
For Goddes love, tak al in pacience
Oure prisoun, for it may non other be;   1085

Behind her back, a full yard long, I guess. 1050
And as the sun rose up, out in the garden,
Up and down she walks there; as she likes then, 195
She gathers flowers, some white and some red,
To make a woven garland for her head;
And like an angel's, heavenly her song.
     The great tower, that was so thick and strong
And of the castle served as the chief dungeon 200
(It was there the knights were kept in prison
As I told you and will tell more withal):
This was adjacent to the garden wall 1060
Where fair Emily did all her playing.
Bright was the sun and clear upon that morning, 205
And Palamon, this woeful prisoner,
As was his wont, by leave of his jailer,
Arose and roamed about his chamber so
That he could see the city far below
And then the garden full of branches green, 210
Where Emily, so fresh and bright, was seen
Roaming up and down, before her walk was done.
This mournful prisoner, this Palamon, 1070
Goes in the chamber, roaming to and fro,
And to himself complaining of his woe. 215
That he was born, he often said, "Alas!"
And so, by chance or luck it came to pass,
That through a window that was thickly barred
With iron like a beam as square and hard,
He cast his eye down upon Emily, 220
And at the sight he blanched, and "Ah!" cried he,
As though he had been stung deep in his heart.
And with that cry, Arcite at once did start 1080
And said, "Oh, now my cousin, what does ail
You, for you're a deathly sight and you're so pale? 225
Why did you cry? Who has done you offense?
For love of God, take all now in patience
Our prison; for otherwise, it cannot be.

Fortune hath yeven us this adversitee.
Som wikke aspect or disposicioun
Of Saturne, by sum constellacioun,
Hath yeven us this, although we hadde it sworn:
So stood the hevene whan that we were born. 1090
We moste endure it; this is the short and pleyn."
   This Palamon answerde and seyde ageyn,
"Cosyn, for sothe, of this opinioun
Thou hast a veyn imaginacioun.
This prison caused me nat for to crye, 1095
But I was hurt right now thurghout myn yë
Into myn herte, that wol my bane be.
The fairnesse of that lady that I see
Yond in the gardin romen to and fro
Is cause of al my crying and my wo. 1100
I noot wher she be womman or goddesse,
But Venus is it soothly, as I gesse."
And therwithal on kneës doun he fil,
And seyde: "Venus, if it be thy wil
Yow in this gardin thus to transfigure 1105
Bifore me, sorweful wrecched creature,
Out of this prisoun help that we may scapen.
And if so be my destinee be shapen
By eterne word to dyen in prisoun,
Of oure linage have som compassioun, 1110
That is so lowe y-broght by tirannye."
And with that word Arcite gan espye
Wher as this lady romed to and fro;
And with that sighte hir beautee hurte him so,
That, if that Palamon was wounded sore, 1115
Arcite is hurt as muche as he, or more.
And with a sigh he seyde pitously:
"The fresshe beautee sleeth me sodeynly

Fortune has given us this adversity.
Some wicked aspect or disposition   230
Sent from Saturn, by some constellation,
Brought us this, though the opposite we'd sworn;
So stood the heavens when we both were born.   1090
We must endure; this is the long and short."
      Palamon answered back with this retort,   235
"In truth, Cousin, here in this opinion
You have now a misguided conception.
This prison here was not what made me cry,
But I was hurt right now straight through my eye
Into my heart,[5] so my death it will be.   240
The fairness of that lady whom I see
In yonder garden, roaming to and fro,
Is cause of all my crying and my woe.   1100
I don't know if she's woman or goddess,
But she is Venus, truly, as I guess."   245
And with those words, he fell down on his knees,
And said, "Venus, if now it may you please
In this garden yourself to transfigure
Before me, a mournful, wretched creature,
Out of this prison, help us to escape.   250
And should it be my destiny is shaped,
By divine word, to die here in this prison,
On our lineage, have some compassion,   1110
That now is brought so low by tyranny."
And with that word, Arcite began to see   255
Where this lady roamed then to and fro,
And with that sight, her beauty hurt him so
That, if this Palamon was wounded sore,
Arcite is hurt as much as he, or more.
And with a sigh, he said piteously,   260
"The fresh beauty slays me suddenly

---

   5 **straight through my eye / Into my heart**: This reaction is typical of courtly love, which
believed that one fell in love at first sight.

Of hire that rometh in the yonder place;
And, but I have hir mercy and hir grace,   1120
That I may seen hire atte leeste weye,
I nam but deed; ther nis namore to seye."
      This Palamon, whan he tho wordes herde,
Dispitously he loked and answerde:
"Whether seistow this in ernest or in pley?"   1125
      "Nay," quod Arcite, "in ernest, by my fey!
God help me so, me list ful yvele pleye."
      This Palamon gan knitte his browes tweye:
"It nere," quod he, "to thee no greet honour
For to be fals, ne for to be traytour   1130
To me, that am thy cosin and thy brother
Y-sworn ful depe, and ech of us til other,
That nevere, for to dyen in the peyne,
Til that the deeth departe shal us tweyne,
Neither of us in love to hindre other,   1135
Ne in non other cas, my leve brother;
But that thou sholdest trewely forthren me
In every cas, as I shal forthren thee.
This was thyn ooth, and myn also, certeyn;
I wot right wel, thou darst it nat withseyn.   1140
Thus artow of my counseil, out of doute,
And now thou woldest falsly been aboute
To love my lady, whom I love and serve,
And evere shal til that myn herte sterve.
Now certes, false Arcite, thou shalt nat so.   1145
I loved hire first, and tolde thee my wo
As to my counseil and my brother sworn
To forthre me, as I have told biforn.
For which thou art y-bounden as a knight
To helpen me, if it lay in thy might,   1150
Or elles artow fals, I dar wel seyn."
      This Arcite ful proudly spak ageyn:
"Thou shalt," quod he, "be rather fals than I;
But thou art fals, I telle thee outrely;

Of her who's roaming yonder in that place;
Unless I have her mercy and her grace,   1120
So I at least may see her anyway,
I am as good as dead; no more to say."   265
          This Palamon, when he those words had heard,
With cold anger he looked and then answered,
"Do you say this in earnest or in jest?"
          "No," said Arcite, "by my faith, in earnest!
It suits me not to play, God help me now."   270
          This Palamon began to knit his brow.
"It'd be," said he, "to you no great honor
To be so false or else to be a traitor   1130
To me, who am your cousin and your brother
Deeply sworn, each of us to the other,   275
So that never, though we die in torture's pain,
Until death comes and sunders us in twain,
Neither of us in love hinders the other,
Nor in another case, beloved brother,
But always you should truly further me   280
In each case; and I'll help you, certainly—
This was the oath you made, as well as I;
I know right well this you don't dare deny.   1140
Thus you are in my confidence, no doubt,
And yet you would now falsely be about   285
To love my lady, whom I love and serve
Until I die; my heart will never swerve.
No, in truth, false Arcite, you'll not do so.
I loved her first and told you of my woe,
My confidant and brother who once swore   290
To further me, as I have said before.
To which vows you are bound now as a knight
To help me, if it lies within your might,   1150
Or else, I dare well say, you behave falsely."
          This Arcite replied to him quite proudly: 295
"You will," said he, "be false, rather than me:
And you are false, I tell you, utterly.

For paramour I loved hire first er thow.   1155
What wiltow seyn? Thou woost nat yet now
Whether she be a womman or goddesse!
Thyn is affeccioun of holinesse,
And myn is love, as to a creature;
For which I tolde thee myn aventure   1160
As to my cosin and my brother sworn.
I pose that thou lovedest hire biforn:
Wostow nat wel the olde clerkes sawe,
That 'who shal yeve a lovere any lawe?'
Love is a gretter lawe, by my pan,   1165
Than may be yeve to any erthly man.
And therefore positif lawe and swich decree
Is broken al day for love in ech degree.
A man moot nedes love, maugree his heed.
He may nat fleen it, thogh he sholde be deed,   1170
Al be she mayde or widwe or elles wyf.
And eek it is nat lykly al thy lyf
To stonden in hir grace; namore shal I;
For wel thou woost thyselven verraily,
That thou and I be dampned to prisoun   1175
Perpetuelly; us gayneth no raunsoun.
We stryve as dide the houndes for the boon:
They foughte al day, and yet hir part was noon;
Ther cam a kyte, whyl that they were so wrothe,
And bar awey the boon bitwixe hem bothe.   1180
And therfore, at the kinges court, my brother,
Ech man for himself: ther is non other.
Love if thee list; for I love and ay shal;
And soothly, leve brother, this is al.
Here in this prisoun mote we endure,   1185
And everich of us take his aventure."

     Greet was the stryf and long bitwixe hem tweye,

I loved her amorously before you.
What will you say? You don't know if it's true
Whether she's a woman or a goddess!   300
Yours is affection due to holiness,
Mine is the love due to a human creature;[6]
This is why I told you my adventure,   1160
As to my cousin and brother sworn to me.
Suppose you loved her earlier; let's see—   305
Don't you well know that ancient scholars' saw
Of 'who will give a lover any law?'
By my skull, love is a greater law than
May be given to any earthly man.
And therefore man-made laws and their decrees   310
Are breached each day for love in all degrees.
By need, a man must love, despite his head;
He may not flee it, though he should be dead,   1170
Though she's a maiden, widow or else wife.
And also, it's not likely all your life   315
To stand within her grace; no more shall I;
For well you know yourself, it is no lie,
That you and I are condemned to prison
Perpetually; no ransom helps us then.
Like hounds over the bone, we both are striving;   320
They fought all day, and yet their share was nothing.
While they were wrathful, a kite[7] came that day,
And from between them, bore the bone away.   1180
Thus, now at the king's court, my dear brother,
Each man is for himself; there is no other.   325
Love, if you wish, for I shall love her always;
Dear brother, truly, this is all I say.
Here in this prison, we must both endure,
And each must take his chances, that is sure."
        Great was the strife they had, and long as well,   330

6   The distinction Arcite makes here is between the two kinds of courtly love: Platonic and sensual.
7   **kite**: Scavenger bird.

If that I hadde leyser for to seye,
But to th'effect. It happed on a day,
To telle it yow as shortly as I may,   1190
A worthy duk that highte Perotheus,
That felawe was unto duk Theseus
Sin thilke day that they were children lyte,
Was come to Athenes his felawe to visyte,
And for to pleye as he was wont to do;   1195
For in this world he loved no man so,
And he loved him as tendrely ageyn.
So wel they lovede, as olde bokes seyn,
That whan that oon was deed, sothly to telle,
His felawe wente and soghte him doun in helle;   1200
But of that story list me nat to wryte.
Duk Perotheus loved wel Arcite,
And hadde him knowe at Thebes yeer by yere;
And fynally, at requeste and preyere
Of Perotheus, withouten any raunsoun,   1205
Duk Theseus him leet out of prisoun
Freely to goon wher that him liste over al,
In swich a gyse as I you tellen shal.

   This was the forward, pleynly for t'endyte,
Bitwixen Theseus and him Arcite: 1210
That if so were, that Arcite were y-founde
Evere in his lyf, by day or night, o stounde
In any contree of this Theseus,
And he were caught, it was acorded thus,
That with a swerd he sholde lese his heed;   1215
Ther nas non other remedye ne reed;
But taketh his leve, and homward he him spedde;
Let him be war, his nekke lyth to wedde.

   How greet a sorwe suffreth now Arcite!
The deeth he feleth thurgh his herte smyte;   1220
He wepeth, wayleth, cryeth pitously;
To sleen himself he wayteth prively.
He seyde, "Allas that day that I was born!

If only I had leisure now to tell;
But, to the point. It happened then one day,
To tell you this as shortly as I may,   1190
A worthy duke known as Perotheus,
Who was a good friend of Duke Theseus   335
Since the time when they were little children,
Has come to visit his good friend in Athens,
And there to play as he was wont to do;
In this world, he loved no man so, it's true;
Theseus loved him tenderly always.   340
So well they loved, that, as the old books say,
When one of them was dead, truly to tell,
His fellow went and sought him down in hell—   1200
But of that story, I don't wish to write.
Duke Perotheus well loved this Arcite;   345
For many years, he'd known him at Thebes there,
And finally, at the request and prayer
Of Perotheus, and with no ransom's fee
Duke Theseus from prison set him free,
Freely to go where he might like, as well,   350
In such a manner as I shall you tell.
        This was the agreement, plainly now to write,
Made between Theseus and this Arcite: 1210
If it should ever happen that he might,
One moment in his life, by day or night,   355
Be found in any land of Theseus,
And he were caught, it was accorded thus,
That with a sword, then, he would lose his head.
There was no remedy; and he'd be dead.
He takes his leave, and homeward he speeds yet.   360
Let him beware! His neck as pledge lies set.
        How great a sorrow suffers now Arcite!
Throughout his heart, he feels that death does smite;   1220
He weeps and wails, he cries out piteously;
To slay himself, he does wait privately.   365
He said, "The day that I was born, I curse!

Now is my prison worse than biforn;
Now is me shape eternally to dwelle   1225
Noght in purgatorie but in helle.
Allas, that evere knew I Perotheus!
For elles hadde I dwelled with Theseus
Y-fetered in his prisoun everemo.
Than hadde I been in blisse, and nat in wo.   1230
Only the sighte of hire whom that I serve,
Though that I nevere hir grace may deserve,
Wolde han suffised right ynough for me.
O dere cosin Palamon," quod he,
"Thyn is the victorie of this aventure: 1235
Ful blisfully in prison maistow dure.
In prison? certes nay, but in paradys!
Wel hath Fortune y-turned thee the dys,
That hast the sighte of hire, and I th'absence.
For possible is, sin thou hast hire presence,   1240
And art a knight, a worthy and an able,
That by som cas, sin Fortune is chaungeable,
Thou mayst to thy desyr somtyme atteyne.
But I, that am exyled and bareyne
Of alle grace, and in so greet despeir   1245
That ther nis erthe, water, fyr, ne eir,
Ne creature that of hem maked is
That may me helpe or doon confort in this,
Wel oughte I sterve in wanhope and distresse.
Farwel my lyf, my lust, and my gladnesse!   1250
        Allas, why pleynen folk so in commune
On purveyaunce of God, or of Fortune,
That yeveth hem ful ofte in many a gyse
Wel bettre than they can hemself devyse?
Som man desyreth for to han richesse,   1255
That cause is of his mordre or greet siknesse.
And som man wolde out of his prison fayn,
That in his hous is of his meynee slayn.
Infinite harmes been in this matere;

Now has my prison become even worse;
Now I am made eternally to dwell
Not just in purgatory, but in hell.
Alas, I ever knew Perotheus!   370
For then, I could have dwelled with Theseus,
Forever fettered in his prison so.
Then I'd have been in bliss and not in woe.   1230
The sight alone of her, the one I serve,
Although I never may her grace deserve,   375
Would have sufficed right well enough for me.
Oh, dear cousin Palamon," said he,
"Victory is yours in this adventure.
Quite blissfully in prison you endure—
In prison? Surely not! In paradise!   380
Well has Fortune cast for you the dice,
Who has sight of her, and I, the absence.
It's possible, since you have her presence,   1240
And are a knight, a worthy one, and able,
That by some chance, since Fortune is unstable,   385
Sometime, you may get your desire then.
But I, who am exiled and thus barren
Of all grace, and in so great despair
That there is not earth, fire, water, air,
Nor creature who of them all made might be   390
Who, in my plight, may help or comfort me;
In despair I ought to die, and in distress.
Farewell to my life, my love, my gladness!   1250
　　　Alas, why do folks have little patience
With Fortune or else with God's providence,   395
Who can often give, in many a guise,
Much better than they would themselves devise?
For one man could want to have great richness,
Which might cause his murder or his sickness;
And one man would be happy out of prison,   400
Who in his house, his retinue might slay then.
Infinite harms can happen in this way.

We witen nat what thing we preyen here.   1260
We faren as he that dronke is as a mous:
A dronke man wot wel he hath an hous,
But he noot which the righte wey is thider;
And to a dronke man the wey is slider.
And certes, in this world so faren we;   1265
We seken faste after felicitee,
But we goon wrong ful often, trewely.
Thus may we seyen alle, and namely I,
That wende and hadde a greet opinioun   1270
That if I mighte escapen from prisoun,
Than hadde I been in joye and perfit hele,
Ther now I am exyled fro my wele.
Sin that I may nat seen yow, Emelye,
I nam but deed; ther nis no remedye."

          Upon that other syde Palamon,   1275
Whan that he wiste Arcite was agon,
Swich sorwe he maketh that the grete tour
Resouneth of his youling and clamour.
The pure fettres on his shines grete
Weren of his bittre salte teres wete.   1280
"Allas!" quod he, "Arcita, cosin myn,
Of al our stryf, God woot, the fruyt is thyn.
Thow walkest now in Thebes at thy large,
And of my wo thou yevest litel charge.
Thou mayst, sin thou hast wisdom and manhede,   1285
Assemblen alle the folk of our kinrede,
And make a werre so sharp on this citee,
That by som aventure, or some tretee,
Thou mayst have hir to lady and to wyf,
For whom that I moste nedes lese my lyf.   1290
For, as by wey of possibilitee,
Sith thou art at thy large, of prison free,
And art a lord, greet is thyn avauntage
More than is myn, that sterve here in a cage.
For I mot wepe and wayle, whyl I live,   1295

We do not know the thing for which we pray;   1260
We're like the man who is drunk as a mouse.
A drunken man knows well he has a house,   405
But the right way back to it knows not he,
For to a drunken man, the way is slippery.
And certainly, in this world, so fare we;
We seek fast after our felicity,
But we go wrong quite often, it's no lie.   410
Thus all of us may say, and namely I,
Who supposed and had a great opinion
That if I might escape there from this prison,   1270
Then I would be in joy and perfect health,
Whereas now I am exiled from my wealth.   415
Since now I may not see you, Emily,
I'm surely dead; there is no remedy."

     Upon that other side now, Palamon,
When he first knew that this Arcite was gone,
Makes sorrow such that all of that great tower   420
Resounds now with his yowling and his clamor.
And thus upon his shins, the very fetters
Were wet from his tears, salty and bitter.   1280
"Alas, Arcite, oh cousin mine, God knows,
The fruit of our strife," said he, "to you goes.   425
Now in Thebes, you're walking freely there,
And of my woe you take so little care.
Since you have your wisdom and your manhood,
All our kinfolks you assemble could,
And make so sharp a war upon this city   430
That by some circumstance or by some treaty
You may have her as lady and as wife
And for her I, by need, must lose my life.   1290
For there is a good possibility,
Since you are now at large, from prison free,   435
And are a lord, that great is your advantage
More than is mine, who dies here in a cage.
For I must weep and wail, while I may live,

With al the wo that prison may me yive,
And eek with peyne that love me yiveth also,
That doubleth al my torment and my wo."
Therwith the fyr of jalousye up sterte
Withinne his brest, and hente him by the herte   1300
So woodly, that he lyk was to biholde
The boxtree or the asshen dede and colde.
Thanne seyde he: "O cruel goddes, that governe
This world with binding of youre word eterne,
And wryten in the table of athamaunt   1305
Your parlement and youre eterne graunt,
What is mankinde more unto yow holde
Than is the sheep that rouketh in the folde?
For slayn is man right as another beste,
And dwelleth eek in prison and areste,   1310
And hath siknesse and greet adversitee,
And ofte tymes giltelees, pardee!
        What governaunce is in this prescience
That giltelees tormenteth innocence?
And yet encreseth this al my penaunce,   1315
That man is bounden to his observaunce,
For Goddes sake, to letten of his wille,
Ther as a beest may al his lust fulfille.
And whan a beest is deed, he hath no peyne;
But man after his deeth moot wepe and pleyne,   1320
Though in this world he have care and wo.
Withouten doute it may stonden so.
The answere of this I lete to divynis,
But wel I woot, that in this world gret pyne is.
Allas! I see a serpent or a theef,   1325
That many a trewe man hath doon mescheef,
Goon at his large, and where him list may turne.
But I mot been in prison thurgh Saturne,

With all the woe that prison may me give,
And with the pain that love gives me also,   440
Which doubles all my torment and my woe."
With that, the fire of jealousy up starts
Within his breast, and seized him by the heart   1300
So madly that he was then to behold
Like boxwood[8] or like ashes, dead and cold.   445
Then said he, "Oh, you cruel gods who will
Rule this world with binding word eternal
And then write in tablets of adamant
Both your decrees and your eternal grants,
What greater worth for man now do you hold   450
Than for the sheep that cowers in the fold?
For like man, any other beast is slain;
Imprisoned and arrested he remains,   1310
And he suffers sickness and adversity,
And often he is guiltless, certainly.   455
      "What governance lies in this prescience
That can thus torment guiltless innocence?
Yet this increases all my agony;
That man is bound to carry out his duty,
For God's sake, and renouncing his own will,   460
Whereas a beast may all its wants fulfill.
And when a beast is dead, it has no pain;
But man after his death weeps and complains,   1320
Though in this world he had much care and woe.
Without a doubt, it all stands, even so.   465
To answer this, let diviners explain
But well I know in this world is great pain.
Alas, I see a serpent or a thief
Who once has brought a true man to his grief,
Now go at large; where he likes, he may turn.   470
But in prison I must be through Saturn,

8 **boxwood**: Associated with the color white just as ashes are typically associated with the color gray.

And eek thurgh Juno, jalous and eek wood,
That hath destroyed wel ny al the blood   1330
Of Thebes, with his waste walles wyde.
And Venus sleeth me on that other syde
For jalousye, and fere of him Arcite."
          Now wol I stinte of Palamon a lyte,
And lete him to his prison stille dwelle,   1335
And of Arcita forth I wol yow telle.
          The somer passeth, and the nightes longe
Encresen double wyse the peynes stronge
Bothe of the lovere and the prisoner.
I noot which hath the wofullere mester.   1340
For, shortly for to seyn, this Palamoun
Perpetuelly is dampned to prisoun,
In cheynes and in fettres to ben deed;
And Arcite is exyled upon his heed
For evermo as out of that contree,   1345
Ne neveremo ne shal his lady see.
          Yow loveres axe I now this questioun:
Who hath the worse, Arcite or Palamoun?
That oon may seen his lady day by day,
But in prison he moot dwelle alway.   1350
That other wher him list may ryde or go,
But seen his lady shal he neveremo.
Now demeth as yow liste, ye that can,
For I wol telle forth as I bigan.

Explicit prima pars.
Sequitur pars secunda.

          Whan that Arcite to Thebes comen was,   1355
Ful ofte a day he swelte and seyde "allas,"
For seen his lady shal he neveremo.
And shortly to concluden al his wo,
So muche sorwe hadde nevere creature
That is, or shal, whyl that the world may dure. 1360

And through Juno, who's both mad and jealous
And who's destroyed nearly all the blood thus   1330
Of Thebes now, with its wasted walls so wide;
And Venus slays me on the other side   475
For jealousy and fear of this Arcite."
  Now I will cease with Palamon, if I might,
And leave him in his prison still to dwell,
And of Arcite right now I will you tell.
  The summer passes, and the nights so long   480
Increase in double-wise all the pains strong
Both of the lover and the prisoner.
I don't know whose woeful task is harsher.   1340
But, shortly now to tell, this Palamon
Perpetually is condemned to prison,   485
In fetters and in chains until he's dead;
Arcite's exiled, on pain to lose his head,
Forever more outside of that country,
And nevermore his lady will he see.
  To you lovers, I now ask this question: 490
Who has it worse, Arcite or Palamon?
The one may see his lady day by day,
But in prison he is dwelling always;   1350
That other, where he likes may ride or go,
But never see his lady even so.   495
Now judge this as you like, all you who can,
For I'll tell forth the tale that I began.

The first part ends.
The second part follows.

  When Arcite to Thebes had made his way,
Faint he became and said "Alas!" all day,
For nevermore he'll see his lady so,   500
And shortly to conclude about his woe,
So much sorrow never had a creature
Who lives, or will, while the world may endure.   1360

His sleep, his mete, his drink is him biraft,
That lene he wex and drye as is a shaft.
His eyen holwe, and grisly to biholde;
His hewe falow and pale as asshen colde;
And solitarie he was and evere allone,   1365
And waillinge al the night, makinge his mone.
And if he herde song or instrument,
Thanne wolde he wepe, he mighte nat be stent.
So feble eek were his spirits, and so lowe,
And chaunged so, that no man coude knowe   1370
His speche nor his vois, though men it herde.
And in his gere for al the world he ferde
Nat oonly lyk the loveres maladye
Of Hereos, but rather lyk manye
Engendred of humour malencolyk   1375
Biforen, in his celle fantastyk.
And shortly, turned was al up so doun
Bothe habit and eek disposicioun
Of him, this woful lovere daun Arcite.
          What sholde I al day of his wo endyte?   1380
Whan he endured hadde a yeer or two
This cruel torment and this peyne and wo,
At Thebes, in his contree, as I seyde,
Upon a night, in sleep as he him leyde,
Him thoughte how that the winged god Mercurie   1385
Biforn him stood and bad him to be murye.
His slepy yerde in hond he bar uprighte;
An hat he werede upon his heres brighte.
Arrayed was this god, as he took keep,

His sleep, his food, his drink he does deny,
And like a stick, he waxes lean and dry,   505
His eyes hollowed and grisly to behold,
His hue yellow and pale as ashes cold,
Forever solitary and alone,
And wailing all night long, making his moan.
And if he heard an instrument or song,   510
Then would he weep; he could not stop for long.
So feeble, too, his spirits, and so low,
And they were so changed that no man could know   1370
His speech or voice, although he heard him there.
In his manner, for all the world he fared   515
Just like he had the lovers' malady
Of Hereos,⁹ and mania, quite likely,
Engendered by the humor melancholy
In the mind's front cell¹⁰ that governs fantasy.
And, in short, his physical condition   520
Was turned upside down, and the disposition
Of him, this woeful lover Don Arcite.
    What should I all day of his woe now write? 1380
When he had then endured a year or so
This cruel torment and this pain and woe   525
In this country, Thebes, as I have said,
One night as he lay sleeping in his bed,
It seemed to him the winged god Mercury
Before him stood and bade him to be merry.
In his hand, his sleep-filled wand was upright;   530
And his hat he wore on his hair bright.
This god was arrayed, Arcite took notice,

9   malady / Of Hereos: The word *Hereos* is a conflation of "eros" and "hero" in a typical medieval false etymology. The symptoms that Arcite shows are typical of the male courtly lover, who is often represented, in both medieval medical and literary texts, as suffering exactly these kinds of symptoms, emotional excesses, and physical transformations. See the discussion of courtly love in the introduction.

10   front cell: Area of the brain that was thought to control the imagination.

As he was whan that Argus took his sleep;   1390
And seyde him thus: "To Athenes shaltou wende:
Ther is thee shapen of thy wo an ende."
And with that word Arcite wook and sterte.
"Now trewely, how sore that me smerte,"
Quod he, "to Athenes right now wol I fare;   1395
Ne for the drede of deeth shal I nat spare
To see my lady, that I love and serve.
In hire presence I recche nat to sterve."
          And with that word he caughte a greet mirour,
And saugh that chaunged was al his colour,   1400
And saugh his visage al in another kinde.
And right anoon it ran him in his minde,
That, sith his face was so disfigured
Of maladye, the which he hadde endured,
He mighte wel, if that he bar him lowe,   1405
Live in Athenes everemore unknowe,
And seen his lady wel ny day by day.
And right anon he chaunged his array,
And cladde him as a povre laborer,
And al allone, save oonly a squyer   1410
That knew his privetee and al his cas,
Which was disgysed povrely as he was,
To Athenes is he goon the nexte way.
And to the court he wente upon a day,
And at the gate he profreth his servyse   1415
To drugge and drawe, what so men wol devyse.
And shortly of this matere for to seyn,
He fil in office with a chamberleyn,
The which that dwellinge was with Emelye;
For he was wys, and coude soone aspye   1420
Of every servaunt, which that serveth here.
Wel coude he hewen wode and water bere,

Just as when to sleep he had put Argus;[11]   1390
And he said thus: "To Athens you will wend.
And there, for you, your woe's destined to end."   535
And with that word, Arcite did wake and start,
"In truth, however sorely I may smart,"
Said he, "to Athens right now I'll repair,
And for the dread of death, I shall not spare
To see my lady whom I love and serve.   540
In her presence, my death I shall not swerve."
    With that word, he took up a great mirror,
And saw that all transformed had been his color,   1400
And saw his visage changed from its own kind.
And right away, the thought ran through his mind,   545
That, now since his face was so disfigured
By the malady that he'd long endured,
If he bore himself humbly, he might well
Unknown in Athens evermore go dwell,
And see his lady almost every day.   550
And right away, he changed all his array,
And clad himself like a poor laborer,
And all alone, save only with a squire   1410
Who knew his fortune and his privacy,
And was disguised in the same poor clothes as he,   555
To Athens he went by the nearest way.
And to the court he went upon a day,
And at the gate, offers himself for hire,
To drudge and draw—whatever they require.
And shortly now, this matter to explain,   560
He fell in service with a chamberlain,
For the chamberlain dwelled with Emily,
And he was wise and he could quickly see,   1420
Among all the servants, which ones served her.
Well could he hew wood and carry water,   565

---

11 **Argus:** Argus was a mythological character who had a hundred eyes, the better to guard Zeus's lover, Io. Mercury had to put all the eyes to sleep before he could kill this monster.

For he was yong and mighty for the nones,
And therto he was strong and big of bones
To doon that any wight can him devyse.   1425
A yeer or two he was in this servyse,
Page of the chambre of Emelye the brighte;
And Philostrate he seide that he highte.
But half so wel biloved a man as he
Ne was ther nevere in court of his degree;   1430
He was so gentil of condicioun
That thurghout al the court was his renoun.
They seyden that it were a charitee
That Theseus wolde enhauncen his degree
And putten him in worshipful servyse,   1435
Ther as he mighte his vertu excercyse.
And thus withinne a whyle his name is spronge,
Bothe of his dedes and his goode tonge,
That Theseus hath taken him so neer
That of his chambre he made him a squyer,   1440
And gaf him gold to mayntene his degree;
And eek men broghte him out of his contree
From yeer to yeer, ful prively, his rente;
But honestly and slyly he it spente,
That no man wondred how that he it hadde.   1445
And three yeer in this wyse his lyf he ladde,
And bar him so in pees and eek in werre,
Ther was no man that Theseus hath derre.
And in this blisse lete I now Arcite,
And speke I wol of Palamon a lyte.   1450
       In derknesse and horrible and strong prisoun
Thise seven yeer hath seten Palamoun,
Forpyned, what for wo and for distresse;

For he was young and mighty for the chore,[12]
And he was tall and big of bone therefore
To do what any man might tell him to.
In this service, he was a year or two,
The chamber page of lovely Emily,   570
And claimed his name Philostratus[13] to be.
But half so well beloved a man as he
Was never at this court of his degree;   1430
His manner was so gentle that his name
Was known throughout the court to bring him fame.   575
They said that it would be a charity
For Theseus to advance him in degree
And honorable work for him devise,
In which he might his talents exercise.
And thus, within a time, his fame has sprung,   580
Because of both his deeds and his good tongue,
So that Theseus has drawn him closer,
And he made him a squire in his chamber,   1440
And gave him gold to maintain his degree.
To him men brought out from his own country,   585
Year by year, his income privately,
Which he spent honestly and discreetly,
So no one wondered how he had such pay.
And for three years he lead his life this way,
And in both peace and war bore himself thus,   590
That no man dearer was to Theseus.
And in this bliss, I leave Arcite to dwell,
And a little about Palamon, I'll tell.   1450
    In the darkness and the horrible, strong prison
These seven years was sitting Palamon,   595
Pained deeply, what for woe and for distress.

---

12 **mighty for the chore**: It is a paradox of courtly love that, no matter how wasted the man might
be by his love-longing, he retains enough physical prowess to accomplish mighty feats.

13 **Philostratus**: The name literally means "one prostrate in love." Chaucer got the name from
the title of Boccaccio's fourteenth-century work *Il Filostrato*.

Who feleth double soor and hevinesse
But Palamon, that love destreyneth so   1455
That wood out of his wit he gooth for wo?
And eek therto he is a prisoner
Perpetuelly, noght oonly for a yeer.
Who coude ryme in English proprely
His martirdom? For sothe, it am nat I;   1460
Therefore I passe as lightly as I may.
      It fel that in the seventhe yeer, of May
The thridde night, as olde bokes seyn,
That al this storie tellen more pleyn,
Were it by aventure or destinee—   1465
As, whan a thing is shapen, it shal be—
That sone after the midnight Palamoun,
By helping of a freend, brak his prisoun
And fleeth the citee faste as he may go;
For he hadde yive his gayler drinke so   1470
Of a clarree maad of a certeyn wyn,
With nercotikes and opie of Thebes fyn,
That al that night, thogh that men wolde him shake,
The gayler sleep, he mighte nat awake;
And thus he fleeth as faste as evere he may.   1475
The night was short and faste by the day,
That nedes cost he moot himselven hyde,
And til a grove, faste ther bisyde,
With dredful foot thanne stalketh Palamoun.
For, shortly, this was his opinioun: 1480
That in that grove he wolde him hyde al day,
And in the night thanne wolde he take his way
To Thebes-ward, his freendes for to preye
On Theseus to helpe him to werreye;
And shortly, outher he wolde lese his lyf   1485
Or winnen Emelye unto his wyf.
This is th'effect and his entente pleyn.
      Now wol I turne to Arcite ageyn,
That litel wiste how ny that was his care,

Who feels a double sorrow and sadness
But Palamon, whom loving afflicts so
That mad out of his mind he goes for woe?
Moreover, he remains a prisoner   600
Not only for a year now, but forever.
Who could rhyme in English properly
About his martyrdom? Not I, truly;   1460
Therefore, I pass as lightly as I may.

      It happened in the seventh year, in May,   605
On the third night (as old books explain,
Which make all of this story much more plain),
Whether it were by chance or destiny—
As when something is shaped, so it shall be—
That shortly after midnight Palamon,   610
With a friend's help, broke out of his prison
And flees the city fast as he may go.
For he'd given his jailer a drink so   1470
Made from a certain spiced and sweetened wine,
Narcotics and a Theban opium fine,   615
That all night long, though some men should shake him,
The jailer sleeps; for no one might awake him.
Thus Palamon flees as quickly as he may.
The night was short, and quickly came the day,
When he must find a place so he can hide,   620
And to a grove quite close by the roadside,
With fearful foot, now stalks in Palamon.
For, in short, now this was his opinion: 1480
That in the grove, he'd hide himself all day,
And when night came, then he would take his way   625
To Thebes, and to his friends he would pray thus
To help him to wage war on Theseus;
And, in short, either he would lose his life,
Or he'd win Emily to be his wife.
This is his purpose and intention clear.   630

      Now, to Arcite again I will turn here,
Who little knew how close his foe was there,

Til that Fortune had broght him in the snare.   1490
    The bisy larke, messager of day,
Saluëth in hir song the morwe gray;
And fyry Phebus ryseth up so brighte
That al the orient laugheth of the lighte,
And with his stremes dryeth in the greves   1495
The silver dropes hanginge on the leves.
And Arcite, that in the court royal
With Theseus is squyer principal,
Is risen and loketh on the myrie day.
And for to doon his observaunce to May,   1500
Remembringe on the poynt of his desyr,
He on a courser, startlinge as the fyr,
Is riden into the feeldes him to pleye,
Out of the court, were it a myle or tweye;
And to the grove of which that I yow tolde,   1505
By aventure his wey he gan to holde,
To maken him a gerland of the greves,
Were it of wodebinde or hawethorn leves,
And loude he song ageyn the sonne shene:
"May, with alle thy floures and thy grene,   1510
Welcome be thou, faire fresshe May,
In hope that I som grene gete may."
And from his courser, with a lusty herte,
Into the grove ful hastily he sterte,
And in a path he rometh up and doun,   1515
Theras, by aventure, this Palamoun
Was in a bush, that no man mighte him see,
For sore afered of his deeth was he.
Nothing ne knew he that it was Arcite;
God wot he wolde have trowed it ful lyte.   1520
But sooth is seyd, go sithen many yeres,
That "feeld hath eyen and the wode hath eres."

Until Fortune had caught him in her snare.   1490
    The busy lark, the messenger of day,
Saluted in her song the morning gray,   635
And fiery Phoebus rises up so bright
That all the eastern sky laughs with his light,
And with his beams, he dries throughout the copse
On all the leaves, the hanging silver drops.
And Arcite, who in the royal court thus   640
Is squire principal of Theseus,
Has risen and looks on the merry day,
So he might do his homage unto May.   1500
Remembering the point of his desire,
On a charger, cantering like fire,   645
He rides into the fields so he might play,
Out of the court, a mile or so away.
And to the grove, of which I have you told,
And just by chance, his way now he does hold;
A garland from the branches he will weave,   650
Whether of woodbine or of hawthorn leaves,
And loudly to the bright sun, then sang he:
"May, with thy flowers and thy greenery,   1510
Now welcome be to thee, fair and fresh May,
I hope to get some green here,[14] if I may."   655
Down from his charger, with a lusty heart,
Into the grove quite quickly he does start,
And on a path, he roams up and down where,
As chance would have it, Palamon is there
Within a bush so no man might him see,   660
Since sore afraid of his own death was he.
That it was Arcite, not a thing he knew;
God knows he'd not believe that it was true.   1520
But truth be told, as it has been for years,
Which says that "fields have eyes and woods have ears."   665

---

14 **get some green here**: The allusion isn't clear, but the phrase may indicate part of a game or
practice to celebrate May.

It is ful fair a man to bere him evene,

For al day meeteth men at unset stevene.

Ful litel woot Arcite of his felawe,   1525

That was so ny to herknen al his sawe,

For in the bush he sitteth now ful stille.

      Whan that Arcite hadde romed al his fille,

And songen al the roundel lustily,

Into a studie he fil sodeynly,   1530

As doon thise loveres in hir queynte geres,

Now in the croppe, now doun in the breres,

Now up, now doun, as boket in a welle.

Right as the Friday, soothly for to telle,

Now it shyneth, now it reyneth faste,   1535

Right so can gery Venus overcaste

The hertes of hir folk; right as hir day

Is gereful, right so chaungeth she array.

Selde is the Friday al the wyke ylyke.

      Whan that Arcite had songe, he gan to syke,   1540

And sette him doun withouten any more.

"Alas!" quod he, "that day that I was bore!

How longe, Juno, thurgh thy crueltee,

Woltow werreyen Thebes the citee?

Allas! y-broght is to confusioun   1545

The blood royal of Cadme and Amphioun—

Of Cadmus, which that was the firste man

That Thebes bulte, or first the toun bigan,

And of the citee first was crouned king.

Of his lynage am I, and his ofspring   1550

By verray ligne, as of the stok royal;

And now I am so caitif and so thral

That he that is my mortal enemy,

I serve him as his squyer povrely.

For a man to be calm is a fine thing
Since men can often have an unplanned meeting.
And little knew Arcite his fellow here
Heard all his speech, because he was so near,
For in the bush, he's sitting now, quite still.   670
  When Arcite of roaming had his fill,
And his whole roundel had sung lustily,
Into a study he fell suddenly,   1530
As these lovers do with their quaint manners,
Now in the leaves, now down in the briars,   675
Now up, now down, like buckets in a well.
They're just like Friday,[15] truly now to tell:
Now it shines, and now it's raining fast;
Just so can fickle Venus overcast
The hearts of her folk; just as her own day   680
Is changeable, so she will change array.
Friday is seldom like the week gone by.
  When Arcite had first sung, then he did sigh   1540
And sits himself down without more ado.
"Alas," said he, "that I was born, I rue!   685
Oh how long, Juno, through your cruelty,
Will you wage war upon the Theban city?
For, alas, now brought is to confusion
The royal blood of Cadmus and Amphion—
Of Cadmus, he who had been the first man   690
Who built up Thebes, and first the town began,
And of the city first was crowned its king.
Of his lineage am I, and his offspring   1550
In the true line, from royal stock withal;
Now, I'm a wretched captive and a thrall   695
To him who is my mortal enemy;
As squire I serve him with humility.

---

15 **just like Friday:** In these lines, the emphasis is on the alleged changeability of Fridays. Since Friday was Venus's day, and since Venus, as the goddess of love, was notoriously changeable, Fridays were thought to be as changeable as lovers were under Venus's influence.

And yet doth Juno me wel more shame,   1555
For I dar noght biknowe myn owne name;
But ther as I was wont to highte Arcite,
Now highte I Philostrate, noght worth a myte.
Allas, thou felle Mars! allas, Juno!
Thus hath youre ire our lynage al fordo,   1560
Save only me and wrecched Palamoun,
That Theseus martyreth in prisoun.
And over al this, to sleen me outrely,
Love hath his fyry dart so brenningly
Y-stiked thurgh my trewe careful herte,   1565
That shapen was my deeth erst than my sherte.
Ye sleen me with youre eyen, Emelye!
Ye been the cause wherfore that I dye.
Of all the remenant of myn other care
Ne sette I nat the mountaunce of a tare,   1570
So that I coude don aught to your plesaunce!"
And with that word he fil down in a traunce
A longe tyme; and after he up sterte.
        This Palamoun, that thoughte that thurgh his herte
He felte a cold swerd sodeynliche glyde,   1575
For ire he quook, no lenger wolde he byde.
And whan that he had herd Arcites tale,
As he were wood, with face deed and pale,
He sterte him up out of the buskes thikke,
And seyde: "Arcite, false traitour wikke,   1580
Now artow hent, that lovest my lady so,
For whom that I have al this peyne and wo,
And art my blood, and to my counseil sworn,
As I ful ofte have told thee heerbiforn,
And hast byjaped here duk Theseus,   1585
And falsly chaunged hast thy name thus!
I wol be deed, or elles thou shalt dye.

And yet to me Juno does greater shame,
For I dare not acknowledge my own name;
Where I was wont once to be named Arcite,   700
Now I'm Philostratus, not worth a mite.
Alas to you, fierce Mars! Alas, Juno!
Your ire has destroyed our lineage so,   1560
Save only me, and wretched Palamon,
Whom Theseus martyrs in his prison.   705
On top of this, to slay me utterly,
Through my sad, faithful heart, Love burningly
Has his fiery dart straight through it laid;
My death was shaped before my shirt was made.[16]
Emily, you slay me with your eye!   710
For you are the whole reason that I die.
As for the rest of every other care,
I value them no better than a tare,   1570
If I might do something to please you well."
And with that word, down in a trance he fell   715
For a long time, and after up he starts.
        This Palamon, who thought that through his heart
He felt a cold sword gliding suddenly,
With ire he quaked; no longer wait would he.
And after he had heard all Arcite's tale,   720
As though he's mad, with face deathly and pale,
He started up out of the bushy thicket
And said: "Arcite, you false traitor wicked,   1580
Now you are seized, who loves my lady so,
For whom I have had all this pain and woe;   725
You are my blood; to counsel me you swore,
As I have told you many times before,
And here now you have tricked Duke Theseus,
And now falsely you have changed your name thus!
I will be dead, or else you will die, truly.   730

16 **before my shirt was made:** He is suggesting that the gods knew when his death would come even before his first article of clothing had been woven.

Thou shalt nat love my lady Emelye,

But I wol love hire only, and namo;

For I am Palamoun, thy mortal fo.   1590

And though that I no wepne have in this place,

But out of prison am astert by grace,

I drede noght that outher thou shalt dye

Or thou ne shalt nat loven Emelye.

Chees which thou wolt, for thou shalt nat asterte."   1595

      This Arcitë, with ful despitous herte,

Whan he him knew, and hadde his tale herd,

As fiers as leoun pulled out his swerd

And seyde thus: "By God that sit above,

Nere it that thou art sik and wood for love,   1600

And eek that thou no wepne hast in this place,

Thou sholdest nevere out of this grove pace,

That thou ne sholdest dyen of myn hond.

For I defye the seuretee and the bond

Which that thou seyst that I have maad to thee.   1605

What, verray fool, I think wel that love is free,

And I wol love hire maugre al thy might!

But, for as muche thou art a worthy knight,

And wilnest to darreyne hire by batayle,

Have heer my trouthe: tomorwe I wol nat fayle,   1610

Withoute witing of any other wight,

That here I wol be founden as a knight,

And bringen harneys right ynough for thee;

And chees the beste, and leve the worste for me.

And mete and drinke this night wol I bringe   1615

Ynough for thee, and clothes for thy beddinge.

And if so be that thou my lady winne,

And slee me in this wode ther I am inne,

Thou mayst wel have thy lady, as for me."

This Palamon answerde: "I graunte it thee."   1620

And thus they been departed til amorwe,

Whan ech of hem had leyd his feith to borwe.

      O Cupide, out of alle charitee!

You will not love my lady Emily,
I'll be the only one to love her so;
For I am Palamon, your mortal foe. 1590
And though I have no weapon in this place,
For out of prison I've escaped by grace, 735
Either you'll die—there is no doubt in me,
Or else you must cease loving Emily.
Choose, or you won't escape, as I was born!"
        This Arcite, whose heart was so full of scorn,
When he knew him and heard his whole tale, too, 740
Fierce as a lion, out his sword he drew,
And he said thus, "By God who sits above,
Were you not here both sick and mad for love, 1600
And also have no weapon in this place,
Then you would never out of this grove pace, 745
Unless first, by my own hand, you would die.
For any pledge and bond now I defy
That you have said I made you, certainly.
What! Arrant fool, know well that love is free;
I will love her in spite of all your might! 750
But inasmuch as you're a worthy knight,
And for her wish in battle to prevail,
Have here my pledge; tomorrow, I won't fail— 1610
And to know of this, no one else might—
So on my honor as I am a knight, 755
I will bring armor for you; you'll go first,
And choose the best, and for me leave the worst.
And food and drink this very night I'll bring
Enough for you, and some cloth for your bedding.
And if it be that you my lady win, 760
And slay me in these woods that I am in,
You may have your lady, as you wished to do."
This Palamon answered back, "I grant it to you." 1620
And thus they parted until the next day,
When each of them as pledge his faith did lay. 765
        Oh Cupid, lacking in all charity!

O regne, that wolt no felawe have with thee!
Ful sooth is seyd that love ne lordshipe   1625
Wol noght, his thankes, have no felaweshipe;
Wel finden that Arcite and Palamoun.
Arcite is riden anon unto the toun,
And on the morwe, er it were dayes light,
Ful prively two harneys hath he dight,   1630
Bothe suffisaunt and mete to darreyne
The bataille in the feeld bitwix hem tweyne.
And on his hors, allone as he was born,
He carieth al this harneys him biforn;
And in the grove, at tyme and place y-set,   1635
This Arcite and this Palamon ben met.

        To chaungen gan the colour in hir face,
Right as the hunters in the regne of Trace,
That stondeth at the gappe with a spere,
Whan hunted is the leoun or the bere,   1640
And hereth him come russhing in the greves,
And breketh bothe bowes and the leves,
And thinketh, "Heere cometh my mortel enemy!
Withoute faile, he moot be deed or I;
For outher I mot sleen him at the gappe,   1645
Or he mot sleen me, if that me mishappe,"—
So ferden they in chaunging of hir hewe.

        As fer as everich of hem other knewe,
Ther nas no "good day," ne no saluing;
But streight, withouten word or rehersing,   1650
Everich of hem heelp for to armen other
As freendly as he were his owne brother;
And after that, with sharpe speres stronge
They foynen ech at other wonder longe.
Thou mightest wene that this Palamoun   1655
In his fighting were a wood leoun,
And as a cruel tygre was Arcite;
As wilde bores gonne they to smyte,
That frothen whyte as foom for ire wood.

Oh ruler, who wants no partner with thee!
Truly it's said neither love nor lordship
Wants willingly to have a partnership.
They found that out, Arcite and Palamon. 770
Arcite then rode into the town anon,
And the next day, before it was light there,
In private, suits of armor did prepare, 1630
That were sufficient and appropriate
For battle on the field when they are met; 775
And on his horse, as he was born, alone,
He carried all the armor on his own.
In the grove, at the time and place they set,
This Arcite and this Palamon have met.

To change began the color in their face; 780
Just as with hunters in the land of Thrace,
Who stand and guard the gap with a spear there,
When hunted is the lion or the bear, 1640
And hear it in the groves rush at a run,
And break the leaves and branches, every one, 785
And think, "Here comes my mortal enemy!
Without fail, either he must die, or me,
For either at the gap I must him slay,
Or he slays me, if luck won't go my way."
So fared they in the changing of their hue. 790

As far as each of them the other knew,
There was no "Good day," and no conversing.
Straight away, without word or rehearsing, 1650
Each of them did help to arm the other,
Friendly as though he were his own brother; 795
And after that, with both their sharp spears strong,
They thrust at each other wondrously long.
You might suppose then that this Palamon
In his fighting were a maddened lion,
And like a cruel tiger was Arcite; 800
Like wild boars, so they begin to smite
That in mad rage froth foamed white as a flood.

Up to the ancle foghte they in hir blood.   1660
And in this wyse I lete hem fighting dwelle,
And forth I wole of Theseus yow telle.
        The destinee, ministre general,
That executeth in the world over al
The purveyaunce that God hath seyn biforn,   1665
So strong it is that, though the world had sworn
The contrarie of a thing by ye or nay,
Yet somtyme it shal fallen on a day
That falleth nat eft withinne a thousand yere.
For certeinly, oure appetytes here,   1670
Be it of werre, or pees, or hate, or love,
Al is this reuled by the sighte above.
This mene I now by mighty Theseus,
That for to hunten is so desirous,
And namely at the grete hert in May,   1675
That in his bed ther daweth him no day
That he nis clad and redy for to ryde
With hunte and horn and houndes him bisyde.
For in his hunting hath he swich delyt
That it is al his joye and appetyt   1680
To been himself the grete hertes bane;
For after Mars he serveth now Diane.
        Cleer was the day, as I have told er this,
And Theseus, with alle joye and blis,
With his Ipolita, the fayre quene,   1685
And Emelye, clothed al in grene,
On hunting be they riden royally.
And to the grove that stood ful faste by,
In which ther was an hert, as men him tolde,
Duk Theseus the streighte wey hath holde.   1690
And to the launde he rydeth him ful right,
For thider was the hert wont have his flight,

Up to the ankle fought they in their blood.   1660

And fighting in this way, I let them dwell,

And now of Theseus, I will you tell.   805

     Destiny, that general minister,

Which will execute the wide world over

The providence that God has seen before,

So strong it is, that though the whole world swore

The opposite of some thing, "yea" or "nay,"   810

Yet sometimes something happens on a day

That would not happen in a thousand years.

For certainly, all our desires here,   1670

Be they for war or peace or hate or love,

They are all ruled by foresight from above.   815

This I say now of mighty Theseus,

Who to go hunt is so desirous,

And namely for the worthy hart in May,

That in his bed there dawns for him no day

That he's not clad, and ready out to ride   820

With huntsmen, horns, and hounds there by his side.

For in his hunting he has such delight

That all his joy and hope is that he might   1680

Become himself the bane of the great hart,

For after Mars, he serves Diana's part.[17]   825

     Clear was the day, as I've told before this,

And Theseus with all due joy and bliss,

With his Hippolyta, with his fair queen,

And Emily, who is all clothed in green,

Out hunting have they ridden royally.   830

To the grove that stood nearby quite closely,

In which there was a hart, as men them told,

Duke Theseus the straight way now did hold.   1690

To the clearing, he rides with all his might,

For there the hart was wont to take his flight,   835

17 **Mars . . . Diana:** Mars is the god of war under whose banner Theseus rides into battle, and when he is freed from his military obligations he serves Diana, the goddess of hunting.

And over a brook, and so forth on his weye.
This duk wol han a cours at him or tweye,
With houndes swiche as that him list comaunde.   1695
   And whan this duk was come unto the launde,
Under the sonne he loketh, and anon
He was war of Arcite and Palamon,
That foughten breme as it were bores two.
The brighte swerdes wenten to and fro   1700
So hidously that with the leeste strook
It seemed as it wolde felle an ook;
But what they were, no thing he ne woot.
This duk his courser with his spores smoot,
And at a stert he was bitwix hem two,   1705
And pulled out a swerd and cryed, "Ho!
Namore, up peyne of lesinge of youre heed!
By mighty Mars, he shal anon be deed
That smyteth any strook that I may seen.
But telleth me what mister men ye been,   1710
That been so hardy for to fighten here
Withouten juge or other officere,
As it were in a listes royally?"
   This Palamon answerde hastily,
And seyde: "Sire, what nedeth wordes mo?   1715
We have the deeth deserved bothe two.
Two woful wrecches been we, two caytyves,
That been encombred of our owne lyves;
And as thou art a rightful lord and juge,
Ne yeve us neither mercy ne refuge,   1720
But slee me first, for seynte charitee.
But slee my felawe eek as wel as me,
Or slee him first: for though thou knowest it lyte,
This is thy mortal fo, this is Arcite,
That fro thy lond is banished on his heed,   1725
For which he hath deserved to be deed.
For this is he that cam unto thy gate
And seyde that he highte Philostrate.

Leaping a brook as it went on its way.
This duke will have a run at him this day
With good hounds such as he likes to command.
        When in the clearing this duke came to stand,
Toward the sun he looks, and then anon   840
Right there he saw Arcite and Palamon,
Who fiercely fought as though they were two boars.
The bright swords went so fast to make their scores   1700
So hideously that with their mildest stroke
It seemed as if the thrust could fell an oak.   845
But who they were, he did not know a bit.
This duke now with his spurs his charger hit,
And with a bound, he was between them so,
And he unsheathed his sword and cried out, "Ho!
No more, on penalty to lose your head!   850
By mighty Mars, he will at once be dead
Who smites a single stroke that I might see.
But tell what kind of men you both might be,   1710
Who are so foolhardy to fight right here
And have no judge or officer stand near,   855
As it would be proper in lists royally."
        This Palamon then answered hastily,
And he said, "Sir, what need would more words serve?
For both of us our deaths so well deserve.
Two such woeful wretches both are we,   860
Whom our own lives encumber, certainly;
And since as rightful lord and judge you live,
Mercy or refuge to us, do not give,   1720
So slay me first, by holy charity!
But slay my fellow, too, as well as me;   865
Or slay him first, for little do you know,
This is Arcite, this is your mortal foe,
Banned from your land at the price of his head,
For which cause, he deserves now to be dead.
For he it is, who came right to your gate thus   870
And said that he was called Philostratus.

Thus hath he japed thee ful many a yeer,
And thou hast maked him thy chief squyer;   1730
And this is he that loveth Emelye.
For sith the day is come that I shal dye,
I make pleynly my confessioun
That I am thilke woful Palamoun
That hath thy prison broken wikkedly.   1735
I am thy mortal fo, and it am I
That loveth so hote Emelye the brighte
That I wol dye present in hir sighte.
Wherfore I axe deeth and my juwyse;
But slee my felawe in the same wyse,   1740
For bothe han we deserved to be slayn."
          This worthy duk answerde anon agayn,
And seyde, "This is a short conclusioun.
Youre owne mouth, by your confessioun,
Hath dampned you, and I wol it recorde;   1745
It nedeth noght to pyne yow with the corde.
Ye shul be deed, by mighty Mars the rede!"
          The quene anon, for verray wommanhede,
Gan for to wepe, and so dide Emelye,
And alle the ladies in the companye.   1750
Gret pitee was it, as it thoughte hem alle,
That ever swich a chaunce sholde falle;
For gentil men they were of greet estat,
And no thing but for love was this debat;
And sawe hir blody woundes wyde and sore,   1755
And alle cryden, bothe lasse and more,
"Have mercy, lord, upon us wommen alle!"
And on hir bare knees adoun they falle,
And wolde have kist his feet ther as he stood,
Til at the laste aslaked was his mood;   1760
For pitee renneth sone in gentil herte.
And though he first for ire quook and sterte,

He's tricked you all these years since you did hire

Him and made him into your chief squire;   1730

And this is he who does love Emily.

Since on this day my death will come to me,   875

I plainly make here my own confession

That I am the same woeful Palamon

Who has escaped your prison wickedly.

I am your mortal foe; it's I, you see,

Who loves so hotly Emily the bright   880

That now I will die right here in her sight.

Therefore, I seek my sentence and my death;

But slay my fellow within the same breath,   1740

For both of us deserve to be slain then."

    This worthy duke answered at once again,   885

And said, "Now, this brings a short conclusion.

Your own mouth, right here by your confession,

Has damned you, and I will it so record;

Around your heads no need to twist the cord.[18]

By mighty Mars the red, you both will die!"   890

    At this, the queen at once began to cry,

From true womanhood; and so did Emily,

And all the ladies in the company.   1750

Great pity was it, as they all thought then,

That such an event would ever happen,   895

For they were gentlemen of great estate,

And love alone had caused their whole debate.

When they saw bloody wounds so sore and wide,

The greater and the less together cried,

"Have mercy, Lord, upon us women all!"   900

And then on their bare knees right down they fall

And would have kissed his feet there where he stood;

Until, at last, his mood was calmed for good,   1760

For pity runs soon in a gentle heart.

Though first from ire he might quake and start,   905

---

18 **twist the cord**: Get a confession through torture.

He hath considered shortly, in a clause,
The trespas of hem bothe, and eek the cause,
And although that his ire hir gilt accused,   1765
Yet in his resoun he hem bothe excused,
As thus: he thoghte wel that every man
Wol helpe himself in love, if that he can,
And eek delivere himself out of prisoun.
And eek his herte had compassioun   1770
Of wommen, for they wepen evere in oon.
And in his gentil herte he thoghte anoon,
And softe unto himself he seyde: "Fy
Upon a lord that wol have no mercy,
But been a leoun, bothe in word and dede,   1775
To hem that been in repentaunce and drede
As well as to a proud despitous man
That wol maynteyne that he first bigan!
That lord hath litel of discrecioun
That in swich cas can no divisioun,   1780
But weyeth pryde and humblesse after oon."
        And shortly, whan his ire is thus agoon,
He gan to loken up with eyen lighte,
And spak thise same wordes al on highte:
"The god of love, a, *benedicite*,   1785
How mighty and how greet a lord is he!
Ayeins his might ther gayneth none obstacles.
He may be cleped a god for his miracles,
For he can maken at his owne gyse
Of everich herte as that him list devyse.   1790
Lo heere, this Arcite and this Palamoun,
That quitly weren out of my prisoun,
And mighte han lived in Thebes royally,
And witen I am hir mortal enemy
And that hir deeth lyth in my might also;   1795
And yet hath love, maugree hir eyen two,
Broght hem hider bothe for to dye!
Now loketh, is nat that an heigh folye?

He has considered briefly, in a clause,
The trespass of them both, and then the cause,
And even though his wrath their guilt accused,
Yet, with his reason, he them both excused,
Like this: he thought well that every man   910
Will help himself in love, if he so can,
And deliver himself too from prison,
And also, his heart there had compassion   1770
For women, who weep continually,
And in his gentle heart he thought quickly   915
And softly to himself, and then said, "Fie
Upon a lord who mercy will deny—
And who's a lion, both in word and deed—
To men who to repent and dread take heed,
As he would to a proud and scornful man   920
Who will persist in what he first began.
For such a lord has little discretion,
Who, in such a case, knows no distinction   1780
But weighs pride and humility the same."
          And shortly, when he'd quenched his ire's flame,   925
He looked up with a light within his eye
And spoke these words to those who were nearby:
"The god of love, ah, blessed may we be!
How mighty and how great a lord is he!
Against his might avail no obstacles.   930
A god he's called, for all his miracles,
For after his own fashion, he can make
Hearts, as he likes, his own command to take.   1790
Lo! Here—this Arcite and this Palamon,
Who were free and outside of my prison,   935
And might have both lived in Thebes royally;
They know that I'm their mortal enemy,
And know that in my power their death lies too,
And yet love has, for all that they might do,
Brought both of them to die right here, truly.   940
Now, look here: is that not highest folly?

Who may been a fool but if he love?
Bihold, for Goddes sake that sit above,   1800
Se how they blede! be they noght wel arrayed?
Thus hath hir lord, the god of love, y-payed
Hir wages and hir fees for hir servyse!
And yet they wenen for to been ful wyse
That serven love, for aught that may bifalle.   1805
But this is yet the beste game of alle:
That she, for whom they han this jolitee,
Can hem therfore as muche thank as me;
She woot namore of al this hote fare,
By God, than woot a cokkow or an hare!   1810
But al mot been assayed, hoot and cold;
A man mot been a fool, or yong or old;
I woot it by myself ful yore agoon,
For in my tyme a servant was I oon.
And therefore, sin I knowe of loves peyne,   1815
And woot how sore it can a man distreyne,
As he that hath ben caught ofte in his las,
I yow foryeve al hoolly this trespas,
At requeste of the quene that kneleth here,
And eek of Emelye, my suster dere.   1820
And ye shul bothe anon unto me swere
That neveremo ye shul my contree dere,
Ne make werre upon me night ne day,
But been my freendes in al that ye may.
I yow foryeve this trespas every del."   1825
And they him swore his axing fayre and wel,
And him of lordshipe and of mercy preyde,
And he hem graunteth grace, and thus he seyde:
        "To speke of royal linage and richesse,
Though that she were a quene or a princesse,   1830
Ech of yow bothe is worthy, doutelees,
To wedden whan tyme is, but nathelees—
I speke as for my suster Emelye,
For whom ye have this stryf and jalousye—

Who is a fool unless he is in love?
Behold now, for God's sake who sits above, 1800
See how they bleed! Are they not well arrayed?
Thus has their lord, the god of love, well paid 945
Their wages and their fees for all their service!
Yet they suppose they are quite wise in this,
Those who serve love, whatever may befall.
But this is yet the best game of them all:
That she for whom they have this gaiety 950
Gives them as many thanks as she gives me.
She knows no more about all this hot fare,
By God, than knows a cuckoo or a hare! 1810
But all must be assayed, both hot and cold;
A man must be a fool, though young or old— 955
I know it by myself, from long ago;
For in my time, I was love's servant also.
And therefore, since I know about love's pain
And how sorely it can a man constrain,
As one who's been there in his snare, alas, 960
I forgive you wholly for this trespass,
At the plea of the queen, who now kneels here,
And Emily, my sister-in-law dear. 1820
At once, you both shall make to me this vow
That never more you'll harm my country now, 965
Nor war upon me, either night or day,
But be my friends in every way you may.
Your trespass I do forgive completely."
They swore to his asking well and fairly,
And prayed his protection and his mercy, 970
And he granted them grace, and thus said he:
          "To speak of royal lineage and richness,
Although she were a queen or else a princess, 1830
Each of you both is worthy, doubtless,
To wed her at the right time; nonetheless— 975
I speak now for my sister Emily,
For whom you have this strife and jealousy—

Ye woot yourself she may not wedden two   1835
Atones, though ye fighten everemo:
That oon of yow, al be him looth or leef,
He moot go pypen in an ivy leef;
This is to seyn, she may nat now han bothe,
Al be ye never so jalous ne so wrothe.   1840
And forthy I yow putte in this degree,
That ech of yow shal have his destinee
As him is shape, and herkneth in what wyse;
Lo heer your ende of that I shal devyse.

      My wil is this, for plat conclusioun,   1845
Withouten any replicacioun—
If that yow lyketh, tak it for the beste:
That everich of yow shal gon wher him leste
Frely, withouten raunson or daunger;
And this day fifty wykes, fer ne ner,   1850
Everich of yow shal bringe an hundred knightes
Armed for listes up at alle rightes,
Al redy to darreyne hire by bataille.
And this bihote I yow withouten faille,
Upon my trouthe, and as I am a knight,   1855
That whether of yow bothe that hath might—
This is to seyn, that whether he or thou
May with his hundred, as I spak of now,
Sleen his contrarie or out of listes dryve—
Thanne shal I yeve Emelya to wyve   1860
To whom that Fortune yeveth so fair a grace.
The listes shal I maken in this place,
And God so wisly on my soule rewe,
As I shal even juge been and trewe.
Ye shul non other ende with me maken,   1865
That oon of yow ne shal be deed or taken.
And if yow thinketh this is wel y-sayd,

You know yourself she may not wedded be
To you both, though you fight eternally,
And one of you, despite his joy or grief,   980
Might as well whistle in an ivy leaf;[19]
She may not have you both, it's plain to see,
No matter if you're jealous now or angry.   1840
I therefore put you under this decree,
That each of you will have the destiny   985
That's shaped for him, and listen in what guise;
Lo, hear the end of what I will devise.
          My will is thus, in this plain conclusion,
And there will be here no refutation—
If you like it, then take it for the best so,   990
Wherever you choose, each of you will go
Freely, without ransom or resistance,
And on this very day, fifty weeks hence,   1850
Each of you will bring a hundred knights
Armed for the lists, in all respects by rights,   995
In battle ready to decide who wins her,
And without fail, to you I here aver,
Upon my word, and as I am a knight:
That whichever of you two may have the might—
Whichever of you two, to make this clear,   1000
May with his hundred, of whom I spoke here,
Slay his foe or drive him from the strife,
To him I shall give Emily as wife,   1860
To him whom Fortune gives so fair a grace.
The lists I shall have made right in this place;   1005
May wise God have mercy on my soul, too,
So as a judge I shall be fair and true.
You'll no other ending with me make then,
So one of you will not be dead or taken.
And if you think that this plan is well laid,   1010

---

19   ... **ivy leaf**: That is, for all the consolation or satisfaction he'll get. Equivalent to the modern expression "You may as well go whistle."

Seyeth your avys, and holdeth yow apayd.
This is your ende and youre conclusioun."
      Who loketh lightly now but Palamoun?   1870
Who springeth up for joye but Arcite?
Who couthe telle, or who couthe it endyte,
The joye that is maked in the place
Whan Theseus hath doon so fair a grace?
But doun on knees wente every maner wight,   1875
And thanked him with al hir herte and might,
And namely the Thebans often sythe.
And thus with good hope and with herte blythe
They take hir leve, and homward gonne they ryde
To Thebes, with his olde walles wyde.   1880

Explicit secunda pars.
Sequitur pars tercia.

      I trowe men wolde deme it necligence
If I foryete to tellen the dispence
Of Theseus, that goth so bisily
To maken up the listes royally,
That swich a noble theatre as it was,   1885
I dar wel seyn that in this world ther nas.
The circuit a myle was aboute,
Walled of stoon, and diched al withoute.
Round was the shap, in manere of compas,
Ful of degrees, the heighte of sixty pas,   1890
That whan a man was set on o degree,
He letted nat his felawe for to see.
      Estward ther stood a gate of marbel whyt,
Westward right swich another in the opposit.
And shortly to concluden, swich a place   1895
Was noon in erthe, as in so litel space;
For in the lond ther was no crafty man
That geometrie or ars-metrike can,
Ne purtreyour, ne kervere of images,

Speak your accord, and consider yourselves paid.
All this is your end and your conclusion."
    Who looks lightly now but Palamon?   1870
Who springs up for joy now but Arcite?
Who could tell it, or who could endite,   1015
The joy that was made then throughout that place
When Theseus has moved with such fair grace?
Down on their knees went everyone in sight,
And they thanked him with all their heart and might,
And especially the Thebans many times.   1020
And thus with blissful heart as their hope climbs,
They take their leave, and homeward they do ride
On back toward Thebes, with its walls old and wide.   1880

The second part ends.
The third part follows.

    I believe men would deem it negligence
If I forgot to tell all the expense   1025
Of Theseus, who goes so busily
In making up the lists quite royally,
So that truly such a noble theater
I dare well say in this world was never.
Its circuit measured a mile overall,   1030
Surrounded by a ditch and a stone wall.
And formed just like a ring, its shape was round;
Tiers of seats, sixty paces high, were found,   1890
So when a man on one tier was sitting,
His neighbor he did not prevent from seeing.   1035
    On the east stood a white gate of marble,
And on the west a gate identical.
And shortly to conclude, no single place
On earth was like this, in so little space.
There was no skillful man throughout the land,   1040
With geometry or arithmetic in hand,
No painter or carver of images

That Theseus ne yaf him mete and wages   1900
The theatre for to maken and devyse.
And for to doon his ryte and sacrifyse,
He estward hath, upon the gate above,
In worshipe of Venus, goddesse of love,
Don make an auter and an oratorie;   1905
And on the gate westward, in memorie
Of Mars, he maked hath right swich another,
That coste largely of gold a fother.
And northward, in a touret on the wal,
Of alabastre whyt and reed coral,   1910
An oratorie riche for to see,
In worshipe of Dyane of chastitee,
Hath Theseus don wroght in noble wyse.
        But yet hadde I foryeten to devyse
The noble kerving and the portreitures,   1915
The shap, the countenaunce, and the figures,
That weren in thise oratories three.
        First in the temple of Venus maystow see
Wroght on the wal, ful pitous to biholde,
The broken slepes and the sykes colde,   1920
The sacred teres and the waymentinge,
The fyry strokes of the desiringe
That loves servaunts in this lyf enduren;
The othes that hir covenants assuren;
Plesaunce and Hope, Desyr, Foolhardinesse,   1925
Beautee and Youthe, Bauderie, Richesse,
Charmes and Force, Lesinges, Flaterye,
Dispense, Bisynesse, and Jalousye,
That wered of yelwe goldes a gerland,
And a cokkow sittinge on hir hand;   1930
Festes, instruments, caroles, daunces,
Lust and array, and alle the circumstaunces

Whom Theseus did not give food and wages   1900
The theater to design and to build, too.
So rites and sacrifices he might do,   1045
On the eastward side, up on the gate above,
In worship of Venus, goddess of love,
He made an altar and an oratory;
And on the westward gate, in memory
Of Mars, just such another he has made,   1050
And for them a cartload of gold he paid.
On the north side, in a turret on a wall,
Of alabaster white and of red coral,   1910
An oratory that was rich to see,
For Diana, goddess of chastity,   1055
Theseus, there in noble form, had set.
        And yet, to describe I'll not forget
The noble carvings and the portraitures,
The shape, the appearance, and the figures
That were there in these oratories three.   1060
        First, in the temple of Venus, you may see
Wrought on the wall, piteous to behold,
The broken sleep, and all the sighs so cold,   1920
The sacred tears, and all the lamenting,
The fiery strokes of all the desiring   1065
That love's servants in this life endure;
And the oaths that their covenants assure;
Pleasure, Hope, Desire, Foolhardiness,
Beauty and Youth, and Bawdry and Richness,
Charms and Force, Falsehoods and Flattery,   1070
Expenses, Business, and here Jealousy
Wore of yellow marigolds[20] a garland,
And had a cuckoo[21] sitting on her hand.   1930
Feasts, carols, instruments, and dances,
Pleasure and dress and all the circumstances   1075

20 **yellow marigolds**: Yellow was a color linked with jealousy in the Middle Ages.
21 **cuckoo**: Bird associated with cuckolding.

Of love, whiche that I rekned and rekne shal,
By ordre weren peynted on the wal,
And mo than I can make of mencioun.   1935
For soothly, al the mount of Citheroun,
Ther Venus hath hir principal dwellinge,
Was shewed on the wal in portreyinge,
With al the gardin and the lustinesse.
Nat was foryeten the porter, Ydelnesse,   1940
Ne Narcisus the faire of yore agon,
Ne yet the folye of king Salamon,
Ne yet the grete strengthe of Hercules,
Th'enchauntements of Medea and Circes,
Ne of Turnus, with the hardy fiers corage,   1945
The riche Cresus, caytif in servage.
Thus may ye seen that wisdom ne richesse,
Beautee ne sleighte, strengthe ne hardinesse,
Ne may with Venus holde champartye,
For as hir list the world than may she gye.   1950
Lo, alle thise folk so caught were in hir las,
Til they for wo ful ofte seyde "Allas!"
Suffyceth heer ensamples oon or two,
And though I coude rekne a thousand mo.
       The statue of Venus, glorious for to see,   1955
Was naked fletinge in the large see,
And fro the navele doun all covered was
With wawes grene, and brighte as any glas.
A citole in hir right hand hadde she,
And on hir heed, ful semely for to see,   1960
A rose gerland, fresh and wel smellinge;
Above hir heed hir dowves flikeringe.
Biforn hir stood hir sone Cupido,
Upon his shuldres winges hadde he two,
And blind he was, as it is ofte sene.   1965
A bowe he bar and arwes brighte and kene.

Of love, if I could reckon up them all,
In order here were painted on the wall,
And many more than I can ever count.
For truly all of Cithaeron's mount,[22]
Where Venus has her principal dwelling,   1080
Was shown on the walls there in the painting,
With all the garden and its lustiness.
Nor was forgotten the porter, Idleness,   1940
Nor Narcissus, from time past the fair one,
Nor yet the folly of King Solomon,   1085
Nor yet the mighty strength of Hercules—
The enchantments of Medea and of Circes—
Nor Turnus, with courage fierce and hardy,
Rich Croesus, abased in captivity.
Thus you see: neither wisdom nor richness,   1090
Beauty nor trickery, strength nor braveness,
May with Venus be partners in power,
For as she likes, she guides the world each hour.   1950
Lo, all these folks were caught in her snare so,
Till they quite often said "Alas!" from woe.   1095
Suffice for now examples one or two,
Although a thousand more I could tell you.
        The statue of Venus, glorious to see,
Was naked, floating there on the wide sea.
From the navel down, her covering did pass,   1100
Made of green waves, as bright as any glass.
A zither then in her right hand held she,
And on her head, quite seemly there to see,   1960
A rose garland, fresh and sweetly smelling;
Above her head, her doves all fluttering.   1105
Her son Cupid stood right there before her,
And he had two wings upon his shoulders,
But he was blind, as is quite often seen;
A bow he bore, and arrows bright and keen.

---

22 **Cithaeron's mount:** A conflation with Cytherea, the island associated with Venus.

Why sholde I noght as wel eek telle yow al
The portreiture that was upon the wal
Withinne the temple of mighty Mars the rede?
Al peynted was the wal, in lengthe and brede,   1970
Lyk to the estres of the grisly place
That highte the grete temple of Mars in Trace,
In thilke colde frosty regioun
Ther as Mars hath his sovereyn mansioun.

   First on the wal was peynted a foreste,   1975
In which ther dwelleth neither man ne beste,
With knotty knarry bareyne treës olde,
Of stubbes sharpe and hidouse to biholde,
In which ther ran a rumbel in a swough,
As though a storm sholde bresten every bough.   1980
And downward from an hille, under a bente,
Ther stood the temple of Mars armipotente,
Wroght al of burned steel, of which the entree
Was long and streit, and gastly for to see.
And therout cam a rage and such a vese   1985
That it made al the gate for to rese.
The northren light in at the dores shoon,
For windowe on the wal ne was ther noon,
Thurgh which men mighten any light discerne.
The dore was al of adamant eterne,   1990
Y-clenched overthwart and endelong
With iren tough; and for to make it strong,
Every piler, the temple to sustene,
Was tonne-greet, of iren bright and shene.

   Ther saugh I first the derke imagining   1995
Of Felonye, and al the compassing;
The cruel Ire, reed as any glede;
The pykepurs, and eek the pale Drede;
The smylere with the knyf under the cloke;
The shepne brenning with the blake smoke;   2000

And why then should I now not tell you all   1110
The painting that was there upon the wall
In the temple of mighty Mars the red?
On its length and breadth, the wall was painted,   1970
Just like the inside of that grisly place
That's called the great temple of Mars in Thrace,   1115
In that very same cold, frosty region
There where Mars has set his sovereign mansion.
    On the wall first painted was a forest,
In which to dwell not man nor beast thought best,
With gnarled and knotted barren trees so old,   1120
With sharp stumps, quite hideous to behold,
Through which there ran a rapid rumbling now,
As though a storm would break off every bough.   1980
And downward from a hill, where the slope bent
Stood the temple of Mars-in-arms-all-potent,   1125
Wrought all of burnished steel, of which the entry
Was narrow, long, and quite ghastly to see.
And from it came a roar and such a blast
It made the gate shake like it couldn't last.
The northern light in at the doorways shone,   1130
For not one window did the walls there own,
Through which men might any light discern well.   1989
The door was made from adamant eternal,
Clinched lengthwise and both its ends along
With iron tough; and thus to make it strong,   1135
Every pillar, the temple sustaining,
Was tun-great,[23] of iron bright and shining.
    There saw I first the dark imaginings
Of Felony, and all of his schemings;
The cruel Ire, like a glowing coal so red;   1140
The pickpocket, and also the pale Dread;
The smiler with the knife under the cloak;
The stable burning down with its black smoke;   2000

23 **tun-great**: As wide around as the circumference of a large barrel.

The treson of the mordring in the bedde;
The open werre, with woundes al bibledde;
Contek, with blody knyf and sharp manace.
Al ful of chirking was that sory place.
The sleere of himself yet saugh I ther: 2005
His herte-blood hath bathed al his heer;
The nayl y-driven in the shode a-night;
The colde deeth, with mouth gaping upright.
Amiddes of the temple sat Meschaunce,
With disconfort and sory contenaunce.   2010
Yet saugh I Woodnesse laughing in his rage,
Armed Compleint, Outhees, and fiers Outrage;
The careyne in the bush, with throte y-corve;
A thousand slayn, and nat of qualm y-storve;
The tiraunt, with the prey by force y-raft;   2015
The toun destroyed, ther was nothing laft.
Yet saugh I brent the shippes hoppesteres;
The hunte strangled with the wilde beres;
The sowe freten the child right in the cradel;
The cook y-scalded, for al his longe ladel—   2020
Noght was foryeten by the infortune of Marte—
The carter overriden with his carte,
Under the wheel ful lowe he lay adoun.
Ther were also, of Martes divisioun,
The barbour and the bocher and the smith,   2025
That forgeth sharpe swerdes on his stith.
And al above, depeynted in a tour,
Saw I Conquest, sitting in greet honour,
With the sharpe swerde over his heed
Hanginge by a sotil twynes threed.   2030
Depeynted was the slaughtre of Julius,
Of grete Nero, and of Antonius;
Al be that thilke tyme they were unborn,
Yet was hir deeth depeynted ther-biforn
By manasinge of Mars, right by figure.   2035
So was it shewed in that portreiture,

The treason of the murdering in the bed;
The open war, where grievous wounds have bled;   1145
Strife, with bloody knife and its sharp menace;
Full of groaning was this sorry place for this.
The slayer of himself yet I saw there—
Whose very heart-blood had bathed all his hair—
With the nail driven in his head at night;   1150
And cold death, with its mouth gaping upright.
In the middle of the temple, in her place
Sat pained Misfortune with her wretched face.   2010
Yet saw I Madness, laughing in his rage,
Armed Complaint and Outcry and fierce Outrage;   1155
The corpse down in the bushes with throat carved;
A thousand slain, and not from plague they starved;
The tyrant with his prey by force obtained;
The town destroyed, and not a thing remained.
Ships dancing on the seas I saw burned there;   1160
The hunter strangled to death by wild bears;
The sow eating the child right in the cradle;
The cook scalded, despite his long ladle.   2020
No ill fate was forgotten on Mars's part:
The carter here run over by his cart—   1165
Under the wheel quite low he lay and sank.
There were also those who were of Mars's ranks:
Barber and butcher, and the smith as well,
Who forges such sharp swords upon his anvil.
Above them all, and painted in a tower,   1170
I saw Conquest, sitting in great honor,
With the sharpened sword over his head
Hanging by a thinly entwined thread.   2030
There Caesar's slaughter was painted to see,
Also great Nero's and Marc Antony's;   1175
Although at that time they were not born yet,
Still their deaths as painted had been set
In their horoscopes by Mars's menacings;
So it was depicted in these paintings,

As is depeynted in the sterres above
Who shal be slayn or elles deed for love.
Sufficeth oon ensample in stories olde:
I may not rekene hem alle, thogh I wolde.   2040
      The statue of Mars upon a carte stood
Armed, and loked grim as he were wood;
And over his heed ther shynen two figures
Of sterres, that been cleped in scriptures
That oon Puella, that other Rubeus: 2045
This god of armes was arrayed thus.
A wolf ther stood biforn him at his feet
With eyen rede, and of a man he eet.
With sotil pencel was depeynted this storie
In redoutinge of Mars and of his glorie.   2050
      Now to the temple of Diane the chaste,
As shortly as I can, I wol me haste
To telle yow al the descripcioun.
Depeynted been the walles up and doun
Of hunting and of shamfast chastitee.   2055
Ther saugh I how woful Calistopee,
Whan that Diane agreved was with here,
Was turned from a womman til a bere,
And after was she maad the lode-sterre;
Thus was it peynted, I can say yow no ferre;   2060
Hir sone is eek a sterre, as men may see.
Ther saugh I Dane, y-turned til a tree—
I mene nat the goddesse Diane,
But Penneus doughter, which that highte Dane.
Ther saugh I Attheon an hert y-maked,   2065
For vengeaunce that he saugh Diane al naked;
I saugh how that his houndes have him caught

As it is painted in the stars above,   1180
Who will be slain or else be dead for love.
One example from old histories must do;
I can't count them all, though I wanted to.   2040
      Mars's statue, on a cart, in armor clad,
Stood with a grim look as though he were mad;   1185
And there over his head two figures shining
Of the stars that were named in old writings,
Puella one, the other Rubeus[24]—
Mars, this god of arms was all arrayed thus.
A wolf stood there before him at his feet   1190
With such red eyes, and a man he did eat;
A subtle pencil has portrayed this story
In honoring of Mars and of his glory.   2050
      Now to the temple of Diana chaste,
As shortly as I can, I will make haste   1195
Here to tell you all of the description.
The walls' scenes are painted in this fashion
To show hunting and modest chastity.
There saw I how Callisto[25] woefully,
When Diana was with her aggrieved there,   1200
Was changed then from a woman to a bear,
And she was made into the pole star after.
Thus it was shown; I can tell you no further.   2060
Her son too is a star, as men may see.
There saw I Daphne turned into a tree—   1205
I do not mean Diana the goddess,
But Daphne,[26] called daughter of Penneus.
Acteon I saw changed to a hart there,
For vengeance since he saw Diana bare;
There I saw how his hounds all have him got   1210

---

24 **Puella . . . Rubeus:** Figures associated with astrological divination, composed of a pattern of dots that taken together signify Mars.

25 **Callisto:** She was transformed by Diana because she gave up her virginity to Jupiter.

26 **Daphne:** When Apollo chased her, Diana changed her into the laurel tree.

And freten him, for that they knewe him naught.
Yet peynted was a litel forther moor,
How Atthalante hunted the wilde boor,   2070
And Meleagre, and many another mo,
For which Diane wroghte him care and wo.
Ther saugh I many another wonder storie,
The whiche me list nat drawen to memorie.

   This goddesse on an hert ful hye seet,   2075
With smale houndes al aboute hir feet;
And undernethe hir feet she hadde a mone,
Wexinge it was, and sholde wanie sone.
In gaude grene hir statue clothed was,
With bowe in honde, and arwes in a cas.   2080
Hir eyen caste she ful lowe adoun,
Ther Pluto hath his derke regioun.
A womman travailinge was hir biforn,
But for hir child so longe was unborn,
Ful pitously Lucyna gan she calle,   2085
And seyde, "Help, for thou mayst best of alle."
Wel koude he peynten lyfly that it wroghte;
With many a florin he the hewes boghte.

   Now been thise listes maad, and Theseus,
That at his grete cost arrayed thus   2090
The temples and the theatre every del,
Whan it was doon, him lyked wonder wel.
But stinte I wole of Theseus a lyte,
And speke of Palamon and of Arcite.

   The day approcheth of hir retourninge,   2095
That everich sholde an hundred knightes bringe
The bataille to darreyne, as I yow tolde;
And til Athenes, hir covenant for to holde,

And devoured him, because they knew him not.
There's painted further on a little more,
How Atalanta hunted the wild boar,   2070
With Meleager and the others also,
For which Diana brought him care and woe.   1215
There did I see many a strange story,
Which I don't wish to keep in memory.

    High on a hart, this goddess had her seat,
With many small hounds all about her feet,
And underneath her feet she had a moon—   1220
Waxing it was, but would be waning soon.
Her statue was clothed in a greenish yellow,
With bow in hand, and in a case, her arrows.   2080
And her eyes she was casting down quite low
To where in his dark region there lives Pluto.   1225
A woman before her labored in great pain;
Since still unborn her child so long remained,
Quite piteously Lucina[27] she did call
And said, "Help me, for you may best of all!"
Well could he paint it lifelike who this wrought;   1230
With many florins, he the pigments bought.

    Now are the lists all made, and Theseus—
Who at his own great cost had arrayed thus   2090
The temples and the theater so completely—
When it was done, was pleased enormously.   1235
I'll leave now Theseus and will move on,
To speak of Arcite and of Palamon.

    The day approaches now for their returning,
When each of them one hundred knights should bring
To join the battle, as I have you told.   1240
And toward Athens, their covenant to hold,

---

27 **Lucina:** The name of Diana when she assumed her function as the goddess of childbirth. The
attribution of this epithet to her may have derived from a conflation/confusion of Diana with Lucina,
a Roman goddess of childbirth, perhaps through their shared association with the moon or Diana's
association as the goddess of hunting with nature, and thus fertility.

Hath everich of hem broght an hundred knightes

Wel armed for the werre at alle rightes.   2100

And sikerly, ther trowed many a man

That never, sithen that the world bigan,

As for to speke of knighthod of hir hond,

As fer as God hath maked see or lond,

Nas of so fewe so noble a companye.   2105

For every wight that lovede chivalrye,

And wolde, his thankes, han a passant name,

Hath preyed that he mighte ben of that game;

And wel was him that therto chosen was.

For if ther fille tomorwe swich a cas,   2110

Ye knowen wel that every lusty knight

That loveth paramours and hath his might,

Were it in Engelond or elleswhere

They wolde, hir thankes, wilnen to be there.

To fighte for a lady, *benedicite!*   2115

It were a lusty sighte for to see.

     And right so ferden they with Palamon.

With him ther wenten knightes many oon;

Som wol ben armed in an habergeoun,

And in a brest plate and a light gipoun;   2120

And som wol have a peyre plates large;

And som wol have a Pruce sheeld or a targe;

Som wol ben armed on his legges weel,

And have an ax, and som a mace of steel.

Ther nis no newe gyse that it nas old.   2125

Armed were they, as I have you told,

Everich after his opinioun.

     Ther maistow seen, coming with Palamoun,

Ligurge himself, the grete king of Trace.

Blak was his berd, and manly was his face.   2130

The cercles of his eyen in his heed,

They gloweden bitwixen yelow and reed;

And lyk a griffon loked he aboute,

With kempe heres on his browes stoute;

Each of them has brought one hundred knights,
In all ways well armed for the war by rights. 2100
Certainly it seemed to many a man
That never once, since the world first began, 1245
In terms of knighthood and prowess at hand,
As far as God has made the sea or land,
Was of so few, so noble a company.
For every man who loved well chivalry
And would, by choice, have a surpassing name, 1250
Has prayed them that he might join in that game;
It went well for him who has gained a place,
For if there came tomorrow such a case, 2110
You know well that every hardy knight
Who loves with passion and who has such might, 1255
Whether it's here in England or elsewhere,
They would, by choice, quite eagerly be there—
To fight for a lady, now God bless me!
It was a pleasing sight for one to see.
            And just so with Palamon it did fare. 1260
With him full many good knights arrived there;
Some will be armed in coat of mail to fight,
And in a breastplate and a tunic light; 2120
Some will wear a full set of plate armor;
And some of them a Prussian shield prefer; 1265
Some will have legs all well armed in this place,
And have an ax, and some, of steel a mace—
There is no fashion new that is not old.
Armed were they all, as now I have you told,
Each according to his own opinion. 1270
            There may you see, coming with Palamon,
Lycurgus himself, the great king of Thrace.
Black was his beard, and manly was his face; 2130
The circles of the eyes set in his head,
Their color glowed between yellow and red, 1275
And like a griffin he looked all about,
With shaggy hairs upon his eyebrows stout;

His limes grete, his braunes harde and stronge,   2135
His shuldres brode, his armes rounde and longe;
And as the gyse was in his contree,
Ful hye upon a char of gold stood he,
With foure whyte boles in the trays.
In stede of cote-armure over his harnays,   2140
With nayles yelewe and brighte as any gold
He hadde a beres skin, col-blak for old.
His longe heer was kembd bihinde his bak—
As any ravenes fethere it shoon for blak;
A wrethe of gold arm-greet, of huge wighte,   2145
Upon his heed, set ful of stones brighte,
Of fyne rubies and of dyamaunts.
Aboute his char ther wenten whyte alaunts,
Twenty and mo, as grete as any steer,
To hunten at the leoun or the deer,   2150
And folwed him with mosel faste y-bounde,
Colered of gold, and tourettes fyled rounde.
An hundred lordes hadde he in his route,
Armed ful wel, with hertes sterne and stoute.
        With Arcita, in stories as men finde,   2155
The grete Emetreus, the king of Inde,
Upon a steede bay trapped in steel,
Covered in cloth of gold diapred weel,
Cam ryding lyk the god of armes, Mars.
His cote-armure was of cloth of Tars,   2160
Couched with perles whyte and rounde and grete.
His sadel was of brend gold newe y-bete;
A mantelet upon his shuldre hanginge
Bret-ful of rubies rede as fyr sparklinge.
His crispe heer lyk ringes was y-ronne,   2165
And that was yelow, and glitered as the sonne.
His nose was heigh, his eyen bright citryn,
His lippes rounde, his colour was sangwyn;

His limbs were great, his muscles hard and strong,
His shoulders broad, his arms so round and long;
And as was the custom in his country,   1280
High on a chariot of gold stood he,
And in the traces, he had white bulls four.
No tunic over his armor he wore,   2140
But, with claw-nails yellow and bright as gold,
A bearskin, all coal black since it was old.   1285
And his long hair was combed behind his back;
As any raven's feathers, it shone black;
Upon his head, a wreath of gold, arm-great,
Was full of brightest stones and of huge weight,
With fine diamonds and rubies all set round.   1290
And, around his chariot, white wolfhounds,
Twenty or more, as great as any steer,
Ready to hunt for the lion or the deer;   2150
They followed him with muzzles tightly bound,
Collared with gold, and leash-rings filed all round. 1295
A hundred lords were in his company,
With hearts stern and stout, and armed completely.
   With Arcite, as men in stories find thus,
India's king, the great Emetreus,
On a bay steed covered with steel trappings,   1300
Cloaked in cloth of gold with crisscross quilting,
Rode in just like Mars, the god of arms, then.
His heraldic vest of Tarsian[28] cloth was woven,   2160
Set with pearls white and round, great to behold;
His saddle newly trimmed with burnished gold;   1305
A short cloak upon his shoulder hanging,
Brimful of rubies red as fire sparkling.
In style, his curly hair like rings did run;
It was yellow and glittered like the sun.
His nose arched high, and his eyes bright amber,   1310
His lips were round, and ruddy was his color;

28 **Tarsian**: From Turkestan.

A fewe frakenes in his face y-spreynd,

Betwixen yelow and somdel blak y-meynd;   2170

And as a leoun he his loking caste.

Of fyve and twenty yeer his age I caste:

His berd was wel bigonne for to springe.

His voys was as a trompe thunderinge.

Upon his heed he wered of laurer grene   2175

A gerland fresh and lusty for to sene.

Upon his hand he bar for his deduyt

An egle tame, as any lilie whyt.

An hundred lordes hadde he with him there,

Al armed, sauf hir heddes, in al hir gere,   2180

Ful richely in alle maner thinges.

For trusteth wel that dukes, erles, kinges

Were gadered in this noble companye

For love and for encrees of chivalrye.

Aboute this king ther ran on every part   2185

Ful many a tame leoun and leopart.

And in this wyse thise lordes, alle and some,

Ben on the Sonday to the citee come

Aboute pryme, and in the toun alight.

This Theseus, this duk, this worthy knight,   2190

Whan he had broght hem into his citee,

And inned hem, everich in his degree,

He festeth hem, and dooth so greet labour

To esen hem and doon hem al honour,

That yet men wenen that no mannes wit   2195

Of noon estat ne coude amenden it.

The minstralcye, the service at the feste,

The grete yiftes to the moste and leste,

The riche array of Theseus paleys,

Ne who sat first ne last upon the deys,   2200

What ladies fairest been or best daunsinge,

Or which of hem can dauncen best and singe,

Ne who most felingly speketh of love;

What haukes sitten on the perche above,

A few freckles on his face were sprinkled,
Their color of black and yellow mingled;   2170
Like a lion, he cast his glances here.
His age I'd put at five and twenty years.   1315
By now, his beard had well begun to spring;
His voice was like a trumpet thundering.
Upon his head he wore of laurel green
A garland, fresh and pleasing to be seen.
Upon his hand, he bore for his delight   1320
An eagle tame, and like a lily, white.
A hundred lords now he had with him here,
All armed, except their heads, in all their gear,   2180
Very richly in all manner of things.
For trust it well, that dukes and earls and kings   1325
Were gathered in this noble company,
For love and the increase of chivalry.
About India's king, on every side, there run
Many a tame leopard and tame lion.
And these great lords, one and all, in this way,   1330
Came into this city on a Sunday
In the morning, and in town they alight.
      This Theseus, this duke, this worthy knight,   2190
When he had brought them all into his city,
And lodged them all, according to degree,   1335
He feasts them, and goes to such great labor
To put them at ease and to do them honor
That men proclaim that no one else's wit
Of any rank could improve upon it.
The minstrelsy, the service at the feast,   1340
The large gifts for the greatest and the least,
The rich array of Theseus's palace,
Nor who sat first or last upon the dais,   2200
What ladies fairest were or best at dancing,
Or which of them could carol best or sing,   1345
Nor who most feelingly could speak of love;
What hawks were sitting on the perch above,

What houndes liggen on the floor adoun—   2205
Of al this make I now no mencioun;
But al th'effect, that thinketh me the beste.
Now comth the poynt, and herkneth if yow leste.
     The Sonday night, er day bigan to springe,
When Palamon the larke herde singe   2210
(Although it nere nat day by houres two,
Yet song the larke) and Palamon right tho
With holy herte and with an heigh corage,
He roos to wenden on his pilgrimage
Unto the blisful Citherea benigne—   2215
I mene Venus, honurable and digne.
And in hir houre he walketh forth a pas
Unto the listes ther hir temple was,
And doun he kneleth, and with humble chere
And herte soor, he seyde as ye shul here: 2220
     "Faireste of faire, O lady myn, Venus,
Doughter to Jove and spouse of Vulcanus,
Thou gladere of the mount of Citheroun.
For thilke love thou haddest to Adoun,
Have pitee of my bittre teres smerte,   2225
And tak myn humble preyere at thyn herte.
Allas! I ne have no langage to telle
Th'effectes ne the torments of myn helle;
Myn herte may myne harmes nat biwreye;
I am so confus that I can noght seye   2230
But mercy, lady bright, that knowest weele
My thought, and seest what harmes that I feele.
Considere al this, and rewe upon my sore,
As wisly as I shal for everemore,
Emforth my might, thy trewe servant be,   2235
And holden werre alwey with chastitee.
That make I myn avow, so ye me helpe.
I kepe noght of armes for to yelpe,
Ne I ne axe nat tomorwe to have victorie,
Ne renoun in this cas, ne veyne glorie   2240

What hounds were lying down upon the floor—
All this, I will not mention any more,
Just the effect; to me, that's the best way.   1350
Now comes the point, and listen, I you pray.
        That Sunday night, before the day did spring,
When Palamon had heard the lark first sing   2210
(Two hours yet before the day's begun,
Still the lark sang) and right then Palamon,   1355
With holy heart and with lofty courage,
He rose to wend upon his pilgrimage
To the benign Citherea blissful—
I mean Venus, who is so worshipful.
In the lists, at the hour of Venus,   1360
He slowly walks to where her temple is,
And down he kneels, and with a humble cheer
And with sore heart, he said as you will hear: 2220
        "Fairest of the fair, my lady Venus,
Daughter of Jove, and spouse of Hephaestus,   1365
You made the mount of Cithaeron glad
With all the love you for Adonis had,
Have pity on my bitter tears that smart,
And take my humble prayer into your heart.
Alas! I have no language now to tell   1370
The effects or the torments of my hell;
And my heart may not all my hurt betray;
I'm so confused that I can nothing say   2230
But 'Mercy, lady bright, for well you know
My thoughts. See now how I feel such sorrow!'   1375
Ponder all this; on my pain take pity,
As surely as I shall eternally,
With all my might, your truest servant be,
And always I'll wage war on chastity.
That is the vow I make, if me you'll help!   1380
About armed prowess, I don't care to yelp,
Tomorrow I don't ask for victory,
Nor renown in this case, nor vainglory,   2240

Of pris of armes blowen up and doun,

But I wolde have fully possessioun

Of Emelye, and dye in thy servyse.

Find thou the manere how, and in what wyse:

I recche nat but it may bettre be   2245

To have victorie of hem, or they of me,

So that I have my lady in myne armes.

For though so be that Mars is god of armes,

Youre vertu is so greet in hevene above,

That if yow list, I shal wel have my love.   2250

Thy temple wol I worshipe everemo,

And on thyn auter, where I ryde or go,

I wol don sacrifice and fyres bete.

And if ye wol nat so, my lady swete,

Than preye I thee, tomorwe with a spere   2255

That Arcita me thurgh the herte bere.

Thanne rekke I noght, whan I have lost my lyf,

Though that Arcita winne hire to his wyf.

This is th'effect and ende of my preyere:

Yif me my love, thou blisful lady dere."   2260

      Whan the orison was doon of Palamon,

His sacrifice he dide, and that anon,

Ful pitously, with alle circumstaunces,

Al telle I noght as now his observaunces.

But atte laste the statue of Venus shook,   2265

And made a signe, wherby that he took

That his preyere accepted was that day.

For thogh the signe shewed a delay,

Yet wiste he wel that graunted was his bone;

And with glad herte he wente him hoom ful sone.   2270

      The thridde houre inequal that Palamon

Bigan to Venus temple for to goon,

Up roos the sonne, and up roos Emelye,

And to the temple of Diane gan hye.

Hir maydens, that she thider with hir ladde,   2275

Ful redily with hem the fyr they hadde,

With praise for my deeds trumpeted loudly;
But I wish to have possession fully   1385
Of Emily, and die in your service.
You must find the way for me to do this:
I do not care if it may better be
To have victory from them, or they from me,
If I can have my lady in my arms.   1390
Though it may be that Mars is god of arms,
Your strength is so great in heaven above
That if you wish it, I will have my love.   2250
I'll worship your temple ever more so,
And on your altar, where I ride or go,   1395
I'll make a sacrifice and kindle fire.
If this, my lady sweet, you don't desire,
Then I pray you, tomorrow with a spear
That Arcite pierce me through the heart right here.
I do not care, when I have lost my life,   1400
If then Arcite should win her for his wife.
This, the effect and ending of my prayer:
Give me my love, you blissful lady fair."   2260
        When Palamon had made his orison,
His sacrifice he did, and that anon,   1405
Quite piteously, with propriety;
I won't tell about the ceremony;
But at last the statue of Venus shook,
And made a sign to him, by which he took
It that his prayer accepted was that day.   1410
For though the sign at first showed some delay,
Yet he knew well that granted was his boon,
And with glad heart, he went back home quite soon.   2270
        In the third hour after which Palamon
To the temple of Venus had then gone,   1415
Up rose the sun, and up rose Emily,
And to Diana's temple hastened she.
Her maidens, who did her accompany,
All brought the fire with them readily;

Th'encens, the clothes, and the remenant al
That to the sacrifyce longen shal;
The hornes fulle of meth, as was the gyse,
Ther lakked noght to doon hir sacrifyse.   2280
Smokinge the temple, full of clothes faire,
This Emelye, with herte debonaire,
Hir body wessh with water of a welle,
But how she dide hir ryte I dar nat telle,
But it be any thing in general;   2285
And yet it were a game to heren al;
To him that meneth wel it were no charge,
But it is good a man ben at his large.
Hir brighte heer was kembd, untressed al;
A coroune of a grene ook cerial   2290
Upon hir heed was set ful fair and mete.
Two fyres on the auter gan she bete,
And dide hir thinges, as men may biholde
In Stace of Thebes and thise bokes olde.
Whan kindled was the fyr, with pitous chere   2295
Unto Diane she spak as ye may here:
      "O chaste goddesse of the wodes grene,
To whom bothe hevene and erthe and see is sene,
Quene of the regne of Pluto derk and lowe,
Goddesse of maydens, that myn herte hast knowe   2300
Ful many a yeer, and woost what I desire,
As keepe me fro thy vengeaunce and thyn ire,
That Attheon aboughte cruelly.
Chaste goddesse, wel wostow that I
Desire to been a mayden al my lyf,   2305
Ne never wol I be no love ne wyf.
I am, thou woost, yet of thy companye,
A mayde, and love hunting and venerye,
And for to walken in the wodes wilde,
And noght to been a wyf and be with childe.   2310
Noght wol I knowe companye of man.
Now help me, lady, sith ye may and can,

The incense, clothes, and such they brought along   1420
That to their sacrifices do belong;
Horns full of mead as was the custom, too—
Nothing they lacked their sacrifice to do.   2280
Censing the temple, full of hangings rare,
Was Emily, with heart gentle and fair,   1425
Her body washed with water from a well.
But how she did her rites, I dare not tell,
Unless it were to speak in general;
And yet it were a game to hear it all.
It wouldn't matter to him who means well;   1430
But it is good to choose what one should tell.
Her bright hair was combed and all unbraided;
A coronet was set upon her head   2290
Of evergreen oak, so fair and fitting.
Two fires on the altar she was kindling,   1435
And did her duties, as men may behold
In Statius of Thebes and these books old.
The fire kindled, and with piteous cheer
To Diana she spoke as you may hear:
        "Oh you chaste goddess of the woodlands green,   1440
By whom sea, earth, and heaven can be seen,
Queen of Pluto's kingdom, dark below,
Goddess of maidens, whom my heart does know,   2300
And through these years has known what I desire,
Keep me from both your vengeance and your ire,   1445
That Actaeon had paid for cruelly.
Chaste goddess, you know full well that for me—
I want to be a maiden all my life,
I never wish to be lover or wife.
I am, you know, still in your company,   1450
A maiden who loves hunting, as you see,
And to go walking out in the woods wild,
And not to be a wife and be with child.   2310
I don't wish to hold congress with a man.
Now help me, lady, since you may and can,   1455

For tho thre formes that thou hast in thee.
And Palamon, that hath swich love to me,
And eek Arcite, that loveth me so sore,   2315
This grace I preye thee withoute more:
As sende love and pees bitwixe hem two,
And fro me turne awey hir hertes so
That al hir hote love and hir desyr,
And al hir bisy torment and hir fyr,   2320
Be queynt or turned in another place.
And if so be thou wolt not do me grace,
Or if my destinee be shapen so,
That I shal nedes have oon of hem two,
As sende me him that most desireth me.   2325
Bihold, goddesse of clene chastitee,
The bittre teres that on my chekes falle.
Sin thou art mayde and kepere of us alle,
My maydenhede thou kepe and wel conserve,
And whyl I live a mayde, I wol thee serve."   2330
        The fyres brenne upon the auter clere,
Whyl Emelye was thus in hir preyere.
But sodeinly she saugh a sighte queynte,
For right anon oon of the fyres queynte,
And quiked agayn, and after that anon   2335
That other fyr was queynt, and al agon;
And as it queynte, it made a whistelinge,
As doon thise wete brondes in hir brenninge,
And at the brondes ende out ran anoon
As it were blody dropes many oon;   2340
For which so sore agast was Emelye
That she was wel ny mad, and gan to crye,
For she ne wiste what it signifyed;
But only for the fere thus hath she cryed,
And weep, that it was pitee for to here.   2345

Because of those three forms²⁹ that you contain.
Palamon has such love for me and pain,
And Arcite, too, whose love for me's so sore.
This grace I pray of you, and then no more:
Now send love and peace between those two,   1460
And have them turn their hearts from me, please do,
So that all of their hot love and desire,
All their painful torment and their fire   2320
Be quenched, or focused in another place.
And if perchance you won't do me this grace,   1465
Or if my destiny's so shaped, indeed,
That one of these two I must have by need,
Send me the one who most desires me.
Behold, you goddess of clean chastity,
The bitter tears that on my cheeks now fall.   1470
Since you're a maiden, keeper of us all,
My maidenhood, keep well now and conserve,
And while I live, as maiden, I'll you serve."   2330
         The fires burn clearly on the altar there,
While Emily was thus saying her prayer.   1475
But then she saw a sight so strange and quaint,
For suddenly, one of the fires grew faint
And went out, and quickened once again;
The other fire was extinguished then;
And as it died there, it made a whistling,   1480
As wet firewood will in its burning.
And the firewood's end ran without stop
What seemed to her like many bloody drops;   2340
By which so sorely scared was Emily
That well nigh mad and crying there was she,   1485
For she did not know what it signified,
But only out of fear thus has she cried
And weeps so it a pity was to hear.

29 **three forms:** Diana's three forms are goddess of the underworld (Hecate), of the hunt (Diana),
and of childbirth (Lucina/Luna).

And therwithal Diane gan appere,
With bowe in hond, right as an hunteresse,
And seyde: "Doghter, stint thyn hevinesse.
Among the goddes hye it is affermed,
And by eterne word writen and confermed,   2350
Thou shalt ben wedded unto oon of tho
That han for thee so muchel care and wo;
But unto which of hem I may nat telle.
Farwel, for I ne may no lenger dwelle.
The fyres which that on myn auter brenne   2355
Shulle thee declaren, er that thou go henne,
Thyn aventure of love, as in this cas."
And with that word, the arwes in the cas
Of the goddesse clateren faste and ringe,
And forth she wente, and made a vanisshinge;   2360
For which this Emelye astoned was,
And seyde, "What amounteth this, allas!
I putte me in thy proteccioun,
Diane, and in thy disposicioun."
And hoom she gooth anon the nexte weye.   2365
This is th'effect, ther is namore to seye.
        The nexte houre of Mars folwinge this,
Arcite unto the temple walked is
Of fierse Mars, to doon his sacrifyse,
With alle the rytes of his payen wyse.   2370
With pitous herte and heigh devocioun,
Right thus to Mars he seyde his orisoun:
        "O stronge god, that in the regnes colde
Of Trace honoured art and lord y-holde,
And hast in every regne and every lond   2375
Of armes al the brydel in thyn hond,
And hem fortunest as thee list devyse,
Accepte of me my pitous sacrifyse.
If so be that my youthe may deserve,
And that my might be worthy for to serve   2380
Thy godhede, that I may be oon of thyne,

At that, Diana started to appear,
With bow in hand, garbed just like a huntress,   1490
And said, "Daughter, cease now in your sadness.
Among the gods on high, it is affirmed,
And eternal word has written and confirmed,   2350
You will be wed to one of them, now know,
Who for you has had so much care and woe,   1495
But now to which of them, I may not tell.
Farewell, for here I may no longer dwell.
The fires here that on my altar burn
Will declare to you, before you do return,
Which outcome to you love will deliver."   1500
And with that word, the arrows in the quiver
Of the goddess clatter fast and ring,
And forth she went her way then, vanishing;   2360
All these events astonished Emily.
"Oh, what does this amount to?" then said she.   1505
"Diana, I am in your protection,
And also under your dispensation."
At once, she goes home by the nearest way.
This, the effect; there is no more to say.
        The hour after this, to Mars belonging,   1510
Arcite now comes to the temple walking
Of fierce Mars to do sacrifice this day
With all the rites there of his pagan ways.   2370
With piteous heart and high devotion,
This way to Mars he said his orison: 1515
        "Oh you strong god, who in the regions cold
Of Thrace is honored, which as lord you hold,
And have in every kingdom and each land
The bridle of all arms within your hand,
And shape men's fortunes as it pleases you,   1520
Take this piteous sacrifice I do.
If it might be my youth is deserving,
And my strength is worthy here for serving   2380
Your godhead, since I am one of your own,

Thanne preye I thee to rewe upon my pyne.

For thilke peyne and thilke hote fyr

In which thou whylom brendest for desyr,

Whan that thou usedest the beautee   2385

Of fayre yonge fresshe Venus free,

And haddest hir in armes at thy wille—

Although thee ones on a tyme misfille

Whan Vulcanus hadde caught thee in his las,

And fond thee ligginge by his wyf, allas!—   2390

For thilke sorwe that was in thyn herte,

Have routhe as wel upon my peynes smerte.

I am yong and unkonning, as thou wost,

And, as I trowe, with love offended most

That evere was any lyves creature;   2395

For she that dooth me al this wo endure,

Ne reccheth nevere wher I sinke or flete.

And wel I woot, er she me mercy hete,

I moot with strengthe winne hire in the place;

And wel I woot, withouten help or grace   2400

Of thee, ne may my strengthe noght availle.

Than help me, lord, tomorwe in my bataille,

For thilke fyr that whylom brente thee,

As wel as thilke fyr now brenneth me;

And do that I tomorwe have victorie.   2405

Myn be the travaille, and thyn be the glorie!

Thy soverein temple wol I most honouren

Of any place, and alwey most labouren

In thy plesaunce and in thy craftes stronge,   2410

And in thy temple I wol my baner honge,

And alle the armes of my companye;

And everemo, unto that day I dye,

Eterne fyr I wol biforn thee finde.

And eek to this avow I wol me binde: 2415

My berd, myn heer, that hongeth long adoun,

That never yet ne felte offensioun

Of rasour nor of shere, I wol thee yive,

I pray for pity on the pain I've known.   1525
Because this same pain and this same hot fire
In which you once did burn with true desire,
When you yourself enjoyed all of the beauty
Of the fair, youthful Venus, fresh and free,
And at your will, you held her in your arms—   1530
Although there was one time you came to harm,
When Vulcan's net had caught you in its snare,
When he found you lying by his wife there—   2390
For that same sorrow that was in your heart,
Have pity now upon how my pains smart.   1535
I am young and ignorant, as you know,
And, I think, with love offended more so
Than ever was any living creature,
For she who makes me all this woe endure,
Whether I sink or float she does not care,   1540
I know well, before she grants mercy there,
With my strength, I must win her in this place,
And well I know that, without help or grace   2400
Sent from you, my own strength will not avail.
Then help me, lord, in battle to prevail,   1545
Given that fire that burned you formerly,
As well as that same fire that now burns me,
Ensure tomorrow I'll have victory.
Mine, the labor, but yours be the glory!
Your sovereign temple I will most honor   1550
Of any place, and always most labor
Both for your pleasure and in your arts strong.
In your temple, my banner will hang long,   2410
And all the arms, too, of my company,
And evermore, until death comes to me,   1555
Eternal flame you will here always find.
Also to this vow I myself do bind:
My beard and hair, which I have left to grow,
And which do not the injury yet know
Of razor nor of shears, to you I'll give,   1560

And ben thy trewe servant whyl I live.
Now lord, have routhe upon my sorwes sore:
Yif me the victorie, I aske thee namore."   2420
      The preyere stinte of Arcita the stronge,
The ringes on the temple dore that honge,
And eek the dores, clatereden ful faste,
Of which Arcita somwhat him agaste.
The fyres brenden up on the auter brighte,   2425
That it gan al the temple for to lighte;
And swete smel the ground anon up yaf,
And Arcita anon his hand up haf,
And more encens into the fyr he caste,
With othere rytes mo; and atte laste   2430
The statue of Mars bigan his hauberk ringe.
And with that soun he herde a murmuringe
Ful lowe and dim, that sayde thus, "Victorie,"
For which he yaf to Mars honour and glorie.
And thus with joye and hope wel to fare,   2435
Arcite anon unto his in is fare,
As fayn as fowel is of the brighte sonne.
      And right anon swich stryf ther is bigonne,
For thilke graunting, in the hevene above,
Bitwixe Venus, the goddesse of love,   2440
And Mars, the sterne god armipotente,
That Jupiter was bisy it to stente;
Til that the pale Saturnus the colde,
That knew so manye of aventures olde,
Fond in his olde experience an art   2445
That he ful sone hath plesed every part.
As sooth is sayd, elde hath greet avantage;
In elde is bothe wisdom and usage;
Men may the olde atrenne and noght atrede.
Saturne anon, to stinten stryf and drede,   2450
Al be it that it is agayn his kynde,
Of al this stryf he gan remedie fynde.
      "My dere doghter Venus," quod Saturne,

And be your servant true while I may live.
Now, lord, take pity on my sorrows sore;
Give me the victory; I ask no more."   2420
        The prayer ends now of Arcite, strong and young;
The rings that on the temple door there hung,   1565
And the door also, clattered very fast,
By which then Arcite somewhat was aghast.
The fires burned upon the altar bright,
And throughout the whole temple cast their light;
A sweet smell then the ground at once gave up,   1570
And Arcite quickly did his hand heave up.
And more incense into the fire he cast,
And did some other rites; and then at last,   2430
Mars's statue its coat of mail did ring,
And with that sound, he heard a murmuring   1575
All low and dim, which said thus, "Victory!"
For which he gave to Mars honor and glory.
And thus with joy and hope that well he'd fare,
Arcite at once went to his lodgings there,
As happy as a bird is for bright sun.   1580
        Immediately, such strife was begun
From these promises, up in heaven above,
Between fair Venus, the goddess of love,   2440
And Mars, the stern god in-arms-all-potent,
Which Jupiter himself could not prevent,   1585
Until, by need, grim Saturn, pale and cold,
Who knew so much about adventures old,
Found in his old experience an art
So that quite soon he has pleased every heart.
Old age has great advantage, in this sense: 1590
In wisdom, truly, and experience;
Men may the old outrun, but not outwit.
Saturn now, to ease the strife and end it,   2450
Though it was not his nature to be kind,
For all this strife, a remedy did find.   1595
        "My dear daughter Venus," then said Saturn,

"My cours, that hath so wyde for to turne,
Hath more power than wot any man: 2455
Myn is the drenching in the see so wan;
Myn is the prison in the derke cote;
Myn is the strangling and hanging by the throte;
The murmure and the cherles rebelling,
The groyninge and the pryvee empoysoning.   2460
I do vengeance and pleyn correccioun
Whyl I dwelle in the signe of the leoun.
Myn is the ruine of the hye halles,
The falling of the toures and of the walles
Upon the mynour or the carpenter.   2465
I slow Sampsoun, shakinge the piler;
And myne be the maladyes colde,
The derke tresons, and the castes olde;
My loking is the fader of pestilence.
Now weep namore, I shal doon diligence   2470
That Palamon, that is thyn owne knight,
Shal have his lady, as thou hast him hight.
Though Mars shal helpe his knight, yet nathelees
Bitwixe yow ther moot be som tyme pees,
Al be ye noght of o complexioun,   2475
That causeth al day swich divisioun.
I am thin ayel, redy at thy wille;
Weep now namore, I wol thy lust fulfille."
          Now wol I stinten of the goddes above,
Of Mars and of Venus, goddesse of love,   2480
And telle yow as pleynly as I can
The grete effect for which that I bigan.

Explicit tercia pars.

"My orbit, which goes so wide in its turn,
Has more power than any man can mark.[30]
Mine is the drowning in the sea so dark.
Mine is the prison in dark cell remote;   1600
Mine, the strangling and hanging by the throat,
The murmuring and peasants' rebelling,[31]
The complaining and secret poisoning;   2460
I seek vengeance and take full correction
While I dwell in the sign of the lion.[32]   1605
Mine is ruining of the highest halls,
Collapsing of the towers and the walls
Upon the miner or the carpenter.
I slew Sampson, shaking down the pillar;
And mine are all the maladies so cold,   1610
The darkest treasons, and the plots of old;
My glance is the father of pestilence.
Now, weep no more; I'll use my diligence   2470
So Palamon, who is your own true knight,
As you promised, will have his lady bright.   1615
Though Mars will help his knight, yet nonetheless,
Between you two, there must be peacefulness,
Though you two aren't of the same complexion,
Which, all day long, causes such division.
I am your grandfather, ready to do your will;   1620
Weep now no more; your pleasure, I'll fulfill."

        Now, I will cease about the gods above,
About Mars and Venus, goddess of love,   2480
And tell you now as plainly as I can
The great outcome of that which I began.   1625

The third part ends.

    30 **My orbit . . . mark:** Chaucer here is deliberately conflating the planet Saturn and the god
Saturn.
    31 **peasants' rebelling:** Perhaps this phrase refers to the Peasants' Revolt of 1381. If so, it is one of
the few times Chaucer mentions this event in his writing.
    32 **sign of the lion:** Zodiacal sign Leo.

Sequitur pars quarta.

     Greet was the feste in Athenes that day,
And eek the lusty seson of that May
Made every wight to been in swich plesaunce,   2485
That al that Monday justen they and daunce,
And spenden it in Venus heigh servyse.
But by the cause that they sholde ryse
Erly, for to seen the grete fight,
Unto hir reste wenten they at night.   2490
And on the morwe, whan that day gan springe,
Of hors and harneys noyse and clateringe
Ther was in hostelryes al aboute;
And to the paleys rood ther many a route
Of lordes upon stedes and palfreys.   2495
Ther maystow seen devysing of harneys
So uncouth and so riche, and wroght so weel
Of goldsmithrie, of browdinge, and of steel;
The sheeldes brighte, testeres, and trappures;
Gold-hewen helmes, hauberkes, cote-armures;   2500
Lordes in paraments on hir courseres,
Knightes of retenue, and eek squyeres
Nailinge the speres, and helmes bokelinge;
Gigginge of sheeldes with layneres lacinge—
Ther as need is, they weren no thing ydel;   2505
The fomy steedes on the golden brydel
Gnawinge, and faste the armurers also
With fyle and hamer prikinge to and fro;
Yemen on foote and communes many oon
With shorte staves, thikke as they may goon;   2510
Pypes, trompes, nakers, clariounes
That in the bataille blowen blody sounes,
The paleys ful of peple up and doun,
Heer three, ther ten, holding hir questioun,
Divyninge of thise Thebane knightes two.   2515
Somme seyden thus, somme seyde it shal be so;

The fourth part follows.

Great was the feasting in Athens that day,
And too, the merry season known as May
Made everyone feel then such great delight
That, all Monday, joust and dance they might,
And spend it in high service made to Venus.   1630
But, because every one of them must thus
Rise early, in time to see the great fight,
They all went off to take their rest that night.   2490
And next morning, when day began to spring,
From horse and harness, noise and clattering   1635
There sounded out from all the hostelries;
To the palace rode many companies
Of these lords upon their steeds and palfries.
Such armor you may see prepared on these
That is exotic, rich, and strange in making   1640
By gold- and steelsmiths and embroidering;
Their bright horse armor and shields of the best,
Gold helmets, mail coats, and heraldic vests;   2500
Lords in robes richly decked upon their coursers,
Knights in their retinues and then the squires   1645
Nailing heads on spears and helmets buckling;
Fitting shields with straps; the straps then lacing—
Where the need arose, they were not idle;
Foaming steeds here on the golden bridle
Gnawing, and quickly armorers also   1650
With file and hammer pricking to and fro;
Yeomen on foot, and common soldiers go
With short staves, they're thickly crowding also;   2510
Pipes, trumpets, drums, and bugles all around,
Which in the battle blow their bloody sound;   1655
The palace full of people who are going,
Here three, there ten, one question all debating,
Conjecturing about these Theban knights.
Some said thus, "That one now will show his might";

Somme helden with him with the blake berd,
Somme with the balled, somme with the thikke herd;
Somme sayde he loked grim, and he wolde fighte—
"He hath a sparth of twenty pound of wighte."   2520
Thus was the halle ful of divyninge,
Longe after that the sonne gan to springe.

     The grete Theseus, that of his sleep awaked
With minstralcye and noyse that was maked,
Held yet the chambre of his paleys riche,   2525
Til that the Thebane knightes, bothe yliche
Honoured, were into the paleys fet.
Duk Theseus was at a window set,
Arrayed right as he were a god in trone.
The peple preesseth thiderward ful sone   2530
Him for to seen, and doon heigh reverence,
And eek to herkne his heste and his sentence.

     An heraud on a scaffold made an "Oo!
Til al the noyse of peple was ydo;
And whan he saugh the peple of noyse al stille,   2535
Thus showed he the mighty dukes wille:

     "The lord hath of his heigh discrecioun
Considered that it were destruccioun
To gentil blood to fighten in the gyse
Of mortal bataille now in this empryse.   2540
Wherfore, to shapen that they shal not dye,
He wol his firste purpos modifye.
No man therfore, up peyne of los of lyf,
No maner shot, ne polax, ne short knyf
Into the listes sende, or thider bringe;   2545
Ne short swerd, for to stoke with poynt bytinge,
No man ne drawe ne bere it by his syde.
Ne no man shal unto his felawe ryde
But o cours with a sharp y-grounde spere;

Some favored the black-bearded one right there, 1660
Some the bald one or the one with thick hair;
Some said that one would fight, for he looked grim:
"A twenty-pound battle-ax he has with him." 2520
Thus was the hall full of such speculating,
Long after the sun had had its rising. 1665
     The great Theseus, who from his sleep did wake
With all the noise and minstrelsy they make,
In his rich palace chamber does delay
Till the Theban knights, both of them that day
Honored alike, did to the palace get. 1670
Duke Theseus was at a window set,
Arrayed just like a god upon a throne,
The people crowded to him on their own 2530
To see him and to pay high reverence,
And to hear both his behest and sentence. 1675
     A herald on a scaffold loudly yelled,
Till all the noise the people made was quelled,
And when he saw the people all were still,
Then he proclaimed the mighty duke's own will:
     "The lord has now, with his great discretion, 1680
Considered that it would be destruction
Of gentle blood to fight under the guise
Of mortal combat in this enterprise. 2540
Thus, to arrange it so they will not die,
He will his first intention modify. 1685
No man, therefore, on pain of loss of life,
A battle-ax, crossbow bolt, or short knife
Into the lists may either send or bring,
Or short sword with biting point for stabbing,
No man can draw, or bear it by his side. 1690
No man against his enemy may ride
More than one charge with his sharply ground spear;[33]

33 **More than one charge**, etc.: While it might seem that deadly damage could be inflicted with a "sharply ground spear," the point here is that Theseus does not want the tournament to involve mortal combat.

Foyne, if him list, on fote, himself to were.   2550
And he that is at meschief shal be take,
And noght slayn, but be broght unto the stake
That shal ben ordeyned on either syde;
But thider he shal by force, and ther abyde.
And if so falle the chieftayn be take   2555
On either syde, or elles sleen his make,
No lenger shal the turneyinge laste.
God spede yow! goth forth, and ley on faste.
With long swerd and with mace fighteth youre fille.
Goth now youre wey—this is the lordes wille."   2560
        The voys of peple touchede the hevene,
So loude cryde they with mery stevene:
"God save swich a lord, that is so good,
He wilneth no destruccioun of blood!"
        Up goon the trompes and the melodye,   2565
And to the listes rit the companye,
By ordinaunce, thurghout the citee large,
Hanged with cloth of gold and nat with sarge.
Ful lyk a lord this noble duk gan ryde,
Thise two Thebans upon either syde;   2570
And after rood the quene and Emelye,
And after that another companye
Of oon and other, after hir degree.
And thus they passen thurghout the citee,
And to the listes come they bytyme.   2575
It nas not of the day yet fully pryme
Whan set was Theseus ful riche and hye,
Ipolita the quene and Emelye,
And othere ladies in degrees aboute.
Unto the seetes preesseth al the route.   2580
        And westward, thurgh the gates under Marte,
Arcite, and eek the hundred of his parte,
With baner reed is entred right anon;
And in that selve moment Palamon
Is under Venus, estward in the place,   2585

Thrust, if he like, on foot, in defense here. 2550
And he who's in distress will then be taken
And not slain, but be brought to the stake then 1695
That will be ordained for either side;
He'll be taken by force, and there abide.
If it befalls that the chieftain today
Of either side is seized, or his foe slays,
No longer will this tournament then last. 1700
God speed you now! Go forth, and lay on fast!
With long sword and with mace, now fight your fill.
Go on your way now. This is the lord's will." 2560
      People's voices touched heaven on each side,
So loudly with a merry shout they cried, 1705
"Now God save such a lord and give him joy,
Who wants no gentle blood here to destroy!"
      Up go the trumpets and the melody,
And to the lists ride both the companies,
In proper order, through the city large 1710
Adorned with cloths of gold, and not with serge.
Just like a lord this noble duke did ride;
The Theban knights were with him on each side, 2570
And after rode the queen and Emily,
And after that, another company 1715
Of attendants, according to degree.
Thus they make their way throughout the city,
And at the lists arriving in good time.
The day had not yet fully reached its prime;
Theseus was seated on high richly, 1720
With Queen Hippolyta and Emily,
And other ladies with them in the tiers.
Into the seats the whole crowd presses here. 2580
      On the west, through the gates of Mars so wide,
Arcite and the hundred knights of his side 1725
With banner red have entered there anon.
At that same moment, entered Palamon
Through Venus's gate, east now of that place,

With baner whyt, and hardy chere and face.
In al the world, to seken up and doun,
So evene withouten variacioun,
Ther nere swiche companyes tweye.
For ther was noon so wys that coude seye   2590
That any hadde of other avauntage
Of worthinesse, ne of estaat ne age,
So evene were they chosen, for to gesse.
And in two renges faire they hem dresse.
Whan that hir names rad were everichoon,   2595
That in hir nombre gyle were ther noon,
Tho were the gates shet, and cryed was loude:
"Do now your devoir, yonge knightes proude!"
        The heraudes lefte hir priking up and doun;
Now ringen trompes loude and clarioun.   2600
Ther is namore to seyn, but west and est
In goon the speres ful sadly in th'arest;
In goth the sharpe spore into the syde.
Ther seen men who can juste and who can ryde;
Ther shiveren shaftes upon sheeldes thikke;   2605
He feleth thurgh the herte-spoon the prikke.
Up springen speres twenty foot on highte;
Out goon the swerdes as the silver brighte.
The helmes they tohewen and toshrede;
Out brest the blood, with sterne stremes rede.   2610
With mighty maces the bones they tobreste.
He thurgh the thikkeste of the throng gan threste;
Ther stomblen stedes stronge, and doun goth al;
He rolleth under foot as dooth a bal.
He foyneth on his feet with his tronchoun,   2615
And he him hurtleth with his hors adoun.
He thurgh the body is hurt and sithen y-take,
Maugree his heed, and broght unto the stake.
As forward was, right ther he moste abyde;
Another lad is on that other syde.   2620
And som tyme dooth hem Theseus to reste,

With banner white, and with brave mien and face.
In the whole world, if you sought all around,   1730
So evenly matched might nowhere be found
Any other two such companies,
For there was no one so wise he could see   2590
One had over other an advantage
In worthiness or in estate or age,   1735
They were chosen so evenly, one guessed.
In two fair ranks, each other they addressed.
And when the names were read of everyone
So in their number, guile there would be none,
The gates were shut, and it was cried aloud: 1740
"Do now your duty, all you young knights proud!"
        The heralds up and down cease from their pricking;
Loudly the trumpets and the bugles ring.   2600
There is no more to say, but east and west,
In go the spears quite firmly in their rests;   1745
In go the spurs quite sharply in the sides.
Men now see who can joust and who can ride;
There shiver shafts upon the shields so thick;
Through the breastbone, a man can feel the prick.
Up spring the spears to twenty feet of height;   1750
Out flash the swords that shine like silver bright;
Through the helmets they hack and hew and shred;
Out bursts the blood in stern, strong streams so red;   2610
With massive maces, bones to bits they burst.
One through the thickest of the throng thrusts first;   1755
There stumble the strong steeds, and down goes all,
This one rolls under foot just like a ball;
That one on his feet stabs hard with his spear,
And hurls another down with his horse here;
He through the body is hurt and then taken;   1760
For all his pains, he is brought to the stake then,
As they agreed and there he must abide.
Another one's led to the other side.   2620
And sometimes Theseus does make them rest,

Hem to refresshe and drinken, if hem leste.

      Ful ofte a day han thise Thebanes two

Togidre y-met, and wroght his felawe wo;

Unhorsed hath ech other of hem tweye.   2625

Ther nas no tygre in the vale of Galgopheye,

Whan that hir whelp is stole whan it is lyte,

So cruel on the hunte as is Arcite

For jelous herte upon this Palamoun.

Ne in Belmarye ther nis so fel leoun   2630

That hunted is, or for his hunger wood,

Ne of his praye desireth so the blood,

As Palamon to sleen his foo Arcite.

The jelous strokes on hir helmes byte;

Out renneth blood on bothe hir sydes rede.   2635

      Som tyme an ende ther is of every dede.

For er the sonne unto the reste wente,

The stronge king Emetreus gan hente

This Palamon, as he faught with Arcite,

And made his swerd depe in his flesh to byte;   2640

And by the force of twenty is he take

Unyolden and y-drawe unto the stake.

And in the rescus of this Palamoun

The stronge king Ligurge is born adoun;

And king Emetreus, for al his strengthe,   2645

Is born out of his sadel a swerdes lengthe,

So hitte him Palamon er he were take.

But al for noght: he was broght to the stake.

His hardy herte mighte him helpe naught;

He moste abyde, whan that he was caught,   2650

By force and eek by composicioun.

Who sorweth now but woful Palamoun,

That moot namore goon agayn to fighte?

      And whan that Theseus had seyn this sighte,

Refresh themselves and drink, as they think best.   1765
      Often that day, have these two Thebans so
Met together and brought each other woe;
Twice already they've unhorsed each other.
In Gargaphia,[34] there was no tiger,
When her small cub has been stolen away,   1770
So cruel to hunters as Arcite that day
Was, with his jealous heart, to Palamon.
In Benmarin,[35] there is no cruel lion,   2630
That's hunted or stalks from hunger madly,
Or from his prey wants the blood so badly,   1775
As Palamon, who wants to slay Arcite.
The jealous strokes upon their helmets bite;
Out runs the blood on both their sides so red.
      A time comes when each deed must be ended.
Before the sun went to its rest and ease,   1780
The strong king Emetreus there did seize
This Palamon, as he fought with Arcite,
And made his sword deep into his flesh bite,   2640
And by the force of twenty he is taken,
Unyielding, and he's brought to the stake then.   1785
In his effort Palamon to rescue,
The strong king Lycurgus is brought down too,
And King Emetreus, for all his strength,
Is borne from his saddle by a sword's length;
Palamon hit him before he's taken.   1790
All for nothing—he went to the stake then.
His hardy heart there brings him help for naught;
For he must stay there once he has been caught,   2650
By force and also by this agreement.
Who but woeful Palamon does lament,   1795
Who must no more again go to the fight?
      And now when Theseus has seen this sight,

34 **Gargaphia**: Valley in Greece.
35 **Benmarin**: In North Africa.

Unto the folk that foghten thus echoon   2655
He cryde, "Ho! namore, for it is doon!
I wol be trewe juge, and nat partye.
Arcite of Thebes shal have Emelye,
That by his fortune hath hir faire y-wonne."
Anon ther is a noyse of peple bigonne   2660
For joye of this, so loude and heighe withalle,
It semed that the listes sholde falle.
           What can now faire Venus doon above?
What seith she now? what dooth this quene of love
But wepeth so, for wanting of hir wille,   2665
Til that hir teres in the listes fille?
She seyde, "I am ashamed, doutelees."
           Saturnus seyde, "Doghter, hold thy pees.
Mars hath his wille: his knight hath al his bone;
And, by myn heed, thou shalt ben esed sone."   2670
           The trompours with the loude minstralcye,
The heraudes that ful loude yelle and crye,
Been in hir wele for joye of daun Arcite.
But herkneth me, and stinteth noyse a lyte,
Which a miracle ther bifel anon.   2675
           This fierse Arcite hath of his helm y-don,
And on a courser, for to shewe his face,
He priketh endelong the large place,
Loking upward upon this Emelye;
And she agayn him caste a freendlich yë   2680
(For wommen, as to speken in comune,
They folwen alle the favour of fortune)
And she was al his chere, as in his herte.
           Out of the ground a furie infernal sterte,
From Pluto sent at requeste of Saturne,   2685
For which his hors for fere gan to turne
And leep asyde, and foundred as he leep;
And er that Arcite may taken keep,
He pighte him on the pomel of his heed,
That in the place he lay as he were deed,   2690

To all the folks who fought thus, every one,
He cried, "Whoa! No more here, for it is done!
I'm no partisan, but will judge truly.   1800
Arcite of Thebes now will have Emily,
Who, by his fortune, has her fairly won."
At once shouts from the people have begun   2660
For joy at this, so loud and high withal
It seemed their shouting would make these lists fall.   1805
          What now can fair Venus do up above?
What says she now? What does this queen of love
But weep—she did not get her will at all—
Until her tears into the lists did fall?
She said, "Doubtless, I'm in disgrace today."   1810
          Saturn said, "Daughter, hold your peace, I pray!
Mars has his will; his knight's received his boon,
And, by my head, you will be eased quite soon."   2670
          The trumpeters, with their loud minstrelsy,
The heralds, who yell and cry so loudly,   1815
To Don Arcite's gladness add their joys.
But listen now, and cease a bit this noise:
Hear what a miracle has happened yet.
          This fierce Arcite has removed his helmet,
And on his courser there, to show his face,   1820
He pricks from end to end of this large place,
Looking upward at Emily on high;
And toward him, she cast a friendly eye   2680
(For women, to speak in general, soon
They'll follow all the favor of Fortune);   1825
She was the source of pleasure in his heart.
          Out of the ground, an infernal fury starts,
Sent by Pluto at the charge of Saturn,
Because of which, his horse in fear did turn,
And leaped aside, stumbling as he leaped there;   1830
And before Arcite might take proper care,
He struck himself on the crown of his head,
So in that place he lay like he were dead;   2690

His brest tobrosten with his sadel-bowe.
As blak he lay as any cole or crowe,
So was the blood y-ronnen in his face.
Anon he was y-born out of the place,
With herte soor, to Theseus paleys.   2695
Tho was he corven out of his harneys,
And in a bed y-brought ful faire and blyve,
For he was yet in memorie and alyve,
And alway crying after Emelye.

      Duk Theseus, with al his companye,   2700
Is comen hoom to Athenes his citee,
With alle blisse and greet solempnitee.
Al be it that this aventure was falle,
He nolde noght disconforten hem alle.
Men seyde eek that Arcite shal nat dye;   2705
He shal ben heled of his maladye.
And of another thing they were as fayn:
That of hem alle was ther noon y-slayn,
Al were they sore y-hurt, and namely oon,
That with a spere was thirled his brest-boon.   2710
To othere woundes and to broken armes
Some hadden salves, and some hadden charmes;
Fermacies of herbes, and eek save
They dronken, for they wolde hir limes have.
For which this noble duk, as he wel can,   2715
Conforteth and honoureth every man,
And made revel al the longe night
Unto the straunge lordes, as was right.
Ne ther was holden no disconfitinge
But as a justes or a tourneyinge;   2720
For soothly ther was no disconfiture,
For falling nis nat but an aventure.
Ne to be lad with fors unto the stake
Unyolden, and with twenty knightes take,
O persone allone, withouten mo,   2725
And haried forth by arme, foot, and to,

His breast was broken from his saddle's bow.
He lay quite black then, like coal or a crow,   1835
For thus the blood was running in his face.
At once then, he was carried from this place,
To Theseus's palace, with heart sore.
And then he was carved out of his armor;
To bed he was brought quickly and fairly,   1840
For he still had his life and memory,
And always crying out for Emily.

Duke Theseus, with all his company,   2700
Has come home to Athens, to his city,
With all bliss and great solemnity.   1845
For although this adventure did befall,
He didn't want to incommode them all.
Men also said that Arcite will not die;
He'll be healed of his sickness by and by.
Another thing made them as glad withal: 1850
That there was no one slain out of them all,
Though they were sorely hurt, namely one here,
Whose breast bone had been pierced through with a spear.   2710
For other wounds, and too for broken arms,
Some had salves, and others here had charms;   1855
Their teas of sage and also herbal brews
They all drank up, so limbs they would not lose.
And thus this noble duke, as best he can,
Comforts here and honors every man,
And he made revelry through the long night   1860
To all these foreign lords, as it was right.
And to dishonor was no one's intent
Save what one finds at jousts or tournaments.   2720
For surely, there was no dishonor meant.
Falling off a horse is just an accident,   1865
And to be led by force off to the stake then,
Unyielding, by twenty knights there taken,
One person all alone, with no help though,
And dragged away by arm and foot and toe,

And eek his steede driven forth with staves
With footmen, bothe yemen and eek knaves—
It nas aretted him no vileinye,
Ther may no man clepen it cowardye.   2730
      For which anon duk Theseus leet crye,
To stinten alle rancour and envye,
The gree as wel of o syde as of other,
And either syde ylyk as otheres brother;
And yaf hem yiftes after hir degree,   2735
And fully heeld a feste dayes three;
And conveyed the kinges worthily
Out of his toun a journee largely.
And hoom wente every man the righte way.
Ther was namore but "Farewel, have good day!"   2740
Of this bataille I wol namore endyte,
But speke of Palamon and of Arcite.
      Swelleth the brest of Arcite, and the sore
Encreesseth at his herte more and more.
The clothered blood, for any lechecraft,   2745
Corrupteth and is in his bouk y-laft,
That neither veyne-blood, ne ventusinge,
Ne drinke of herbes may ben his helpinge.
The vertu expulsif, or animal,
Fro thilke vertu cleped natural   2750
Ne may the venim voyden ne expelle.
The pypes of his longes gonne to swelle,
And every lacerte in his brest adoun
Is shent with venim and corrupcioun.
Him gayneth neither, for to gete his lyf,
Vomyt upward ne dounward laxatif;
Al is tobrosten thilke regioun.
Nature hath now no dominacioun;

And to have his steed with staves forth driven   1870
By footmen, the servants and the yeomen—
He would deserve no shame or blame for this;
No man thereby might call it cowardice.   2730
      To this end, Duke Theseus did proclaim—
So he might end rancor, ill will, or blame—   1875
His esteem for one side and the other—
Both alike and similar as brothers;
And he gave them gifts according to degree,
And held a feast that lasted for days three,
And accompanied the two kings nobly   1880
Out of town a good day's journey fully.
And every man went home the quickest way.
There was no more but "Farewell, have good day!"   2740
Of this battle, I will no longer write,
But speak now of Palamon and Arcite.   1885
      Now swells the breast of Arcite, and the sore
Around his heart increases more and more.
The clotted blood, despite leech-craft quite deft,
Becomes infected and in his trunk is left,
So that neither bloodletting nor cupping,[36]   1890
Nor herbal drinks now give any helping.
The expulsive power, that's termed "animal,"
From that same power, that's called "natural,"[37]   2750
The poison there cannot void or expel.
Thus the pipes of his lungs begin to swell,   1895
And every muscle in the breast of him
Is destroyed with both decay and venom.
Now neither profits him to make him live:
Upward vomit, or downward laxative.
All has burst completely in this region;   1900
Nature now no longer has dominion.

36 **cupping**: Drawing blood to the surface with a heated cup for curative purposes.

37 "**animal**" . . . "**natural**": The forces in the body believed to be able to expel infection and
illness.

And certeinly, ther nature wol nat wirche,

Farewel, phisyk; go ber the man to chirche.   2760

This al and som, that Arcita mot dye;

For which he sendeth after Emelye

And Palamon, that was his cosin dere.

Than seyde he thus, as ye shul after here:

       "Naught may the woful spirit in myn herte   2765

Declare o poynt of alle my sorwes smerte

To yow, my lady, that I love most;

But I biquethe the service of my gost

To yow aboven every creature,

Sin that my lyf may no lenger dure.   2770

Allas, the wo! allas, the peynes stronge,

That I for yow have suffred, and so longe!

Allas, the deeth! allas, myn Emelye!

Allas, departinge of oure companye!

Allas, myn hertes quene! allas, my wyf!   2775

Myn hertes lady, endere of my lyf!

What is this world? what asketh men to have?

Now with his love, now in his colde grave

Allone, withouten any companye.

Farewel, my swete fo, myn Emelye!   2780

And softe tak me in your armes tweye,

For love of God, and herkneth what I seye:

       I have heer with my cosin Palamon

Had stryf and rancour many a day agon,

For love of yow and for my jalousye.   2785

And Jupiter so wis my soule gye,

To speken of a servant proprely,

With alle circumstaunces trewely—

That is to seyn, trouthe, honour, knighthede,

Wisdom, humblesse, estaat, and heigh kinrede,   2790

Fredom, and al that longeth to that art—

So Jupiter have of my soule part,

As in this world right now ne knowe I non

So worthy to ben loved as Palamon,

And certainly, when Nature's in the lurch,
Farewell physic! Go bear the man to church! 2760
The sum of this is that Arcite must die;
He sends for Emily to come nearby, 1905
And Palamon, who is his cousin dear.
And he said thus, as you will after hear:
      "The woeful spirit that in my heart goes
Can't declare one point of all my sorrows
To you, my lady, whom I love the most, 1910
But I bequeath the service of my ghost
To you above any living creature,
Since now my life no longer may endure. 2770
Alas, the woe! Alas, the pains so strong,
That I have suffered for you for so long! 1915
Alas, now death! Alas, my Emily!
Alas, the parting of our company!
Alas, queen of my heart! Alas, my wife,
My heart's lady and ender of my life!
What is this world? What can a man here crave? 1920
Now with his love, and now in his cold grave
Alone, and without any company.
Farewell, now, my sweet foe, my Emily! 2780
And gently take me in your arms, I pray,
For love of God, and now hear what I say. 1925
      I have here with my cousin Palamon
Strife and rancor long ago begun
From jealousy, and for the love of you.
May Jupiter guide my soul, wisely too,
To speak about love's servant properly, 1930
In all of his circumstances truly—
That is, knighthood, honor, humility,
Wisdom, lofty lineage, and degree, 2790
Generosity, and all of love's art—
May Jupiter now here take my soul's part, 1935
In this world right now, I know of no one
As worthy to be loved as Palamon,

That serveth yow and wol don al his lyf.   2795
And if that evere ye shul been a wyf,
Foryet nat Palamon, the gentil man."
And with that word his speche faille gan,
For from his feet up to his brest was come
The cold of deeth, that hadde him overcome,   2800
And yet moreover, in his armes two
The vital strengthe is lost and al ago.
Only the intellect, withouten more,
That dwelled in his herte syk and sore,
Gan faillen when the herte felte deeth.   2805
Dusked his eyen two, and failled breeth,
But on his lady yet caste he his yë;
His laste word was, "Mercy, Emelye!"
His spirit chaunged hous and wente ther
As I cam never, I can nat tellen wher.   2810
Therfor I stinte, I nam no divinistre;
Of soules finde I nat in this registre,
Ne me ne list thilke opiniouns to telle
Of hem, though that they wryten wher they dwelle.
Arcite is cold, ther Mars his soule gye.   2815
Now wol I speken forth of Emelye.
        Shrighte Emelye and howleth Palamon,
And Theseus his suster took anon
Swowninge, and bar hire fro the corps away.
What helpeth it to tarien forth the day   2820
To tellen how she weep bothe eve and morwe?
For in swich cas wommen have swich sorwe,
Whan that hir housbondes been from hem ago,
That for the more part they sorwen so,
Or elles fallen in swich a maladye   2825
That at the laste certeinly they dye.
        Infinite been the sorwes and the teres
Of olde folk and folk of tendre yeres

Who serves you and will do so all his life.
And if it happens you should be a wife,
Forget not Palamon, this gentle man."   1940
And with that word, his speech to fail began,
For from his feet up to his breast had come
The cold of death, which had him overcome,   2800
And moreover now in both his arms so
The vital strength is lost, and it did go.   1945
Only the intellect, with nothing more,
Which dwelled within his heart so sick and sore,
Began to falter when his heart felt death.
His eyes grew dusky, and then failed his breath,
But on his lady, still his eyes cast he;   1950
His last words were, "Now, mercy, Emily!"
His spirit houses changed, and it went there,
Since I've not seen it, I can't tell you where.   2810
Thus, I stop; I am not a minister;
Of souls, I find not in this register,[38]   1955
Nor those opinions do I want to tell
Of authors who would write where souls do dwell.
Arcite is cold, where Mars guides his spirit!
Now will I speak of Emily a bit.
          Shrieks Emily, and howls Palamon.   1960
Theseus his sister-in-law anon
Takes and bears swooning from the corpse away.
What would it help now to prolong the day   2820
To tell how she wept both eve and morrow?
In such cases women have such sorrow,   1965
When time comes that their husbands from them go,
That for the most part, they have such sorrow,
Or else fall into such a malady
That, at the last, they will die certainly.
          Infinite are the sorrows and the tears   1970
Of both old folks and folks of tender years

38 **register**: Text, book.

In al the toun, for deeth of this Theban;
For him ther wepeth bothe child and man.   2830
So greet weping was ther noon, certayn,
Whan Ector was y-broght, al fresh y-slayn,
To Troye. Allas, the pitee that was ther:
Cracchinge of chekes, renting eek of heer.
"Why woldestow be deed," thise wommen crye,   2835
"And haddest gold ynough, and Emelye?"
          No man mighte gladen Theseus
Savinge his olde fader Egeus,
That knew this worldes transmutacioun,
As he had seyn it chaunge bothe up and doun—   2840
Joye after wo, and wo after gladnesse—
And shewed hem ensamples and lyknesse.
          "Right as ther deyed nevere man," quod he,
"That he ne livede in erthe in some degree,
Right so ther livede never man," he seyde,   2845
"In al this world, that som tyme he ne deyde.
This world nis but a thurghfare ful of wo,
And we ben pilgrimes, passinge to and fro:
Deeth is an ende of every worldly sore."
And over al this yet seyde he muchel more   2850
To this effect, ful wysely to enhorte
The peple that they sholde hem reconforte.
          Duk Theseus, with al his bisy cure,
Caste now wher that the sepulture
Of goode Arcite may best y-maked be,   2855
And eek most honurable in his degree.
And at the laste he took conclusioun,
That ther as first Arcite and Palamoun
Hadden for love the bataille hem bitwene,
That in that selve grove, swote and grene,   2860
Ther as he hadde his amorouse desires,
His compleynte, and for love his hote fires,
He wolde make a fyr, in which the office
Funeral he mighte al accomplice;

In all the town for the death of this Theban.
For him, in truth, there weeps each child and man;   2830
Surely, such great weeping did not obtain
When Hector was brought home, just freshly slain,   1975
To Troy. Alas, the pity that was there,
Scratching of cheeks, and rending, too, of hair.
"Now why would you be dead," these women rue.
"You had enough gold, and Emily, too?"
          Here no man now might comfort Theseus,   1980
Except for his old father, Egeus,
Who well knew all this world's transmutation—
He'd seen it change on many occasions,   2840
Woe after gladness, and joy after woe—
Many examples of this he could show.   1985
          "Just as no man has ever died," said he,
"Who did not live on earth in some degree,
Just so, no man has ever lived," he said,
"In all this world, who won't some day be dead.
This world is but a thoroughfare full of woe,   1990
And we are pilgrims passing to and fro.
Death is an end to earthly misery."
And also beyond this, much more said he   2850
To this effect, quite wisely to exhort
The people so they would take some comfort.   1995
          Now Duke Theseus had to consider
With proper care where the sepulcher
Of good Arcite may best constructed be,
And most honorable to his degree.
Finally he came to this conclusion,   2000
That there where first Arcite and Palamon
Had made, for love, the battle them between,
That in the selfsame grove, so sweet and green,   2860
There where he had his amorous desires,
His complainings, and for love, his hot fires,   2005
He'd build a fire in which the funeral
Office he might accomplish there in full.

And leet comaunde anon to hakke and hewe   2865
The okes olde, and leye hem on a rewe
In colpons wel arrayed for to brenne.
His officers with swifte feet they renne
And ryde anon at his comaundement.
And after this, Theseus hath y-sent   2870
After a bere, and it al overspradde
With cloth of gold, the richeste that he hadde;
And of the same suyte he cladde Arcite.
Upon his hondes hadde he gloves whyte,
Eek on his heed a croune of laurer grene,   2875
And in his hond a swerd ful bright and kene.
He leyde him, bare the visage, on the bere;
Therwith he weep that pitee was to here.
And for the people sholde seen him alle,
Whan it was day he broghte him to the halle,   2880
That roreth of the crying and the soun.
        Tho cam this woful Theban Palamoun,
With flotery berd and ruggy, asshy heres,
In clothes blake, y-dropped al with teres;
And, passinge othere of weping, Emelye,   2885
The rewfulleste of al the companye.
In as muche as the service sholde be
The more noble and riche in his degree,
Duk Theseus leet forth three stedes bringe,
That trapped were in steel al gliteringe   2890
And covered with the armes of daun Arcite.
Upon thise stedes, that weren grete and whyte,
Ther seten folk, of which oon bar his sheeld,
Another his spere up in his hondes heeld,
The thridde bar with him his bowe Turkeys—   2895
Of brend gold was the cas and eek the harneys;
And riden forth a pas with sorweful chere
Toward the grove, as ye shul after here.

And he ordered men at once to hack and hew
The old oaks, and lay them in a row, too,
In piles quite well arranged so they would burn.   2010
To this, with swift feet, his officers turn
And they ride at once at his commandment.
And after this, soon Theseus has sent   2870
For a bier, on top of which he has thrown
A cloth of gold, the richest he did own.   2015
And in the same cloth, he had clad Arcite;
Upon his hands, he had put gloves of white,[39]
And on his head a crown of laurel green,
And in his hand, a sword quite bright and keen.
He laid him, with face bare, upon the bier;   2020
He wept so it a pity was to hear.
So that people might see him, one and all,
When daylight came, he bore him to the hall,   2880
Which roars when all their crying they began.
            Then came Palamon, this woeful Theban,   2025
With flowing beard and shaggy, ash-filled hair,
Dripping with tears, and black clothes he did wear;
Surpassing all in weeping, Emily,
The most pitiful of all the company.
Inasmuch as the services should be   2030
The nobler and the more rich in degree,
Duke Theseus then had them three steeds bring,
All equipped with glittering steel trappings,   2890
Covered with the coat of arms of Arcite.
Upon these steeds, which all were great and white,   2035
Were seated folks, and one his shield did bear,
Another his spear raised in his hands there,
A third one carried Arcite's Turkish bow
(Burnished gold its case and fittings also);
They ride forth slowly with sorrowful cheer   2040
Toward the grove, as you will after hear.

39 **gloves of white**: White gloves were burial garb for an unmarried person.

The nobleste of the Grekes that ther were
Upon hir shuldres carieden the bere,   2900
With slakke pas and eyen rede and wete,
Thurghout the citee by the maister strete,
That sprad was al with blak; and wonder hye
Right of the same is the strete y-wrye.
Upon the right hond wente old Egeus,   2905
And on that other syde duk Theseus,
With vessels in hir hand of gold ful fyn,
Al ful of hony, milk, and blood, and wyn;
Eek Palamon, with ful greet companye;
And after that cam woful Emelye,   2910
With fyr in honde, as was that tyme the gyse,
To do the office of funeral servyse.
        Heigh labour and ful greet apparaillinge
Was at the service and the fyr-makinge,
That with his grene top the hevene raughte,   2915
And twenty fadme of brede the armes straughte—
This is to seyn, the bowes were so brode.
Of stree first ther was leyd ful many a lode;
But how the fyr was maked upon highte,
Ne eek the names how the treës highte—   2920
As ook, firre, birch, aspe, alder, holm, popler,
Wilow, elm, plane, ash, box, chasteyn, lind, laurer,
Mapul, thorn, beech, hasel, ew, whippeltree—
How they weren feld shal nat be told for me;
Ne how the goddes ronnen up and doun,   2925
Disherited of hire habitacioun,
In which they woneden in reste and pees—
Nymphes, faunes, and amadrides,
Ne how the bestes and the briddes alle
Fledden for fere whan the wode was falle,   2930
Ne how the ground agast was of the light,
That was nat wont to seen the sonne bright;

The noblest of the Greeks honorably
On their shoulders Arcite's bier they carry,   2900
With their eyes red and wet and with slow feet,
Throughout the whole city on the main street;   2045
Black cloth the funeral bier overspread,
The street draped in the same way overhead.
On the right hand there went old Egeus,
And on the other side went Theseus,
With vessels in their hands of pure gold fine,   2050
All full of honey, milk and blood and wine;
Palamon, too, with a great company;
And after that came woeful Emily,   2910
With fire in her hand to do the office,
By their custom, for the funeral service.   2055
     Much great labor and much great preparing
Were at the service and the fire-making.
The pyre reached heaven with its top of green;
To twenty fathoms stretched the sides between—
The trees' boughs were so broad, that is to say.   2060
First there, many a load of straw they lay.
But how the fire was built to be so tall,
Nor even the names that the trees were called,   2920
Oak, birch, alder, holly, poplar, aspen,
Willow, elm, plane, ash, box, laurel, linden,   2065
Maple, thorn, beech, yew, hazel, dogwood tree—
How they were felled will not be told by me;
Nor how the wood gods up and down all run,
Disinherited of their dominion,
Where once in rest and peace they all dwelled glad,   2070
The nymphs and the fauns and hamadryads,[40]
Nor how the beasts and how the birds then all
Fled for fear, once the woods began to fall;   2930
Nor how the ground was frightened by the light,
Which was not used to seeing the sun bright;   2075

40 **hamadryads:** Wood nymphs.

Ne how the fyr was couched first with stree,
And thanne with drye stikkes cloven a three,
And thanne with grene wode and spycerye,   2935
And thanne with cloth of gold and with perrye,
And gerlandes hanginge with ful many a flour,
The mirre, th'encens, with al so greet odour;
Ne how Arcite lay among al this,
Ne what richesse aboute his body is;   2940
Ne how that Emelye, as was the gyse,
Putte in the fyr of funeral servyse;
Ne how she swowned whan men made the fyr,
Ne what she spak, ne what was hir desyr;
Ne what jeweles men in the fyr caste,   2945
Whan that the fyr was greet and brente faste;
Ne how som caste hir sheeld, and som hir spere,
And of hire vestiments whiche that they were,
And cuppes ful of milk and wyn and blood,
Into the fyr that brente as it were wood;   2950
Ne how the Grekes with an huge route
Thryës riden al the fyr aboute
Upon the left hand, with a loud shoutinge,
And thryës with hir speres clateringe;
And thryës how the ladies gonne crye;   2955
Ne how that lad was homward Emelye;
Ne how Arcite is brent to asshen colde;
Ne how that liche-wake was y-holde
Al thilke night; ne how the Grekes pleye
The wake-pleyes, ne kepe I nat to seye—   2960
Who wrastleth best naked with oille enoynt,
Ne who that bar him best in no disjoynt.
I wol nat tellen eek how that they goon
Hoom til Athenes whan the pley is doon;
But shortly to the poynt than wol I wende,   2965

Nor how the fire with straw's laid carefully,
And then with dry tree trunks cloven in three,
And then with green wood and with many spices,
Then with golden cloth and jeweled devices,
And garlands, all hung around with flowers,   2080
Myrrh and incense, with their mighty odors;
Nor how Arcite lay among all of this,
Nor what richness around his body is;   2940
Nor how Emily, with the wonted rite,
The fire of the funeral then did light;   2085
Nor how she swooned when men stoked up the fire,
Nor what she spoke, nor what was her desire;
Nor what jewels in the fire men might cast,
When the fire was great and burning fast;
Nor how some cast their shields, and some their spears,   2090
And some the robes that they were wearing here,
And cups of milk and wine and blood some had
Cast in the fire, which burned like it were mad;   2950
Nor how the Greeks, in their huge band precise,
There all around the fire, they ride thrice   2095
On the left hand with all their loud shouting,
And then thrice too with their spears clattering;
And thrice how ladies cried out sorrowfully;
And how then homeward led was Emily;
Nor how Arcite was burned to ashes cold;   2100
Nor how the funeral wake they did hold
All that night; nor how the Greeks do play
Their funeral games;[41] I don't care to say   2960
Who wrestles best, nude with oil anointed,
Nor who won and was not disappointed.   2105
Nor will I tell how they then go, each one,
Homeward to Athens when the games are done;
But shortly to the point then will I wend,

41 **funeral games:** Throughout classical literature are descriptions of the elaborate athletic contests held after heroes' funerals to honor them. See Homer's *Iliad* and Virgil's *Aeneid* for examples.

And maken of my longe tale an ende.
    By processe and by lengthe of certeyn yeres
Al stinted is the moorninge and the teres
Of Grekes, by oon general assent.
Thanne semed me ther was a parlement   2970
At Athenes, upon certeyn poynts and cas;
Among the whiche poynts y-spoken was
To have with certeyn contrees alliaunce,
And have fully of Thebans obeisaunce.
For which this noble Theseus anon   2975
Leet senden after gentil Palamon,
Unwist of him what was the cause and why;
But in his blake clothes sorwefully
He cam at his comaundement in hye.
Tho sente Theseus for Emelye.   2980
Whan they were set, and hust was al the place,
And Theseus abiden hadde a space
Er any word cam from his wyse brest,
His eyen sette he ther as was his lest,
And with a sad visage he syked stille,   2985
And after that right thus he seyde his wille:
    "The Firste Moevere of the cause above,
Whan he first made the faire cheyne of love,
Greet was th'effect, and heigh was his entente.
Wel wiste he why, and what thereof he mente,   2990
For with that faire cheyne of love he bond
The fyr, the eyr, the water, and the lond
In certeyn boundes, that they may nat flee.
That same Prince and that Moevere," quod he,
"Hath stablissed in this wrecched world adoun   2995

And of my long tale I will make an end.

    In the course of things and through the length of years,   2110

There has ceased all the mourning and the tears

Of the Greeks, by one general assent.

It seems to me there was a parliament   2970

At Athens, held on certain cases there;

Among which cases, it was then declared   2115

With some countries they would make alliance,

And from the Thebans have obedience.

This noble Theseus, when this was done,

He sent at once for gentle Palamon,

Although the cause of all this knew not he,   2120

But in his black clothes, then, quite sorrowfully,

At this command, forward he came quickly.

Then Theseus sent after Emily.   2980

When they were settled, and hushed was the place,

And Theseus had waited for a space   2125

Before a word came forth from his wise breast,

Where he liked then, he let his eyes soon rest.

And with sad face, he sighed softly and still,

And after that, right thus he said his will:

    "The First Mover[42] then of the cause above,   2130

When he had first made the fair Chain of Love,[43]

Great the effect, and high was his intent.

Well knew he why, and what by it he meant,   2990

For with the fair Chain of love in his hand,

He bound the fire, air, water, and land   2135

In certain limits, so they cannot flee.

That same Prince, and that same Mover," said he,

"Established in this wretched world below

---

42 **First Mover**: God, within Chaucer's own Christian context. But since Theseus is not Christian, and given the classical setting of the story, the First Mover is designated as Jupiter. Theseus is nevertheless allowed a prominent monotheism in this important speech.

43 **Chain of Love**: The notion of the Great Chain of Being was Platonic in its origins and adopted by Christian thinkers to represent the hierarchical arrangement of all things in the universe, as that arrangement was intended by God. Love as a force soldered together the links of the chain.

Certeyne dayes and duracioun
To al that is engendred in this place,
Over the whiche day they may nat pace,
Al mowe they yet tho dayes wel abregge.
Ther needeth non auctoritee to allegge,   3000
For it is preved by experience,
But that me list declaren my sentence.
Than may men by this ordre wel discerne
That thilke Moevere stable is and eterne.
Wel may men knowe, but it be a fool,   3005
That every part deryveth from his hool.
For nature hath nat taken his beginning
Of no partye or cantel of a thing,
But of a thing that parfit is and stable,
Descendinge so til it be corrumpable.   3010
And therfore, of his wyse purveyaunce,
He hath so wel biset his ordinaunce
That speces of thinges and progressiouns
Shullen enduren by successiouns
And nat eterne, withouten any lye.   3015
　　　　This maistow understonde and seen at eye:
Lo, the ook that hath so long a norisshinge
From tyme that it first biginneth springe,
And hath so long a lyf, as we may see,
Yet at the laste wasted is the tree.   3020
Considereth eek, how that the harde stoon
Under oure feet, on which we trede and goon,
Yet wasteth it, as it lyth by the weye.
The brode river somtyme wexeth dreye;
The grete tounes see we wane and wende.   3025
Than may ye see that al this thing hath ende.
　　　　Of man and womman seen we wel also
That nedes, in oon of thise termes two,
This is to seyn, in youthe or elles age,

A limit of days and duration so
For all that is engendered in this place,   2140
Beyond which limit they may never race,
Although their length of days abridge they might.
There is no need authorities to cite,   3000
For it is proven by experience,
Except they help me clarify my sentence.   2145
By this order, men may all discern well
This Mover is stable and eternal.
A man may know well, unless he's a fool,
The part comes from the whole, and that's the rule;
Nature has not taken its beginning   2150
From any part or portion of a thing,
But from a thing that is perfect and stable,
Descending down till it's corruptible.[44]   3010
And therefore now, through his wise providence,
He has so well set with his ordinance   2155
That species and natural progressions
Will endure and follow in succession,
And not last, it's no lie, eternally.
        This you understand and see quite plainly.
Lo, the oak, that needs such long nurturing   2160
Back from the time it first begins to spring,
And has so long a life, as we may see,
Yet, in the long run, wasted is the tree.   3020
Consider now how the hard stone also
Under our feet, on which we tread and go,   2165
It wastes away as by the road it lies.
And the broad river sometimes waxes dry;
Great towns, too, we see wane and pass away.
Then may you see all things have their last day.
        With man and woman, you may also see,   2170
At one of two times, by necessity—
That is to say, in youth or else in age—

---

44 **corruptible:** In this context, transient, mortal, emphemeral.

He moot be deed, the king as shal a page;   3030
Som in his bed, som in the depe see,
Som in the large feeld, as men may see.
Ther helpeth noght: al goth that ilke weye.
Thanne may I seyn that al this thing moot deye.
      What maketh this but Jupiter the king,   3035
That is prince and cause of alle thing,
Convertinge al unto his propre welle
From which it is deryved, sooth to telle?
And here-agayns no creature on lyve,
Of no degree, availleth for to stryve.   3040
      Thanne is it wisdom, as it thinketh me,
To maken vertu of necessitee,
And take it wel that we may nat eschue,
And namely that to us alle is due.
And whoso gruccheth ought, he dooth folye,   3045
And rebel is to him that al may gye.
And certeinly a man hath most honour
To dyen in his excellence and flour,
Whan he is siker of his gode name;
Than hath he doon his freend ne him no shame.   3050
And gladder oghte his freend ben of his deeth
Whan with honour up yolden is his breeth,
Than whan his name apalled is for age,
For al forgeten is his vasselage.
Than is it best, as for a worthy fame,   3055
To dyen whan that he is best of name.
      The contrarie of al this is wilfulnesse.
Why grucchen we, why have we hevinesse,
That goode Arcite, of chivalrye flour,
Departed is with duetee and honour   3060
Out of this foule prison of this lyf?
Why grucchen heer his cosin and his wyf
Of his welfare, that loveth hem so weel?
Can he hem thank? Nay, God wot, never a deel,
That bothe his soule and eek hemself offende,   3065

He must be dead, the king just like the page; 3030
Some in their bed, and some in the deep sea,
And some in the large field, as men may see; 2175
Nothing helps then; and therefore now say I,
All goes that way, and everything must die.

       Who causes this but Jupiter, the king,
Who is the prince and cause of everything,
Making all go back to its origin, 2180
From which it did derive and did begin?
Against this, for no creature that's alive,
Of any rank, avails it then to strive. 3040

       Then is it wisdom, as it seems to me,
To make a virtue of necessity, 2185
And take well that which we may not escape,
Namely the fate that for us all is shaped.
He who complains does folly too besides,
And rebels against him who all may guide.
And certainly a man has most honor 2190
To die in youth's flower and in valor,
When he may be certain of his good name;
To himself and his friend he's done no shame. 3050
And gladder should his friend be of his death,
When with honor he's yielded up his breath, 2195
Than when his name has become pale with age,
For then forgotten is his vassalage.
Then it is best, to keep a worthy name,
To die when one is at the height of fame.

       The contrary of this is willfulness. 2200
Why then complain, why have we now sadness,
That Arcite, of chivalry the flower,
Has departed with respect and honor 3060
Out of the foul prison of this life?
Why complain here his cousin and his wife 2205
About his welfare, they who loved him so?
Can he thank them? Never a bit, God knows,
Who both his soul and himself too offend,

And yet they mowe hir lustes nat amende.
    What may I conclude of this longe serie,
But after wo I rede us to be merie,
And thanken Jupiter of al his grace;
And er that we departen from this place,   3070
I rede that we make of sorwes two
O parfyt joye, lastinge everemo;
And loketh now, wher most sorwe is herinne,
Ther wol we first amenden and biginne.
    Suster," quod he, "this is my fulle assent,   3075
With al th'avys heer of my parlement:
That gentil Palamon, your owne knight,
That serveth yow with wille, herte, and might,
And ever hath doon sin ye first him knewe,
That ye shul of your grace upon him rewe,   3080
And taken him for housbonde and for lord.
Leene me your hond, for this is our acord.
Lat see now of youre wommanly pitee.
He is a kinges brother sone, pardee;
And though he were a povre bacheler,   3085
Sin he hath served yow so many a yeer,
And had for yow so greet adversitee,
It moste been considered, leveth me;
For gentil mercy oghte to passen right."
    Than seyde he thus to Palamon the knyght: 3090
"I trowe ther nedeth litel sermoning
To make yow assente to this thing.
Com neer, and tak your lady by the hond."
Bitwixen hem was maad anon the bond
That highte matrimoigne or marriage,   3095
By al the counseil and the baronage.
And thus with alle blisse and melodye
Hath Palamon y-wedded Emelye.
And God, that al this wyde world hath wroght,
Sende him his love that hath it dere aboght.   3100
For now is Palamon in alle wele,

And yet their own desires they can't amend.

      What may I conclude from this commentary?   2210

After woe, I advise us to be merry

And to thank Jupiter for all his grace.

And before we depart now from this place,   3070

I advise we make from two sorrows sore

One perfect joy that lasts forever more.   2215

And let's look now where most sorrow descends:

There we will first begin to make amends.

      Sister," said he, "this is my full intent,

With all the advice of my parliament,

That gentle Palamon, your own true knight,   2220

Who serves you with his whole will, heart, and might,

And who has done so since you first him knew,

You will from your grace now upon him rue,   3080

And take him for your husband and your lord.

Give me your hand, for this is our accord.   2225

Show to us now your womanly pity.

He is a king's brother's son, certainly;

And even though a poor young knight he might be,

For many years he's served you faithfully,

And for you suffered great adversity,   2230

He should be considered now, believe me.

Gentle mercy should trump all claims and rights."

      Then he said thus to Palamon the knight: 3090

"I think there needs little sermonizing

To convince you to assent to this thing.   2235

Come here, and by the hand, your lady take."

Between them both at once the bond he makes

That is called matrimony or marriage,

Witnessed by the counsel and baronage.

And thus with all bliss and all melody   2240

Palamon has now wedded Emily.

And God, who all of this wide world has wrought,

Send him his love who has it dearly bought;   3100

For now is Palamon in happiness,

Livinge in blisse, in richesse, and in hele,
And Emelye him loveth so tendrely,
And he hir serveth so gentilly
That nevere was ther no word hem bitwene   3105
Of jalousye or any other tene.
Thus endeth Palamon and Emelye;
And God save al this faire companye! Amen.

Heere is ended the Knyghtes Tale.

Living in health and in bliss and richness,   2245
And Emily loves him so tenderly,
And he in his turn serves her so gently,
That never between them a single word
Of annoyance or jealousy was heard.
Thus now end Palamon and Emily;
And God save all of this fair company! Amen.

Here is ended the Knight's Tale.

THE MILLER'S PROLOGUE

Heere folwen the wordes bitwene the Hoost and the Millere.

Whan that the Knight had thus his tale y-told,
In al the route nas ther yong ne old   3110
That he ne seyde it was a noble storie,
And worthy for to drawen to memorie,
And namely the gentils everichoon.
Oure Hoste lough and swoor, "So moot I goon, laughed
This gooth aright; unbokeled is the male.   3115
Lat see now who shal telle another tale,
For trewely, the game is wel bigonne.
Now telleth ye, sir Monk, if that ye conne,
Sumwhat to quyte with the Knightes tale."
The Miller, that fordronken was al pale,   3120
So that unnethe upon his hors he sat,
He nolde avalen neither hood ne hat,
Ne abyde no man for his curteisye,
But in Pilates vois he gan to crye,
And swoor, "By armes and by blood and bones,   3125
I can a noble tale for the nones,
With which I wol now quyte the Knightes tale."
Oure Hoste saugh that he was dronke of ale,
And seyde, "Abyd, Robin, my leve brother,

THE MILLER'S PROLOGUE

Here follow the words between the Host and the Miller.

When the Knight had thus his whole tale told,
In all the group was no one, young or old   3110
Who didn't say it was a noble story,
One worthy to be kept in memory,
And namely, the gentlefolk, even more.   5
"So help me now," our Host then laughed and swore,
"The wallet is untied; this will not fail.
Now let's see who will tell another tale;
For certainly, quite well this game began.
Now, come, sir Monk, you tell one if you can,   10
Tell something to requite the Knight's own tale."
The Miller was so drunk he was all pale,   3120
And just barely upon his horse he sat,
He wouldn't take off either hood or hat,
And no man's courtesy would he abide,   15
But in the voice of Pilate,[1] loud he cried,
And swore, "By Christ's blood, and by Christ's bones, too,
I know a noble tale I could tell you,
With which right now I'll pay back the Knight's tale."
Our Host saw just how drunk he was on ale,   20
And said, "Robin, wait now, my dear brother;

---

1   **voice of Pilate**: A loud, ranting voice. In medieval mystery plays, Pilate was traditionally characterized with such a voice.

Som bettre man shal telle us first another: 3130
Abyd, and lat us werken thriftily."
        "By Goddes soul," quod he, "that wol nat I;
For I wol speke or elles go my wey."
Oure Hoste answerde, "Tel on, a devel wey!
Thou art a fool, thy wit is overcome."   3135
        "Now herkneth," quod the Miller, "alle and some!
But first I make a protestacioun
That I am dronke, I knowe it by my soun.
And therfore, if that I misspeke or seye,
Wyte it the ale of Southwerk, I yow preye;   3140
For I wol telle a legende and a lyf
Bothe of a carpenter and of his wyf,
How that a clerk hath set the wrightes cappe."
        The Reve answerde and seyde, "Stint thy clappe!
Lat be thy lewed dronken harlotrye.   3145
It is a sinne and eek a greet folye
To apeiren any man, or him diffame,
And eek to bringen wyves in swich fame.
Thou mayst ynogh of othere thinges seyn."
        This dronken Miller spak ful sone ageyn,   3150
And seyde, "Leve brother Osewold,
Who hath no wyf, he is no cokewold.
But I sey nat therfore that thou art oon;
Ther been ful gode wyves many oon,
And ever a thousand gode ayeyns oon badde.   3155
That knowestow wel thyself, but if thou madde.
Why artow angry with my tale now?
I have a wyf, pardee, as well as thou,
Yet nolde I, for the oxen in my plogh,
Take upon me more than ynogh,   3160
As demen of myself that I were oon;
I wol beleve wel that I am noon.
An housbond shal nat been inquisitif

Some better man will tell us first another.   3130
Wait now, and let us move on properly."
      "By God's soul, I will not do that," said he,
"For I will speak, or else be on my way."   25
Our Host replied, "Tell, by the Devil's way!
You are a fool; your reason's all undone."
      "Now listen," said the Miller, "everyone!
But first, before we go, I must admit
That I am drunk. By my voice, I know it.   30
And so now, should I mis-speak or mis-say,
Go blame the ale of Southwark, I do pray.   3140
For I will tell the legend and the life
Both of a carpenter, and of his wife,
And how a clerk could set him on his ear."   35
      The Reeve spoke up and said, "Shut up! You hear?
Now stop your stupid, drunken ribaldry.
It is both a sin and a great folly
To injure any man, or him defame,
And also to besmirch a good wife's name.   40
There are stories enough for you to try."
      The drunken Miller spoke soon in reply,   3150
And said to him, "Beloved brother Oswald,
He who has no wife is not a cuckold.
But I'm not saying, therefore, you are one;   45
For there are quite good wives, many a one,
And a thousand good ones for every bad.
You know that well yourself, unless you're mad.
Why are you angry now with my tale, too?
I have a wife, by God, as well as you.   50
Yet, for the very oxen in my plow,
I would not presume so far right now   3160
As to believe that I myself am one;[2]
Instead, I will believe that I am none.
Inquisitive a husband should not be,   55

2 **one**: That is, a cuckold.

Of Goddes privetee, nor of his wyf.
So he may finde Goddes foyson there,   3165
Of the remenant nedeth nat enquere."
      What sholde I more seyn, but this Millere
He nolde his wordes for no man forbere,
But tolde his cherles tale in his manere.
M'athynketh that I shal reherce it here.   3170
And therfore every gentil wight I preye,
For Goddes love, demeth nat that I seye
Of evel entente, but that I moot reherce
Hir tales alle, be they bettre or werse,
Or elles falsen som of my matere.   3175
And therfore, whoso list it nat y-here,
Turne over the leef, and chese another tale;
For he shal finde ynowe, grete and smale,
Of storial thing that toucheth gentillesse,
And eek moralitee and holinesse.   3180
Blameth nat me if that ye chese amis.
The Millere is a cherl, ye knowe wel this;
So was the Reve eek and othere mo,
And harlotrye they tolden bothe two.
Avyseth yow and putte me out of blame;   3185
And eek men shal nat maken ernest of game.

To pry in God's or his wife's privacy.
So long as there he may God's plenty find,
About the rest he doesn't need to mind."
      But this Miller—why should I now say more—
For no man living, he his words forbore,   60
But in his own way told his churlish tale.
It seems that to repeat it I can't fail.   3170
Therefore, to every gentle man, I pray,
For the love of God, judge not what I say
As my own rude intent; I must rehearse   65
All of their tales, the better and the worse,
Or else, my matter falsify and lose.
Therefore, to hear it, who does not so choose,
Turn over the leaf, and pick another tale.
Of great and small, he'll find what will avail   70
Of history's things that touch gentility,
And holiness and then morality.   3180
But don't blame me if you should choose amiss.
The Miller is a churl; you well know this.
So was the Reeve, and more of them, as well,   75
And ribaldry they both did choose to tell.
Consider this, and keep me out of blame;
For men should not make earnestness from game.

THE MILLER'S TALE

Heere bigynneth the Millere his tale.

Whylom ther was dwellinge at Oxenford
A riche gnof, that gestes heeld to bord,
And of his craft he was a carpenter.
With him ther was dwellinge a povre scoler,   3190
Hadde lerned art, but al his fantasye
Was turned for to lerne astrologye,
And coude a certeyn of conclusiouns
To demen by interrogaciouns,
If that men asked him in certein houres   3195
Whan that men sholde have droghte or elles shoures,
Or if men asked him what sholde bifalle
Of every thing, I may nat rekene hem alle.
   This clerk was cleped hende Nicholas.
Of derne love he coude and of solas;   3200
And therto he was sleigh and ful privee,
And lyk a mayden meke for to see.
A chambre hadde he in that hostelrye
Allone, withouten any companye,
Ful fetisly y-dight with herbes swote;   3205

THE MILLER'S TALE

Here the Miller begins his tale.

    Long ago, there was, dwelling at Oxford,

A rich churl who took lodgers in to board,   80

And, in his craft, he was a carpenter.

With him, there was dwelling a poor scholar,   3190

Who'd done his studies, but his fantasy

Was focused now to learn astrology,

He knew astrological operations,   85

So he could answer, with his calculations,

If men should ask, at which of the stars' hours

There should be coming either drought or showers,

Or if men asked him what next should befall

About anything; I can't reckon them all.   90

    This young clerk was called handy[3] Nicholas.

He knew well both secret love and solace;   3200

And to that end, he was private and sly,

And like a maid, meek looking to the eye.

A chamber had he in that hostelry,   95

Alone, without a bit of company,

Quite elegantly hung with herbs so sweet;

---

3   **handy**: The Middle English word used as an epithet to describe Nicholas throughout is *hende*. *Hende* simultaneously means handy, near-at-hand, handsome, with the additional implication of "grabby." Since no one Modern English word can suggest all these meanings, I have settled on "handy," but Chaucer's epithet is meant to evoke them all.

And he himself as swete as is the rote
Of licorys, or any cetewale.
His Almageste and bokes grete and smale,
His astrelabie, longinge for his art,
His augrim-stones layen faire apart   3210
On shelves couched at his beddes heed;
His presse y-covered with a falding reed.
And al above ther lay a gay sautrye,
On which he made a-nightes melodye
So swetely, that al the chambre rong,   3215
And *Angelus ad virginem* he song,
And after that he song the kinges note;
Ful often blessed was his mery throte.
And thus this swete clerk his tyme spente
After his freendes finding and his rente.   3220
      This carpenter hadde wedded newe a wyf
Which that he lovede more than his lyf;
Of eightetene yeer she was of age.
Jalous he was, and heeld hire narwe in cage,
For she was wilde and yong, and he was old   3225
And demed himself ben lyk a cokewold.
He knew nat Catoun, for his wit was rude,
That bad man sholde wedde his similitude.
Men sholde wedden after hire estaat,
For youthe and elde is often at debaat.   3230
But sith that he was fallen in the snare,
He moste endure, as other folk, his care.
Fair was this yonge wyf, and therwithal

As sweet he was as is the root complete
Of licorice or zedoary[4] withal.
His *Almageste*[5] and books both great and small,   100
His astrolabe[6] he needed for his art,
His counting stones there,[7] laying far apart,   3210
On shelves were all arranged by his bed's head;
His cupboard decked with coarse wool cloth of red;
Above them all, there lay a gay psaltery,[8]   105
On which, at night, he made his melody
So sweetly, then, that all the chamber rang;
And *Angelus ad Virginem*,[9] he sang;
And after that, he sang out "The King's Note."[10]
Quite often blessed thus was his merry throat.   110
And so this sweet clerk could his time well spend,
Living on gifts and income from his friends.   3220
      This carpenter had just wedded a wife;
He loved her more than he did his own life;
And only eighteen years she was in age.   115
Jealous he was, and kept her closely caged,
For she was wild and young, and he was old
And he feared he could become a cuckold.
He knew not Cato, for his wit was rude,
Who said men should wed their similitude.   120
And men should wed according to their state,
For youth and age are often in debate.   3230
But since he was now fallen in that snare,
Like other folks, he must endure his care.
Fair then was this young wife, and moreover   125

---

4   **zedoary**: Ginger-like spice.

5   *Almageste*: Astrological book attributed to Ptolemy, the second-century C.E. astronomer and mathematician.

6   **astrolabe**: Astronomical instrument for determining the stars' positions.

7   **counting stones**: Stones used for making mathematical calculations.

8   **Psaltery**: Harp.

9   *Angelus ad Virginem*: The angel to the Virgin, a song about the annunciation.

10   **"The King's Note"**: Name of a song whose identity isn't clear.

As any wesele hir body gent and smal.

A ceynt she werede barred al of silk;   3235

A barmclooth eek as whyt as morne milk

Upon hir lendes, ful of many a gore.

Whyt was hir smok, and broyden al bifore

And eek bihinde, on hir coler aboute,

Of col-blak silk, withinne and eek withoute.   3240

The tapes of hir whyte voluper

Were of the same suyte of hir coler;

Hir filet brood of silk and set ful hye.

And sikerly she hadde a likerous yë.

Ful smale y-pulled were hire browes two,   3245

And tho were bent, and blake as any sloo.

She was ful more blisful on to see

Than is the newe pere-jonette tree;

And softer than the wolle is of a wether.

And by hir girdel heeng a purs of lether   3250

Tasseled with silk, and perled with latoun.

In al this world, to seken up and doun,

There nis no man so wys that coude thenche

So gay a popelote, or swich a wenche.

Ful brighter was the shyning of hir hewe   3255

Than in the Tour the noble y-forged newe.

But of hir song, it was as loude and yerne

As any swalwe sittinge on a berne.

Therto she coude skippe and make game,

As any kide or calf folwinge his dame.   3260

Hir mouth was swete as bragot or the meeth,

Or hord of apples leyd in hey or heeth.

Winsinge she was, as is a joly colt,

Long as a mast, and upright as a bolt.

A brooch she baar upon hir lowe coler,   3265

As brood as is the bos of a bocler;

Her body like a weasel's, slim and slender.
A girdle wore she, striped and all of silk,
An apron, just as white as morning milk
Upon her loins, and frills it did not lack.
White was her shift, embroidered all in back   130
And in front, on her collar round about
With coal-black silk, within and then without.   3240
The ribbons hanging from her white cap fine
Were, like her collar, of the same design;
Her broad headband of silk was set quite high.   135
And certainly, she had a flirting eye;
Quite finely plucked her eyebrows were also,
And they were curved and black just like a sloe.[11]
She was a good deal more pleasing to see
Than is the newly blossoming pear tree,   140
And softer than the wool atop a wether.
From her girdle hung a purse of leather,   3250
Tasselled with silk; with bright brass it was pearled.
If he looked high and low throughout the world,
No wise man could his fantasy so wrench   145
To picture such a gay doll or a wench.
Much brighter was the shining of her hue
Than in the Tower,[12] gold coins forged all new.
Her song, so loud and eagerly she sang,
That, just like a barn swallow's, out it rang.   150
And thus she knew both how to skip and play,
Like kids or calves behind their dams all day.   3260
Her mouth was sweet as honeyed ale or mead,
Or a hoard of apples laid in hay, indeed.
Skittish she was, just like a pretty colt,   155
Long as a mast, straight as a crossbow bolt.
The broach, which she pinned low upon her collar,
Was broad as the boss[13] upon a buckler.

11   **sloe**: Blackthorn berry.
12   **Tower**: Coins were minted in the Tower of London.
13   **boss**: Raised metal circular center on a shield.

Hir shoes were laced on hir legges hye.
She was a prymerole, a piggesnye,
For any lord to leggen in his bedde,
Or yet for any good yeman to wedde.   3270
      Now sire, and eft sire, so bifel the cas,
That on a day this hende Nicholas
Fil with this yonge wyf to rage and pleye,
Whyl that hir housbond was at Oseneye,
As clerkes ben ful subtile and ful queynte.   3275
And prively he caughte hire by the queynte,
And seyde, "Ywis, but if ich have my wille,
For derne love of thee, lemman, I spille,"
And heeld hire harde by the haunche-bones,
And seyde, "Lemman, love me al atones,   3280
Or I wol dyen, also God me save!"
And she sprong as a colt doth in the trave,
And with hir heed she wryed faste awey,
And seyde, "I wol nat kisse thee, by my fey.
Why, lat be," quod she, "lat be, Nicholas,   3285
Or I wol crye 'out, harrow' and 'allas.'
Do wey your handes for your curteisye!"
      This Nicholas gan mercy for to crye,
And spak so faire, and profred him so faste,
That she hir love him graunted atte laste,   3290
And swoor hir ooth, by Seint Thomas of Kent,
That she wol been at his comandement,
Whan that she may hir leyser wel espye.
"Myn housbond is so ful of jalousye,
That but ye wayte wel and been privee,   3295
I woot right wel I nam but deed," quod she.
"Ye moste been ful derne, as in this cas."
      "Nay, therof care thee noght," quod Nicholas.

Her shoes were laced up on her legs quite high.
She was a primrose and a blooming pigs' eye,[14]   160
For any lord to lay down in his bed,
And yet for any good yeoman to wed.   3270
      Now, sir, and again, sir, it happened thus
That, on a day, this handy Nicholas
Began with this young wife to romp and play   165
While at Osney,[15] her husband was away,
Like clerks who are subtle and ingenious;
Privately he grabbed her Mount of Venus,
And said, "In truth, unless my will have I,
For secret love of you, sweetheart, I'll die."   170
And by her haunchbones he held her so fast,
And said, "My sweetheart, love me now, at last,   3280
Or I will surely die, so help me God!"
And she sprang like a colt that won't be shod,
And with her head, she made a rapid twist,   175
And said, "On my faith, you will not be kissed.
Why, let go!" said she, "Let go, Nicholas,
Or I will cry 'Out, harrow' and 'Alas'!
Drop your hands, in the name of courtesy!"
      Nicholas began to cry for mercy,   180
Spoke so fairly, and pressed himself so fast
That she her love him granted at the last,   3290
And swore her oath, by Saint Thomas of Kent,[16]
That she now would act by his commandment,
When she might spy the opportunity.   185
"My husband is so full of jealousy,
Unless you wait and be private," she said,
"I know quite well that I could then be dead.
You must be very secretive in this."
      "No, don't fret about that," said Nicholas.   190

---

14 **pigs' eye**: Name of a wildflower.

15 **Osney**: Town close to Oxford.

16 **Saint Thomas of Kent**: Thomas Becket, to whose shrine the pilgrims, of course, are riding.

"A clerk had litherly biset his whyle,
But if he coude a carpenter bigyle."   3300
And thus they been acorded and y-sworn
To wayte a tyme, as I have told biforn.
Whan Nicholas had doon thus everydeel,
And thakked hire aboute the lendes weel,
He kiste hire swete, and taketh his sautrye,   3305
And pleyeth faste, and maketh melodye.

       Thanne fil it thus, that to the parish chirche,
Cristes owene werkes for to wirche,
This gode wyf wente on an haliday;
Hir forheed shoon as bright as any day,   3310
So was it wasshen whan she leet hir werk.

       Now was ther of that chirche a parish clerk,
The which that was y-cleped Absolon.
Crul was his heer, and as the gold it shoon,
And strouted as a fanne large and brode;   3315
Ful streight and evene lay his joly shode.
His rode was reed, his eyen greye as goos;
With Powles window corven on his shoos,
In hoses rede he wente fetisly.
Y-clad he was ful smal and properly,   3320
Al in a kirtel of a light waget—
Ful faire and thikke been the poyntes set—
And therupon he hadde a gay surplys
As whyt as is the blosme upon the rys.
A mery child he was, so God me save.   3325
Wel coude he laten blood and clippe and shave,
And make a chartre of lond or acquitaunce.
In twenty manere coude he trippe and daunce

"A clerk has wasted his time all the while,
If he cannot a carpenter beguile."   3300
And thus they were accorded and they swore
To wait a while, as I have told before.
When Nicholas had thus said and rejoined   195
And thumped her thoroughly about her loins,
He kissed her sweetly, and he took his psaltery,
And played it fast, and made his melody.

      Then, at the parish church, it thus befell,
So that Christ's own works she could do as well,   200
This good wife entered on a holy day.
Her forehead shone as bright as any day,   3310
So well she washed it when she left her work.

      Now there was in that church a parish clerk,
And this clerk was called Absolon by name.   205
Curled was his hair; like gold it shone the same;
Like a fan it spread out large and broad there.
All even lay his pretty, parted hair.
His eyes gray as a goose, his skin was red.
Saint Paul's windows,[17] his shoes decorated;   210
In his red hose, he walked elegantly.
For he was clad finely and properly   3320
All in a tight-fit tunic of light blue;
Quite fair and close its laces were set, too.
Over it, a gay surplice he wore now   215
As white as is a blossom on the bough.
A merry lad he was, so God me save.
And well he could let blood, clip hair, and shave,[18]
Make a deed for land or else a quittance.[19]
In twenty fashions, he could trip and dance   220

---

17 **Saint Paul's windows**: Designs shaped like the windows in Saint Paul's Cathedral, which were cut into shoe leather in order to show colored stockings.

18 **let blood**, etc.: Letting blood was a medical practice thought to cure certain diseases. Because of their skill with razors, barbers were entrusted with bloodletting during the Middle Ages and the Renaissance.

19 **quittance**: A deed legally releasing property.

After the scole of Oxenforde tho,
And with his legges casten to and fro,   3330
And pleyen songes on a small rubible,
Therto he song som tyme a loud quinible;
And as wel coude he pleye on a giterne.
In al the toun nas brewhous ne taverne
That he ne visited with his solas,   3335
Ther any gaylard tappestere was.
But sooth to seyn, he was somdel squaymous
Of farting, and of speche daungerous.
        This Absolon, that jolif was and gay,
Gooth with a sencer on the haliday,   3340
Sensinge the wyves of the parish faste,
And many a lovely look on hem he caste,
And namely on this carpenteres wyf:
To loke on hire him thoughte a mery lyf.
She was so propre and swete and likerous,   3345
I dar wel seyn, if she had been a mous,
And he a cat, he wolde hire hente anon.
This parish clerk, this joly Absolon,
Hath in his herte swich a love-longinge,
That of no wyf ne took he noon offringe;   3350
For curteisye, he seyde, he wolde noon.
        The mone, whan it was night, ful brighte shoon,
And Absolon his giterne hath y-take;
For paramours he thoghte for to wake.
And forth he gooth, jolif and amorous,   3355
Til he cam to the carpenteres hous
A litel after cokkes hadde y-crowe,
And dressed him up by a shot-windowe
That was upon the carpenteres wal.
He singeth in his vois gentil and smal,   3360
"Now, dere lady, if thy wille be,

In the mode of Oxford; he would go
Casting his legs about fast, to and fro,   3330
And playing songs upon a rebec fiddle;[20]
Sometimes he'd sing loud in his high treble,
And he was accomplished on the cithern.[21]   225
In the town was no brewhouse or tavern
Where he'd not visited and entertained,
So long as merry barmaids there remained.
But, truth to tell, he was somewhat squeamish
About farting, and in speech, fastidious.   230
        This Absolon, who pretty was and gay,
Went with the censer on this holiday,   3340
Censing the parish wives all quick and fast;
Many a lovely look on them he cast,
And namely on the carpenter's own wife.   235
To look at her, it seemed a merry life,
So proper, sweet, and desirable this spouse.
I dare well say, if she had been a mouse,
And he a cat, he would have made quick work.
This pretty Absolon, this parish clerk   240
Had, in his heart, caught such a love-longing
That from no wife took he the offering;   3350
From courtesy, he said, he would decline.
        The moon, when it was night, quite bright did shine,
And Absolon now did his cithern take;   245
For love's sake, he thought he would stay awake.
And forth he went, so amorous and gay,
Till, to the carpenter's house, he found his way,
A little while after it was cock's crow,
And pressed himself up close to the hinged window   250
That was there in the carpenter's house wall.
He sings in his voice high, gentle, and small: 3360
"Now, dearest lady, if your will it be,

---

20 **rebec fiddle**: Stringed instrument much like a modern fiddle.
21 **cithern**: Stringed instrument much like a modern guitar.

I preye yow that ye wol rewe on me,"
Ful wel acordaunt to his giterninge.
This carpenter awook and herde him singe,
And spak unto his wyf, and seyde anon,   3365
"What, Alison, herestow nat Absolon
That chaunteth thus under oure boures wal?"
And she answerde hir housbond therwithal,
"Yis, God wot, John, I here it every deel."
          This passeth forth; what wol ye bet than wel?   3370
Fro day to day this joly Absolon
So woweth hire, that him is wo bigon.
He waketh al the night and al the day;
He kembeth hise lokkes brode, and made him gay;
He woweth hire by menes and brocage,   3375
And swoor he wolde been hir owene page;
He singeth, brokkinge as a nightingale;
He sente hire piment, meeth, and spyced ale,
And wafres, pyping hote out of the glede;
And for she was of toune, he profred mede.   3380
For som folk wol ben wonnen for richesse,
And som for strokes, and som for gentillesse.
          Somtyme, to shewe his lightness and maistrye,
He pleyeth Herodes on a scaffold hye.
But what availleth him as in this cas?   3385
She loveth so this hende Nicholas,
That Absolon may blowe the bukkes horn;
He ne hadde for his labour but a scorn.
And thus she maketh Absolon hire ape,
And al his ernest turneth til a jape.   3390
Ful sooth is this proverbe, it is no lye,
Men seyn right thus, "Alwey the nye slye
Maketh the ferre leve to be looth."

I pray you that you'll start to pity me,"
Quite nicely with his cithern harmonizing.   255
The carpenter awoke and heard him sing,
And he said to his wife, "What, Alison,
Wake up! Aren't you now hearing Absolon?
Right there outside our bedroom wall, he sings."
And she said to her husband, answering,   260
"Yes, God knows, John, I hear it, every bit."

      This passes forth. Would you want more of it?   3370
From day to day, this pretty Absolon
Woos her so hard for he is woebegone.
He stays awake throughout the night and day;   265
He combs his locks out wide; his dress is gay;
He woos her with both go-between and agent
And swears that he will always be her servant;
He sings with trillings like a nightingale;
He sends her sweetened wine and mead and ale,   270
And, straight from the fire, hot cakes with honey;
And since she was from town, he offered money;   3380
For some folks will be won by shows of richness,
And some by blows, and some by gentleness.

      Sometimes, to show his skill and mastery,   275
Up on the stage, King Herod's part plays he.[22]
But what does it avail if he acts thus?
For she so loves this handy Nicholas
That Absolon can go blow the buck's horn.[23]
He got, to pay his labor, only scorn.   280
And thus she makes of Absolon her ape;
His earnestness she turns into a jape.   3390
Quite true this proverb is—it is no lie;
Men say: "Always the sly one who's nearby
Will make the farther lover loathed to be."   285

---

22 **King Herod's part**: The part of King Herod in the mystery plays; see also footnote 1, *Miller's Tale*, above. Herod, like Pilate, was supposed to be a loud, forceful character.

23 **go blow the buck's horn**: Go whistle.

For though that Absolon be wood or wrooth,
By cause that he fer was from hir sighte,   3395
This nye Nicholas stood in his lighte.
        Now bere thee wel, thou hende Nicholas!
For Absolon may waille and singe "allas."
And so bifel it on a Saterday,
This carpenter was goon til Osenay,   3400
And hende Nicholas and Alisoun
Acorded been to this conclusioun,
That Nicholas shal shapen him a wyle
This sely jalous housbond to bigyle;
And if so be the game wente aright,   3405
She sholde slepen in his arm al night,
For this was his desyr and hire also.
And right anon, withouten wordes mo,
This Nicholas no lenger wolde tarie,
But doth ful softe unto his chambre carie   3410
Bothe mete and drinke for a day or tweye,
And to hire housbonde bad hire for to seye,
If that he axed after Nicholas,
She sholde seye she niste where he was,
Of al that day she saugh him nat with yë;   3415
She trowed that he was in maladye,
For for no cry hir mayde coude him calle
He nolde answere, for thing that mighte falle.
        This passeth forth al thilke Saterday,
That Nicholas stille in his chambre lay,   3420
And eet and sleep, or dide what him leste,
Til Sonday, that the sonne gooth to reste.
This sely carpenter hath greet merveyle
Of Nicholas, or what thing mighte him eyle,
And seyde, "I am adrad, by Seint Thomas,   3425
It stondeth nat aright with Nicholas.
God shilde that he deyde sodeynly!
This world is now ful tikel, sikerly:
I saugh to-day a cors y-born to chirche

So if Absolon were mad or angry,
Because he was now farther from her sight,
This nearby Nicholas stood in his light.

   Now bear you well, you handy Nicholas,
For Absolon may wail and sing, "Alas!"   290
And so it happened on a Saturday,
At Osney was the carpenter away;   3400
And handy Nicholas and Alison
Reached accord and came to this conclusion:
That Nicholas himself will plot some wile   295
This hapless, jealous husband to beguile;
And if it happened that the game went right,
Then she would sleep within his arms all night,
Because this was his desire—and hers, too.
With no more words and no further ado,   300
This Nicholas would no longer tarry,
But to his chamber privately does carry   3410
Both meat and drink to last a couple days,
And to her husband told her what to say,
If it chanced he asked after Nicholas,   305
She should just say she knew not where he was;
For all day long, nowhere in sight was he;
She did believe he'd caught some malady,
For, no matter how loud her maid might call,
He didn't answer, come what might befall.   310

   It goes on like this all that Saturday.
Nicholas, quiet, in his chamber lay,   3420
He ate and slept and did what pleased him best,
Till Sunday, when the sun went to its rest.
This foolish carpenter began to wonder   315
What ailment it was Nicholas was under,
And said, "I'm afraid, now, by Saint Thomas,
That things do not go right with Nicholas.
God forbid he should die all suddenly!
This world is now quite ticklish, certainly.   320
I saw a corpse borne to the church today

That now, on Monday last, I saugh him wirche.   3430
Go up," quod he unto his knave anoon,
"Clepe at his dore, or knokke with a stoon,
Loke how it is, and tel me boldely."
          This knave gooth him up ful sturdily,
And at the chambre dore, whyl that he stood,   3435
He cryde and knokked as that he were wood:
"What! how! what do ye, maister Nicholay?
How may ye slepen al the longe day?"
But al for noght, he herde nat a word.
          An hole he fond, ful lowe upon a bord,   3440
Ther as the cat was wont in for to crepe;
And at that hole he looked in ful depe,
And at the laste he hadde of him a sighte.
This Nicholas sat evere caping uprighte,
As he had kyked on the newe mone.   3445
Adoun he gooth, and tolde his maister sone
In what array he saugh this ilke man.
          This carpenter to blessen him bigan,
And seyde, "Help us, Seinte Frideswyde!
A man woot litel what him shal bityde.   3450
This man is falle, with his astromye,
In som woodnesse or in som agonye;
I thoghte ay wel how that it sholde be!
Men sholde nat knowe of Goddes privetee.
Ye, blessed be alwey a lewed man   3455
That noght but oonly his bileve can!
So ferde another clerk with astromye:
He walked in the feeldes for to prye
Upon the sterres, what ther sholde bifalle,
Til he was in a marle-pit y-falle—   3460
He saugh nat that. But yet, by Seint Thomas,
Me reweth sore of hende Nicholas.
He shal be rated of his studying,

That I saw up and working this past Monday.   3430
Go up now," to his serving boy said he,
"Call at the door, or with a stone knock loudly.
See what goes on, and tell me directly."   325
      The serving boy climbed the stairs quite boldly;
Standing at the chamber door, he hit it,
And cried and knocked, like he had lost his wits,
"What, how! Lo! Master Nicholas, I say!
How are you sleeping all the livelong day?"   330
But all for nought; he didn't hear a sound.
      Low down upon a board, a hole he found,   3440
Through which the cat was often wont to creep,
And through the hole, he took a good long peep.
And at last, what he saw was quite a sight.   335
Nicholas, gaping skyward, sat bolt upright,
Like he'd been gazing on the brand-new moon.
He goes right down and tells his master soon
In what condition he had found this man.
      This carpenter to cross himself began,   340
And said, "Oh, help us now, Saint Frideswide![24]
Full little knows a man what will betide.   3450
This man has fallen, through astrology,
Into some mad fit or some agony.
I always knew that this is how it'd be!   345
Men shouldn't know about God's privacy.
Yes, blessed is the unschooled man indeed
Who doesn't know much more than just his creed!
With astrology, another clerk so fared:
He walked out in the fields so he could stare   350
Up at the stars, to see what might happen,
Till down in a clay pit he had fallen;   3460
He didn't see that. But, by good Saint Thomas,
I feel sorry for handy Nicholas.
He will be scolded for his studying,   355

24 **Saint Frideswide:** The patron saint of Oxford, she was associated with healing.

If that I may, by Jesus, hevene king!
Get me a staf, that I may underspore,   3465
Whyl that thou, Robin, hevest up the dore.
He shal out of his studying, as I gesse."
And to the chambre dore he gan him dresse.
His knave was a strong carl for the nones,
And by the haspe he haf it up atones;   3470
Into the floor the dore fil anon.
This Nicholas sat ay as stille as stoon,
And ever caped upward into the eir.
This carpenter wende he were in despeir,
And hente him by the sholdres mightily,   3475
And shook him harde, and cryde spitously,
"What, Nicholay! what, how! what, loke adoun!
Awake, and thenk on Cristes passioun!
I crouche thee from elves and fro wightes!"
Therwith the night-spel seyde he anon-rightes   3480
On foure halves of the hous aboute,
And on the threshfold of the dore withoute:
"Jesu Crist, and Seynte Benedight,
Blesse this hous from every wikked wight,
For nightes verye, the white *pater-noster!*   3485
Where wentestow, seynt Petres soster?"
     And atte laste this hende Nicholas
Gan for to syke sore, and seyde, "Allas!
Shal al the world be lost eftsones now?"
     This carpenter answerde, "What seystow?   3490
What! thenk on God, as we don, men that swinke!"
     This Nicholas answerde, "Fecche me drinke;
And after wol I speke in privitee
Of certeyn thing that toucheth me and thee;

If I can do it, by the heaven's king!
Get me a staff, so I can pry up more,
While you, Robin, are heaving off the door.
He'll snap out of his studying, I guess."
To the chamber door, he himself addressed.   360
His servant was a strong churl for this chore,
And off its hinge, at once, he heaved the door;   3470
Onto the floor the door went falling flat.
Still as a stone, this Nicholas just sat,
Forever gaping straight up in the air.   365
This carpenter thought he was in despair,
And grabbed him by the shoulders mightily,
And shook him hard and cried vigorously,
"What! Nicholas! Come, look down! Lo! What, how!
Awake, and think upon Christ's passion, now!   370
I bless you against elves' and creatures' harms."
With that, first, he started saying night charms   3480
Around the house, on all of the four sides,
And he said one on the threshhold outside:
"Oh, Saint Benedict and Lord, Christ Jesus,   375
Bless this house! From wicked spirits, save us,
Against night's creatures, a white *pater-noster!*[25]
Where have you gone, good Saint Peter's sister?"[26]
        And then, at last, this handy Nicholas
Began sorely to sigh, and said, "Alas!   380
Shall the world be lost a second time now?"
        This carpenter answered, "What say you? How?   3490
As we do, men who work, on God now think."
        Nicholas answered back, "First, fetch me drink,
And after, I will speak in privacy   385
Of something now that touches you and me.

---

25 white *pater-noster*: A charm or spell not connected to the traditional Pater Noster ("Our Father"), designated "white" to show its association with good magic.

26 **Saint Peter's sister**: Saint Petronilla, who was mentioned in a charm such as the ones John is saying.

I wol telle it non other man, certeyn."   3495
    This carpenter goth doun and comth ageyn,
And broghte of mighty ale a large quart;
And whan that ech of hem had dronke his part,
This Nicholas his dore faste shette,
And doun the carpenter by him he sette.   3500
    He seyde, "John, myn hoste lief and dere,
Thou shalt upon thy trouthe swere me here,
That to no wight thou shalt this conseil wreye;
For it is Cristes conseil that I seye,
And if thou telle it man, thou art forlore;   3505
For this vengeaunce thou shalt han therfore,
That if thou wreye me, thou shalt be wood!"
"Nay, Crist forbede it, for his holy blood!"
Quod tho this sely man, "I nam no labbe,
Ne, though I seye, I nam nat lief to gabbe.   3510
Sey what thou wolt, I shal it nevere telle
To child ne wyf, by him that harwed helle!"
    "Now John," quod Nicholas, "I wol nat lye.
I have y-founde in myn astrologye,
As I have loked in the mone bright,   3515
That now, a Monday next, at quarter night,
Shal falle a reyn and that so wilde and wood,
That half so greet was nevere Noës flood.
This world," he seyde, "in lasse than in an hour
Shal al be dreynt, so hidous is the shour;   3520
Thus shal mankynde drenche and lese hir lyf."
    This carpenter answerde, "Allas, my wyf!
And shal she drenche? allas, myn Alisoun!"
For sorwe of this he fil almost adoun,
And seyde, "Is ther no remedie in this cas?"   3525
    "Why, yis, for Gode," quod hende Nicholas,

To no one else I'll tell it, that is certain."

This carpenter goes down, and comes again,

And brought with him a quart of mighty ale,

And when, to drink their share, each did not fail,   390

Nicholas closed his door and shut it fast

And by the carpenter sat down at last.   3500

He said, "Now, John, my host, beloved and dear,

You shall, upon your word, swear to me here

This counsel you won't tell in any way   395

To anyone—it's Christ's counsel I say;

You are lost if you tell any man.

For on this vengeance, you can surely plan:

You will go mad if you do betray me."

"Christ forbid it, by his blood so holy!"   400

This foolish man said. "No! I am no blab.

Although I talk, I do not like to gab.   3510

Say what you want, I will it never tell

To child nor wife, by him who harrowed hell!"[27]

"John," said Nicholas, "I won't lie, truly;   405

I have found out, through my astrology,

As I have looked upon the moon so bright,

Come next Monday, a quarter through the night,

A rain will fall, and that so wild and mad

That Noah's flood was never half so bad.   410

This world," he said, "in well less than an hour

Will be drowned, so hideous the shower.   3520

Thus mankind will all drown and lose their lives."

This carpenter answered, "Alas, my wife!

Alas, my Alison! And will she drown?"   415

For sorrowing, he almost fell right down,

And said, "Is there no remedy for this?"

"Why, yes, by God," said handy Nicholas,

---

27 **by him who harrowed hell**: It was believed that Christ went down to hell and harrowed (plowed) it on Easter Saturday to release the redeemable souls trapped there because of Adam and Eve's transgression.

"If thou wolt werken after lore and reed;
Thou mayst nat werken after thyn owene heed;
For thus seith Salomon, that was ful trewe,
'Werk al by conseil, and thou shalt nat rewe.'   3530
And if thou werken wolt by good conseil,
I undertake, withouten mast and seyl,
Yet shal I saven hire and thee and me.
Hastow nat herd how saved was Noë,
Whan that Oure Lord hadde warned him biforn   3535
That al the world with water sholde be lorn?"
          "Yis," quod this carpenter, "ful yore ago."
          "Hastow nat herd," quod Nicholas, "also
The sorwe of Noë with his felawshipe?
Er that he mighte gete his wyf to shipe,   3540
Him hadde be levere, I dar wel undertake,
At thilke tyme than alle hise wetheres blake
That she hadde had a ship hirself allone.
And therfore, wostou what is best to done?
This asketh haste, and of an hastif thing   3545
Men may nat preche or maken tarying.
          Anon go gete us faste into this in
A kneding trogh or elles a kymelyn
For ech of us, but loke that they be large,
In whiche we mowe swimme as in a barge,   3550
And han therinne vitaille suffisant
But for a day; fy on the remenant!
The water shal aslake and goon away
Aboute pryme upon the nexte day.
But Robin may nat wite of this, thy knave,   3555
Ne eek thy mayde Gille I may nat save.
Axe nat why, for though thou aske me,
I wol nat tellen Goddes privetee.
Suffiseth thee, but if thy wittes madde,

"If you'll follow on advice that's learnèd,
And not work according to your own head;   420
For thus says Solomon, and it's quite true:
'Work well by counsel, and you will not rue.'   3530
And if you work so good counsel prevails,
I promise you that, without mast or sails,
Yet still I will save her and me and you.   425
Have you not heard how Noah was saved, too,
When our Lord had warned him well beforehand
That water soon would cover all the land?"

    "Yes," said the Carpenter, "some time ago."
    Said Nicholas, "And haven't you heard also   430
Of Noah's sorrow with his fellowship,
Before he could get his wife on the ship?[28]   3540
For at that moment, he would have preferred
More than all his black wethers, by my word,
That she had had a ship of her own, too.   435
And therefore, do you know what's best to do?
This demands haste, and with a hasty thing
Men shouldn't preach or stall with tarrying.

    Now, go on fast, and bring to your house here
A kneading trough or tub for brewing beer   440
For each of us, but make sure that they're large,
In which we each can float, as in a barge,   3550
And in them each, sufficient food you'll store
To last a day—and fie on any more!
The water will subside and go away   445
Sometime around midmorning the next day.
Of this, your servant Robin must not know,
Or your maid Gille; I can't save her also.
Don't ask why, for even though you ask me,
I will not tell things of God's privacy.   450
It should suffice, unless your wits are mad,

---

28 **his wife on the ship**: In medieval mystery plays, a traditional comic scene in the Noah story presented his perpetually complaining wife as intransigently reluctant to board the ark.

To han as greet a grace as Noë hadde.   3560
Thy wyf shal I wel saven, out of doute.
Go now thy wey, and speed thee heer-aboute.
      But whan thou hast, for hire and thee and me,
Y-geten us thise kneding tubbes three,
Than shaltow hange hem in the roof ful hye,   3565
That no man of oure purveyaunce espye.
And whan thou thus hast doon, as I have seyd,
And hast oure vitaille faire in hem y-leyd,
And eek an ax, to smyte the corde atwo
When that the water comth, that we may go,   3570
And breke an hole an heigh upon the gable
Unto the gardin-ward, over the stable,
That we may frely passen forth our way
Whan that the grete shour is goon away—
Than shaltow swimme as myrie, I undertake,   3575
As doth the whyte doke after hire drake.
Thanne wol I clepe, 'How, Alison! how, John!
Be myrie, for the flood wol passe anon!'
And thou wolt seyn, 'Hayl, maister Nicholay!
Good morwe, I se thee wel, for it is day.'   3580
And thanne shul we be lordes al oure lyf
Of al the world, as Noë and his wyf.
      But of o thyng I warne thee ful right:
Be wel avysed on that ilke night
That we ben entred into shippes bord   3585
That noon of us ne speke nat a word,
Ne clepe, ne crye, but been in his preyere;
For it is Goddes owene heste dere.
      Thy wyf and thou mote hange fer atwinne,
For that bitwixe yow shal be no sinne   3590
No more in looking than ther shal in dede;
This ordinance is seyd, go, God thee spede!
Tomorwe at night, whan men ben alle aslepe,
Into oure kneding tubbes wol we crepe,
And sitten ther, abyding Goddes grace.   3595

To have as great a grace as Noah had.   3560
Your wife I'll save, so there is no worry.
Go on your way. And about this, hurry.
  But when you have, for her and you and me,   455
Gotten for us these kneading troughs all three,
Then you will hang them from the roof on high
So no one can our preparations spy.
And when you thus have done all that I bade,
And when, in them, our food you've fairly laid,   460
And add an ax to cut the cord also,
So when the water comes, then we may go   3570
And break a hole up high in the gable,
On the garden side, over the stable,
So we may freely pass forth on our way,   465
As soon as the great shower's gone away.
Then merrily you'll swim, make no mistake,
As does the white duck following her drake.
Then, I will call, 'How, Alison! How, John!
Be merry, for the flood will soon pass on.'   470
'Hail, Master Nicholas,' you then will say,
'Good morning! I see you well, for it's day.'   3580
And then we will be lords for our whole life
Of all the world, like Noah and his wife.
  But of one thing, I'm warning you outright: 475
Be well aware that on that very night
When we have into our three ships entered,
No one of us must speak a single word,
Nor call, nor cry, but be quite still in prayer;
This is God's own dear bidding for us there.   480
  Your wife and you must both hang far apart,
So that between you both no sin might start,   3590
No more in looking than shall be in deed.
Now this command is said. Go, with God speed!
Tomorrow at night, when men are asleep,   485
Into our kneading tubs we three will creep,
And we'll sit there, all waiting for God's grace.

Go now thy wey, I have no lenger space
To make of this no lenger sermoning.
Men seyn thus, 'Send the wyse, and sey no thing.'
Thou art so wys, it nedeth thee nat teche;
Go, save oure lyf, and that I thee biseche."   3600
      This sely carpenter goth forth his wey.
Ful ofte he seith "allas" and "weylawey,"
And to his wyf he tolde his privetee;
And she was war, and knew it bet than he,
What al this queynte cast was for to seye.   3605
But nathelees she ferde as she wolde deye,
And seyde, "Allas! go forth thy wey anon,
Help us to scape, or we ben dede echon.
I am thy trewe verray wedded wyf;
Go, dere spouse, and help to save oure lyf."   3610
      Lo, which a greet thyng is affeccioun!
Men may dyen of imaginacioun,
So depe may impressioun be take.
This sely carpenter biginneth quake;
Him thinketh verraily that he may see   3615
Noës flood come walwing as the see
To drenchen Alisoun, his hony dere.
He wepeth, weyleth, maketh sory chere,
He syketh with ful many a sory swogh.
He gooth and geteth him a kneding trogh,   3620
And after that a tubbe and a kymelyn,
And prively he sente hem to his in,
And heng hem in the roof in privetee.
His owene hand he made laddres three,
To climben by the ronges and the stalkes   3625
Unto the tubbes hanginge in the balkes,
And hem vitailled, bothe trogh and tubbe,
With breed and chese, and good ale in a jubbe,
Suffysinge right ynogh as for a day.
But er that he had maad al this array,   3630
He sente his knave and eek his wench also

Go your way now, for I have no more space
To give any longer sermonizing.
Men say thus, 'Send the wise, and say nothing.'   490
You are so wise, there is no need to teach.
Go, save our lives, and this I do beseech."   3600
     This foolish carpenter goes on his way.
Often he said, "Alas and well away,"
To his wife, he revealed this privately;   495
And she knew all of it well more than he,
And all of what this quaint plan might portend.
Still, as though she would die, she did pretend;
"Alas, go on your way at once," she said,
"Help us escape, or we will all be dead!   500
I am your true and faithful wedded wife;
Go, dear spouse, fast, and help to save our life."   3610
     Lo, now, what a great thing is emotion!
Men may soon die of imagination,
So deep is the impression it might take.   505
This foolish carpenter begins to shake;
It seems to him that he can surely see
Noah's flood surging up there like the sea
To drown his Alison, his honey dear.
He weeps and wails; he's in a sorry cheer;   510
He sighs aloud, and he makes sorry groan;
He gets a kneading trough all of his own,   3620
A tub and then a vat for brewing meant,
And privately to his house, these he sent,
And hung them from the roof in privacy.   515
With his own hand, he then made ladders three,
For climbing on the uprights and the rungs
Up to the beams, there where the tubs were hung;
With food enough, the trough and tubs he stocked,
With bread and cheese and good ale in a crock,   520
Sufficing right enough to last a day.
Before he could prepare, he sent away   3630
His serving boy, and then his maid also;

Upon his nede to London for to go.
And on the Monday, whan it drow to night,
He shette his dore withoute candel-light,
And dressed al thing as it sholde be.   3635
And shortly, up they clomben alle three;
They sitten stille wel a furlong-way.
          "Now, *Pater-noster*, clom!" seyde Nicholay,
And "clom," quod John, and "clom," seyde Alisoun.
This carpenter seyde his devocioun,   3640
And stille he sit, and biddeth his preyere,
Awaytinge on the reyn, if he it here.
          The dede sleep, for wery bisinesse,
Fil on this carpenter right as I gesse
Aboute corfew-tyme, or litel more;   3645
For travail of his goost he groneth sore,
And eft he routeth, for his heed mislay.
Doun of the laddre stalketh Nicholay,
And Alisoun, ful softe adoun she spedde;
Withouten wordes mo, they goon to bedde   3650
Theras the carpenter is wont to lye.
Ther was the revel and the melodye;
And thus lyth Alison and Nicholas
In bisinesse of mirthe and of solas,
Til that the belle of Laudes gan to ringe,   3655
And freres in the chauncel gonne singe.
          This parish clerk, this amorous Absolon,
That is for love alwey so wo bigon,
Upon the Monday was at Oseneye
With compaignye him to disporte and pleye,   3660
And axed upon cas a cloisterer
Ful prively after John the carpenter;

To London, on his business they did go.
And on that Monday, when it drew toward night,   525
He shut his door, and without candlelight,
He arranged all now just as it should be.
And shortly, they climbed up there, all these three;
A little while, quite still they all sat thus.

    "Now, *Pater-noster!* [29] Clam up!" said Nicholas,   530
"Clam up!" said John. "Clam up!" said Alison.
The carpenter does all his devotions;   3640
He says his prayers, and then still he does sit,
Waiting for rain, if he'll ever hear it.

    A dead sleep, from all of his busyness,   535
Fell right upon this carpenter, I guess,
Around dusk's curfew time, or a bit more;
From the travail of his spirit, he groans sore;
Then, too, he snores since his head lay amiss.
Right down the ladder then stalks Nicholas,   540
And Alison, all softly down, she sped;
And without one word more, they go to bed,   3650
There where the carpenter is wont to be.
Now there was revelry and melody,
And thus lie Alison and Nicholas   545
In the business of their mirth and solace,
Until the bell for lauds[30] began to ring,
And friars to the chancel went to sing.

    This parish clerk, this amorous Absolon,
Who is for love always so woebegone,   550
Was at Osney upon that same Monday,
With company to sport himself and play;   3660
By chance he asked a certain cloisterer
Privately about John the carpenter;

---

29 *Pater-noster*: Here, the prayer is the traditional "Our Father," which Nicholas is bidding them say silently.

30 **lauds**: In the sequence of Benedictine hours that structure the monastic day, Lauds was the first service, which came before dawn.

And he drough him apart out of the chirche,
And seyde, "I noot, I saugh him here nat wirche
Sin Saterday. I trow that he be went   3665
For timber, ther oure abbot hath him sent,
For he is wont for timber for to go,
And dwellen at the grange a day or two;
Or elles he is at his hous, certeyn.
Wher that he be, I can nat sothly seyn."   3670
  This Absolon ful joly was and light,
And thoghte, "Now is tyme to wake al night;
For sikirly I saugh him nat stiringe
Aboute his dore sin day bigan to springe.
So moot I thryve, I shal, at cokkes crowe,   3675
Ful prively knokken at his windowe
That stant ful lowe upon his boures wal.
To Alison now wol I tellen al
My love-longing, for yet I shal nat misse
That at the leste wey I shal hire kisse.   3680
Som maner confort shal I have, parfay.
My mouth hath icched al this longe day;
That is a signe of kissing atte leste.
Al night me mette eek, I was at a feste.
Therfore I wol gon slepe an houre or tweye,   3685
And al the night than wol I wake and pleye."
  Whan that the firste cok hath crowe, anon
Up rist this joly lovere Absolon,
And him arrayeth gay, at point-devys.
But first he cheweth greyn and lycorys   3690
To smellen swete, er he had kembd his heer.
Under his tonge a trewe-love he beer,
For therby wende he to ben gracious.
He rometh to the carpenteres hous,
And stille he stant under the shot-windowe—   3695

And outside of the church, he drew the clerk   555
And said, "I don't know; I've not seen him work
Since Saturday. I do believe he went
For timber, where our abbot has him sent;
Since, often, out for timber he will go
And stay there at the farm a day or so;   560
Or else he's at his own house, certainly.
I cannot say for sure where he might be."   3670
      Now Absolon was glad; his heart was light,
And he thought, "Now it's time to wake all night,
Certainly, I didn't see him stirring   565
About his door, since day began to spring.
As I may thrive, I shall, when the cocks crow,
Privately start knocking at his window
That stands so low upon his bedroom wall.
To Alison, now surely I'll tell all   570
My love-longing; this chance I shall not miss,
And at the very least, I'll get a kiss.   3680
Some kind of comfort I shall have, I say.
My mouth has itched me through this whole long day;
That is a sign of kissing, at the least.   575
All night I dreamed that I was at a feast.
Therefore, I'll sleep an hour or two today,
And all tonight, then will I wake and play."
      As soon as he had heard the first cocks' crows,
This pretty lover Absolon up rose;   580
He dresses gay, and each detail is nice.
Licorice, he chews and Grain of Paradise,[31]   3690
So he'd smell sweet, before he combed his hair.
Under his tongue, a true-love leaf[32] he bears;
He thinks it will make him more alluring.   585
To the carpenter's house, he comes roaming,
And stands still beneath the bedroom window—

31 **Grain of Paradise**: Cardamom.
32 **true-love leaf**: Four-leaf clover.

Unto his brest it raughte, it was so lowe—
And softe he cougheth with a semi-soun:
"What do ye, hony-comb, swete Alisoun,
My faire brid, my swete cinamome?
Awaketh, lemman myn, and speketh to me!   3700
Wel litel thenken ye upon my wo,
That for youre love I swete ther I go.
No wonder is thogh that I swelte and swete;
I moorne as doth a lamb after the tete.
Ywis, lemman, I have swich love-longinge,   3705
That lyk a turtel trewe is my moorninge;
I may nat ete na more than a mayde."
        "Go fro the window, Jakke fool," she sayde,
"As help me God, it wol nat be 'com pa me.'
I love another, and elles I were to blame,   3710
Wel bet than thee, by Jesu, Absolon!
Go forth thy wey or I wol caste a ston,
And lat me slepe, a twenty devel wey!"
        "Allas," quod Absolon, "and weylawey,
That trewe love was evere so yvel biset!   3715
Thanne kisse me, sin it may be no bet,
For Jesus love and for the love of me."
        "Wiltow thanne go thy wey therwith?" quod she.
        "Ye, certes, lemman," quod this Absolon.
        "Thanne make thee redy," quod she, "I come anon;"   3720
And unto Nicholas she seyde stille,
"Now hust, and thou shalt laughen al thy fille."
        This Absolon doun sette him on his knees,
And seyde, "I am a lord at alle degrees;
For after this I hope ther cometh more.   3725
Lemman, thy grace, and swete brid, thyn ore!"
        The window she undoth, and that in haste,
"Have do," quod she, "com of, and speed thee faste,
Lest that oure neighebores thee espye."
        This Absolon gan wype his mouth ful drye: 3730
Derk was the night as pich, or as the cole,

Down to his breast it reached, it was so low.
With a thin sound, he starts softly coughing:
"Honeycomb, my sweet, what art thou doing,   590
My sweet cinnamon, fair little birdie?
Awake now, belovèd mine, and speak to me!   3700
Full little doth thou think upon my woe.
For thy love, I sweat wherever I go.
I melt and sweat. There is no wonder to it;   595
I mourn just like a lamb after the tit.
Sure, sweetheart, in love I have such longing—
Like a turtledove's, true is my mourning.
I can't eat a bit more than a maiden."
    "Leave the window, you Jack fool," she said then;   600
"So help me God, it won't be 'come kiss me.'
I love another—blame me, certainly—   3710
Better, by Jesus, Absolon, than you.
Now, go away! I'll cast a stone or two!
Now let me sleep, for twenty devils' ways!"   605
    "Alas," said Absolon, "and well away,
That true love was ever beset so sore!
Then kiss me now, since it may be no more,
For Jesus's love, and for the love of me."
    "Will you be on your way with that?" said she.   610
    "Yes, certainly, my sweetheart," then said he.
    "I come right now," she said. "So get ready."   3720
And then to Nicholas, she said quite still,
"Now hush, my love, and you will laugh your fill."
    Absolon set himself down on his knees   615
And said, "I am your lord in all degrees;
For, after this, I hope more comes to me.
Belovèd, your grace, and sweet bird, your mercy."
    The window she undoes, and that in haste.
"Hurry up," she said, "There is no time to waste,   620
Lest here some of our neighbors should you spy."
    This Absolon then wiped his mouth all dry.   3730
Dark was the night as pitch, or just like coal,

And at the window out she putte hir hole,
And Absolon, him fil no bet ne wers,
But with his mouth he kiste hir naked ers
Ful savourly, er he was war of this.   3735
      Abak he stirte, and thoghte it was amis,
For wel he wiste a womman hath no berd;
He felte a thing al rough and long y-herd,
And seyde, "Fy! allas, what have I do?"
      "Tehee!" quod she, and clapte the window to;   3740
And Absolon goth forth a sory pas.
      "A berd, a berd!" quod hende Nicholas,
"By Goddes *corpus*, this goth faire and weel!"
      This sely Absolon herde every deel,
And on his lippe he gan for anger byte;   3745
And to himself he seyde, "I shal thee quyte."
      Who rubbeth now, who froteth now his lippes
With dust, with sond, with straw, with clooth, with chippes,
But Absolon, that seith ful ofte, "Allas!
My soule bitake I unto Sathanas,   3750
But me wer levere than al this toun," quod he,
"Of this despyt awroken for to be.
Allas!" quod he, "allas, I ne hadde y-bleynt!"
His hote love was cold and al y-queynt;
For fro that tyme that he had kiste hir ers,   3755
Of paramours he sette nat a kers,
For he was heeled of his maladye.
Ful ofte paramours he gan deffye,
And weep as dooth a child that is y-bete.
A softe paas he wente over the strete   3760
Until a smith men cleped daun Gerveys,
That in his forge smithed plough harneys:
He sharpeth shaar and culter bisily.
This Absolon knokketh al esily,
And seyde, "Undo, Gerveys, and that anon."   3765
      "What, who artow?" "It am I, Absolon."
"What, Absolon! for Cristes swete tree,

And at the window, she stuck out her hole,
And Absolon got no better or worse, 625
But with his mouth, he kissed her naked arse
Savouringly, before he knew of this.

     He started back and thought it was amiss:
A woman has no beard—this he well knew.
He felt a thing all rough and long haired, too, 630
And said, "Fie! Alas! What did I just do?"

     "Teehee!" said she, and slammed the window to, 3740
And Absolon goes with a sorry tread.

     "A beard! A beard!" handy Nicholas then said,
"By God's body, fair and well now goes it." 635

     This foolish Absolon heard every bit,
And on his lips from anger, he did bite,
And to himself, he said, "You, I'll requite."

     Oh, who now rubs, and who now scrapes his lips
With dust, with sand, with straw, with cloth, with chips, 640
But Absolon, who "Alas!" said often,
"My soul I hereby promise unto Satan, 3750
If, rather than own this whole town," said he,
"For this insult I now avenged would be.
Alas," said he, "oh, if abstained had I!" 645
His hot love was all cold and quenched thereby;
For, from the time that he had kissed her arse,
He reckoned that this loving was a curse,
For he was all healed of his malady,
And often times this loving denounced he; 650
He wept as does a child when it is beaten.
With a soft step, he went across the street then 3760
To a smith whom men did call Don Gervais,
Who, for plows, in his forge made the harness;
Plowshares and colters he sharpens busily. 655
This Absolon starts knocking easily,
And said, "Open, Gervais! Do it quickly."

     "What? Who are you?" "It's Absolon; it's me."
"What, Absolon! On Christ's cross, is it true?

Why ryse ye so rathe, ey, *benedicite!*
What eyleth yow? som gay gerl, God it woot,
Hath broght yow thus upon the viritoot;   3770
By Seynt Note, ye woot wel what I mene."
      This Absolon ne roghte nat a bene
Of al his pley. No word agayn he yaf;
He hadde more tow on his distaf
Than Gerveys knew, and seyde, "Freend so dere,   3775
That hote culter in the chimenee here,
As lene it me: I have therwith to done,
And I wol bringe it thee agayn ful sone."
      Gerveys answerde, "Certes, were it gold,
Or in a poke nobles alle untold,   3780
Thou sholdest have, as I am trewe smith.
Ey, Cristes foo! what wol ye do therwith?"
      "Therof," quod Absolon, "be as be may:
I shal wel telle it thee tomorwe day,"
And caughte the culter by the colde stele.   3785
Ful softe out at the dore he gan to stele,
And wente unto the carpenteres wal.
He cogheth first, and knokketh therwithal
Upon the windowe, right as he dide er.
      This Alison answerde, "Who is ther   3790
That knokketh so? I warante it a theef."
      "Why, nay," quod he, "God woot, my swete leef,
I am thyn Absolon, my dereling.
Of gold," quod he, "I have thee brought a ring—
My moder yaf it me, so God me save—   3795
Ful fyn it is, and therto wel y-grave.
This wol I yeve thee, if thou me kisse!"
      This Nicholas was risen for to pisse,
And thoghte he wolde amenden al the jape;
He sholde kisse his ers er that he scape.   3800

Why rise up so early? Hey, God bless you! 660

What ails you now? Some gay girl, God knows,

Has made it that so early you arose. 3770

By Saint Neot,[33] you know well what I mean."

      Absolon didn't care a single bean

For all his play; he would not speak or laugh; 665

He had more flax waiting on his distaff [34]

Than Gervais knew, and he said, "Friend so dear,

That hot colter right in the chimney here,

Lend it to me; I have something to do,

And very soon, I'll bring it back to you." 670

      Gervais answered, "For sure, if it were gold,

Or gold coins in a bag with count untold, 3780

You should have it, as I'm a smith so true.

Hey, by Christ's foe! With it, what will you do?"

      "Of that," said Absolon, "be as be may. 675

I'll tell it all to you another day"—

Catching the colter's handle of cold steel.

Quite softly out the door, then, he did steal,

And went right to the carpenter's own wall.

He coughs first, and then knocks with a sound small 680

At the window, as earlier he'd done.

      This Alison answered, "Who is the one 3790

Who knocks so loud? It is a thief, I swear."

      "Why, no," said he, "God knows, my sweetheart there.

It is I, your Absolon, my darling. 685

Of gold," he said, "I have brought you a ring,

So God me save, my mother gave to me;

Quite fine, it is, and all engraved, you'll see.

I'll give you this, if you'll give me a kiss."

      This Nicholas got up to take a piss, 690

And thought he would improve upon the jape;

He'd kiss his arse before he could escape. 3800

---

33 **Saint Neot**: An English saint associated with Glastonbury.

34 **more flax waiting on his distaff**: In other words, he had more to do.

And up the windowe dide he hastily,
And out his ers he putteth prively
Over the buttok, to the haunche-bon;
And therwith spak this clerk, this Absolon,
"Spek, swete brid, I noot nat wher thou art."   3805
        This Nicholas anon leet fle a fart,
As greet as it had been a thonder-dent,
That with the strook he was almost y-blent;
And he was redy with his iren hoot,
And Nicholas amidde the ers he smoot.   3810
Of gooth the skin an hande-brede aboute,
The hote culter brende so his toute,
And for the smert he wende for to dye.
As he were wood, for wo he gan to crye—
"Help! water! water! help, for Goddes herte!"   3815
        This carpenter out of his slomber sterte,
And herde oon cryen "water" as he were wood,
And thoghte, "Allas! now comth Nowelis flood!"
He sit him up withouten wordes mo,
And with his ax he smoot the corde atwo,   3820
And doun goth al; he fond neither to selle
Ne breed ne ale, til he cam to the celle
Upon the floor; and ther aswowne he lay.
        Up sterte hire Alison and Nicholay,
And cryden "out" and "harrow" in the strete.   3825
The neighebores, bothe smale and grete,
In ronnen for to gauren on this man,
That yet aswowne lay, bothe pale and wan;
For with the fal he brosten hadde his arm.
But stonde he moste unto his owene harm.   3830
For whan he spak, he was anon bore doun
With hende Nicholas and Alisoun.
They tolden every man that he was wood,
He was agast so of "Nowelis flood"
Thurgh fantasye, that of his vanitee   3835
He hadde y-boght him kneding tubbes three,

He opened up the window hastily,
And he stuck out his arse all privately;
Past buttocks up to haunchbone, out it poked;   695
And so this clerk, this Absolon then spoke:
"Speak now, sweet bird, I know not where thou art."
        This Nicholas at once let fly a fart
As great as if it were a thunder blast;
It nearly blinded him till it had passed;   700
And he was ready with his iron hot—
A smack right on the arse Nicholas got.   3810
        Off goes the skin, a handbreadth, and for what?
The hot colter had so burned up his butt,   705
And for the pain, he thought that he would die.
In his woe like a madman he did cry,
"Help! Water! Water! Help, for God's good heart!"
        This made the carpenter from slumber start;
He heard some madman "Water!" crying out,   710
And thought, "Lo! Noah's flood has come about!"
He sits up then, with no words or ado,   3820
And with his ax, he cuts the cord in two,
And down goes all; he didn't stop to sell
Much bread or ale, as to the floor he fell,   715
And he lay in a swoon when it was done.
        Up started Nicholas and Alison,
And in the street, "Out" and "Harrow" they cried.
The neighbors, great and small, from every side,
Came running in upon this man to stare,   720
Who, pale and wan, still lay in his swoon there,
For with the fall, he broken had his arm.   3830
But stand he must, for he brought his own harm;
For when he spoke, then up piped Alison
And handy Nicholas, like they were one.   725
They said to every man that he was mad;
So great a fear of Noah's flood he had
That, in his folly, with this fantasy,
He had bought kneading tubs for them, all three,

And hadde hem hanged in the roof above;
And that he preyed hem, for Goddes love,
To sitten in the roof, *par compaignye*.
    The folk gan laughen at his fantasye;   3840
Into the roof they kyken and they cape,
And turned al his harm unto a jape.
For what so that this carpenter answerde,
It was for noght; no man his reson herde.
With othes grete he was so sworn adoun,   3845
That he was holden wood in al the toun.
For every clerk anonright heeld with other:
They seyde, "The man is wood, my leve brother;"
And every wight gan laughen at this stryf.
    Thus swyved was this carpenteres wyf   3850
For al his keping and his jalousye;
And Absolon hath kist hir nether yë;
And Nicholas is scalded in the toute.
This tale is doon, and God save al the route!

Heere endeth the Millere his tale.

And had them hanging from the roof above;   730
And he had prayed to them, for God's own love,
To sit up there and keep him company.
      The folks then laughed at his strange fantasy;   3840
Up at the roof, they all do stare and gape,
And they turned all his harm into a jape.   735
For whatever the carpenter answered,
It was for nought; no man his reason heard.
With great oaths, there he loudly was sworn down
So he was thought quite mad throughout the town;
Every clerk agreed then with the other.   740
They said, "This man's mad now, my dear brother";
And every man did laugh at all this strife.
      And thus screwed was the carpenter's own wife,   3850
For all the jealous guarding he might try,
And Absolon has kissed her nether eye,   745
And scalded in the butt is Nicholas.
This tale is done, and God save all of us!

Here the Miller ends his tale.

THE REEVE'S PROLOGUE

Whan folk had laughen at this nyce cas   3855
Of Absolon and hende Nicholas,
Diverse folk diversely they seyde,
But, for the more part, they loughe and pleyde;
Ne at this tale I saugh no man him greve,
But it were only Osewold the Reve.   3860
By cause he was of carpenteres craft,
A litel ire is in his herte y-laft.
He gan to grucche and blamed it a lyte.
    "So theek," quod he, "ful wel coude I thee quyte
With blering of a proud milleres yë,   3865
If that me liste speke of ribaudye.
But ik am old; me list not pley for age;
Gras-tyme is doon, my fodder is now forage,
This whyte top wryteth myne olde yeres.
Myn herte is also mowled as myne heres,   3870
But if I fare as dooth an open-ers;
That ilke fruit is ever lenger the wers,
Til it be roten in mullok or in stree.
We olde men, I drede, so fare we:
Til we be roten, can we nat be rype;   3875
We hoppen alwey whyl that the world wol pype.
For in oure wil ther stiketh evere a nayl,
To have an hoor heed and a grene tayl

THE REEVE'S PROLOGUE

When folks had laughed at this silly business
Of Absolon and handy Nicholas,
Then diverse folks diversely did say,
But for the most part, they did laugh and play.
Nor at this tale did I see one man grieve,   5
Except only for Oswald the Reeve.   3860
Because he was a carpenter by craft,
A little ire in his heart is left.
He groused some, and some blame he tried to lay.
　　　"So help me," said he, "I could well repay   10
You and make a miller's proud eye bleary,
If I wanted to speak of ribaldry.
But I'm old and don't like to play from age—
My grass time's done, my fodder now is forage;
This white top writes about all my old years;   15
My heart is moldy just like my hair here,   3870
Unless I fare like that fruit, the open-arse[1]—
For that same fruit just keeps on getting worse,
Till it rots stored in straw or rubbish there.
In the same way, I fear, we old men fare: 20
Until we're rotten, we cannot be ripe;
And we'll keep hopping if the world will pipe.
For in our will there always sticks a nail—
To have a hoary head and a green tail

1　**open-arse**: Fruit of the medlar tree, which is not edible until it starts to rot.

As hath a leek, for thogh our might be goon,
Oure wil desireth folie evere in oon.   3880
For whan we may nat doon, than wol we speke;
Yet in oure asshen olde is fyr y-reke.
　　　　Foure gledes han we, whiche I shal devyse:
Avaunting, lying, anger, coveityse.
Thise foure sparkles longen unto elde.   3885
Our olde lemes mowe wel been unwelde,
But wil ne shal nat faillen, that is sooth.
And yet ik have alwey a coltes tooth,
As many a yeer as it is passed henne
Sin that my tappe of lyf bigan to renne.   3890
For sikerly, whan I was bore, anon
Deeth drogh the tappe of lyf and leet it gon;
And ever sithe hath so the tappe y-ronne,
Til that almost al empty is the tonne.
The streem of lyf now droppeth on the chimbe.   3895
The sely tonge may wel ringe and chimbe
Of wrecchednesse that passed is ful yore;
With olde folk, save dotage, is namore."
　　　　Whan that oure Host hadde herd this sermoning,
He gan to speke as lordly as a king.   3900
He seide, "What amounteth al this wit?
What shul we speke alday of Holy Writ?
The devel made a reve for to preche,
Or of a soutere a shipman or a leche.
Sey forth thy tale, and tarie nat the tyme;   3905
Lo, Depeford, and it is half-way pryme!
Lo, Grenewich, ther many a shrewe is inne!
It were al tyme thy tale to biginne."
　　　　"Now, sires," quod this Osewold the Reve,

Just like a leek; although our might's past prime,   25

Our will desires folly all the time.   3880

For when we may not do, then will we speak.

Old ash still covers fire if you seek.

　　"Four live coals have we, as I fashion this—

They're boasting, lying, anger, avarice.   30

These four sparks to the elderly belong.

Our old limbs may well not be very strong,

But the will won't fail, and that's the truth.

And now I still do have a young colt's tooth,[2]

No matter all the years now passed and done   35

Since the tap of my life began to run.   3890

For truly, when I was born long ago,

Death drew the tap of life and let it go,

And ever since, the tap so sure has run

That now almost all empty is the tun.   40

The stream of life drops on the rim this time.

The silly tongue may now well ring and chime

About wickedness passed by long before;

With old folks, save for dotage, there's no more!"

　　When our Host had heard this sermonizing,   45

He began to speak as lordly as a king.   3900

He said, "What is the worth of all this wit?

Why should we speak all day of Holy Writ?

Now the devil made a reeve a preacher,

Or a doctor or a shipman from a cobbler.   50

Speak forth your tale, and do not waste the time.

Lo, Deptford,[3] and it's now half way through prime.

Lo, Greenwich,[4] the town that scoundrels live in.

Now it is high time your tale to begin."

　　"Now, sires," then said this Oswald the Reeve,   55

　　2　**young colt's tooth**: Young person's sexual desires.

　　3　**Deptford**: About five miles from London.

　　4　**Greenwich**: About half a mile beyond Deptford. It's in Kent, where Chaucer was living when he began to write *The Tales*.

"I pray yow alle that ye nat yow greve,   3910
Thogh I answere and somdel sette his howve;
For leveful is with force force of-showve.
      This dronke millere hath y-told us heer
How that bigyled was a carpenteer,
Peraventure in scorn for I am oon.   3915
And, by youre leve, I shal him quyte anoon;
Right in his cherles termes wol I speke.
I pray to God his nekke mote tobreke—
He can wel in myn yë seen a stalke,
But in his owne he can nat seen a balke."   3920

"I pray you all now that you do not grieve 3910
If, answering, I somewhat tip his hood;[5]
You can shove force with force, it's understood.

     "Here now to us has this drunken Miller
Told how beguiled had been a carpenter, 60
Perhaps out of contempt since I am one.
By your leave, I'll pay him back before I'm done;
Right in his churl's terms I will speak today.
May his neck break in pieces, God I pray;
He can see a straw if it's in my eye, 65
But not a beam in his,[6] and that's no lie." 3920

---

5   **tip his hood:** Make a fool of him (the Miller).
6   **straw . . . beam:** A reference to Matthew 7:3.

THE REEVE'S TALE

    At Trumpyngtoun, nat fer fro Cantebrigge,
Ther goth a brook and over that a brigge;
Upon the whiche brook ther stant a melle;
And this is verray soth that I yow telle.
A millere was ther dwelling many a day;   3925
As eny pecok he was proud and gay.
Pypen he coude and fisshe, and nettes bete,
And turne coppes, and wel wrastle and shete;
Ay by his belt he baar a long panade,
And of a swerd ful trenchant was the blade.   3930
A joly popper baar he in his pouche—
Ther was no man for peril dorste him touche—
A Sheffeld thwitel baar he in his hose.
Round was his face, and camus was his nose;
As piled as an ape was his skulle.   3935
He was a market-betere atte fulle.
Ther dorste no wight hand upon him legge,
That he ne swoor he sholde anon abegge.
A theef he was for sothe of corn and mele,
And that a sly, and usaunt for to stele.   3940

THE REEVE'S TALE

Here begins the Reeve's Tale.

At Trumpington, not too far from Cambridge,
There runs a brook, and over that, a bridge;
Upon the brook, there stands a mill as well;
And this is downright truth that I you tell.   70
There a miller had dwelled many a day;
Like any peacock, he was proud and gay.
He could play bagpipes, fish, mend nets to boot,
Play bottoms up[7] and wrestle well and shoot.
On his belt a long cutlass he displayed,   75
And of his sword well sharpened was the blade.   3930
In his pouch, he bore a dashing dagger—
None dared touch him for fear of the danger.
A Sheffield[8] knife did he wear in his hose.
Round was his face, and pug flat was his nose;   80
As balding as an ape's was all his skull.
He was a bully and a thug as well.
And no man dared a hand on him to lay,
Or else he swore that man would surely pay.
In truth, he was a thief of corn and meal,   85
A sly one who accustomed was to steal.   3940

---

7   **bottoms up**: A drinking game.
8   **Sheffield**: Town historically known for the quality of its steel.

His name was hote deynous Simkin.
A wyf he hadde, y-comen of noble kin:
The person of the toun hir fader was.
With hire he yaf ful many a panne of bras,
For that Simkin sholde in his blood allye.   3945
She was y-fostred in a nonnerye
For Simkin wolde no wyf, as he sayde,
But she were wel y-norissed and a mayde,
To saven his estaat of yomanrye.
And she was proud, and pert as is a pye.   3950
A ful fair sighte was it upon hem two;
On halydayes biforn hire wolde he go
With his tipet wounde about his heed,
And she cam after in a gyte of reed;
And Simkin hadde hosen of the same.   3955
Ther dorste no wight clepen hire but "Dame."
Was noon so hardy that wente by the weye
That with hir dorste rage or ones pleye,
But if he wolde be slayn of Simkin
With panade, or with knyf, or boydekin,   3960
For jalous folk ben perilous everemo—
Algate they wolde hire wyves wenden so.
And eek, for she was somdel smoterlich,
She was as digne as water in a dich,
And ful of hoker and of bisemare.   3965
Hir thoughte that a lady sholde hire spare,
What for hire kinrede and hir nortelrye
That she had lerned in the nonnerye.
      A doghter hadde they bitwixe hem two
Of twenty yeer, withouten any mo,   3970
Savinge a child that was of half-yeer age;

And his name was called conceited Symkin.[9]
A wife he had, who came from noble kin;
The parson of the town was her own father.
He gave many a pan of brass[10] with her,   90
So Symkin with his blood allied should be.
She had been fostered in a nunnery;
For Symkin wanted no wife, he said then,
Unless she were well raised and a virgin,
To save his rank as yeoman,[11] I don't lie.   95
She was as proud and pert as any magpie.   3950
Quite the fair sight the two of them were so;
On holidays in front of her he'd go
With his hood's tip wound up around his head,
And she came after in a gown of red;   100
And Symkin had hose colored all the same.
No one dared call her anything but "dame";
No man was so bold who passed by that way
Who ever dared to flirt with her or play,
Unless he wanted to be slain by Symkin   105
With his knife, his cutlass, or his bodkin.[12]   3960
For jealous folks are perilous, we know—
Or they're wishing that their wives suppose so.
And since she was besmirched by just a snitch,
She was as proud as water in a ditch,   110
And full of scorn and of snobbish reproof.
Ladies, she thought, should hold themselves aloof,
What with all her kindred and her nurture
That she'd learned in the nunnery, for sure.

    A daughter from the two of them they bore,   115
Who's twenty years of age, and no child more,   3970
Except a boy child, half a year in age,

---

9 **Symkin:** Nickname for Simon.

10 **many a pan of brass:** For her dowry. Despite her father-the-priest's upper-class pretensions, pans of brass for a dowry are not exactly silver or gold vessels.

11 **rank as yeoman:** As freeman rather than serf.

12 **bodkin:** Dagger.

In cradel it lay and was a propre page.
This wenche thikke and wel y-growen was,
With camuse nose and eyen greye as glas,
With buttokes brode and brestes rounde and hye;   3975
But right fair was hire heer, I wol nat lye.
   The person of the toun, for she was feir,
In purpos was to maken hire his heir
Bothe of his catel and his messuage,
And straunge he made it of hir mariage.   3980
His purpos was for to bistowe hire hye
Into som worthy blood of auncetrye;
For holy chirches good moot been despended
On holy chirches blood, that is descended.
Therfore he wolde his holy blood honoure,   3985
Though that he holy chirche sholde devoure.
   Gret soken hath this miller, out of doute,
With whete and malt of al the land aboute;
And nameliche ther was a greet collegge
Men clepen the Soler Halle at Cantebregge;   3990
Ther was hir whete and eek hir malt y-grounde.
And on a day it happed, in a stounde,
Sik lay the maunciple on a maladye:
Men wenden wisly that he sholde dye,
For which this millere stal bothe mele and corn   3995
An hundred tyme more than biforn;
For ther-biforn he stal but curteisly,
But now he was a theef outrageously.
For which the wardeyn chidde and made fare,
But therof sette the millere nat a tare;   4000
He craketh boost, and swoor it was nat so.
   Than were ther yonge povre scolers two
That dwelten in this halle of which I seye.
Testif they were, and lusty for to pleye,

Who, in its cradle lay, a proper page.
This wench thick was, and she was well grown too,
With pug-flat nose, and eyes like glass as blue,   120
With buttocks broad and breasts round and up high.
But right fair was her hair,[13] I will not lie.

      This parson of the town, since she was fair,
Now had in mind to take her for his heir
Of his chattel and of his house and land,   125
And made fuss if a marriage were at hand.   3980
His purpose was to bestow her nobly
On some old blood of worthy ancestry;
For Holy Church's goods must be expended
On blood that is from Holy Church descended.   130
Therefore, his holy blood he would empower,
Though Holy Church itself he should devour.

      The sole rights had this miller, without doubt,
To grind wheat and malt in all the land about;
And namely, there was then a great college   135
That is called by men King's Hall at Cambridge;   3990
And right there was their wheat and malt both ground.
On a day it chanced, as it was found,
Sick lay the manciple with a malady;
All the men supposed he would die surely.   140
Corn and wheat the miller stole then from their stores
A hundred times more than he had before;
For earlier, he stole courteously,
But now he was a thief outrageously.
The master chided, and he fussed indeed.   145
The miller valued all this not a weed;   4000
He cracked a boast, and swore it wasn't true.

      Among the young, poor scholars there were two,
Who dwelled there in this hall, as I shall say.
Testy they were, and hankering to play,   150

---

13 **pug-flat nose…hair**: Symkin's daughter shows the mixed-class background of her parentage
in features that combine stereotypes of the peasant woman with stereotypes of the courtly lady.

And, only for hire mirthe and revelrye,   4005
Upon the wardeyn bisily they crye
To yeve hem leve but a litel stounde
To goon to mille and seen hir corn y-grounde;
And hardily they dorste leye hir nekke,
The millere shold nat stele hem half a pekke   4010
Of corn by sleighte, ne by force hem reve;
And at the laste the wardeyn yaf hem leve.
John highte that oon, and Aleyn highte that other;
Of o toun were they born, that highte Strother,
Fer in the north—I can nat telle where.   4015
      This Aleyn maketh redy al his gere,
And on an hors the sak he caste anon.
Forth goth Aleyn the clerk, and also John,
With good swerd and with bokeler by hir syde.
John knew the wey, hem nedede no gyde,   4020
And at the mille the sak adoun he layth.
Aleyn spak first, "Al hayl, Symond, y-fayth!
How fares thy faire doghter and thy wyf?"
      "Aleyn, welcome," quod Simkin, "by my lyf!
And John also, how now, what do ye heer?"   4025
      "Symond," quod John, "by God, nede has na peer.
Him boes serve himselve that has na swayn,
Or elles he is a fool, as clerkes sayn.
Oure manciple, I hope he wil be deed,
Swa werkes ay the wanges in his heed.   4030
And forthy is I come, and eek Alayn,

And because of their mirth and revelry,
They cried out to the master busily
To let them, in the free time they have found,
Go to the mill and there see their corn ground;
And boldly, they would dare to bet their neck   155
From them the miller won't steal half a peck   4010
Of corn by sleight of hand or else by force;
At last the master let them go, of course.
John was named one, and Alan was the other;
In one town they were born, which was named Strother,[14]   160
Far in the north, but I cannot tell where.

      This Alan readied all of his gear there,
And then their horse the sack he cast upon.
Forth goes Alan the clerk, and also John
With buckler and good sword right by their side.   165
John knew the way—there's no need for a guide—   4020
And at the mill lays down the sack indeed.
Alan spoke first: "'Ail, Symkin, by yer creed!
'ow fares now yer fair daughter and yer wife?"[15]

      "Alan, welcome," Symkin said, "upon my life!   170
And how now, John, what are you doing here?"

      "Symkin," said John, "by God, need 'as no peer.
'e mus' serve 'imself that 'as no swain,
Or else 'e is a fool, the clerks make plain.
Our manciple, I think 'e will be dead,   175
So work the teeth all achin' in 'is 'ead;   4030
And straightaway I come, and so do Alan,

14   **Strother**: Town in the north of England. The Reeve and his two student characters are all
northerners.

15   "**'Ail, Symkin ... yer wife?**": Because both the Reeve and the students are from the north of
England, they are represented as rustic provincials. To make this representation more realistic, Chau-
cer has the students speak in a northern dialect of Middle English. This is the first known example in
the history of English literature of an author using dialect in speech in order to heighten characteriza-
tion. The dialect in Chaucer's original text is signaled both by the form of the words and by grammar.
I have tried to capture both by dropping initial *h*'s and terminal *g*'s and by changing some spellings
in order to give the sense that the two clerks, for all their cleverness, are meant to be seen as country
bumpkins.

To grinde our corn and carie it ham agayn;
I pray yow spede us hethen that ye may."
       "It shal be doon," quod Simkin, "by my fay.
What wol ye doon whyl that it is in hande?"   4035
       "By God, right by the hopur will I stande,"
Quod John, "and se how that the corn gas in.
Yet saugh I never, by my fader kin,
How that the hopur wagges til and fra."
       Aleyn answerde, "John, and wiltow swa?   4040
Than wil I be bynethe, by my croun,
And se how that the mele falles doun
Into the trough; that sal be my disport.
For John, in faith, I may been of youre sort:
I is as ille a millere as are ye."   4045
       This miller smyled of hir nycetee,
And thoghte, "Al this nis doon but for a wyle.
They wene that no man may hem bigyle,
But, by my thrift, yet shal I blere hire yë
For al the sleighte in hir philosophye.   4050
The more queynte crekes that they make,
The more wol I stele whan I take.
In stide of flour, yet wol I yeve hem bren.
'The gretteste clerkes been noght wysest men,'
As whylom to the wolf thus spak the mare;   4055
Of al hir art counte I noght a tare."
       Out at the dore he gooth ful prively,
Whan that he saugh his tyme, softely;
He loketh up and doun til he hath founde
The clerkes hors, ther as it stood y-bounde   4060
Bihinde the mille, under a levesel.
And to the hors he gooth him faire and wel;

To grind our corn, and take it 'ome again;

I pray now get us 'ence quick as you may."

   "It will be done," said Symkin, "right, today!   180

What will you do while the milling is in hand?"

   "By God, right by the 'opper[16] will I stand,"

Said John, "and see then 'ow the corn goes in.

I never saw yet, by my father's kin,

Just 'ow that 'opper's waggin' to and fro."   185

   Alan answered, "John, and will you do so?   4040

Then I'll be underneath, by my 'ead's crown,

To see jus' 'ow 'ere all that meal falls down

Into the trough; that will be some good sport.

Now, John, in faith, I may be of your sort: 190

I'm as bad a miller as you, by my guess."

   The miller smiled at all their foolishness,

And he thought, "All of this is just some trick.

They think that no man can beguile them quick,

Yet, by my skill, I'll blear their eye, you'll see,   195

For all the sleights of their philosophy.   4050

The more clever and quaint the tricks they make,

The more I'll steal from them what I do take.

Instead of flour, I'll give them just bran then.

'The greatest clerks are not the wisest men,'   200

As the mare once told the wolf[17] indeed.

Now all their art I don't count worth a weed."

   Out at the door he went all privately;

When he saw his time, he went out softly.

And he looks up and down till he has found   205

The clerks' horse, right there where it stood bound 4060

Behind the mill, underneath an arbor;

And there toward the horse he now moves closer;

---

 16 'opper: Hopper, part of the mill.

 17 **As the mare once told the wolf**: Refers to an adage from a story in the medieval Reynard the
Fox collection of beast fables in which a mare tells a wolf that wants to buy her colt that its price is on
her back hoof, with the predictable result.

He strepeth of the brydel right anon.
And whan the hors was laus, he ginneth gon
Toward the fen, ther wilde mares renne,   4065
Forth with "wehee," thurgh thikke and thurgh thenne.
    This miller gooth agayn, no word he seyde,
But dooth his note, and with the clerkes pleyde,
Til that hir corn was faire and wel y-grounde.
And whan the mele is sakked and y-bounde,   4070
This John goth out and fynt his hors away,
And gan to crye "harrow" and "weylaway!
Oure hors is lorn! Alayn, for goddes banes
Step on thy feet! com of, man, al atanes!
Allas, our wardeyn has his palfrey lorn!"   4075
This Aleyn al forgat bothe mele and corn;
Al was out of his mynde his housbondrye.
"What, whilk way is he geen?" he gan to crye.
    The wyf cam lepinge inward with a ren;
She seyde, "Allas! youre hors goth to the fen   4080
With wilde mares, as faste as he may go.
Unthank come on his hand that boond him so,
And he that bettre sholde han knit the reyne."
    "Allas," quod John, "Aleyn, for Cristes peyne,
Lay doun thy swerd, and I will myn alswa.   4085
I is ful wight, God waat, as is a raa;
By Goddes herte he sal nat scape us bathe!
Why ne had thou pit the capul in the lathe?
Il-hayl, by God, Aleyn, thou is a fonne!"
    This sely clerkes han ful faste y-ronne   4090
Toward the fen, bothe Aleyn and eek John.
    And whan the millere saugh that they were gon,
He half a busshel of hir flour hath take,
And bad his wyf go knede it in a cake.
He seyde, "I trowe the clerkes were aferd,   4095
Yet can a millere make a clerkes berd

He strips the bridle off the horse right so.
And when the horse was loose, then, he did go   210
Where all the wild mares run down in the fen,
Forth with "weehee," through thick and thin again.

  The miller goes back; no word did he say,
But does his task, and with the clerks does play
Until their corn was well and fairly ground,   215
And when the meal is all bagged up and bound,   4070
John goes and finds the horse has run away,
And starts to cry out, "'arrow! Wey-la-way!
By God's bones, our 'orse is now lost, Alan!
Step on yer feet! Come on! 'urry up, man!   220
Our master's lost 'is palfrey in this deal."
This Alan forgot all—both corn and meal;
Straight out of his mind flew such husbandry.
He began to cry: "Which way now went he?"

  The wife came leaping inward at a run then.   225
She said, "Alas! Your horse goes to the fen   4080
With wild mares, now as fast as he can go.
Bad luck goes to the hand that bound him so,
For he more tightly should have tied the reins!"

  "Alas," said John, "Alan, fer all Christ's pains,   230
Lay down yer sword, and me, I will also.
I'm right strong, God knows, like a buck or roe;
By God's 'eart, us 'e won't escape for long!
Whyn't put 'im in the barn where 'e belongs?
Curse fer you, Alan! You're a fool at last!"   235

  These silly clerks have now then run so fast,   4090
Both Alan and John, straight toward the fen.

  When the miller saw that they had gone again,
Half a bushel of their flour he did take,
And bade his wife go knead it in a cake.   240
He said, "I think the clerks got what they feared.
A miller still can pull on a clerk's beard,[18]

---

18 **pull on a clerk's beard**: Trick him; make him look foolish.

For al his art; now lat hem goon hir weye.
Lo, wher he gooth! ye, lat the children pleye.
They gete him nat so lightly, by my croun!"

      Thise sely clerkes rennen up and doun   4100
With "Keep! keep! stand! stand! jossa! warderere!
Ga whistle thou, and I shal kepe him here!"
But shortly, til that it was verray night,
They coude nat, though they dide al hir might,
Hir capul cacche, he ran alwey so faste,   4105
Til in a dich they caughte him atte laste.

      Wery and weet, as beest is in the reyn,
Comth sely John, and with him comth Aleyn.
"Allas," quod John, "the day that I was born!
Now are we drive til hething and til scorn.   4110
Oure corn is stole, men wil us foles calle,
Bathe the wardeyn and our felawes alle,
And namely the millere, weylaway!"

      Thus pleyneth John as he goth by the way
Toward the mille, and Bayard in his hond.   4115
The millere sitting by the fyr he fond,
For it was night, and forther mighte they noght.
But for the love of God they him bisoght
Of herberwe and of ese, as for hir peny.

      The millere seyde agayn, "If ther be eny,   4120
Swich as it is, yet shal ye have youre part.
Myn hous is streit, but ye han lerned art:
Ye conne by argumentes make a place
A myle brood of twenty foot of space.
Lat see now if this place may suffyse—   4125
Or make it roum with speche, as is youre gyse."

For all his art! Let them go on their way!
Look where he goes! Yes, let the children play.
They won't catch him soon now, by my head's crown."   245

    These silly clerks were running up and down   4100
With "Keep! Keep! Stand! Stand! Look out in the rear,
Go whistle, you. I'll try to keep 'im 'ere!"
But to tell shortly, until it was night,
They could not, though they tried with all their might,   250
Catch their nag, for he ran away so fast,
Till in a ditch they caught him there at last.

    Weary and wet, like beasts in the rain then,
Comes silly John, and with him comes Alan.
"Alas," said John, "the day that I was born!   255
Now we're both drove to mockin' and to scorn.   4110
Our corn is stolen. Fools they'll sure us call,
Our master and our fellows, one and all,
And namely this miller, wey-la-way!"

    Thus John complains, as he goes by the way,   260
With Bayard[19] in hand, back toward the mill.
He found the miller by the fire still,
And they could not then leave, since it was night;
For the love of God, they asked then if they might
Have food and shelter and they'd pay their penny.   265

    The miller answered them, "If there is any,   4120
Such as it is, still you can have your part.
My house's tight, but you know logic's art;[20]
You know, by arguments, to make a place
A mile broad out of twenty feet of space.   270
Let's see if this place can be sufficient,
Made roomy by your speech and argument."

---

19 **Bayard**: Their horse, called by a name usually associated with a knight's charger.

20 **logic's art**: Symkin here refers to the kinds of logical disputation Alan and John would have learned as university students. Symkin's implication is that intellectual arguments end up only seeming to make something out of nothing.

"Now, Symond," seyde John, "by Seint Cutberd,
Ay is thou mery, and this is faire answerd.
I have herd seyd, 'man sal taa of twa thinges:
Slyk as he fyndes, or taa slyk as he bringes.'   4130
But specially, I pray thee, hoste dere,
Get us som mete and drinke and make us chere,
And we will payen trewely atte fulle;
With empty hand men may na haukes tulle.
Lo, here oure silver, redy for to spende."   4135
    This millere into toun his doghter sende
For ale and breed, and rosted hem a goos,
And bond hir hors, it sholde namoore go loos;
And in his owene chambre hem made a bed
With shetes and with chalons faire y-spred,   4140
Noght from his owene bed ten foot or twelve.
His doghter hadde a bed, al by hirselve,
Right in the same chambre, by and by.
It mighte be no bet, and cause why,
Ther was no roumer herberwe in the place.   4145
They soupen and they speke, hem to solace,
And drinken evere strong ale atte beste.
Aboute midnight wente they to rest.
    Wel hath this millere vernisshed his heed:
Ful pale he was fordronken, and nat reed;   4150
He yexeth, and he speketh thurgh the nose
As he were on the quakke, or on the pose.
To bedde he gooth, and with him gooth his wyf—
As any jay she light was and jolyf,
So was hir joly whistle wel y-wet.   4155
The cradel at hir beddes feet is set,
To rokken, and to yeve the child to souke.
And whan that dronken al was in the crouke,

"Now," said John, "by good Saint Cuthbert,[21] Symkin,
Merrily 'ow you've answered back again.
I 'ave 'eard said: 'A man'll take two things: 275
Take like 'e finds, and take jus' like 'e brings.'   4130
But now I pray you special, my 'ost dear,
Get us some meat and drink, and make good cheer,
And we'll pay you up truly, that's fer sure.
With empty 'and, no 'awks can a man lure;   280
Lo, 'ere's our silver, waitin' to be spent."
      This miller into town his daughter sent,
For ale and bread, and roasted them a goose,
And tied their horse so it would not get loose.
In his own chamber, he made up their bed,   285
Right there with sheets and blankets fairly spread   4140
Not ten feet from his own, or twelve instead.
All by herself, his daughter had a bed,
Right in that selfsame chamber and nearby.
It was no better, and the reason why?   290
In that place was no lodging roomier.
For amusement, they talk and eat supper,
And drink the strong ale that is very best.
Around midnight, they all went to their rest.
      Well had the miller varnished up his head;[22]   295
He was quite pale from drinking, and not red.   4150
He belches, and he's speaking through his nose,
Like he's got a cold or quacking, I suppose.
To bed he goes, and with him goes his wife.
She was as light and jolly, by my life,   300
As any jay. Her jolly whistle's wet.
The cradle at their bed's foot now she set,
To give the child suck and the cradle rock.
And when they'd drunk up all that's in the crock,

---

21 **Saint Cuthbert**: A popular saint from the north of England, who had been bishop of Lindisfarne in the seventh century.
22 **varnished up his head**: Drunk a lot.

To bedde went the doghter right anon;
To bedde gooth Aleyn and also John;   4160
Ther nas na more, hem nedede no dwale.
This millere hath so wisly bibbed ale,
That as an hors he fnorteth in his sleep,
Ne of his tayl bihinde he took no keep.
His wyf bar him a burdon, a ful strong: 4165
Men mighte hir routing here two furlong;
The wenche routeth eek *par compaignye.*
          Aleyn the clerk, that herd this melodye,
He poked John, and seyde, "Slepestow?
Herdestow evere slyk a sang er now?   4170
Lo, swilk a compline is y-mel hem alle!
A wilde fyr upon thair bodyes falle!
Wha herkned ever slyk a ferly thing?
Ye, they sal have the flour of il ending.
This lange night ther tydes me na reste;   4175
But yet, na fors, al sal be for the beste.
For John," seyde he, "als evere moot I thryve,
If that I may, yon wenche wil I swyve.
Som esement has lawe y-shapen us.
For John, ther is a lawe that says thus,   4180
That gif a man in a point be agreved,
That in another he sal be releved.
Oure corn is stoln, sothly, it is na nay,
And we han had an il fit al this day.
And sin I sal have neen amendement   4185
Agayn my los, I wil have esement.
By Goddes saule, it sal neen other be!"
          This John answerde, "Alayn, avyse thee,
The miller is a perilous man," he seyde,
"And gif that he out of his sleep abreyde,   4190
He mighte doon us bathe a vileinye."
          Aleyn answerde, "I count him nat a flye."

To bed went the daughter right away then.   305

To bed goes John, and to bed goes Alan—   4160

That's all: no sleeping potion did they need.

This miller swigged his ale so well indeed

That like a horse, he's snorting in his sleep;

Nor of his tail behind did he take keep.   310

His wife took up the bass line loud and strong;

Their snoring carried two furlongs along;

The wench snores, too, to keep them company.

    Alan, the clerk, who heard this melody,

Poked John and said: "Can you sleep any more?   315

Now did you 'ear of such a song before?   4170

Lo! 'ear what a compline's²³ sung among 'em all;

May a wild fire on all 'er bodies fall!

Whoever 'arkened suchlike bloody thing?

Sure, they'll all meet up with some bad ending.   320

This livelong night, I won't get any rest;

No matter; it'll all be fer the best.

Fer, John," said he, "may I thrive if I do—

If I can, sure that wench there I will screw.

Some compensation the law makes fer us,   325

Fer, John, this 'ere law, it does make clear, thus: 4180

That if a man in one point is aggrieved,

Then in another point, 'e'll be relieved.

Our corn is stolen, it's true, as I say,

And we 'ave 'ad an ill time 'ere all day;   330

There's no return in this situation

For my loss, so I'll 'ave compensation.

By God's soul now, it shan't be otherwise!"

    John answered, "Alan, take care, I'd advise!

This miller is a perilous man," he said,   335

"And if 'e should wake up out of 'is bed,   4190

'e might do to us both some villainy."

    Alan said, "'e won't count a fly with me."

---

23 **compline:** Last evening service of the day sung in monasteries and convents.

And up he rist, and by the wenche he crepte.
This wenche lay upright, and faste slepte
Til he so ny was, er she mighte espye,   4195
That it had been to late for to crye,
And shortly for to seyn, they were aton;
Now pley, Aleyn! for I wol speke of John.

      This John lyth stille a furlong-wey or two,
And to himself he maketh routhe and wo: 4200
"Allas!" quod he, "this is a wikked jape.
Now may I seyn that I is but an ape.
Yet has my felawe somwhat for his harm:
He has the milleris doghter in his arm.
He auntred him, and has his nedes sped,   4205
And I lye as a draf-sak in my bed.
And when this jape is tald another day,
I sal been halde a daf, a cokenay!
I wil aryse and auntre it, by my fayth!
Unhardy is unsely, thus men sayth."   4210
And up he roos and softely he wente
Unto the cradel, and in his hand it hente,
And baar it softe unto his beddes feet.

      Sone after this the wyf hir routing leet,
And gan awake, and wente hir out to pisse,   4215
And cam agayn, and gan hir cradel misse,
And groped heer and ther, but she fond noon.
"Allas!" quod she, "I hadde almost misgoon;
I hadde almost gon to the clerkes bed—
Ey, *benedicite*, thanne hadde I foule y-sped!"   4220
And forth she gooth til she the cradel fond;
She gropeth alwey forther with hir hond,
And fond the bed, and thoghte noght but good,
By cause that the cradel by it stood,
And niste wher she was, for it was derk;   4225
But faire and wel she creep in to the clerk,
And lyth ful stille, and wolde han caught a sleep.
Withinne a whyl this John the clerk up leep,

And up he rose, and to the wench he crept.
This wench lay on her back and soundly slept;   340
He was so close, before she did him spy,
That it'd have been too late for her to cry.
To tell it fast, right there they got it on.
Now, play, Alan, for I will speak of John.

     This John lies still a minute there or so;   345
He's pitying himself and feeling woe.   4200
"Alas," said he, "this is one wicked jape;
Now I can see I'm nothin' but an ape.
My friend got somethin' to repay his 'arms;
He's got the miller's daughter in 'is arms.   350
'e took 'is chance, and 'e 'as succeeded,
While, like a sack of dung 'ere, I'm in bed;
When this jape's told again, no matter what,
I'll be 'eld up as a daft idiot!
Now I'll rise up and chance it, by my creed!   355
'Unhardy is unlucky,' it's agreed."   4210
Up he rose, and quietly went to stand
Near the cradle and took it in his hand,
And to his bed's foot quietly it bore.

     Soon after this, the wife did cease to snore,   360
And she awoke and went outside to piss,
And came back in and did her cradle miss,
Groped here and there, but found it in no way.
"Alas!" said she, "I almost went astray;
I almost went to the clerks' bed, indeed.   365
God bless me, that'd be no way to succeed!"   4220
She goes till she finds the cradle near her.
With her hand, she is then groping further,
And found the bed, and thought it only good,
Because the cradle right near by it stood,   370
And knew not where she was, for it was dark;
But fair and well she crept into the clerk,
And lies all still and would have caught some sleep.
Within a while, this clerk John up did leap,

And on this gode wyf he leyth on sore.

So mery a fit ne hadde she nat ful yore;   4230

He priketh harde and depe as he were mad.

This joly lyf han thise two clerkes lad

Til that the thridde cok bigan to singe.

      Aleyn wex wery in the daweninge,

For he had swonken al the longe night,   4235

And seyde, "Fare weel, Malyne, swete wight!

The day is come; I may no lenger byde;

But everemo, wher so I go or ryde,

I is thyn awen clerk, swa have I seel!"

      "Now, dere lemman," quod she, "go, far weel!   4240

But er thou go, o thing I wol thee telle:

Whan that thou wendest homward by the melle,

Right at the entree of the dore bihinde,

Thou shalt a cake of half a busshel finde

That was y-maked of thyn owene mele,   4245

Which that I heelp my sire for to stele.

And, gode lemman, God thee save and kepe!"

And with that word almost she gan to wepe.

      Aleyn up rist, and thoughte, "Er that it dawe,

I wol go crepen in by my felawe,"   4250

And fond the cradel with his hand anon.

"By God," thoghte he, "al wrang I have misgon.

Myn heed is toty of my swink tonight:

That maketh me that I go nat aright.

I woot wel by the cradel I have misgo—   4255

Heere lyth the miller and his wyf also."

And forth he goth, a twenty devel way,

Unto the bed ther as the miller lay—

He wende have cropen by his felawe John—

And by the millere in he creep anon,   4260

And caughte hym by the nekke, and softe he spak.

He seyde, "Thou, John, thou swynes-heed, awak

And on this good wife strongly then he lays. 375
Such a merry fit she'd lacked for many days; 4230
He pricks then hard and deep like he's gone mad.
And thus this jolly life these two clerks had
Until the third cock had begun to sing.[24]
      Alan waxed weary as the day was dawning, 380
Who that long night his labor did endure.
He said, "Farewell, Molly, my sweet creature!
The day is come; no longer can I stay;
But, evermore, wherever go I may,
I am your own clerk, may I prosper so!" 385
      "Oh, dear lover," said she, "farewell, now go! 4240
But first there's one thing I will tell you still:
When you wend your way homeward by the mill,
Right at the entrance and the door behind,
You shall a cake of half a bushel find 390
That was made up right out of your own meal,
Which I have helped my sire from you steal.
And, good lover, may God you save and keep!"
With those words, she began almost to weep.
      Alan rose and thought, "Before dawn comes on, 395
I will go creep in right by my friend John." 4250
With his hand, he found the cradle before long.
"By God," thought he, "now I 'ave gone all wrong.
My 'ead's all muzzy from my work tonight,
It's makin' me so I'm not goin' right. 400
By the cradle there I know wrong I did go;
'ere the miller lies and 'is wife also."
Forth he goes—twenty devils take their way—
Straight to the bed right where the miller lay.
He thought he crept into his friend John's bed, 405
But by the miller in he crept instead, 4260
And caught him by the neck and softly said,
"You, John," said he, "wake up, you old swine's 'ead,

---

24 **third cock began to sing:** Right before dawn.

For Cristes saule, and heer a noble game.
For by that lord that called is Seint Jame,
As I have thryes in this shorte night   4265
Swyved the milleres doghter bolt upright,
Whyl thow hast as a coward been agast.
     "Ye, false harlot," quod the millere, "hast?
A! false traitour! false clerk!" quod he,
"Thou shalt be deed, by Goddes dignitee!   4270
Who dorste be so bold to disparage
My doghter, that is come of swich linage?"
And by the throte-bolle he caughte Alayn;
And he hente hym despitously agayn,
And on the nose he smoot him with his fest—   4275
Doun ran the blody streem upon his brest.
And in the floor, with nose and mouth tobroke,
They walwe as doon two pigges in a poke.
And up they goon, and doun agayn anon,
Til that the miller sporned at a stoon,   4280
And doun he fil bakward upon his wyf,
That wiste no thing of this nyce stryf,
For she was falle aslepe a lyte wight
With John the clerk, that waked hadde al night;
And with the fal, out of hir sleep she breyde.   4285
"Help, holy croys of Bromeholm," she seyde,
"*In manus tuas!* Lord, to thee I calle!
Awak, Symond! the feend is on me falle,
Myn herte is broken, help, I nam but deed:
There lyth oon upon my wombe and on myn heed.   4290
Help, Simkin, for the false clerkes fighte."
     This John sterte up as faste as ever he mighte,
And graspeth by the walles to and fro,
To finde a staf; and she sterte up also,
And knew the estres bet than dide this John,   4295

For Christ's soul, and 'ear of some noble games.
For by the good lord who is called Saint James,   410
Three times this night I 'ave in short order
Screwed, flat on her back, the miller's daughter,
While, coward, you've been frightened in your bed."
           "Yeah, false harlot, you did?" the miller said.
"Ah! False traitor! Ah, you false clerk!" said he,   415
"You shall be dead, by God's own dignity!   4270
Who'd dare be so bold as to disparage
My daughter, who comes from such high lineage?"
By the Adam's apple he caught Alan,
And he hit him angrily again,   420
And on the nose he smote him with his fist.
Down ran the bloody stream upon his breast;
On the floor, with nose and mouth all broken,
They wallow just like two pigs in a poke then;
Up they go, and down again they tumbled,   425
Till upon a stone the miller stumbled,   4280
And backward he fell down upon his wife,
Who knew nothing of all this stupid strife;
For she'd fallen asleep as it got light
By John the clerk, who had been up all night;   430
With that fall, out of her sleep she started.
"Oh holy cross of Bromholm, help!"[25] she said,
"*In manus tuas!*[26] Lord, to you I call!
Awake, Symkin! The fiend on me did fall.
My heart is broken; help! I'm nearly dead!   435
There lies one on my womb and on my head.   4290
Help me, Symkin, for now the false clerks fight!"
           John started up just as fast as he might,
And gropes along the walls, both to and fro,
To find a staff; and she starts up also,   440
And knew the room's nooks better than John could,

---

25 **holy cross of Bromholm**: Site in England where there was allegedly a piece of Christ's cross.
26 *In manus tuas*: Into your hands.

And by the wal a staf she fond anon,
And saugh a litel shimering of a light—
For at an hole in shoon the mone bright—
And by that light she saugh hem bothe two,
But sikerly she niste who was who, 4300
But as she saugh a whyt thing in hir yë
And whan she gan this whyte thing espye,
She wende the clerk hadde wered a volupeer,
And with the staf she drough ay neer and neer,
And wende han hit this Aleyn at the fulle, 4305
And smoot the millere on the pyled skulle
That doun he gooth and cryde, "Harrow! I dye!"
Thise clerkes bete him weel and lete him lye,
And greythen hem, and toke hir hors anon,
And eek hire mele, and on hir wey they gon. 4310
And at the mille yet they toke hir cake
Of half a busshel flour, ful wel y-bake.

      Thus is the proude millere wel y-bete,
And hath y-lost the grinding of the whete,
And payed for the soper everideel 4315
Of Aleyn and of John, that bette him weel;
His wyf is swyved, and his doghter als.
Lo, swich it is a millere to be fals!
And therefore this proverbe is seyd ful sooth,
"Him thar nat wene wel that yvel dooth; 4320
A gylour shal himself bigyled be."
And God, that sitteth heighe in magestee,
Save al this compaignye grete and smale!
Thus have I quit the Millere in my tale.

Heere is ended the Reves Tale.

And by the wall, she found where a staff stood,
And saw a little shimmering of light,
For at a hole, in shone the moon so bright,
And by that light, she saw them both, those two,   445
But, in truth, she did not know who was who,   4300
Except she saw a white thing with her eye.
And when this same white thing there she did spy,
She thought the clerk had worn a nightcap, so
With the staff, close and closer she did go,   450
And thought she'd hit Alan square on the head,
And smote the miller's smooth bald skull instead,
And down he goes, and cried, "Harrow! I die!"
These clerks both beat him well and let him lie,
And they got dressed and quickly grabbed their horse,   455
And their meal, too, and then they took their course.   4310
And at the mill, they also took the cake
From half a bushel of flour she did bake.
          Thus is the proud miller quite well beaten,
And has lost the grinding of his wheat then,   460
And he paid for the supper every bit
Of John and Alan, who him beat and hit.
His wife is screwed, and his daughter also.
Lo, such it is to be a miller false so!
And thus this proverb's said because it's true,   465
"Do not expect good if you evil do."   4320
A guiler shall himself beguiled then be.
And God, who sits on high in majesty,
Let this company, both great and small, prevail!
Thus, I've repaid the Miller in my tale.   470

Here is ended the Reeve's Tale.

THE COOK'S PROLOGUE

The Cook of London, whyl the Reve spak,
For joye him thoughte he clawed him on the bak.
"Ha ha!" quod he, "for Cristes passioun,
This millere hadde a sharp conclusioun
Upon his argument of herbergage!"
Wel seyde Salomon in his langage,
'Ne bringe nat every man into thyn house.'
For herberwinge by nighte is perilous.
Wel oghte a man avysed for to be
Whom that he broughte into his privetee.
I pray to God, so yeve me sorwe and care
If ever, sith I highte Hogge of Ware,
Herde I a millere bettre y-set a-werk.
He hadde a jape of malice in the derk.
But God forbede that we stinten here,
And therfore, if ye vouchesauf to here
A tale of me, that am a povre man,
I wol you telle as wel as evere I can
A little jape that fil in our citee."
  Our Host answerde and seide, "I graunte it thee;
Now telle on, Roger, loke that it be good;
For many a pastee hastow laten blood,

THE COOK'S PROLOGUE

After the Reeve spoke, the Cook of London
Felt like his back'd been scratched, he'd had such fun.
"Ha! Ha!" said he, "Now, by Christ's own passion,
This Miller reached a painful conclusion
To arguing for giving board and bed!   5
In his own language, Solomon well said,   4330
'Don't bring every man into your house thus,'
For sheltering by night is perilous.
A careful man now well advised would be
About who came to share his privacy.   10
I pray God to give me sorrow and care
If ever, as I'm called Roger of Ware,[1]
I heard a miller made a better mark.
He had a dirty joke there in the dark.
But God forbid that we should stop it here;   15
And therefore, if you will agree to hear   4340
A tale from me, who's only a poor man,
I will tell you, as well now as I can,
A small joke that happened in our city."
        Our Host answered and said, "Then, I agree.   20
Tell on, Roger. To make it good, now try,
For you've let blood from many a meat pie,[2]

---

1 **Ware:** Town thirty miles from London.
2 **let blood from many a meat pie:** Taken out some of their fillings to make them skimpier.

And many a Jakke of Dover hastow sold
That hath been twyes hoot and twyes cold.
Of many a pilgrim hastow Cristes curs,
For of thy persly yet they fare the wors,   4350
That they han eten with thy stubbel-goos,
For in thy shoppe is many a flye loos.
Now telle on, gentil Roger, by thy name.
But yet I pray thee, be nat wrooth for game.
A man may seye ful sooth in game and pley."   4355
      "Thou seist ful sooth," quod Roger, "by my fey,
But 'sooth pley, quaad pley,' as the Fleming seith.
And therfore, Herry Bailly, by thy feith,
Be thou nat wrooth, er we departen heer,
Though that my tale be of an hostileer.   4360
But nathelees I wol nat telle it yit,
But er we parte, ywis, thou shalt be quit."
And therwithal he lough and made chere,
And seyde his tale, as ye shul after here.

And many stale Jack of Dovers[3] you have sold
That twice have been hot and twice have been cold.
On you have many pilgrims wished Christ's curse,   25
Since from your parsley they have fared the worse,   4350
Which they ate with your tough, stubble-fed goose,
For in your shop, many a fly is loose.
Now, tell on, gentle Roger, by your name.
I pray you; don't be angry at a game;   30
A man can tell the truth in game and play."
        "By my faith," said Roger, "you truly say!
But 'true joke, no joke,' the Flemish[4] have agreed.
And therefore, Harry Bailley,[5] by your creed,
Before we separate—don't be angry—   35
My tale about an innkeeper will be.   4360
But now, that's not the one I want to tell.
Before we part, you'll be repaid quite well."
And with that, he did laugh and made good cheer,
And told his tale, as you will later hear.   40

---

3 **Jack of Dovers**: Pies or pastries.
4 **the Flemish**: The proverb originated in Flanders.
5 **Harry Bailley**: The host of the Tabard Inn in Southwark where the pilgrimage started, who is riding with them to Canterbury and serving as judge of the tales. This is the first time he's named in *The Tales*. Interestingly, there are records of an historical Harry Bailley who was an innkeeper in Southwark. It is not known whether Chaucer knew him or, if he did, what the point of the reference to him in *The Tales* would be.

THE COOK'S TALE

Heere bigynneth the Cookes Tale.

A prentis whylom dwelled in our citee,   4365
And of a craft of vitaillers was he.
Gaillard he was as goldfinch in the shawe,
Broun as a berie, a propre short felawe,
With lokkes blake, y-kempt ful fetisly.
Dauncen he coude so wel and jolily   4370
That he was cleped Perkin Revelour.
He was as ful of love and paramour
As is the hyve ful of hony swete;
Wel was the wenche with him mighte mete.
At every brydale wolde he singe and hoppe.   4375
He loved bet the taverne than the shoppe.
For whan ther any ryding was in Chepe,
Out of the shoppe thider wolde he lepe.
Til that he hadde al the sighte y-seyn
And daunced wel, he wolde nat come ageyn.   4380
And gadered him a meinee of his sort
To hoppe and singe and maken swich disport.
And ther they setten steven for to mete
To pleyen at the dys in swich a strete,
For in the toune nas ther no prentys   4385

THE COOK'S TALE

Here begins the Cook's Tale.

An apprentice once dwelled in our city,
And one of the victualers' guild was he.
Like a goldfinch in the woods as merry,
A handsome short one, brown just like a berry,
With his black locks, combed all elegantly;   45
And he could dance so well and merrily   4370
That he was called Perkin⁶ the Reveler.
He was as full of love, this paramour,
As the hive that's all filled with honey sweet—
Well was it with the wench who him might meet.   50
At every wedding, he'd dance, sing and hop.
He loved the tavern better than the shop,
When in Cheapside⁷ there was a parade,
Out of the shop to it he leaped and played—
Until he had seen all the sights and then   55
Danced well, he would not come back in again—   4380
And he drew to him a crew of this sort
To hop and sing and dance and make such sport;
And there they all set up a time to meet,
So they could play at dice in such a street.   60
For in the town no apprentice was more fair

---

6 **Perkin:** Nickname for Peter.
7 **Cheapside:** Market street in London.

That fairer coude caste a paire of dys
Than Perkin coude, and therto he was free
Of his dispense, in place of privetee.
That fond his maister wel in his chaffare,
For often tyme he fond his box ful bare.   4390
For sikerly a prentis revelour
That haunteth dys, riot, or paramour,
His maister shal it in his shoppe abye,
Al have he no part of the minstralcye.
For thefte and riot, they ben convertible,   4395
Al conne he pleye on giterne or ribible.
Revel and trouthe, as in a low degree,
They been ful wrothe al day, as men may see.
        This joly prentis with his maister bood,
Til he were ny out of his prentishood,   4400
Al were he snibbed bothe erly and late,
And somtyme lad with revel to Newgate.
But atte laste his maister him bithoghte,
Upon a day whan he his paper soghte,
Of a proverbe that seith this same word: 4405
"Wel bet is roten appel out of hord
Than that it rotie al the remenaunt."
So fareth it by a riotous servaunt—
It is ful lasse harm to lete him pace,
Than he shende alle the servants in the place.   4410
Therefore his maister yaf him acquitance,
And bad him go, with sorwe and with meschance.
And thus this joly prentis hadde his leve.
Now lat him riote al the night or leve.
        And for ther is no theef withoute a louke,   4415
That helpeth him to wasten and to souke
Of that he brybe can or borwe may,

Than Perkin was, who could well cast a pair
Of dice, and for this reason, he was free
With spending, in a place of privacy.
His master found this in his business there,   65
For oftentimes, he found his strongbox bare.   4390
For, sure, with an apprentice reveler
Haunting dice, debauchery, and paramours,
In his shop, his master buys it handily,
Though he has not enjoyed the minstrelsy.   70
Theft and debauching are interchangeable,
Though the master plays guitar or fiddle.[8]
Revels and truth, in man of low degree,
All day they are at odds, as men can see.
          This jolly apprentice stayed with his master,   75
Till his apprenticeship was almost over,   4400
Though he was scolded both early and late, then
Sometimes led with revels to Newgate prison.
But at last to himself his master thought,
When his indenture papers Perkin sought,   80
Of a proverb that should not be ignored:
"The rotten apple's best outside the hoard
Rather than bring rot into the remnant."
So it fares with a dissolute servant;
It's less harm to let him leave and then have space   85
Than let him ruin each servant in the place.   4410
His master thus released him from indenture—
Go with sorrow and bad luck to be sure!
This jolly apprentice got his chance to leave.
Let him carouse all night or take his leave.   90
          And since there's no thief without an accomplice
Who helps him to suck dry and waste with malice
Anything he can steal or borrow may,

---

8   master . . . guitar or fiddle: An ambiguous line. Either the master hasn't been able to join the
revelry even though he can play musical instruments, or else the master himself is a reveler, but still
can't keep up with Perkin's antics.

Anon he sente his bed and his array
Unto a compeer of his owne sort,
That lovede dys and revel and disport,   4420
And hadde a wyf that heeld for countenance
A shoppe, and swyved for hir sustenance.

At once he sent his bedding and array
To a companion who was just his sort,   95
Who loved dice and much revelry and sport,   4420
And had a wife, who kept a shop for giving
A good appearance, but she screwed for a living....

[*The Cook's Tale* is unfinished. It's not clear whether Chaucer ever intended to finish it or whether he got bored with it and left it deliberately incomplete.]

THE WIFE OF BATH'S PROLOGUE

"Experience, though noon auctoritee
Were in this world, is right ynough for me
To speke of wo that is in mariage:
For, lordinges, sith I twelf yeer was of age,
Thonked be God that is eterne on lyve,   5
Housbondes at chirche dore I have had fyve
(If I so ofte myghte have y-wedded be)
And alle were worthy men in hir degree.
But me was told, certeyn, nat longe agon is,
That sith that Crist ne wente nevere but onis   10
To wedding in the Cane of Galilee,
That by the same ensample taughte he me
That I ne sholde wedded be but ones.
Herkne eek, lo, which a sharp word for the nones
Besyde a welle, Jesus, God and man,   15

THE WIFE OF BATH'S PROLOGUE

"Experience, though no authority
Were in this world, is right enough for me
To speak of the woe that is in marriage;
For, my lords, since I was twelve years of age,
Thanks be to God, eternally alive,   5*
Husbands at the church door, I have had five—
If quite so often I might wedded be—
And all were worthy men in their degree.
But it was told me not so long ago,[1]
That since just once our Christ did ever go   10
To a wedding, in Cana in Galilee,[2]
That by that same example, he taught me
That only one time I should wedded be.
Lo, listen, what a sharp word then spoke he,
Beside a well when Jesus, God and man,   15

*Throughout this volume, an absence of combined lineation numbers indicates the beginning of what, in most medieval manuscripts, is a new part or fragment of *The Canterbury Tales*.

1 **But it was told me not so long ago**: The Wife of Bath cites a number of biblical sources as she constructs her argument in support of her many marriages. The vast majority of these sources and of the position on marriage that she's rebutting can be found in Saint Jerome's *Adversus Jovinianum* (392 C.E.), a work that Chaucer uses frequently throughout *The Tales*. In this work, Saint Jerome, a Father of the Church known for, among other things, his asceticism, challenges Jovinian's more liberal views toward marriage and remarriage and toward women, views that did not find favor with the Church in the fourth century. Chaucer also took many aspects of the Wife of Bath's personality, even as he wrought his own changes on them, from the figure of the Old Woman in Jean de Meun's continuation of *The Romance of the Rose*.

2 **wedding...Galilee**: John 2:1.

Spak in repreve of the Samaritan:
'Thou hast y-had fyve housbondes,' quod he,
'And that ilke man that now hath thee
Is noght thyn housbond'—thus seyde he certeyn.
What that he mente therby, I can nat seyn,   20
But that I axe, why that the fifthe man
Was noon housbond to the Samaritan?
How manye mighte she have in mariage?
Yet herde I nevere tellen in myn age
Upon this nombre diffinicioun.   25
Men may devyne and glosen up and doun,
But wel I woot expres, withoute lye,
God bad us for to wexe and multiplye:
That gentil text can I wel understonde.
Eek wel I woot he seyde, myn housbonde   30
Sholde lete fader and moder, and take to me;
But of no nombre mencioun made he,
Of bigamye or of octogamye.
Why sholde men thanne speke of it vileinye?
        Lo, here the wyse king, daun Salomon;   35
I trowe he hadde wyves mo than oon.
As wolde God it leveful were unto me
To be refresshed half so ofte as he!
Which yifte of God hadde he for alle his wyvis!
No man hath swich that in this world alyve is.   40
God woot this noble king, as to my wit,
The firste night had many a mery fit
With ech of hem, so wel was him on lyve!
Blessed be God that I have wedded fyve,
Of whiche I have pyked out the beste,   44a
Bothe of here nether purs and of here cheste.
Diverse scoles maken parfyt clerkes,
And diverse practyk in many sondry werkes

Spoke in reproof of the Samaritan:[3]
'Thou hast had five husbands,' then said he,
'And so that same man here who now hath thee
Is not thy husband,' said he by the well.
But what he meant thereby, I cannot tell;   20
Except I ask, why is it the fifth man
Was not husband to the Samaritan?
How many might she have in marriage?
Yet I've never heard tell, in all my age,
About this, any number definite.   25
Up and down, men gloss and guess about it,
But well I know, expressly, it's no lie,
That God bade us to wax and multiply;[4]
This gentle text, I can well understand.
Also, well I know, he said my husband   30
Should leave mother and father and cleave to me.
But of no number a mention made he,
Of bigamy, or of octogamy;
Why then should men speak of it villainy?
　　　　Lo, here is the wise king, Don Solomon;   35
I think he had some wives, well more than one.
Now would to God it lawful were for me
To be refreshed here half so much as he!
A gift from God had he with all his wives!
No man has such a gift who's now alive.   40
This noble king, God knows, as I would judge it,
That first night had many a merry fit
With each of them, so well was he alive.
Blessèd be God that I have wedded five!
Of whom I have picked out the very best,   44a
For both their nether purse and money chest.
Different schools can turn out perfect clerks,
And different practices in sundry works

3　**Samaritan:** John 4:5.
4　**wax and multiply:** Genesis 1:28.

Maketh the werkman parfyt sekirly:

Of fyve husbondes scoleiyng am I.   44f

Welcome the sixte, whan that evere he shall!   45

For sothe I wol nat kepe me chast in al.

Whan myn housbond is fro the world y-gon,

Som Cristen man shal wedde me anon;

For thanne th'Apostle seith that I am free

To wedde, a Goddes half, where it lyketh me.   50

He seith that to be wedded is no sinne:

Bet is to be wedded than to brinne.

What rekketh me thogh folk seye vileinye

Of shrewed Lameth and his bigamye?

I woot wel Abraham was an holy man,   55

And Jacob eek, as ferforth as I can;

And ech of hem hadde wyves mo than two,

And many another holy man also.

Wher can ye seye, in any manere age,

That hye God defended mariage   60

By expres word? I pray you, telleth me.

Or where comanded he virginitee?

I woot as wel as ye, it is no drede,

Th'Apostel, whan he speketh of maydenhede,

He seyde that precept therof hadde he noon.   65

Men may conseille a womman to been oon,

But conseilling is no comandement:

He putte it in oure owene jugement.

For hadde God comanded maydenhede,

Thanne hadde he dampned wedding with the dede.   70

And certes, if ther were no seed y-sowe,

Virginitee, thanne wherof sholde it growe?

Poul dorste nat comanden, atte leste,

Make the workman perfect, it's no lie;

From my five husbands, studying am I.   44f

Welcome the sixth, when he shall come along.   45

In truth, I won't keep chaste for very long.

And when my husband from this world has passed,

Another Christian man will wed me fast;

Then the apostle[5] says that I am free

To wed, by God, where it most pleases me.   50

He says to be wedded is not sinning;

Better to be wedded than be burning.

What do I care if folks speak villainy

About accursed Lamech's[6] bigamy?

Abraham was a holy man, I know;   55

And as I understand it, Jacob also;

And each of them had wives now, more than one,

As many other holy men have done.

Where, can you say, in any kind of age,

That our high God has forbidden marriage   60

Expressly, in a word? I pray, tell me.

Or where did he command virginity?

I know as well as you, or else you should,

The apostle,[7] when he speaks of maidenhood,

Said that a precept for it he had none.[8]   65

Men may counsel a woman to be one,

But counseling does not make a commandment.

All of it he left to our own judgment;

For if our God commanded maidenhood,

Then wedding with the deed, he'd damn for good.   70

And surely, if no seed were ever sown,

From what, then, would virginity be grown?

And at the least, Paul never dared demand

---

5   the apostle: Saint Paul.

6   Lamech: First bigamist in the Bible, Genesis 4:19.

7   the apostle: Again, Saint Paul.

8   a precept . . . none: 1 Corinthians 7, here and following, as the Wife takes on this strain of argument.

A thing of which his maister yaf noon heste.
The dart is set up for virginitee;   75
Cacche who so may: who renneth best lat see.
      But this word is nat take of every wight,
But ther as God list give it of his might.
I woot wel that th'Apostel was a mayde,
But natheless, thogh that he wroot and sayde   80
He wolde that every wight were swich as he,
Al nis but conseil to virginitee,
And for to been a wyf, he yaf me leve
Of indulgence. So nis it no repreve
To wedde me, if that my make dye,   85
Withoute excepcioun of bigamye,
Al were it good no womman for to touche—
He mente as in his bed or in his couche—
For peril is bothe fyr and tow t'assemble;
Ye knowe what this ensample may resemble.   90
This al and som: he heeld virginitee
More parfit than wedding in freletee.
Freletee clepe I, but if that he and she
Wolde leden al hir lyf in chastitee.
      I graunte it wel, I have noon envye   95
Thogh maydenhede preferre bigamye.
Hem lyketh to be clene, body and goost.
Of myn estaat I nil nat make no boost:
For wel ye knowe, a lord in his houshold
He hath nat every vessel al of gold;   100
Somme been of tree, and doon hir lord servyse.
God clepeth folk to him in sondry wyse,
And everich hath of God a propre yifte,
Som this, som that, as Him lyketh shifte.

A thing that his own Master won't command.
The prize is set up for virginity;   75
Catch it who may; who runs the best, let's see.
        To everyone, this word does not apply,
But only where God's might wants it to lie.
I know the apostle was a virgin;
Nonetheless, although he wrote and said then   80
He wished that everyone was such as he,
This is but counsel to virginity.
He gave me leave to be a wife, all the same,
With his permission, so it is no shame,
If my mate dies, to go then and wed me,   85
Without objections about bigamy.
Though it may be good not to touch women—
In his bed or on his couch, he meant then—
Fire and flax together make peril so—
What this example resembles, you all know.   90
The sum is this: he held virginity
More perfect than to wed from frailty.
Frailty I call it, unless he and she
Wished to lead all their lives in chastity.
        I grant it well that I have no envy,   95
Though maidenhood's preferred to bigamy.⁹
To be clean pleases them, body and spirit;
Of my state, I make no boast about it,
For you well know, a lord in his household,
He has not every vessel made of gold;¹⁰   100
Some come from wood, and serve their lord withal.
In sundry ways, folks to him God does call,
Each has God's special gift while he must live,
Some this, some that, it pleases God to give.

---

9   **bigamy**: Here and elsewhere, it's important to note that, as the Wife of Bath uses the term "bigamy" in her fourteenth-century context and in relation to her own marital history, the word can mean marriage to or of someone whose previous spouse has died, and not just having more than one spouse at the same time, though it sometimes bore that latter meaning, too.

10   **vessel made of gold**: 2 Timothy 2:20.

Virginitee is greet perfeccioun,   105
And continence eek with devocioun.
But Crist, that of perfeccioun is welle,
Bad nat every wight he sholde go selle
All that he hadde and give it to the pore,
And in swich wyse folwe him and his fore.   110
He spak to hem that wolde live parfitly,
And lordinges, by youre leve, that am nat I.
I wol bistowe the flour of al myn age
In the actes and in fruit of mariage.

    Telle me also, to what conclusioun   115
Were membres maad of generacioun
And of so parfit wys a wright y-wroght?
Trusteth right wel, they were nat maad for noght.
Glose whoso wole, and seye bothe up and doun
That they were maked for purgacioun   120
Of urine, and oure bothe thinges smale
Were eek to knowe a femele from a male,
And for noon other cause: sey ye no?
The experience woot wel it is noght so.
So that the clerkes be nat with me wrothe,   125
I sey this, that they maked been for bothe—
This is to seye, for office, and for ese
Of engendrure, ther we nat God displese.
Why sholde men elles in hir bokes sette
That man shal yelde to his wyf hire dette?   130
Now wherwith sholde he make his payement
If he ne used his sely instrument?
Thanne were they maad upon a creature
To purge uryne, and eek for engendrure.

    But I seye noght that every wight is holde,   135
That hath swich harneys as I to yow tolde,
To goon and usen hem in engendrure:
Thanne sholde men take of chastitee no cure.
Crist was a mayde and shapen as a man,
And many a seint, sith that the world bigan,   140

Virginity thus is great perfection,   105
And also continence spurred by devotion,
But Christ, who of perfection is the well,
Bade not that every person should go sell
All that he has and give it to the poor,
And follow in his footsteps thus, for sure.   110
He spoke to those who would live perfectly,
And my lords, by your leave, that is not me.
I will bestow the flower of my life
In married acts and fruits, and be a wife.

  Tell me, for what purpose and conclusion   115
Were the members made for generation,
And by so perfectly wise a maker wrought?
Trust it well now: they were not made for nought.
Say what you will, or hedge it by glossing,
That they were made simply for the purging   120
Of urine; and both our small things also
Were made so male from female we could know,
And for no other cause—do you say no?
Experience well knows it is not so.
So the clerks will not be angry at me,   125
They were made for both: I say this truly.
That is, to do our business and for ease
In engendering, where God we don't displease.
Why should men otherwise in their books set
It down that man should yield his wife her debt?   130
Now how to her should he make his payment,
Unless he'd used his silly instrument?
Thus, they were bestowed upon a creature
To purge urine, and so we could engender.

  But I don't say that each one's obligated,   135
Who has the harness that I've just related,
To go and use it for engendering.
Then for chastity, men wouldn't care a thing.
Christ was a maiden and shaped like a man,
And many saints, since first the world began;   140

Yet lived they evere in parfit chastitee.

I nil envye no virginitee:

Lat hem be breed of pured whete-seed,

And lat us wyves hoten barly-breed.

And yet with barly-breed, Mark telle can,   145

Oure Lord Jesu refresshed many a man.

In swich estaat as God hath cleped us

I wol persevere, I nam nat precious.

In wyfhode I wol use myn instrument

As frely as my Makere hath it sent.   150

If I be daungerous, God yeve me sorwe!

Myn housbond shal it have bothe eve and morwe,

Whan that him list com forth and paye his dette.

An housbonde I wol have, I wol nat lette,

Which shal be bothe my dettour and my thral,   155

And have his tribulacioun withal

Upon his flessh, whyl that I am his wyf.

I have the power duringe al my lyf

Upon his propre body, and noght he:

Right thus th' Apostel tolde it unto me,   160

And bad oure housbondes for to love us weel.

Al this sentence me lyketh every deel."

     Up sterte the Pardoner, and that anon.

"Now dame," quod he, "by God and by Seint John,

Ye been a noble prechour in this cas!   165

I was aboute to wedde a wyf. Allas,

What sholde I bye it on my flesh so dere?

Yet hadde I levere wedde no wyf to-yere!"

     "Abyde!" quod she, "my tale is nat bigonne.

Nay, thou shalt drinken of another tonne   170

Er that I go, shal savoure wors than ale.

And whan that I have told thee forth my tale

Of tribulacioun in mariage,

Of which I am expert in al myn age—

This to seyn, myself have been the whippe—   175

Than maystow chese whether thou wolt sippe

They lived forever in perfect chastity.
I won't envy any virginity.
Let them be bread of wheat that's been refined,
As barley bread, let us wives be defined;
And yet, with barley bread, as Mark can tell,   145
Our Lord has refreshed many men quite well.
In whatever rank God's called to us,
I'll persevere; I'm not fastidious.
In wifehood, I will use my instrument
As freely as my Maker has it sent.   150
If I'm aloof, then God send me dismay!
My husband can well have it, night and day,
When it pleases him to come and pay his debt.
A husband I will have—I won't stop yet—
Who shall be both my debtor and my slave,   155
With tribulation, unless he behaves,
Upon his flesh while I may be his wife.
I have the power, during all my life
Over his own body, and not he.
Thus the Apostle has told this to me,   160
And bade our husbands they should love us well.
This meaning, I like more than I can tell—"
        Up the Pardoner starts, immediately;
"Now, Madame, by God and Saint John," said he,
"You are a noble preacher on this strife.   165
Alas! I was about to wed a wife.
Why on my flesh now pay a price so dear?
I'd rather not wed any wife this year!"
        "Just wait! My tale is not begun," said she.
"No, you'll drink from another cask, you'll see,   170
Before I go, that will taste worse than ale.
And when I will have told you all my tale
Of the tribulation that's in marriage—
About which I'm an expert in my age—
That is to say that I have been the whip—   175
Then you can choose if you might want to sip

Of thilke tonne that I shal abroche.

Be war of it, er thou to ny approche,

For I shall telle ensamples mo than ten.

'Whoso that nil be war by othere men,   180

By him shul othere men corrected be.'

The same wordes wryteth Ptholomee:

Rede in his Almageste, and take it there."

        "Dame, I wolde praye yow, if youre wil it were,"

Seyde this Pardoner, "as ye bigan,   185

Telle forth youre tale, spareth for no man,

And teche us yonge men of youre praktike."

        "Gladly," quod she, "sith it may yow lyke.

But yet I praye to al this companye,

If that I speke after my fantasye,   190

As taketh not agrief of that I seye;

For myn entente nis but for to pleye.

        Now sires, now wol I telle forth my tale.

As evere mote I drinken wyn or ale,

I shal seye sooth, tho housbondes that I hadde,   195

As three of hem were gode and two were badde.

The three men were gode, and riche, and olde;

Unnethe mighte they the statut holde

In which that they were bounden unto me.

Ye woot wel what I mene of this, pardee!   200

As help me God, I laughe whan I thinke

How pitously a-night I made hem swinke,

And by my fey, I tolde of it no stoor.

They had me yeven hir lond and hir tresoor;

Me neded nat do lenger diligence   205

To winne hir love, or doon hem reverence.

They loved me so wel, by God above,

That I ne tolde no deyntee of hir love!

A wys womman wol bisye hire evere in oon

Out of the cask that I will open here.
Beware of it, before you come too near;
For I shall give examples, more than ten.
'Whoever won't be warned by other men,   180
By him will other men corrected be.'
Those same words were written by Ptolemy;[11]
Read his *Almageste*, and there you'll find it still."
        "Madame, I pray you, if it be your will,"
Said this Pardoner, "now as you began,   185
Tell forth your tale, and don't spare any man;
Teach us young men all about your practice."
        "Gladly," said she, "since you might well like this;
But yet I pray to all this company,
If I speak after my own fantasy,   190
Do not be aggrieved by what I say,
For my intent is only now to play.
        And now, sir, now I'll tell on with my tale.
As ever I might drink of wine or ale,
I'll tell the truth; those husbands that I had,   195
Some three of them were good, and two were bad.
The three who were good men were rich and old;
And so they barely could the statute hold
Through which they all had bound themselves to me.
By God, you know what I mean, certainly!   200
So help me God, I laugh to remember
How pitifully at night I made them labor!
In faith, I set no store by their pleasure.
To me, they had given land and treasure;
No longer need I use my diligence   205
To win their love or do them reverence.
They loved me so well that, by God above,
I set no value then upon their love!
A wise woman will be the busy one

11 **Ptolemy**: the second-century astronomer and mathematician. His work *The Almageste* was
mistakenly believed to contain, in addition to its astrological lore, a collection of proverbs.

To gete hire love, ye, ther as she hath noon.   210
But sith I hadde hem hoolly in myn hond,
And sith they hadde me yeven all hir lond,
What sholde I taken keep hem for to plese,
But it were for my profit and myn ese?
I sette hem so a-werke, by my fey,   215
That many a night they songen 'weilawey!'
The bacoun was nat fet for hem, I trowe,
That som men han in Essex at Dunmowe.
I governed hem so wel after my lawe
That ech of hem ful blisful was and fawe   220
To bringe me gaye thinges fro the fayre.
They were ful glad whan I spak to hem fayre,
For God it woot, I chidde hem spitously.
        Now herkneth how I bar me proprely:
Ye wyse wyves, that can understonde,   225
Thus shul ye speke and bere hem wrong on honde,
For half so boldely can ther no man
Swere and lyen as a womman can.
I sey nat this by wyves that ben wyse,
But if it be whan they hem misavyse.   230
A wys wyf, if that she can hir good,
Shal beren him on hond the cow is wood,
And take witnesse of hir owene mayde
Of hir assent. But herkneth how I sayde:
        'Sire olde kaynard, is this thyn array?   235
Why is my neighebores wyf so gay?
She is honoured over al ther she goth:
I sitte at hoom, I have no thrifty cloth.
What dostow at my neighebores hous?
Is she so fair? artow so amorous?   240

To get herself love, yes, where she has none.   210
But since I had them wholly in my hand,
And since to me they'd given all their land,
Why should I take care that I should them please
Unless it were for my profit and my ease?
I set them so to hard work, by my lights,   215
That they sung 'Wey-la-way!' on many nights.
I don't think the bacon was meant for them now
That some men win in Essex at Dunmowe.[12]
I governed them so well, after my law,
That each of them was eager, as I saw,   220
To bring me home some gay things from the fair.
They were glad when my speech to them was fair;
I scolded them, as God knows, spitefully.

     Now, listen how I acted properly,
You wise wives, who can so well understand.   225
Thus should you accuse falsely, out of hand.
For half so boldly knows no living man
How to swear and lie just as a woman can.
This statement about wise wives, I don't make—
Unless it be when they've made some mistake.   230
A wise wife, who knows what's good for her,
Will swear the tattling crow[13] is mad for sure,
And make sure that her maid has assented
As her witness. But hear now what I said:

     'Sir old dotard, is this your array?   235
Why is it that my neighbor's wife's so gay?
She is honored everywhere she goes;
I sit at home; I have no decent clothes.
What do you do at my neighbor's house there?
Are you so amorous? Is she so fair?   240

---

12   **the bacon ... Dunmowe:** A side of bacon was the prize given to the husband and wife who'd avoided quarreling for a year.

13   **tattling crow:** The talking crow who sees his mistress's transgressions and squeals about them. A proverbial figure also found in Ovid and at the center of the plot in Chaucer's *Manciple's Tale*.

What rowne ye with oure mayde? *benedicite!*
Sire olde lechour, lat thy japes be!
And if I have a gossib or a freend,
Withouten gilt, thou chydest as a feend,
If that I walke or pleye unto his hous!   245
Thou comest hoom as dronken as a mous,
And prechest on thy bench, with yvel preef!
Thou seist to me, it is a greet meschief
To wedde a povre womman, for costage.
And if that she be riche, of heigh parage,   250
Thanne seistow that it is a tormentrye
To suffre hire pryde and hire malencolye.
And if that she be fair, thou verray knave,
Thou seyst that every holour wol hire have:
She may no whyle in chastitee abyde   255
That is assailled upon ech a syde.

     Thou seyst som folk desyren us for richesse,
Somme for oure shap, and somme for oure fairnesse,
And som for she can outher singe or daunce,
And som for gentillesse and daliaunce,   260
Som for hir handes and hir armes smale;
Thus goth al to the devel, by thy tale.
Thou seyst men may nat kepe a castel wal,
It may so longe assailled been over al.

     And if that she be foul, thou seist that she   265
Coveiteth every man that she may se;
For as a spaynel she wol on him lepe,
Til that she finde som man hire to chepe.
Ne noon so grey goos goth ther in the lake
As, seistow, that wol been withoute make.   270
And seyst, it is an hard thing for to welde
A thing that no man wol, his thankes, helde.
Thus seistow, lorel, whan thow goost to bedde,
And that no wys man nedeth for to wedde,
Ne no man that entendeth unto hevene.   275
With wilde thonder-dint and firy levene

What do you whisper to our maid? Bless me!

Sir old lecher, now let your jokes be!

If, without guilt, I have a chum or friend,

Just like a fiend, you scold me without end

If I should play or walk down to his house!   245

But you come home as drunken as a mouse,

And then preach from your bench, no proof from you!

And it's great mischief, as you tell me too,

A poor woman to wed, for the expense;

If she's rich and born to lofty parents,   250

Then you say that a torment it will be

To bear her pride and sullen melancholy.

And if she should be fair, you horrid cur,

You say every lecher soon will have her;

For she can't long in chastity abide,   255

Who is always assailed on every side.

      You say some folk want us for our richness,

Some for our figure, and some for our fairness,

Some because she can either dance or sing,

Some for gentility and socializing;   260

And some because their hands and arms are small;

By your lights, to the devil thus goes all.

You say men can't defend a castle wall

When it's so long assailed by large and small.

      And if she should be ugly, you say she   265

Will covet every man that she may see,

For like a spaniel, she will on him leap

Until she finds a man to buy her cheap.

No goose goes out there on the lake so gray

That she will be without a mate, you say.   270

You say it's hard for men to have controlled

A thing that no man willingly would hold.

Thus you say, scoundrel, when you go to bed,

That no wise man has any need to wed,

Nor one who toward heaven would aspire.   275

With wild thunder claps and lightning's fire

Mote thy welked nekke be to-broke!
    Thow seyst that dropping houses and eek smoke
And chyding wyves maken men to flee
Out of hir owene hous; a, *benedicite!*   280
What eyleth swich an old man for to chyde?
Thow seyst we wyves wol oure vyces hyde
Til we be fast, and thanne we wol hem shewe—
Wel may that be a proverbe of a shrewe!
    Thou seist that oxen, asses, hors, and houndes,   285
They been assayed at diverse stoundes;
Bacins, lavours, er that men hem bye,
Spones and stoles, and al swich housbondrye,
And so been pottes, clothes, and array;
But folk of wyves maken noon assay   290
Til they be wedded. Olde dotard shrewe!
And thanne, seistow, we wol oure vices shewe.
    Thou seist also that it displeseth me
But if that thou wolt preyse my beautee,
And but thou poure alwey upon my face,   295
And clepe me "faire dame" in every place;
And but thou make a feste on thilke day
That I was born, and make me fresh and gay,
And but thou do to my norice honour,
And to my chamberere withinne my bour,   300
And to my fadres folk and his allyes—
Thus seistow, olde barel ful of lyes!
    And yet of oure apprentice Janekyn,
For his crispe heer, shyninge as gold so fyn,
And for he squiereth me bothe up and doun,   305
Yet hastow caught a fals suspecioun.
I wol hym noght, thogh thou were deed tomorwe.

May your old withered neck break right in two!
    You say that leaky houses, and smoke too,
And scolding wives all cause a man to flee
Out of his own house; ah now, God bless me!   280
What can ail such an old man, who must chide?
You say that we wives will our vices hide
Till we're hitched, and then we show them to you—
Well may that be the proverb of a shrew!
    You say horses, hounds, asses, and oxen   285
At different times can be tried out by men;
Wash bowls and basins, spoons and stools, you say,
All household things men try before they pay;
The same thing goes for clothes and gear and pots;
But to try out a wife, a man may not   290
Till they are wedded—you old dotard shrew!—
And then we show our vices, so say you.
    You say also that it displeases me
Unless you will always praise my beauty,
Or else always pore over my face,   295
And call me "Fair Madame" in every place.
Unless you make a feast upon the day
That I was born, and dress me fresh and gay;
Unless to my nurse,[14] you do all honor,
And to the chambermaid within my bower,   300
And to my father's folk and kin all day—
Old barrelful of lies, all this you say!
    Yet of Jenkin, who is our apprentice,
Whose curly hair shines just like gold—for this,
And because he will squire me around,   305
A cause for false suspicions, you have found.
I don't want him, though you should die tomorrow!

---

14 **nurse:** Although the Wife and Shakespeare's Juliet are of different classes (Juliet is an aristo-
crat, while the Wife is middle class), we should construe "nurse" here to be a figure like Juliet's "nurse":
in other words, an older woman who may once have been a wetnurse but has subsequently become a
close companion since the younger person's childhood.

But tel me this, why hydestow, with sorwe,
The keyes of thy cheste awey fro me?
It is my good as wel as thyn, pardee.   310
What, wenestow make an idiot of oure dame?
Now by that lord that called is Seint Jame,
Thou shalt nat bothe, thogh that thou were wood,
Be maister of my body and of my good;
That oon thou shalt forgo, maugree thyne yën;   315
What helpith thee of me to enquere or spyën?
I trowe, thou woldest loke me in thy chiste!
Thou sholdest seye, "Wyf, go wher thee liste;
Tak your disport, I wol nat leve no talis.
I knowe yow for a trewe wyf, dame Alis."   320
We love no man that taketh kepe or charge
Wher that we goon; we wol ben at oure large.
     Of alle men y-blessed moot he be,
The wyse astrologien Daun Ptholome,
That seith this proverbe in his Almageste   325
 "Of alle men his wisdom is the hyeste,
That rekketh nevere who hath the world in honde."
By this proverbe thou shalt understonde,
Have thou ynogh, what thar thee recche or care
How merily that othere folkes fare?   330
For certeyn, olde dotard, by youre leve,
Ye shul have queynte right ynough at eve.
He is to greet a nigard that wol werne
A man to lighte a candle at his lanterne;
He shal have never the lasse light, pardee.   335
Have thou ynough, thee thar nat pleyne thee.
     Thou seyst also that if we make us gay
With clothing and with precious array,
That it is peril of oure chastitee;
And yet, with sorwe, thou most enforce thee,   340
And seye thise wordes in th'Apostles name:

Tell me: why do you hide, to my sorrow,
The keys now of your chest away from me?
They are my goods as well as yours, bless me!   310
Will you make an idiot of your dame?
Now, by that good lord who is called Saint James,
You will not, though it might make you crazy,
Be master of both my goods and body;
One of them you'll forgo, to spite your eyes.   315
What good is it to ask around and spy?
I think you want to lock me in your chest!
You should say, "Wife, go where you think is best;
Enjoy yourself; I'll believe no tales of this.
I know you for my own true wife, Dame Alice."   320
We love no man who will take heed or charge
Of where we go; we want to be at large.

     And of all men, quite blessèd must he be,
That wise astrologer, Don Ptolemy,
Who says this proverb in his *Almageste*,[15]   325
"Of all men, his wisdom is the highest
Who never cares who holds the world in hand."
By this proverb, you should well understand,
If you have enough, why then should you care
How merrily some other folks might fare?   330
For certainly, old dotard, by your leave,
You'll have some quaint things sure enough come eve.
He is too great a niggard who would spurn
A man to light a candle at his lantern;
By God, from that, he doesn't have less light.   335
If you've enough, complaining isn't right.

     You also say if we make ourselves gay
With our clothing and with precious array,
That it is peril to our chastity;
Woe to you—you then enforce it for me,   340
And say these words in the Apostle's name:

15 *Almageste*: Again, this proverb is not found in Ptolemy's work.

"In habit maad with chastitee and shame,
Ye wommen shul apparaille yow," quod he,
"And noght in tressed heer and gay perree,
As perles, ne with gold, ne clothes riche."   345
After thy text, ne after thy rubriche
I wol nat wirche as muchel as a gnat.
        Thou seydest this, that I was lyk a cat:
For whoso wolde senge a cattes skin,
Thanne wolde the cat wel dwellen in his in;   350
And if the cattes skin be slyk and gay,
She wol nat dwelle in house half a day,
But forth she wole, er any day be dawed,
To shewe hir skin and goon a-caterwawed.
This is to seye, if I be gay, sire shrewe,   355
I wol renne out, my borel for to shewe.
        Sire olde fool, what helpeth thee to spyën?
Thogh thou preye Argus, with his hundred yën,
To be my warde-cors, as he can best,
In feith, he shal nat kepe me but me lest;   360
Yet coude I make his berd, so moot I thee.
        Thou seydest eek that ther ben thinges three,
The whiche thinges troublen al this erthe,
And that no wight ne may endure the ferthe.
O leve sire shrewe, Jesu shorte thy lyf!   365
Yet prechestow and seyst an hateful wyf
Y-rekened is for oon of thise meschances.
Been ther none othere maner resemblances
That ye may lykne youre parables to,
But if a sely wyf be oon of tho?   370
        Thou lykenest eek wommanes love to helle,
To bareyne lond, ther water may not dwelle;

"In clothing made from chastity and shame
You women all should dress yourselves," said he,
"Not with well-coifed hair and with gay jewelry,
Not with rich clothes, with pearls, or else with gold."   345
With your text and your rubric,[16] I don't hold,
Or follow them as much as would a gnat.

    You said this: that I was just like a cat;
Whoever wanted to singe a cat's skin
He could be sure the cat would then stay in;   350
And if the cat's skin were so sleek and gay,
She'd not stay in the house for half a day;
Forth she'd go, before the day was dawning,
To show her skin and to go caterwauling.
That is to say, if I am gay, sir shrew,   355
I'll run to put my poor old clothes on view.

    Sir old fool, what help is it if you spy?
Though you prayed Argus[17] with his hundred eyes
To be my bodyguard, as he'd know best,
He'd not guard me till I let him, I'll be blessed.   360
I'd hoodwink him, as I am prospering!

    Yet you also say that there are three things,
And that these same things trouble all this earth,
And that no man might yet endure the fourth.
Oh, dear sir shrew, Jesus shorten your life!   365
Yet you will preach and say a hateful wife
Is one of these misfortunes that you reckon.
Aren't there other kinds of comparison
That, for all your parables, you could use,
Unless a poor wife were the one you'd choose?   370

    You liken, too, a woman's love to hell,
To barren land where water may not dwell.

---

16 **rubric:** Refers here either to the red letters that began sections of medieval manuscripts or to words written in red in manuscripts to signify their importance.

17 **Argus:** Argus was a mythological character who had one hundred eyes, the better to guard Zeus's lover, Io. Mercury had to put all the eyes to sleep before he could kill this monster.

Thou lyknest it also to wilde fyr.
The more it brenneth, the more it hath desyr
To consume every thing that brent wol be.   375
Thou seyst that right as wormes shende a tree,
Right so a wyf destroyeth hire housbonde;
This knowe they that been to wyves bonde.'
        Lordinges, right thus, as ye have understonde,
Bar I stifly myne olde housbondes on honde   380
That thus they seyden in hir dronkenesse;
And al was fals, but that I took witnesse
On Janekin and on my nece also.
O Lord, the peyne I dide hem and the wo,
Ful giltelees, by Goddes swete pyne!   385
For as an hors I coude byte and whyne.
I coude pleyne, thogh I were in the gilt,
Or elles often tyme hadde I ben spilt.
Whoso that first to mille comth, first grint.
I pleyned first: so was oure werre y-stint.   390
They were ful glad to excusen hem ful blyve
Of thing of which they nevere agilte hir lyve.
Of wenches wolde I beren hem on honde,
Whan that for syk unnethes mighte they stonde.
        Yet tikled I his herte, for that he   395
Wende that I hadde of him so greet chiertee.
I swoor that al my walkinge out by nighte
Was for t'espye wenches that he dighte.
Under that colour hadde I many a mirthe,
For al swich wit is yeven us in oure birthe.   400
Deceite, weping, spinning God hath yive
To wommen kindely whyl they may live.
And thus of o thing I avaunte me:
Atte ende I hadde the bettre in ech degree,
By sleighte, or force, or by som maner thing,   405
As by continuel murmur or grucching.
Namely abedde hadden they meschaunce:
Ther wolde I chyde and do hem no plesaunce;

You liken it also to a wild fire;
The more it burns, the more it has desire
To consume everything that burned will be.   375
You say that just as worms destroy a tree,
A wife destroys her husband, you have found;
This, they well know who to wives have been bound.'
      My lords, right thus, as you can understand,
I stiffly kept my old husbands in hand   380
And swore they said thus in their drunkenness;
And all was false; except I took witness
On Jenkin there, and on my niece, also.
Oh Lord! The pain I did them and the woe.
And, by God's sweet pain, they were not guilty!   385
For, like a horse, I could bite and whinny.
I knew how to complain well even when
I had the guilt, or I'd been ruined then.
Whoever comes first to the mill, first grinds;
Complaining first, our war stopped, I did find.   390
They were glad to excuse themselves quite quickly
For things of which they never had been guilty.
Of wenches, I'd accuse them out of hand
When, in their sickness, they could hardly stand.
      Yet it tickled his heart, because then he   395
Thought that I had for him such great fancy!
I swore that all my walking out at night
Was to spy on wenches he was holding tight;
Using that cover, I enjoyed much mirth.
For all such wit is given us at birth;   400
Deceit, weeping, and spinning God did give
To women by nature, all the time they live.
And thus of one thing, I can surely boast:
In the end, I'm the one who won the most
By tricks or force or by some other thing   405
As much as constant grumbling and grousing.
Namely, then, they would have bad luck in bed:
I did them no pleasure, and I chided;

I wolde no lenger in the bed abyde,

If that I felte his arm over my syde,   410

Til he had maad his raunson unto me;

Thanne wolde I suffre him do his nycetee.

And therfore every man this tale I telle,

Winne whoso may, for al is for to selle.

With empty hand men may none haukes lure.   415

For winning wolde I al his lust endure,

And make me a feyned appetyt—

And yet in bacon hadde I nevere delyt.

That made me that evere I wolde hem chyde.

For thogh the Pope had seten hem biside,   420

I wolde nat spare hem at hir owene bord.

For by my trouthe, I quitte hem word for word.

As help me verray God omnipotent,

Thogh I right now sholde make my testament,

I ne owe hem nat a word that it nis quit.   425

I broghte it so aboute, by my wit,

That they moste yeve it up, as for the beste,

Or elles hadde we nevere been in reste.

For thogh he loked as a wood leoun,

Yet sholde he faille of his conclusioun.   430

        Thanne wolde I seye, 'Godelief, tak keep

How mekely loketh Wilkin oure sheep!

Com neer, my spouse, lat me ba thy cheke!

Ye sholde been al pacient and meke,

And han a swete spyced conscience,   435

Sith ye so preche of Jobes pacience.

Suffreth alwey, sin ye so wel can preche;

And but ye do, certein we shal yow teche

That it is fair to have a wyf in pees.

Oon of us two moste bowen, doutelees,   440

And sith a man is more resonable

I would no longer in the bed abide,
If I felt his arm come over my side,   410
Till he had paid his ransom down to me;
Then I'd suffer him to do his foolery.
Therefore, to every man this tale I tell:
Win whoso may, for all is there to sell;
With empty hands men may no hawks then lure.   415
For profit, I would all their lust endure,
And I would fake it with feigned appetite;
And yet in bacon,[18] I had no delight.
That was the reason I would always chide them,
For though the pope were sitting right beside them,   420
At their own table, I would never spare.
In truth, I repaid them word for word there.
So help me, oh true God omnipotent,
If now I made my will and testament,
There was not one unpaid word I did owe.   425
By my own wit, I brought it all about so
That they must give it up, and for the best,
Or otherwise, we never would have rest;
Though he looked as crazy as a lion,
He would fail at gaining his conclusion.   430
          Then I would say to him, 'Sweetheart, take heed—
See how meek our sheep Willie looks, indeed!
Come near, my spouse, and let me kiss your cheek!
Truly you should be all patient and meek,
And have, too, a carefully spiced conscience,   435
Since you always preach about Job's patience.
Suffer always, since you can so well preach;
Unless you do, for sure we shall you teach
That it's nice to have a wife in peace now.
Doubtless, one of the two of us must bow,   440
And so, since man is more reasonable

---

18 **bacon:** Perhaps a reference to the prize at Dunmow, but as preserved, salted meat, also a
sexual double entendre.

Than womman is, ye moste been suffrable.
What eyleth yow to grucche thus and grone?
Is it for ye wolde have my queynte allone?
Why taak it al! lo, have it every-deel!   445
Peter! I shrewe yow but ye love it weel!
For if I wolde selle my *bele chose*,
I coude walke as fresh as is a rose;
But I wol kepe it for your owene tooth.
Ye be to blame. By God, I sey yow sooth.'   450
Swiche manere wordes hadde we on honde.
Now wol I speken of my fourthe housbonde.

　　　My fourthe housebonde was a revelour—
This is to seyn, he hadde a paramour—
And I was yong and ful of ragerye,   455
Stiborn and strong, and joly as a pye.
Wel coude I daunce to an harpe smale,
And singe, ywis, as any nightingale,
Whan I had dronke a draughte of swete wyn.
Metellius, the foule cherl, the swyn,   460
That with a staf birafte his wyf hir lyf
For she drank wyn, thogh I hadde been his wyf,
He sholde nat han daunted me fro drinke!
And after wyn on Venus moste I thinke,
For al so siker as cold engendreth hayl,   465
A likerous mouth moste han a likerous tayl.
In wommen vinolent is no defence—
This knowen lechours by experience.

　　　But, Lord Crist! whan that it remembreth me
Upon my yowthe, and on my jolitee,   470
It tikleth me aboute myn herte rote.
Unto this day it dooth myn herte bote

Than woman, to suffer you are able.
What ails you now that thus you grouse and groan?
Do you just want my quaint thing for your own?
Why, take it all! Lo, have it through and through!   445
You love it well, by Peter,[19] curse on you;
For if I wanted to sell my *belle chose*,[20]
Then I could walk as fresh as is a rose;
But I will keep it just for your own tooth.
You are to blame, by God! I tell the truth.'   450
These are the kinds of words I had on hand.
And now I will speak of my fourth husband.

        My fourth husband was a reveler—
That is to say, he had a paramour—
And young and full of wantonness was I,   455
Stubborn, strong and jolly as a magpie.
How I'd dance when the small harp was playing;
Like a nightingale's was all my singing,
When I had drunk my draught of fine sweet wine!
Metellius,[21] the foul churl, the swine,   460
Who, with a staff, bereft his wife of life,
Because she drank wine, if I were his wife,
He wouldn't frighten me away from drink!
And after wine, on Venus I must think,
For just as sure as cold engenders hail,   465
A lecherous mouth must have lecherous tail.
In wine-drunk women, there is no defence—
This, lechers know from their experience.

        But—Lord Christ!—when memories come back to me,
About my youth and all my jollity,   470
It tickles me right down to my heart's root.
To this day, it does my heart good, to boot,

19 **Peter**: Saint Peter, but perhaps also perhaps a double entendre on the male sex organ.
20 *belle chose*: Literally, "pretty thing," an obvious euphemism.
21 **Metellius**: The husband in a common exemplum from a compendium of anecdotes assembled
by Valerius Maximus (first century); it was a popular medieval schoolbook.

That I have had my world as in my tyme.
But age, allas! that al wol envenyme,
Hath me biraft my beautee and my pith.   475
Lat go, farewel! the devel go therwith!
The flour is goon, ther is namore to telle:
The bren, as I best can, now moste I selle;
But yet to be right mery wol I fonde.
Now wol I tellen of my fourthe housbonde.   480
        I seye, I hadde in herte greet despyt
That he of any other had delyt.
But he was quit, by God and by Seint Joce!
I made him of the same wode a croce—
Nat of my body in no foul manere,   485
But certeinly, I made folk swich chere
That in his owene grece I made him frye
For angre and for verray jalousye.
By God, in erthe I was his purgatorie,
For which I hope his soule be in glorie.   490
For God it woot, he sat ful ofte and song
Whan that his shoo ful bitterly him wrong.
Ther was no wight, save God and he, that wiste
In many wyse how sore I him twiste.
He deyde whan I cam fro Jerusalem,   495
And lyth y-grave under the rode-beem,
Al is his tombe noght so curious
As was the sepulcre of him Darius,
Which that Appelles wroghte subtilly;
It nis but wast to burie him preciously.   500
Lat him farewel, God yeve his soule reste!

That I have had my world right in my time.
But age, alas, that poisons what is prime,
Has bereft me of my beauty and my pith.   475
Let it go. Farewell! The devil go therewith!
The flower's gone; there is no more to tell;
The bran, as I best can, now must I sell;
But yet to be right merry I have planned.
And now I will tell of my fourth husband.   480
        I say, I had in my heart a great spite
That he in any other took delight.
By God and Saint Judocus,²² he's repaid!
Of the same wood, a cross for him I made;
Not in a foul manner with my body,   485
But I made folks such cheer that certainly
I made him fry enough in his own grease
Because his jealous anger would not cease.
By God, on earth I was his purgatory,
For which, I hope his soul will be in glory.   490
God knows, he often sat and sang "Alack"
When his shoe so bitterly pinched him back.
There was no man who knew, save God and he,
In what ways I twisted him so sorely.
When I came from Jerusalem,²³ he died;   495
Buried beneath the cross's beam,²⁴ he lies.
His tomb is not fancy or curious
As was the sepulcher of Darius,²⁵
Which Appelles²⁶ had formed so skillfully;
A waste to bury him expensively.   500
Let him fare well. God rest his soul, I ask it!

22 **Saint Judocus:** Also known as Saint Josse, a Breton saint whose sign was the pilgrim's staff.
23 **Jerusalem:** The Wife is a great fan of making pilgrimages, and the one to Jerusalem was the most venerated, and also, for an English person in the fourteenth century, the most difficult to make.
24 **cross's beam:** He is buried inside the church, under a beam bearing the crucifix.
25 **Darius:** King of ancient Persia.
26 **Appelles:** Jewish craftsman credited with allegedly building Darius's elaborate tomb (sixth century).

He is now in the grave and in his cheste.

      Now of my fifthe housbond wol I telle—

God lete his soule nevere come in helle!

And yet was he to me the moste shrewe.   505

That fele I on my ribbes al by rewe,

And evere shal unto myn ending day.

But in oure bed he was so fresh and gay,

And therwithal so wel coude he me glose

Whan that he wolde han my *bele chose*,   510

That thogh he hadde me bet on every boon,

He coude winne agayn my love anoon.

I trowe I loved him beste for that he

Was of his love daungerous to me.

We wommen han, if that I shal nat lye,   515

In this matere a queynte fantasye:

Wayte what thing we may nat lightly have,

Thereafter wol we crye al day and crave.

Forbede us thing, and that desyren we;

Prees on us faste, and thanne wol we flee.   520

With daunger oute we al oure chaffare:

Greet prees at market maketh dere ware,

And to greet cheep is holde at litel prys.

This knoweth every womman that is wys.

      My fifthe housbonde, God his soule blesse!   525

Which that I took for love and no richesse,

He som tyme was a clerk of Oxenford,

And had left scole, and wente at hoom to bord

With my gossib, dwellinge in oure toun—

God have hir soule! hir name was Alisoun.   530

She knew myn herte and eek my privetee

Bet than oure parisshe preest, so moot I thee!

To hire biwreyed I my conseil al,

For had myn housebonde pissed on a wal,

Or doon a thing that sholde han cost his lyf,   535

To hire and to another worthy wyf,

And to my nece, which that I loved weel,

He is now in his grave and in his casket.
      Now of my fifth husband I will tell.
May God let his soul never go to hell!
Yet to me he was the biggest scoundrel;   505
On my whole row of ribs, I feel it still,
And ever shall until my dying day.
But in our bed, he was so fresh and gay,
And he knew so well just how to gloss me
When he wanted my *belle chose*, as you'll see;   510
Although he'd beaten me on every bone,
Quickly he'd win back my love for his own.
I believe that I loved him best since he
Could be standoffish with his love for me.
We women have, and no lie this will be,   515
In this matter, our own quaint fantasy:
Whatever thing won't lightly come our way,
Then after it we'll cry and crave all day.
Forbid us something, and that desire we;
Press on us fast, and then we're sure to flee.   520
With standoffishness, we spread out all our wares;
Great crowds at market make the goods dear there,
Too great a bargain isn't thought a prize;
And this knows every woman who is wise.
      My fifth husband—now God his soul should bless—   525
Whom I took for love and not for richness,
Formerly, he was a clerk at Oxford,
And had left school, and went back home to board
With my close friend who in our town did dwell.
God save her! Her name's Alison, as well.   530
She knew both my heart and my privacy
More than our parish priest did, so help me!
With her, I shared my secrets one and all.
For had my husband pissed upon a wall,
Or done a thing that should have cost his life,   535
To her and to another worthy wife,
And to my niece, whom I did love so well,

I wolde han told his conseil every deel.
And so I dide ful often, God it woot,
That made his face ful often reed and hoot   540
For verray shame, and blamed himself for he
Had told to me so greet a privetee.

      And so bifel that ones in a Lente—
So often tymes I to my gossib wente,
For evere yet I lovede to be gay,   545
And for to walke in March, Averille, and May,
Fro hous to hous, to here sondry talis—
That Jankin clerk and my gossib dame Alis
And I myself into the feldes wente.
Myn housbond was at London al that Lente: 550
I hadde the bettre leyser for to pleye,
And for to see, and eek for to be seye
Of lusty folk. What wiste I wher my grace
Was shapen for to be, or in what place?
Therefore I made my visitaciouns,   555
To vigilies and to processiouns,
To preching eek and to thise pilgrimages,
To pleyes of miracles, and mariages,
And wered upon my gaye scarlet gytes.
Thise wormes, ne thise motthes, ne thise mytes,   560
Upon my peril, frete hem never a deel;
And wostow why? for they were used weel.

      Now wol I tellen forth what happed me.
I seye that in the feeldes walked we,
Til trewely we hadde swich daliance,   565
This clerk and I, that of my purveyance
I spak to him and seyde him how that he,
If I were widwe, sholde wedde me.
For certeinly, I sey for no bobance,

All of his secrets I'd be sure to tell.
God knows too that I did this quite often
So I made his face both red and hot then   540
From shame itself. He blamed himself that he
Had ever shared with me his privacy.
      And so it happened that one time in Lent—
For often times to my close friend I went,
Because I always did love being gay,   545
And to walk out in March, April, and May,
From house to house, and sundry tales to hear—
Jenkin the clerk, Alison, my friend dear,
And I myself, into the fields all went.
My husband was at London all that Lent;   550
More leisure for my playing, I then had,
To see and to be seen (and I was glad)
By lusty folks. Did I know where good grace
Was destined to find me, or in what place?
Therefore, I made all my visitations   555
To vigils and also to processions,
To preachings and to these pilgrimages,
To miracle plays²⁷ and to marriages,
And always wore my gowns of scarlet bright.
Neither the worms nor moths nor any mites,   560
On my soul's peril, had my gowns abused.
Do you know why? Because they were well used.
      Now I'll tell you what happened then to me.
I say that out into the fields walked we,
Till truly, we had such a flirtation,   565
This clerk and I, that I made due provision
And spoke to him, and said to him how he,
Were I a widow, should be wed to me.
For certainly—and I'm not boasting here—

---

27 **miracle plays**: A medieval dramatic form, performed generally on religious holidays, which
were festive public occasions. As their name suggests, they were focused on religious topics, but they
could also at times be humorous in their representations of the foibles of their characters.

Yet was I nevere withouten purveyance   570
Of mariage, n'of othere thinges eek.
I holde a mouses herte nat worth a leek
That hath but oon hole for to sterte to,
And if that faille, thanne is al y-do.
          I bar him on honde he hadde enchanted me—   575
My dame taughte me that soutiltee—
And eek I seyde I mette of him al night:
He wolde han slayn me as I lay upright,
And al my bed was ful of verray blood;
But yet I hope that he shal do me good,   580
For blood bitokeneth gold, as me was taught.
And al was fals—I dremed of it right naught,
But as I folwed ay my dames lore
As wel of this as of othere thinges more.
          But now sire, lat me see, what I shal seyn?   585
Aha! by God, I have my tale ageyn.
          Whan that my fourthe housbond was on bere,
I weep algate, and made sory chere
As wyves moten, for it is usage,
And with my coverchief covered my visage;   590
But for that I was purveyed of a make,
I wepte but smal, and that I undertake.
          To chirche was myn housbond born a-morwe
With neighebores, that for him maden sorwe;
And Jankin oure clerk was oon of tho.   595
As help me God! whan that I saugh him go
After the bere, me thoughte he hadde a paire
Of legges and of feet so clene and faire,
That al myn herte I yaf unto his hold.
He was, I trowe, twenty winter old,   600
And I was fourty, if I shal seye sooth;
But yet I hadde alwey a coltes tooth.

I have not ever lacked provisions clear   570
For marriage, or for such things, so to speak.
I hold a mouse's heart not worth a leek
Who's only got one hole where it can run,
And if that fails, then everything is done.
     I made him think he had enchanted me—   575
My mother taught me all that subtlety—
And said I had dreamed this of him all night:
As I lay on my back, he'd slain me quite,
And I dreamed full of blood then was my bed;
'But yet I hope you'll do me good,' I said,   580
'For blood betokens gold, as was taught me.'
And all was false; I had no dream, you see,
But I always followed my mother's lore,
In this as well as other things before.
     But now, sirs, let's see what I shall say then.   585
Aha! By God, I've got my tale again.
     When my fourth husband lay up on his bier,
I wept quite long and made a sorry cheer,
As wives must, for it is common usage.
With my coverchief, I hid my visage,   590
But since I was provided with my next mate,
I didn't weep much—this to you I'll state.
     To church was my husband borne next morning
With the neighbors, who for him were mourning;
And there Jenkin, our clerk, was one of those.   595
So help me God, when I saw how he goes
Behind the bier, I thought he had a pair
Of legs and feet that were so clean and fair,
I gave him all my heart for him to hold.
He was, I think, just twenty winters old,   600
And I was forty, if I tell the truth;
But yet I always had a coltish tooth

Gat-tothed I was, and that bicam me weel;

I hadde the prente of Seynte Venus seel.

As help me God, I was a lusty oon,   605

And faire, and riche, and yong, and wel bigoon;

And trewely, as myne housbondes tolde me,

I had the beste *quoniam* mighte be.

For certes, I am al Venerien

In felinge, and myn herte is Marcien: 610

Venus me yaf my lust, my likerousnesse,

And Mars yaf me my sturdy hardinesse;

Myn ascendent was Taur, and Mars therinne.

Allas! allas! that evere love was sinne!

I folwed ay myn inclinacioun   615

By vertu of my constellacioun;

That made me I coude noght withdrawe

My chambre of Venus from a good felawe.

Yet have I Martes mark upon my face,

And also in another privee place.   620

For, God so wis be my savacioun,

I ne loved nevere by no discrecioun,

But evere folwede myn appetyt:

Al were he short or long, or blak or whyt,

I took no kepe, so that he lyked me,   625

How pore he was, ne eek of what degree.

　　　What sholde I seye but, at the monthes ende,

This joly clerk Jankin, that was so hende,

Hath wedded me with greet solempnitee,

Gap toothed[28] was I, and that became me well;
With Venus's seal[29] I'm printed, I can tell.
So help me God, I was a lusty one, 605
And fair and rich and young and well begun,
And truly, as my husbands all told me,
I had the best *quoniam*[30] there might be.
For certainly, I'm all Venerian
In feeling, and my heart is Martian. 610
Venus gave me my love and lecherousness,
And Mars gave me my sturdy hardiness;
My ascendant sign's Taurus, with Mars therein.
Alas! Alas! That ever love was sin!
I always followed my inclination 615
By virtue of my stars' constellation;
Thus I could not withdraw—I was made so—
My chamber of Venus from a good fellow.
Yet I have Mars's mark upon my face,
And also in another private place. 620
For as God so wise is my salvation,
I have never loved in moderation,
But I always followed my appetite,
Should he be long or short or black or white;
I took no heed, so long as he liked me, 625
Of how poor he was, or of what degree.
　　　What should I say, but at the month's end, he,
This pretty clerk, this Jenkin, so handy,[31]
Has wedded me with great solemnity,

---

28 **Gap toothed**: The Wife had a space between her teeth; this was considered a sign of being highly sexed in the Middle Ages.

29 **Venus's seal**: A birthmark. She says that her temperament can be understood because she was born under the warring zodiacal signs of Venus and Mars: Venus makes her interested in sex, and Mars gives her her bellicosity.

30 *quoniam*: In Latin, literally, "because" or "whereas." Used here as another euphemism for female genitals.

31 **handy**: Chaucer here uses the same adjective, *hende*, to describe Jenkin as he does to describe Nicholas in *The Miller's Tale*. It means simultaneously "handsome," "near-at-hand," "handy," and "grabby."

And to him yaf I al the lond and fee   630
That evere was me yeven therbifore.
But afterward repented me ful sore;
He nolde suffre nothing of my list.
By God, he smoot me ones on the list
For that I rente out of his book a leef,   635
That of the strook myn ere wex al deef.
Stiborn I was as is a leonesse,
And of my tonge a verray jangleresse,
And walke I wolde, as I had doon biforn,
From hous to hous, although he had it sworn.   640
For which he often tymes wolde preche,
And me of olde Romayn gestes teche,
How he Simplicius Gallus lefte his wyf,
And hire forsook for terme of al his lyf,
Noght but for open-heveded he hir say   645
Lokinge out at his dore upon a day.
            Another Romayn tolde he me by name,
That, for his wyf was at a someres game
Withoute his witing, he forsook hire eke.
And thanne wolde he upon his Bible seke   650
That ilke proverbe of Ecclesiaste
Wher he comandeth and forbedeth faste
Man shal nat suffre his wyf go roule aboute;
Thanne wolde he seye right thus, withouten doute:
            'Whoso that buildeth his hous al of salwes,   655
And priketh his blinde hors over the falwes,
And suffreth his wyf to go seken halwes,
Is worthy to been hanged on the galwes!'
But al for noght; I sette noght an hawe
Of his proverbes n'of his olde sawe,   660

And I gave him all the land and property   630
That ever had been given me before.
But after, I was made to rue that sore;
My desires he would not suffer to hear.
By God, he hit me once upon the ear,
Because, out of his book, a leaf I rent,   635
And from that stroke, my ear all deaf then went.
But, like a lionness, I was stubborn,
And with my tongue, I was a jangler³² born,
And I would walk around, as I once did,
From house to house, although he did forbid;   640
Because of this, quite often he would preach,
And from old Roman stories, he would teach;
How one Simplicius Gallus³³ left his wife,
And her forsook for the rest of his life,
Because one day, and for no reason more,   645
Bareheaded she was looking out the door.
          Another Roman he told me by name,
Who, since his wife was at a summer's game
Without his knowledge, he then her forsook.
And then he would into his Bible look   650
For the proverb of Ecclesiasticus³⁴
Where he commands, and he does forbid thus:
That man shall not suffer wife to roam about.
Then would he say right thus, without a doubt:
          'Whoever builds his house up all from willow   655
And pricks his blind horse over fields so fallow,
And lets his wife go seeking shrines so hallowed,
Is worthy to be hanging on the gallows!'³⁵
But all for nought: I didn't give a straw
For all his old proverbs or for his saws,   660

32 **jangler**: Avid talker.
33 **Simplicius Gallus**: Another exemplum, also mentioned in Valerius Maximus.
34 **Ecclesiasticus**: An apocryphal book of the Bible, not to be confused with Ecclesiastes.
35 **"Whoever builds ... gallows"**: The Wife here is quoting from conventional misogynist lore.

Ne I wolde nat of him corrected be.
I hate him that my vices telleth me,
And so do mo, God woot, of us than I.
This made him with me wood al outrely:
I nolde noght forbere him in no cas.   665
　　　　Now wol I seye yow sooth, by Seint Thomas,
Why that I rente out of his book a leef,
For which he smoot me so that I was deef.
　　　　He hadde a book that gladly, night and day,
For his desport he wolde rede alway.   670
He cleped it Valerie and Theofraste,
At which book he lough alwey ful faste.
And eek ther was somtyme a clerk at Rome,
A cardinal, that highte Seint Jerome,
That made a book agayn Jovinian;   675
In which book eek ther was Tertulan,
Crisippus, Trotula, and Helowys,
That was abbesse nat fer fro Parys;
And eek the Parables of Salomon,
Ovydes Art, and bokes many on,   680
And alle thise were bounden in o volume.
And every night and day was his custume,
Whan he hadde leyser and vacacioun
From other worldly occupacioun,

Nor by him would I then corrected be.
I hate him who my vices tells to me,
And so do more of us, God knows, than me.
This drove him mad about me, utterly;
For I wouldn't bear with any of this.   665
　　　I'll tell you the truth now, by Saint Thomas,
Why once out of his book a leaf I rent,
For which he hit me so that deaf I went.
　　　He had a book that, gladly, night and day,
For his pleasure, he would be reading always;   670
It's called Valerius and Theophrastus;[36]
He always laughed as he read it to us.
And also there was once a clerk at Rome,
A cardinal, who was called Saint Jerome,[37]
Who made a book against Jovinian;[38]   675
In which book was also Tertullian,
Crisippus,[39] Trotula,[40] and Heloise,[41]
An abbess near to Paris, if you please,
And too the Parables of Solomon,
Ovid's Ars,[42] and more books, many a one,   680
And all of these in one volume were bound,
And every night and day, some time he found
When he had some leisure and vacation
From his other worldly occupation,

36 **Valerius and Theophrastus**: Two writers of texts against marriage. Jenkin's volume, his "book of wicked wives," whose contents the Wife describes in the following lines, is actually an anthology of antifeminist writings by various classical and Christian authors. Such anthologies were common in the Middle Ages; they may have served to promote celibacy among the clergy.

37 **Saint Jerome**: Church Father.

38 **Jovinian**: A monk whose ideas about marriage and virginity were more permissive than Jerome's.

39 **Tertullian, Crisippus**: Two misogynist writers.

40 **Trotula**: At the time, Trotula was believed to be an eleventh-century Italian woman physician who wrote a gynecological treatise; she has since been determined to be legendary.

41 **Heloise**: Abelard's lover who, in the twelfth century, became a famous abbess after his castration because of their love affair.

42 **Ovid's Ars**: The book on love, the Ars Amatoria, or Art of Love, by Ovid, the great first-century Roman poet, who was a central influence on Chaucer's writing.

To reden on this book of wikked wyves.   685
He knew of hem mo legendes and lyves
Than been of gode wyves in the Bible.
For trusteth wel, it is an impossible
That any clerk wol speke good of wyves,
But if it be of holy seintes lyves,   690
Ne of noon other womman never the mo.
Who peyntede the leoun, tel me, who?
By God, if wommen hadde writen stories,
As clerkes han withinne hir oratories,
They wolde han writen of men more wikkednesse   695
Than all the mark of Adam may redresse.
The children of Mercurie and of Venus
Been in hir wirking ful contrarious:
Mercurie loveth wisdom and science,
And Venus loveth ryot and dispence;   700
And, for hire diverse disposicioun,
Ech falleth in otheres exaltacioun,
And thus, God woot, Mercurie is desolat
In Pisces wher Venus is exaltat,
And Venus falleth ther Mercurie is reysed;   705
Therfore no womman of no clerk is preysed.
The clerk, whan he is old and may noght do
Of Venus werkes worth his olde sho—
Thanne sit he doun and writ in his dotage
That wommen can nat kepe hir mariage!   710
          But now to purpos why I tolde thee
That I was beten for a book, pardee.
Upon a night Jankin, that was our syre,
Redde on his book as he sat by the fyre
Of Eva first, that for hir wikkednesse   715
Was al mankinde broght to wrecchednesse,
For which that Jesu Crist himself was slayn,

To read then in this book of wicked wives.   685
He knew of them more legends and more lives
Then there are of good wives in the Bible.
For trust it well, it is impossible
For any clerk to speak some good of wives,
Unless he speaks about holy saints' lives: 690
This for no other women will he do.
Now who painted the lion, tell me who?
By God, if women had written stories,
Like clerks do within their oratories,
They would have written of men more wickedness   695
Than all the mark of Adam could redress.
The children of Venus and Mercury[43]
In their actions are always contrary;
Mercury loves both wisdom and science;
Venus, revelry and extravagance.   700
Because of their different dispositions,
Each falls in the other sign's exaltation.
And thus, God knows, Mercury's despondent
In Pisces, when Venus is ascendant,
And Venus falls where Mercury is raised.   705
Therefore, no woman by a clerk is praised.
The clerk, when he is old and may not do
Of Venus's work what's worth his old shoe,
Then he sits down and writes in his dotage
That women cannot keep up their marriage!   710
          But now to my purpose, why I told you
That I was beaten for a book, it's true!
One night Jenkin, who was our lord and sire,
Read in this book, as he sat by the fire,
Of Eve first: because of her wickedness,   715
All mankind was brought into wretchedness,
And thus Jesus Christ himself was slain then,

43 **Venus and Mercury**: Venus, of course, is involved with love, while Mercury is involved with
learning.

That boghte us with his herteblood agayn.
Lo, here expres of womman may ye finde
That womman was the los of all mankinde.   720
     Tho redde he me how Sampson loste his heres:
Slepinge, his lemman kitte hem with hir sheres,
Thurgh whiche tresoun loste he bothe his yën.
     Tho redde he me, if that I shal nat lyen,
Of Hercules and of his Dianyre,   725
That caused him to sette himself afyre.
     Nothing forgat he the sorwe and the wo
That Socrates had with hise wyves two—
How Xantippa caste pisse upon his heed:
This sely man sat stille, as he were deed;   730
He wyped his heed; namore dorste he seyn
But 'Er that thonder stinte, comth a reyn.'
     Of Phasipha that was the quene of Crete—
For shrewednesse him thoughte the tale swete—
Fy! spek namore, it is a grisly thing,   735
Of hire horrible lust and hir lyking.
     Of Clitermistra, for hire lecherye,
That falsly made hire housbond for to dye,
He redde it with ful good devocioun.
     He tolde me eek for what occasioun   740
Amphiorax at Thebes loste his lyf.
Myn housbond hadde a legende of his wyf,
Eriphilem, that for an ouche of gold
Hath prively unto the Grekes told
Wher that hir housbonde hidde him in a place,   745
For which he hadde at Thebes sory grace.
     Of Lyvia tolde he me, and of Lucye.

Who bought us with his own heart's blood again.
Lo, here, expressly, of woman you find
That woman was the loss of all mankind.   720
        He read to me how Samson[44] lost his hair:
His lover cut it while he did sleep there;
And through this treason, he lost both his eyes.
        And then he read to me, if I don't lie,
About Dianyra and Hercules;   725
She made him set himself on fire, if you please.
        Nor forgot he the woe throughout his life
That Socrates endured from his two wives,
How Xantippa cast piss upon his head.
This foolish man sat still like he were dead;   730
He wiped his head and no more dared say plain,
But 'Before thunder stops, there comes the rain!'
        Of Pasiphaë,[45] who was the queen of Crete,
From evilness, the tale seemed to him sweet;
Fie! Speak no more—it is a grisly thing—   735
Of her lust and horrible desiring.
        Of Clytemnestra,[46] who, from lechery,
Falsely made her husband die, you see,
He read out that tale with great devotion.
        He told me also on what occasion   740
Amphiaraus at Thebes had lost his life.
My husband had a legend of his wife,
Eriphyle, who, for a brooch of gold
Has privately unto the Greeks then told
Where her husband had kept his hiding place,   745
And thus at Thebes he suffered sorry grace.
        Of Livia and Lucia, then heard I:

---

44 **Samson:** What follows is a list of disastrous love affairs and marriages that warn against
women's treachery. Footnotes are provided if the meaning is not clear from the context.

45 **Pasiphaë:** Fell in love with a bull and, as a result, gave birth to the Minotaur, a creature in
Greek mythology that is half man, half bull.

46 **Clytemnestra:** With her lover, Aegisthus, murdered her husband, Agamemnon, when he
came home from the Trojan War.

They bothe made hir housbondes for to dye,
That oon for love, that other was for hate.
Lyvia hir housbond, on an even late,   750
Empoysoned hath, for that she was his fo.
Lucya, likerous, loved hire housbond so,
That, for he sholde alwey upon hire thinke,
She yaf him swich a manere love-drinke,
That he was deed er it were by the morwe;   755
And thus algates housbondes han sorwe.
        Thanne tolde he me how oon Latumius
Compleyned unto his felawe Arrius,
That in his gardin growed swich a tree
On which he seyde how that his wyves three   760
Hanged hemself for herte despitous.
'O leve brother,' quod this Arrius,
'Yif me a plante of thilke blissed tree,
And in my gardin planted shal it be!'
        Of latter date, of wyves hath he red   765
That somme han slayn hir housbondes in hir bed,
And lete hir lechour dighte hire al the night
Whyl that the corps lay in the floor upright.
And somme han drive nayles in hir brayn
Whyl that they slepte, and thus they han hem slayn.   770
Somme han hem yeve poysoun in hire drinke.
He spak more harm than herte may bithinke,
And therwithal he knew of mo proverbes
Than in this world ther growen gras or herbes.
'Bet is,' quod he, 'thyn habitacioun   775
Be with a leoun or a foul dragoun,
Than with a womman usinge for to chyde.
Bet is,' quod he, 'hye in the roof abyde
Than with an angry wyf doun in the hous;
They been so wikked and contrarious   780
They haten that hir housbondes loveth ay.'
He seyde, 'A womman cast hir shame away
Whan she cast of hir smok;' and forthermo,

How both of them had made their husbands die,
The one for love, the other one for hate.
This Livia, for sure, one evening late,   750
Poisoned her husband for she was his foe;
Lecherous Lucia loved her husband so
That, to make sure he'd always on her think,
She gave to him such a kind of love-drink
He was dead before it was tomorrow;   755
And thus, always, husbands have had sorrow.
        Then he told me how one Latumius
Complained once to his fellow Arrius
That in his garden there grew such a tree
On which, he said, that all of his wives three   760
Hung themselves with spite, one then another.
Said this Arrius, 'Beloved brother,
Give me a shoot from off that blessèd tree,
And in my garden, planted it will be.'
        And later on, about wives he has read,   765
And some had slain their husbands in their bed,
And let their lechers hump them all the night,
While on the floor the corpses lay upright.
And some have driven nails into the brain,
While they did sleep, and thus they had them slain.   770
And some did give them poison in their drink.
He spoke more slander than the heart can think,
And on top of it, he knew more proverbs
Than in this world there can grow grass and herbs.
'Better,' he said, 'that your habitation   775
Be either with a lion or foul dragon,
Than with a woman who is used to chide.
Better,' said he, 'high on the roof abide,
Than down in the house with an angry wife;
They're so wicked and contrary all their lives,   780
That they hate what their husbands love always.'
He said, 'A woman casts her shame away,
When she casts off her shift.' He spoke more so:

'A fair womman, but she be chaast also,
Is lyk a gold ring in a sowes nose.'   785
Who wolde wene, or who wolde suppose
The wo that in myn herte was, and pyne?
        And whan I saugh he wolde nevere fyne
To reden on this cursed book al night,
Al sodeynly three leves have I plight   790
Out of his book, right as he radde, and eke
I with my fist so took him on the cheke
That in oure fyr he fil bakward adoun.
And he upstirte as dooth a wood leoun,
And with his fist he smoot me on the heed   795
That in the floor I lay as I were deed.
And when he saugh how stille that I lay,
He was agast, and wolde han fled his way,
Til atte laste out of my swogh I breyde.
'O! hastow slayn me, false theef ?' I seyde,   800
'And for my land thus hastow mordred me?
Er I be deed, yet wol I kisse thee.'
        And neer he cam, and kneled faire adoun,
And seyde, 'Dere suster Alisoun,
As help me God, I shall thee nevere smyte;   805
That I have doon, it is thyself to wyte.
Foryeve it me, and that I thee biseke'—
And yet eftsones I hitte him on the cheke
And seyde, 'Theef! thus muchel am I wreke.
Now wol I dye: I may no lenger speke.'   810
But atte laste, with muchel care and wo,
We fille acorded by us selven two.
He yaf me al the brydel in myn hond,
To han the governance of hous and lond,
And of his tonge and of his hond also;   815
And made him brenne his book anon right tho.
And whan that I hadde geten unto me,
By maistrie, al the soveraynetee,
And that he seyde, 'Myn owene trewe wyf,

'A fair woman, unless she's chaste also,
Is just like a gold ring in a sow's nose.'   785
Who would imagine, or who would suppose
The woe that in my heart was, and the pain?

      And when I saw he never would refrain
From reading on this cursèd book all night,
Then suddenly, three leaves I have ripped right   790
Out of his book, as he read, and also
With my fist, I took him on the cheek so
That backward in our fire, right down fell he.
He starts up like a lion who's gone crazy,
And with his fist, he hit me on the head   795
So on the floor I lay like I were dead.
And when he saw how still it was I lay,
He was aghast, and would have fled away,
Till, at last, out of my swoon I awoke.
'Oh! Hast thou slain me, false thief?' then I spoke,   800
'And for my land, hast thou now murdered me?
Before I'm dead, yet will I still kiss thee.'

      And fairly he knelt down when he came near,
And he said, 'Alison, my sister dear,
Never more will I hit you, in God's name!   805
If I've done so, you are yourself to blame.
I pray you, your forgiveness now I seek.'
And right away, I hit him on the cheek,
And said, 'Thief, now this much avenged am I;
I may no longer speak, now I will die.'   810
But then, at last, after much woe and care,
We two fell into an agreement there,
He gave me all the bridle in my hand
To have the governing of house and land,
And of his tongue, and of his hands, then, too;   815
I made him burn his book without ado.
And when I had then gotten back for me,
By mastery, all the sovereignty,
And when he said to me, 'My own true wife,

Do as thee lust the terme of al thy lyf;   820
Keep thyn honour, and keep eek myn estaat'—
After that day we hadden never debaat.
God help me so, I was to him as kinde
As any wyf from Denmark unto Inde,
And also trewe, and so was he to me.   825
I prey to God that sit in magestee,
So blesse his soule for his mercy dere!
Now wol I seye my tale, if ye wol here."

Biholde the wordes bitween the Somonour and the Frere.

        The Frere lough whan he hadde herd al this.
"Now, dame," quod he, "so have I joye or blis,   830
This is a long preamble of a tale!"
And whan the Somnour herde the Frere gale,
"Lo," quod the Somnour, "Goddes armes two,
A frere wol entremette him everemo!
Lo, gode men, a flye and eek a frere   835
Wol falle in every dish and eek matere.
What spekestow of preambulacioun?
What! amble, or trotte, or [pace,] or go sit doun!
Thou lettest oure disport in this manere."
        "Ye, woltow so, sire Somnour?" quod the Frere;   840
"Now by my feith, I shal, er that I go,
Telle of a somnour swich a tale or two
That alle the folk shal laughen in this place."
        "Now elles, Frere, I wol bishrewe thy face,"
Quod this Somnour, "and I bishrewe me   845
But if I telle tales two or thre
Of freres, er I come to Sidingborne,
That I shal make thyn herte for to morne—
For wel I woot thy pacience is goon."
        Oure Hoste cryde "Pees! and that anoon!"   850

Do as you like the rest of all your life;   820
Keep your honor, and keep my rank and state'—
After that day, we never had debate.
God help me so, there's no wife you would find
From Denmark to India who was so kind,
And also true, and so was he to me.   825
I pray to God, who sits in majesty,
To bless his soul with all his mercy dear.
Now will I tell my tale, if you will hear."

Behold the words between the Summoner and the Friar.

     The Friar laughed, when he had heard all this;
"Madame," said he, "so have I joy or bliss,   830
This is a long preamble to a tale!"
The Summoner had heard his windy gale,
"By God's two arms," the Summoner said, "lo!
Always will a friar interfere so.
Lo, good men, a fly and then a friar   835
Will both fall in every dish and matter.
Of preambulation, what's to say of it?
What! Amble, trot, keep still, or just go sit!
You're hindering our sport in this manner."
     "You say so, sir Summoner?" said the Friar;   840
"Now, by my faith, I shall, before I go,
Tell a tale of a summoner, you know,
That all the folks will laugh at in this place."
     "Now, elsewise, Friar, I do curse your face,"
Said this Summoner. "And I curse myself, too,   845
Unless I tell some tales, at least a few,
Of friars before I come to Sittingbourne[47]
So that, be sure, I will make your heart mourn.
I know full well that you're out of patience."
     Our Host cried out, "Peace now! And that at once!"   850

---

47 **Sittingbourne:** A town forty miles from London on the road to Canterbury.

And seyde, "Lat the womman telle hire tale.
Ye fare as folk that dronken been of ale.
Do, dame, tel forth youre tale, and that is best."
    "Al redy, sire," quod she, "right as yow lest,
If I have licence of this worthy Frere."   855
    "Yis, dame," quod he, "tel forth, and I wol here."

Heere endeth the Wyf of Bathe hir Prologe.

And he said, "Let the woman tell her tale.
You act like folks who are all drunk on ale.
Do, madame, tell your tale, and all the rest."
          "All ready, sir," said she, "as you think best,
If I have license of this worthy Friar."   855
          "Yes, madame," said he, "tell on. I will hear."

Here the Wife of Bath ends her Prologue.

THE WIFE OF BATH'S TALE

Heere bigynneth the Tale of the Wyf of Bathe.

In th'olde dayes of the King Arthour,
Of which that Britons speken greet honour,
All was this land fulfild of fayerye.
The elf-queen with hir joly companye   860
Daunced ful ofte in many a grene mede.
This was the olde opinion, as I rede—
I speke of manye hundred yeres ago—
But now can no man see none elves mo.
For now the grete charitee and prayeres   865
Of limitours and othere holy freres,
That serchen every lond and every streem,
As thikke as motes in the sonne-beem,
Blessinge halles, chambres, kichenes, boures,
Citees, burghes, castels, hye toures,   870
Thropes, bernes, shipnes, dayeryes—
This maketh that ther been no fayeryes.
For ther as wont to walken was an elf,
Ther walketh now the limitour himself
In undermeles and in morweninges,   875
And seyth his Matins and his holy thinges
As he goth in his limitacioun.

THE WIFE OF BATH'S TALE

Here begins the Tale of the Wife of Bath.

In the olden days of good King Arthur,
Of whom Britons still speak with great honor,
This whole land was all filled up with fairies.
The elf queen, with her pretty company,   860
Went dancing then through many a green mead.
I think this was the old belief, indeed;
I speak of many hundred years ago.
But now no one sees elves and fairies go,
For now all the charity and prayers   865
Of limitors[48] and other holy friars,
Who haunt through every land and every stream
As thick as motes floating in a sun beam,
Blessing halls and chambers, kitchens, bowers,
Cities, boroughs, castles, and high towers,   870
Barns and villages, cowsheds and dairies—
This is the reason why there are no fairies.
For there where once was wont to walk an elf,
Now there the begging friar walks himself
In the afternoons and in the mornings,   875
He says his matins and his holy things
As he walks all throughout his begging grounds.

---

48 **limitors**: Friars who paid for the rights to beg in a specific territory. See the *General Prologue*'s
friar, line 209.

Wommen may go now saufly up and doun:
In every bush or under every tree
Ther is noon other incubus but he,   880
And he ne wol doon hem but dishonour.
     And so bifel that this King Arthour
Hadde in his hous a lusty bacheler,
That on a day cam rydinge fro river;
And happed that, allone as he was born,   885
He saugh a mayde walkinge him biforn,
Of whiche mayde anon, maugree hir heed,
By verray force he rafte hire maydenheed.
For which oppressioun was swich clamour
And swich pursute unto the King Arthour,   890
That dampned was this knight for to be deed
By cours of lawe, and sholde han lost his heed—
Paraventure swich was the statut tho—
But that the quene and othere ladies mo
So longe preyeden the king of grace   895
Til he his lyf him graunted in the place,
And yaf him to the quene al at hir wille,
To chese whether she wolde him save or spille.
     The quene thanketh the king with al hir might,
And after this thus spak she to the knight   900
Whan that she saugh hir tyme, upon a day:
"Thou standest yet," quod she, "in swich array
That of thy lyf yet hastow no suretee.
I grante thee lyf, if thou canst tellen me
What thing is it that wommen most desyren.   905
Be war, and keep thy nekke-boon from yren.
And if thou canst nat tellen it anon,
Yet wol I yeve thee leve for to gon
A twelf-month and a day, to seche and lere
An answere suffisant in this matere.   910

Now women may go safely all around.
In every bush and under every tree,
There is no other incubus[49] but he,   880
And he'll do them no harm but dishonor.

So it happened that this good King Arthur
Once had a lusty knight, a bachelor,
Who, one day, came riding from the river,
And it chanced that, as he was born, alone,   885
He saw a maiden walking on her own,
From which maid, then, no matter what she said,
By very force, he took her maidenhead;
This oppressive violence caused such clamor,
And such a suit for justice to King Arthur   890
That soon this knight was sentenced to be dead,
By the course of law, and should have lost his head—
By chance that was the law back long ago—
Except the queen and other ladies also
So long had then prayed to the king for grace   895
Till he had granted his life in that place,
And gave him to the queen, to do her will,
To choose whether she would him save or kill.

The queen then thanked the king with all her might,
And after this, thus spoke she to the knight,   900
When, on a day, she saw that it was time.
"You stand," she said, "in this state for your crime:
That of your life, you've no security.
I grant you life, if you can tell to me
What thing it is that women most desire.   905
Keep your neck-bone from the ax now, sire!
And if, at once, the answer you don't know,
Still, I will give you leave so you can go
A twelvemonth and a day, to search and learn
Sufficient answer before you return;   910

49 **incubus:** Evil spirits believed to have intercourse with human women that always ended in pregnancy.

And suretee wol I han, er that thou pace,
Thy body for to yelden in this place."
　　　　Wo was this knight and sorwefully he syketh.
But what! he may nat do al as him lyketh,
And at the laste he chees him for to wende,　　　　　　　　915
And come agayn, right at the yeres ende,
With swich answere as God wolde him purveye;
And taketh his leve and wendeth forth his weye.
　　　　He seketh every hous and every place
Wheras he hopeth for to finde grace,　　　　　　　　　　920
To lerne what thing wommen loven most;
But he ne coude arryven in no cost
Wheras he mighte finde in this matere
Two creatures accordinge in-fere.
　　　　Somme seyde wommen loven best richesse,　　　　925
Somme seyde honour, somme seyde jolynesse;
Somme riche array, somme seyden lust abedde,
And ofte tyme to be widwe and wedde.
　　　　Somme seyde that oure hertes been most esed
Whan that we been y-flatered and y-plesed.　　　　　　930
He gooth ful ny the sothe, I wol nat lye:
A man shal winne us best with flaterye;
And with attendance and with bisinesse
Been we y-lymed, bothe more and lesse.
　　　　And somme seyn how that we loven best　　　　　935
For to be free and do right as us lest,
And that no man repreve us of oure vyce,
But seye that we be wyse, and no thing nyce.
For trewely, ther is noon of us alle,
If any wight wol clawe us on the galle,　　　　　　　　940
That we nil kike for he seith us sooth:
Assay, and he shal finde it that so dooth.
For be we never so vicious withinne,
We wol been holden wyse, and clene of sinne.
　　　　And somme seyn that greet delyt han we　　　　945
For to ben holden stable and eek secree,

Before you leave, I'll have security
That here you'll surrender up your body."
   Woe was this knight, and he sighs sorrowfully;
But what! He can't do all he likes completely.
And at last, he decided that he'd wend   915
His way and come back home at the year's end,
With such an answer as God would convey;
He takes his leave and goes forth on his way.
   He seeks in every house and every place
Where he has hopes that he'll find some good grace 920
To learn the thing that women love the most,
But he could not arrive on any coast
Where he might find out about this matter,
Two creatures who agreed on it together.
   Some said that all women best loved richness, 925
Some said honor, and some said jolliness,
Some, rich array, and some said lust in bed,
And often times to be widowed and wed.
   Some said that our hearts were most often eased
When we could be both flattered and well pleased. 930
He got quite near the truth, it seems to me.
A man shall win us best with flattery,
Solicitude, and eager busyness.
Thus we are captured, both the more and less.
   And some said that the best of all love we   935
To do what pleases us, and to be free,
And that no man reproves us for our folly,
But says that we are wise and never silly.
For truly, there is not one of us all,
If any one will claw us where it galls,   940
That we won't kick when what he says is true.
Try, and he'll find it so who will so do;
For, be we ever so vicious within,
We want to be held wise and clean of sin.
   And some say that we find it very sweet   945
To be thought dependable and discreet,

And in o purpos stedefastly to dwelle,
And nat biwreye thing that men us telle—
But that tale is nat worth a rake-stele.
Pardee, we wommen conne nothing hele: 950
Witnesse on Myda—wol ye here the tale?
        Ovyde, amonges othere thinges smale,
Seyde Myda hadde under his longe heres,
Growinge upon his heed two asses eres,
The whiche vyce he hidde as he best mighte   955
Ful subtilly from every mannes sighte,
That, save his wyf, ther wiste of it namo.
He loved hire most, and trusted hire also;
He preyede hire that to no creature
She sholde tellen of his disfigure.   960
        She swoor him nay, for al this world to winne,
She nolde do that vileinye or sinne,
To make hir housbond han so foul a name.
She nolde nat telle it for hir owene shame.
But nathelees, hir thoughte that she dyde   965
That she so longe sholde a conseil hyde.
Hir thoughte it swal so sore aboute hir herte
That nedely som word hire moste asterte,
And sith she dorste telle it to no man,
Doun to a mareys faste by she ran.   970
Til she came there hir herte was afyre,
And as a bitore bombleth in the myre,
She leyde hir mouth unto the water doun:
"Biwreye me nat, thou water, with thy soun,"
Quod she, "to thee I telle it, and namo;   975
Myn housbond hath longe asses eres two!
Now is myn herte all hool, now is it oute.
I mighte no lenger kepe it, out of doute."
Heer may ye se, thogh we a tyme abyde,
Yet out it moot, we can no conseil hyde.   980

And in one purpose steadfastly to dwell,
And not betray a thing that men us tell.
A rake handle isn't worth that story.
We women can't keep secrets, by God's glory; 950
See Midas—will you hear the tale withal?
      Once Ovid, among some other things small,
Said Midas covered up with his long hair,
On his head two ass's ears that grew there,
And this flaw he did hide as best he might 955
Quite cleverly from every mortal's sight,
So that, save for his wife, no one did know.
He loved her most, and trusted her also;
He prayed her that to no other creature
She would tell how he was so disfigured. 960
      She swore to him, "No"; all this world to win,
She would not do that villainy or sin,
To make her husband have so foul a name.
She wouldn't tell because of her own shame.
But, nonetheless, it seemed to her she died 965
Because so long she must that secret hide;
She thought it swelled so sorely near her heart
That some word from her must, by needs, depart;
Since she dared not tell it to any man,
Down to the marsh that was nearby, she ran— 970
Until she got there, her heart was on fire—
And as a bittern⁵⁰ bellows in the mire,
Down by the water, she did her mouth lay:
"Thou water, with your sound do not betray:
To thee I tell, and no one else," she said; 975
"My husband has long ass ears on his head!
Now is my heart all whole; now is it out.
I could no longer keep it, without doubt."
Here you see, if a time we might abide,
Yet it must out; we can no secret hide. 980

---

50 **bittern:** A bird that lives in marshes and whose voice resembles that of a bellowing ox.

The remenant of the tale if ye wol here,
Redeth Ovyde, and ther ye may it lere.
　　　This knight of which my tale is specially,
Whan that he saugh he mighte nat come therby,
This is to seye, what wommen loven moost,   985
Withinne his brest ful sorweful was the goost,
But hoom he gooth, he mighte nat sojourne.
The day was come that hoomward moste he tourne,
And in his wey it happed him to ryde
In al this care under a forest-syde,   990
Wheras he saugh upon a daunce go
Of ladies foure and twenty and yet mo;
Toward the whiche daunce he drow ful yerne,
In hope that som wisdom sholde he lerne.
But certeinly, er he came fully there,   995
Vanisshed was this daunce, he niste where.
No creature saugh he that bar lyf,
Save on the grene he saugh sittinge a wyf—
A fouler wight ther may no man devyse.
Agayn the knight this olde wyf gan ryse,   1000
And seyde, "Sire knight, heerforth ne lyth no wey.
Tel me what that ye seken, by youre fey!
Paraventure it may the bettre be:
Thise olde folk can muchel thing," quod she.
　　　"My leve mooder," quod this knight, "certeyn   1005
I nam but deed, but if that I can seyn
What thing it is that wommen most desyre.
Coude ye me wisse, I wolde wel quyte your hyre."
　　　"Plighte me thy trouthe, heer in myn hand," quod she,
"The nexte thing that I requere thee,   1010
Thou shalt it do, if it lye in thy might,
And I wol telle it yow er it be night."
　　　"Have heer my trouthe," quod the knight, "I grante."
　　　"Thanne," quod she, "I dar me wel avante
Thy lyf is sauf, for I wol stonde therby.   1015
Upon my lyf, the queen wol seye as I.

If of this tale you want to hear the rest,
Read Ovid, and there you will learn it best.
  This knight, about whom my tale is concerned,
Seeing that the answer he'd not learned—
That is to say, what women love the best— 985
Sorrowful was the spirit in his breast.
But home he goes; no more might he sojourn;
The day had come when homeward he must turn.
And on his way, it happened he did ride,
With all his cares, near to a forest's side, 990
Where he saw come together for a dance,
Some four and twenty ladies there by chance;
Toward which dance he eagerly did turn,
In hopes some wisdom from them he might learn.
But truly, before he had arrived there, 995
The dancing ladies vanished—who knew where.
No creature saw he left there who bore life,
Save on the green, he saw sitting a wife—
A fouler creature, none imagine might.
This old wife then arose to meet the knight. 1000
"Sir knight, there's no road out of here," said she.
"What you are seeking, by your faith, tell me.
Perhaps, then, you'll be better prospering."
She said, "These old folks can know many things."
  "Beloved mother," said this knight, "it's fate 1005
That I am dead unless I can relate
What thing it is that women most desire.
Could you tell me, I'd well repay your hire."
  "Pledge me your troth," said she, "here in my hand,
And swear to me the next thing I demand, 1010
You shall do it if it lies in your might,
And I'll tell you the answer before night."
  "I grant," he said, "you have this pledge from me."
  "Then, sire, I dare well boast to you," said she,
"Your life is safe, and I will stand thereby; 1015
Upon my life, the queen will say as I.

Lat see which is the proudeste of hem alle,
That wereth on a coverchief or a calle,
That dar seye nay of that I shal thee teche.
Lat us go forth withouten lenger speche." 1020
Tho rouned she a pistel in his ere,
And bad him to be glad and have no fere.

     Whan they be comen to the court, this knight
Seyde he had holde his day, as he hadde hight,
And redy was his answere, as he sayde. 1025
Ful many a noble wyf, and many a mayde,
And many a widwe—for that they ben wyse—
The quene hirself sittinge as a justyse,
Assembled been, his answere for to here;
And afterward this knight was bode appere. 1030

     To every wight comanded was silence,
And that the knight sholde telle in audience
What thing that worldly wommen loven best.
This knight ne stood nat stille as doth a best,
But to his questioun anon answerde 1035
With manly voys, that al the court it herde:

     "My lige lady, generally," quod he,
"Wommen desyren to have sovereyntee
As wel over hir housbond as hir love,
And for to been in maistrie him above. 1040
This is youre moste desyr, thogh ye me kille.
Doth as yow list—I am heer at your wille."
In al the court ne was ther wyf, ne mayde,
Ne widwe that contraried that he sayde,
But seyden he was worthy han his lyf. 1045
And with that word up stirte the olde wyf,
Which that the knight saugh sittinge in the grene:
"Mercy," quod she, "my sovereyn lady quene!
Er that youre court departe, do me right.
I taughte this answere unto the knight; 1050
For which he plighte me his trouthe there,
The firste thing I wolde of him requere

Let see who is the proudest of them yet
Who wears either a coverchief or hairnet
Who dares say 'Nay' to what I will you teach.
Let us go forth without a longer speech." 1020
Then she whispered a message in his ear,
And bade him to be glad, and have no fear.

When they came to the court, this knight did say
That, as he'd pledged, he had held to his day,
And he said his answer was ready then. 1025
Many noble wives and many maidens
And many widows, because wise are they,
With the queen sitting as the judge that day,
Were all assembled, his answer to hear;
And then this knight was told he should appear. 1030

It was commanded that there should be silence
And that the knight should tell in audience
The thing that worldly women love the best.
The knight did not stand like a beast at rest;
At once to his question then he answered 1035
With manly voice, so all the court it heard:

"My liege lady, generally," said he,
"Women desire to have sovereignty
As well over their husbands as their loves,
And to be in mastery them above. 1040
This is your greatest desire, though me you kill.
Do as you like; I am here at your will."
In all the court, there was no wife or maiden
Nor widow who denied what he had said then,
But they said he was worthy of his life. 1045
And with that word, then, up jumps the old wife,
Whom the knight had seen sitting on the green:
"Mercy," said she, "my sovereign lady queen!
Before your court departs, by me do right.
I taught this very answer to this knight; 1050
For which he pledged to me his troth and hire,
So that the first thing I'd of him require,

He wolde it do, if it lay in his might.
Bifore the court thanne preye I thee, sir knight,"
Quod she, "that thou me take unto thy wyf,   1055
For wel thou wost that I have kept thy lyf.
If I sey fals, sey nay, upon thy fey!"
          This knight answerde, "Allas and weylawey!
I woot right wel that swich was my biheste.
For Goddes love, as chees a newe requeste: 1060
Tak al my good, and lat my body go."
          "Nay thanne," quod she, ' "I shrewe us bothe two!
For thogh that I be foul and old and pore,
I nolde for al the metal ne for ore
That under erthe is grave or lyth above   1065
But if thy wyf I were, and eek thy love."
          "My love?" quod he, "Nay, my dampnacioun!
Allas! that any of my nacioun
Sholde evere so foule disparaged be!"
But al for noght, the ende is this, that he   1070
Constreyned was: he nedes moste hire wedde,
And taketh his olde wyf and gooth to bedde.
          Now wolden som men seye, paraventure,
That for my necligence I do no cure
To tellen yow the joye and al th'array   1075
That at the feste was that ilke day.
To whiche thing shortly answere I shal:
I seye ther nas no joye ne feste at al;
Ther nas but hevinesse and muche sorwe,
For prively he wedded hire on morwe,   1080
And al day after hidde him as an oule,
So wo was him, his wyf looked so foule.
          Greet was the wo the knight hadde in his thoght,
Whan he was with his wyf abedde y-broght;
He walweth, and he turneth to and fro.   1085
His olde wyf lay smylinge everemo,
And seyde, "O dere housbond, *benedicite!*
Fareth every knight thus with his wyf as ye?

This he would do, if it lay in his might.
Before the court, then I pray you, sir knight,"
Said she, "that you now take me for your wife,   1055
For well you know that I have saved your life.
Upon my faith, if I say false, say 'nay.' "
        This knight answered, "Alas, and well away!
I know that was my promise, I'll be blessed.
But for God's love now, choose a new request!   1060
Take all my goods, and let my body go."
        "Oh no," said she, "I curse us both then so!
For though I may be foul and poor and old,
I'd not want all the metal, ore, or gold
That's buried in the earth or lies above,   1065
Unless I were your lady and your love."
        "My love?" said he, "oh, no, my damnation!
Alas, that one of my birth and station
Ever should so foully disparaged be!"
But all for naught; the end is this, that he   1070
Constrained was here; by needs, he must her wed,
And take his old wife, and go off to bed.
        Now here some men would want to say perhaps
That I take no care—so it is a lapse—
To tell you all the joy and the array   1075
That at the wedding feast was on that day:
To which, my answer here is short and small:
I say there was no joy or feast at all.
Only sorrow and heaviness, I say.
For privately he wedded her next day,   1080
And all day after, he hid like an owl,
For woe was he that his wife looked so foul.
        Great was the woe the knight had in his thoughts,
When he was with his wife to their bed brought;
He wallows and he writhes there, to and fro.   1085
His old wife just lay smiling, even so,
And said, "Oh husband dear, God save my life!
Like you, does every knight fare with his wife?

Is this the lawe of King Arthures hous?
Is every knight of his so dangerous?   1090
I am youre owene love and eek youre wyf;
I am she which that saved hath youre lyf;
And certes yet dide I yow nevere unright.
Why fare ye thus with me this firste night?
Ye faren lyk a man had lost his wit!   1095
What is my gilt? for Goddes love, tel me it,
And it shal been amended, if I may."
          "Amended?" quod this knight, "allas! nay, nay!
It wol nat been amended nevere mo!
Thou art so loothly, and so old also,   1100
And therto comen of so lowe a kinde,
That litel wonder is thogh I walwe and winde.
So wolde God myn herte wolde breste!"
          "Is this," quod she, "the cause of youre unreste?"
          "Ye, certainly," quod he, "no wonder is."   1105
          "Now, sire," quod she, "I coude amende al this,
If that me liste, er it were dayes three,
So wel ye mighte bere yow unto me.
          But for ye speken of swich gentillesse
As is descended out of old richesse—   1110
That therfore sholden ye be gentil men—
Swich arrogance is nat worth an hen.
Loke who that is most vertuous alway,
Privee and apert, and most entendeth ay
To do the gentil dedes that he can,   1115
And tak him for the grettest gentil man.
Crist wol we clayme of him oure gentillesse,
Nat of oure eldres for hire old richesse.
For thogh they yeve us al hir heritage—
For which we clayme to been of heigh parage—   1120
Yet may they nat biquethe, for no thing,
To noon of us hir vertuous living
That made hem gentil men y-called be,
And bad us folwen hem in swich degree.

Is this the law here in the house of Arthur?
Is each knight to his wife aloof with her?   1090
I am your own love, and I am your wife;
And I am she who has just saved your life.
Surely, toward you I have done only right;
Why fare you thus with me on this first night?
You're faring like a man who's lost his wits!   1095
What's my guilt? For love of God, now tell it,
And it will be amended if I may."

     "Amended?" said this knight, "alas! No way!
It will not be amended, this I know.
You are so loathly, and so old also,   1100
And come from such low lineage, no doubt,
Small wonder that I wallow and writhe about.
I would to God my heart burst in my breast!"

     "Is this," said she, "the cause of your unrest?"
     "Yes," said he, "no wonder is, that's certain."   1105

     "Sir," said she, "I could mend this again,
If I liked, before there'd passed days three,
If you might now behave well toward me.

     But since you speak now of such gentleness
As descends to you down from old richness,   1110
So that, because of it, you're gentle men,
Such arrogance is just not worth a hen.
See who is most virtuous all their lives,
In private and in public, and most strives
To always do what gentle deeds he can: 1115
Now take him for the greatest gentle man.
Christ wills we claim from him our gentleness,
Not from our elders and from their old richness.
Though they leave us their worldly heritage,
And we claim that we're from high lineage,   1120
Yet they may not bequeath a single thing
To us here of their virtuous living,
Which is what made them be called gentle men;
This is the path they bade us follow then.

Wel can the wyse poete of Florence,   1125
That highte Dant, speken in this sentence;
Lo, in swich maner rym is Dantes tale:
'Ful selde up ryseth by his branches smale
Prowesse of man, for God of his goodnesse
Wol that of him we clayme oure gentillesse;'   1130
For of oure eldres may we no thing clayme
But temporel thing, that man may hurte and mayme.
      Eek every wight wot this as wel as I,
If gentillesse were planted naturelly
Unto a certeyn linage doun the lyne,   1135
Privee and apert, than wolde they nevere fyne
To doon of gentillesse the faire offyce—
They mighte do no vileinye or vyce.
      Tak fyr, and ber it in the derkeste hous
Bitwix this and the Mount of Caucasus,   1140
And lat men shette the dores and go thenne,
Yet wol the fyr as faire lye and brenne,
As twenty thousand men mighte it biholde:
His office naturel ay wol it holde,
Up peril of my lyf, til that it dye.   1145
      Heer may ye see wel how that genterye
Is nat annexed to possessioun,
Sith folk ne doon hir operacioun
Alwey, as dooth the fyr, lo, in his kinde.
For, God it woot, men may wel often finde   1150
A lordes sone do shame and vileinye;
And he that wol han prys of his gentrye
For he was boren of a gentil hous,
And hadde his eldres noble and vertuous,
And nil himselven do no gentil dedis,   1155

Well can he, the wise poet of Florence,   1125
Who's named Dante,[51] speak forth with this sentence.
Lo, Dante's tale is in this kind of rhyme:
'Seldom up his family tree's branches climbs
A man's prowess, for God in his goodness,
Wills that from him we claim our gentleness';   1130
For, from our elders, we may no thing claim
But temporal things that may hurt us and maim.
    And every man knows this as well as me,
If gentleness were planted naturally
In a certain lineage down the line, yet   1135
They'd not cease in public or in private,
From gentleness, to do their fair duty;
They might not then do vice or villainy.
    Take fire and bring it in the darkest house,
From here to mountains of the Caucasus,   1140
And let men shut the doors and go return;
Yet still the fire will lie as fair and burn
Like twenty thousand men might it behold;
Its natural duty it will always hold,
On my life, till extinguished it may be.   1145
    Here, may you well see how gentility
Is not connected to one's possessions,
Since folks don't follow its operation
Always, as does the fire, lo, in its kind.
For, God knows it, men may well often find   1150
That a lord's son does shame and villainy;
And he who wants praise for his gentility,
Since a gentle house he was born into,
And had elders full of noble virtue,
And who will not himself do gentle deeds,   1155

---

51 **Dante:** Dante Alighieri (1265–1321), the prominent Florentine poet whose works elevating the vernacular for the purposes of sophisticated literary expression were important to the shape of Chaucer's career. There are similarities here between the old woman's ideas about intrinsic virtue and those found in Dante's *Convivio*; but these ideas are also widespread and found in many sources in Chaucer's time.

Ne folwe his gentil auncestre that deed is,
He nis nat gentil, be he duk or erl;
For vileyns sinful dedes make a cherl.
For gentillesse nis but renomee
Of thyne auncestres, for hire heigh bountee,   1160
Which is a straunge thing to thy persone.
Thy gentillesse cometh fro God allone.
Thanne comth oure verray gentillesse of grace:
It was nothing biquethe us with oure place.
        Thenketh how noble, as seith Valerius,   1165
Was thilke Tullius Hostilius,
That out of povert roos to heigh noblesse.
Redeth Senek, and redeth eek Boëce:
Ther shul ye seen expres that it no drede is
That he is gentil that doth gentil dedis.   1170
And therfore, leve housbond, I thus conclude:
Al were it that myne auncestres were rude,
Yet may the hye God, and so hope I,
Grante me grace to liven vertuously.
Thanne am I gentil, whan that I biginne   1175
To liven vertuously and weyve sinne.
        And ther as ye of povert me repreve,
The hye God, on whom that we bileve,
In wilful povert chees to live his lyf.
And certes every man, mayden, or wyf,   1180
May understonde that Jesus, hevene king,
Ne wolde nat chese a vicious living.
Glad povert is an honest thing, certeyn;
This wol Senek and othere clerkes seyn.
Whoso that halt him payd of his poverte,   1185
I holde him riche, al hadde he nat a sherte.

And dead gentle ancestors hardly heeds,
He is not gentle, be he duke or earl;
A villain's sinful deeds do make a churl.
For such gentleness is only fame
From your elders' high goodness and their name,   1160
Which is a thing your person does not own.
Your gentleness must come from God alone.
Thus our true gentleness must come from grace;
It's not a thing bequeathed us with our place.
Think how noble, as says Valerius,[52]   1165
Was this one Tullius Hostillius,[53]
Nobility did poverty succeed.
Read Seneca, and Boethius[54] read;
There you shall see expressly that, indeed,
The man is gentle who does gentle deeds.   1170
And therefore, my dear husband, I conclude:
Though my ancestors were humble and rude,
Yet may the high God, and for this I pray,
Grant me grace to live virtuously each day.
I am gentle, whenever I begin,   1175
To live virtuously and to waive sin.

You reproach me for poverty, indeed,
High God above, on whom we base our creed,
In willing poverty did live his life.
And certainly each man, maiden, or wife   1180
May understand that Jesus, heaven's king,
Would not choose a vicious way of living.
Glad poverty's an honest thing, it's true;
Thus Seneca and other clerks say, too.
He who sees he's well paid by poverty,   1185
Though he had no shirt, he seems rich to me.

52 **Valerius**: Valerius Maximus, Roman author, early first century.
53 **Tullius Hostellius**: Third king of Rome, who rose to great heights from humble beginnings.
54 **Boethius**: Early Christian philosopher from Rome, late fifth through early sixth century, author of *The Consolation of Philosophy*, a work he wrote when he was imprisoned in Pavia and that Chaucer translated; it influenced Chaucer's ideas about free will.

He that coveyteth is a povre wight,

For he wolde han that is nat in his might.

But he that noght hath, ne coveyteth have,

Is riche, although ye holde him but a knave.   1190

Verray povert, it singeth proprely.

Juvenal seith of povert merily:

'The povre man, whan he goth by the weye,

Bifore the theves he may singe and pleye.'

Poverte is hateful good, and as I gesse,   1195

A ful greet bringere out of bisinesse;

A greet amendere eek of sapience

To him that taketh it in pacience.

Poverte is this, although it seme elenge,

Possessioun that no wight wol chalenge;   1200

Poverte ful ofte, whan a man is lowe,

Maketh his God and eek himself to knowe;

Poverte a spectacle is, as thinketh me,

Thurgh which he may his verray frendes see.

And therfore, sire, sin that I noght yow greve,   1205

Of my povert namore ye me repreve.

  Now, sire, of elde ye repreve me:

And certes, sire, thogh noon auctoritee

Were in no book, ye gentils of honour

Seyn that men sholde an old wight doon favour   1210

And clepe him fader, for youre gentillesse;

And auctours shal I finden, as I gesse.

  Now ther ye seye that I am foul and old,

Than drede you noght to been a cokewold,

For filthe and elde, also moot I thee,   1215

Been grete wardeyns upon chastitee.

But nathelees, sin I knowe youre delyt,

I shal fulfille youre worldly appetyt.

  Chese now," quod she, "oon of thise thinges tweye:

To han me foul and old til that I deye   1220

He is a poor man who can only covet,
For he wants what he lacks power to get;
He who has naught, and does not covet, too,
Is rich, though he a peasant seems to you.   1190
True poverty, it sings out properly;
Now Juvenal[55] says of it merrily:
'The poor man, when he should go by the way,
Before the thieves, this man can sing and play.'
Poverty is a hateful good, I guess,   1195
A great encouragement to busyness;
Great improver of wisdom and good sense
For him who can suffer it with patience.
Poverty, though miserable seems its name,
Is a possession no one else will claim.   1200
Poverty often, when a man is low,
Can make him both his God and himself know.
Poverty's an eyeglass, it seems to me,
Through which he might his good and true friends see.
And sire, now, if I don't grieve you, therefore   1205
For poverty don't blame me anymore.
      Now, sire, with old age you have reproached me;
And truly, sire, though no authority
Were in books, you gentlemen of honor
Say folks to an old man should show favor   1210
And call him father, in your gentleness;
And I shall find authorities, I guess.
      Now, since you say that I am foul and old,
You don't have to fear to be a cuckold;
For filth and age, so far as I can see,   1215
Are great wardens upon one's chastity.
But, nonetheless, since I know your delight,
I shall fulfill your worldly appetite.
      Choose now," said she, "of these things, one of two:
Till I die, to have me foul and old, too,   1220

---

55 **Juvenal**: Roman poet (first to second century), who was most famous for his *Satires*.

And be to yow a trewe humble wyf,
And nevere yow displese in al my lyf,
Or elles ye wol han me yong and fair,
And take youre aventure of the repair
That shal be to youre hous, by cause of me,   1225
Or in som other place, may wel be.
Now chese yourselven whether that yow lyketh."
       This knight avyseth him and sore syketh,
But atte laste he seyde in this manere:
"My lady and my love, and wyf so dere,   1230
I put me in youre wyse governance:
Cheseth youreself which may be most plesance
And most honour to yow and me also.
I do no fors the whether of the two,
For as yow lyketh, it suffiseth me."   1235
       "Thanne have I gete of yow maistrye," quod she,
"Sin I may chese and governe as me lest?"
       "Ye, certes, wyf," quod he, "I holde it best."
       "Kis me," quod she. "We be no lenger wrothe,
For by my trouthe, I wol be to yow bothe,   1240
This is to seyn, ye, bothe fair and good.
I prey to God that I mot sterven wood,
But I to yow be also good and trewe
As evere was wyf, sin that the world was newe.
And but I be to-morn as fair to sene   1245
As any lady, emperyce, or quene,
That is bitwixe the est and eke the west,
Doth with my lyf and deeth right as yow lest.
Cast up the curtin: loke how that it is."
       And whan the knight saugh verraily al this,   1250
That she so fair was and so yong therto,
For joye he hente hire in his armes two;
His herte bathed in a bath of blisse.
A thousand tyme a-rewe he gan hire kisse,
And she obeyed him in every thing   1255
That mighte doon him plesance or lyking.

And be to you a true and humble wife,
And never displease you in all my life,
Or else you can have now a fair, young thing,
And take your chances with the visiting
That happens at your house because of me,   1225
Or in some other place, as well may be.
Choose yourself whichever one will please you."
        This knight now ponders and sighs sorely, too,
But finally, he said in this way here:
"My lady and my love and wife so dear,   1230
I put myself in your wise governing;
Choose yourself which one may be most pleasing
And most honor to both you and me too.
I do not care now which one of the two;
What pleases you suffices now for me."   1235
        "Then have I got mastery from you," said she,
"Since I may choose and govern all the rest?"
        "Yes, truly, wife," said he, "I think it best."
        "Kiss me," said she, "we are no longer angry,
For, by my troth, to you I will both be—   1240
Yes, now both fair and good, as will be plain.
I pray to God that I might die insane,
Unless to you I'm also good and true
As any wife's been, since the world was new.
Unless tomorrow I'm as fair to see   1245
As any queen or empress or lady,
Who is between the east and then the west,
Do with my life and death as you think best.
Cast up the curtain; how it is, now see."
        And when the knight saw all this verily,   1250
That she now was so fair and so young, too,
For joy he seized her within his arms two,
His heart was all bathed in a bath of bliss.
A thousand times in a row, he did her kiss,
And she obeyed him then in everything   1255
That was to his pleasure or his liking.

And thus they live unto hir lyves ende
In parfit joye. And Jesu Crist us sende
Housbondes meke, yonge, and fresshe abedde,
And grace t'overbyde hem that we wedde.   1260
And eek I preye Jesu shorte hir lyves
That noght wol be governed by hir wyves;
And olde and angry nigardes of dispence,
God sende hem sone verray pestilence.

And thus they both lived until their lives' end
In perfect joy; and Jesus Christ us send,
Husbands meek and young and fresh in bed,
And the grace to outlive those whom we wed;   1260
I pray that Jesus may shorten the lives
Of those who won't be governed by their wives;
And old and stingy niggards who won't spend,
To them may God a pestilence soon send!

THE CLERK'S PROLOGUE

Heere folweth the Prologe of the Clerkes Tale of Oxenford.

"Sir Clerk of Oxenford," our Hoste sayde,
"Ye ryde as coy and stille as dooth a mayde
Were newe spoused, sittinge at the bord.
This day ne herde I of your tonge a word.
I trowe ye studie aboute som sophyme,   5
But Salomon seith, 'every thing hath tyme.'
        For Goddes sake, as beth of bettre chere.
It is no tyme for to studien here.
Telle us som mery tale, by youre fey!
For what man that is entred in a pley,   10
He nedes moot unto the pley assente.
But precheth nat, as freres doon in Lente,
To make us for our olde sinnes wepe,
Ne that thy tale make us nat to slepe.
        Telle us som mery thing of aventures.   15
Youre termes, youre colours, and youre figures,
Kepe hem in stoor til so be ye endyte
Heigh style, as whan that men to kinges wryte.
Speketh so pleyn at this time, we yow preye,
That we may understonde what ye seye."   20
        This worthy Clerk benignely answerde:
"Hoste," quod he, "I am under your yerde;
Ye han of us as now the governaunce,
And therfor wol I do yow obeisaunce
As fer as reson axeth, hardily.   25

THE CLERK'S PROLOGUE

Here follows the Prologue of the Clerk of Oxford's Tale.

"Now, Sir Clerk of Oxford," our Host said then,
"You ride shy and still as does a maiden
Newly wed, who's sitting at the banquet;
Today, no word from your tongue I've heard yet.
Some sophism, I believe, you study on;
But 'each thing has its time,' says Solomon.   6
        For God's sake, now, come be of better cheer!
This is no time to be studying here.
So, by your faith, some merry tale now say!
For when one undertakes a game to play,   10
To the game's rules one must then assent.
But do not preach, as friars do in Lent;
For our old sins now, do not make us weep,
And make sure your tale won't put us to sleep.
        Tell some merry thing about adventures.   15
Your terms and your rhetorical figures,
Keep them in storage till you can indite
In high style, as when men to kings do write.
Just speak quite plainly at this time, we pray,
So we can understand what you might say."   20
        This worthy clerk answered him benignly:
"Host, I am under your authority,"
Said he, "of us, you have now governance;
Therefore to you I owe obedience,
As far as reason asks, it is no lie.   25

367

I wol yow telle a tale which that I
Lerned at Padowe of a worthy clerk,
As preved by his wordes and his werk.
He is now deed and nayled in his cheste;
I prey to God so yeve his soule reste!   30
        Fraunceys Petrark, the laureat poete,
Highte this clerk, whos rethoryke sweete
Enlumined al Itaille of poetrye,
As Linian dide of philosophye
Or lawe, or other art particuler;   35
But deeth, that wol nat suffre us dwellen heer
But as it were a twinkling of an yë,
Hem bothe hath slayn, and alle shul we dye.
        But forth to tellen of this worthy man
That taughte me this tale, as I bigan,   40
I seye that first with heigh style he endyteth,
Er he the body of his tale wryteth,
A proheme, in the which discryveth he
Pemond, and of Saluces the contree,
And speketh of Apennyn, the hilles hye,   45
That been the boundes of West Lumbardye,
And of Mount Vesulus in special,
Where as the Poo, out of a welle smal,
Taketh his firste springing and his sours,
That estward ay encresseth in his cours   50
To Emelward, to Ferrare, and Venyse:
The which a long thing were to devyse,
And trewely, as to my jugement,
Me thinketh it a thing impertinent,
Save that he wol conveyen his matere.   55
But this his tale, which that ye may here."

I will tell you a tale now, one that I
Learned at Padua from a worthy clerk,
As proven by his words and by his work.
He is now dead and nailed in his coffin;
I pray God that his soul's rest he dwells in!   30
       Frances Petrarch,[1] the laureate poet,
This clerk is named, whose sweet rhetoric yet
Illumines Italy with poetry,
As Lignano[2] did with philosophy,
Canon law, or studies particular.   35
But to dwell here, Death will not us suffer;
As it were in the twinkling of an eye,
Death slew them both, and all of us will die.
       But to tell on about this worthy man
Who did teach me this tale, as I began,   40
I say that, first, in high style he indites,
Before the body of his tale he writes,
A proem, and then in it describes he
Piedmont and of Saluzzo the country,
And of the Apennines' high hills speaks he—   45
They're the boundaries of West Lombardy—
And especially of Monte Viso,
Where, from a small pool, the great river Po
Does take its first springing and its source,
And to the east increases in its course   50
Toward Emilia, Ferrara, and Venice;
It would be a long thing to describe this.
Certainly, as it stands in my judgment,
It is, I think, a thing irrelevant,
Save to begin his tale, it does appear;   55
But this is his tale, which you now may hear."

---

   1   **Frances Petrarch**: The great Italian poet (1304–1374), who was crowned with laurel for his poetry by the Senate in Rome in 1341. Although the Clerk credits Petrarch with the story of Griselde, Petrarch's version itself is actually an adaptation in Latin of Boccaccio's Italian vernacular redaction of the tale in *The Decameron*. In composing *The Clerk's Tale*, Chaucer used a French translation of Petrarch's story, along with Petrarch's story itself. All of these versions, interestingly, are in prose.

   2   **Lignano**: John of Lignano (c. 1320–1383), a famous professor of canon law at the University of Bologna.

THE CLERK'S TALE

Ther is, at the west syde of Itaille,
Doun at the rote of Vesulus the colde,
A lusty playne, habundant of vitaille,
Wher many a tour and toun thou mayst biholde   60
That founded were in tyme of fadres olde,
And many another delitable sighte,
And Saluces this noble contree highte.

A markis whylom lord was of that londe,
As were his worthy eldres him bifore;   65
And obeisant, ay redy to his honde
Were alle his liges, bothe lasse and more.
Thus in delyt he liveth, and hath don yore,
Biloved and drad, thurgh favour of Fortune,
Bothe of his lordes and of his commune.   70

Therwith he was, to speke as of linage,
The gentilleste y-born of Lumbardye,
A fair persone, and strong, and yong of age,
And ful of honour and of curteisye;
Discreet ynogh his contree for to gye—   75
Save in somme thinges that he was to blame—
And Walter was this yonge lordes name.

THE CLERK'S TALE

Here begins the Tale of the Clerk of Oxford.

There is, on the west side of Italy,
Down at the foot of Monte Viso cold,
With abundant crops, a plain that's comely,
With many towns and towers to behold,   60
That founded were in times of fathers old,
And many more delightful sights to see:
And Saluzzo was named this fine country.

A marquis once the lord was of that land,
As were his worthy elders, one and all;   65
Obedient and always right at hand
Were all his liegemen, both the great and small.
Thus in delight he lives, as years do fall,
Beloved and feared, through Fortune's high rewards,
Both by his common subjects and his lords.   70

And thus he was, to speak of lineage,
The most gently born man of Lombardy,
A handsome person, strong and young in age,
And full of honor and of courtesy;
Discreet enough to govern all his country,   75
Save in some things, in which he was to blame;
And Walter was this gentle young lord's name.

I blame him thus, that he considered noght
In tyme cominge what mighte him bityde,
But on his lust present was al his thoght,   80
As for to hauke and hunte on every syde;
Wel ny alle othere cures leet he slyde,
And eek he nolde—and that was worst of alle—
Wedde no wyf, for noght that may bifalle.

Only that point his peple bar so sore   85
That flokmele on a day they to him wente,
And oon of hem, that wysest was of lore,
Or elles that the lord best wolde assente
That he sholde telle him what his peple mente,
Or elles coude he shewe wel swich matere,   90
He to the markis seyde as ye shul here.

"O noble markis, your humanitee
Assureth us and yeveth us hardinesse,
As ofte as tyme is of necessitee,
That we to yow mowe telle our hevinesse.   95
Accepteth, lord, now of youre gentillesse,
That we with pitous herte unto yow pleyne,
And lete youre eres nat my voys disdeyne.

Al have I noght to done in this matere
More than another man hath in this place,   100
Yet for as muche as ye, my lord so dere,
Han alwey shewed me favour and grace,
I dar the better aske of yow a space
Of audience, to shewen our requeste,
And ye, my lord, to doon right as yow leste.   105

I blame him thus: that he considered nought
In the future all that might him betide,
But on his present pleasure was his thought, 80
To go hunting and hawking on each side.
Almost all other cares he did let slide;
Also he wouldn't—this was worst of all—
A woman wed, whatever might befall.

His people so badly bore this spurning 85
That in a group one day they to him went.
One of them, who wisest was in learning—
Either because the lord best would assent
That he should tell him what the people meant,
Or else the matter well argue could he— 90
As you will hear, he said to the marquis:

"Oh noble marquis, your humanity
Assures us and gives to us the boldness,
As often as it is necessity,
To tell you, as we must, of our sadness. 95
Accept, our lord, now, through your gentleness
What we, with piteous hearts, here do complain,
And, pray, let your ears not my voice disdain.

Though I have no stake in this matter here
More than the other men do in this place, 100
Yet, insofar as you, my lord so dear,
Have always shown me your favor and grace
I dare the more to ask you for the space
Of an audience to give our request,
And you, my lord, should do as you think best. 105

For certes, lord, so wel us lyketh yow
And al your werk, and ever han doon, that we
Ne coude nat us self devysen how
We mighte liven in more felicitee,
Save o thing, lord, if it youre wille be,   110
That for to been a wedded man yow leste:
Than were your peple in sovereyn hertes reste.

Boweth youre nekke under that blisful yok
Of soveraynetee, noght of servyse,
Which that men clepeth spousaille or wedlok;   115
And thenketh, lord, among your thoghtes wyse,
How that oure dayes passe in sondry wyse;
For though we slepe or wake, or rome, or ryde,
Ay fleeth the tyme, it nil no man abyde.

And though youre grene youthe floure as yit,   120
In crepeth age alwey, as stille as stoon,
And deeth manaceth every age, and smit
In each estaat, for ther escapeth noon.
And al so certein as we knowe echoon
That we shul deye, as uncerteyn we alle   125
Been of that day whan deeth shal on us falle.

Accepteth than of us the trewe entente,
That never yet refuseden youre heste,
And we wol, lord, if that ye wol assente,
Chese yow a wyf in short tyme, atte leste,   130
Born of the gentilleste and of the meste
Of al this lond, so that it oghte seme
Honour to God and yow, as we can deme.

For truly, lord, so well you please us now,
And your work, as you've always done, that we
Could not among ourselves imagine how
We might live now in more felicity,
Save one thing, lord, if your will it might be: 110
To be a wedded man you might think best;
Then people's hearts would be in perfect rest.

Bow your neck now under that blissful yoke,
Not of service, but of sovereignty,
Whose name, wedlock or marriage, men invoke;   115
And think, our lord, for so wise you may be,
How, in sundry ways, our days pass quickly,
For though we sleep, wake, roam, ride while we can,
Time always flees; it will wait for no man.

And though you flower now in green youth's might,   120
Age creeps in always, silent as a stone,
And death menaces every age, and smites
Each rank, for not one man escapes alone;
And just as surely as to all it's known
That we shall die, as uncertain we all   125
Are of that day when death will on us fall.

Accept then now from us this true intent,
Who never yet have refused your behest,
And we will, lord, if you wish to assent,
Choose you a wife, in short time, as is best,   130
Born of the highest and the gentlest
Of all this land, so that it should well seem
Honor to God and you, as we can deem.

Delivere us out of al this bisy drede
And tak a wyf, for hye Goddes sake;   135
For if it so bifelle, as God forbede,
That thurgh your deeth your lyne sholde slake,
And that a straunge successour sholde take
Youre heritage, O, wo were us alyve!
Wherfor we pray you hastily to wyve."   140

Hir meke preyere and hir pitous chere
Made the markis herte han pitee.
"Ye wol," quod he, "myn owene peple dere,
To that I never erst thoghte streyne me.
I me rejoysed of my libertee   145
That selde tyme is founde in mariage;
Ther I was free, I moot been in servage.

But nathelees I see your trewe entente,
And truste upon youre wit, and have don ay;
Wherfore of my free wil I wole assente   150
To wedde me, as sone as evere I may.
But theras ye han profred me today
To chese me a wyf, I yow relesse
That choys, and prey yow of that profre cesse.

For God it woot, that children ofte been   155
Unlyk hir worthy eldres hem bifore;
Bountee comth al of God, nat of the streen
Of which they been engendred and y-bore.
I truste in Goddes bountee and therfore
My mariage and myn estaat and reste   160
I him bitake; he may don as him leste.

Deliver us from all this constant fear,
And marry soon, for love of God on high! 135
For, God forbid, if it should happen here,
That your line should diminish when you die,
And thus a strange successor would come by
Your heritage. Oh, woe would be our life!
Therefore, we pray you, quickly take a wife." 140

Their meek prayer and all their piteous cheer
Made the marquis in his heart have pity.
"You wish," said he, "now my own people dear,
What I never wanted to constrain me.
I did rejoice in all my liberty, 145
And that quite seldom is in marriage found;
Where I was free, to serve I must be bound.

But nonetheless, I see your true intent
And trust your wisdom, as I have always;
Therefore, of my free will, I will assent 150
To marry, as soon as ever I may.
But whereas you have offered me today
To choose my wife, here I now you release
From that choice, and pray that this offer cease.

God knows it, surely children can remain 155
Unlike worthy elders who came before;
All virtue comes from God, not from the strain
Which did engender them and which them bore.
I trust in all God's bounty, and therefore
My marriage and estate and all the rest 160
I entrust to him to do as he thinks best.

Lat me alone in chesinge of my wyf—
That charge upon my bak I wol endure;
But I yow preye, and charge upon youre lyf,
That what wyf that I take, ye me assure   165
To worshipe hire whyl that hir lyf may dure,
In word and werk, bothe here and everywhere,
As she an emperoures doghter were.

And forthermore this shal ye swere, that ye
Agayn my choys shul neither grucche ne stryve;   170
For sith I shal forgoon my libertee
At your requeste, as ever moot I thryve,
Ther as myn herte is set, ther wol I wyve.
And but ye wole assente in swich manere,
I prey yow, speketh namore of this matere."   175

With hertely wil they sworen and assenten
To al this thing—ther seyde no wight nay—
Bisekinge him of grace, er that they wenten,
That he wolde graunten hem a certein day
Of his spousaille, as sone as evere he may;   180
For yet alwey the peple somwhat dredde
Lest that this markis no wyf wolde wedde.

He graunted hem a day, swich as him leste,
On which he wolde be wedded sikerly,
And seyde he dide al this at hir requeste.   185
And they, with humble entente, buxomly,
Knelinge upon hir knees ful reverently,
Him thanken alle; and thus they han an ende
Of hire entente, and hoom agayn they wende.

Leave to me alone the choosing of my wife—
That burden on my back I will endure.
But I pray you, and charge it on your life,
Whatever wife I take, you do assure   165
Me worship of her, while her life endures,
Everywhere, in word and work surely,
As though an emperor's daughter were she.

And furthermore, this too you'll swear to me:
Against my choice, you'll never grudge or strive;   170
For since I shall forego my liberty
At your request, as ever must I thrive,
I will marry where my heart does arrive.
Unless you'll assent in such a manner,
I pray you, speak no more of this matter."   175

With hearty will, they swear and they assent
To all this thing—and not one man said, "Nay"—
Beseeching him, by grace, before they went,
That he would name for them a certain day
For his wedding, soon as ever he may;   180
For yet, always, the people had some dread,
Lest still the young marquis no wife would wed.

He granted them a day, at their request,
On which he would be wed then certainly,
And said he did all this at their behest.   185
With humble intent, obediently,
Kneeling upon their knees reverently,
They all thank him, and thus they have an end
To their request, and home again they wend.

And heerupon he to his officeres   190
Comaundeth for the feste to purveye,
And to his privee knightes and squyeres
Swich charge yaf as him liste on hem leye;
And they to his comandement obeye,
And ech of them doth al his diligence   195
To doon unto the feste reverence.

Explicit pars prima.
Incipit secunda pars.

Noght fer fro thilke paleys honurable
Wheras this markis shoop his mariage,
Ther stood a throp, of site delitable,
In which that povre folk of that village   200
Hadden hir bestes and hir herbergage,
And of hire labour took hir sustenance
After that the erthe yaf hem habundance.

Amonges thise povre folk ther dwelte a man
Which that was holden povrest of hem alle;   205
But hye God somtyme senden can
His grace into a litel oxes stalle.
Janicula men of that throp him calle;
A doghter hadde he, fair ynogh to sighte,
And Grisildis this yonge mayden highte.   210

And thereupon, he bids his officers   190
Prepare the wedding feast without delay,
And then to his own private knights and squires
Gives such charges, as he would on them lay;
And they to his commands at once obey,
And each of them does all his diligence   195
To make the wedding feast with reverence.

The first part ends.
The second part begins.

Not too far from that palace beautiful,
Where the marquis made plans for his marriage,
Stood a hamlet on a site delightful,
In which all the poor folk of that village   200
Did keep their beasts, and also, there they lodge,
And from their labor took their sustenance,
As the earth would give them its abundance.

Among these poor folk there did dwell a man
Who was then thought the poorest of them all;   205
But there are times our highest Lord send can
His grace into a little oxen's stall;³
The village men Janicula him call.
A daughter had he, in appearance fair;
Griselda this young maiden was called there.   210

---

3   **oxen's stall**: It is customary to note that here and elsewhere in *The Clerk's Tale* (e.g., lines 274
ff.), Chaucer has added imagery of the Annunciation and the Nativity and other associations with the
Virgin Mary to his characterization of Griselda.

But for to speke of vertuous beautee,
Than was she oon the faireste under sonne;
For povreliche y-fostred up was she,
No likerous lust was thurgh hire herte y-ronne.
Wel ofter of the welle than of the tonne   215
She drank; and for she wolde vertu plese,
She knew wel labour, but non ydel ese.

But thogh this mayde tendre were of age,
Yet in the brest of hir virginitee
Ther was enclosed rype and sad corage;   220
And in greet reverence and charitee
Hir olde povre fader fostred she.
A fewe sheep, spinninge, on feeld she kepte;
She wolde noght been ydel til she slepte.

And whan she hoomward cam, she wolde bringe   225
Wortes or othere herbes tymes ofte,
The whiche she shredde and seeth for hir livyng,
And made hir bed ful harde and nothing softe;
And ay she kepte hir fadres lyf on lofte
With everich obeisaunce and diligence   230
That child may doon to fadres reverence.

Upon Grisilde, this povre creature,
Ful ofte sythe this markis sette his yë
As he on hunting rood paraventure;
And whan it fil that he mighte hire espye,   235
He noght with wantoun loking of folye
His eyen caste on hire, but in sad wyse
Upon hir chere he wolde him ofte avyse,

But to speak of her virtuous beauty,
Of the fairest, she was beneath the sun;
For, since she was brought up in poverty,
No lustful longing through her heart did run.
More often from the well than from the tun
She drank, and since she wished virtue to please,   216
She well knew labor, but not idle ease.

But though this maiden was of tender age,
Yet in the breast of her virginity
Was enclosed a ripe and sober courage;   220
And with such great respect and charity
Her poor old father gladly tended she.
While spinning, a few sheep, in field she kept,
And she would not be idle till she slept.

And when she came back homeward, she would bring   225
Cabbages or other herbs quite often,
Which she'd shred and stew to make their living;
The hard bed she made nothing could soften;
Always she her father's life sustained then
With the obedience and diligence   230
A child shows to do a father reverence.

Yet upon Griselda, this poor creature,
Quite often this marquis has set his eye
When out on his hunting he would venture;
And when it happened that he might her spy,   235
He not with wanton looking cast an eye
For folly on her, but with somber guise
On her aspect, he would himself advise,

Commendinge in his herte hir wommanhede,
And eek hir vertu, passinge any wight   240
Of so yong age, as wel in chere as dede.
For thogh the peple have no greet insight
In vertu, he considered ful right
Hir bountee, and disposed that he wolde
Wedde hire only, if ever he wedde sholde.   245

The day of wedding cam, but no wight can
Telle what womman that it sholde be;
For which merveille wondred many a man,
And seyden, whan they were in privetee,
"Wol nat our lord yet leve his vanitee?   250
Wol he nat wedde? allas, allas the whyle!
Why wol he thus himself and us bigyle?"

But natheles this markis hath don make
Of gemmes, set in gold and in asure,
Broches and ringes, for Grisildis sake,   255
And of hir clothing took he the mesure
By a mayde, lyk to hire stature,
And eek of othere ornamentes alle
That unto switch a wedding sholde falle.

The tyme of undern of the same day   260
Approcheth, that this wedding sholde be;
And al the paleys put was in array,
Bothe halle and chambres, ech in his degree;
Houses of office stuffed with plentee
Ther maystow seen, of deyntevous vitaille   265
That may be founde as fer as last Itaille.

Commending in his heart her womanhood,
And far beyond her youth, the stalwart might   240
Of her virtue, in look and deeds all good.
For though the people have no great insight
Into virtue, he pondered, as is right,
Her graciousness and decided he would
Wed only her, if wed he ever should.   245

The wedding day soon came, but no one can
Tell what woman to him should married be;
At this marvel wondered many a man,
And some said to each other privately,
"Will not our lord yet leave his vanity?   250
Will he not wed? Alas! Alas, the while!
Why will he thus himself and us beguile?"

But nonetheless, the marquis had men make
From his gems, set all in gold and azure,
Both rings and brooches for Griselda's sake;   255
Of her clothing, he has taken measure
From a maiden quite like her in stature,
And also, of all kinds the ornaments
That then for such a wedding would be meant.

The middle morning of the very day   260
Approaches, when his wedding there should be;
All the palace was decked in its array,
Both hall and chambers, as was fit to see,
Both kitchen and pantry stuffed with plenty
Of each and every great delicacy   265
That may be found in all of Italy.

This royal markis, richely arrayed,
Lordes and ladyes in his companye,
The whiche unto the feste were y-prayed,
And of his retenue the bachelrye,   270
With many a soun of sondry melodye,
Unto the village of the which I tolde,
In this array the righte wey han holde.

Grisilde of this, God woot, ful innocent
That for hire shapen was al this array,   275
To fecchen water at a welle is went,
And cometh hoom as sone as ever she may.
For wel she hadde herd seyd that thilke day
The markis sholde wedde, and, if she mighte,
She wolde fayn han seyn some of that sighte.   280

She thoghte, "I wol with othere maydens stonde,
That been my felawes, in our dore and see
The markisesse, and therfor wol I fonde
To doon at hoom as sone as it may be
The labour which that longeth unto me;   285
And than I may at leyser hire biholde,
If she this wey unto the castel holde."

And as she wolde over hir threshfold goon,
The markis cam and gan hire for to calle,
And she sette doun hir water pot anoon   290
Bisyde the threshfold, in an oxes stalle,
And doun upon hir knees she gan to falle,
And with sad contenance kneleth stille
Til she had herd what was the lordes wille.

This royal marquis, so richly arrayed,
The lords and ladies in his company,
Whose presence at his wedding feast he'd prayed,
And all the young knights there in his meinie,[4]
With many sounds of sundry melodies,   271
To the village of which I have you told
In this array the nearest way they hold.

Griselda, as God knows, all innocent,
That for her now was shaped all this array—   275
Out to fetch water at a well, she went,
And she comes home then as soon as she may;
For she had heard it said that this same day
The young marquis would wed, and if she might,
She would be glad to see some of that sight.   280

She thought, "I will with other maidens stand,
Who are my fellows, in our door and see
The new marchioness, and thus I've planned
To do at home, as quickly as may be,
All the labor that does belong to me,   285
And then I may at leisure her behold,
If toward the castle this way she may hold."

But before her threshold she had passed,
The marquis came, and for her he did call;
And then her water pot she set down fast,   290
Beside the threshold, in an ox's stall,
And down upon her knees then she did fall;
With sober countenance she kneels all still,
Until she had heard what was the lord's will.

---

4   **meinie**: Feudal retinue or followers.

This thoghtful markis spak unto this mayde   295
Ful sobrely, and seyde in this manere:
"Wher is your fader, Grisildis?" he sayde,
And she with reverence, in humble chere,
Answerde, "Lord, he is al redy here."
And in she gooth withouten lenger lette,   300
And to the markis she hir fader fette.

He by the hond than took this olde man,
And seyde thus whan he him hadde asyde,
"Janicula, I neither may ne can
Lenger the plesance of myn herte hyde.   305
If that thou vouche sauf, what so bityde,
Thy doghter wol I take er that I wende
As for my wyf, unto hir lyves ende.

Thou lovest me, I woot it wel, certeyn,
And art my feithful lige man y-bore;   310
And al that lyketh me, I dar wel seyn
It lyketh thee; and specially therfore
Tel me that poynt that I have seyd bifore:
If that thou wolt unto that purpos drawe
To take me as for thy sone-in-lawe."   315

This sodeyn cas this man astoned so
That reed he wex; abayst and al quaking
He stood. Unnethes seyde he wordes mo,
But only thus: "Lord," quod he, "my willinge
Is as ye wole, ne ayeines your lykinge   320
I wol no thing, ye be my lord so dere.
Right as yow lust governeth this matere."

This pensive marquis spoke then to this maiden   295
Quite soberly, and said to her so clear:
"Where is your father, Griselda?" he asked then.
And she with reverence and humble cheer,
Answered him, "Lord, he is already here."
Without tarrying longer, in goes she,   300
And she her father fetched for the marquis.

Right by the hand, he then took this old man,
And said thus, when he'd taken him aside:
"Janicula, I neither may nor can
A moment longer my heart's pleasure hide.   305
If you vouchsafe, whatever may betide,
Your daughter I will take before I wend,
To be my wife, until her life may end.

You love me well, I know it certainly,
And are my faithful liege man furthermore,   310
And I dare say that all that pleases me,
It pleases you. Especially therefore
Answer the point that I have said before,
If you should wish to that purpose to draw,
And take me here to be your son-in-law."   315

This new event astonished so this man,
He waxed red; embarrassed and all quaking
He stood; and hardly one word speak he can,
But only thus: "Lord," said he, "my willing
Is as you will, nor against your liking   320
Do I will one thing, you are my lord so dear;
Just as you like, govern this matter here."

"Yet wol I," quod this markis softely,
"That in thy chambre I and thou and she
Have a collacion, and wostow why?   325
For I wol axe if it hire wille be
To be my wyf, and reule hire after me.
And al this shal be doon in thy presence—
I wol noght speke out of thyn audience."

And in the chambre whyl they were aboute   330
Hir tretis, which as ye shal after here,
The peple cam unto the hous withoute,
And wondred hem in how honest manere
And tentifly she kepte hir fader dere.
But outerly Grisildis wondre mighte,   335
For never erst ne saugh she swich a sighte.

No wonder is thogh that she were astoned
To seen so greet a gest come in that place;
She never was to swiche gestes woned,
For which she loked with ful pale face.   340
But shortly forth this matere for to chace,
Thise arn the wordes that the markis sayde
To this benigne, verray, feithful mayde.

"Grisilde," he seyde, "ye shul wel understonde
It lyketh to your fader and to me   345
That I yow wedde, and eek it may so stonde,
As I suppose, ye wol that it so be.
But thise demandes axe I first," quod he,
"That sith it shal be doon in hastif wyse,
Wol ye assente, or elles yow avyse?   350

Then said this marquis softly, "Yet wish I
That in your chamber I and you and she
Should have a colloquy. Do you know why?   325
For I will ask if her will it might be
To be my wife and to be ruled by me.
All this will be done within your presence;
I won't speak without you as audience."

In the chamber, while they then were making   330
Their agreement, which you will hear after,
The people came and outside they were standing,
And marveled in how virtuous a manner
Attentively she cared for her dear father.
But utterly Griselda wonder might,   335
For she never before saw such a sight.

If she were astonished, then no wonder,
To see so great a guest come in that place;
To such guests, accustomed was she never,
And thus she looked around with a pale face.   340
But shortly now, this matter forth to chase,
These are the words that the marquis said then
To this true, benign, and faithful maiden:

"Griselda," he said, "you should understand
It's pleasing to your father and to me   345
That I wed you, and too, it may so stand,
As I suppose, you wish that it may be,
But these questions I ask you first," said he,
"Since this all will be done quite hastily.
Will you think on it, or assent to me?   350

I seye this, be ye redy with good herte
To al my lust, and that I frely may,
As me best thinketh, do yow laughe or smerte,
And never ye to grucche it, night ne day?
And eek whan I sey 'ye,' ne sey nat 'nay,'   355
Neither by word ne frowning contenance?
Swere this, and here I swere our alliance."

Wondringe upon this word, quakinge for drede,
She seyde, "Lord, undigne and unworthy
Am I to thilke honour that ye me bede;   360
But as ye wol yourself, right so wol I.
And heer I swere that nevere willingly
In werk ne thoght I nil yow disobeye,
For to be deed, though me were looth to deye."

"This is ynogh, Grisilde myn!" quod he.   365
And forth he gooth with a ful sobre chere
Out at the dore, and after that cam she,
And to the peple he seyde in this manere:
"This is my wyf," quod he, "that standeth here.
Honoureth hire and loveth hire I preye   370
Whoso me loveth; ther is namore to seye."

And for that nothing of hir olde gere
She sholde bringe into his hous, he bad
That wommen sholde dispoilen hire right there;
Of which thise ladyes were nat right glad   375
To handle hir clothes wherinne she was clad.
But natheles, this mayde bright of hewe
Fro foot to heed they clothed han al newe.

I say this: are you ready with good heart
To do all I wish, so that I freely may,
As I think best, make you laugh or else smart,
And you will not begrudge it, night or day?
Also, when I say 'Yea,' you won't say 'Nay,'   355
Neither with word nor frowning countenance?
Swear, and here I will swear our alliance."

Wondering at his words, quaking for fear,
She said, "Lord, unsuitable and unworthy
Am I to this honor you offer here.   360
As you yourself wish, so it goes with me.
And here I swear that never willingly,
In work or thought, disobey will not I,
Though I'd be dead, and I am loathe to die."

"This is enough, Griselda mine," said he.   365
And thus now he goes forth with sober cheer
Out through the door, and after that came she,
And to the people, said for all to hear,
"This is my wife," said he, "who's standing near.
Now honor her and love her, I you pray,   370
You who love me; there is no more to say."

And so that nothing then of her old gear
She should bring into his house, he had
Women who would undress her now right here;
For sure, these ladies were not very glad   375
To handle her clothes in which she was clad.
But nonetheless, this maiden bright of hue
From head to foot they dressed in clothes all new.

Hir heres han they kembd, that lay untressed
Ful rudely, and with hir fingres smale   380
A corone on hire heed they han y-dressed,
And sette hire ful of nowches grete and smale.
Of hire array what sholde I make a tale?
Unnethe the peple hir knew for hire fairnesse,
Whan she translated was in swich richesse.   385

This markis hath hire spoused with a ring
Broght for the same cause, and thanne hire sette
Upon an hors, snow-whyt and wel ambling,
And to his paleys, er he lenger lette,
With joyful peple that hire ladde and mette,   390
Conveyed hire; and thus the day they spende
In revel, til the sonne gan descende.

And shortly forth this tale for to chace,
I seye that to this newe markisesse
God hath swich favour sent hire of his grace,   395
That it ne semed nat by lyklinesse
That she was born and fed in rudenesse,
As in a cote or in an oxe-stalle,
But norished in an emperoures halle.

To every wight she woxen is so dere   400
And worshipful, that folk ther she was bore
And from hire birthe knewe hire yeer by yere,
Unnethe trowed they—but dorste han swore—
That to Janicle, of which I spak bifore,
She doghter were, for, as by conjecture,   405
Hem thoughte she was another creature.

They have combed her hair, which lay unbraided
All roughly, and then with their fingers small   380
A nuptial garland they set on her head,
And decked her with jeweled brooches, great and small.
Of her new array, why should I tell all?
These folks hardly knew her for her fairness
When translated was she to such richness.   385

This marquis has her married with a ring
Brought for this purpose, and then he her set
On a horse, snow white and gently ambling;
To his palace—he would not tarry yet—
With joyful people, who her led and met,   390
He conveyed her; and thus the day they spend
In revelry till the sun did descend.

And shortly now, this whole tale forth to chase,
I say that to this new marchioness
God has sent her such favor by his grace   395
It did seem like a true unlikeliness
That she was born and fostered in such rudeness,
As in a peasant's hut or oxen's stall,
But rather nurtured in an emperor's hall.

To each person she has become so dear   400
And worshipped that folks where she had been born,
And who, from her birth, knew her year by year,
Hardly they believed—but they would have sworn—
To Janicula, whom I named before,
She daughter was, for, by their conjecture,   405
It seemed to them she was another creature.

For thogh that evere vertuous was she,
She was encressed in swich excellence
Of thewes gode, y-set in heigh bountee,
And so discreet and fair of eloquence,   410
So benigne and so digne of reverence,
And coude so the peples herte embrace,
That ech hire lovede that loked on hir face.

Noght only of Saluces in the toun
Publiced was the bountee of hir name,   415
But eek bisyde in many a regioun:
If oon seyde wel, another seyde the same.
So spradde of hire heighe bountee the fame
That men and wommen, as wel yonge as olde,
Gon to Saluce upon hire to biholde.   420

Thus Walter lowly—nay but royally—
Wedded with fortunat honestetee,
In Goddes pees liveth ful esily   425
At hoom, and outward grace ynogh had he;
And for he saugh that under low degree
Was ofte vertu hid, the peple him helde
A prudent man, and that is seyn ful selde.

Nat only this Grisildis thurgh hir wit
Coude al the feet of wyfly hoomlinesse,
But eek, whan that the cas requyred it,   430
The commune profit coude she redresse.
Ther nas discord, rancour, ne hevinesse
In al that lond that she ne coude apese,
And wysly bringe hem alle in reste and ese.

For although always virtuous was she,
She had increased in showing excellence
In all good traits, set within great bounty,
And so discreet and fair in eloquence,   410
So benign and worthy of reverence,
And she could so the people's hearts embrace
That all loved her who looked upon her face.

Not only in the town of Saluzzo
Was published all the bounty of her name,   415
But in many other regions also,
If one spoke well, the other spoke the same;
So far of her great bounty spread the fame
That men and women, both the young and old,
All to Saluzzo go her to behold.   420

Thus Walter lowly—no, but royally—
Has wed thus with fortunate honesty,
Now in God's peace he does live easily
At home, and outward grace enough had he;
And since he saw that under low degree   425
Virtue can hide, his people held him then
A prudent man, and this is not said often.

Not only did Griselda through her wit
Know all the skills that a good housewife should,
But also, when the case required it,   430
She knew how to promote the common good.
No rancor or discord then, but she could
In all that land such heavyness appease,
And wisely bring them all to rest and ease.

Though that hire housbonde absent were, anoon   435
If gentil men or othere of hire contree
Were wrothe, she wolde bringen hem atoon;
So wyse and rype wordes hadde she,
And jugements of so greet equitee,
That she from heven sent was, as men wende,   440
Peple to save and every wrong t'amende.

Nat longe tyme after that this Grisild
Was wedded, she a doughter hath y-bore.
Al had hire levere have born a knave child,
Glad was this markis and the folk therfore;   445
For though a mayde child come al bifore,
She may unto a knave child atteyne
By lyklihed, sin she nis nat bareyne.

Explicit secunda pars.
Incipit tercia pars.

Ther fil, as it bifalleth tymes mo,
Whan that this child had souked but a throwe,   450
This markis in his herte longeth so
To tempte his wyf, hir sadnesse for to knowe,
That he ne mighte out of his herte throwe
This merveillous desyr, his wyf t'assaye;
Needless, God woot, he thoughte hire for t'affraye.   455

He hadde assayed hire ynogh bifore
And fond hire evere good. What needed it
Hire for to tempte and alwey more and more,
Though som men preise it for a subtil wit?
But as for me, I seye that yvel it sit   460
T'assaye a wyf whan that it is no nede,
And putten hire in anguish and in drede.

Although at times her husband absent were,   435
If gentlemen or folk of her country
Were wrathful, she'd bring them all together;
Such wise and such ripe words always had she,
And judgments sure of such great equity,
That men supposed that heaven did her send   440
People to save and every wrong to mend.

This Griselda, not a long time after
She had been wed, a baby daughter bore,
Even though a boy child she'd prefer;
Glad was this marquis and the folk therefore,   445
For although now a girl child came before,
Still she may yet attain a boy child then
By likelihood, since she was not barren.

The second part ends.
The third part begins.

It befell, as happens many times though,
When this child had sucked a short time so,   450
The marquis in his heart felt longing go
To test his wife, her constancy to know,
Because he might not out of his heart throw
This strange desire to go test his wife, then;
Needless, God knows, he thought her he'd frighten.   455

For he had her assayed enough before,
And found her always good; what need was it
To test her now, and always more and more,
Though some men might see it as clever wit?
But as for me, I say it ill befits   460
One to assay a wife when there's no need,
And make her feel anguish and dread, indeed.

For which this markis wroghte in this manere:
He cam alone a-night, ther as she lay,
With sterne face and with ful trouble chere,   465
And seyde thus: "Grisilde," quod he, "that day
That I yow took out of your povre array
And putte yow in estaat of heigh noblesse,
Ye have nat that forgeten, as I gesse.

I seye, Grisild, this present dignitee,   470
In which that I have put yow, as I trowe,
Maketh yow nat foryetful for to be
That I yow took in povre estaat ful lowe.
For any wele ye moot yourselven knowe,
Take hede of every word that I yow seye: 475
Ther is no wight that hereth it but we tweye.

Ye woot yourself wel how that ye cam here
Into this hous, it is nat longe ago,
And though to me that ye be lief and dere,
Unto my gentils ye be no thing so;   480
They seyn, to hem it is greet shame and wo
For to be subgets and ben in servage
To thee, that born art of a smal village.

And namely sith thy doghter was y-bore
Thise wordes han they spoken, doutelees;   485
But I desyre, as I have doon bifore,
To live my lyf with hem in reste and pees;
I may nat in this caas be recchelees.
I moot don with thy doghter for the beste,
Nat as I wolde, but as my peple leste.   490

To this end, he acted in this manner:
He came alone at night, there where she lay,
With stern face and with troubled demeanor,   465
And to her, "Griselda," said he, "that day
That I took you out of your poor array,
And in rank of nobility you dressed—
You have not that forgotten, I would guess?

I say, Griselda, this high dignity,   470
In which, I believe, I have put you so,
Does not make you forgetful thus to be
That I took you from poor estate quite low,
Despite whatever wealth you now might know.
Take heed of every word I say to you;   475
There is no one who hears us but we two.

You yourself know full well how you came here
Into this house, it is not long ago;
And though to me you are beloved and dear,
To my nobles, you are not at all so.   480
They say, to them, it is great shame and woe
To be subjects and be in servitude
To you, who were born in a village rude.

Especially, since your daughter you bore
These very words they have spoken, doubtless.   485
But I desire, as I have done before,
To live with them in rest and peace, regardless.
For in this case, I may not be careless;
I must do with my daughter what is best,
Not what I want, but what people request.   490

And yet, God wot, this is ful looth to me.
But nathelees withoute your witing
I wol nat doon; but this wol I," quod he,
"That ye to me assente as in this thing.
Shewe now youre pacience in youre werking   495
That ye me highte and swore in your village
That day that maked was oure mariage."

Whan she had herd al this, she noght ameved
Neither in word or chere or countenaunce;
For as it semed, she was nat agreved.   500
She seyde, "Lord, al lyth in youre plesaunce;
My child and I with hertely obeisaunce
Ben youres al, and ye mowe save or spille
Youre owene thing: werketh after youre wille.

Ther may no thing, God so my soule save,   505
Lyken to yow that may displese me;
Ne I desyre no thing for to have,
Ne drede for to lese, save only ye;
This wil is in myn herte and ay shal be.
No lengthe of tyme or deeth may this deface,   510
Ne chaunge my corage to another place."

Glad was this markis of hire answering,
But yet he feyned as he were nat so;
Al drery was his chere and his loking
Whan that he sholde out of the chambre go.   515
Sone after this, a furlong wey or two,
He prively hath told al his entente
Unto a man, and to his wyf him sente.

And yet, God knows, this is loathsome to me;
But nonetheless, sure, without your knowing,
I won't do it; but this I wish," said he,
"That you assent to me about this thing.
The same patience show in your behaving, 495
Which you swore and promised in your village
On that day when we did make our marriage."

When she had heard all this, she changed not yet,
Either in speech, or cheer, or countenance,
For, as it seemed, she was not now upset. 500
She said, "Lord, it lies in your preference.
My child and I, with true obedience,
Are yours wholly, and you can save or kill
Your own things; and so work now as you will.

There is nothing, may God now my soul bless, 505
Pleasing to you that may displease me, too;
Nor do I desire one thing to possess,
Nor dread to lose one thing—save only you.
This will is in my heart, forever, too;
No length of time or death may this deface, 510
Nor steer my heart into another place."

Glad was this marquis at her answering,
But yet he feigned as if he were not so;
Dreary was his manner and his looking,
When he should then out of the chamber go. 515
After this, a furlong away or so,
He privately has told all his intent
To a man, whom to his wife he sent.

A maner sergeant was this privee man,
The which that feithful ofte he founden hadde   520
In thinges grete, and eek swich folk wel can
Don execucioun in thinges badde.
The lord knew wel that he him loved and dradde;
And whan this sergeant wiste his lordes wille,
Into the chambre he stalked him ful stille.   525

"Madame," he seyde, "ye mote foryeve it me,
Thogh I do thing to which I am constreyned.
Ye ben so wys that ful wel knowe ye
That lordes hestes mowe nat been y-feyned;
They mowe wel been biwailled or compleyned,   530
But men mot nede unto hire lust obeye,
And so wol I; ther is na more to seye.

This child I am comanded for to take"—
And spak na more, but out the child he hente
Despitously, and gan a chere make   535
As though he wolde han slayn it er he wente.
Grisildis mot al suffren and al consente;
And as a lamb she sitteth meke and stille,
And leet this cruel sergeant doon his wille.

Suspecious was the diffame of this man,   540
Suspect his face, suspect his word also;
Suspect the tyme in which he this bigan.
Allas! hir doghter that she lovede so,
She wende he wolde han slawen it right tho.
But natheles she neither weep ne syked,   545
Conforminge hire to that the markis lyked.

A kind of sergeant was this private servant,
Whom often the marquis faithful found had   520
In great things. And also such folks are meant
To do the execution of things bad.
The lord knew the love and fear he for him had;
When this sergeant learned all his lord's will,
Into the chamber he stalked and stood still.   525

"Madame," he said, "you must now forgive me,
Though I do things to which I am constrained.
You are so wise you know as well as me
That lords' commands must never be disdained;
About them, we may wail or else complain,   530
But men must always their desire obey,
And so will I; there is no more to say.

This child I am commanded now to take"—
He spoke no more, but from her, the child rent
Spitefully, and began motions to make   535
As though he'd slay it there before he went.
Now Griselda must suffer and consent,
And like a lamb, she sits so meek and still,
And she lets this cruel sergeant do his will.

Suspicious was the bad name of this man,   540
Suspect his face, suspect his words also;
Suspect the time at which he this began.
Alas! Her daughter whom she did love so,
She thought he would slay her before he'd go.
But for this, neither weep nor sigh did she,   545
Conforming to the will of the marquis.

But atte laste speken she bigan,
And mekely she to the sergeant preyde,
So as he was a worthy gentil man,
That she moste kisse hire child er that it deyde;   550
And in hir barm this litel child she leyde
With ful sad face, and gan the child to blisse
And lulled it, and after gan it kisse.

And thus she seyde in hire benigne voys,
"Far weel, my child; I shal thee nevere see.   555
But, sith I thee have marked with the croys
Of thilke Fader, blessed mote he be,
That for us deyde upon a croys of tree,
Thy soule, litel child, I him bitake,
For this night shaltow dyen for my sake."   560

I trowe that to a norice in this cas
It had ben hard this rewthe for to se;
Wel mighte a mooder than han cryed "allas!"
But nathelees so sad stedfast was she
That she endured all adversitee,   565
And to the sergeant mekely she sayde,
"Have heer agayn your litel yonge mayde.

Goth now," quod she, "and dooth my lordes heste.
But o thing wol I preye yow of youre grace,
That, but my lord forbad yow, atte leste   570
Burieth this litel body in som place
That bestes ne no briddes it torace."
But he no word wol to that purpos seye,
But took the child and wente upon his weye.

But, finally, to speak then she began,
And meekly to the sergeant she did pray,
Because he was a worthy gentleman,
To kiss her child before it died that day.   550
This little child on her breast she did lay
With face so sad, and prayed for the child's bliss,
And lulled it so, and then she did it kiss.

And thus she said, in her voice so benign,
"Farewell, my child! I shall you never see.   555
But since I marked you with the cross's sign
Of this Father—now blessed must he be!—
Who died for us upon the cross's tree,
Your soul here, little child, may he now take,
For on this night you shall die for my sake."   560

I think that if a nurse came to this pass,
This pitiful case would be hard to see;
Well might a mother then have cried "Alas!"
So squarely steadfast nonetheless was she
That she endured all this adversity,   565
And to the sergeant she said meekly then,
"Have here again your young, little maiden.

Go now," said she, "and do my lord's behest;
But one thing will I pray you of your grace.
Unless my lord forbade you, I request: 570
Bury this little body in some place
Where neither beasts nor birds might it deface."
But he no word will to that bidding say,
But took the child and went upon his way.

This sergeant cam unto his lord ageyn,   575
And of Grisildis wordes and hire chere
He tolde him point for point, in short and playn,
And him presenteth with his doghter dere.
Somwhat this lord hath rewthe in his manere,
But nathelees his purpos heeld he stille,   580
As lordes doon whan they wol han hir wille.

And bad this sergeant that he prively
Sholde this child softe winde and wrappe
With alle circumstances tendrely,
And carie it in a cofre or in a lappe;   585
But, upon peyne his heed of for to swappe,
That no man sholde knowe of his entente,
Ne whenne he cam, ne whider that he wente;

But at Boloigne to his suster dere,
That thilke tyme of Panik was countesse,   590
He sholde it take, and shewe hire this matere,
Bisekinge hire to don hire bisinesse
This child to fostre in alle gentilesse;
And whos child that it was he bad hire hyde
From every wight, for oght that may bityde.   595

The sergeant gooth, and hath fulfild this thing;
But to this markis now retourne we.
For now goth he ful faste imagining
If by his wyves chere he mighte see,
Or by hire word aperceyve, that she   600
Were chaunged; but he never hire coude finde
But ever in oon ylyke sad and kinde.

This sergeant came back to his lord again;   575
Of Griselda's words and her demeanor,
Soon point by point, he quickly told him then,
And he presents him with his dear daughter.
This lord had some pity in his manner,
But nonetheless, his purpose he held still,   580
As lords will do, when they will have their will;

And bade this sergeant that quite privately
This child now he should softly swathe and wrap,
With all attention due quite tenderly,
And carry it in a box or in a wrap;   585
And upon pain his head should meet some mishap,
No man alive should know of his intent,
Nor whence he came, nor whither that he went;

But to Bologna, to his dear sister,
Who back then of Panico[5] was the countess,   590
He should take it and tell of this matter,
Beseeching her to take on the business
This child to foster in all gentleness;
And whose child it was, he bid her to hide
From everyone, whatever might betide.   595

The sergeant goes, and he fulfills this thing;
But to this marquis now return must we.
For now he goes closely examining
If by his wife's demeanor he might see,
Or by her words he might perceive that she   600
Were changed at all; but never could he find
Her anything but steadfast, calm, and kind.

5 **Panico**: Near Bologna.

As glad, as humble, as bisy in servyse,
And eek in love as she was wont to be,
Was she to him in every manner wyse;   605
Ne of hir doghter noght a word spak she.
Non accident for noon adversitee
Was seyn in hire, ne never hir doghter name
Ne nempned she, in ernest nor in game.

Explicit tercia pars.
Sequitur pars quarta.

In this estaat ther passed been foure yeer   610
Er she with childe was; but, as God wolde,
A knave child she bar by this Walter,
Ful gracious and fair for to biholde.
And whan that folk it to his fader tolde,
Nat only he, but al his contree, merie   615
Was for this child, and God they thanke and herie.

When it was two yeer old and fro the brest
Departed of his norice, on a day
This markis caughte yet another lest
To tempte his wyf yet ofter, if he may.   620
O needles was she tempted in assay!
But wedded men ne knowe no mesure
Whan that they finde a pacient creature.

"Wyf," quod this markis, "ye han herd er this,
My peple sikly berth oure mariage,   625
And namely, sith my sone y-boren is,
Now is it worse than ever in al our age.
The murmur sleeth myn herte and my corage,
For to myne eres comth the voys so smerte
That it wel ny destroyed hath myn herte.   630

As busy in service, as humble, as glad,
As busy in love as she was wont to be,
Was she to him in every way she had;   605
And of her daughter, not a word spoke she;
And not one change brought by adversity
Was seen in her, nor once her daughter's name
Did she mention, in earnestness or game.

The third part ends.
The fourth part follows.

In this manner, four years had passed before   610
She was with child again. As God's will holds,
A boy child by this Walter she now bore,
Who was quite fair and gracious to behold.
And when the folk this to his father told,
Not just he, but all his country merry   615
Was for this child. To God their praise they carry.

When it was two years old, and from the breast
Of its nurse had been weaned, there came a day
When in the marquis the desire to test
His wife again caught hold, if so he may.   620
O needless was she tried in this assay!
But wed men can no moderation measure,
When once they have found a patient creature.

"Wife," said this marquis, "as you heard before,
My people approve not of our marriage;   625
Especially since now my son you bore,
It is worse than when we first made our pledge.
Their murmurings slay my heart and courage.
All their sharp voices do make my ears smart
So that almost they have destroyed my heart.   630

Now sey they thus, 'Whan Walter is agoon,
Thanne shal the blood of Janicle succede
And been our Lord, for other have we noon;'
Swiche wordes seith my peple, out of drede.
Wel oughte I of swich murmur taken hede, 635
For certeinly, I drede swich sentence,
Though they nat pleyn speke in myn audience.

I wolde live in pees if that I mighte;
Wherfor I am disposed outerly,
As I his suster servede by nighte, 640
Right so thenke I to serve him prively.
This warne I yow, that ye nat sodeynly
Out of youreself for no wo sholde outraye:
Beth pacient, and therof I yow preye."

"I have," quod she, "seyd thus, and ever shal, 645
I wol no thing ne nil no thing, certayn,
But as yow list; noght greveth me at al,
Thogh that my doghter and my sone be slayn—
At your comandement, this is to sayn.
I have noght had no part of children tweyne 650
But first siknesse, and after wo and peyne.

Ye been oure lord, doth with youre owene thing
Right as yow list; axeth no reed at me.
For as I lefte at hoom al my clothing
Whan I first cam to yow, right so," quod she, 655
"Left I my wil and al my libertee,
And took your clothing. Wherfore I yow preye,
Doth your plesaunce; I wol youre lust obeye.

Now they say thus: 'When Walter's time is done,
The blood of Janicula will succeed
And be our lord, for others have we none.'
Such words my people say from fear indeed.
Well ought I of such murmuring take heed;   635
Surely such ideas I should be fearing,
Though they don't speak plainly in my hearing.

I wish to live in peace here, if I might;
Therefore, I am disposed now utterly,
Just as I did his sister serve by night,   640
Just so I mean to serve him privately.
This I warn you: you should not suddenly
For woe erupt, and thus yourself betray;
But patient be. Now, this of you I pray."

"I have," said she, "said always, you recall: 645
I will or do not will a thing, certain,
But as you wish. It grieves me not at all,
Though my daughter and my son are slain, when
Your command it is, as you do say then.
For no part of two children did I know   650
But sickness first, and after, pain and woe.

You are our lord; thus, do with your own things
Just as you like; ask no advice of me.
As I left at home all of my clothing,
When I first came to you, just so," said she,   655
"Left I my will and all my liberty,
And took your clothing; therefore, I you pray,
Do your pleasure; I will your will obey.

And certes, if I hadde prescience
Your will to knowe er ye youre lust me tolde,   660
I wolde it doon withouten necligence.
But now I woot youre lust and what ye wolde,
Al youre plesaunce ferme and stable I holde;
For wiste I that my deeth wolde do yow ese,
Right gladly wolde I dyen, yow to plese.   665

Deth may noght make no comparisoun
Unto youre love." And whan this markis sey
The constance of his wyf, he caste adoun
His eyen two, and wondreth that she may
In pacience suffre al this array.   670
And forth he gooth with drery contenaunce,
But to his herte it was ful greet plesaunce.

This ugly sergeant, in the same wyse
That he hire doghter caughte, right so he—
Or worse, if men worse can devyse—   675
Hath hent hire sone that ful was of beautee.
And evere in oon so pacient was she
That she no chere made of hevinesse,
But kiste hir sone, and after gan it blesse.

Save this: she preyede him that if he mighte   680
Hir litel sone he wolde in erthe grave,
His tendre limes, delicat to sighte,
Fro foules and fro bestes for to save.
But she non answer of him mighte have.
He wente his wey, as him nothing ne roghte,   685
But to Boloigne he tendrely it broghte.

And certainly, if I had the prescience
To know your will before you had me told,   660
I would then do it without negligence;
Now that I know how your will does unfold,
All your pleasure firm and stable I hold;
For if I knew my death would do you ease,
Quite gladly would I die, then, you to please.   665

Death can make no comparison, I own,
To your love." And thus when this lord marquis
Saw all the constancy his wife had shown,
He casts his eyes down, and wonders how she
Can suffer all such treatment patiently;   670
He leaves looking dreary beyond measure,
But to his heart, it was such a great pleasure.

This ugly sergeant then in the same guise
He used to seize her daughter, just so he—
Or looking worse, if men can so devise—   675
Has seized her son, who's so full of beauty.
And steadfastly, so patient then was she
That she showed no sign of unhappiness,
But kissed her son, and after did him bless;

Save this, to him she prayed that, if he might,   680
He should in earth dig to make her son's grave;
His tender limbs, so delicate a sight,
From all the birds and beasts he then could save.
But there no answer to her plea he gave.
He went his way, like he did care for nought,   685
But to Bologna tenderly him brought.

This markis wondreth evere lenger the more
Upon hir pacience, and if that he
Ne hadde soothly knowen ther-bifore
That parfitly hir children loved she,   690
He wolde have wend that of som subtiltee,
And of malice or for cruel corage,
That she had suffred this with sad visage.

But wel he knew that next himself, certayn,
She loved hir children best in every wyse.   695
But now of wommen wolde I axen fayn,
If thise assayes mighte nat suffyse?
What coude a sturdy housbond more devyse
To preve hir wyfhod and hir stedfastnesse,
And he continuinge evere in sturdinesse?   700

But ther ben folk of swich condicioun
That, whan they have a certein purpos take,
They can nat stinte of hire entencioun;
But right as they were bounden to a stake,
They wol nat of that firste purpos slake.   705
Right so this markis fulliche hath purposed
To tempte his wyf as he was first disposed.

He waiteth if by word or contenance
That she to him was changed of corage,
But never coude he finde variance: 710
She was ay oon in herte and in visage.
And ay the forther that she was in age,
The more trewe, if that it were possible,
She was to him in love, and more penible.

As time went on, this marquis wondered more
About her patience, and surely if he
Had not for certain known quite well before
That she did love her children perfectly,   690
He would have thought that from some treachery,
Or either from a cruel heart or from malice,
She had with steadfast mien suffered all this.

Well he knew that, next to himself, truly,
In every way, she loved her children best.   695
But of women now I would ask gladly:
Has she not here endured sufficient test?
What more could a harsh husband now request
To prove her womanhood and steadfastness,
While he continues ever in his harshness?   700

There are folks of such a constitution
That, when they do a certain purpose take,
They can't stop short of their full intention,
But, just as if they were bound to a stake,
From their initial purpose, they won't break.   705
Just so, this marquis fully has proposed
To test his wife, as he was first disposed.

He waits to see if in word or expression
Her heart toward him had changed in any way,
But never could he find a variation.   710
In heart and face, she was the same each day,
And as she further grew in age, always
More true to him, if there were such a thing,
In her love was she, and more painstaking.

For which it semed thus, that of hem two   715
Ther nas but o wil; for, as Walter leste,
The same lust was hire plesance also;
And, God be thanked, al fil for the beste.
She shewed wel for no worldly unreste
A wyf, as of hirself, no thing ne sholde   720
Wille in effect but as hir housbond wolde.

The sclaundre of Walter ofte and wyde spradde
That of a cruel herte he wikkedly,
For he a povre womman wedded hadde,
Hath mordred bothe his children prively.   725
Swich murmur was among hem comunly.
No wonder is, for to the peples ere
Ther cam no word but that they mordred were.

For which, wher as his peple therbifore
Had loved him wel, the sclaundre of his diffame   730
Made hem that they him hatede therfore:
To been a mordrer is an hateful name.
But natheles, for ernest ne for game,
He of his cruel purpos nolde stente.
To tempte his wyf was set al his entente.   735

Whan that his doghter twelf yeer was of age,
He to the court of Rome, in subtil wyse
Enformed of his wil, sente his message,
Comaundinge hem swiche bulles to devyse
As to his cruel purpos may suffyse: 740
How that the Pope, as for his peples reste,
Bad him to wedde another if him leste.

For this reason it seemed that in these two 715
There was one will. As Walter did request,
The same desire was her pleasure to do.
And, God be thanked, it all fell for the best.
She showed that in spite of earthly unrest
A wife, on her own, nothing ever should 720
Desire, in fact, but as her husband would.

The evil fame of Walter widely spread:
That, from a cruel heart, he wickedly,
Because it was a poor woman he'd wed,
Had murdered both his children privately. 725
Such murmurs were among them commonly.
No wonder, because to the people's ear
Came no word but that they were murdered here.

And thus, whereas his people had before
Loved him well, the scandal of his ill fame 730
Made it so now they hated him therefore.
To be called murderer's a hateful name;
Nonetheless, not for earnestness nor game,
Would he from his cruel purpose yet relent;
To test his wife was all of his intent. 735

When twelve years of age became his daughter,
He to the court at Rome, in secret guise
Informed of his will, sent his messenger,
Such papal bulls[6] commanding they devise
To let him his cruel purpose realize: 740
How that the pope, to calm people's unrest,
Bade him to wed another, if he thought best.

---

6   ... Such papal bulls: In the Middle Ages, the Church forbade divorce. Nonetheless, marriages, especially those of the nobility or aristocracy, could be annulled for just cause by the papacy through bulls, or decrees. Such causes could range from consanguinity or nonconsummation of the marriage to trumped up causes like the one Walter invokes here. Of course, all of this is just a charade, as the next stanzas make clear, because the bulls aren't real and the papacy is not really dissolving the marriage of Walter and Griselda.

I seye, he bad they sholde countrefete
The Popes bulles, makinge mencioun
That he hath leve his firste wyf to lete,   745
As by the Popes dispensacioun,
To stinte rancour and dissencioun
Bitwixe his peple and him—thus seyde the bulle,
The which they han publiced atte fulle.

The rude peple, as it no wonder is,   750
Wenden ful wel that it had been right so;
But whan thise tydinges cam to Grisildis,
I deme that hire herte was ful wo.
But she, ylyke sad for evermo,
Disposed was, this humble creature,   755
Th'adversitee of Fortune al t'endure,

Abydinge evere his lust and his plesaunce,
To whom that she was yeven herte and al,
As to hire verray worldly suffisaunce.
But shortly if this storie I tellen shal,   760
This markis writen hath in special
A lettre in which he sheweth his entente,
And secrely he to Boloigne it sente.

To the Erl of Panik, which that hadde tho
Wedded his suster, preyde he specially   765
To bringen hoom agayn his children two
In honurable estaat al openly.
But o thing he him preyede outerly,
That he to no wight, though men wolde enquere,
Sholde nat telle whos children that they were,   770

I say, he bade that they should counterfeit
The pope's bulls, so that they would make mention
That he has leave his first wife to forfeit, 745
Because of a papal dispensation,
To stop all the rancor and dissension
Between his people and him, thus said the bull;
And then they publicized it all in full.

The unlearned people, it's no wondering, 750
Believed full well that it had been just so;
But when to Griselda came these tidings,
I judge that then her heart was full of woe.
But she, constantly steadfast even so,
Disposed was, this ever humble creature, 755
The adversity of Fortune to endure,

Awaiting always his will and his pleasure,
To whom, whole heart and all, given was she,
As though he were her only earthly measure.
But if I shall tell this story shortly, 760
This marquis has now written specially
A letter, in which he shows his intent,
And to Bologna secretly it's sent.

To the Earl of Panico, who had then
Married his sister, he prayed especially 765
To bring back home his two children again
With honorable display, quite publicly.
But one thing he prayed to him fervently,
That he to no one, though men would inquire,
Would tell at all who was the children's sire, 770

But seye the mayden sholde y-wedded be
Unto the Markis of Saluce anon.
And as this erl was preyed, so dide he,
For at day set he on his wey is goon
Toward Saluce, and lordes many oon   775
In riche array, this mayden for to gyde,
Hir yonge brother rydinge hire bisyde.

Arrayed was toward hir mariage
This fresshe mayde, ful of gemmes clere;
Hir brother, which that seven yeer was of age,   780
Arrayed eek ful fresh in his manere.
And thus in greet noblesse and with glad chere,
Toward Saluces shaping hir journey,
Fro day to day they ryden in hir wey.

Explicit quarta pars.
Sequitur quinta pars.

Among al this, after his wikke usage,   785
This markis yet his wyf to tempte more
To the uttereste preve of hir corage,
Fully to han experience and lore
If that she were as stedfast as bifore,
He on a day in open audience   790
Ful boistously hath seyd hire this sentence:

"Certes, Grisilde, I hadde ynough plesaunce
To han yow to my wyf for youre goodnesse—
As for youre trouthe and for youre obeisaunce—
Nought for youre linage ne for your richesse.   795
But now knowe I in verray soothfastnesse
That in gret lordshipe, if I wel avyse,
Ther is gret servitute in sondry wyse.

But he should say the maiden wed will be
At once to the Marquis of Saluzzo,
And as this earl was asked, then so did he;
At daybreak, he sets on his way to go
To Saluzzo, and many lords also 775
In rich array, this young maiden to guide,
With her young brother riding by her side.

Then she was arrayed thus for her marriage,
This fresh maiden, all covered with gems clear;
Her brother, who was seven years of age, 780
Arrayed quite freshly in his own way here.
In great nobility, and with glad cheer,
Toward Saluzzo they all shape their way,
And ride upon their journey day by day.

The fourth part ends.
The fifth part begins.

Meanwhile, following his wicked usage, 785
This marquis, still to test his wife yet more
To the utmost proof of all her courage,
To know sure and experience therefore
If she were yet as steadfast as before,
He, one day there, in public audience 790
Quite harshly pronounced to her this sentence:

"Truly, Griselda, I've had pleasure since
Taking you as my wife for your goodness,
For your loyalty and obedience,
Not for your lineage or for richness; 795
But now I know that, in all truthfulness,
If I judge right, in great lordship always
There is great servitude in sundry ways.

I may nat don as every plowman may.
My peple me constreyneth for to take   800
Another wyf, and cryen day by day;
And eek the Pope, rancour for to slake,
Consenteth it, that dar I undertake,
And treweliche thus muche I wol yow seye,
My newe wyf is coming by the weye.   805

Be strong of herte, and voyde anon hir place;
And thilke dowere that ye broghten me
Tak it agayn, I graunte it of my grace.
Retourneth to your fadres hous," quod he.
"No man may alwey han prosperitee;   810
With evene herte I rede yow t'endure
The strook of Fortune or of aventure."

And she agayn answerde in pacience,
"My lord," quod she, "I woot, and wiste alway,
How that bitwixen youre magnificence   815
And my poverte no wight can ne may
Maken comparison; it is no nay.
I ne heeld me nevere digne in no manere
To be youre wyf, no, ne youre chamberere.

And in this hous ther ye me lady made—   820
The heighe God take I for my witnesse,
And also wisly he my soule glade—
I nevere heeld me lady ne maistresse,
But humble servant to youre worthinesse,
And ever shal, whyl that my lyf may dure,   825
Aboven every worldly creature.

I may not do as every plowman may.
My people are constraining me to take   800
Another wife, and they cry day by day;
Also the pope, all their rancor to break,
Consents to it—that dare I undertake—
And truly then this much to you I'll say:
My new wife is now coming on her way.   805

Be strong of heart; at once, vacate her place;
And that same dowry that you brought to me,
Take it again; I grant it through my grace.
Return now to your father's house," said he;
"No man may always have prosperity.   810
I advise you, with tranquil heart, endure
Fortune's stroke, or else her chance adventure."

And she answered him again with patience:
"My lord," said she, "I know, and knew always,
How yet between your own magnificence   815
And my poverty no man can or may
Make comparison; there's no more to say.
Unworthy am I in any manner
To be your wife or a maid in your chamber.

In this house where you made me a lady—   820
The high God I now take for my witness,
And also may he gladden my soul wisely—
I never held myself lady or mistress,
But humble servant to your worthiness,
And ever shall, while my life may endure,   825
Hold you above any earthly creature.

That ye so longe of youre benignitee
Han holden me in honour and nobleye,
Wher as I was noght worthy for to be,
That thonke I God and yow, to whom I preye   830
Foryelde it yow. There is namore to seye.
Unto my fader gladly wol I wende,
And with him dwelle unto my lyves ende.

Ther I was fostred of a child ful smal,
Til I be deed, my lyf ther wol I lede: 835
A widwe clene, in body, herte, and al.
For sith I yaf to yow my maydenhede,
And am youre trewe wyf, it is no drede,
God shilde swich a lordes wyf to take
Another man to housbonde or to make.   840

And of youre newe wyf, God of his grace
So graunte yow wele and prosperitee!
For I wol gladly yelden hire my place,
In which that I was blisful wont to be.
For sith it lyketh yow, my lord," quod she,   845
"That whylom weren al myn hertes reste,
That I shal goon, I wol gon whan yow leste.

But ther as ye me profre swich dowaire
As I first broghte, it is wel in my minde
It were my wrecched clothes, nothing faire,   850
The which to me were hard now for to finde.
O gode God! how gentil and how kynde
Ye semed by youre speche and youre visage
The day that maked was oure mariage!

That you so long from your benignity
Held me in honor and in noble ways,
When I was not then worthy thus to be,
For this, thank you and God, to whom I pray   830
He may repay you; there's no more to say.
To my father now gladly will I wend,
And with him I will dwell till my life's end.

Where I was fostered as a child so small,
There I will lead my life till I am dead,   835
A widow clean in body, heart, and all.
For since I gave to you my maidenhead,
And am your true wife, there is naught to dread;
God forbid such a lord's wife should take
Another man, and him her husband make!   840

And with your new wife, God of his true grace
So grant you all wealth and prosperity!
For I will gladly yield to her my place,
In which I was wont so blissful to be.
For since it pleases you, my lord," said she,   845
"Who formerly were all of my heart's rest,
That I shall go, I'll go when you think best.

But whereas you proffer such dowry
As I first brought, it seems that to my mind
It was my wretched clothes, not fair to see,   850
Which now would be quite hard for me to find.
Oh good God! Both how gentle and how kind
You seemed by your speech and by your visage
On that day when you had made our marriage!

But sooth is seyd—algate I finde it trewe,   855
For in effect it preved is on me—
Love is noght old as whan that it is newe.
But certes, lord, for noon adversitee,
To dyen in the cas, it shal nat be
That evere in word or werk I shal repente   860
That I yow yaf myn herte in hool entente.

My lord, ye woot that in my fadres place
Ye dide me strepe out of my povre wede,
And richely me cladden, of youre grace.
To yow broghte I noght elles, out of drede,   865
But feyth and nakednesse and maydenhede.
And here agayn your clothing I restore,
And eek your wedding ring, for everemore.

The remenant of your jewels redy be
Inwith your chambre, dar I saufly sayn.   870
Naked out of my fadres hous," quod she,
"I cam, and naked moot I turne agayn.
Al youre plesaunce wol I folwen fayn.
But yet I hope it be nat youre entente
That I smoklees out of youre paleys wente.   875

Ye coude nat doon so dishoneste a thing
That thilke wombe in which youre children leye
Sholde biforn the peple, in my walking,
Be seyn al bare; wherfore I yow preye,
Lat me nat lyk a worm go by the weye.   880
Remembre yow, myn owene lord so dere,
I was youre wyf, thogh I unworthy were.

But truth be told—surely I find it true,   855
For, in effect, it proven is on me—
Old love is not the same as when it's new.
But truly, lord, in no adversity,
Even were I to die, it will not be
Ever in word or works I shall repent   860
That I gave you my heart with good intent.

My lord, you know that at my father's place
You stripped me of my poor clothes. In their stead,
You had me richly clad, out of your grace.
And nothing else I brought you, out of dread,   865
But faith, and nakedness, and maidenhead;
Thus here, once more, your clothing I restore,
And too your wedding ring, for evermore.

The rest of your jewels are there already
Within your chamber, I dare safely swear.   870
Naked out of my father's house," said she,
"I came, and naked I must return there.
Your pleasure will I gladly do with care;
But yet I hope it was not your intent
That I, smockless, forth from your palace went.   875

You couldn't do so dishonorable a thing
That the same womb in which your children lay
Should before the people, as I'm walking,
Be seen all bare; and therefore, I you pray,
Let me not like a worm go by the way.   880
Remember, my own lord so dear to me,
I was your wife, although I was unworthy.

Wherfore in guerdon of my maydenhede,
Which that I broghte, and noght agayn I bere,
As voucheth sauf to yeve me to my mede   885
But swich a smok as I was wont to were,
That I therwith may wrye the wombe of here
That was youre wyf. And heer take I my leve
Of yow, myn owene lord, lest I yow greve."

"The smok," quod he, "that thou hast on thy bak,   890
Lat it be stille, and bere it forth with thee."
But wel unnethes thilke word he spak
But wente his wey for rewthe and for pitee.
Biforn the folk hirselven strepeth she,
And in hir smok, with heed and foot al bare,   895
Toward hir fader hous forth is she fare.

The folk hire folwe wepinge in hir weye,
And Fortune ay they cursen as they goon.
But she fro weping kepte hire eyen dreye,
Ne in this tyme word ne spak she noon.   900
Hir fader, that this tydinge herde anoon,
Curseth the day and tyme that nature
Shoop him to been a lyves creature.

For out of doute this olde povre man
Was evere in suspect of hir mariage;   905
For evere he demed, sith that it bigan,
That whan the lord fulfild hadde his corage,
Him wolde thinke it were a disparage
To his estaat so lowe for t'alighte,
And voyden hire as sone as ever he mighte.   910

In compensation for my maidenhead,
Which I brought here, but home I cannot bear,
Vouchsafe to give, as my reward, instead 885
Just such a smock as I was wont to wear,
That with it I may cover the womb there
Of her who was your wife. Now I take leave
Of you, my own lord, lest now I you grieve."

"The smock that's on your back, I will allow 890
To stay there. Take it with you," then said he.
But barely could he speak forth those words now,
But went away, with sorrow and pity.
Before the folk themselves, now does strip she,
And in her smock, with head and feet all bare, 895
Toward her father's house she does repair.

Weeping, the folk follow her on her way;
Fortune they all curse as they are going.
But from tears she kept her eyes dry always;
All this time, not one word was she speaking. 900
Her father, who had heard all these tidings,
Curses both the day and time when Nature
Had shaped him into a living creature.

For, it's without a doubt, this poor old man
Was always suspicious of her marriage; 905
For he judged always, since it first began,
With lust sated, the lord would encourage
Himself to think that it did disparage
His rank because so lowly he did plight,
And he'd dismiss her as soon as he might. 910

Agayns his doghter hastilich goth he,
For he by noyse of folk knew hire cominge,
And with hire old cote, as it mighte be,
He covered hire ful sorwefully wepinge.
But on hire body mighte he it nat bringe,   915
For rude was the cloth and she more of age
By dayes fele than at hire mariage.

Thus with hire fader for a certeyn space
Dwelleth this flour of wyfly pacience,
That neither by hire wordes ne hire face   920
Biforn the folk, ne eek in hire absence,
Ne shewed she that hire was doon offence;
Ne of hire heighe estaat no remembraunce
Ne hadde she, as by hire countenaunce.

No wonder is, for in hire grete estaat   925
Hire goost was evere in pleyn humylitee:
No tendre mouth, noon herte delicaat,
No pompe, no semblant of royaltee,
But ful of pacient benignitee,
Discreet and prydeles, ay honurable,   930
And to hire housbonde evere meke and stable.

Men speke of Job and most for his humblesse,
As clerkes, whan hem list, can wel endyte,
Namely of men; but as in soothfastnesse,
Thogh clerkes preyse wommen but a lyte,   935
Ther can no man in humblesse him acquyte
As womman can, ne can ben half so trewe
As wommen been, but it be falle of newe.

Toward his daughter hastily goes he.
From the folk's noise, he knew of her coming;
With her old coat, as well as it might be
He covered her, while with sorrow weeping.
But on her body, he might not it bring,   915
For rude was the cloth, and she more in age
By many days than she was at her marriage.

Thus with her father for a certain space
Dwells now this flower of wifely patience,
So that neither by her words or her face,   920
Before the folk, or yet in their absence,
Does she show that she had suffered offense;
Nor of high estate had she remembrance,
If one were judging by her countenance.

No wonder, for when she had great status,   925
Her spirit lived in plain humility;
No tender mouth,[7] no heart fastidious,
No pomp and no semblance of royalty,
Always full of patient benignity,
Discreet, prideless, always honorable,   930
To her husband, ever meek and stable.

Men speak of Job and his humility;
Of this, clerks, when they like, can write quite well,
Namely of men, but it is clear to see,
Though clerks but little praise of women tell,   935
In humility, no man does so well
As woman can, nor can be half so true
As women are—or this is something new.

7   **tender mouth:** Finicky tastes.

[*Pars Sexta.*]

Fro Boloigne is this Erl of Panik come,
Of which the fame up sprang to more and lesse,   940
And in the peples eres alle and some
Was couth eek that a newe markisesse
He with him broghte, in swich pompe and richesse,
That never was ther seyn with mannes yë
So noble array in al West Lumbardye.   945

The markis, which that shoop and knew al this,
Er that this erl was come sente his message
For thilke sely povre Grisildis;
And she with humble herte and glad visage,
Nat with no swollen thoght in hire corage,   950
Cam at his heste, and on hire knees hire sette,
And reverently and wysly she him grette.

"Grisild," quod he, "my wille is outrely
This mayden, that shal wedded been to me,
Receyved be tomorwe as royally   955
As it possible is in myn hous to be,
And eek that every wight in his degree
Have his estaat in sitting and servyse
And heigh plesaunce, as I can best devyse.

I have no wommen suffisaunt, certayn,   960
The chambres for t'arraye in ordinaunce
After my lust, and therfor wolde I fayn
That thyn were al swich maner governaunce;
Thou knowest eek of old al my plesaunce.
Though thyn array be badde and yvel biseye,   965
Do thou thy devoir at the leeste weye."

[Part Six]*

From Bologna, Panico's earl has come.
His fame sprang up among the great and small,   940
And in the people's ears there, all and some,
Was known that a new marchioness withal
Came in such pomp and richness overall
That never might a man's eye come to see
So grand array in all West Lombardy.   945

This marquis, who all this both shaped and knew,
Before this earl arrived, sent his message
Out to poor, innocent Griselda too;
And she, with humble heart and glad visage,
Not with swollen thoughts to give her courage,   950
Came at his command and knelt on her knees,
Greeting him reverently, so as to please.

"Griselda," said he, "my will's utterly
That this maiden, who shall be wed to me,
Should be received tomorrow royally   955
As is possible in my house to be,
And each man should, according to degree,
Have his rank in service and in seating
And high pleasure of my best devising.

Certainly, I have no able women   960
The chambers to array in proper measure
After my taste, and I would thus wish then
That you would manage this with manner sure.
From times past, you know what gives me pleasure;
Though your clothes are bad and evil to see,   965
At the very least, now do your duty."

*This section is marked inconsistently in the medieval manuscripts of *The Canterbury Tales*.

"Nat only, lord, that I am glad," quod she,
"To doon youre lust, but I desyre also
Yow for to serve and plese in my degree
Withouten feynting, and shal everemo.   970
Ne nevere, for no wele ne no wo,
Ne shal the gost withinne myn herte stente
To love yow best with al my trewe entente."

And with that word she gan the hous to dighte,
And tables for to sette and beddes make;   975
And peyned hir to doon al that she mighte,
Preying the chambereres, for Goddes sake,
To hasten hem, and faste swepe and shake.
And she, the most servisable of alle,
Hath every chambre arrayed and his halle.   980

Abouten undern gan this erl alighte,
That with him broghte thise noble children tweye,
For which the peple ran to seen the sighte
Of hire array, so richely biseye;
And thanne at erst amonges hem they seye   985
That Walter was no fool thogh that him leste
To chaunge his wyf, for it was for the beste.

For she is fairer, as they demen alle,
Than is Grisild, and more tendre of age,
And fairer fruit bitwene hem sholde falle,   990
And more plesant, for hire heigh linage;
Hir brother eek so fair was of visage
That hem to seen the peple hath caught plesaunce,
Commendinge now the markis governaunce.

"Not only, lord, am I quite glad," said she,
"To do your will, but I desire also
To serve and please you, after my degree
Without flagging, and always will, you know;   970
And never, despite any wealth or woe,
Shall the spirit within my heart relent
To love you best with all my true intent."

And with that word, the house she did prepare,
She did set tables, and the beds did make,   975
And pained herself to do all she might there,
Praying the chambermaids now, for God's sake,
To hasten them, and quickly sweep and shake;
And she, the most attentive of them all,
Has every chamber readied and his hall.   980

About midmorning this earl did alight,
Who had brought both these noble children here,
And so the people ran to see the sight
Of their array, so splendid they appear;
For the first time, they said that it was clear   985
That Walter was no fool in his request
To change his wife, for it was for the best.

For she is fairer, they deem, one and all,
Than Griselda, and more tender in age,
And fairer fruit between them sure would fall,   990
And more pleasant, given her high lineage.
Her brother, too, was so fair in visage
That the folk have such pleasure them to see,
They now commend the acts of the marquis.

"O stormy peple! unsad and evere untrewe!   995
Ay undiscreet and chaunging as a vane!
Delytinge evere in rumbel that is newe,
For lyk the mone ay wexe ye and wane!
Ay ful of clapping, dere ynogh a jane!
Youre doom is fals, youre constance yvel preveth,   1000
A ful greet fool is he that on yow leveth!"

Thus seyden sadde folk in that citee,
Whan that the peple gazed up and doun,
For they were glad, right for the noveltee,
To han a newe lady of hir toun.   1005
Namore of this make I now mencioun,
But to Grisilde agayn wol I me dresse,
And telle hir constance and hir bisinesse.

Ful bisy was Grisilde in every thing
That to the feste was apertinent;   1010
Right noght was she abayst of hire clothing,
Though it were rude and somdel eek torent.
But with glad chere to the yate is went
With other folk, to grete the markisesse,
And after that doth forth hire bisinesse.   1015

With so glad chere his gestes she receyveth,
And so conningly, everich in his degree,
That no defaute no man aperceyveth;
But ay they wondren what she mighte be
That in so povre array was for to see,   1020
And coude swich honour and reverence;
And worthily they preisen hire prudence.

"Stormy people! Unstable and untrue! 995
Thoughtless and changing like a weather vane!
Delighting so in rumors that are new,
For like the moon, you always wax and wane!
Full of chattering whose worthlessness is plain!
Your judgment's false; your constancy proves ill; 1000
A great fool he, who would believe you still."

Thus the sober folk said in that city,
When there the people had gazed up and down,
For they were quite glad of the novelty,
Of having a new lady in their town. 1005
No more about this now will I expound,
But to Griselda now myself address,
And tell her constancy and busyness.

Busy was Griselda with each thing
That to the wedding feast was pertinent. 1010
Nor was she abashed by her own clothing,
Though it were rough, and somewhat torn and rent;
But with glad cheer, out to the gate she went
With others, the new marchioness to greet, 1015
And after did her business, as was meet.[8]

With glad cheer, all his guests she now receives
So skillfully, each one in his degree,
That any flaw in this, no man perceives,
But ever wonders who then she might be
Who in such poor array was there to see, 1020
And yet knew such honor and reverence,
And worthily, they all praise her prudence.

8 **meet**: Fitting, appropriate.

In al this mene whyle she ne stente
This mayde and eek hir brother to commende
With al hir herte, in ful benigne entente,   1025
So wel that no man coude hir prys amende.
But atte laste, whan that thise lordes wende
To sitten doun to mete, he gan to calle
Grisilde, as she was bisy in his halle.

"Grisilde," quod he, as it were in his pley,   1030
"How lyketh thee my wyf and hire beautee?"
"Right wel," quod she, "my lord, for in good fey,
A fairer say I nevere noon than she.
I prey to God yeve hire prosperitee,
And so hope I that he wol to yow sende   1035
Plesance ynogh unto youre lyves ende.

O thing biseke I yow, and warne also,
That ye ne prikke with no tormentinge
This tendre mayden, as ye han don mo.
For she is fostred in hire norishinge   1040
More tendrely, and to my supposinge,
She coude nat adversitee endure
As coude a povre fostred creature."

And whan this Walter saugh hire pacience,
Hir glade chere and no malice at al—   1045
And he so ofte had doon to hire offence,
And she ay sad and constant as a wal,
Continuinge evere hire innocence overal—
This sturdy markis gan his herte dresse
To rewen upon hire wyfly stedfastnesse.   1050

In the meantime, not once did she relent
This maiden and her brother to commend
With all her heart and all benign intent,   1025
So well that no man could her praise amend.
But at the last, when all these lords did wend
Their way to dinner, Walter then did call
Griselda, who was busy in his hall.

"Griselda," said he, as though he meant to play,   1030
"Do you like my new wife and her beauty?"
"Quite well, my lord," said she, "in faith, I say,
I've never seen a maid fairer than she.
I pray that God grant her prosperity;
Also I hope that he to you will send   1035
Pleasure enough to last till your life's end.

One thing I beseech, and I warn you, too,
That you not prick with any tormenting
This tender maid, as you were wont to do;
For she is fostered in her nurturing   1040
More tenderly, and to my supposing,
Adversity she could not well endure
As could a poorly fostered creature."

And when now this Walter saw her patience,
With her glad cheer and no malice at all,   1045
Though he so often had done her offense,
And she steadfast and constant as a wall,
Maintaining still her innocence withal,
This cruel marquis did his heart address
To pity now her wifely steadfastness.   1050

"This is ynogh, Grisilde myn," quod he,
"Be now namore agast ne yvel apayed;
I have thy feith and thy benignitee,
As wel as ever womman was, assayed.
In greet estaat, and povreliche arrayed,   1055
Now knowe I, dere wyf, thy stedfastnesse,"
And hire in armes took and gan hire kesse.

And she for wonder took of it no keep;
She herde nat what thing he to hire seyde;
She ferde as she had stert out of a sleep,   1060
Til she out of hir masednesse abreyde.
"Grisilde," quod he, "by God that for us deyde,
Thou art my wyf, ne noon other I have,
Ne never hadde, as God my soule save!

This is thy doghter which thou hast supposed   1065
To be my wyf; that other feithfully
Shal be myn heir, as I have ay disposed;
Thou bare him in thy body trewely.
At Boloigne have I kept hem prively;
Tak hem agayn, for now maystow nat seye   1070
That thou hast lorn non of thy children tweye.

And folk that otherweyes han seyd of me,
I warne hem wel that I have doon this dede
For no malice ne for no crueltee,
But for t'assaye in thee thy wommanhede,   1075
And nat to sleen my children, God forbede!
But for to kepe hem prively and stille,
Til I thy purpos knewe and al thy wille."

"This is enough, Griselda mine," said he;
"Be afraid no more nor evilly paid.
I have your faith and your benignity,
As well as ever woman's was, assayed,
In high estate and when poorly arrayed. 1055
Now I know, dear wife, that you are steadfast"—
And took her in his arms and kissed her fast.

And she, from wonder, took of it no keep;
She heard then not a thing he to her spoke;
She fared as though she'd started out of sleep, 1060
Until from dazedness she then awoke.
"Griselda, as God died for us," he spoke,
"You are my wife; no other I elect,
Nor ever will, so God my soul protect!

This is your daughter, whom you have supposed 1065
To be my wife; that other faithfully
Will be my heir, as I always proposed;
Yet you bore him in your body truly.
At Bologna, I kept them privately;
Take them again, for now you may not say 1070
You've lost any of your children today.

And folk who otherwise have said of me,
I warn them well that all these deeds I did
Not from malice nor from cruelty,
But to assay in you your womanhood, 1075
Not slay my children—as God would forbid!—
But rather keep them privately and still,
Till I your purpose knew, and all your will."

Whan she this herde, aswowne doun she falleth
For pitous joye, and after hire swowninge   1080
She bothe hire yonge children to hire calleth,
And in hire armes, pitously wepinge,
Embraceth hem, and tendrely kissinge,
Ful lyk a mooder, with hire salte teres
She batheth bothe hire visage and hire heres.   1085

O, which a pitous thing it was to see
Hir swowning, and hire humble voys to here!
"Grauntmercy, lord, God thanke it yow," quod she,
"That ye han saved me my children dere!
Now rekke I never to ben deed right here;   1090
Sith I stonde in youre love and in youre grace,
No fors of deeth, ne whan my spirit pace!

O tendre, o dere, o yonge children myne,
Your woful mooder wende stedfastly
That cruel houndes or som foul vermyne   1095
Hadde eten yow; but God of his mercy,
And youre benigne fader, tendrely
Hath doon yow kept;" and in that same stounde
Al sodeynly she swapte adoun to grounde.

And in her swough so sadly holdeth she   1100
Hire children two, whan she gan hem t'embrace,
That with greet sleighte and greet difficultee
The children from hire arm they gonne arace.
O many a teer on many a pitous face
Doun ran of hem that stoden hire bisyde;   1105
Unnethe abouten hire mighte they abyde.

When she had heard this, swooning down she falls
From piteous joy, and after her swooning, 1080
She both of her young children to her calls,
And, in her arms, piteously weeping,
Embraces them, and tenderly kissing,
Quite like a mother, with her salty tears,
She did bathe both their hair and faces here. 1085

O! what a piteous thing then to see
Her swooning, and her humble voice to hear!
"Grant mercy, lord, God thank you now," said she,
"That you have saved for me my children dear!
Now care I not if I should die right here; 1090
Since I stand in your grace and in your love,
No matter when death calls my soul above!

Oh tender, oh dear, oh my young children!
Your woeful mother supposed steadfastly
That some cruel hounds or else some foul vermin 1095
Had eaten you; but God in his mercy
And too your benign father tenderly
Have kept you safe"—and in that same moment
All suddenly down to the ground she went.

And in her swooning so tightly holds she 1100
Her children both, when she them did embrace,
That with great care and great difficulty
The children from her arms they did unlace.
O! the tears on many a pitying face
Ran down from those who there stood her beside; 1105
Around her they could hardly bear abide.

Walter hire gladeth and hire sorwe slaketh;
She ryseth up, abaysed, from hire traunce,
And every wight hire joye and feste maketh
Til she hath caught agayn hire contenaunce.   1110
Walter hire dooth so feithfully plesaunce
That it was deyntee for to seen the chere
Bitwixe hem two, now they ben met yfere.

Thise ladyes, whan that they hir tyme say,
Han taken hire and into chambre goon,   1115
And strepen hire out of hire rude array,
And in a cloth of gold that brighte shoon,
With a coroune of many a riche stoon
Upon hire heed, they into halle hire broghte,
And ther she was honoured as hire oghte.   1120

Thus hath this pitous day a blisful ende,
For every man and womman dooth his might
This day in murthe and revel to dispende
Til on the welkne shoon the sterres light.
For more solempne in every mannes sight   1125
This feste was, and gretter of costage,
Than was the revel of hire mariage.

Ful many a yeer in heigh prosperitee
Liven thise two in concord and in reste,
And richely his doghter maried he   1130
Unto a lord, oon of the worthieste
Of al Itaille; and than in pees and reste
His wyves fader in his court he kepeth,
Til that the soule out of his body crepeth.

Walter cheers her and her sorrow lessens;
She rises up, abashed then, from her trance.
Everyone to bid her joy now hastens
Till, to compose herself, she had some chance.   1110
Walter seeks to please her in each circumstance
So it delightful was to see the cheer
Between them now that they're together here.

These ladies, when they saw their time that day,
Into a chamber did take her alone,   1115
And they stripped her out of her rough array,
And in a cloth of gold that brightly shone.
With a crown decked by many a rich stone
Upon her head, they to the hall her brought,
And there she received honor, as she ought.   1120

This piteous day has a blissful end,
For every man and woman did their might
This day in mirth and revelry to spend
Till in the heavens shone the stars so bright.
For more solemn in every person's sight   1125
This feast was, and greater in cost, at least,
Than were the revels for their wedding feast.

For many years in high prosperity
These two did live in concord and at rest,
And richly, then, his daughter married he   1130
To a lord, who's one of the worthiest
In Italy, and then in peace and rest
His wife's father in his court he keeps,
Until the soul out of his body creeps.

His sone succedeth in his heritage,   1135
In reste and pees, after his fader day,
And fortunat was eek in mariage,
Al putte he nat his wyf in greet assay.
This world is nat so strong, it is no nay,
As it hath been in olde tymes yore.   1140
And herkneth what this auctour seith therfore:

This storie is seyd, nat for that wyves sholde
Folwen Grisilde as in humilitee,
For it were importable, though they wolde;
But for that every wight in his degree   1145
Sholde be constant in adversitee
As was Grisilde. Therfore Petrark wryteth
This storie, which with heigh style he endyteth.

For sith a womman was so pacient
Unto a mortal man, wel more us oghte   1150
Receyven al in gree that God us sent.
For greet skile is he preve that he wroghte,
But he ne tempteth no man that he boghte—
As seith Seint Jame, if ye his pistel rede.
He preveth folk al day, it is no drede,   1155

And suffreth us, as for our excercyse,
With sharpe scourges of adversitee
Ful ofte to be bete in sondry wyse,
Nat for to knowe oure wil; for certes he,
Er we were born, knew al oure freletee.   1160
And for our beste is al his governaunce:
Lat us than live in vertuous suffraunce.

His son succeeds him in this heritage,   1135
In rest and peace, after his father's day,
And he was fortunate in his marriage,
Although his wife he put to no assay.
It's no lie that the world's not strong today
As it has been in times of old before.   1140
Hearken to what my author[9] says therefore.

This story is told not because wives should
Follow Griselda in humility—
It would be intolerable if they would—
But so that every man in his degree,   1145
Should be constant in his adversity
As was Griselda; therefore Petrarch writes
This story, which in high style he indites.[10]

For since a woman was so patient
To a mortal man, the more we ought   1150
Receive all graciously what God has sent;
It's reasonable he test what he has wrought.
He tempts no man whom his redemption bought,
As says Saint James; in his epistle read;
For he proves[11] folks all day in word and deed,

And suffers us, to exercise us always,
With these sharp scourges of adversity
Often to be beaten in many ways,
Not just to know our will, for surely he,
Before our birth, knew all our frailty;   1160
And for the best is all his governance.
Let us live in virtuous forbearance.

9   **my author**: Petrarch, the source the Clerk has named for his tale.
10   **indites**: Writes.
11   **proves**: Tests.

But o word, lordinges, herkneth er I go:
It were ful hard to finde now-a-dayes
In al a toun Grisildes three or two;   1165
For if that they were put to swiche assayes,
The gold of hem hath now so badde alayes
With bras, that thogh the coyne be fair at yë,
It wolde rather breste a-two than plye.

For which heer, for the Wyves love of Bathe—   1170
Whos lyf and al hire secte God mayntene
In heigh maistrye, and elles were it scathe—
I wol with lusty herte fresshe and grene
Seyn yow a song to glade yow, I wene,
And lat us stinte of ernestful matere.   1175
Herkneth my song, that seith in this manere:

Lenvoy de Chaucer

Grisilde is deed, and eek hire pacience,
And bothe atones buried in Itaille.
For which I crye in open audience:
No wedded man so hardy be t'assaille   1180
His wyves pacience, in hope to finde
Grisildes, for in certein he shall faille!

O noble wyves, ful of heigh prudence,
Lat noon humilitee your tonge naille,
Ne lat no clerk have cause or diligence   1185
To wryte of yow a storie of swich mervaille
As of Grisildis, pacient and kinde,
Lest Chichevache yow swelwe in hire entraille!

But one word, lords, hearken before I'm through:
It were quite hard to find here nowadays
Throughout a town, Griseldas three or two;   1165
For if women were put to such assays,
Their gold now has such bad alloys, I say,
With brass, that though the coin looks fair, the end
Is that it'd rather break in two than bend.

Thus, for the Wife of Bath's love here, you see—   1170
Whose life and all her sect God keep serene
In high mastery, or else it's a pity—
I will with lusty heart, so fresh and green,
Sing a song now to gladden you, I mean;
And let's cease from all this earnest matter.   1175
Hear my song, for it goes in this manner:

The Envoy of Chaucer[12]

Griselda's dead, and also her patience;
In Italy they're buried without fail;
For which I cry in open audience
No wedded man be so cruel to assail   1180
His wife's patience, in the hope then to find
Griselda, for sure, he will not prevail.

Oh you noble wives full of high prudence,
Let no humility your tongues now nail,
And let no clerks have cause or diligence   1185
To write of you so marvelous a tale
As of Griselda, who's patient and kind,
Lest Chichevache[13] you swallow in her entrails!

12 *The Envoy of Chaucer*: The Envoy, or Epilogue, to *The Clerk's Tale* is so designated in man-
uscripts by a scribe. It is labeled as Chaucer's because it has no source in Petrarch's tale of patient
Griselda or in the French version of it that Chaucer also used. While it is not clear whether we should
imagine this spoken by the Clerk or in Chaucer's own voice, it certainly could be read in either way.
13 **Chichevache**: In medieval French legend, the cow who was always lean and hungry because its
diet consisted of patient wives.

Folweth Ekko, that holdeth no silence,
But evere answereth at the countretaille;   1190
Beth nat bidaffed for your innocence,
But sharply tak on yow the governaille.
Emprinteth wel this lesson in youre minde
For commune profit, sith it may availle.

Ye archewyves, stondeth at defence—   1195
Sin ye be stronge as is a greet camaille—
Ne suffreth nat that men yow doon offence.
And sclendre wyves, feble as in bataille,
Beth egre as is a tygre yond in Inde;
Ay clappeth as a mille, I yow consaille.   1200

Ne dreed hem nat, doth hem no reverence;
For though thyn housbonde armed be in maille,
The arwes of thy crabbed eloquence
Shal perce his brest, and eek his aventaille.
In jalousye I rede eek thou him binde,   1205
And thou shalt make him couche as dooth a quaille.

If thou be fair, ther folk ben in presence
Shew thou thy visage and thyn apparaille;
If thou be foul, be free of thy dispence;
To gete thee freendes ay do thy travaille.   1210
Be ay of chere as light as leef on linde,
And lat him care, and wepe, and wringe, and waille!

Follow Echo, who will hold no silence,
But always answers back and without fail.   1190
Don't be made daft because of innocence,
But make sure that your governance prevails.
Imprint here well this lesson in your mind,
For common profit, since it may avail.

And you archwives, now stand at your defense,   1195
Since, strong as the great camel,[14] you assail;
Nor suffer that men do to you offense.
And slender wives, who may in battle fail,
Be fierce as tigers men in India find;
Now chatter like a mill so you'll prevail.   1200

Dread him not; and do him no reverence,
For though your husband were armed all in mail.
The arrows of your crabbed eloquence
Will pierce his breast and neck as you assail.
In jealousy, I suggest you him bind,   1205
And you will make him cringe just like a quail.

If you are fair, when folks are in your presence,
With your visage and your good clothes, them regale;
If you are ugly, gifts freely dispense;
For to get friends, you must do your travail;   1210
In cheer, be light as linden leaves in sail,
And let him weep and wring his hands and wail!

14   **the great camel**: The medieval imagination saw the camel as a fearsome beast.

Bihoold the murye wordes of the Hoost.

This worthy Clerk, whan ended was his tale,   1212a
Our Hoste seyde and swoor, "By Goddes bones,
Me were lever than a barel ale
My wyf at hoom had herd this legende ones.
This is a gentil tale for the nones,
As to my purpos, wiste ye my wille;
But thing that wol nat be, lat it be stille."   1212g

Heere endeth the Tale of the Clerk of Oxenford.

Behold the merry words of the Host.

This worthy clerk, when ended was his tale,   1212a
"By God's bones," our Host then said and swore,
"I'd rather than a barrelful of ale
My wife had heard this legend once or more!
This is a gentle tale to set the score,
For my own purpose, if you knew my will;
But things that will not be, let them be still."   1212g

Here ends the Tale of the Clerk of Oxford.

THE MERCHANT'S PROLOGUE

"Weping and wayling, care and other sorwe
I know ynogh, on even and a-morwe,"
Quod the Marchant, "and so doon othere mo   1215
That wedded been. I trowe that it be so,
For wel I woot it fareth so with me.
I have a wyf, the worste that may be;
For thogh the feend to hir y-coupled were,
She wolde him overmacche, I dare wel swere.   1220
What sholde I yow reherce in special
Hir hye malice? She is a shrewe at al.
There is a long and large difference
Bitwix Grisildis grete pacience
And of my wyf the passing crueltee.   1225
Were I unbounden, also moot I thee,
I wolde nevere eft comen in the snare.
We wedded men live in sorwe and care.
Assaye whoso wol, and he shal finde
That I seye sooth, by Seint Thomas of Inde,   1230
As for the more part—I sey nat alle.
God shilde that it sholde so bifalle!
        A! Goode sire Host, I have y-wedded be
Thise monthes two—and more nat, pardee—
And yet, I trowe, he that all his lyve   1235

THE MERCHANT'S PROLOGUE

"Weeping, wailing, care and other sorrowing
I know enough, at night and in the morning,"
Said the Merchant, "and many more do, too,
Who married are. This, I believe, is true,
For I know well that it fares thus with me.   5
I have a wife, the worst one that may be;
For if the fiend himself coupled with her,
She would outmatch him; this, I do aver.   1220
Why should I tell in great detail to you
Her high-pitched malice? She's a total shrew.   10
There is a large and lengthy difference
Between Griselda's overwhelming patience
And all my wife's surpassing cruelty.
I'd prosper so, were I unbound and free.
Never again would I fall in that snare.   15
We wedded men live in sorrow and care.
He shall find, whoever might want to try,
By Saint Thomas of India,[1] I don't lie   1230
About the greater part—I don't say all.
For God forbid that thus it should befall!   20
    Ah, good sir Host, now I have wedded been
These past two months—no more, by God and men;
Yet, I believe, the man who, all his life,

---

1   **Saint Thomas of India**: The Apostle. His legend maintained that he traveled to India, where
he effected mass conversions.

Wyflees hath been, though that men wolde him ryve
Unto the herte, ne coude in no manere
Tellen so muchel sorwe as I now heere
Coude tellen of my wyves cursednesse."

    "Now," quod our Hoost, "Marchaunt, so God yow blesse,   1240
Sin ye so muchel knowen of that art,
Ful hertely I pray yow telle us part."

    "Gladly," quod he, "but of myn owene sore,
For sory herte, I telle may namore."

Wifeless has been, though stabbed through with a knife
Right in his heart, he still could in no way   25
Tell as much sorrow as I could now say
About my own wife's very cursedness!"

    "Now," said our Host, "Merchant, may God you bless,   1240
Since you do know so much about that art,
Quite heartily, I pray you, tell us part."   30

    "Gladly," said he, "but about my own sore,
Since my heart's sorry, I will say no more."

THE MERCHANT'S TALE

    Whylom ther was dwellinge in Lumbardye   1245
A worthy knight that born was of Pavye,
In which he lived in greet prosperitee.
And sixty yeer a wyflees man was he,
And folwed ay his bodily delyt
On wommen, ther as was his appetyt,   1250
As doon thise foles that ben seculeer.
And whan that he was passed sixty yeer—
Were it for holinesse or for dotage
I can nat seye—but swich a greet corage
Hadde this knight to been a wedded man   1255
That day and night he dooth al that he can
T'espyen where he mighte wedded be,
Preyinge our Lord to graunten him that he
Mighte ones knowe of thilke blisful lyf
That is bitwixe an housbond and his wyf,   1260
And for to live under that holy bond
With which that first God man and womman bond.
"Non other lyf," seyde he, "is worth a bene,
For wedlok is so esy and so clene
That in this world it is a paradys."   1265
Thus seyde this olde knight, that was so wys.
      And certeinly, as sooth as God is king,
To take a wyf it is a glorious thing,

THE MERCHANT'S TALE

Here begins the Merchant's Tale.

Long ago, there did dwell in Lombardy
A worthy knight; at Pavia born was he,
And there he lived in great prosperity;   35
For sixty years, a wifeless man was he,
Who followed always bodily delight
With women there; thus was his appetite,   1250
Like all these fools among the laity.
When his years had numbered more than sixty,   40
Whether in his holiness or dotage,
I can't say, but surely such great courage
Pricked in this knight to be a wedded man
That, day and night, he does all that he can
To spy out just where he might wedded be;   45
He prayed our Lord to grant to him that he
Might for once know of that same blissful life
That lies between a husband and a wife,   1260
And live beneath that holy bond profound
Through which God first both man and woman bound.   50
"No other life," said he, "is worth a bean,
For wedlock is so easy and so clean
That, on this earth, it is a paradise."
Thus said this old knight, for he was so wise.
    And certainly, as sure as God is king,   55
To take a wife is a glorious thing,

461

And namely whan a man is old and hoor;
Thanne is a wyf the fruit of his tresor. 1270
Thanne sholde he take a yong wyf and a feir,
On which he mighte engendren him an heir,
And lede his lyf in joye and in solas,
Wheras thise bacheleres singe "Allas!"
Whan that they finden any adversitee 1275
In love, which nis but childish vanitee.
And trewely it sit wel to be so,
That bacheleres have often peyne and wo:
On brotel ground they builde, and brotelnesse
They finde whan they wene sikernesse. 1280
They live but as a brid or as a beest,
In libertee and under non arreest,
Ther as a wedded man in his estaat
Liveth a lyf blisful and ordinaat,
Under the yok of mariage y-bounde. 1285
Wel may his herte in joye and blisse habounde.
For who can be so buxom as a wyf?
Who is so trewe and eek so ententyf
To kepe him, syk and hool, as is his make?
For wele or wo she wol him nat forsake. 1290
She nis nat wery him to love and serve,
Thogh that he lye bedrede til he sterve.
And yet somme clerkes seyn it nis nat so,
Of whiche he, Theofraste, is oon of tho.
What force though Theofraste liste lye? 1295
"Ne take no wyf," quod he, "for housbondrye,
As for to spare in houshold thy dispence.
A trewe servant dooth more diligence
Thy good to kepe than thyn owene wyf,
For she wol clayme half part al hir lyf. 1300

More so when a man is old and hoary;
His wife's the fruit then of his treasury.   1270
Then he should take a wife who's young and fair,
On whom he might beget himself an heir,   60
Leading his life in pleasure and solace,
While bachelors go singing "Alas" thus,
Whenever they come to adversity
In love—and it's just childish vanity.
And, truly, it is fitting that it's so—   65
That bachelors have frequent pain and woe.
On brittle ground they build, and brittleness
They find when they were sure of steadfastness.   1280
They live just like a bird or like a beast,
In liberty, from all restraint released,   70
Whereas a man within the married state
Lives a life blissful, ordered, and sedate
Because under the marriage yoke he's bound.
Well may his heart in joy and bliss abound,
For who but a wife can be so pliant?   75
Who is so true, and who so diligent
To tend him, sick or well, as his mate will?
Him she will not forsake, for good or ill;   1290
To love and serve him best she never tires,
Though bedridden he lies till he expires.   80
And yet some learned clerks say it's not thus,
Of whom one of them's named Theophrastus.[2]
What are Theophrastus's lies to me?
"Take no wife, for your home's economy,"
He says, "And spare your household the expense.   85
A true servant will show more diligence
To guard your goods for you than your own wife,
For she'll claim half of them throughout her life.   1300

2   **Theophrastus:** Greek philosopher (c. fourth century), disciple of Aristotle, to whom the
Middle Ages attributed the lost work *The Golden Book of Marriage,* a tract arguing against marriage.
The Middle Ages knew of this work only through Jerome's *Adversus Jovinianum.*

And if that thou be syk, so God me save,
Thy verray frendes or a trewe knave
Wol kepe thee bet than she that waiteth ay
After thy good and hath don many a day.
And if thou take a wyf unto thyn hold,   1305
Ful lightly maystow been a cokewold."
This sentence and an hundred thinges worse
Wryteth this man—ther God his bones corse!
But take no kepe of al swich vanitee.
Deffye Theofraste and herke me.   1310
          A wyf is Goddes yifte, verraily.
Alle other maner yiftes, hardily,
As londes, rentes, pasture, or commune,
Or moebles, alle ben yiftes of Fortune,
That passen as a shadwe upon a wal.   1315
But dredelees, if pleynly speke I shal,
A wyf wol laste and in thyn hous endure,
Wel lenger than thee list, paraventure.
          Marriage is a ful gret sacrement.
He which that hath no wyf, I holde him shent: 1320
He liveth helplees and al desolat
(I speke of folk in seculer estaat).
And herke why—I sey nat this for noght—
That womman is for mannes help y-wroght:
The hye God, whan he hadde Adam maked   1325
And saugh him al allone, bely-naked,
God of his grete goodnesse seyde than,
"Lat us now make an helpe unto this man
Lyk to himself," and thanne he made him Eve.
Heer may ye se, and heerby may ye preve,   1330
That wyf is mannes help and his confort,
His paradys terrestre and his disport.
So buxom and so vertuous is she,
They moste nedes live in unitee.
O flesh they been, and o flesh as I gesse   1335
Hath but on herte, in wele and in distresse.

And, if you become sick, so God me save,
Your own true friends or else a faithful knave   90
Tends you better than she who waits always
To grab your goods; that's how she spends her days.
If you take a wife into your household,
In a wink, you may become a cuckold."
This sentence, and a hundred things much worse,   95
This man writes down, and may God his bones curse!
But take no heed of all such vanity;
Defy Theophrastus. Listen now to me.   1310
        A gift from God a wife is, verily;
All other sorts of gifts, then, certainly—   100
Lands or pastures, or usage rights or rents
Or movables—are gifts from Fortune sent,
Which pass just like a shadow on a wall.
Fear not, though I speak plainly, all in all:
A wife will last and in your house endure   105
Much longer than you'd like, you may be sure.
        Marriage is a sacrament in this life.
I think him ruined, he who has no wife,   1320
Alone and desolate without a mate—
I speak of folks of secular estate.   110
And hearken why: I don't say this for naught,
That woman for the help of man is wrought.
When first God on high Adam created,
And saw him all alone there, belly naked,
Then God in his great goodness had a plan: 115
"Let us now make a helpmate for this man
Like to himself," and he therefore made Eve.
Thus you may prove, and thus you may believe: 1330
Woman is man's helpmate and his comfort,
His paradise terrestrial and his consort.   120
So pliant and so virtuous is she
That they must live their lives in unity.
One flesh they are, and one flesh, I would guess,
Has but one heart in joy and in distress.

A wyf—a, Seinte Marie, *benedicite!*
How mighte a man han any adversitee
That hath a wyf? Certes, I can nat seye.
The blisse which that is bitwixe hem tweye   1340
Ther may no tonge telle or herte thinke.
If he be povre, she helpeth him to swinke.
She kepeth his good and wasteth never a deel.
Al that hir housbonde lust hir lyketh weel.
She seith not ones "nay" whan he seith "ye."   1345
"Do this," seith he; "Al redy, sir," seith she.
O blisful ordre of wedlok precious,
Thou art so mery and eek so vertuous,
And so commended and appreved eek,
That every man that halt him worth a leek   1350
Upon his bare knees oghte al his lyf
Thanken his God that him hath sent a wyf,
Or elles preye to God him for to sende
A wyf to laste unto his lyves ende,
For thanne his lyf is set in sikernesse.   1355
He may nat be deceyved, as I gesse,
So that he werke after his wyves reed.
Than may he boldly beren up his heed.
They been so trewe and therwithal so wyse,
For which, if thou wolt werken as the wyse,   1360
Do alwey so as wommen wol thee rede.
    Lo, how that Jacob, as thise clerkes rede,
By good conseil of his moder Rebekke,
Bond the kides skin aboute his nekke,
Thurgh which his fadres benisoun he wan.   1365
    Lo Judith, as the storie eek telle can,
By wys conseil she Goddes peple kepte,

A wife, oh, God bless you, by Saint Mary,   125
How might a man then have adversity
Who has a wife? Truly, I cannot say.
The bliss that is between them both each day,   1340
No tongue may tell, and no heart may conjure.
If he's poor, she helps him in his labor;   130
She guards his goods, and not a bit she wastes;
And what her husband wants is to her taste;
Not once does she say "nay" when he says "yea."
"Do this," says he. "All ready, sir," she'll say.
Blissful order of wedlock so precious,   135
You are so merry, yet so virtuous,
So commended and approved by all who speak
That every man who thinks he's worth a leek,   1350
Upon his bare knees, this man all his life
Should thank his God who has sent him a wife,   140
Or else he should pray that God will him send
A wife to last him until his life's end,
For then his life's set in assuredness.
He may not be deceived, as I would guess,
So long as he follows his wife's counsel.   145
Then he may boldly hold his head up well—
They are so true, and therefore, so wise, too.
Thus, if you'll work as you know how to do,   1360
Do always just as women will advise.
    Lo, see how Jacob, as the clerks advise,   150
With counsel from Rebecca,³ his mother,
Won himself the blessing of his father,
When a kid's skin around his neck he bound.
    Lo, Judith, as in her story it's found,
By her wise counsel, she God's people kept,   155

---

3   **Rebecca**, etc.: What follows is a list of biblical women who are taken as examples of women's ingenuity and resourcefulness, despite the violence involved in their stories: Rebecca (Genesis 27:1–29), Judith (Book of Judith, chapters 10–13), Abigail (1 Samuel 25:1–35), Esther (Book of Esther, chapters 7–8).

And slow him Olofernus whyl he slepte.
     Lo Abigayl, by good conseil how she
Saved hir housbonde Nabal whan that he   1370
Sholde han be slayn; and loke, Ester also
By good conseil delivered out of wo
The peple of God, and made him Mardochee
Of Assuere enhaunced for to be.
     Ther nis no thing in gree superlatyf,   1375
As seith Senek, above an humble wyf.
     Suffre thy wyves tonge, as Caton bit;
She shal comande and thou shalt suffren it,
And yet she wol obeye of curteisye.
A wyf is keper of thyn housbondrye.   1380
Wel may the syke man biwaille and wepe,
Ther as ther nis no wyf the hous to kepe.
I warne thee, if wisely thou wolt wirche,
Love wel thy wyf, as Crist loveth his chirche.
If thou lovest thyself, thou lovest thy wyf.   1385
No man hateth his flesh, but in his lyf
He fostreth it, and therfore bidde I thee
Cherisse thy wyf, or thou shalt never thee.
Housbond and wyf, what so men jape or pleye,
Of worldly folk holden the siker weye.   1390
They been so knit ther may noon harm bityde,
And namely upon the wyves syde.
For which this Januarie, of whom I tolde,
Considered hath, inwith his dayes olde,
The lusty lyf, the vertuous quiete,   1395
That is in mariage hony-swete;
And for his freendes on a day he sente,
To tellen hem th'effect of his entente.
     With face sad his tale he hath hem told.
He seyde, "Freendes, I am hoor and old   1400
And almost, God wot, on my pittes brinke.

And she slew Holofernus while he slept.

Lo, Abigail, for by good counsel, she
Rescued Nabal, her husband, although he   1370
Should have been slain. Look at Esther also,
Who, by good counsel, delivered up from woe   160
God's people, and then Mordechai she thus
Exalted through her husband Ahasuerus.

There's nothing of superlative degree,
Says Seneca, more than humble wives will be.

Suffer your wife's tongue, Cato did adjure;   165
Whatever she commands, you will endure,
And yet, she will obey through courtesy.
A wife is keeper of your husbandry.[4]   1380
The sick man may bewail himself and weep
When he's without a wife his house to keep.   170
If you seek to work wisely, in your search,
Then love your wife as Christ did love his church.
And if you love yourself, you love your wife.
No man can hate his flesh, but in his life
He fosters it; thus to you I aver,   175
Cherish your wife, or you'll never prosper.
Husband and wife—let who will joke or play—
Among lay folk, they hold the safer way.   1390
They are so close knit no harm can occur,
And namely, on the wife's side, to be sure.   180
Thus, this January, of whom I've told,
Has well considered, now that he is old,
The pleasing life, with virtue's calm replete
That dwells within a marriage, honey sweet,
And for his close friends one fine day he sent   185
To tell them all the gist of his intent.

With sober face, his tale he has them told.
He said, "My friends, now I am hoar and old,   1400
And almost, God knows, just at my pit's brink;

4   **husbandry**: Household management.

Upon my soule somwhat moste I thinke.
I have my body folily despended—
Blessed be God that it shal been amended!
For I wol be, certeyn, a wedded man,   1405
And that anoon in al the haste I can,
Unto som mayde fair and tendre of age.
I prey yow, shapeth for my mariage
Al sodeynly, for I wol nat abyde,
And I wol fonde t'espyen, on my syde,   1410
To whom I may be wedded hastily.
But forasmuche as ye ben mo than I,
Ye shullen rather swich a thing espyen
Than I, and wher me best were to allyen.
        But o thing warne I yow, my freendes dere,   1415
I wol non old wyf han in no manere.
She shal nat passe twenty yeer, certayn.
Old fish and yong flesh wolde I have fayn.
Bet is," quod he, "a pyk than a pikerel,
And bet than old boef is the tendre veel.   1420
I wol no womman thritty yeer of age;
It is but bene-straw and greet forage.
And eek thise olde widwes, God it woot,
They conne so muchel craft, on Wades boot,
So muchel broken harm, whan that hem leste,   1425
That with hem sholde I never live in reste.
For sondry scoles maken sotil clerkis;
Womman of manye scoles half a clerk is.
But certeynly, a yong thing may men gye,
Right as men may warm wex with handes plye.   1430
Wherfore I sey yow pleynly, in a clause,
I wol non old wyf han right for this cause.
For if so were I hadde swich mischaunce
That I in hir ne coude han no plesaunce,

Somewhat on my soul now I must think. 190
My body I have foolishly expended.
Blessed be God that it may be amended;
I wish to be, in truth, a wedded man,
And that, at once, in all the haste I can,
To some maiden of tender age and fair. 195
I pray you, for my marriage now prepare
At once. Any delay I won't abide,
And I will try to spy out, on my side, 1410
To whom I may be wedded hastily.
And because there are more of you than me, 200
You can better spy out such a thing
And where it's best I do my marrying.
      But, my dear friends, I warn you, on my life,
I will in no way marry an old wife.
She won't be over twenty, certainly. 205
Old fish and young flesh I will have gladly.
Pike is better than pickerel,⁵ I feel,
And better than old beef is tender veal. 1420
No thirty-year-old woman will I try;
They're only fodder coarse and bean stalks dry. 210
Moreover, these old widows, God take note,
Know such craftiness, upon Wade's boat,⁶
And so much harm they do when they think best,
That, with them all, I'd never have a rest.
For sundry schools can all make subtle clerks; 215
Women, of many schools, are half-baked clerks.
But, certainly, a young thing men may guide,
Just as they, with their hands, warm wax have plied. 1430
Therefore, I tell you plainly, in a clause,
That I will not have an old wife because 220
If I had such bad luck beyond measure
That I could not take in her my pleasure,

---

5 **pickerel**: Young pike.
6 **Wade's boat**: An allusion that remains obscure.

Thanne sholde I lede my lyf in avoutrye   1435
And go streight to the devel whan I dye,
Ne children sholde I none upon hir geten.
Yet were me levere houndes had me eten
Than that myn heritage sholde falle
In straunge hand, and this I tell yow alle.   1440
I dote nat. I woot the cause why
Men sholde wedde, and forthermore woot I
Ther speketh many a man of mariage
That woot namore of it than woot my page
For whiche causes man sholde take a wyf: 1445
If he ne may nat liven chast his lyf,
Take him a wyf with greet devocioun
By cause of leveful procreacioun
Of children to th'onour of God above,
And nat only for paramour or love;   1450
And for they sholde lecherye eschue
And yelde hir dettes whan that they ben due;
Or for that ech of hem sholde helpen other
In meschief, as a suster shal the brother,
And live in chastitee ful holily.   1455
But sires, by your leve, that am nat I.
For God be thanked, I dar make avaunt,
I fele my limes stark and suffisaunt
To do al that a man bilongeth to.
I woot myselven best what I may do.   1460
Though I be hoor, I fare as dooth a tree
That blosmeth er that fruyt y-woxen be,
And blosmy tree nis neither drye ne deed.
I fele me nowher hoor but on myn heed.
Myn herte and alle my limes been as grene   1465
As laurer thurgh the yeer is for to sene.
And sin that ye han herd al myn entente,
I prey yow to my wil ye wole assente."
          Diverse men diversely him tolde
Of mariage manye ensamples olde.   1470

Then in adultery my life would lie;
And I'd go to the devil when I die.
No children would I beget on her then;   225
I'd prefer that hounds would have me eaten
Rather than that my whole estate should fall
To strangers' hands. And this I tell you all: 1440
I am no fool, I know the reason why
That men should wed, and furthermore know I   230
That many men there are who speak of marriage
Who know no more good causes than my page
And reasons why a man should take a wife.
If he cannot live chaste throughout his life,
Let him take a wife with great devotion   235
For the cause of lawful procreation
Of children, to honor our God above,
And not only for pleasure or for love;   1450
And so that they will lechery eschew
And pay their marriage debt when it is due;   240
Or so each of them should help the other
In misfortune, like sister and brother,
And live quite blessedly in chastity—
But, sires, now by your leave, that's not for me.
For, God be thanked, if boasting isn't wrong,   245
I feel my limbs sufficient now and strong
To do those things it behooves a man to;
For I myself know best what I can do.   1460
Though I am hoary, I fare like a tree
That blossoms first before the fruit you'll see;   250
A blossoming tree is not dry nor dead.
Nowhere do I feel hoar but on my head;
My heart and all my limbs are quite as green
As any laurel that you've ever seen.
And since you now have heard all my intent,   255
I pray that to my will you will assent."
        Diverse men there diversely to him told
About marriage, many examples old.   1470

Somme blamed it, somme preysed it, certeyn.
But atte laste, shortly for to seyn,
As al day falleth altercacioun
Bitwixen freendes in disputisoun,
Ther fil a stryf bitwixe his bretheren two,   1475
Of whiche that oon was cleped Placebo;
Justinus soothly called was that other.
          Placebo seyde, "O Januarie, brother,
Ful litel nede had ye, my lord so dere,
Conseil to axe of any that is here,   1480
But that ye been so ful of sapience
That yow ne lyketh, for your heighe prudence,
To weyven fro the word of Salomon.
This word seyde he unto us everichon:
'Wirk alle thing by conseil,' thus seyde he,   1485
'And thanne shaltow nat repente thee.'
But though that Salomon spak swich a word,
Myn owene dere brother and my lord,
So wisly God my soule bringe at reste,
I hold your owene conseil is the beste.   1490
For, brother myn, of me tak this motyf:
I have now been a court-man al my lyf,
And God it woot, though I unworthy be,
I have stonden in ful greet degree
Abouten lordes of ful heigh estaat,   1495
Yet hadde I never with noon of hem debaat.
I never hem contraried, trewely.
I woot wel that my lord can more than I.
What that he seith, I holde it ferme and stable.
I seye the same or elles thing semblable.   1500
A ful gret fool is any conseillour
That serveth any lord of heigh honour
That dar presume or elles thenken it

Some condemned it, some praised it, certainly,
But at last, to tell the story quickly,   260
As always befalls an altercation
Between friends who are in disputation,
There happened strife between his brothers so,
Of whom the first one was called Placebo.[7]
Justinus,[8] in truth, was named the other.   265
    Placebo said, "January, brother,
Full little need have you, my lord so dear,
Counsel to ask of any who are here,   1480
Except that, with your wise intelligence,
You do not wish, given your great prudence,   270
To waiver from the word of Solomon.
This word he said unto us, every one:
'If by counsel you will work all things,
You will have no reason for repenting.'
But though King Solomon said such a word,   275
As, my lord and dear brother, you have heard,
So wisely may God my soul bring to rest,
I hold that your own counsel is the best.   1490
For, my brother, take my advice right here,
Since all my life I've been a courtier,   280
And God knows, although I am unworthy,
I have stood high within my own degree
Amid lords who are of quite great estate;
And yet with none of them had I debate.
I never contradicted them, it's true;   285
I know well my lords know more than I do.
What they might say, I deem firm and stable;
I say the same, as near as I am able.   1500
A quite great fool is any counselor,
In service to a lord of such high honor,   290
Who dares presume, or else even think it,

---

7 **Placebo**: The name means: "I shall please." Placebo is a sychophant.
8 **Justinus**: The name means: "The just one." Justinus is the voice of hard-edged truth.

That his conseil sholde passe his lordes wit.
Nay, lordes been no fooles, by my fay.   1505
Ye han yourselven shewed heer today
So heigh sentence, so holily and weel,
That I consente and conferme everydeel
Your wordes alle and your opinioun.
By God, ther nis no man in al this toun   1510
Ne in Itaille that coude bet han sayd.
Crist halt him of this conseil wel apayd.
And trewely, it is an heigh corage
Of any man that stapen is in age
To take a yong wyf. By my fader kin,   1515
Your herte hangeth on a joly pin!
Doth now in this matere right as yow leste,
For finally I holde it for the beste."
          Justinus, that ay stille sat and herde,
Right in this wyse he to Placebo answerde: 1520
"Now, brother myn, be pacient, I preye,
Sin ye han seyd, and herkneth what I seye.
Senek, among his othere wordes wyse,
Seith that a man oghte him right wel avyse
To whom he yeveth his lond or his catel.   1525
And sin I oghte avyse me right wel
To whom I yeve my good awey fro me,
Wel muchel more I oghte avysed be
To whom I yeve my body for alwey.
I warne yow wel, it is no childes pley   1530
To take a wyf withoute avysement.
Men moste enquere—this is myn assent—
Wher she be wys or sobre or dronkelewe,
Or proud or elles otherweys a shrewe,
A chydester or wastour of thy good,   1535
Or riche or poore, or elles mannish wood.
Al be it so that no man finden shal

That his advice should outweigh his lord's wit.
No, lords are no one's fools, my faith would own.
Right here today, you have yourselves all shown,
Blessedly and well, such stable judgment 295
That I confirm each last bit and consent
To your view and to your words one and all.
No man in this town whom I can recall 1510
Nor in all Italy has talked so well!
Christ deems himself well paid by good counsel. 300
And truly, it is an act of courage
For any man steeped well along in age
To take a young wife. By my father's kin,
Your heart is hung up on a jolly pin!⁹
Do now as you like about this matter. 305
Finally, I think that that is better."

       Justinus, who sat still and all this heard,
In this way, he to Placebo answered: 1520
"Now, brother mine, be patient here, I pray.
You've said your piece; now hearken what I say. 310
Once Seneca, among his words so wise,
Said that a man would well himself advise
To whom he gives both his land and chattel.
And since I should advise myself quite well
To whom I send my goods away from me, 315
Then even more I should well counseled be
To whom I give my body through my days.
I warn you well that it is no child's play 1530
To take a wife *sans* deliberation.
Men must inquire—this is my opinion— 320
If wise or sober or a drinker, too,
She be, or proud, or else, in ways, a shrew,
A scold or waster of your goods, or lazy,
Or rich, or poor, or else perhaps man crazy.
Although it is true that no man can see 325

9   **hung up on a jolly pin:** Your heart is merry or frisky.

Noon in this world that trotteth hool in al—
Ne man ne beest, swich as men coude devyse—
But nathelees it oghte ynough suffise   1540
With any wyf if so were that she hadde
Mo goode thewes than hir vyces badde;
And al this axeth leyser for t'enquere.
For God it woot, I have wept many a tere
Ful prively sin I have had a wyf.   1545
Preyse whoso wole a wedded mannes lyf,
Certein I finde in it but cost and care
And observances of alle blisses bare.
And yet, God woot, my neighebores aboute,
And namely of wommen many a route,   1550
Seyn that I have the moste stedefast wyf
And eek the mekeste oon that bereth lyf.
But I wot best wher wringeth me my sho.
Ye mowe, for me, right as yow lyketh do.
Avyseth yow—ye been a man of age—   1555
How that ye entren into mariage,
And namely with a yong wyf and a fair.
By Him that made water, erthe, and air,
The yongest man that is in al this route
Is bisy ynogh to bringen it aboute   1560
To han his wyf allone. Trusteth me,
Ye shul nat plese hir fully yeres three
(This is to seyn, to doon hir ful plesaunce).
A wyf axeth ful many an observaunce.
I prey yow that ye be nat yvel apayd."   1565
　　　　"Wel," quod this Januarie, "and hastow sayd?
Straw for thy Senek and for thy proverbes!
I counte nat a panier ful of herbes
Of scole-termes. Wyser men than thow,
As thou hast herd, assenteden right now   1570
To my purpos. Placebo, what sey ye?"

One in this world who can trot perfectly,
Neither man nor beast, as men imagine,
Nonetheless, it should suffice enough, then,   1540
For any wife, if you were sure she had
More of good qualities than she had bad.   330
All this asks leisure for an inquiry.
God knows, I have myself wept privately
Many a tear since I have had a wife.
Though praise whoever will the wed man's life,
In truth, I find there only cost and care,   335
And in it duties of all real bliss bare.
And yet, God knows, my neighbors close at hand—
Namely, of the women, many a band—   1550
All say that mine is the most steadfast wife,
And, too, the meekest one who may bear life—   340
But I know best where I'm pinched by my shoe.
For all I care, do as you want to do.
But heed yourself—you're a man of some age—
How you start to enter into marriage,
And namely with a wife who's young and fair.   345
By him who made the water, earth, and air,
In all this company, the youngest man
Is busy enough making up a plan   1560
To have his wife for himself. Now trust me,
You won't please her more than three years fully—   350
That's to say, to fully do her pleasure.
Wives want obeisance beyond measure.
In this, may you not be displeased, I pray."
          Said this January, "Have you had your say?
A straw for Seneca and for your proverbs!   355
Now I don't care a basketful of herbs
For your school talk.[10] Much wiser men than you,
As you have heard, now have assented to   1570
My purpose. What do you say, Placebo?"

10   **school talk**: Language of philosophical argumentation.

"I seye it is a cursed man," quod he,
"That letteth matrimoine, sikerly."
And with that word they rysen sodeynly,
And been assented fully that he sholde   1575
Be wedded whanne him list and wher he wolde.
    Heigh fantasye and curious bisinesse
Fro day to day gan in the soule impresse
Of Januarie aboute his mariage.
Many fair shape and many a fair visage   1580
Ther passeth thurgh his herte, night by night.
As whoso toke a mirour polished bright
And sette it in a commune market-place,
Than sholde he see many a figure pace
By his mirour; and in the same wyse   1585
Gan Januarie inwith his thoght devyse
Of maydens whiche that dwelten him bisyde.
He wiste nat wher that he mighte abyde,
For if that oon have beaute in hir face,
Another stant so in the peples grace   1590
For hir sadnesse and hir benignitee
That of the peple grettest voys hath she.
And somme were riche and hadden badde name.
But nathelees, bitwixe ernest and game,
He atte laste apoynted him on oon,   1595
And leet alle othere from his herte goon,
And chees hir of his owene auctoritee;
For love is blind al day and may nat see.
And whan that he was in his bed y-broght,
He purtreyed in his herte and in his thoght   1600
Hir fresshe beautee and hir age tendre,
Hir myddel smal, hir armes longe and sclendre,
Hir wyse governaunce, hir gentillesse,
Hir wommanly beringe and hir sadnesse.
And whan that he on hir was condescended,   1605
Him thoughte his chois mighte nat ben amended.
For whan that he himself concluded hadde,

"It is," said he, "a cursed man, I know,   360
Who hinders matrimony, certainly."
And with that word, they rose up suddenly,
And fully they were all agreed he should
Be wedded when he wants and where he would.
      Keen fantasies and curious busyness   365
From day to day their marks did well impress
In January about his marriage.
Many fair shapes and many a fair visage   1580
There pass then through his heart, night by night.
Just as one takes a mirror, polished bright,   370
And sets it in the common marketplace,
Then he would see many a figure pace
By his mirror, and in the same way, then,
Did January in his thoughts imagine
All the maidens who lived nearby him yet.   375
He knew not where his sights were best to set.
If one of them has beauty in her face,
Another stands so in the people's grace   1590
For calm composure and benignity
That from the people greatest praise had she;   380
And some were rich and yet had a bad name.
Nonetheless, between earnestness and game,
He finally decided on one, so
He let all the others from his heart go.
He chose her of his own authority—   385
For love is blind all day and may not see.
At night when he was into his bed brought,
He pictured in his mind and in his thought   1600
Her fresh beauty and her age so tender,
Her middle slim, her arms so long and slender,   390
Her wise demeanor, her gentility,
Womanly bearing and solemnity.
When upon her his choice had descended,
He saw no way it might be amended.
And when he for himself decided had,   395

Him thoughte ech other mannes wit so badde
That inpossible it were to replye
Agayn his chois—this was his fantasye.   1610
His freendes sente he to at his instaunce
And preyed hem to doon him that plesaunce,
That hastily they wolden to him come.
He wolde abregge hir labour, alle and some:
Nedeth namore for him to go ne ryde;   1615
He was apoynted ther he wolde abyde.
Placebo cam and eek his freendes sone,
And alderfirst he bad hem alle a bone,
That noon of hem none argumentes make
Agayn the purpos which that he hath take,   1620
Which purpos was plesant to God, seyde he,
And verray ground of his prosperitee.
      He seyde ther was a mayden in the toun,
Which that of beautee hadde greet renoun.
Al were it so she were of smal degree,   1625
Suffyseth him hir youthe and hir beautee.
Which mayde, he seyde, he wolde han to his wyf,
To lede in ese and holinesse his lyf,
And thanked God that he mighte han hire al,
That no wight his blisse parten shal,   1630
And preyed hem to laboure in this nede
And shapen that he faille nat to spede.
For thanne, he seyde, his spirit was at ese.
"Thanne is," quod he, "no thing may me displese,
Save o thing priketh in my conscience,   1635
The which I wol reherce in your presence.
      I have," quod he, "herd seyd ful yore ago
Ther may no man han parfite blisses two,
This is to seye, in erthe and eek in hevene.
For though he kepe him fro the sinnes sevene,   1640
And eek from every branche of thilke tree,
Yet is ther so parfit felicitee
And so greet ese and lust in mariage

He thought all other men's wits were so bad,
To argue were impossibility
Against his choice—this was his fantasy.   1610
To his friends he sent; then at his request,
He begged their favor that they'd do their best   400
And hastily upon him they would call;
He would abridge their labor, one and all.
No more need was there they should walk or ride;
He was all settled where he would decide.
Placebo came, and other friends quite soon,   405
But first of all, he asked from them this boon:
That none of them an argument would make
Against the very purpose he would take,   1620
Which was both pleasing unto God, said he,
And the true ground of his prosperity.   410
        He said there was a maiden in the town,
And for her beauty, she had great renown.
Although this maiden came of low degree,
For him sufficed both her youth and beauty.
Which maiden, he said, he'd have for a wife,   415
To lead in ease and holiness his life;
Since, he would, thank God, have her wholly, there
Would never be a man his bliss to share.   1630
He prayed them labor to fulfill his need
And make it so he'd fail not to succeed;   420
For then, he said, his spirit was at ease.
"Then not a thing," said he, "could me displease,
Except one thing pricks me in my conscience,
Which I'll now rehearse within your presence.
        I have," said he, "heard many years ago,   425
That no man has two perfect joys just so—
That is to say, on earth and in heaven.
Though he shuns the deadly sins, those seven,   1640
And every branch upon that selfsame tree,
Yet is there such perfect felicity   430
And great ease and pleasure within marriage,

That ever I am agast now in myn age

That I shal lede now so mery a lyf,   1645

So delicat, withouten wo and stryf,

That I shal have myn hevene in erthe here.

For sith that verray hevene is boght so deere

With tribulacioun and greet penaunce,

How sholde I thanne, that live in swich plesaunce   1650

As alle wedded men don with hir wyvis,

Come to the blisse ther Crist eterne on lyve is?

This is my drede, and ye, my bretheren tweye,

Assoilleth me this questioun, I preye."

      Justinus, which that hated his folye,   1655

Answerde anon, right in his japerye,

And for he wolde his longe tale abregge,

He wolde noon auctoritee allegge

But seyde, "Sire, so ther be noon obstacle

Other than this, God of his hye miracle   1660

And of his mercy may so for yow wirche

That, er ye have your right of holy chirche,

Ye may repente of wedded mannes lyf,

In which ye seyn ther is no wo ne stryf.

And elles, God forbede but he sente   1665

A wedded man him grace to repente

Wel ofte rather than a sengle man!

And therfore, sire, the beste reed I can:

Dispeire yow noght, but have in your memorie,

Paraunter she may be your purgatorie!   1670

She may be Goddes mene and Goddes whippe.

Than shal your soule up to hevene skippe

Swifter than dooth an arwe out of the bowe.

I hope to God herafter shul ye knowe

That ther nis no so greet felicitee   1675

In mariage, ne never mo shal be,

That yow shal lette of your savacioun,

So that ye use, as skile is and resoun,

The lustes of your wyf attemprely,

That I am terrified in my old age
That I shall now lead such a merry life,
So delightful, and without woe and strife,
That I shall have my heaven on earth here.   435
Because heaven itself is bought so dear
With both great penance and tribulation,
How should I, who'll live in such elation,   1650
As must each wedded man do with his wife,
To bliss in Christ come in eternal life?   440
This is my dread, and my dear brothers two,
Solve this problem for me, now I pray you."
        Justinus, who hated all this folly,
Then answered him right back with mockery;
He sought to shorten his tale if he might,   445
So he wished no authorities to cite,
But said, "Sire, so there'll be no obstacle
Other than this, God, through high miracle   1660
And his endless mercy, may well function
So before you receive extreme unction,   450
You may rue having lived a wed man's life,
In which, you say, there is no woe and strife.
Now God forbid that he should not have sent
To a wed man the full grace to repent
Rather more often than the single man!   455
Therefore, sire—I advise as best I can—
Do not despair, but keep in memory
That perhaps she'll be your purgatory!   1670
And she may well be God's means and God's whip;
Then shall your soul right up to heaven skip   460
Swifter than flies the arrow from the bow.
I hope to God that after this you'll know
There is not such a great felicity
Within marriage, nor will there ever be,
So that it will keep you from salvation,   465
If, lead by propriety and reason,
In her you take pleasure temperately,

And that ye plese hir nat to amorously,   1680
And that ye kepe yow eek from other sinne.
My tale is doon, for my wit is thinne.
Beth nat agast herof, my brother dere.
But lat us waden out of this matere.
The Wyf of Bathe, if ye han understonde,   1685
Of mariage, which we have on honde,
Declared hath ful wel in litel space.
Fareth now wel; God have yow in his grace."
          And with this word this Justin and his brother
Han take hir leve, and ech of hem of other.   1690
For whan they sawe it moste nedes be,
They wroghten so by sly and wys tretee
That she, this mayden which that Mayus highte,
As hastily as ever that she mighte
Shal wedded be unto this Januarie.   1695
I trowe it were to longe yow to tarie
If I yow tolde of every scrit and bond
By which that she was feffed in his lond,
Or for to herknen of hir riche array.
But finally y-comen is the day   1700
That to the chirche bothe be they went
For to receyve the holy sacrement.
Forth comth the preest, with stole aboute his nekke,
And bad hir be lyk Sarra and Rebekke
In wisdom and in trouthe of mariage,   1705
And seyde his orisons as is usage,
And croucheth hem, and bad God sholde hem blesse,
And made al siker ynogh with holinesse.
          Thus been they wedded with solempnitee,
And at the feste sitteth he and she   1710
With other worthy folk upon the deys.
Al ful of joye and blisse is the paleys,

And you don't please her too amorously,   1680
And if you keep yourself from other sin.
My tale is now done, for my wit is thin.   470
Do no now fear these things, my dear brother,
But let us now wade out of this matter.
The Wife of Bath, as you can understand,
About marriage, the subject now at hand,
Has pronounced quite well in a little space.   475
Now fare you well. God have you in his grace."
        With this word, Justinus and his brother
Now took their leave, each one of the other.   1690
For when they saw that this all needs must be,
By sly, wise dealing, they made it so she,   480
This young maiden who, by name, was called May,
As hastily as they could pick the day,
Shall wedded be unto January.
I think it would be too long to tarry,
If I told you of every writ and deed,   485
Which to enfeoff[11] her with his land they need,
Or if I told you of her rich array.
But finally there has arrived the day   1700
When to the church the both of them then went
There to receive the holy sacrament.   490
Forth comes the priest, the stole on his neck laid;
To be like Sarah and Rebecca,[12] he bade
Her, both in fidelity and wisdom.
He says his orisons, as is his custom;
He signs them with the cross, bids God them bless,   495
And makes it sure enough with holiness.
        Thus are they wedded with solemnity,
And at the marriage feast sit he and she   1710
With other worthy folks upon the dais.
All filled with joy and bliss now is the palace,   500

11 **enfeoff**: Term for legally endowing with land.
12 **Sarah and Rebecca**: Biblical women who exemplified wifely virtues.

And ful of instruments and of vitaille,
The moste deyntevous of al Itaille.
Biforn hem stoode instruments of swich soun   1715
That Orpheus ne of Thebes Amphioun
Ne maden never swich a melodye.
At every cours than cam loud minstralcye
That never tromped Joab for to here,
Nor he Theodomas yet half so clere   1720
At Thebes whan the citee was in doute.
Bacus the wyn hem skinketh al aboute,
And Venus laugheth upon every wight—
For Januarie was bicome hir knight
And wolde bothe assayen his corage   1725
In libertee and eek in mariage—
And with hir fyrbrond in hir hand aboute
Daunceth biforn the bryde and al the route.
And certeinly, I dar right wel seyn this,
Ymeneus, that god of wedding is,   1730
Saugh never his lyf so mery a wedded man.
Hold thou thy pees, thou poete Marcian,
That wrytest us that ilke wedding murie
Of hir, Philologye, and him, Mercurie,
And of the songes that the Muses songe.   1735
To smal is bothe thy penne and eek thy tonge
For to descryven of this mariage.
Whan tendre youthe hath wedded stouping age,
Ther is swich mirthe that it may nat be writen.

With instruments and food for all to see,
The most delicious in all Italy.
Before them all, such instruments stood thus
That Amphion of Thebes[13] or Orpheus[14]
Could never hope to make such melody.   505
At every course came such loud minstrelsy
That Joab[15] never trumpeted to hear
Nor Theodomas[16] either half as clear   1720
At Thebes then when its safety was in doubt.
Soon Bacchus[17] to them all the wine pours out,   510
And Venus laughs on every man in sight
For January has become her knight
And wants to test the rigor of his courage
Both in bachelorhood and now in marriage;
And with her firebrand[18] in her hand, she   515
Danced for the bride and all the company.
And certainly, I dare well say this, then,
He who is the god of weddings, Hymen,   1730
Saw never wedded man so merry thus.
Hold your peace, you poet, Martianus,[19]   520
Who for us wrote of that wedding merry
Between Philology and Mercury,
And all about the songs the Muses sung!
For far too small is both your pen and tongue
For you to portray all of this marriage.   525
When tender youth has wedded stooping age,
There is such mirth that it cannot be written.

---

13 **Amphion of Thebes**: The king of Thebes who was also a renowned musician.

14 **Orpheus**: Mythical Greek musician who sought his wife Eurydice in the underworld.

15 **Joab**: Biblical trumpeter in King David's army.

16 **Theodomus**: Theban trumpeter and seer.

17 **Bacchus**: Roman god of wine.

18 **firebrand**: Hymen, the Greek god of marriage, was often depicted leading the wedding procession with a lit torch. Here, Venus is given the honor.

19 **Martianus**: Martianus Capella was the author of the allegorical poem about the marriage of Philology and Mercury, which is a far more auspicious event than the wedding scene in *The Merchant's Tale*.

Assayeth it yourself; than may ye witen   1740
If that I lye or noon in this matere.
      Mayus, that sit with so benigne a chere,
Hir to biholde it semed fayerye.
Quene Ester loked never with swich an yë
On Assuer, so meke a look hath she.   1745
I may yow nat devyse al hir beautee,
But thus muche of hir beautee telle I may,
That she was lyk the brighte morwe of May,
Fulfild of alle beautee and plesaunce.
      This Januarie is ravisshed in a traunce   1750
At every time he loked on hir face;
But in his herte he gan hir to manace
That he that night in armes wolde hir streyne
Harder than ever Paris dide Eleyne.
But nathelees yet hadde he greet pitee   1755
That thilke night offenden hir moste he,
And thoughte, "Allas! O tendre creature,
Now wolde God ye mighte wel endure
Al my corage, it is so sharp and kene.
I am agast ye shul it nat sustene.   1760
(But God forbede that I dide al my might!)
Now wolde God that it were woxen night
And that the night wolde lasten evermo.
I wolde that al this peple were ago."
And finally he doth al his labour   1765
As he best mighte, savinge his honour,
To haste hem fro the mete in subtil wyse.
      The tyme cam that reson was to ryse,
And after that men daunce and drinken faste,
And spyces al aboute the hous they caste,   1770
And ful of joye and blisse is every man—

Try it for yourself, and you'll admit then 1740
If I lie or not about this matter.

     May sits there with such benign demeanor, 530
Enchanting as a fairy to behold her.
Never with such an eye looked Queen Esther[20]
On Ahasuerus, so meek a look has she.
For you, I cannot describe her beauty.
But this much of her beauty tell I may, 535
That she was like a bright morning in May,
Filled so full with all delight and beauty.

     Ravished in a trance is January 1750
Every time that he looked on her face;
But in his heart, he threatened to embrace 540
Her that same night and in his arms to press
Her more than ever Helen was by Paris.[21]
But nonetheless, still he had great pity
That this very night offend her must he,
And thought, "Alas! Oh, you tender creature, 545
Now, would to God that you might well endure
All my ardor; it is so sharp and plain!
I am afraid that it you can't sustain. 1760
But God forbid that I did all I might!
Now would to God that day would turn to night, 550
And that the night would last well beyond dawn.
I wish that all these people were long gone."
And at last, he finished up his labor,
As best he might while saving his honor,
To rush them from the feast in subtle guise. 555

     At last, then, it was reasonable to rise;
And after that, men danced and drank up fast,
And spices all about the house they cast, 1770
And full of joy and bliss is every man—

20 **Esther**: One of the prime biblical examples of the extraordinary wife.
21 **Helen was by Paris**: Paris's abduction of Helen, the world's most beautiful woman, from her husband, Menelaus, caused the Trojan War.

All but a squyer highte Damian,
Which carf biforn the knight ful many a day.
He was so ravisshed on his lady May
That for the verray peyne he was ny wood.   1775
Almost he swelte and swowned ther he stood,
So sore hath Venus hurt him with hir brond,
As that she bar it daunsinge in hir hond;
And to his bed he wente him hastily.
Namore of him at this tyme speke I,   1780
But ther I lete him wepe ynough and pleyne,
Til fresshe May wol rewen on his peyne.

      O perilous fyr that in the bedstraw bredeth!
O famulier foo that his servyce bedeth!
O servant traitour, false hoomly hewe,   1785
Lyk to the naddre in bosom sly untrewe,
God shilde us alle from your aqueyntaunce!
O Januarie, dronken in plesaunce
Of mariage, see how thy Damian,
Thyn owene squyer and thy borne man,   1790
Entendeth for to do thee vileinye.
God graunte thee thyn hoomly fo t'espye,
For in this world nis worse pestilence
Than hoomly foo al day in thy presence.

      Parfourned hath the sonne his ark diurne.   1795
No lenger may the body of him sojurne
On th'orisonte as in that latitude.
Night with his mantel that is derk and rude
Gan oversprede the hemisperie aboute,
For which departed is this lusty route   1800
Fro Januarie, with thank on every syde.
Hom to hir houses lustily they ryde,

All but a squire who's named Damian;   560
Who before the knight carved²² many a day.
He was so ravished by his lady May
That, from the pain, he was quite close to mad.
Almost he'd swooned, and almost fainted had,
So sore had Venus hurt him with her brand²³   565
As she bore it, while dancing, in her hand;
And to his bed he went then, hastily.
Right now you'll hear no more of him from me;   1780
I leave him there to weep and to complain
Until fresh May finds pity for his pain.   570
            Oh, perilous fire, that in bedstraw breeds!
Oh, familiar foe, his services who cedes!
Oh, traitor servant, false with humble hue,
The adder in the bosom, sly, untrue,
God protect us all from your acquaintance!   575
Oh January, drunk in the pleasing trance
Of marriage, see now how your Damian,
Your own squire, since he was first born, your man,   1790
Intends to do you villainy close by.
God grant you that your household foe you'll spy!   580
For in this world is no worse pestilence
Than a household foe always in your presence.
            The sun has now performed his arc diurnal;
No longer may his body stay withal
On the horizon, in that latitude.   585
Night with his mantle, which is dark and rude,
To cloak this whole hemisphere has started;
Now this merry company's departed   1800
From January, with thanks on each side.
Home to their houses merrily they ride,   590

---

22 **squire . . . carved**: One of the roles of a squire was to carve the meat for his lord. See the portrait of the Squire in *The General Prologue*, who carves for his father, the Knight.

23 **brand**: Firebrand or torch; earlier, Venus has been depicted carrying the wedding torch (usually reserved for Hymen) at the wedding feast of January and May.

Wher as they doon hir thinges as hem leste,
And whan they sye hir tyme, goon to reste.
Sone after that this hastif Januarie   1805
Wolde go to bedde—he wolde no lenger tarie.
He drinketh ipocras, clarree, and vernage
Of spyces hote, t'encresen his corage,
And many a letuarie hadde he, ful fyn,
Swiche as the cursed monk dan Constantyn   1810
Hath writen in his book, *De Coitu*.
To eten hem alle he nas no thing eschu.
And to his privee freendes thus seyde he:
"For Goddes love, as sone as it may be,
Lat voyden al this hous in curteys wyse."   1815
And they had doon right as he wol devyse.
Men drinken, and the travers drawe anon.
The bryde was broght abedde as stille as stoon,
And whan the bed was with the preest y-blessed,
Out of the chambre hath every wight him dressed,   1820
And Januarie hath faste in armes take
His fresshe May, his paradys, his make.
He lulleth hir, he kisseth hir ful ofte.
With thikke bristles of his berd unsofte—
Lyk to the skin of houndfish, sharp as brere,   1825
For he was shave al newe in his manere—
He rubbeth hir aboute hir tendre face
And seyde thus: "Allas! I moot trespace
To yow, my spouse, and yow gretly offende,
Er tyme come that I wil doun descende.   1830
But nathelees, considereth this," quod he,
"Ther nis no werkman, whatsoever he be,

Where they all do the things that they like best,
And when they see their time, they take their rest.
Soon after that, eager January
Wished to go to bed; he would not tarry.
He drinks claret, hippocras, and vernage[24]   595
Spiked with hot spices to increase his courage;
And many medicines has he so fine,
Such as that cursed monk, Don Constantine,[25]   1810
Has recorded in his book *De Coitu*;
And not a one of them would he eschew.   600
To his close friends in private thus said he:
"For love of God, as soon as it can be,
Clear this house out in some courteous way."
And they thus followed all that he did say.
Men drink and draw the traverse curtain[26] taut;   605
To bed, the bride as still as stone is brought;
And when the marriage bed the priest had blessed,
Out of the chamber withdrew every guest,   1820
And January did not hesitate
To grab fresh May, his paradise, his mate.   610
He lulls her and he kisses her quite often.
With thick bristles of his beard unsoft then—
Just like dogfish's skin,[27] sharp as a burr,
For he was newly shaven in his manner—
He rubs around her tender face. "Alas!"   615
He said to her thus, "I must now trespass
Against you, my spouse, and greatly offend
You before the time comes when I'll down descend.   1830
But nonetheless, consider this," said he,
"There's no workman, whoever he may be,   620

---

24 **claret, hippocras, and vernage**: Varieties of spiced wines that January is using as aphrodisiacs.

25 **Constantine**: Constantinus Africanus (eleventh century), who wrote a treatise *De Coitus* (*On Intercourse*) that included sections on virility and recipes for the aphrodisiacs to enhance it.

26 **traverse curtain**: In the Middle Ages, even wealthy homes often lacked private sleeping quarters. They were formed by drawing a traverse curtain across a larger room in order to create a bedroom.

27 **dogfish's skin**: Skin of a small shark.

That may bothe werke wel and hastily.
This wol be doon at leyser parfitly.
It is no fors how longe that we pleye.   1835
In trewe wedlok coupled be we tweye,
And blessed be the yok that we been inne,
For in our actes we mowe do no sinne.
A man may do no sinne with his wyf,
Ne hurte himselven with his owene knyf,   1840
For we han leve to pleye us by the lawe."
Thus laboureth he til that the day gan dawe,
And than he taketh a sop in fyn clarree,
And upright in his bed than sitteth he,
And after that he sang ful loude and clere,   1845
And kiste his wyf and made wantoun chere.
He was al coltish, ful of ragerye,
And ful of jargon as a flekked pye.
The slakke skin aboute his nekke shaketh
Whyl that he sang, so chaunteth he and craketh.   1850
But God wot what that May thoughte in hir herte,
Whan she him saugh up sittinge in his sherte,
In his night-cappe, and with his nekke lene.
She preyseth nat his pleying worth a bene.
Than seide he thus, "My reste wol I take.   1855
Now day is come, I may no lenger wake."
And doun he leyde his heed and sleep til pryme.
And afterward, whan that he saugh his tyme,
Up ryseth Januarie; but fresshe May
Held hir chambre unto the fourthe day,   1860
As usage is of wyves for the beste.
For every labour somtyme moot han reste,
Or elles longe may he nat endure—
This is to seyn, no lyves creature,
Be it of fish or brid or beest or man.   1865
      Now wol I speke of woful Damian,

Who does his work both well and hastily;
This will be done at leisure, perfectly.
It doesn't matter how long we might play;
In true wedlock we coupled are today.
Blessed be the yoke we find ourselves within,   625
For in our actions we can do no sin.
A married man cannot sin with his wife,
Nor can he hurt himself on his own knife,   1840
For by the law, we're given leave to play."
Thus labors he till dawn arrives next day;   630
He takes a sop of claret[28] from a cup,
And then there in his bed he sits right up,
And after that he sang out loud and clear,
And kissed his wife, and made a wanton leer.
He was all coltish, full of lechery,   635
And like a spotted magpie chattered he.
About his neck, the slack skin shifts and shakes
As he sings and croaks, so loud a sound he makes.   1850
But God knows what May thought then in her heart,
When, there in just his shirt, she saw him start   640
Up in his nightcap, and with his neck lean;
She didn't praise his playing worth a bean.
Then he said thus, "My rest here I will take;
Now day has come, I cannot stay awake."
And down he laid his head and slept till nine,   645
And after, when he saw the time was fine,
Up rises January. But fresh May
Kept to her chamber until the fourth day,   1860
As custom is for wives, as is the best.
For every labor sometimes must have rest,   650
Or else for long, the labor can't endure;
This is true for every living creature,
Should it be fish or bird or beast or man.
    Now I will speak of woeful Damian,

---

28 **sop of claret:** Bread soaked in wine, not uncommon as a medieval breakfast.

That languissheth for love, as ye shul here.
Therfore I speke to him in this manere:
I seye, "O sely Damian, allas!
Answere to my demaunde, as in this cas.   1870
How shaltow to thy lady, fresshe May,
Telle thy wo? She wole alwey seye 'nay.'
Eek if thou speke, she wol thy wo biwreye.
God be thyn help—I can no bettre seye."
      This syke Damian in Venus fyr   1875
So brenneth that he dyeth for desyr,
For which he putte his lyf in aventure.
No lenger mighte he in this wyse endure,
But prively a penner gan he borwe,
And in a lettre wroot he al his sorwe,   1880
In manere of a compleynt or a lay,
Unto his faire, fresshe lady May.
And in a purs of silk, heng on his sherte,
He hath it put and leyde it at his herte.
The mone that at noon was thilke day   1885
That Januarie hath wedded fresshe May
In two of Taur, was into Cancre gliden.
So longe hath Maius in hir chambre biden,
As custume is unto thise nobles alle.
A bryde shal nat eten in the halle   1890
Til dayes foure, or three dayes atte leste,
Y-passed been; than lat hir go to feste.
The fourthe day compleet fro noon to noon,
Whan that the heighe masse was y-doon,
In halle sit this Januarie and May,   1895
As fresh as is the brighte someres day.
And so bifel how that this gode man
Remembred him upon this Damian
And seyde, "Seinte Marie! How may this be

Who languishes, you'll hear, for love of her;   655
Therefore, I speak to him in this manner:
I say, "Alas, oh silly Damian!
Now answer here my question, if you can.   1870
How shall you, to your lady, the fresh May,
Tell of your woe? She will say no all day.   660
And if you speak, she will your woe betray.
God be your help! No better can I say."
          This Damian, sick in Venus's fire,
Burns so much that he's dying from desire;
Thus he risks his life in this adventure—   665
No longer can he in this way endure.
Privately a pen case he did borrow,
And wrote in a letter all his sorrow,   1880
Using the style of a complaint or lay,²⁹
Addressed to his fair lady, his fresh May;   670
In a purse of silk that hung from his shirt's part
He placed it, and he laid it by his heart.
In the second degree of Taurus was the moon
On January's wedding day at noon;
Now that same moon had into Cancer strayed,   675
So long within her chamber had May stayed,
As was the custom of the nobles all.
A bride shall not take meals within the hall   1890
Till four days later, or three days at least
Have passed; then let her join in with the feast.   680
The fourth day was complete from sun to sun,
And when the high mass then was also done,
January sits in the hall with May,
As fresh as is the sunny summer's day.
And so it happened now that this good man   685
Quite suddenly remembered Damian,
And said, "Saint Mary! Now, how can this be,

---

29 **complaint or lay:** Two forms of short, courtly love poems; the first is a lament, and the second is a short courtly narrative like *The Franklin's Tale*.

That Damian entendeth nat to me?   1900
Is he ay syk, or how may this bityde?"
His squyeres whiche that stoden ther bisyde
Excused him bycause of his siknesse,
Which letted him to doon his bisinesse.
Noon other cause mighte make him tarie.   1905
      "That me forthinketh," quod this Januarie,
"He is a gentil squyer, by my trouthe!
If that he deyde, it were harm and routhe.
He is as wys, discreet, and as secree
As any man I woot of his degree,   1910
And therto manly and eek servisable,
And for to been a thrifty man right able.
But after mete, as sone as ever I may,
I wol myself visyte him, and eek May,
To doon him al the confort that I can."   1915
And for that word him blessed every man,
That of his bountee and his gentillesse
He wolde so conforten in siknesse
His squyer, for it was a gentil dede.
"Dame," quod this Januarie, "tak good hede,   1920
At after-mete ye with your wommen alle,
Whan ye han been in chambre out of this halle,
That alle ye go see this Damian.
Doth him disport—he is a gentil man—
And telleth him that I wol him visyte,   1925
Have I no thing but rested me a lyte;
And spede yow faste, for I wole abyde
Til that ye slepe faste by my syde."
And with that word he gan to him to calle
A squyer that was marchal of his halle,   1930
And tolde him certeyn thinges what he wolde.
      This fresshe May hath streight hir wey y-holde,
With alle hir wommen, unto Damian.
Doun by his beddes syde sit she than,
Confortinge him as goodly as she may.   1935

That Damian's not here to wait on me? 1900
How may this happen? Is he always sick?"
His squires who were standing there were quick 690
To excuse him then because of sickness,
Which kept him from attending to his business;
There was no other reason he would tarry.
      "I'm sorry for him," said this January,
"For on my word, a gentle squire is he! 695
If he died, it'd be a shame and pity.
For he is as wise, discreet, and private
As any man of his rank that I've met, 1910
And what's more, he's manly and attentive,
A man, in short, who can be quite effective. 700
After the meal, just as soon as I may,
I'll visit him myself, just as will May,
To give him all the comfort that I can."
For those words, then, blessed him every man
That, with his gentility and goodness 705
He would offer such comfort in sickness
Thus to his squire; it was a gentle deed.
"My dame," said January, "take good heed, 1920
That after dinner, with your women all,
When you go to your chamber from this hall, 710
All of you should go visit Damian.
Amuse him well—he is a gentle man.
Tell him that I will pay him a visit,
Once I have had time to rest up a bit;
And hurry fast, for my time I will bide 715
Till you are sleeping fast right by my side."
And with those words, then, he began to call
A squire who was marshal of the hall, 1930
And what he wished now, certain things he told.
      This fair, fresh May then straight her way did hold 720
With all her women right to Damian.
Down by his bedside did she sit right then,
Comforting him as nicely as she may.

This Damian, whan that his tyme he say,
In secree wise his purs and eek his bille,
In which that he y-writen hadde his wille,
Hath put into hir hand, withouten more,
Save that he syketh wonder depe and sore,   1940
And softely to hir right thus seyde he:
"Mercy—and that ye nat discovere me!
For I am deed if that this thing be kid."
This purs hath she inwith hir bosom hid,
And wente hir wey; ye gete namore of me.   1945
But unto Januarie y-comen is she,
That on his beddes syde sit ful softe.
He taketh hir and kisseth hir ful ofte
And leyde him doun to slepe, and that anon.
She feyned hir as that she moste gon   1950
There as ye woot that every wight mot nede.
And whan she of this bille hath taken hede,
She rente it al to cloutes atte laste,
And in the privee softely it caste.
        Who studieth now but faire fresshe May?   1955
Adoun by olde Januarie she lay,
That sleep til that the coughe hath him awaked.
Anon he preyde hir strepen hir al naked.
He wolde of hir, he seyde, han som plesaunce,
And seyde hir clothes dide him encombraunce,   1960
And she obeyeth, be hir lief or looth.
But lest that precious folk be with me wrooth,
How that he wroghte I dar nat to yow telle,
Or whether hir thoughte it paradys or helle;
But here I lete hem werken in hir wyse   1965
Til evensong rong and that they moste aryse.
        Were it by destinee or aventure,
Were it by influence or by nature
Or constellacion, that in swich estat
The hevene stood that tyme fortunat   1970
Was for to putte a bille of Venus werkes

Damian, when the right time came his way,

Both his purse and his letter secretly, 725

In which all his desire penned had he,

He put into her hand with no words more,

Save that he heaved a sigh so deep and sore, 1940

And softly to her right thus then said he:

"Have mercy! Pray, do not discover me, 730

For I'd be dead if such a thing you did."

This purse has she down in her bosom hid

And gone her way; you'll get no more from me.

But then to January come is she,

Who on his bedside quietly sits then. 735

He takes her and kisses her so often,

And lays right down to sleep without delay.

And she feigned then that she must make her way 1950

To that place which, as you know, we all need;

And when she of this letter did take heed, 740

She tore it all in tiny bits at last,

And in the privy, quietly it cast.

     Who's ruminating now but this fresh May?

Down by old January she did lay,

Who slept until his cough awoke him there. 745

He prayed her that she strip herself all bare;

He'd have with her, he said, some dalliance,

And said her clothes were for him an encumbrance; 1960

Whether she likes it or not, she does obey.

Lest finicky folk be irked at what I say, 750

How he performed, I do not dare to tell—

Whether she thought it paradise or hell.

But here I let them work as they deem wise

Till vespers rang, and then up they must rise.

     Were it by destiny, were it by chance, 755

By nature or the planets' influence,

Or constellations in locations thus

In the heavens so it was propitious 1970

To make petition for Venus's works—

(For alle thing hath tyme, as seyn thise clerkes)
To any womman, for to gete hir love,
I can nat seye—but grete God above,
That knoweth that non act is causelees,   1975
He deme of al, for I wol holde my pees.
But sooth is this: how that this fresshe May
Hath take swich impression that day
For pitee of this syke Damian
That from hir herte she ne dryve can   1980
The remembraunce for to doon him ese.
"Certeyn," thoghte she, "whom that this thing displese
I rekke noght, for here I him assure
To love him best of any creature,
Though he namore hadde than his sherte."   1985
Lo, pitee renneth sone in gentil herte.
       Heer may ye se how excellent franchyse
In wommen is whan they hem narwe avyse.
Som tyrant is, as ther be many oon
That hath an herte as hard as any stoon,   1990
Which wolde han lete him sterven in the place
Wel rather than han graunted him hir grace;
And hem reioysen in hir cruel pryde,
And rekke nat to been an homicyde.
       This gentil May, fulfilled of pitee,   1995
Right of hir hande a lettre made she,
In which she graunteth him hir verray grace.
Ther lakketh noght but only day and place
Wher that she mighte unto his lust suffyse,
For it shal be right as he wol devyse.   2000
And whan she saugh hir time upon a day,
To visite this Damian goth May,
And sotilly this lettre doun she threste
Under his pilwe—rede it if him leste.
She taketh him by the hand and harde him twiste   2005
So secrely that no wight of it wiste,
And bad him been al hool, and forth she wente

For all things have their time, as say these clerks—   760
To any woman thus to get some love,
I cannot say, but dearest God above,
Who knows no act without cause can unfold,
Let him be judge; I wish my peace to hold.
The truth amounts to this: how this fresh May   765
Such an impression has taken that day
Of pity for this poor, sick Damian
That from her heart, she cannot drive the plan   1980
Nor the idea that she must give him ease.
"Surely," she thought, "whom now this might displease,   770
I do not care, for here him I'll assure
Now to love him best of any creature,
Though he only a shirt had for his part."
Lo, pity soon runs in the gentle heart!
       Here you may see what generosity   775
Women have when they ponder carefully.
Tyrants there are, and not just one alone,
Who have hearts that are hard as any stone,   1990
And would have let him perish in that place
Instead of granting him some of their grace,   780
And then rejoiced in showing their cruel pride,
Not caring if they practice homicide.
       This gentle May, so filled full with pity,
By her own hand, a letter then wrote she,
In which she granted him her very grace.   785
Nothing lacked now except the day and place
Where she might do what will ease his desire,
For it will be just as he does require.   2000
And when she sees the chance, a certain day,
To visit Damian now goes this May,   790
And subtly, then, her letter down she thrust
Beneath his pillow; read it if he must.
She takes him by the hand and hard did twist
So secretly the act might well be missed,
And told him to get well, and forth she went   795

To Januarie, whan that he for hir sente.

      Up ryseth Damian the nexte morwe.

Al passed was his siknesse and his sorwe.   2010

He kembeth him, he proyneth him and pyketh,

He dooth al that his lady lust and lyketh,

And eek to Januarie he gooth as lowe

As ever dide a dogge for the bowe.

He is so plesant unto every man   2015

(For craft is al, whoso that do it can)

That every wight is fayn to speke him good,

And fully in his lady grace he stood.

Thus lete I Damian aboute his nede,

And in my tale forth I wol procede.   2020

      Somme clerkes holden that felicitee

Stant in delyt, and therefor certeyn he,

This noble Januarie, with al his might,

In honest wyse, as longeth to a knight,

Shoop him to live ful deliciously.   2025

His housinge, his array, as honestly

To his degree was maked as a kinges.

Amonges othere of his honest thinges

He made a gardin, walled al with stoon.

So fair a gardin woot I nowher noon.   2030

For out of doute, I verraily suppose

That he that wroot the Romance of the Rose

Ne coude of it the beautee wel devyse;

Ne Priapus ne mighte nat suffyse,

Though he be god of gardins, for to telle   2035

To January, when he for her sent.

    Up gets Damian on the next morning;

All passed was his sickness and his sorrowing.   2010

He combs himself, he preens, and he does primp;

On what his lady fancies he won't skimp,   800

And then to January goes as low

As do dogs trained for hunting with a bow.

He's so pleasant to every single man—

For craft is all; whoever does it, can—

That of him everyone speaks only good,   805

And fully in his lady's grace he stood.

Thus leave I Damian to tend his need,

And further in my tale I will proceed.   2020

    Some clerks believe that true felicity

Lies in earthly pleasure,[30] and therefore he,   810

This noble January, with all his might,

Honorably, as it behooves a knight,

Shaped it so that he'd live deliciously.

His household and array as honorably

Were made to suit his rank as is a king's.   815

Among his other honorable things,

He made a garden, walled around with stone;

So fair a garden nowhere have I known.   2030

Without a doubt, I verily suppose

That he who wrote *The Romance of the Rose*[31]   820

Could not well describe the beauty of it;

And Priapus[32] would lack sufficient wit,

Though he is god of gardens, now to tell

---

30 **...clerks...earthly pleasure**: A reference here to the philosophies of Epicurus, the Greek philosopher (fourth to third century B.C.E.), who advocated living the good life as the route to happiness. His positions became associated with hedonism by the Middle Ages.

31 *The Romance of the Rose*: Thirteenth-century French allegorical romance begun by Guillaume de Lorris and finished, in a distinctly more satirical vein, by Jean de Meun. It is one of the most widely read and influential secular literary works of the high Middle Ages, and an important source for Chaucer's writing. The Chaucer canon includes an incomplete translation of *The Romance of the Rose*, although it is acknowledged that it is not entirely the work of Chaucer.

32 **Priapus**: Roman fertility god often represented with a large erection.

The beautee of the gardin and the welle
That stood under a laurer alwey grene.
Ful ofte tyme he Pluto and his quene
Proserpina and al hir fayerye
Disporten hem and maken melodye   2040
Aboute that welle, and daunced, as men tolde.
     This noble knight, this Januarie the olde,
Swich deintee hath in it to walke and pleye
That he wol no wight suffren bere the keye
Save he himself—for of the smale wiket   2045
He bar alwey of silver a smal cliket,
With which, whan that him leste, he it unshette.
And whan he wolde paye his wyf hir dette
In somer seson, thider wolde he go,
And May his wyf, and no wight but they two.   2050
And thinges whiche that were nat doon abedde
He in the gardin parfourned hem and spedde.
And in this wyse many a mery day
Lived this Januarie and fresshe May.
But worldly joye may nat alwey dure   2055
To Januarie, ne to no creature.
     O sodeyn hap! O thou Fortune unstable,
Lyk to the scorpion so deceivable,
That flaterest with thyn heed when thou wolt stinge;
Thy tayl is deeth thurgh thyn enveniminge.   2060
O brotil joye! O swete venim queynte!
O monstre, that so subtilly canst peynte
Thy yiftes under hewe of stedfastnesse,
That thou deceyvest bothe more and lesse!
Why hastow Januarie thus deceyved,   2065
That haddest him for thy ful frend receyved?
And now thou hast biraft him bothe hise yën,
For sorwe of which desyreth he to dyen.

The beauty of the garden and the well
That stood under a laurel, always green. 825
And often the god Pluto and his queen,
Proserpina,³³and their fairy company,
Amused themselves, and they made melody 2040
About the well, and they danced, as men told.

      This noble knight, this January old, 830
To walk and play there such pleasure takes he,
That he will let no person bear the key
But himself. To the small gate, the wicket,
He bore the silver latchkey made to fit it,
Which, when he liked, he in the gate would set. 835
When he wished to pay his wife her marriage debt
In the summer to the garden he would go,
And May his wife, and no one else would know; 2050
And those things that could not be done in bed
He performed, and he succeeded there instead. 840
In this manner, many a merry day,
This January lived with his fresh May.
But earthly joy may not always endure
For January or for any creature.

      Oh, sudden chance! Oh, Fortune unstable, 845
Like the scorpion, to deceive so able,
Who flatters with your head when you would sting!
Your tail is death through all your poisoning. 2060
Oh, brittle joy! Oh, sweet venom quaint,
Oh, monster that so subtly can paint 850
Your gifts beneath the hue of constancy,
So that both great and small deceived will be,
Why have you January thus deceived,
When him as full-fledged friend you had received?
Of both his eyes you've left him now bereft; 855
He wants to die of sorrow from your theft.

---

33 ...Pluto...and Proserpina: The Roman god who is king of Hades, the underworld, and his
queen. See below, footnote 40 at line 1017.

Allas! this noble Januarie free,
Amidde his lust and his prosperitee   2070
Is woxen blind, and that al sodeynly.
He wepeth and he wayleth pitously,
And therwithal the fyr of jalousye—
Lest that his wyf sholde falle in som folye—
So brente his herte that he wolde fayn   2075
That som man bothe him and hir had slayn.
For neither after his deeth nor in his lyf
Ne wolde he that she were love ne wyf,
But ever live as widwe in clothes blake,
Soul as the turtle that lost hath hir make.   2080
But atte laste, after a monthe or tweye
His sorwe gan aswage, sooth to seye;
For whan he wiste it may noon other be,
He paciently took his adversitee,
Save, out of doute, he may nat forgoon   2085
That he nas jalous evermore in oon.
Which jalousye it was so outrageous
That neither in halle n'in noon other hous,
Ne in noon other place, neverthemo
He nolde suffre hir for to ryde or go   2090
But if that he had hand on hir alway.
For which ful ofte wepeth fresshe May,
That loveth Damian so benignely
That she mot outher dyen sodeynly
Or elles she mot han him as hir leste.   2095
She wayteth whan hir herte wolde breste.
      Upon that other syde Damian
Bicomen is the sorwefulleste man
That ever was, for neither night ne day
Ne mighte he speke a word to fresshe May   2100
As to his purpos, of no swich matere,
But if that Januarie moste it here,
That hadde an hand upon hir evermo.
But nathelees, by wryting to and fro

Oh, this noble, generous January,

Amidst his solace and prosperity,   2070

Finds that he has become blind suddenly.

He weeps out loud and wails piteously;   860

And thereupon, the fire of jealousy—

Lest his wife should fall into some folly—

So burned his heart that he'd gladly prefer

That some man would now slay both him and her.

Neither after his death nor in his life   865

Would he have her be another's love or wife,

But in black clothes always, in widowed state,

Lone as the turtledove who's lost her mate.   2080

But then at last, after a month or two,

His sorrow lessened, to say what is true.   870

For when he knew that this way it must be,

He patiently bore his adversity,

Except that, doubtless, he may never cease

To have his jealousy always increase.

Which jealousy was so extreme in all   875

That in another house or other hall,

Or any other spots around beside

He would not suffer her to walk or ride   2090

Unless he had a hand on her all day;

And often therefore weeps now his fresh May   880

Who loved Damian so graciously

That either she must now die suddenly

Or else she must have him when she likes best.

She waits for her heart to burst within her breast.

      Upon the other side now, Damian   885

Has become the most sorrowful of men

Who ever lived, for neither night nor day

He might not speak a word to his fresh May,   2100

In any way to make his purpose clear,

Since January would surely overhear —   890

His hand's on her wherever she might go.

But nonetheless, by writing to and fro,

And privee signes, wiste he what she mente,   2105
And she knew eek the fyn of his entente.
     O Januarie, what mighte it thee availle
Thou mightest see as fer as shippes saille?
For as good is blind deceyved be
As to be deceyved whan a man may se.   2110
Lo Argus, which that hadde an hondred yën,
For al that ever he coude poure or pryen,
Yet was he blent, and God wot so ben mo
That wenen wisly that it be nat so.
Passe over is an ese; I sey namore.   2115
     This fresshe May, that I spak of so yore,
In warme wex hath emprented the cliket
That Januarie bar of the smale wiket
By which into his gardin ofte he wente.
And Damian, that knew al hir entente,   2120
The cliket countrefeted prively.
Ther nis namore to seye, but hastily
Som wonder by this cliket shal bityde,
Which ye shul heren if ye wole abyde.
     O noble Ovyde, ful sooth seystou, God woot!   2125
What sleighte is it, thogh it be long and hoot,
That he nil finde it out in som manere?
By Piramus and Tesbee may men lere:
Thogh they were kept ful longe streite overal,
They been accorded, rouninge thurgh a wal,   2130
Ther no wight coude han founde out swich a sleighte.
     But now to purpos: er that dayes eighte
Were passed er the monthe of Juil, bifil
That Januarie hath caught so greet a wil—
Thurgh egging of his wyf—him for to pleye   2135

And private signs, he did know what she meant,
And she knew, too, the end of his intent.

    Oh, January, what might it avail,   895
Though you could see as far as ships can sail?
For it's as good blind and deceived to be,
As then to be deceived when one can see.   2110
Lo, Argus,[34] he who had a hundred eyes,
For all that in his time he pokes and pries,   900
He's blinded, as were others, God does know,
Who always think that it could not be so.
Not knowing can bring ease; no more I'll say.

    She of whom I have spoken, this fresh May
Imprinted in warm wax the key that fit,   905
Which January bore, for the small wicket,[35]
Through which often he to his garden went;
And Damian, who knew all her intent,   2120
The key he counterfeited privately.
There is no more to say, but presently   910
Some marvel through this little key will happen,
Which, if you wait a bit, you will hear then.

    O, Ovid, you speak truth, as God does know:
Though long and hot it is, what trick might go
That Love will not discover in some way?   915
Learn from Pyramus and Thisbe,[36] let me say;
Though they were watched quite strictly overall,
They made their pact with whispers through a wall,   2130
Where none could have found out a trick so great.

    But to the purpose now: before days eight   920
Could fully in the month of June expire,
January has caught such a desire,
Through his wife's egging on, to go and play

---

34 **Argus**: Argus was a mythological character who had one hundred eyes, the better to guard Zeus's lover, Io. Mercury had to put all the eyes to sleep before he could kill this monster.

35 **wicket**: A garden gate.

36 **Pyramus and Thisbe**: Ovid in *The Metamorphosis* writes the story of the two lovers who were kept separated and who talked to each other through a crack in a wall between their properties.

In his gardin, and no wight but they tweye,
That in a morwe unto this May seith he:
"Rys up, my wyf, my love, my lady free!
The turtles vois is herd, my douve swete.
The winter is goon, with alle his reynes wete.   2140
Com forth now, with thyn eyen columbyn.
How fairer been thy brestes than is wyn.
The gardin is enclosed al aboute;
Com forth, my whyte spouse. Out of doute
Thou hast me wounded in myn herte, o wyf.   2145
No spot of thee ne knew I al my lyf.
Com forth, and lat us taken our disport.
I chees thee for my wyf and my confort."
    Swiche olde lewed wordes used he.
On Damian a signe made she   2150
That he sholde go biforen with his cliket.
This Damian thanne hath opened the wiket
And in he stirte, and that in swich manere
That no wight mighte it see neither y-here,
And stille he sit under a bush anoon.   2155
    This Januarie, as blind as is a stoon,
With Maius in his hand and no wight mo,
Into his fresshe gardin is ago
And clapte to the wiket sodeynly.
    "Now, wyf," quod he, "heer nis but thou and I,   2160
That art the creature that I best love.
For, by that Lord that sit in heven above,
Lever ich hadde dyen on a knyf
Than thee offende, trewe dere wyf !
For Goddes sake, thenk how I thee chees: 2165
Noght for no coveityse, doutelees,
But only for the love I had to thee.

In his garden, the two of them, some day,
That on one morning to his May says he: 925
"Rise, my wife,[37] my love, my noble lady!
The turtledove's voice is heard, my sweet dove;
The winter's gone with wet rains from above.   2140
Come forth here now! How dovelike your eyes shine!
How fairer are your breasts than any wine!   930
The garden is enclosed all round about;
Come forth, my white[38] spouse! For, without a doubt,
You've wounded me right in my heart, oh wife.
No spot[39] in you knew I in all my life.
Come forth, and here let us ourselves disport;   935
I chose you for my wife and for my comfort."

      Such ignorant and rude old words used he.
To Damian right then a sign made she   2150
So he'd go first and bring his key that fit.
Damian then opens up the wicket   940
And there, in such a manner in starts he
That no man could the movement hear or see,
And he sits still, beneath a bush, alone.

      This January, blind as is a stone,
With May in hand, and with no others so,   945
Right into his fresh garden now did go,
And he clapped shut the wicket suddenly.

      "Now wife, here is just you and I," said he.   2160
"You are the creature whom the best I love.
For by the Lord who sits on high above   950
I would much rather die upon a knife
Than offend you, my true and dearest wife.
For God's sake, think, since it is all doubtless,
How I chose you not for covetousness,
But only for the love of you in me.   955

---

37 **Rise, my wife**: January's speech that begins here is filled with allusions to the Song of Songs.
38 **white**: In the sense of radiantly beautiful and fair.
39 **spot**: Flaw, imperfection.

And though that I be old and may nat see,
Beth to me trewe, and I shal telle yow why.
Three thinges, certes, shul ye winne therby: 2170
First, love of Crist, and to yourself honour,
And al myn heritage, toun and tour,
I yeve it yow, maketh chartres as yow leste.
This shal be doon tomorwe er sonne reste,
So wisly God my soule bringe in blisse.   2175
I prey yow first in covenant ye me kisse,
And thogh that I be jalous, wyte me noght.
Ye been so depe enprented in my thoght
That whan that I considere your beautee
And therwithal the unlykly elde of me,   2180
I may nat, certes, thogh I sholde dye,
Forbere to been out of your companye
For verray love—this is withouten doute.
Now kis me, wyf, and lat us rome aboute."
      This fresshe May, whan she thise wordes herde,   2185
Benignely to Januarie answerde,
But first and forward she bigan to wepe.
"I have," quod she, "a soule for to kepe
As wel as ye, and also myn honour,
And of my wyfhod thilke tendre flour   2190
Which that I have assured in your hond
Whan that the preest to yow my body bond.
Wherfore I wole answere in this manere
By the leve of yow, my lord so dere:
I prey to God that never dawe the day   2195
That I ne sterve as foule as womman may,
If ever I do unto my kin that shame,
Or elles I empeyre so my name
That I be fals. And if I do that lakke,
Do strepe me and put me in a sakke   2200
And in the nexte river do me drenche.
I am a gentil womman and no wenche.
Why speke ye thus? But men ben ever untrewe,

And although I am old and may not see,
Be true to me, and I will tell you why:
Three things, for certain, you will win thereby.   2170
First, the love of Christ, and your own honor,
And all my estate, both town and tower —   960
I give to you; make deeds as you think best
Before tomorrow's sun can find its rest,
So that God wisely brings my soul to bliss.
First, pray, seal the covenant with a kiss;
Do not blame me although I am jealous.   965
You're so deeply printed in my thoughts thus
That when I consider all your beauty
And the unsuitable old age of me,   2180
I may not, though it'd be the death of me,
Endure not being in your company   970
For true love's sake. This is without doubt.
Now kiss me, wife, and let us roam about."
        This fresh May, when these words of his she'd heard,
Graciously to January answered,
But first and foremost, she began to weep.   975
"I have," said she, "a soul to guard and keep
As well as you; also, there's my honor,
And of my womanhood, that tender flower   2190
Which I placed in your hand, as you have found,
That day the priest to you my body bound.   980
Therefore, I'll answer in this manner here,
By your leave now, my lord who is so dear:
I pray to God that never dawns the day
When I'd die foully as a woman may,
If ever I do to my kin that shame,   985
Or else if I should so impair my name,
By being false; if truthfulness I lack,
Then strip me here and put me in a sack,   2200
And in the river make me drowned and drenched.
I am a gentle woman and no wench.   990
Why speak you thus? Men are ever untrue,

And wommen have repreve of yow ay newe.
Ye han non other contenance, I leve,   2205
But speke to us of untrust and repreve."
          And with that word she saugh wher Damian
Sat in the bush, and coughen she bigan,
And with hir finger signes made she
That Damian sholde climbe upon a tree   2210
That charged was with fruit; and up he wente,
For verraily he knew al hir entente
And every signe that she coude mak
Wel bet than Januarie, hir owene make.
For in a lettre she had told him al   2215
Of this matere, how he werchen shal.
And thus I lete him sitte upon the pyrie,
And Januarie and May rominge myrie.
          Bright was the day, and blew the firmament.
Phebus hath of gold his stremes doun y-sent   2220
To gladen every flour with his warmnesse.
He was that tyme *in Geminis*, as I gesse,
But litel fro his declinacioun
Of Cancer, Jovis exaltacioun.
And so bifel that brighte morwe-tyde   2225
That in that gardin, in the ferther syde,
Pluto, that is the king of Fayerye,
And many a lady in his companye
Folwinge his wyf, the quene Proserpyna,
Which that he ravysshed out of Ethna   2230
Whil that she gadered floures in the mede.
(In Claudian ye may the story rede,
How in his grisly carte he hir fette.)

And women always reproach you anew.
You have no other recourse, if you must,
Except to speak of reproof and mistrust."
          And with that word, she saw where Damian   995
Sat in the bush, and to cough she began,
And with her finger then some signs made she
That Damian should climb up in a tree   2210
That heavy was with fruit, and up he went.
For truly now, he knew all her intent,   1000
And every private sign she could create,
Better than January, her own mate,
For she'd told him all within a letter
How he should go work it in this matter.
Thus I leave him sitting in a pear tree,   1005
And January and May roam merrily.
          Bright was the day, and blue the firmament.
And Phoebus has his streams of gold down sent,   2220
Bringing to each flower warmth and gladness.
Right then, he was in Gemini, I guess,   1010
A small distance from the declination
Of Cancer, where Jove has his exaltation.
That bright morning time, it did so happen
That further on in January's garden,
Pluto, who is the king of Fairy,   1015
And many ladies in his company,
Following his wife, Queen Proserpina—[40]
He had ravished her down from Mount Etna   2230
While she gathered flowers in the meadow;
In Claudian,[41] the tales you may follow,   1020
How in his grisly cart he had her fetched—

    40 **Queen Proserpina**, etc.: The following lines give a thumbnail sketch of the rape or abduction
of Proserpina by Pluto, who took her to the underworld to be his wife. Her mother, Ceres, goddess
of agriculture, was so heartbroken that she brought permanent winter to the earth until Pluto was
made to return Proserpina to her mother for half of each year, which became the seasons of spring and
summer.
    41 **Claudian**: Fourth-century Roman author of *The Rape of Proserpina*.

This king of Fairye thanne adoun him sette
Upon a bench of turves fresh and grene,   2235
And right anon thus seyde he to his quene:
  "My wyf," quod he, "ther may no wight sey nay.
Th'experience so preveth every day
The tresons whiche that wommen doon to man.
Ten hondred thousand stories telle I can   2240
Notable of your untrouthe and brotilnesse.
O Salomon, wys, richest of richesse,
Fulfild of sapience and of worldly glorie,
Ful worthy been thy wordes to memorie
To every wight that wit and reson can.   2245
Thus preiseth he yet the bountee of man:
'Amonges a thousand men yet fond I oon,
But of wommen alle fond I noon.'
  Thus seith the king that knoweth your wikkednesse.
And Jesus *filius Syrak*, as I gesse,   2250
Ne speketh of yow but selde reverence.
A wilde fyr and corrupt pestilence
So falle upon your bodies yet tonight!
Ne see ye nat this honurable knight?
Bycause, allas, that he is blind and old,   2255
His owene man shal make him cokewold.
Lo, heer he sit, the lechour, in the tree.
Now wol I graunten, of my magestee,
Unto this olde, blinde, worthy knight
That he shal have ayeyn his eyen sight,   2260
Whan that his wyf wold doon him vileinye.
Than shal he knowen al his harlotrye
Both in repreve of hir and othere mo."
  "Ye shal?" quod Proserpyne. "Wol ye so?

This king of Fairy then himself down stretched
On a bench made of turf, all fresh and green,
And right away, he said thus to his queen,
          "My wife," said he, "no man could well gainsay—   1025
For experience so proves it every day—
The treasons women perpetrate on man.
Ten hundred thousand stories tell I can   2240
That note your treachery and brittleness.
O Solomon, wise and richest in his richness,   1030
Filled with wisdom and with earthly glory,
Your words are worthy to hold in memory
By each man of wit and reason, if he can.
Thus does he praise the goodness found in man:
'Among a thousand men, yet I found one,   1035
But among all the women, I've found none.'
          Thus says the king who knows your wickedness.
Jesus, *filius Syrak*,[42] as I guess,   2250
But seldom speaks of you with reverence.
Fiery rashes and corrupting pestilence—   1040
May they fall on your bodies yet tonight!
Nor do you see this honorable knight,
Who, since, alas, he is both blind and old,
His own man will now make him a cuckold.
Look where he sits, the lecher, in a tree!   1045
Now I will grant, through my high majesty,
Here to this old and blind and worthy knight
That he once again will have his eyesight   2260
When his wife will treat him treacherously.
Then all her wickedness he'll clearly see,   1050
To reprove her and other women, too."
          "Yes?" said Proserpina, "This you will do?

---

42 **Jesus,** *filius Syrak*: Jesus, son of Sirach, the alleged author of the apocryphal biblical book of
Ecclesiasticus (not to be confused with Ecclesiastes).

Now, by my modres sires soule, I swere   2265
That I shal yeven hir suffisant answere—
And alle wommen after, for hir sake—
That though they be in any gilt y-take,
With face bold they shulle hemself excuse,
And bere hem doun that wolden hem accuse.   2270
For lakke of answer noon of hem shal dyen.
Al hadde man seyn a thing with bothe his yën,
Yit shul we wommen visage it hardily
And wepe and swere and chyde subtilly,
So that ye men shul been as lewed as gees.   2275
          What rekketh me of your auctoritees?
I woot wel that this Jew, this Salomon,
Fond of us wommen foles many oon.
But though that he ne fond no good womman,
Yet hath ther founde many another man   2280
Wommen ful trewe, ful gode and vertuous.
Witnesse on hem that dwelle in Cristes hous:
With martirdom they preved hir constance.
The Romayn gestes eek maken remembrance
Of many a verray, trewe wyf also.   2285
But sire—ne be nat wrooth—al be it so
Though that he seyde he fond no good womman,
I prey yow take the sentence of the man.
He mente thus: that in sovereyn bontee
Nis noon but God, but neither he ne she.   2290
          Ey! For verray God that nis but oon,
What make ye so muche of Salomon?
What though he made a temple, Goddes hous?
What though he were riche and glorious?
So made he eek a temple of false goddis.   2295
How mighte he do a thing that more forbode is?
Pardee, as faire as ye his name emplastre,

Now by my mother's sire's soul[43] I swear,
I will give her sufficient answer there,
And for her sake, to women all around,   1055
So that if in some guilty deed they're found,
With bold expressions, they'll themselves excuse,
So that no one can ever them accuse.   2270
For lack of answer, not a woman dies.
Though a man saw something with both eyes,   1060
Yet we women shall face him down boldly,
And weep and swear and scold him cleverly;
You men shall stay as ignorant as geese.
      What do I care for your authorities?
I know well that this Jew, this Solomon,   1065
Found fools among us women, many a one.
But though he could not find one good woman,
Yet certainly, many another man   2280
Found women true and good and virtuous.
Witness the ones who dwell in Christ's house, thus;   1070
With martyrdom, they proved their constancy.
Roman history reminds you and me
Of many true and faithful wives also.
Sir, don't be angry, though it may be so
That he said he found not one good woman;   1075
I pray—find the true meaning of this man.
He meant: in sovereign goodness, as you see,
There's only God, but neither he nor she.   2290
      Ah! By the true God who's triune in one,
Why do you make so much of Solomon?   1080
What if he built a temple, God's house, thus?
What if he were both rich and glorious?
He made a temple, too, to false gods, then;
How could he do something more forbidden?
No matter how his name you patch and plaster,   1085

---

43 **mother's sire's soul**: Saturn, father of Jupiter, Neptune, and Pluto, and thus the patriarch of the gods. See *The Knight's Tale* for examples of his influence and power.

He was a lechour and an ydolastre,
And in his elde he verray God forsook.
And if that God ne hadde, as seith the book,   2300
Y-spared him for his fadres sake, he sholde
Have lost his regne rather than he wolde.
I sette right noght, of al the vileinye
That ye of wommen wryte, a boterflye.
I am a womman—nedes moot I speke   2305
Or elles swelle til myn herte breke.
For sithen he seyde that we ben jangleresses,
As ever hool I mote brouke my tresses,
I shal nat spare, for no curteisye,
To speke him harm that wolde us vileinye."   2310
        "Dame," quod this Pluto, "be no lenger wrooth.
I yeve it up. But sith I swoor myn ooth
That I wolde graunten him his sighte ageyn,
My word shal stonde, I warne yow, certeyn.
I am a king; it sit me noght to lye."   2315
        "And I," quod she, "a queene of Fayerye.
Hir answere shal she have, I undertake.
Lat us namore wordes heerof make,
For sothe I wol no lenger yow contrarie."
        Now lat us turne agayn to Januarie,   2320
That in the gardin with his faire May
Singeth ful merier than the papejay,
"Yow love I best, and shal, and other noon."
So longe aboute the aleyes is he goon
Til he was come agaynes thilke pyrie   2325
Wher as this Damian sitteth ful myrie
An heigh among the fresshe leves grene.
        This fresshe May, that is so bright and shene,
Gan for to syke and seyde, "Allas, my syde!
Now sir," quod she, "for aught that may bityde,   2330

He was a lecher and idolator,
Who, in his old age, God himself forsook;
If God hadn't, as it says in the Book,   2300
Spared him there for his father's sake, he should
Have lost his reign much sooner than he would.   1090
I do not count all of the calumny
You write of women worth one butterfly.
I am a woman; to speak I have need,
Or else swell until my heart breaks indeed.
Since we're chatterers, so he professes—   1095
As ever, unharmed, I'll enjoy my tresses[44]—
I won't spare for the sake of courtesy
To badmouth him who wills our infamy."   2310
      "Dame," Pluto said, "now be angry no more.
I give it up! But since my oath I swore   1100
That I would grant to him his sight again,
My word shall stand, I warn you for certain.
I am a king; it suits me not to lie."
      "A queen of Fairy, too," said she, "am I.
She'll have her answer; this I undertake.   1105
And let us no more words about this make.
To you no more will I be contrary."
      Now let us turn again to January,   2320
Who in the garden there with his fair May
Sings more merrily than the popinjay,   1110
"I love you best for always, without doubt."
So long the garden paths he's walked about
Till he comes in front of that same pear tree
In which this Damian sits quite merrily,
On high among the leaves all fresh and green.   1115
      Fresh May, bright and beautiful to be seen,
Began to sigh, and said, "My side! Alas!
Sire," said she, "whatever comes to pass,   2330

---

44 **enjoy my tresses**: Idiomatic expression meaning to enjoy one's hair, whole and unharmed, or, roughly, to stay whole, undamaged, or alive.

I moste han of the peres that I see
Or I mot dye, so sore longeth me
To eten of the smale peres grene.
Help, for hir love that is of hevene quene!
I telle yow wel, a womman in my plyt   2335
May han to fruit so greet an appetyt
That she may dyen but she of it have."

      "Allas," quod he, "that I ne had heer a knave
That coude climbe! Allas, allas," quod he,
"That I am blind!" "Ye, sir, no fors," quod she,   2340
"But wolde ye vouchesauf, for Goddes sake,
The pyrie inwith your armes for to take
(For wel I woot that ye mistruste me),
Thanne sholde I climbe wel ynogh," quod she,
"So I my foot mighte sette upon your bak."   2345

      "Certes," quod he, "theron shal be no lak,
Mighte I yow helpen with myn herte blood."
He stoupeth doun, and on his bak she stood,
And caughte hir by a twiste, and up she gooth—
Ladies, I prey yow that ye be nat wrooth;   2350
I can nat glose; I am a rude man—
And sodeynly anon this Damian
Gan pullen up the smok, and in he throng.

      And whan that Pluto saugh this grete wrong,
To Januarie he gaf agayn his sighte   2355
And made him see as wel as ever he mighte.
And whan that he hadde caught his sighte agayn,
Ne was ther never man of thing so fayn.
But on his wyf his thoght was evermo;
Up to the tree he caste his eyen two   2360
And saugh that Damian his wyf had dressed
In swich manere it may nat ben expressed
But if I wolde speke uncurteisly.
And up he yaf a roring and a cry
As doth the moder whan the child shal dye.   2365
"Out! Help! Allas! Harrow!" he gan to crye.

I must have the pears that I see hanging,
Or I must die, so sore is my longing   1120
To eat some of those pears there, small and green.
Help—for her love, who is of heaven queen.
I tell you well: a woman in my plight
May have for fruit so great an appetite,
She'll die if she can't have what she does crave."   1125
      "Alas," said he, "here I'm without my knave
Who could climb up! Alas, alas," said he,
"That I am blind!" "No matter, sire," said she,   2340
"But would you now vouchsafe, for God's own sake,
The pear tree's trunk right in your arms to take—   1130
For well I know how much you mistrust me—
Then I should climb up well enough," said she,
"If I might set my foot upon your back."
      "Surely," said he, "in this will be no lack,
For with my heart's own blood, help you I would."   1135
Then he stoops down, and on his back she stood,
And caught herself a branch, and up she goes—
Ladies, now don't be angry. Heaven knows   2350
I can't gloss over this; I'm a rude man—
And suddenly at once this Damian   1140
Pulled up her smock right there, and in he thrust.
      And when Pluto saw this great breach of trust,
To January he gave again his sight,
And made him see just as well as he might.
And when his sight back once again he had,   1145
Never was man of anything so glad,
But on his wife his thoughts were settled fast.
So up into the tree, his eyes he cast   2360
And saw that Damian his wife addressed
In such a way it cannot be expressed   1150
Unless I would speak discourteously;
At once a roaring and a cry made he,
As does a mother when her child will die.
"Out! Help! Alas! Help!" he began to cry,

"O stronge lady store, what dostow?"
　　　　And she answerde, "Sir, what eyleth yow?
Have pacience and reson in your minde.
I have yow holpe on bothe your eyen blinde.　　　　　　　　　2370
Up peril of my soule I shal nat lyen:
As me was taught, to hele with your yën
Was nothing bet to make yow to see
Than strugle with a man upon a tree.
God woot I dide it in ful good entente."　　　　　　　　　　2375
　　　　"Strugle?" quod he. "Ye, algate in it wente!
God yeve yow bothe on shames deeth to dyen!
He swyved thee! I saugh it with myne yën,
And elles be I hanged by the hals!"
　　　　"Thanne is," quod she, "my medicyne al fals.　　　2380
For certeinly, if that ye mighte see,
Ye wolde nat seyn this wordes unto me.
Ye han som glimsing and no parfit sighte."
　　　　"I see," quod he, "as wel as ever I mighte,
Thonked be God, with bothe myne eyen two,　　　　　　　2385
And by my trouthe, me thoughte he dide thee so."
　　　　"Ye maze, maze, gode sire," quod she.
"This thank have I for I have maad yow see.
Allas," quod she, "that ever I was so kinde!"
　　　　"Now, dame," quod he, "lat al passe out of minde.　　2390
Com doun, my lief, and if I have missayd,
God help me so, as I am yvel apayd.
But by my fader soule, I wende han seyn
How that this Damian had by thee leyn,
And that thy smok had leyn upon his brest."　　　　　　　2395
　　　　"Ye, sire," quod she, "ye may wene as yow lest;
But, sire, a man that waketh out of his sleep,
He may nat sodeynly wel taken keep
Upon a thing, ne seen it parfitly
Til that he be adawed verraily.　　　　　　　　　　　　　2400
Right so a man that longe hath blind y-be
Ne may nat sodeynly so wel y-see

"Oh brazen lady bold, what do you do?"   1155
     And she answered to him, "Sire, what ails you?
Keep both patience and reason in your mind.
I've helped you now when both your eyes were blind.   2370
At my soul's risk here, I will tell no lies,
For it was taught me that to heal your eyes,   1160
There was no better way to make you see
Than struggling with a man up in a tree.
God knows, I did it with the best intent."
     "Struggle!" said he, "Oh no—right in it went!
One shameful death to you both for your lies!   1165
He screwed you; I saw it with my own two eyes;
By the neck I'll hang if you did something else."
     "Then," said she, "alas, my medicine is false.   2380
For certainly, if you could clearly see,
You would not utter now such words to me.   1170
You have some glimpsing, but not perfect sight."
     "I see," said he, "just as well as I might,
Thanks be to God, right here with both eyes too.
By my word, it seemed to me he had you."
     "Oh, you're dazed, just dazed, good sire," said she.   1175
"Such thanks I get, I who have made you see.
Alas," said she, "I was ever so kind!"
     "Now, dame," said he, "let this pass from your mind.   2390
Come down, my love. If I'm wrong, don't worry.
God help me; if I misspoke, I'm sorry.   1180
By my father's soul, I thought I saw plain
And clear that by you Damian had lain,
And that your smock had lain upon his breast."
     "Now, sire," said she, "suppose as you think best.
But, sire, a man who wakes up from his sleep,   1185
Then he cannot all of a sudden keep
Something quite clear, nor see it perfectly,
Till he finds himself awakened fully.   2400
In the same way, a man who blind might be
A long while may not suddenly then see   1190

First, whan his sighte is newe come ageyn,
As he that hath a day or two y-seyn.
Til that your sighte y-satled be a whyle,   2405
Ther may ful many a sighte yow bigyle.
Beth war, I prey yow, for by hevene king,
Ful many a man weneth to seen a thing,
And it is al another than it semeth.
He that misconceyveth, he misdemeth."   2410
And with that word she leep doun fro the tree.
          This Januarie, who is glad but he?
He kisseth hir and clippeth hir ful ofte,
And on hir wombe he stroketh hir ful softe,
And to his palays hoom he hath hir lad.   2415
Now, gode men, I pray yow to be glad.
Thus endeth heer my tale of Januarie.
God bless us, and his moder Seinte Marie!

Heere is ended the Marchantes Tale of Januarie.

THE EPILOGUE

          "Ey! Goddes mercy!" seyde our Hoste tho.
"Now swich a wyf I pray God kepe me fro!   2420
Lo, whiche sleightes and subtilitees
In wommen been, for ay as bisy as bees
Ben they, us sely men for to deceyve,
And from a sothe ever wol they weyve.
By this Marchauntes tale it preveth weel.   2425
But doutelees, as trewe as any steel
I have a wyf, though that she povre be;
But of hir tonge a labbing shrewe is she,
And yet she hath an heep of vyces mo.
Therof no fors—lat alle swiche thinges go.   2430
But wite ye what? In conseil be it seyd,
Me reweth sore I am unto hir teyd.

Well when his sight has just returned all new
As he will see within a day or two.
Until your sight is settled for awhile,
There may be many sights that you beguile.
Beware, I pray you, for by heaven's king,   1195
Many men can suppose they see a thing,
And it is something other than it seems.
He who conceives amiss, amiss he deems."   2410
And with that word, she leaped down from the tree.

   This January, who's more glad than he?   1200
He kisses her and cuddles her so often,
And upon her womb he strokes her soft then,
And to his palace led her home he had.
And now, good men, I pray you to be glad.
Thus here ends my tale of January.   1205
Now God bless us, and his mother Saint Mary.

Here is ended the Merchant's Tale of January.

THE EPILOGUE

   "Ah," said our Host, "God's mercy, by my life,
Now I pray God save me from such a wife!   2420
Now see what sly ways and what subtleties
In women are; always busy as bees   1210
They are so they us silly men deceive,
And so far from the truth their ways they weave;
This Merchant's tale right now proves this is real.
Without a doubt, as true as any steel,
I have a wife, although she poor may be,   1215
But with her tongue, a blabbing shrew is she,
And yet she has a heap of vices, too—
No matter. Let such things go as they do.   2430
Do you know what? In confidence, I say,
I sorely rue I'm tied to her today;   1220

For and I sholde rekenen every vyce
Which that she hath, ywis I were to nyce.
And cause why? It sholde reported be   2435
And told to hir of somme of this meynee,
Of whom it nedeth nat for to declare,
Sin wommen connen outen swich chaffare.
And eek my wit suffyseth nat therto
To tellen al, wherfor my tale is do."   2440

For if each of her vices I reckoned,
Quite truly, I would meet a foolish end.
The reason why? It would reported be
To her by someone in this company—
Just who that is, I need not here declare   1225
Since women know how to spread out their wares.
And my wit won't suffice in this matter
To tell all; therefore, my tale is over."   2440

THE FRANKLIN'S PROLOGUE

Thise olde gentil Britons in hir dayes
Of diverse aventures maden layes,
710
Rymeyed in hir firste Briton tonge;
Which layes with hir instruments they songe,
Or elles redden hem for hir plesaunce;
And oon of hem have I in remembraunce,
Which I shal seyn with good wil as I can.
715
But, sires, by cause I am a burel man,
At my biginning first I yow biseche
Have me excused of my rude speche.
I lerned nevere rethoryk, certeyn:
Thing that I speke, it moot be bare and pleyn.
720
I sleep nevere on the Mount of Pernaso,
Ne lerned Marcus Tullius Cithero.
Colours ne knowe I none, withouten drede,
But swiche colours as growen in the mede,
Or elles swiche as men dye or peynte.
725
Colours of rethoryk ben to me queynte:
My spirit feleth noght of swich matere.
But if yow list, my tale shul ye here.

THE FRANKLIN'S PROLOGUE

These old gentle Bretons,[1] in their days,
Of diverse adventures they composed their lays,   710
Which they rhymed in an early Breton tongue,
And these lays with their instruments they sung,
Or they read them for pleasure otherwise;   5
And one of these lays I did memorize,
Which I'll tell with good will the best I can.
    But, sires, since I'm an unlettered man,
As I begin, I will first you beseech:
Excuse me please for my unpolished speech.   10
Rhetoric's colors I never learned, I swear.
For what I speak, it must be plain and bare.   720
I never slept on Mount Parnasus,[2] so
I learned no Marcus Tullius Cicero.[3]
Doubtless, the only colors that I know   15
Are such colors that in a meadow grow,
Or else such colors as men dye or paint.
Rhetoric to me is curious and quaint;
Nothing of this matter moves my spirit.
Here's my tale, though, if you want to hear it.   20

---

  1 **Bretons:** People of Brittany whose roots and language were Celtic.
  2 **Mount Parnasus:** Home of the Muses in Roman mythology.
  3 **Marcus Tullius Cicero:** The great Roman writer and politician (106–43 B.C.E.) whose works
were famous as exemplifications of refined rhetorical usage.

THE FRANKLIN'S TALE

Heere bigynneth the Frankeleyns Tale.

    In Armorik, that called is Britayne,
Ther was a knight that loved and dide his payne   730
To serve a lady in his beste wyse;
And many a labour, many a greet empryse
He for his lady wroghte, er she were wonne.
For she was oon the faireste under sonne,
And eek therto come of so heigh kinrede,   735
That wel unnethes dorste this knight, for drede,
Telle hire his wo, his peyne, and his distresse.
But atte laste she, for his worthinesse,
And namely for his meke obeysaunce,
Hath swich a pitee caught of his penaunce   740
That prively she fil of his accord
To take him for hir housbonde and hir lord,
Of swich lordshipe as men han over hir wyves.
And for to lede the more in blisse hir lyves,
Of his free wil he swoor hire as a knight   745
That nevere in al his lyf he, day ne night,
Ne sholde upon him take no maistrye
Agayn hir wil, ne kythe hire jalousye,
But hire obeye and folwe hir wil in al
As any lovere to his lady shal—   750
Save that the name of soveraynetee,
That wolde he have for shame of his degree.

THE FRANKLIN'S TALE

Here begins the Franklin's Tale

In Armorica, now called Brittany,
There lived a knight who loved, and pains took he   730
To serve his lady all in his best manner;
Many a great enterprise and labor
He did perform for her so she'd be won,   25
For she's among the fairest beneath the sun,
And also from a line of such high kindred
That this knight hardly dared, out of his dread,
To tell her of his woe, pain, and distress.
But she, at last, for all his worthiness,   30
And namely for all his meek obeying,
Such pity took then on his suffering,   740
That privately with him she did accord
To take him for her husband and her lord,
The kind of lordship men have over wives.   35
And so that more in bliss they'd lead their lives,
Of his free will, he swore to her, as knight,
In all his life, that never, day or night,
Would he upon himself take mastery
Against her will, nor show his jealousy,   40
But heed her will and also obey her,
As his lady, just like any lover,   750
Except that the title of sovereignty,
To save his rank from shame, that would keep he.

537

She thanked him, and with ful greet humblesse
She seyde, "Sire, sith of youre gentillesse
Ye profre me to have so large a reyne,   755
Ne wolde nevere God bitwixe us tweyne,
As in my gilt, were outher werre or stryf.
Sire, I wol be youre humble trewe wyf:
Have heer my trouthe, til that myn herte breste."
Thus been they bothe in quiete and in reste.   760
        For o thing, sires, saufly dar I seye,
That frendes everich other moot obeye,
If they wol longe holden companye.
Love wol nat ben constreyned by maistrye.
When maistrie comth, the God of Love anon   765
Beteth hise winges, and farewel, he is gon!
Love is a thing as any spirit free.
Wommen of kinde desiren libertee,
And nat to ben constreyned as a thral;
And so don men, if I soth seyen shal.   770
Loke who that is most pacient in love:
He is at his avantage al above.
Pacience is an heigh vertu, certeyn,
For it venquisseth, as thise clerkes seyn,
Thinges that rigour sholde never atteyne.   775
For every word men may nat chyde or pleyne.
Lerneth to suffre, or elles, so moot I goon,
Ye shul it lerne, wher so ye wole or noon.
For in this world, certein, ther no wight is
That he ne dooth or seith somtyme amis.   780
Ire, siknesse, or constellacioun,
Wyn, wo, or chaunginge of complexioun
Causeth ful ofte to doon amis or speken.
On every wrong a man may nat be wreken:
After the tyme moste be temperaunce   785
To every wight that can on governaunce.
And therfore hath this wyse worthy knight,
To live in ese, suffrance hire bihight,

She thanked him with quite great humility,   45
And said, "Sire, since, with your gentility,
You offer to let me have such free rein,
Pray God, between us never will remain,
Through my own fault here, either war or strife.
Sire, I will be your true and humble wife—   50
Have my word—till my heart bursts in my breast."
Thus they are both in quiet and at rest.   760
    For one thing now, sires, I dare safely say
That friends each other always must obey,
If they for long want to hold company.   55
Love will not be constrained by mastery.
When mastery comes, the God of Love anon
Beats his wings, and then farewell, he is gone.
Love is a thing, like any spirit, free.
Women, by nature, desire liberty,   60
And not to be constrained or held in thrall;
And so do men, if I speak true for all.   770
The one who is the most patient above
All others has advantages in love.
A lofty virtue patience is each day,   65
For it vanquishes, as these clerks all say,
Some things that rigor never would attain.
At every word, men can't chide and complain.
Learn to endure, or else, I tell you now,
Whether you like it or not, you will learn how.   70
For in this world, certainly, there is no one
Who has not sometimes wrongly said or done.   780
Ire, sickness, or some astral influence,
Wine, woe, shifting in the humors' balance
Can make one often do amiss, or speak.   75
For every wrong, a man can't vengeance seek.
For every thing, there must be toleration
In everyone who knows of moderation.
And therefore then had this wise, worthy knight
Promised her patience, so in ease they might   80

And she to him ful wisly gan to swere
That nevere sholde ther be defaute in here.   790
   Heere may men seen an humble wys accord:
Thus hath she take hir servant and hir lord,
Servant in love, and lord in mariage;
Thanne was he bothe in lordship and servage.
Servage? Nay, but in lordshipe above,   795
Sith he hath bothe his lady and his love;
His lady, certes, and his wyf also,
The which that lawe of love acordeth to.
And whan he was in this prosperitee,
Hoom with his wyf he gooth to his contree,   800
Nat fer fro Pedmark, ther his dwelling was,
Where as he liveth in blisse and in solas.
   Who coude telle, but he hadde wedded be,
The joye, the ese, and the prosperitee
That is bitwixe an housbonde and his wyf ?   805
A yeer and more lasted this blisful lyf,
Til that the knight of which I speke of thus,
That of Kayrrud was cleped Arveragus,
Shoop him to goon and dwelle a yeer or tweyne
In Engelond, that cleped was eek Briteyne,   810
To seke in armes worshipe and honour—
For al his lust he sette in swich labour—
And dwelled ther two yeer; the book seith thus.
   Now wol I stinten of this Arveragus,
And speken I wole of Dorigene his wyf,   815
That loveth hire housbonde as hire hertes lyf.
For his absence wepeth she and syketh,
As doon thise noble wyves whan hem lyketh.
She moorneth, waketh, wayleth, fasteth, pleyneth;
Desyr of his presence hire so distreyneth   820
That al this wyde world she sette at noght.

Live now, and to him wisely ˌhe did swear
That never would he find fault in her there.   790
    Here may men see a humble, wise accord;
She's taken him for servant and for lord—
Servant in love and lord in marriage thus.   85
He lived both in lordship and in service.
In service? No, but in lordship above,
Since he has both his lady and his love;
His lady, surely, and his wife also,
In an accord which law's love let them know.   90
And when he had found such prosperity,
With his wife he goes home to his country,   800
Not far from Penmarch,⁴ there where he does dwell,
And lives in pleasure and in bliss as well.
    Now who could tell, unless he wedded be,   95
The joy, the ease, and the prosperity
That exists between a husband and a wife?
A year and more lasted this blissful life,
Until the knight of whom I've spoken thus,
Who was from Karru⁵ and called Arveragus,   100
Reckoned to go and dwell a year or two then
In England, which also was called Britain,   810
To seek in arms good repute and honor—
All his desire was fixed on such labor—
And two years he dwelled there, my source says thus.   105
    Now here I will leave this Arveragus,
And I will speak of Dorigen, his wife,
Who loved her husband like her heart's own life.
For his absence, she weeps and she sighs, too,
As, when it pleases them, noble wives do.   110
She mourns, she sobs, she fasts, she wakes, she wails;
Her desire for his presence so assails   820
Her that to her the whole, wide world means nought.

    4 **Penmarch**: Location on the rocky coast of Brittany.
    5 **Karru**: Perhaps the name of a village.

Hire frendes, whiche that knewe hir hevy thoght,
Conforten hire in al that ever they may:
They prechen hire, they telle hire night and day,
That causelees she sleeth hirself, allas!   825
And every confort possible in this cas
They doon to hire with al hire bisinesse,
Al for to make hire leve hire hevinesse.

      By proces, as ye knowen everichoon,
Men may so longe graven in a stoon   830
Til som figure therinne emprented be.
So longe han they conforted hire til she
Receyved hath, by hope and by resoun,
The emprenting of hire consolacioun,
Thurgh which hir grete sorwe gan aswage: 835
She may nat alwey duren in swich rage.

      And eek Arveragus, in al this care,
Hath sent hire lettres hoom of his welfare,
And that he wol come hastily agayn;
Or elles hadde this sorwe hir herte slayn.   840

      Hire freendes sawe hir sorwe gan to slake,
And preyde hire on knees, for Goddes sake,
To come and romen hire in companye,
Awey to dryve hire derke fantasye.
And finally, she graunted that requeste,   845
For wel she saugh that it was for the beste.

      Now stood hire castel faste by the see,
And often with hire freendes walketh she
Hire to disporte upon the bank an heigh,
Where as she many a ship and barge seigh   850
Seilinge hir cours, where as hem liste go.
But thanne was that a parcel of hire wo,
For to hirself ful ofte "Allas!" seith she,
"Is ther no ship, of so manye as I see,
Wol bringen hom my lord? Thanne were myn herte   855
Al warisshed of his bittre peynes smerte."

      Another tyme ther wolde she sitte and thinke,

Her friends, who knew the whole weight of her thought,
Give her comfort the very best they may.   115
They preach to her and tell her, night and day,
She slays herself for no cause in this case!
And all possible comforts they embrace
To offer her with all due eagerness,
Thus to make her leave her heavy sadness.   120
      With time's passage, as each of you has known,
Men can so long engrave upon a stone,   830
Some figure on it will imprinted be.
Thus, so long have they comforted her that she
Has received, both from hope and from reason,   125
The imprinting of their consolation,
So that they her great sorrow did assuage;
She can't endure forever passion's rage.
      And Arveragus, amid all her care,
Sent her letters home about his welfare,   130
And said he would come hastily again;
Or else, this sorrow would have slain her then.   840
      Her friends all saw her sorrow start to ease,
And, for God's sake, they prayed her, on their knees,
To come and roam some in their company,   135
So she could drive off her dark fantasy.
And finally, she granted that request,
For she saw well that it was for the best.
      Now, since her castle stood fast by the sea,
Quite often there, with all her friends, walks she   140
Thus to amuse herself on that bank high
Where she saw ships and barges going by,   850
Sailing their course, wherever they would go.
But that became a portion of her woe,
For to herself often, "Alas," says she,   145
"Is there no ship of all the ones I see
That will bring home my lord? Then my poor heart
Would be cured of its pains and cease to smart."
      At other times, she would sit there and think

And caste hir eyen dounward fro the brinke.
But whan she saugh the grisly rokkes blake,
For verray fere so wolde hir herte quake   860
That on hire feet she mighte hire noght sustene.
Than wolde she sitte adoun upon the grene,
And pitously into the see biholde,
And seyn right thus, with sorweful sykes colde:
          "Eterne God, that thurgh thy purveyaunce   865
Ledest the world by certein governaunce,
In ydel, as men seyn, ye no thing make.
But Lord, thise grisly feendly rokkes blake,
That semen rather a foul confusioun
Of werk, than any fair creacioun   870
Of swich a parfit wys God and a stable,
Why han ye wroght this werk unresonable?
For by this werk, south, north, ne west, ne eest,
Ther nis y-fostred man, ne brid, ne beest.
It dooth no good, to my wit, but anoyeth.   875
See ye nat, Lord, how mankinde it destroyeth?
An hundred thousand bodies of mankinde
Han rokkes slayn, al be they nat in minde:
Which mankinde is so fair part of thy werk
That thou it madest lyk to thyn owene merk.   880
Thanne semed it ye hadde a greet chiertee
Toward mankinde; but how thanne may it be
That ye swiche meenes make it to destroyen,
Which meenes do no good, but evere anoyen?
I woot wel clerkes wol seyn as hem leste,   885
By arguments, that al is for the beste,
Though I ne can the causes nat y-knowe.
But thilke God that made wind to blowe,
As kepe my lord! This my conclusioun.
To clerkes lete I al disputisoun,   890
But wolde God that alle thise rokkes blake
Were sonken into helle for his sake!
Thise rokkes sleen myn herte for the fere."

As she cast her eyes downward from the brink, 150
When at the grisly black rocks she would look.
For very fear, her heart so quaked and shook, 860
That on her feet she couldn't stand up steady.
To sit down on the green then she was ready;
The vast sea she'd piteously behold, 155
And say right thus, with sorrowful sighs cold:
   "Eternal God, who, through your providence,
Leads all the world with steadfast governance,
Men have said you have made nothing idly.
Lord, these black rocks so fiendish and grisly, 160
Seem rather to be a foul confusion
In their work and not a fair creation 870
Of a perfect God who's wise and stable.
Why make a work that's so unreasonable?
For by this work, not south, west, north, nor east, 165
Is fostered either man or bird or beast;
It does no good, to my mind, just annoys.
Don't you see, Lord, how mankind it destroys?
A hundred thousand bodies of mankind
Such rocks have slain, though numbers one won't find; 170
Of your work, mankind is a part so fair,
You fashioned him in your own image there. 880
Then it seemed you felt a great charity
Toward mankind; but how then may it be
That you've made such a means man to destroy, 175
And these means do no good, but just annoy?
I know that clerks will think they should suggest,
With arguments, that all is for the best,
Though I myself may not the causes know.
But that same God who made the four winds blow, 180
Protect my lord! This is my conclusion.
To clerks, I leave logical disputation. 890
O! that God now all these black rocks would make
Sink deep down into hell here for his sake!
These rocks do slay my heart because of fear." 185

Thus wolde she seyn, with many a pitous tere.

     Hire freendes sawe that it was no disport   895
To romen by the see, but disconfort,
And shopen for to pleyen somewher elles.
They leden hire by riveres and by welles,
And eek in othere places delitables;
They dauncen, and they pleyen at ches and tables.   900
     So on a day, right in the morwe-tyde,
Unto a gardin that was ther bisyde,
In which that they hadde maad hir ordinaunce
Of vitaille and of other purveyaunce,
They goon and pleye hem al the longe day.   905
And this was on the sixte morwe of May,
Which May had peynted with his softe shoures
This gardin ful of leves and of floures;
And craft of mannes hand so curiously
Arrayed hadde this gardin, trewely,   910
That nevere was ther gardin of swich prys,
But if it were the verray Paradys.
The odour of floures and the fresshe sighte
Wolde han maked any herte lighte
That evere was born, but if to gret siknesse   915
Or to gret sorwe helde it in distresse,
So ful it was of beautee with plesaunce.
At after-diner gonne they to daunce,
And singe also, save Dorigen allone,
Which made alwey hir compleint and hir mone,   920
For she ne saugh him on the daunce go,
That was hir housbonde and hir love also.
But nathelees she moste a tyme abyde,
And with good hope lete hir sorwe slyde.
     Upon this daunce, amonges othere men,   925
Daunced a squyer biforen Dorigen,
That fressher was and jolyer of array,
As to my doom, than is the monthe of May.
He singeth, daunceth, passinge any man

Thus she'd say, with many a piteous tear.

      Her friends then saw that it was no good sport

To roam by the sea, but just discomfort,

And they arranged to play elsewhere instead.

By rivers and by wellsprings they her led,   190

And other lovely places, as I guess;

They dance; they play at backgammon and chess.   900

      So on one day, right in the morning then,

They all went into a nearby garden,

Where, according to prior decisions,   195

They arranged for both food and provisions,

And there they played for the entire day.

And this was on the sixth morning in May,

And May had painted with its soft showers

This garden filled with both leaves and flowers;   200

The craft of man's hand so curiously

Had arranged all of this garden, truly,   910

No garden had such value or such price

Unless it were the one, true paradise.

Of flowers, the sweet scent and the fresh sight   205

Would have made any heart to feel so light

That had been born, unless a great sickness,

Or some great sorrow held it in distress,

It was so full of beauty that enchants.

And after dinner, they began to dance,   210

And to sing, too, save Dorigen alone,

Who could do nothing but complain and moan,   920

For in the dance there she did not see go

He who was her lover and her husband also.

But nonetheless, her time she must bide,   215

And with good hope, she must let sorrow slide.

      In this dance, then, among the other men,

A squire danced in front of Dorigen,

Fresher and more charming in his array,

As I would pledge, than is the month of May.   220

He'd dance and sing, surpassing any man

That is, or was, sith that the world bigan.   930
Therwith he was, if men sholde him discryve,
Oon of the beste faringe man on lyve:
Yong, strong, right vertuous, and riche and wys,
And wel biloved, and holden in gret prys.
And shortly, if the sothe I tellen shal,   935
Unwiting of this Dorigen at al,
This lusty squyer, servant to Venus,
Which that y-cleped was Aurelius,
Hadde loved hire best of any creature
Two yeer and more, as was his aventure,   940
But never dorste he telle hire his grevaunce:
Withouten coppe he drank al his penaunce.
He was despeyred; no thing dorste he seye,
Save in his songes somwhat wolde he wreye
His wo, as in a general compleyning;   945
He seyde he lovede, and was biloved no thing.
Of swich matere made he manye layes,
Songes, compleintes, roundels, virelayes,
How that he dorste nat his sorwe telle,
But languissheth as a furie dooth in helle;   950
And dye he moste, he seyde, as dide Ekko
For Narcisus, that dorste nat telle hir wo.
In other manere than ye here me seye,
Ne dorste he nat to hire his wo biwreye,
Save that, paraventure, somtyme at daunces,   955
Ther yonge folk kepen hir observaunces,
It may wel be he loked on hir face
In swich a wyse as man that asketh grace,
But nothing wiste she of his entente.
Nathelees, it happed, er they thennes wente,   960
By cause that he was hire neighebour,
And was a man of worshipe and honour,

Who is, or has been, since the world began.   930
If now to describe him, one did strive.
He was one of the most handsome men alive;
Young, strong, quite virtuous, and rich and wise,   225
And well beloved, considered a great prize.
And if I shall tell the whole truth shortly,
All unknown to Dorigen completely,
This hardy squire, servant unto Venus,
The same one who was named Aurelius,   230
Now loved her the best of any creature
Two years and more; it was his lot, for sure,   940
That, to her, he'd never tell his grievance.
Instead, for love, he drank up all his penance.
He was in despair; nothing dared he say,   235
But in his songs, somewhat he would betray
His woe through a general complaining;
He said he loved, but love was not returning.
Of such matter, then, he made many lays,
Songs and complaints, roundels and virelays,   240
About how he'd not dare his sorrow tell,
But like a Fury,[6] languishes in hell;   950
Die he must, he said, just as did Echo
For Narcissus, who dared not tell her woe.
In any way other than you hear me say,   245
He did not dare his woe to her betray,
Except, truth to tell, sometimes at dances,
Where young folk make courtly observances,
It may well be he looked upon her face
Just like a man who'd ask her for her grace;   250
But nothing did she know of his intent.
It chanced once when they to the garden went,   960
Because Aurelius was her neighbor,
And a man of good repute and honor,

---

6   **Fury:** One of three avenging female deities from Roman mythology, with whom Chaucer may
have been most familiar through Dante's *Inferno*.

And hadde y-knowen him of tyme yore,
They fille in speche; and forth more and more
Unto his purpos drough Aurelius,   965
And when he saugh his tyme, he seyde thus:
      "Madame," quod he, "by God that this world made,
So that I wiste it mighte youre herte glade,
I wolde that day that youre Arveragus
Wente over the see, that I, Aurelius,   970
Had went ther nevere I sholde have come agayn.
For wel I woot my service is in vayn:
My guerdon is but bresting of myn herte.
Madame, reweth upon my peynes smerte,
For with a word ye may me sleen or save.   975
Heere at your feet God wolde that I were grave!
I ne have as now no leyser more to seye:
Have mercy, swete, or ye wol do me deye!"
      She gan to loke upon Aurelius:
"Is this youre wil," quod she, "and sey ye thus?   980
Nevere erst," quod she, "ne wiste I what ye mente.
But now, Aurelie, I knowe youre entente,
By thilke God that yaf me soule and lyf,
Ne shal I nevere been untrewe wyf,
In word ne werk, as fer as I have wit.   985
I wol ben his to whom that I am knit:
Tak this for fynal answere as of me."
But after that in pley thus seyde she:
      "Aurelie," quod she, "by heighe God above,
Yet wolde I graunte yow to been youre love,   990
Sin I yow see so pitously complayne.
Loke what day that, endelong Britayne,
Ye remoeve alle the rokkes, stoon by stoon,
That they ne lette ship ne boot to goon—
I seye, whan ye han maad the coost so clene   995
Of rokkes, that ther nis no stoon y-sene—
Thanne wol I love yow best of any man;
Have heer my trouthe, in al that evere I can."

And because she had known of him before,   255
They talked, and after, forward, more and more
Toward his own purpose drew Aurelius,
And when he saw a good time, he said thus:
        "Madame," said he, "by God who made this world then,
If I knew that it might your heart gladden,   260
I wish the day when your Arveragus
Went out to sea, that I, Aurelius,   970
Went to that place where I'd need to remain.
For well I know my service is in vain;
My reward is the bursting of my heart.   265
Madame, take pity on my pains that smart;
For, with a word, you may me slay or save.
At your feet, would that I could have my grave!
Right now I have no leisure more to say;
Have mercy, sweetheart, or else me you'll slay!"   270
        She then looked upon Aurelius;
"Is this your will," said she, "and say you thus?   980
Never before did I know what you meant.
But now, Aurelius, I know your intent.
By that same God who gave me soul and life,   275
Then shall I never be an untrue wife
In word nor works, to the end of my wit;
I will belong to him to whom I'm knit.
This is the final answer now from me."
But after that, in play, to him said she: 280
        "Aurelius," said she, "by God above,
I might still grant to you to be your love,   990
Since I see you lament piteously.
On that day when, the length of Brittany,
You remove all the rocks there, stone by stone,   285
So that they will leave ships and boats alone—
I say, when you have made the coast so clean
Of rocks that there is no stone to be seen,
Then will I love you best of any man;
Have here my word; I've done the best I can."   290

"Is ther non other grace in yow?" quod he.

"No, by that Lord," quod she, "that maked me!   1000
For wel I woot that it shal never bityde.
Lat swiche folies out of youre herte slyde.
What deyntee sholde a man han in his lyf
For to go love another mannes wyf,
That hath hir body whan so that him lyketh?"   1005

　　Aurelius ful ofte sore syketh;
Wo was Aurelie, whan that he this herde,
And with a sorweful herte he thus answerde:

　　"Madame," quod he, "this were an inpossible!
Than moot I dye of sodein deth horrible."   1010
And with that word he turned him anoon.
Tho come hir othere freendes many oon,
And in the aleyes romeden up and doun,
And nothing wiste of this conclusioun;
But sodeinly bigonne revel newe   1015
Til that the brighte sonne loste his hewe,
For th'orisonte hath reft the sonne his light—
This is as muche to seye as it was night—
And hoom they goon in joye and in solas,
Save only wrecche Aurelius, allas!   1020
He to his hous is goon with sorweful herte.
He seeth he may nat fro his deeth asterte:
Him semed that he felte his herte colde.
Up to the hevene his handes he gan holde,
And on his knowes bare he sette him doun,   1025
And in his raving seyde his orisoun.
For verray wo out of his wit he breyde.
He niste what he spak, but thus he seyde;
With pitous herte his pleynt hath he bigonne
Unto the goddes, and first unto the sonne: 1030

　　He seyde, "Appollo, god and governour
Of every plaunte, herbe, tree and flour,
That yevest, after thy declinacioun,
To ech of hem his tyme and his sesoun,

"Is there no other grace in you?" said he.

"No, there is not," said she, "as God made me! 1000

Well I know that it shall never happen.

Let such follies slip out of your heart then.

What relish should a man take in his life 295

To go and love another man's own wife,

Who has her body when it strikes his fancy?"

　　Aurelius began to sigh sorely.

Woe was Aurelius when this he heard.

With a sorrowful heart, he thus answered: 300

　　"Madame," said he, "this is impossible!

I must die a sudden death so horrible." 1010

And with that word, he turned himself away.

Their other friends came up to her to play,

And on the garden paths they roamed about, 305

They knew not what had happened, without doubt,

But suddenly their revels did renew,

Till the bright sun began to lose his hue;

From the sun, the horizon stole his light—

This is as much to say as it was night— 310

And home they go, after joy and solace,

Except, alas, wretched Aurelius! 1020

With sorrowful heart, his way home he made.

He sees that he cannot his death evade;

It seemed to him he felt his heart grow cold. 315

Up to the heavens, his hands he did hold,

And he knelt down upon his knees all bare,

And in his raving, he sent up his prayer.

Because of woe, he went out of his head.

He knew not what he spoke, but thus he said; 320

With piteous heart, his lament's begun

To all the gods, but first thing, to the sun: 1030

　　He said, "Apollo, god and governor,

Of each plant and herb and tree and flower,

You give, according to your declination, 325

To each of them, both its time and season,

As thyn herberwe chaungeth lowe or hye,   1035
Lord Phebus, cast thy merciable yë
On wrecche Aurelie, which that am but lorn.
Lo, lord! my lady hath my deeth y-sworn
Withoute gilt, but thy benignitee
Upon my dedly herte have som pitee!   1040
For wel I woot, lord Phebus, if yow lest,
Ye may me helpen, save my lady, best.
Now voucheth sauf that I may yow devyse
How that I may been holpe and in what wyse.
    Youre blisful suster, Lucina the shene,   1045
That of the see is chief goddesse and quene—
Though Neptunus have deitee in the see,
Yet emperesse aboven him is she—
Ye knowen wel, lord, that right as hir desyr
Is to be quiked and lighted of youre fyr,   1050
For which she folweth yow ful bisily,
Right so the see desyreth naturelly
To folwen hire, as she that is goddesse
Bothe in the see and riveres more and lesse.
Wherfore, lord Phebus, this is my requeste: 1055
Do this miracle—or do myn herte breste—
That now, next at this opposicioun,
Which in the signe shal be of the Leoun,
As preyeth hire so greet a flood to bringe
That fyve fadme at the leeste it overspringe   1060
The hyeste rokke in Armorik Briteyne;
And lat this flood endure yeres tweyne.
Thanne certes to my lady may I seye:
'Holdeth youre heste, the rokkes been aweye.'
    Lord Phebus, dooth this miracle for me!   1065

Shifting in the zodiac from low to high,
Lord Phoebus,[7] now cast your merciful eye
On poor Aurelius, lost and forlorn.
Lo, lord, my lady has my death here sworn   330
Through no guilt of mine, unless you'll pity   1040
My mortal wound, through your benignity.
For, lord Phoebus, no one else can help me,
I know, but you, except for my lady.
Now, pray, vouchsafe that to you I may say   335
Just how I can be helped and in what way.
    Lucina,[8] filled with beauty's blissfulness,
Your sister, and the sea's chief queen and goddess—
Though Neptune's divine power rules the sea,
Yet above him, as empress there is she—   340
You know well, lord, that just as her desire
Is to be lit and kindled by your fire,   1050
And thus she follows you so busily,
Just so, the sea desires naturally
To follow her, because goddess is she   345
Of big and little rivers and the sea.
Therefore, lord Phoebus, this is my request—
This miracle lest my heart burst in my breast—
When sun and moon are in opposition,[9]
Which will occur in the sign of the Lion,[10]   350
Pray that your sister a great flood brings down
So by at least five fathoms it will drown   1060
The highest rocks along this Breton shore;
And let this flood endure two years or more.
Then, surely, to my lady, I may say,   355
'Keep your promise, for the rocks have gone away.'
    Lord Phoebus, this miracle for me do.

---

7   **Phoebus**: Another name for Apollo, the sun god.
8   **Lucina**: Another name for Diana in her aspect as goddess of the moon and of childbirth.
9   **opposition**: The highest tides occur when the sun and the moon are in the position of being opposite to one another.
10 **Lion**: The zodiacal sign Leo.

Preye hire she go no faster cours than ye;
I seye, preyeth your suster that she go
No faster cours than ye thise yeres two.
Than shal she been evene atte fulle alway,
And spring-flood laste bothe night and day.   1070
And but she vouche sauf in swiche manere
To graunte me my sovereyn lady dere,
Prey hire to sinken every rok adoun
Into hir owene derke regioun
Under the ground, ther Pluto dwelleth inne,   1075
Or nevere mo shal I my lady winne.
Thy temple in Delphos wol I barefoot seke.
Lord Phebus, see the teres on my cheke,
And of my peyne have som compassioun."
And with that word in swowne he fil adoun,   1080
And longe tyme he lay forth in a traunce.
          His brother, which that knew of his penaunce,
Up caughte him and to bedde he hath him broght.
Dispeyred in this torment and this thoght
Lete I this woful creature lye: 1085
Chese he, for me, wher he wol live or dye.
          Arveragus, with hele and greet honour,
As he that was of chivalrye the flour,
Is comen hoom, and othere worthy men.
O blisful artow now, thou Dorigen,   1090
That hast thy lusty housbonde in thyne armes,
The fresshe knight, the worthy man of armes,
That loveth thee as his owene hertes lyf.
No thing list him to been imaginatyf
If any wight hadde spoke, whyl he was oute,   1095
To hire of love; he hadde of it no doute.

Pray her that she'll go the same speed as you;
I say, pray to your sister that she go
No faster than you for two years or so.   360
Then, at high tide so long she'll make her way,
And the spring flood will last both night and day.   1070
Unless she in this manner will agree
To grant to me my dear sovereign lady,
Pray her to sink all those rocks, every one,   365
Down below into her own dark region[11]
Underground, the one that Pluto dwells in,
Or never more shall I my lady win.
Barefoot in Delphi,[12] I'll your temple seek.
Lord Phoebus, see the tears upon my cheek,   370
And for my pain, show some compassion soon."
And with that word, he fell down in a swoon,   1080
And for a long while, he lay in this trance.
        His brother, who knew all this circumstance,
Picked him up, and to his bed has him brought.   375
Despairing in his torment and his thought
Will I now let this woeful creature lie;
Let him choose, for all I care, to live or die.
        Arveragus, with all wealth and honor,
Like one who is of chivalry the flower,   380
Has come home with the other worthy men.
O, blissful are you now, you Dorigen,   1090
Who has your eager husband in your arms,
Your own fresh knight, that worthy man of arms,
Who loves you as much as his own heart's life.   385
And he need not imagine that his wife
Had someone speak to her, while he was out,
Of love; because of this, he had no doubt.

---

11 **her own dark region:** A reference to Diana's other aspect as Hecate, where with Pluto, she resides as one of the gods of Hades, the underworld.

12 **Delphi:** The most important shrine in Greece, seat of the Delphic oracle, it was central to the worship of Apollo but did not have any connection with Diana.

He noght entendeth to no swich matere,
But daunceth, justeth, maketh hire good chere;
And thus in joye and blisse I lete hem dwelle,
And of the syke Aurelius wol I telle.   1100
            In langour and in torment furious
Two yeer and more lay wrecche Aurelius,
Er any foot he mighte on erthe goon.
Ne confort in this tyme hadde he noon,
Save of his brother, which that was a clerk: 1105
He knew of al this wo and al this werk,
For to non other creature, certeyn,
Of this matere he dorste no word seyn.
Under his brest he bar it more secree
Than evere dide Pamphilus for Galathee.   1110
His brest was hool withoute for to sene,
But in his herte ay was the arwe kene;
And wel ye knowe that of a sursanure
In surgerye is perilous the cure,
But men mighte touche the arwe, or come therby.   1115
His brother weep and wayled prively,
Til atte laste him fil in remembraunce,
That whiles he was at Orliens in Fraunce,
As yonge clerkes that been likerous
To reden artes that been curious   1120
Seken in every halke and every herne
Particuler sciences for to lerne—
He him remembred that, upon a day,
At Orliens in studie a book he say
Of magik naturel, which his felawe,   1125
That was that tyme a bacheler of lawe—
Al were he ther to lerne another craft—

He does not pay heed to such a matter,
But dances, jousts, and makes good cheer with her;   390
And thus, in joy and bliss I let them dwell,
And of poor, sick Aurelius, I'll tell.   1100
      In languor and in torment furious
Two years and more lay poor Aurelius,
Till he could put one foot before the other;   395
No comfort had he but what his brother
Could give him then. His brother was a clerk,
Who knew all of this woe and all this work.
He dared not to any other creature
Say a word of this matter, to be sure.   400
For in his heart he hid it better, thus,
Than for Galatea did Pamphilus.[13]   1110
On the outside, his breast as whole was seen,
But in his heart was stuck the arrow keen.
For wounds, you know, that heal on the surface,   405
The cure in surgery is perilous,
Till one can touch the arrow and withdraw it.
So his brother wept and wailed in private,
Till finally he did recall, by chance,
That while he was at Orleans[14] in France—   410
As these young clerks who are so desirous
To study arts arcane and curious   1120
Will seek in every cranny and each nook
Some occult science to learn by the book—
He remembered in Orleans one day,   415
Within a study hall, a book that lay
There on natural magic,[15] which he saw
And which his friend, a bachelor of law—
Though he was there to learn another craft—

---

13   **Galatea...Pamphilus:** Lovers in an anonymous thirteenth-century Latin poem entitled *Pamphilus de Amore.*

14   **Orleans:** Seat of a famous medieval university.

15   **natural magic:** The designation for studies in the workings of nature, such as astrology.

Had prively upon his desk y-laft:
Which book spak muchel of the operaciouns
Touchinge the eighte and twenty mansiouns   1130
That longen to the mone—and swich folye
As in oure dayes is nat worth a flye;
For holy chirches feith in our bileve
Ne suffreth noon illusion us to greve.
And whan this book was in his remembraunce,   1135
Anon for joye his herte gan to daunce,
And to himself he seyde prively:
"My brother shal be warisshed hastily;
For I am siker that ther be sciences
By whiche men make diverse apparences   1140
Swiche as thise subtile tregetoures pleye.
For ofte at festes have I wel herd seye
That tregetours withinne an halle large
Have maad come in a water and a barge,
And in the halle rowen up and doun;   1145
Somtyme hath semed come a grim leoun;
And somtyme floures springe as in a mede;
Somtyme a vyne, and grapes whyte and rede;
Somtyme a castel, al of lym and stoon—
And whan hem lyked, voyded it anoon.   1150
Thus semed it to every mannes sighte.
          Now thanne conclude I thus, that if I mighte
At Orliens som old felawe y-find
That hadde this mones mansions in minde,
Or other magik naturel above,   1155
He sholde wel make my brother han his love.
For with an apparence a clerk may make
To mannes sighte, that alle the rokkes blake
Of Britaigne weren y-voyded everichon,
And shippes by the brinke comen and gon,   1160
And in swich forme endure a wowke or two.

Privately upon his desk had left;   420
This book spoke much of the operations
Touching all the twenty-eight full mansions[16]   1130
Of the moon, and about other folly
That in our day's not worth a fly, you see—
For Holy Church's faith, which we believe,   425
Won't allow that illusions should us grieve.
And when he had recalled this book by chance,
At once, for joy, his heart began to dance,
And to himself he said then privately:
"My brother shall be all healed hastily;   430
For I am sure that there are sciences
For making illusions and appearances,   1140
Like those with which clever magicians play.
For, at some feasts, I have often heard say
That magicians, within a hall quite large,   435
Have made appear both water and a barge,
And in the hall they would row all around.
Sometimes, too, a grim lion would be found;
Sometimes, flowers spring as in a meadow;
Sometimes, vines and grapes both red and white grow;   440
Sometimes castles, with stone and mortar finished;
And then they'd make it vanish when they wished.   1150
Or thus it did seem there to each one's sight.
        Now, I conclude thus: if only I might
At Orleans some good old fellow find   445
Who had the moon's positions all in mind,
Or natural magic for such things above,
He could well make my brother have his love.
For with a good illusion, a clerk might
Cause all the black rocks that are in man's sight   450
In Brittany, each one, to disappear,
So ships along the coast could venture here,   1160
In such a way to last a week or so.

16 **mansions**: Positions of the moon.

Than were my brother warisshed of his wo;
Than moste she nedes holden hir biheste,
Or elles he shal shame hire atte leste."
          What sholde I make a lenger tale of this?   1165
Unto his brotheres bed he comen is,
And swich confort he yaf him for to gon
To Orliens, that he up stirte anon,
And on his wey forthward thanne is he fare,
In hope for to ben lissed of his care.   1170
          Whan they were come almost to that citee,
But if it were a two furlong or three,
A yong clerk rominge by himself they mette,
Which that in Latin thriftily hem grette,
And after that he seyde a wonder thing: 1175
"I knowe," quod he, "the cause of youre coming."
And er they ferther any fote wente,
He tolde hem al that was in hire entente.
          This Briton clerk him asked of felawes
The whiche that he had knowe in olde dawes;   1180
And he answerde him that they dede were,
For which he weep ful ofte many a tere.
          Doun of his hors Aurelius lighte anon,
And forth with this magicien is he gon
Hoom to his hous, and maden hem wel at ese.   1185
Hem lakked no vitaille that mighte hem plese;
So wel arrayed hous as ther was oon
Aurelius in his lyf saugh nevere noon.
          He shewed him, er he wente to sopeer,
Forestes, parkes ful of wilde deer: 1190
Ther saugh he hertes with hir homes hye,
The gretteste that evere were seyn with yë,
He saugh of hem an hondred slayn with houndes,
And somme with arwes blede of bittre woundes.
He saugh, whan voided were thise wilde deer,   1195
Thise fauconers upon a fair river,
That with hir haukes han the heron slayn.

Then would my brother be cured of his woe;
And then her promise she will have to hold,   455
Or at least he can shame her, truth be told."
      Why should I make this tale any longer?
He comes to the bedside of his brother,
And such encouragement gives to depart
For Orleans that right away he starts,   460
And onward then he makes his way forth there
In hopes to be relieved of all his care.   1170
      When they'd almost come into that city,
Save for a couple furlongs, two or three,
A young clerk roaming by himself they meet,   465
In Latin he them handily did greet,
And after that, he said a wondrous thing:
"I know," he said, "the reason for your coming."
Before even a foot further they went,
He had informed them of their own intent.   470
      This Breton clerk asked after their fellows,
The ones, in the old days, that he did know,   1180
And he was answered back that they were dead,
At which news, often, many tears he shed.
      Down from his horse Aurelius alit;   475
With the magician, he walks forth a bit
Home to his house, and makes himself at ease.
No food was lacking there that might him please.
So well appointed a house as this one,
In his life, Aurelius had seen none.   480
      He showed him, before he had supper here,
Forests and parks all teeming with wild deer: 1190
There saw he harts which had their horns held high,
The greatest ever seen by human eye.
He saw of those a hundred slain by hounds;   485
From arrows' sharp wounds, some bled on the ground.
When these deer vanished, he saw falconers
Setting out to hunt toward fair rivers,
Who, with their hawks, have many heron slain.

Tho saugh he knightes justing in a playn;
And after this he dide him swich plesaunce
That he him shewed his lady on a daunce   1200
On which himself he daunced, as him thoughte.
And whan this maister that this magik wroughte
Saugh it was tyme, he clapte his handes two,
And farewel! al oure revel was ago.
And yet remoeved they nevere out of the hous   1205
Whyl they saugh al this sighte merveillous,
But in his studie, ther as his bookes be,
They seten stille, and no wight but they three.

    To him this maister called his squyer,
And seyde him thus: "Is redy oure soper?   1210
Almost an houre it is, I undertake,
Sith I yow bad oure soper for to make,
Whan that thise worthy men wenten with me
Into my studie, ther as my bookes be."

    "Sire," quod this squyer, "whan it lyketh yow,   1215
It is al redy, though ye wol right now."
"Go we than soupe," quod he, "as for the beste:
This amorous folk somtyme mote han reste."

    At after-soper fille they in tretee
What somme sholde this maistres guerdon be,   1220
To remoeven alle the rokkes of Britayne,
And eek from Gerounde to the mouth of Sayne.

    He made it straunge, and swoor, so God him save,
Lasse than a thousand pound he wolde nat have,
Ne gladly for that somme he wolde nat goon.   1225
    Aurelius with blisful herte anoon
Answerde thus, "Fy on a thousand pound!
This wyde world, which that men seye is round,
I wolde it yeve, if I were lord of it.
This bargayn is ful drive, for we ben knit.   1230
Ye shal be payed trewely, by my trouthe!
But loketh now, for no necligence or slouthe,
Ye tarie us heer no lenger than tomorwe."

Then he did see knights jousting on a plain. 490
Next, he offered such pleasant courtesy
That, in a dance, he showed him his lady, 1200
And he danced with her too, or so he thought.
When the master who forth this magic brought
Saw it was time, he clapped, and one by one, 495
Farewell, and all our revel then was done.
Yet outside the house they had moved never
When they saw this wondrous sight together;
But where his books were, right in his study,
There they sat still, and no one but those three. 500
    Then to him this master called his squire,
And asked him: "Is ready now our supper? 1210
Almost an hour now has passed, I wager,
Since I ordered you to make our supper,
Back when these worthy men both went with me 505
Where I keep my books, into my study."
    "Sire," said he, "whenever you like, I vow,
It's ready, even if you want it now."
"Let us then dine," said he, "it's for the best.
These amorous folks sometime must have rest." 510
    After supper, they both made their accord
About the sum of this master's reward 1220
For removing all the Breton rocks then,
From the Gironde to the mouth of the Seine.
    He made it hard and swore, so God him bless, 515
He'd have a thousand pounds and nothing less;
For that sum, still, he would not gladly go.
    Aurelius, whose heart was blissful so,
Answered him thus: "Fie on a thousand pounds!
All this wide world, which men do say is round, 520
I'd gladly give if I were lord of it.
Our bargain is all driven; it's now knit. 1230
Truly, I pledge your pay with diligence.
But see now, out of sloth or negligence,
Longer than tomorrow, do not delay." 525

"Nay," quod this clerk, "have heer my feith to borwe."

     To bedde is goon Aurelius whan him leste,   1235
And wel ny al that night he hadde his reste:
What for his labour and his hope of blisse,
His woful herte of penaunce hadde a lisse.

     Upon the morwe, whan that it was day,
To Britaigne toke they the righte way,   1240
Aurelius and this magicien bisyde,
And been descended ther they wolde abyde;
And this was, as thise bokes me remembre,
The colde frosty seson of Decembre.

     Phebus wex old, and hewed lyk latoun,   1245
That in his hote declinacioun
Shoon as the burned gold with stremes brighte;
But now in Capricorn adoun he lighte,
Where as he shoon ful pale, I dar wel seyn.
The bittre frostes, with the sleet and reyn,   1250
Destroyed hath the grene in every yerd.
Janus sit by the fyr with double berd,
And drinketh of his bugle-horn the wyn;
Biforn him stant brawen of the tusked swyn,   •
And "Nowel" cryeth every lusty man.   1255

     Aurelius, in al that evere he can,
Doth to this maister chere and reverence,
And preyeth him to doon his diligence
To bringen him out of his peynes smerte,
Or with a swerd that he wolde slitte his herte.   1260

     This subtil clerk swich routhe had of this man
That night and day he spedde him that he can,
To wayten a tyme of his conclusioun;

"No," said this clerk, "have here my pledge today."

Aurelius goes to bed when he thinks best,

And almost all that night he had his rest.

Between his hope of bliss and all his labor,

His sad heart, in respite, did not suffer.   530

In the morning, when light came that day,

To Brittany, they took the shortest way,   1240

Aurelius and the magician as well,

And they dismounted there where they would dwell.

This was, as these books make me remember,   535

The cold, frosty season of December.

Now Phoebus, with a hue like brass, grows old,

He who, when his hot declination holds

In summer shines like burnished gold so bright;

But now, in Capricorn, down he alights,   540

I dare well say where his shining is pale.

The bitter frosts, along with sleet and hail,   1250

Have all destroyed the green in every sward.

By his fire, Janus[17] sits with double beard,

And from his wild ox horn he drinks his wine;   545

Before him stands the head of a tusked swine,[18]

And "Noel" cries out every eager man.

Aurelius does everything he can

To cheer his master and show reverence,

And he prays him that with due diligence,   550

He make an end to all his pains that smart,

Or with a sword, then, he should slit his heart.   1260

This clever clerk did pity so this man

That night and day he planned it so he can

Determine the time for the conclusion;   555

---

17 **Janus**: The god of entries and gates, for which the month January is named. He has two beards because he is represented as having two faces, with one looking back at the old year and one looking ahead to the new year.

18 **head of a tusked swine**: As the medieval Christmas carol "The Boar's Head Carol" demonstrates, the swine's head was associated with Christmas because pigs were slaughtered for the season in December.

This is to seye, to maken illusioun,
By swich an apparence or jogelrye—   1265
I ne can no termes of astrologye—
That she and every wight sholde wene and seye
That of Britaigne the rokkes were aweye,
Or elles they were sonken under grounde.
So atte laste he hath his tyme y-founde   1270
To maken his japes and his wrecchednesse
Of swich a supersticious cursednesse.
His tables Toletanes forth he broght,
Ful wel corrected, ne ther lakked noght,
Neither his collect ne his expans yeres,   1275
Ne his rotes ne his othere geres,
As been his centres and his arguments,
And his proporcionels convenients
For his equacions in every thing.
And by his eighte spere in his wirking   1280
He knew ful wel how fer Alnath was shove
Fro the heed of thilke fixe Aries above
That in the ninthe speere considered is:
Ful subtilly he calculed at this.
      Whan he had founde his firste mansioun,   1285
He knew the remenant by proporcioun,
And knew the arysing of his mone weel,
And in whos face, and terme, and everydeel;
And knew ful weel the mones mansioun,
Acordaunt to his operacioun,   1290
And knew also his othere observaunces
For swiche illusiouns and swiche meschaunces
As hethen folk used in thilke days.

That's to say, to make there the illusion,
By an appearance of such jugglery[19]—
I do not know terms from astrology—
That she and each one should suppose and say
From Brittany the rocks had gone away,   560
Or else they were sunk underneath the ground.
And so, at last, the right moment he found   1270
To make the tricks and all the wretchedness
That went with superstitious cursedness.
His Tolletanes tables[20] forth he brought,   565
Well calibrated, and they lacked for nought,
Neither adjustments made just for this year,
Nor basic root dates,[21] nor his other gear
To calculate the planets' positions
And tables to reveal all their motions   570
So their houses he could be equating.
According to the eighth sphere[22] in its working,   1280
He knew full well how far Alnath[23] did shove
Away from Aries' head fixed up above,
That can be observed there in the ninth sphere;   575
This cleverly he calculated here.
        And when he had found the moon's first mansion,
He did know the rest of the positions,
And he knew well of the moon's arising,
And in which sign's division, and everything;   580
He knew the moon's mansion and position
In accordance with its operation,   1290
And knew all his other observations
To make such cursed procedures and illusions
As heathens used to make back in those days.   585

19 **jugglery**: Magician's tricks
20 **Tolletanes tables**: Astrological tables for calculating planets' positions. They were originally formulated for Toledo in the late thirteenth century during the reign of King Alphonso X of Castile.
21 **root dates**: The foundational dates established for calibrating planetary positions.
22 **eighth sphere**: Sphere of the fixed stars.
23 **Alnath**: Star in constellation of Aries.

For which no lenger maked he delayes,
But thurgh his magik, for a wyke or tweye,   1295
It semed that alle the rokkes were aweye.
        Aurelius, which that yet despeired is
Wher he shal han his love or fare amis,
Awaiteth night and day on this miracle;
And whan he knew that ther was noon obstacle—   1300
That voided were thise rokkes everichon—
Doun to his maistres feet he fil anon
And seyde, "I woful wrecche, Aurelius,
Thanke yow, lord, and lady myn Venus,
That me han holpen fro my cares colde."   1305
And to the temple his wey forth hath he holde,
Where as he knew he sholde his lady see.
And whan he saugh his tyme, anonright he,
With dredful herte and with ful humble chere,
Salewed hath his sovereyn lady dere: 1310
        "My righte lady," quod this woful man,
"Whom I most drede and love as I best can,
And lothest were of al this world displese,
Nere it that I for yow have swich disese
That I moste dyen heer at youre foot anon,   1315
Noght wolde I telle how me is wo bigon.
But certes outher moste I dye or pleyne;
Ye slee me, giltelees, for verray peyne.
But of my deeth, thogh that ye have no routhe,
Avyseth yow, er that ye breke your trouthe.   1320
Repenteth yow, for thilke God above,
Er ye me sleen by cause that I yow love.
For, madame, wel ye woot what ye han hight—
Nat that I chalange any thing of right
Of yow, my sovereyn lady, but youre grace—   1325
But in a gardin yond, at swich a place,
Ye woot right wel what ye bihighten me;
And in myn hand youre trouthe plighten ye
To love me best. God woot, ye seyde so,

And thus no longer did he make delays,
But through his magic, for a week or so,
It seemed that all the rocks away did go.
      Aurelius, who is still in despair
If he will have his love or badly fare,   610
He waits day and night for this miracle;
When he knew that there was no obstacle   590
And all these rocks had disappeared quite well,
Down at his master's feet at once he fell,
And said, "I, woeful wretch, Aurelius,   595
Thank you, my lord, and my lady Venus,
Who helped deliver me from my cares cold."
And to the temple, his path he does hold,
Right where he knew he would his lady see.
And when he saw his opportunity,   600
With humble manner and heart full of fear,
Saluted he his sovereign lady dear: 1310
      "Oh, my dear lady," said this woeful man,
"Whom I most dread and love the best I can,
And for this world, were most loathe to displease,   605
If for you I'd not caught such a disease
That I must die now right here at your feet,
I would not tell how my woe is complete.
But I must lament or die now, certainly;
Through my pain, you slay me guiltlessly.   610
Although upon my death you will not rue,
Consider lest you break your promise, too.   1320
Repent you now, by that same God above,
Before you slay me because you I love.
Madame, you know, the vow you did recite—   615
Not that I challenge you or claim a right
From you, my sovereign lady, just your grace—
But in a garden yonder, at that place,
You know full well what you have promised me;
In my hand, you did vow assuredly   620
To love me best—by God, you have said so,

Al be that I unworthy be therto. 1330
Madame, I speke it for the honour of yow
More than to save myn hertes lyf right now.
I have do so as ye comanded me;
And if ye vouchesauf, ye may go see.
Doth as yow list, have youre biheste in minde, 1335
For, quik or deed, right there ye shul me finde.
In yow lyth al to do me live or deye:
But wel I woot the rokkes been aweye!"
        He taketh his leve, and she astonied stood;
In al hir face nas a drope of blood. 1340
She wende never han come in swich a trappe.
"Allas!" quod she, "that evere this sholde happe!
For wende I nevere, by possibilitee,
That swich a monstre or merveille mighte be!
It is agayns the proces of nature." 1345
And hoom she gooth a sorweful creature.
For verray fere unnethe may she go.
She wepeth, wailleth, al a day or two,
And swowneth, that it routhe was to see;
But why it was, to no wight tolde she, 1350
For out of toune was goon Arveragus.
But to hirself she spak, and seyde thus,
With face pale and with ful sorweful chere,
In hire compleynt, as ye shul after here:
        "Allas," quod she, "on thee, Fortune, I pleyne, 1355
That unwar wrapped has me in thy cheyne,
Fro which t'escape woot I no socour
Save only deeth or elles dishonour;
Oon of thise two bihoveth me to chese.
But nathelees yet have I lever to lese 1360
My lyf, than of my body to have a shame,
Or knowe myselven fals, or lese my name;
And with my deth I may be quit, ywis.
Hath ther nat many a noble wyf er this,
And many a mayde, y-slayn hirself, allas! 1365

Although I am unworthy, as I know.   1330
Madame, I say this for your honor's sake
And not so that my heart and life won't break—
I had to do as you commanded me;   625
And if you will consent, you can go see.
Do as you like; keep your promise in mind.
Alive or dead, right there you will me find.
For you can make me live or die today—
But well I know the rocks have gone away."   630
         He takes his leave, and she astonished stood;
And from her face, the blood has gone for good.   1340
She never dreamed she'd fall in such a trap then.
"Alas!" said she, "that this should ever happen!
I did not see the possibility   635
That such a monstrous marvel well might be!
It is against the process of nature."
And home she goes, a sorrowful creature.
For fear itself, now she can hardly go.
She weeps and then she wails a day or so,   640
And swoons so it a pity was to see.
About all this to no one would speak she,   1350
For out of town had gone Arveragus.
But to herself she spoke, and she said thus.
With pale face and sorrowful demeanor,   645
In her lament, as you will hear later:
         "Alas," said she, "to Fortune, I complain,
Who has wrapped me, unwary, in your chain.
To escape it I can find no succor
Except only death or else dishonor;   650
And one of these, it behooves me to choose.
But nonetheless, still I would rather lose   1360
My life than with my body to cause shame,
Or know myself for false, or lose my name;
With death, I may be acquitted truly.   655
Aren't there many noble wives before me
And maidens who have slain themselves, alas,

Rather than with hir body doon trepas?

     Yis, certes, lo, thise stories beren witnesse;

Whan thretty tyraunts, ful of cursednesse,

Hadde slayn Phidoun in Athenes atte feste,

They commanded his doghtres for t'areste,   1370

And bringen hem biforn hem in despyt

Al naked, to fulfille hir foul delyt,

And in hir fadres blood they made hem daunce

Upon the pavement, God yeve hem mischaunce!

For which thise woful maydens, ful of drede,   1375

Rather than they wolde lese hir maydenhede,

They prively ben stirt into a welle,

And dreynte hemselven, as the bokes telle.

     They of Messene lete enquere and seke

Of Lacedomie fifty maydens eke,   1380

On whiche they wolden doon hir lecherye;

But was ther noon of al that compaignye

That she nas slayn, and with a good entente

Chees rather for to dye than assente

To been oppressed of hir maydenhede.   1385

Why sholde I thanne to dye been in drede?

Lo eek the tiraunt Aristoclides

That loved a mayden, heet Stimphalides,

Whan that hir fader slayn was on a night,

Unto Dianes temple goth she right,   1390

And hente the image in hir handes two,

Fro which image wolde she nevere go.

No wight ne mighte hir handes of it arace,

Til she was slayn right in the selve place.

     Now sith that maydens hadden swich despyt   1395

To been defouled with mannes foul delyt,

Wel oghte a wyf rather hirselven slee

Rather than with their bodies to trespass?
    Yes, surely, their stories all bear witness.[24]
When thirty tyrants full of cursedness   660
Had slain Phidon in Athens at a feast,
They said his daughters should not be released,   1370
But brought before them all out of cruel spite,
All naked, to please their foul appetite,
And in their father's blood, they made them dance   665
On the pavement, God curse those miscreants!
And thus those woeful maidens, full of dread,
Rather than sacrifice their maidenhead,
They privately all jumped into a well
And thus they drowned themselves, as the books tell.   670
    From Sparta came the custom of Messene
Fifty maidens to seek for things obscene,   1380
For on them they would work their lechery.
But not a one amid this company
Was then slain there, for with quite good intent,   675
She'd choose to die first, rather than consent
There to be ravished of her maidenhead.
Why then to die should I have so much dread?
    Lo, there was the tyrant Aristoclides,
Who loved a maiden named Stymphalides,   680
When her father was murdered on one night,
Straight to Diana's temple she goes right   1390
Away and grasped the image to her so
That the image she would never let go.
No one might take it out of her embrace   685
Till she was slain there right in that same place.
    Now, since these maidens felt such intense spite
To be befouled for man's foul delight,
Then certainly a wife herself should slay

---

24 **their stories all bear witness . . . :** What follows is a long list of women who chose to commit suicide in order to preserve their honor, and, specifically, their virginity or their wifely chastity. The whole catalogue of these women comes from one source: Saint Jerome's *Adversus Jovinianum* (392 C.E.).

Than be defouled, as it thinketh me.
What shal I seyn of Hasdrubales wyf,
That at Cartage birafte hirself hir lyf ?   1400
For whan she saugh that Romayns wan the toun,
She took hir children alle, and skipte adoun
Into the fyr, and chees rather to dye
Than any Romayn dide hire vileinye.
Hath nat Lucresse y-slayn hirself, allas!   1405
At Rome, whanne she oppressed was
Of Tarquin, for hire thoughte it was a shame
To liven whan she hadde lost hir name?
The sevene maydens of Milesie also
Han slayn hemself, for verray drede and wo,   1410
Rather than folk of Gaule hem sholde oppresse.
Mo than a thousand stories, as I gesse,
Coude I now telle as touchinge this matere.
When Habradate was slayn, his wyf so dere
Hirselven slow, and leet hir blood to glyde   1415
In Habradates woundes depe and wyde,
And seyde, 'My body, at the leeste way,
Ther shal no wight defoulen, if I may.'
        What sholde I mo ensamples heerof sayn,
Sith that so manye han hemselven slayn   1420
Wel rather than they wolde defouled be?
I wol conclude that it is bet for me
To sleen myself than been defouled thus.
I wol be trewe unto Arveragus,
Or rather sleen myself in som manère—   1425
As dide Demociones doghter dere,
By cause that she wolde nat defouled be.
O Cedasus! it is ful greet pitee
To reden how thy doghtren deyde, allas!
That slowe hemself for swich manere cas.   1430
As greet a pitee was it, or wel more,
The Theban mayden that for Nichanore
Hirselven slow right for swich manere wo.

So she'd not be befouled, I would say.   690
What shall I tell about Hasdrubal's wife,
Who at Carthage deprived herself of life?   1400
When she saw that the Romans won the town,
She took all her children and she skipped down
Into the fire, and she chose to die,   695
The Romans thus her body to deny.
Did not Lucretia slay herself then too
When, in Rome, she was ravished of virtue
By Tarquin, for she thought it only shame
To stay alive when sullied was her name?   700
The seven maidens of Miletus also
Have slain themselves because of dread and woe   1410
And not let the Galatians them oppress.
More than a thousand stories, I would guess,
I could now tell touching this matter here.   705
With Adabrates slain, his wife so dear
Killed herself, and then she let her blood glide
Into Adabrates' wounds, so deep and wide,
And said, 'At least my body, in this way,
No man shall befoul, if I have my say.'   710
          Why should I more examples of this say,
Since many did decide themselves to slay   1420
So that befouled they should not live to be?
I thus conclude that it's better for me
To slay myself than to be befouled thus.   715
I will now be true to Arveragus,
And thus I choose to slay myself right here,
As did Demociones' daughter dear
Because befouled she refused to be.
Oh Scedasus, it is a great pity,   720
Alas, how your dear daughter died, to read,
Who slew herself for such a cause, indeed.   1430
As great a pity was it, if not more,
The Theban maiden who for Nichanore
Had slain herself for just this kind of woe.   725

Another Theban mayden dide right so:
For oon of Macedoine hadde hire oppressed,   1435
She with hire deeth hir maydenhede redressed.
What shal I seye of Nicerates wyf
That for swich cas birafte hirself hir lyf?
How trewe eek was to Alcebiades
His love, that rather for to dyen chees   1440
Than for to suffre his body unburied be!
Lo, which a wyf was Alceste," quod she.
"What seith Omer of gode Penalopee?
Al Grece knoweth of hire chastitee.
Pardee, of Laodomya is writen thus,   1445
That whan at Troye was slayn Protheselaus,
No lenger wolde she live after his day.
The same of noble Porcia telle I may:
Withoute Brutus coude she nat live,
To whom she hadde al hool hir herte yive.   1450
The parfit wyfhod of Arthemesye
Honoured is thurgh al the Barbarye.
O Teuta, queen! thy wyfly chastitee
To alle wyves may a mirour be.
The same thing I seye of Bilia,   1455
Of Rodogone, and eek Valeria."
      Thus pleyned Dorigene a day or tweye,
Purposinge evere that she wolde deye.
But natheless, upon the thridde night,
Hom cam Arveragus, this worthy knight,   1460
And asked hire why that she weep so sore;
And she gan wepen ever lenger the more.
"Allas!" quod she, "that ever was I born!
Thus have I seyd," quod she, "thus have I sworn,"
And told him al as ye han herd bifore;   1465
It nedeth nat reherce it yow namore.
This housbonde, with glade chere, in freendly wyse,
Answerde and seyde as I shal yow devyse.
"Is ther oght elles, Dorigen, but this?"

Then another Theban maiden did so
When her a Macedonian oppressed;
With death she has her maidenhood redressed.
What shall I say of Nicerates' wife,
Who for such cause has taken her own life? 730
How true, also, to Alcibiades
Was his own love, whom to die it did please 1440
Rather than let his corpse unburied be.
Lo, what a wife Alcestis was," said she.
"What says Homer of good Penelope? 735
All of Greece knows about her chastity.
Lord, of Laodamia it's written thus,
That when, at Troy, was slain Protesilaus,
No longer would she live after that day.
The same of noble Portia tell I may; 740
Without her Brutus, she just could not live,
To whom wholly her own heart she did give. 1450
Artemesia's perfect wifehood then did come
To be honored through all of heathendom.
Oh, Queen Teuta, your wifely chastity 745
To all wives now may well a mirror be.
The same thing say I here of Bilia,
Of Rhodogune, and of Valeria."

    A day or two thus did she mourn and cry;
Her purpose always was that she should die. 750
It happened, nonetheless, on the third night,
Home Arveragus came, this worthy knight, 1460
And asked her why so sorely she now wept,
But to her weeping she still longer kept.
"Alas," said she, "that ever I was born! 775
Thus have I said," said she, "thus have I sworn—"
And told him everything you've heard before;
I don't need to rehearse it for you more.
This husband, with kind look and friendly way,
Answered, as I'll relate, and he did say, 760
"Is there nothing else, Dorigen, but this?"

"Nay, nay," quod she, "God help me so as wis;   1470
This is to muche, and it were Goddes wille."
    "Ye, wyf," quod he, "lat slepen that is stille.
It may be wel, paraventure, yet today.
Ye shul youre trouthe holden, by my fay!
For God so wisly have mercy on me,   1475
I hadde wel levere y-stiked for to be,
For verray love which that I to yow have,
But if ye sholde youre trouthe kepe and save.
Trouthe is the hyeste thing that man may kepe."
But with that word he brast anon to wepe,   1480
And seyde, "I yow forbede, up peyne of deeth,
That nevere, whyl thee lasteth lyf ne breeth,
To no wight tel thou of this aventure—
As I may best, I wol my wo endure—
Ne make no contenance of hevinesse,   1485
That folk of yow may demen harm or gesse."
    And forth he cleped a squyer and a mayde:
"Goth forth anon with Dorigen," he sayde,
"And bringeth hire to swich a place anon."
They take hir leve, and on hir wey they gon,   1490
But they ne wiste why she thider wente:
He nolde no wight tellen his entente.
    Paraventure an heep of yow, ywis,
Wol holden him a lewed man in this,
That he wol putte his wyf in jupartye.   1495
Herkneth the tale, er ye upon hire crye.
She may have bettre fortune than yow semeth,
And whan that ye han herd the tale, demeth.
    This squyer, which that highte Aurelius,
On Dorigen that was so amorous,   1500
Of aventure happed hire to mete
Amidde the toun, right in the quikkest strete,
As she was boun to goon the wey forth right
Toward the gardin ther as she had hight;
And he was to the gardinward also,   1505

"No, no," said she, "as God is my soul's bliss!   1470
This is too much, unless it were God's will."

    "Yes, wife," said he, "let sleep now what is still.
Today, perhaps, all may be well with this.   765
By my faith now, you shall keep your promise!
In his wisdom, God have mercy on me,
Since stabbed straight through I would much rather be
For the true love that I hold for you now,
Unless you kept the promise you did vow.   770
A vow's the highest thing a man can keep"—
But with that word, he burst forth and did weep,   1480
And said, "I you forbid, on pain of death,
That never, while in you lasts life or breath,
To no one tell now of this adventure.   775
As I best may, I will my woe endure,
Nor will I make any sign of sadness,
Lest folks of you some harm may judge or guess."

    He called a squire and maid to him then:
"Go forth," he said, "at once with Dorigen   780
To such a place as I'll tell you about."
They take their leave and on their way set out,   1490
But they had no idea why there she went.
For to no one would he tell his intent.

    Perhaps a heap of you, if truth be told,   785
Will, in this case, a stupid man him hold
Because he put his wife in jeopardy.
Before you cry for her, hear the tale, truly.
She may have better fortune than it'd appear.
When you have heard the tale, then judge it here.   790

    This squire, who was named Aurelius,
And for Dorigen was so amorous,   1500
Just by some chance he happened her to meet
In the town, right in its most crowded street,
As she was bound to go directly then,   795
As she'd promised, straight toward the garden.
And garden-ward he was heading also;

For wel he spyed whan she wolde go
Out of hir hous to any maner place.
But thus they mette, of aventure or grace;
And he saleweth hire with glad entente,
And asked of hire whiderward she wente;   1510
And she answerde, half as she were mad,
"Unto the gardin, as myn housbond bad,
My trouthe for to holde, allas! allas!"
        Aurelius gan wondren on this cas,
And in his herte hadde greet compassioun   1515
Of hire and of hire lamentacioun,
And of Arveragus, the worthy knight,
That bad hire holden al that she had hight,
So looth him was his wyf sholde breke hir trouthe.
And in his herte he caughte of this greet routhe,   1520
Consideringe the beste on every syde,
That fro his lust yet were him levere abyde
Than doon so heigh a cherlish wrecchednesse
Agayns franchyse and alle gentillesse;
For which in fewe wordes seyde he thus: 1525
        "Madame, seyth to youre lord Arveragus,
That sith I see his grete gentillesse
To yow, and eek I see wel youre distresse,
That him were levere han shame (and that were routhe)
Than ye to me sholde breke thus youre trouthe,   1530
I have wel levere evere to suffre wo
Than I departe the love bitwix yow two.
I yow relesse, madame, into youre hond,
Quit every serement and every bond
That ye han maad to me as heerbiforn,   1535
Sith thilke tyme which that ye were born.
My trouthe I plighte, I shal yow never repreve
Of no biheste, and here I take my leve,
As of the treweste and the beste wyf
That evere yet I knew in al my lyf.   1540
But every wyf be war of hire biheste!

For he spied out whenever she would go
Out of her house to any kind of place.
And thus they met, either by chance or grace,   800
And he saluted her with glad intent,
And asked of her exactly where she went;   1510
And she answered, as if she were half mad,
"To the garden, as bid my husband had,
My promise now to keep—alas, alas!"   805
          Aurelius wondered how this came to pass,
And in his heart, he had great compassion
Both for her and for her lamentation,
And for the worthy knight, Arveragus,
Who told her that she must keep her promise,   810
So loathe for her to break her word was he.
In his heart, he took on this great pity,   1520
Considering what's best on every side,
So his desire he'd rather have denied
Than to commit such churlish wretchedness   815
Against gentility and noble frankness;
Therefore, in just a few words said he thus:
          "Madame, say to your lord Arveragus
That since I see his great gentility
To you, and also your distress I see,   820
So—it'd be a pity—he'd rather have shame
Than have you break your word and hurt your name,   1530
I would rather suffer woe forever
Than the love between you both now sever.
Madame, I release into your hand,   825
Requited, every oath and bond I planned,
That heretofore you'd made to me and sworn,
Back to the very moment you were born.
I shall you not reproach—my pledge believe—
With any promise, and here take my leave   830
Of the very best and truest wife
Whom I have ever met in all my life.   1540
Let every wife be very cautious when

On Dorigene remembreth atte leste.
Thus can a squyer doon a gentil dede
As well as can a knight, withouten drede."
      She thonketh him upon hir knees al bare,   1545
And hoom unto hir housbond is she fare,
And tolde him al as ye han herd me sayd;
And be ye siker, he was so weel apayd
That it were inpossible me to wryte.
What sholde I lenger of this cas endyte?   1550
      Arveragus and Dorigene his wyf
In sovereyn blisse leden forth hir lyf.
Never eft ne was ther angre hem bitwene:
He cherisseth hire as though she were a quene,
And she was to him trewe for everemore.   1555
Of thise two folk ye gete of me namore.
      Aurelius, that his cost hath al forlorn,
Curseth the tyme that evere he was born:
"Allas," quod he, "allas! that I bihighte
Of pured gold a thousand pound of wighte   1560
Unto this philosophre! How shal I do?
I see namore but that I am fordo.
Myn heritage moot I nedes selle
And been a beggere; heer may I nat dwelle,
And shamen al my kinrede in this place,   1565
But I of him may gete bettre grace.
But natheless, I wol of him assaye
At certeyn dayes, yeer by yeer, to paye,
And thanke him of his grete curteisye;
My trouthe wol I kepe, I wol nat lye."   1570
      With herte soor he gooth unto his cofre,
And broghte gold unto this philosophre
The value of fyve hundred pound, I gesse,
And him bisecheth of his gentillesse
To graunte him dayes of the remenaunt,   1575
And seyde, "Maister, I dar wel make avaunt,
I failled nevere of my trouthe as yit;

She takes oaths. At least, think of Dorigen.
And thus a squire a gentle deed can do   835
As well as can a knight, it's doubtless true."
          She thanks him, down upon her knees all bare,
And back home to her husband she goes there,
And told him all, as you have heard me say;
You may be sure, he was so pleased that day,   840
It's impossible for me to tell it right.
Why should I longer about this case now write?   1550
          Arveragus and Dorigen his wife
In sovereign bliss both went on with their life.
No more did anger rise up them between.   845
He cherishes her as though she were a queen,
And she to him was true for evermore.
Of these two folks, you get from me no more.
          Aurelius now all the fee did forfeit
And cursed the day that he was ever born yet: 850
"Alas," said he, "for my promise does bind
To pay a thousand pounds of gold refined   1560
To this philosopher. What should I do?
I only know that for me it's all through.
For my inheritance I must now sell   855
And be a beggar. Here I may not dwell
And shame all of my kinfolk in this place,
Unless, from him, I get some kind of grace.
But nonetheless, I'll ask if there's a way,
Year by year, on certain days, to pay;   860
For his great courtesy, thank him will I.
My promise will I keep, I will not lie."   1570
          With a sore heart, he went to his coffer,
And he brought gold to this philosopher
Worth five hundred pounds, as it seems to me,   865
And beseeches, from his gentility,
To grant him time to pay the remainder,
And said, "Master, this boast dare I offer:
I never failed to keep my word as yet.

For sikerly my dette shal be quit
Towardes yow, howevere that I fare
To goon a-begged in my kirtle bare.   1580
But wolde ye vouche sauf, upon seuretee,
Two yeer or three for to respyten me,
Than were I wel; for elles moot I selle
Myn heritage; ther is namore to telle."

      This philosophre sobrely answerde,   1585
And seyde thus, whan he thise wordes herde:
"Have I nat holden covenant unto thee?"

        "Yes, certes, wel and trewely," quod he.
        "Hastow nat had thy lady as thee lyketh?"
        "No, no," quod he, and sorwefully he syketh.   1590
        "What was the cause? tel me if thou can."

      Aurelius his tale anon bigan,
And tolde him al, as ye han herd bifore:
It nedeth nat to yow reherce it more.

      He seide, "Arveragus, of gentillesse,   1595
Hadde levere dye in sorwe and in distresse
Than that his wyf were of hir trouthe fals."
The sorwe of Dorigen he tolde him als,
How looth hire was to been a wikked wyf,
And that she levere had lost that day hir lyf,   1600
And that hir trouthe she swoor thurgh innocence:
She nevere erst herde speke of apparence.
"That made me han of hire so greet pitee;
And right as frely as he sente hire me,
As frely sente I hire to him ageyn.   1605
This al and som, ther is namore to seyn."

      This philosophre answerde, "Leve brother,
Everich of yow dide gentilly til other.
Thou art a squyer, and he is a knight;
But God forbede, for his blisful might,   1610
But if a clerk coude doon a gentil dede
As wel as any of yow, it is no drede!

      Sire, I relesse thee thy thousand pound,

For certainly, acquitted will my debt 870
All be to you, however I might fare,
Or I'll go begging in my tunic, bare. 1580
But would you grant, with due security,
A respite of two years or three to me,
Then I'd be fine. Otherwise, I must sell 875
My inheritance; there is no more to tell."
  This philosopher soberly answered,
And he said thus, when these words he had heard,
"Have I not kept my promise to you fully?"
  "Yes," said he, "certainly, well and truly." 880
  "Have you not had the lady you did prize?"
  "No, no," said he, and sorrowfully sighs. 1590
  "What was the reason? Tell me if you can."
  Aurelius at once his tale began,
And told him all, as you have heard before. 985
There's no need to repeat it for you more.
  He said, "Arveragus, from gentility,
In distress and sorrow die would he
Rather than have his wife's word be untrue."
Of Dorigen's sorrow, he told him, too, 890
How loathe she was to be a wicked wife,
And how, instead, she'd rather lose her life, 1600
And how, in innocence, her word she swore,
For she'd never heard of illusions before.
"That made me have for her such great pity; 895
Just as freely as he sent her to me,
Thus freely sent I her to him again.
This is all. There is no more to say, then."
  This philosopher said, "Beloved brother,
Each one behaved gently to the other. 900
You are a squire, and he is a knight;
But God forbid, for all his blissful might, 1610
Unless a clerk a gentle deed can do,
Without a doubt, as well as one of you.
  Sire, I release you from the thousand-pound 905

As thou right now were cropen out of the ground,
Ne nevere er now ne haddest knowen me.   1615
For sire, I wol nat take a peny of thee
For al my craft, ne noght for my travaille.
Thou hast y-payed wel for my vitaille;
It is ynogh. And farewel, have good day."
And took his hors, and forth he gooth his way.   1620
        Lordinges, this question thanne wolde I aske now:
Which was the moste free, as thinketh yow?
Now telleth me, er that ye ferther wende.
I can namore: my tale is at an ende.

Heere is ended the Frankeleyns Tale.

Debt as though you'd crept up out of the ground
Just now, and never had yet known of me.
Sire, from you I will not take a penny
For all my skill and for my work as well.
You have paid good money for my victuals. 910
It is enough. Farewell. Have a good day."
He took his horse and goes forth on his way. 1620
     My lords, this question, then, I'll now ask thus:
Which, do you think, was the most generous?
Now tell me here, before you further wend. 915
I know no more; my tale is at an end.

Here is ended the Franklin's Tale.

THE INTRODUCTION TO THE
PARDONER'S TALE

The wordes of the Hoost to the Phisicien and the Pardoner.

Our Hoste gan to swere as he were wood,
"Harrow!" quod he, "by nayles and by blood!
This was a fals cherl and a fals justyse!
As shameful deeth as herte may devyse   290
Come to thise juges and hir advocats!
Algate this sely mayde is slayn, allas!
Allas, to dere boghte she beautee!
Wherfore I seye al day as men may see
That yiftes of Fortune or of Nature   295
Been cause of deeth to many a creature.
Hir beautee was hir deeth, I dar wel sayn;
Allas! So pitously as she was slayn!
Of bothe yiftes that I speke of now
Men han ful ofte more harm than prow.   300
But trewely, my own maister dere,
This is a pitous tale for to heere.
But nathelees, passe over, is no fors;
I pray to God so save thy gentil cors,
And eek thyne urinals and thy jurdones,   305

THE INTRODUCTION TO THE
PARDONER'S TALE

The words of the Host to the Physician and the Pardoner.

Our Host swore as though he had gone crazy;[1]
"Harrow! Now, by Christ's nails and blood!" said he,
"This was a false churl and a false judge, then.
May death shameful as man can imagine   290
Come to such judges and attorneys too!   5
This innocent maid's slain, alas, it's true!
Alas, too dearly she has bought her beauty!
Therefore, I say always that men can see
That both Fortune's gifts and also Nature's
Bring about the deaths of many creatures.   10
Her beauty was her death, I think it's plain.
Alas, so piteously was she slain!
Of both the gifts that I do speak of now
Men often have more harm than good, I vow.   300
But it's the truth now, my own master dear,[2]   15
This is truly a piteous tale to hear.
But nonetheless, no matter; let it be.
I pray God to save your gentle body,
Your chamber pots and urinals too, then,

---

1 **as though he had gone crazy**: The Pardoner comes after the Physician in the storytelling com-
petition. The Host here, addressing the Physician, responds strongly to the tale the Physician has just
told about a beautiful young maiden, Virginia, who is killed by her own father, Virginius, to save her
from a judge's trickery and salacious designs upon her virtue.

2 **my own master dear**: The Host is addressing the Physician, who told the previous tale.

Thyn ypocras, and eek thy galiones,
And every boyste ful of thy letuarie;
God blesse hem, and our lady Seinte Marie!
So moot I theen, thou art a propre man,
And lyk a prelat, by Seint Ronyan!   310
Seyde I nat wel? I can nat speke in terme;
But wel I woot, thou doost my herte to erme,
That I almost have caught a cardiacle.
        "By corpus bones! but I have triacle,
Or elles a draught of moyste and corny ale,   315
Or but I here anon a mery tale,
Myn herte is lost for pitee of this mayde.
Thou bel amy, thou Pardoner," he seyde,
"Tel us som mirthe or japes right anon."
        "It shall be doon," quod he, "by Seint Ronyon!   320
But first," quod he, "heer at this ale-stake
I wol both drinke and eten of a cake."
        But right anon thise gentils gonne to crye,
"Nay! lat him telle us of no ribaudye;
Tel us som moral thing, that we may lere   325
Som wit, and thanne wol we gladly here."
"I graunte, ywis," quod he, "but I mot thinke
Upon som honest thing whyl that I drinke."

And drinks named for Hippocrates and Galen,   20
And each box filled with electuary;³
God bless them, and our lady Saint Mary!
So may I prosper, you're a proper man,
And just like a prelate, by Saint Ronan!⁴   310
That's not right? I can't speak jargon, I believe;   25
But I know well that you made my heart grieve,
And I almost had a cardiac unrest.⁵

    God's bones! Unless some medicine I test,
Or else a draught of moist and malty ale,
Or unless I now hear a merry tale,   30
My heart's lost for pity of this maiden.
You, *bel ami*,⁶ you Pardoner," he said then,
"Tell us some mirth or jokes now right away."

    "It shall be done, by Saint Ronan, I say!   320
But first, here at this alehouse sign," he said,   35
"I will both drink and eat a loaf of bread."

    But right away out cried the gentle folks,
"No, do not let him tell us dirty jokes!
Tell us some moral thing, so we may learn
Some wisdom; then we'll listen to his turn."   40
"I grant this, sure," said he, "but I must think
Upon some honest thing while here I drink."

3 **electuary**: Medicinal syrup.
4 **Saint Ronan**: Scottish saint.
5 **cardiac unrest**: The Middle English here is *cardynacle*, the Host's malapropism for *cardiacle*, or "heart attack." I have used a malapropism here to indicate the Host's lack of familiarity with medical terminology.
6 *bel ami*: Pretty friend. The phrase could be used to insinuate the Pardoner's effeminacy.

THE PARDONER'S PROLOGUE

Heere folweth the Prologe of the Pardoners Tale.

Radix malorum est Cupiditas. Ad Thimotheum, 6.

"Lordinges," quod he, "in chirches whan I preche,
I peyne me to han an hauteyn speche,   330
And ringe it out as round as gooth a belle,
For I can al by rote that I telle.
My theme is alwey oon, and evere was—
Radix malorum est Cupiditas.
        First I pronounce whennes that I come,   335
And thanne my bulles shewe I, alle and somme.
Oure lige lordes seel on my patente,
That shewe I first, my body to warente,
That no man be so bold, ne preest ne clerk,
Me to destourbe of Cristes holy werk;   340
And after that thanne telle I forth my tales.
Bulles of popes and of cardinales,

THE PARDONER'S PROLOGUE

Here follows the Prologue of the Pardoner's Tale.

*Radix malorum est Cupiditas. Ad
Thimotheum, 6.
[The root of all evil is cupidity.
1 Timothy 6:10]*

"My lords," said he, "in churches when I preach,
I take great pains to form impressive speech,   330
And ring it out as loudly as a bell,   45
For I know all by heart that I do tell.
My one theme is the same and always was—
Radix malorum est Cupiditas.
　　　First, I tell them from whence I have come,
And I show my papal bulls,[7] and then some.   50
Our liege lord's seal on my letters patent,[8]
For protection, I show first as warrant,
So no man is so bold, not priest nor clerk,
To bother me amid Christ's holy work.   340
And afterward, then forth my tales I tell;   55
The bulls of popes and cardinals as well,

　　7　**papal bulls:** Any official papal document, but the Pardoner here refers specifically to indulgences for time off one's allotted span in Purgatory, given to Christians in exchange for monetary donations to charitable groups.
　　8　**liege lord's seal on my letters patent:** Official seal either of pope or bishop on letters authorizing the Pardoner's activities.

Of patriarkes, and bishoppes I shewe,
And in Latyn I speke a wordes fewe,
To saffron with my predicacioun,   345
And for to stire hem to devocioun.
Thanne shewe I forth my longe cristal stones,
Y-crammed ful of cloutes and of bones—
Reliks been they, as wenen they echoon.
Thanne have I in latoun a sholder-boon   350
Which that was of an holy Jewes shepe.
'Goode men,' seye I, 'tak of my wordes kepe:
If that this boon be wasshe in any welle,
If cow, or calf, or sheep, or oxe swelle,
That any worm hath ete, or worm y-stonge,   355
Tak water of that welle, and wash his tonge,
And it is hool anon; and forthermore,
Of pokkes and of scabbe and every sore
Shal every sheep be hool, that of this welle
Drinketh a draughte. Tak kepe eek what I telle: 360
If that the good man that the bestes oweth
Wol every wike, er that the cok him croweth,
Fastinge, drinken of this welle a draughte—
As thilke holy Jewe oure eldres taughte—
His bestes and his stoor shal multiplye.   365
        And, sires, also it heleth jalousye:
For though a man be falle in jalous rage,
Let maken with this water his potage,
And nevere shal he more his wyf mistriste,
Though he the sooth of hir defaute wiste—   370
Al had she taken preestes two or three.

Of bishops and of patriarchs I show,
And I speak some words in Latin so
I can give to my sermons some flavor,
And to stir them to devoted ardor.   60
Then I show cases of long crystal stones,[9]
All crammed tight full of clotted rags and bones —
Relics they are, each one supposes then.
I have a shoulder bone mounted in latten [10]   350
Which came from the sheep of a holy Jew.[11]   65
'My good men,' I say, 'heed my words, now do:
If this bone here is washed in any well,
If cow or calf or sheep or ox should swell
That's eaten any snake, or a snake's stung,
Take water from that well and wash its tongue,   70
And it's all quickly healed; and furthermore,
Of pox and pustules and of every sore
Shall every sheep be healed that of this well
Drinks a draught. Now take heed of what I tell: 360
If the good man who owns the beasts will seek,   75
Right before the cock crows, every week,
To drink from this well, fasting as he ought,
As this same holy Jew our elders taught,
His beasts and his stock sure will multiply.
　　　　Sires, it heals jealousy, if you will try.   80
When a man in a jealous rage will stoop,
With this same water, then, have made his soup;
Mistrust of his wife he'll no longer heed,
Though he did know the truth of her misdeed—   370
Though she'd taken a priest, or two, or three.   85

9　**long crystal stones**: In the Middle Ages, reliquaries were containers for holding relics, pieces
of saints' bodies or clothing, considered sacred and thus the repositories of a special grace to which a
believer could gain access by worshipping or buying the relic. Many reliquaries were made of crystal.
Of course, the relics that the Pardoner sells are fraudulent.

10　**latten**: A brass alloy.

11　**holy Jew**: Scholars have not reached agreement on who this figure is. It may be that Chaucer
meant the phrase to be vague and generic.

Heer is a miteyn eek, that ye may see:
He that his hond wol putte in this miteyn,
He shal have multiplying of his greyn
Whan he hath sowen, be it whete or otes,   375
So that he offre pens, or elles grotes.
  Goode men and wommen, o thing warne I yow:
If any wight be in this chirche now,
That hath doon sinne horrible, that he
Dar nat for shame of it y-shriven be,   380
Or any womman, be she yong or old,
That hath y-maked hir housbonde cokewold,
Swich folk shul have no power ne no grace
To offren to my reliks in this place.
And whoso findeth him out of swich blame,   385
He wol com up and offre a Goddes name,
And I assoille him by the auctoritee
Which that by bulle y-graunted was to me.'
  By this gaude have I wonne, yeer by yeer,
An hundred mark sith I was pardoner.   390
I stonde lyk a clerk in my pulpet,
And whan the lewed peple is doun y-set,
I preche, so as ye han herd bifore,
And telle an hundred false japes more.
Thanne peyne I me to strecche forth the nekke,   395
And est and west upon the peple I bekke
As doth a dowve, sittinge on a berne.
Myn hondes and my tonge goon so yerne
That it is joye to see my bisinesse.
Of avaryce and of swich cursednesse   400
Is al my preching, for to make hem free
To yeven hir pens, and namely unto me.
For myn entente is nat but for to winne,
And nothing for correccioun of sinne:

I have a mitten, too, as you can see.
He who puts his hand inside this mitten
Will have multiplying of his grain then,
Once he's sown it, whether it's wheat or oats,
So long as here he offers pence or groats.[12]   90
    Good men and women, I warn of one thing:
If now, in this church, there is a being
Who's done a sin so horrible that he
Dares not, for shame, absolved of it to be,   380
Or any woman, whether young or old,   95
Who has made her husband be a cuckold,
Such folks will have no power and no grace
To offer for my relics in this place.
Whoever finds himself free from such blame,
He will come up and offer, in God's name.   100
I'll absolve him by the authority
That, through the bull, has been granted to me.'
    Year by year, a hundred marks[13] by this game,
I've won since I a pardoner became.   390
I stand like a clerk up in my pulpit,   105
And when the stupid people down do sit,
I preach just as you heard me say before
And tell a hundred false tricks or some more.
I take pains in stretching forth my neck then;
East and west, to them I nod and beckon,   110
As does a dove that in a barn is sitting.
My hands and tongue so eagerly are flitting
That it's a joy to see my busyness.
Of avarice and such accursedness   400
Is all my preaching, thus to make them free   115
To give their pence, and namely, straight to me.
For my intention is only to win,
And nothing for the correction of sin.

12 **groats**: Silver coins.
13 **marks**: Money worth about two thirds of a pound in Chaucer's day.

I rekke nevere, whan that they ben beried,   405
Though that hir soules goon a-blakeberied!
For certes, many a predicacioun
Comth ofte tyme of yvel entencioun:
Som for plesaunce of folk and flaterye,
To been avaunced by ypocrisye,   410
And som for veyne glorie, and som for hate.
For whan I dar non other weyes debate,
Than wol I stinge him with my tonge smerte
In preching, so that he shal nat asterte
To been defamed falsly, if that he   415
Hath trespased to my brethren or to me.
For, though I telle noght his propre name,
Men shal wel knowe that it is the same
By signes and by othere circumstances.
Thus quyte I folk that doon us displesances;   420
Thus spitte I out my venim under hewe
Of holynesse, to semen holy and trewe.
        But shortly myn entente I wol devyse:
I preche of no thing but for coveityse.
Therfore my theme is yet, and evere was,   425
Radix malorum est cupiditas.
Thus can I preche agayn that same vyce
Which that I use, and that is avaryce.
But though myself be gilty in that sinne,
Yet can I maken other folk to twinne   430
From avaryce, and sore to repente.
But that is nat my principal entente:
I preche nothing but for coveityse.
Of this matere it oughte ynogh suffyse.
        Than telle I hem ensamples many oon   435
Of olde stories longe tyme agoon,

I don't care, once they've had their burying,
If their souls then go blackberrying!   120
Surely, many sermons one could mention
Often times come from evil intention;
Some for pleasing folks, some for flattery,
To be advanced then by hypocrisy,   410
And some for vainglory, and some for hate.   125
When in no other way I dare debate,
Then I will sting him with my tongue so smart
In preaching, so that he can't help but start
To be falsely defamed if perchance he
Has trespassed against my brethren and me.   130
For though I may not speak his proper name,
Men shall well know he is one and the same,
By signs and by certain other measures.
Thus I repay folks who cause us displeasure;   420
My venom I spit out under the hue   135
Of holiness, to seem holy and true.
        But shortly my intention I'll explain:
I preach of naught but avarice and gain.
Therefore my theme is still, and always was,
Radix malorum est Cupiditas.[14]   140
Thus the very same vice that I practice,
I preach against, and that is avarice.
Though I myself am guilty of that sin,
Yet still I can make other folks begin   430
To leave avarice and sorely repent.   145
But that is not my principal intent;
I preach of nothing except avarice.
On that matter, suffice enough of this.
        Then I tell them exempla[15] that I know
From the old stories of quite long ago.   150

---

14 *Radix malorum est Cupiditas*: Greed is the root of all evil (1 Timothy 6:10), used as the epigraph for *The Pardoner's Prologue and Tale*.

15 **exempla**: Stories that illustrate the theme of a sermon.

For lewed peple loven tales olde;
Swich thinges can they wel reporte and holde.
What, trowe ye, the whyles I may preche
And winne gold and silver for I teche,   440
That I wol live in povert wilfully?
Nay, nay, I thoghte it nevere, trewely!
For I wol preche and begge in sondry londes;
I wol nat do no labour with myn hondes,
Ne make baskettes, and live therby,   445
By cause I wol nat beggen ydelly.
I wol non of the Apostles counterfete:
I wol have money, wolle, chese, and whete,
Al were it yeven of the povereste page,
Or of the povereste widwe in a village,   450
Al sholde hir children sterve for famyne.
Nay! I wol drinke licour of the vyne,
And have a joly wenche in every toun.
But herkneth, lordinges, in conclusioun:
Youre lyking is that I shall telle a tale.   455
Now have I dronke a draughte of corny ale,
By God, I hope I shal yow telle a thing
That shal by resoun been at youre lyking.
For though myself be a ful vicious man,
A moral tale yet I yow telle can,   460
Which I am wont to preche for to winne.
Now holde youre pees, my tale I wol beginne."

For stupid people love tales that are old;
Such things they can repeat as their minds hold.
What, do you think that while I may thus preach,
And win gold and silver with what I teach, 440
That I'll live in poverty willfully? 155
No, no, I would never think that, truly!
For I will preach and beg in sundry lands;
And I will do no labor with my hands,
Nor make baskets, to sustain my living,
For I will not idly go out begging. 160
No apostles will I counterfeit yet;
Money and wool, cheese and wheat I will get,
Although by the poorest page they're given,
Or the village's poorest widow, then, 450
Even if her children died from hunger. 165
No, from the vine, I will drink the liquor
And have a jolly wench in every town.
But in conclusion, hark, lords of renown:
Your preference is that I should tell a tale.
Now have I drunk a draught of corny[16] ale, 170
And, by God, I hope I'll tell you something
That, by reason, shall be to your liking.
Though I myself am quite a vicious man,
A moral tale yet to you tell I can, 460
Which I am wont to preach so I can win. 175
Now hold your peace! My tale I will begin."

16 **corny**: Strong ale.

THE PARDONER'S TALE

Heere bigynneth the Pardoners Tale.

    In Flaundres whylom was a compaignye
Of yonge folk, that haunteden folye—
As ryot, hasard, stewes, and tavernes,   465
Where as with harpes, lutes, and giternes,
They daunce and pleyen at dees bothe day and night,
And eten also and drinken over hir might,
Thurgh which they doon the devel sacrifyse
Withinne that develes temple, in cursed wyse,   470
By superfluitee abhominable.
Hir othes been so grete and so dampnable,
That it is grisly for to here hem swere.
Our blissed Lordes body they totere—
Hem thoughte Jewes rente him noght ynough—   475
And ech of hem at otheres sinne lough.
And right anon thanne comen tombesteres
Fetys and smale, and yonge fruytesteres,
Singeres with harpes, baudes, wafereres,
Whiche been the verray develes officeres   480
To kindle and blowe the fyr of lecherye
That is annexed unto glotonye:

THE PARDONER'S TALE

Here begins the Pardoner's Tale.

    In Flanders once there was a company
Of young folk who haunted after folly,
Such as gambling and brothels and taverns,
Where, carousing with harps, lutes, and citterns,[17]   180
They'd dance and play at dice both day and night,
And eat also, and drink beyond their might;
To the devil they make sacrifices
In his temple with their cursed devices   470
By overindulgence abominable.   185
Their oaths are both so great and damnable
That it is grisly just to hear them swear.
Our blessed Lord's body into bits they tear[18]—
They thought the Jews then should have torn him more;
Each laughed hard at the sins the others bore.   190
Right away there came the women tumblers,
Slim and small, and then the young fruit peddlers,
Singers with harps, bawds, sellers of wafers,
Who are the very devil's officers   480
To kindle and blow fires of lechery,   195
Which are annexed quite close to gluttony.

17   **citterns**: A kind of medieval guitar.
18   **…into bits they tear**: There was the belief that oaths inflicted suffering on Christ by increasing the number of wounds and tears his body endured at the Crucifixion.

The Holy Writ take I to my witnesse
That luxurie is in wyn and dronkenesse.
   Lo, how that dronken Loth unkindely   485
Lay by his doghtres two, unwitingly;
So dronke he was, he niste what he wroghte.
   Herodes, whoso wel the stories soghte,
Whan he of wyn was repleet at his feste,
Right at his owene table he yaf his heste   490
To sleen the Baptist John ful giltelees.
   Senek seith a good word douteleess:
He seith, he can no difference finde
Bitwix a man that is out of his minde
And a man which that is dronkelewe,   495
But that woodnesse, y-fallen in a shrewe,
Persevereth lenger than doth dronkenesse.
O glotonye, ful of cursednesse!
O cause first of oure confusioun!
O original of oure dampnacioun,   500
Til Crist had boght us with his blood agayn!
Lo, how dere, shortly for to sayn,
Aboght was thilke cursed vileinye;
Corrupt was al this world for glotonye!
Adam oure fader and his wyf also   505
Fro Paradys to labour and to wo
Were driven for that vyce, it is no drede.
For whyl that Adam fasted, as I rede,
He was in Paradys; and whan that he
Eet of the fruyt defended on the tree,   510
Anon he was outcast to wo and peyne.
O glotonye, on thee wel oghte us pleyne!
   O, wiste a man how manye maladyes
Folwen of excesse and of glotonyes,
He wolde been the more mesurable   515
Of his diete, sitting at his table.
Allas! the shorte throte, the tendre mouth,
Maketh that, est and west, and north and south,

Holy Writ I take here for my witness:
There's lechery in wine and drunkenness.
   Lo, how drunken Lot, unnaturally,
Lay by his daughters two, unwittingly;   200
So drunk was he, he knew not what he wrought.
   Herod, whoever has his stories sought,
When at his feast all filled with wine was he,
At his own table, he gave the decree   490
To slay John the Baptist, who was guiltless.   205
   Seneca too says a good word doubtless;
He says that no difference can he find
Between a man who is out of his mind
And one who's always drunk—and that is true—
Except madness, when it befalls a shrew,   210
Will last much longer than does drunkenness.
O gluttony, so full of cursedness!
O, the first cause of all our confusion!
O, the origin of our damnation,   500
Till Christ had bought us with his blood again!   215
Lo, how dearly, to say it shortly then,
Was bought back this accursed villainy!
Corrupted was this world for gluttony.
Adam, our father, and his wife also,
From Paradise to labor and to woe   220
Were driven for that vice, it is no lie.
For while Adam was fasting, as read I,
He was in Paradise; and when, then, he
Ate of the fruit forbidden from that tree,   510
At once he was cast out to woe and pain.   225
O gluttony, of you we should complain!
O if man knew how many maladies
Follow him from excess and gluttonies,
He'd be as moderate as he was able
About his diet, sitting at his table.   230
Alas, the short throat and the tender mouth
Make it so east and west and north and south,

In erthe, in eir, in water, men to swinke
To gete a glotoun deyntee mete and drinke!   520
Of this matere, O Paul, wel canstow trete:
"Mete unto wombe, and wombe eek unto mete,
Shal God destroyen bothe," as Paulus seith.
Allas! a foul thing is it, by my feith,
To seye this word, and fouler is the dede,   525
Whan man so drinketh of the whyte and rede
That of his throte he maketh his privee,
Thurgh thilke cursed superfluitee.

      The apostel, weping, seith ful pitously,
"Ther walken manye of whiche yow told have I"—   530
I seye it now weping with pitous voys—
"They been enemys of Cristes croys,
Of which the ende is deeth: wombe is her god!"
O wombe! O bely! O stinking cod,
Fulfild of donge and of corrupcioun!   535
At either ende of thee foul is the soun.
How greet labour and cost is thee to finde!
Thise cookes, how they stampe, and streyne, and grinde,
And turnen substance into accident,
To fulfille al thy likerous talent!   540
Out of the harde bones knokke they
The mary, for they caste noght awey
That may go thurgh the golet softe and swote;
Of spicerye of leef, and bark, and rote
Shal been his sauce y-maked by delyt,   545
To make him yet a newer appetyt.
But certes, he that haunteth swich delyces
Is deed, whyl that he liveth in tho vyces.

Men must toil hard in earth, water, and air
So dainty meat and drink gluttons have there! 520
About this matter, O Paul,[19] you well treat: 235
"Meat to belly, and belly then to meat,"
As Paul has said, "God shall destroy them both."
Alas, a foul thing, by my faith and oath,
To say this word, and fouler the deed to dread
When a man drinks so of wines white and red 240
That of his throat he then makes his privy
Through this accursed superfluity.
    The apostle, weeping, piteously says too,
"There walk many about whom I've told you— 530
I say now weeping, with voice piteous— 245
These ones are enemies of Christ's cross thus,
Of whom the end is death; their paunch is God!"
O paunch! O belly! O you stinking cod,[20]
Bag all filled up with corruption and dung!
For your foul sound at either end is sung. 250
Great cost and labor food for you to find!
These cooks, look how they pound, stew, strain, and grind,
So they turn substance into accident,[21]
And fill your greedy need up with their talent! 540
Out from the hard bones' middle knocked have they 255
The marrow, for they throw nothing away
That goes through the gullet soft and sweetly.
Spicings from leaf, bark, and root completely
Shall make his sauces up for his delight,
To stir in him a keener appetite. 260
Sure, he who haunts such delicacies nice
Is dead while he is living in such vice.

19 **Paul**: The Apostle Saint Paul.
20 **cod**: In Middle English, *cod*, meaning bag and therefore used to refer to the belly; it was also used to refer to the scrotum.
21 **substance into accident**: Ironic reference to Platonic terminology of the ideal (substance) and the real (accident), or the perfect essence versus the imperfect material reality that derives from it; "accident" here also refers to the excretions that result from too much indulgence of this kind.

A lecherous thing is wyn, and dronkenesse
Is ful of stryving and of wrecchednesse.   550
O dronke man, disfigured is thy face,
Sour is thy breeth, foul artow to embrace,
And thurgh thy dronke nose semeth the soun
As though thou seydest ay "Sampsoun, Sampsoun";
And yet, God wot, Sampsoun drank nevere no wyn.   555
Thou fallest, as it were a stiked swyn;
Thy tonge is lost, and al thyn honest cure,
For dronkenesse is verray sepulture
Of mannes wit and his discrecioun.
In whom that drinke hath dominacioun,   560
He can no conseil kepe, it is no drede.
Now kepe yow fro the whyte and fro the rede—
And namely fro the whyte wyn of Lepe
That is to selle in Fishstrete or in Chepe.
This wyn of Spaigne crepeth subtilly   565
In othere wynes growinge faste by,
Of which ther ryseth swich fumositee,
That whan a man hath dronken draughtes three
And weneth that he be at hoom in Chepe,
He is in Spaigne, right at the toune of Lepe,   570
Nat at The Rochel, ne at Burdeux toun;
And thanne wol he seye, "Sampsoun, Sampsoun."
      But herkneth, lordinges, o word I yow preye,
That alle the sovereyn actes, dar I seye,
Of victories in the Olde Testament,   575
Thurgh verray God, that is omnipotent,
Were doon in abstinence and in preyere:

A lecherous thing is wine, and drunkenness
Is full of fighting and of wretchedness. 550
O drunken man, disfigured is your face, 265
Sour is your breath, foul are you to embrace,
And through your drunken nose the sound does play
As though "Samson, Samson,"[22] you always say,
And yet, God knows, Samson never drank wine.
You fall just like you were a stuck-through swine; 270
Your tongue is lost, and all decent behavior,
For drunkenness is the true sepulcher
Both of man's wit and of his discretion.
One in whom drink has its domination— 560
He can no secret keep, it must be said. 275
Now keep yourself from wine, both white and red,
Especially, from the white wine of Lepe[23]
That is for sale in Fish Street or in Cheap,[24]
Because this wine from Spain creeps stealthily
Through other wines that grow close by, you see, 280
From which there rises such fumosity[25]
That when a man has drunk draughts, two or three,
And then supposes he's back home in Cheap,
He is in Spain, right in the town of Lepe— 570
He's not in La Rochelle, nor in Bordeaux—[26] 285
And then always, "Samson, Samson!" he'll go.
But hearken, now, my lords; one word, I pray,
That all the sovereign acts, I dare well say,
Of victories in the Old Testament,
Through the one, true God, who's omnipotent, 290
Were done in abstinence and done in prayer.

22 **Samson:** Samson did not drink wine so repetition of his name here, for the nasal, nonsense sound typical of drunken speech, is ironic.
23 **Lepe:** Spain.
24 **Fish Street or in Cheap:** London streets.
25 **fumosity:** Fumes, vapors.
26 **nor in Bordeaux:** The reference is to the practice of diluting superior quality French wines with inferior quality Spanish wines, which evidently produces a nasty form of intoxication.

Loketh the Bible, and ther ye may it lere.

    Loke Attila, the grete conquerour,

Deyde in his sleep, with shame and dishonour,   580

Bledinge ay at his nose in dronkenesse:

A capitayn shoulde live in sobrenesse.

And over al this, avyseth yow right wel

What was comaunded unto Lamuel—

Nat Samuel, but Lamuel, seye I—   585

Redeth the Bible, and finde it expresly

Of wyn-yeving to hem that han justyse.

Namore of this, for it may wel suffyse.

    And now that I have spoke of glotonye,

Now wol I yow defenden hasardrye.   590

Hasard is verray moder of lesinges,

And of deceite and cursed forsweringes,

Blaspheme of Crist, manslaughtre, and wast also

Of catel and of tyme; and forthermo,

It is repreve and contrarie of honour   595

For to ben holde a commune hasardour.

And ever the hyer he is of estaat

The more is he y-holden desolaat:

If that a prince useth hasardrye,

In alle governaunce and policye   600

He is, as by commune opinioun,

Y-holde the lasse in reputacioun.

    Stilbon, that was a wys embassadour,

Was sent to Corinthe in ful greet honour,

Fro Lacidomie to make hire alliaunce.   605

And whan he cam, him happede par chaunce

That alle the grettest that were of that lond,

Pleyinge atte hasard he hem fond.

For which, as sone as it mighte be,

He stal him hoom agayn to his contree,   610

Look in the Bible; you will learn it there.
   Now, look, Attilla,[27] the great conqueror,
Died in his sleep, with shame and dishonor,   580
His nose bleeding from drunkenness, you see.   295
A captain should live in sobriety.
And beyond this, consider now quite well
What commanded was unto Lemuel[28]—
Not Samuel, but Lemuel, I say;
Read the Bible, and find it told this way   300
About wine-giving to those who mete justice.
Suffice what it says there; enough of this.
   Since of gluttony I've finished speaking,
Now I'll turn and I'll forbid you gambling.   3050
Gambling is the true mother of lying,   305
And of deceit and accursed perjuring,
Blasphemy, manslaughter, and waste also
Of goods and time, and further still to go,
It is shameful and contrary to honor
To be thought of as a common gambler.   310
The higher in estate that he stands yet,
The more he is considered desolate.
If a prince himself resorts to gambling,
In all his policies and governing,   600
He is, by common consent and opinion,   315
Held to be less in his reputation.
   Stilbo, who was a wise ambassador,
Was sent into Corinth with great honor
Out of Sparta to make an alliance.
And when he came, it happened then by chance   320
That the greatest men from that land around,
Playing at dice there, all of them he found.
And for this reason, soon as it might be,
He stole home again to his own country,   610

27 **Attilla**: King of the Huns.
28 **Lemuel**: King of Massa, who, in Proverbs, is warned that kings should not drink wine.

And seyde, "Ther wol I nat lese my name,
Ne I wol nat take on me so greet defame,
Yow for to allye unto none hasardours.
Sendeth othere wyse embassadours—
For by my trouthe, me were levere dye   615
Than I yow sholde to hasardours allye.
For ye that been so glorious in honours
Shul nat allyen yow with hasardours
As by my wil, ne as by my tretee."
This wyse philosophre, thus seyde he.   620
        Loke eek that to the king Demetrius
The king of Parthes, as the book seith us,
Sente him a paire of dees of gold in scorn,
For he hadde used hasard ther-biforn;
For which he heeld his glorie or his renoun   625
At no value or reputacioun.
Lordes may finden other maner pley
Honeste ynough to dryve the day awey.
        Now wol I speke of othes false and grete
A word or two, as olde bokes trete.   630
Gret swering is a thing abhominable,
And false swering is yet more reprevable.
The heighe God forbad swering at al—
Witnesse on Mathew—but in special
Of swering seith the holy Jeremye,   635
"Thou shalt swere sooth thyn othes and nat lye,
And swere in dome, and eek in rightwisnesse;"
But ydel swering is a cursednesse.
Bihold and see, that in the first table
Of heighe Goddes hestes honurable,   640
How that the seconde heste of him is this:
"Tak nat my name in ydel or amis."
Lo, rather he forbedeth swich swering

And he said, "There I will not lose my name, 325
Nor in this way will I myself defame;
Never will I ally you with gamblers.
Now send forth other wise ambassadors;
For, by my word here, I would rather die
Than with these gamblers thus you to ally. 330
You, who are so glorious in honors,
Shall not ally yourselves with these gamblers
Through any will of mine or any treaty."
Lo, this wise philosopher, thus said he. 620
  And moreover, to the king Demetrius, 335
The king of Parthia,[29] as the book tells us,
Had sent in scorn a pair of dice of gold,
For he'd used dice before, it had been told;
Thus he held his glory and renown, too,
To have little repute and no value. 340
Lords may well locate other kinds of play
Honest enough to drive the day away.
  Now will I speak of oaths both false and great
A word or two, as these old books relate. 630
Swearing is a thing abominable, 345
And false swearing is more condemnable.
God on high forbade swearing completely,
As witness Matthew;[30] but especially
Of swearing says Jeremiah the holy,
"You shall not lie, but swear all oaths truly, 350
And swear in judgment and in righteousness";
But idle swearing is accursedness.
Behold and see that in the first table
Of high God's commandments honorable, 640
How the second commandment demands this: 355
"Take not my name in vain or else amiss."
Lo, he'd rather forbid us such swearing

29 **Parthia**: Persia.
30 **Matthew**: Saint Matthew.

Than homicyde or many a cursed thing—
I seye that, as by ordre, thus it stondeth—   645
This knoweth, that his hestes understondeth,
How that the second heste of God is that.
And forther over, I wol thee telle al plat
That vengeance shal nat parten from his hous
That of his othes is to outrageous.   650
"By Goddes precious herte," and "By his nayles,"
And "By the blode of Crist that is in Hayles,
Seven is my chaunce, and thyn is cink and treye;"
"By Goddes armes, if thou falsly pleye,
This dagger shal thurghout thyn herte go!"   655
This fruyt cometh of the bicched bones two—
Forswering, ire, falsnesse, homicyde.
Now for the love of Crist that for us dyde,
Lete youre othes, bothe grete and smale.
But, sires, now wol I telle forth my tale.   660
        Thise ryotoures three of which I telle,
Longe erst er pryme rong of any belle,
Were set hem in a taverne for to drinke;
And as they sat, they herde a belle clinke
Biforn a cors was caried to his grave.   665
That oon of hem gan callen to his knave,
"Go bet," quod he, "and axe redily,
What cors is this that passeth heer forby;
And looke that thou reporte his name wel."
        "Sire," quod this boy, "it nedeth never-a-del.   670
It was me told, er ye cam heer two houres.
He was, pardee, an old felawe of youres;
And sodeynly he was y-slayn tonight,
Fordronke, as he sat on his bench upright.
Ther cam a privee theef men clepeth Deeth,   675
That in this contree al the peple sleeth,

Than homicide or other cursed thing;
I say that, in their order, thus it stands;
He knows who the commandments understands,   360
How God's second commandment is just that.
And furthermore, here I will tell you flat
That vengeance will not vacate one's house thus
If one with one's oaths is too outrageous.   650
Now "By God's precious heart," and "By his nails,"   365
And "By the blood of Christ that is at Hales,[31]
Seven's my chance, and yours is five and three!"
"By God's arms, I swear, if you play falsely,
This dagger right through your heart will go!"—
This fruit comes from these two bitched bones[32] so: 370
Perjury, ire, falseness, and homicide.
Now, for the love of Christ who for us died,
Leave all your oaths, both the small and the great.
But, sires, here now my tale I will relate.   660
          Thus, these three debauchers of whom I tell,   375
Long before prime had rung from any bell,
Had sat down in a tavern there to drink;
And as they sat, they all heard a bell clink
And toll, for a corpse was brought to his grave.
Thus, one of them then called out to his knave: 380
"Go at once," he said, "and now ask quickly
What corpse is passing nearby that we see;
Make sure that his name you report clearly."
          "Sire," said this boy, "this isn't necessary;   670
It was told to me just two hours before   385
You came, he was an old fellow of yours,
And suddenly, he was slain here tonight,
Stone drunk as he sat on his bench upright.
There came a secret thief called Death, men say,
Who, in this country, all the people slay,   390

31 **Hales**: Name of an abbey in Gloucestershire.
32 **Bones**: Dice.

And with his spere he smoot his herte atwo,
And wente his wey withouten wordes mo.
He hath a thousand slayn this pestilence.
And maister, er ye come in his presence,   680
Me thinketh that it were necessarie
For to be war of swich an adversarie:
Beth redy for to mete him everemore.
Thus taughte me my dame, I sey namore."
"By Seinte Marie," seyde this taverner,   685
"The child seith sooth, for he hath slayn this yeer,
Henne over a myle, withinne a greet village,
Bothe man and womman, child, and hyne, and page;
I trowe his habitacioun be there.
To been avysed greet wisdom it were,   690
Er that he dide a man a dishonour."
        "Ye, Goddes armes," quod this ryotour,
"Is it swich peril with him for to mete?
I shal him seke by wey and eek by strete,
I make avow to Goddes digne bones!   695
Herkneth felawes, we three been al ones:
Lat ech of us holde up his hond til other,
And ech of us bicomen otheres brother,
And we wol sleen this false traytour Deeth.
He shal be slayn, he that so manye sleeth,   700
By Goddes dignitee, er it be night."
        Togidres han thise three hir trouthes plight
To live and dyen ech of hem for other,
As though he were his owene y-boren brother.
And up they sterte, al dronken in this rage,   705
And forth they goon towardes that village
Of which the taverner hadde spoke biforn,
And many a grisly ooth thanne han they sworn,
And Cristes blessed body they to-rente—

In two he smote his heart then with his spear,
And went away with no more words from here.
He's slain a thousand in this pestilence.[33]
Master, before you come in his presence,   680
It seems to me that it's necessary   395
To be wary of this adversary.
Be prepared to meet him forevermore;
Thus my dame taught me; I can say no more."
"By Saint Mary," the tavern-keep said, too,
"He's slain this year, and thus the child speaks true,   400
In a great village, a mile hence, I'd gauge,
Both man and woman, farmer, child, and page;
I believe that he has his dwelling there.
It'd be great wisdom for you to prepare,   690
Before he did someone a dishonor."   405
        "Yes, by God's arms," then said this debaucher,
"Is it such peril if one with him meets?
I shall seek him in all byways and streets,
So to God's worthy bones I make my vow!
Hark, good fellows, we three are all one now;   410
Let's each hold up his hand to the other,
And each one become the other's brother;
We will slay this false traitor Death today.
He shall be slain who does so many slay,   700
By God's dignity, before it is night!"   415
        These three then pledged their word as best they might
To live and die each one for the other,
As though he were his natural-born brother.
And up they start, in their rage all drunken,
And forth they all go toward that village, then,   420
Of which the tavern-keep did speak before.
And many grisly oaths those three then swore,
And Christ's blessed body they did tear and shred—

---

33 **pestilence:** Plague—a reference to the recurrent episodes of the plague, including the Black
Death, that hit England during Chaucer's lifetime.

Deeth shal be deed, if that they may him hente.   710
     Whan they han goon nat fully half a myle,
Right as they wolde han troden over a style,
An old man and a povre with hem mette.
This olde man ful mekely hem grette,
And seyde thus, "Now, lordes, God yow see!"   715
     The proudest of thise ryotoures three
Answerde agayn, "What, carl, with sory grace!
Why artow al forwrapped save thy face?
Why livestow so longe in so greet age?"
     This olde man gan loke in his visage,   720
And seyde thus, "For I ne can nat finde
A man, though that I walked into Inde,
Neither in citee nor in no village,
That wolde chaunge his youthe for myn age;
And therfore moot I han myn age stille,   725
As longe time as it is Goddes wille.
Ne Deeth, allas! ne wol nat han my lyf.
Thus walke I, lyk a restelees caityf,
And on the ground, which is my modres gate,
I knokke with my staf bothe erly and late,   730
And seye, 'Leve moder, leet me in!
Lo, how I vanish, flesh, and blood, and skin!
Allas! whan shul my bones been at reste?
Moder, with yow wolde I chaunge my cheste
That in my chambre longe tyme hath be,   735
Ye, for an heyre clout to wrappe me!'
But yet to me she wol nat do that grace,
For which ful pale and welked is my face.
     But sires, to yow it is no curteisye
To speken to an old man vileinye,   740

If they can catch him, then Death shall be dead! 710

    When they had gone not fully half a mile, 425

Right where they would have climbed over a stile,

An old and poor man[34] with those three did meet.

There this old man quite meekly did them greet,

And said thus, "Now, my lords, may God you see!"

    The proudest one of these debauchers three 430

Answered him back, "What, churl, with sorry grace!

Why are you all wrapped up, except your face?

Why do you live so long to such great age?"

    This old man did look into his visage, 720

And answered thus: "Since I cannot find a 435

Man, even if I walked to India,

Neither in a city or a village,

Who would exchange his youth for my age,

Therefore, I must have my old age still,

For as long a time as it is God's will. 440

Alas, Death does not want to have my life.

I walk here like a wretch in restless strife,

And on the ground, which is my mother's gate,

I knock with my staff, early and late, 730

And I say, 'Dear mother, let me in! 445

Lo, how I vanish, flesh and blood and skin!

Alas, now when shall my bones find their rest?

Mother, I would exchange my treasure chest

That such a long time in my chamber's been,

Yea, for a haircloth shroud to wrap me in!' 450

But yet, to me, she will not give that grace,

And thus, all pale and withered is my face.

    But, sires, to you it does no courtesy

To speak to an old man with villainy, 740

---

34 **An old and poor man**: Who the old man is, or what exactly he is meant to represent, remains a mystery. Some scholars have suggested that he is meant to represent the Wandering Jew; some have suggested that he is an allegorization of wise old age; and still others have suggested that he is just an old man.

But he trespasse in worde or elles in dede.
In Holy Writ ye may yourself wel rede,
'Agayns an old man, hoor upon his heed,
Ye sholde aryse.' Wherfor I yeve yow reed:
Ne dooth unto an old man noon harm now,   745
Namore than that ye wolde men did to yow
In age, if that ye so longe abyde.
And God be with yow, wher ye go or ryde;
I moot go thider as I have to go."

      "Nay, olde cherl, by God, thou shalt nat so,"   750
Seyde this other hasardour anon;
"Thou partest nat so lightly, by Seint John!
Thou spak right now of thilke traitour Deeth
That in this contree alle oure frendes sleeth.
Have heer my trouthe, as thou art his espye,   755
Telle wher he is, or thou shalt it abye,
By God, and by the holy sacrament!
For soothly thou art oon of his assent
To sleen us yonge folk, thou false theef!"

      "Now, sires," quod he, "if that yow be so leef"   760
To finde Deeth, turne up this croked wey,
For in that grove I lafte him, by my fey,
Under a tree, and there he wol abyde:
Nat for youre boost he wole him nothing hyde.
See ye that ook? right ther ye shul him finde.   765
God save yow, that boghte agayn mankinde,
And yow amende!" Thus seyde this olde man.

      And everich of thise ryotoures ran,
Til he cam to that tree, and ther they founde
Of florins fyne of golde y-coyned rounde   770
Wel ny an eighte busshels, as hem thoughte.
No lenger thanne after Deeth they soughte,
But ech of hem so glad was of that sighte—
For that the florins been so faire and brighte—
That doun they sette hem by this precious hord.   775
The worste of hem he spake the firste word.

Unless he should trespass in word or deed.   455
In Holy Writ, you may yourselves well read:
'Before an old man, hoary on his head,
You should stand up.' Thus I warn you instead:
Unto an old man, no harm must you do
More than you would want men to do to you   460
In old age, if so long you might abide.
Let God be with you, where you walk or ride!
I must go now to where I have to go."
          "Nay, by God, old churl, you will not do so,"   750
This other gambler said to him quickly;   465
"By Saint John, you don't leave so easily!
You spoke now of this traitor Death today,
Who, in this country, all our friends does slay.
Have here my word, as you're his spy, I say,
Tell where he is, or for it you will pay,   470
By God and by the holy sacrament!
For surely, with him now, you do consent
To slay all us young folk, you false old thief!"
          "Sires," he said, "if you're eager, to be brief,   760
To find Death, go turn up this crooked way;   475
By my faith, I left him in that grove today,
Under a tree, and there his time he'll bide;
Nothing in your boast will make him hide.
You see that oak? Right there, him you will find.
May God save you, who bought again mankind,   480
And you amend!" Thus said here this old man;
          And then each one of these debauchers ran
Till he came to that tree, and there they found
Of florins fine of gold, coined new and round   770
Well nigh to eight full bushels' worth, they thought.   485
No longer, then, after Death have they sought,
Each of them so glad was of that sight,
Because the florins were so fair and bright,
That they all sat down by that precious hoard.
The worst of them spoke first of their reward.   490

"Brethren," quod he, "take kepe what that I seye:
My wit is greet, though that I bourde and pleye.
This tresor hath Fortune unto us yiven
In mirthe and jolitee our lyf to liven,   780
And lightly as it comth, so wol we spende.
Ey! Goddes precious dignitee! who wende
Today that we sholde han so fair a grace?
But mighte this gold be caried fro this place
Hoom to myn hous—or elles unto youres—   785
For wel ye woot that al this gold is oures—
Thanne were we in heigh felicitee.
But trewely, by daye it may nat be:
Men wolde seyn that we were theves stronge,
And for oure owene tresor doon us honge.   790
This tresor moste y-caried be by nighte,
As wysly and as slyly as it mighte.
Wherfore I rede that cut among us alle
Be drawe, and lat se wher the cut wol falle;
And he that hath the cut with herte blythe   795
Shal renne to the toune, and that ful swythe,
And bringe us breed and wyn ful prively.
And two of us shul kepen subtilly
This tresor wel; and if he wol nat tarie,
Whan it is night we wol this tresor carie,   800
By oon assent, where as us thinketh best."
That oon of hem the cut broughte in his fest,
And bad hem drawe, and loke wher it wol falle;
And it fil on the yongeste of hem alle,
And forth toward the toun he wente anon.   805
And also sone as that he was agon,
That oon of hem spak thus unto that other:
"Thou knowest wel thou art my sworne brother;
Thy profit wol I telle thee anon.
Thou woost wel that oure felawe is agon,   810

"Brethren," said he, "take heed of what I say;
My wit is great, although I jest and play.
This treasure to us Fortune now did give
In mirth and jolliness our life to live;   780
Easily as it comes, so will we spend.   495
God's precious dignity, what did portend
Today that we would have so much good grace?
If this gold might be carried from this place
Back home to my house, or else home to yours—
You know this gold is ours forevermore—   500
Then we would be in high felicity.
But truly, by day, this might never be.
Men would all say that we're thieves bold and strong;
For our own treasure, we'd hang before long.   790
This treasure must be carried out by night   505
As wisely and as slyly as we might.
Thus, I advise a cut[35] among us all
Be drawn, and then see where the cut will fall;
He who wins the cut, with heart blithely cast,
Shall run to town, and that with speed quite fast,   510
And bring us bread and wine quite privately.
And two of us shall guard all stealthily
This treasure well; if he does not tarry,
When it's night, we will this treasure carry,   800
Where we have all by one accord best thought."   515
Then one of them the cut in his fist brought,
And bade them draw and see where it would fall;
And it fell to the youngest of them all,
Who set out for town immediately.
And just as soon as on his way went he,   520
One of them spoke up thus to the other:
"You know well that you are my sworn brother;
At once about your profit let me tell.
Our fellow now is gone, as you know well.   810

35 **cut**: Drawing a straw or drawing lots.

And heer is gold, and that ful greet plentee,
That shal departed been among us three.
But natheles, if I can shape it so
That it departed were among us two,
Hadde I nat doon a freendes torn to thee?"   815
        That other answerde, "I noot how that may be:
He woot how that the gold is with us tweye.
What shal we doon? what shal we to him seye?"
        "Shal it be conseil?" seyde the firste shrewe;
"And I shal tellen in a wordes fewe   820
What we shal doon, and bringe it wel aboute."
"I graunte," quod that other, "out of doute,
That, by my trouthe, I wol thee nat biwreye."
        "Now," quod the firste, "thou woost wel we be tweye,
And two of us shul strenger be than oon.   825
Looke whan that he is set, that right anoon
Arys as though thou woldest with him pleye;
And I shal ryve him thurgh the sydes tweye
Whyl that thou strogelest with him as in game,
And with thy dagger looke thou do the same;   830
And thanne shall al this gold departed be,
My dere freend, bitwixen me and thee.
Thanne may we bothe oure lustes al fulfille,
And pleye at dees right at oure owene wille."
And thus acorded been thise shrewes tweye   835
To sleen the thridde, as ye han herd me seye.
        This yongest, which that wente unto the toun,
Ful ofte in herte he rolleth up and doun
The beautee of thise florins newe and brighte.
"O Lord!" quod he, "if so were that I mighte   840
Have al this tresor to myself allone,
Ther is no man that liveth under the trone
Of God that sholde live so mery as I!"
And atte laste the feend, our enemy,
Putte in his thought that he shold poyson beye,   845
With which he mighte sleen his felawes tweye—

Here is gold, and that in quite some plenty,   525
Which shall divided be among us three.
But nonetheless, if I can shape it so
It's divided between us two, you know,
Wouldn't I have done a good friend's turn to you?"
    The other said, "I don't know what you'll do.   530
He knows that with us both the gold did stay;
What shall we do? To him, what shall we say?"
    "Shall it be secret?" then said the first shrew.
"And I shall tell you now in words a few   820
What we shall do, and bring it well about."   535
"I grant it," said the other, "without doubt,
By my word, that I will not betray you."
    "Now," said the first, "You know well we are two,
And we two shall be stronger than one yet.
See to it, right away, when he is set,   540
Rise up just as though with him you would play;
I'll stab him through his two sides right away
While you struggle with him as though it's a game,
And with your dagger, see you do the same;   830
And then shall all this gold divided be,   545
My dear friend, only between you and me.
Then may we both all of our lusts fulfill,
And play at dice just as much as we will."
Thus these two shrews have one accord that day
To slay the third, as you have heard me say.   550
    This youngest one, who went into the town,
Quite often in his heart rolls up and down
The beauty of these florins new and bright.
"O Lord!" said he, "if it were so I might   840
Have all this treasure for myself alone,   555
There is no man who lives beneath the throne
Of God who would live quite so merrily!"
At last the fiend, who is our enemy,
Put in his thought that he should poison buy,
With which he might make his two fellows die;   560

For-why the feend fond him in swich lyvinge
That he had leve him to sorwe bringe:
For this was outrely his fulle entente,
To sleen hem bothe, and nevere to repente.   850
And forth he gooth—no lenger wolde he tarie—
Into the toun, unto a pothecarie,
And preyed him that he him wolde selle
Som poyson, that he mighte his rattes quelle,
And eek ther was a polcat in his hawe,   855
That, as he seyde, his capouns hadde y-slawe,
And fayn he wolde wreke him, if he mighte,
On vermin, that destroyed him by nighte.

     The pothecarie answerde, "And thou shalt have
A thing that, also God my soule save,   860
In al this world ther nis no creature,
That ete or dronke hath of this confiture
Noght but the mountance of a corn of whete,
That he ne shal his lyf anon forlete.
Ye, sterve he shal, and that in lasse whyle   865
Than thou wolt goon a paas nat but a myle,
This poyson is so strong and violent."

     This cursed man hath in his hond y-hent
This poyson in a box, and sith he ran
Into the nexte strete unto a man   870
And borwed [of] him large botels three,
And in the two his poyson poured he—
The thridde he kepte clene for his drinke—
For al the night he shoop him for to swinke
In caryinge of the gold out of that place.   875
And whan this ryotour, with sory grace,
Hadde filled with wyn his grete botels three,
To his felawes agayn repaireth he.

     What nedeth it to sermone of it more?
For right as they hadde cast his deeth bifore,   880
Right so they han him slayn, and that anon.
And whan that this was doon, thus spak that oon:

The fiend found him to live in such a way
That him to sorrow he could bring that day.
For this was utterly his full intent,
To slay them both, and never to repent. 850
Forth he goes, no longer would he tarry, 565
Into town, to an apothecary,
And prayed the man that to him he would sell
Some poison that would help to kill rats well;
And in his yard there was a weasel, who,
As he then said, had slain his capons, too. 570
He'd happily take vengeance, if he might,
On vermin that destroyed him in the night.
  Said the apothecary, "I will give
You something here, as God lets my soul live, 860
Such that, in this world, there's no single creature 575
Who has drunk or eaten of this mixture
One little grain or just the smallest bit,
Who won't find at once that his life's forfeit;
Yes, he will die, and in a shorter while
Than it will take you to walk but a mile, 580
This poison is so violent and strong."
  This cursed man in his hand took along
This poison in a box, and then he ran
Into a nearby street right to a man, 870
And borrowed from him there large bottles three, 585
And this poison in two of them poured he;
The third one he kept clean for his own drink.
For all that night, to work hard he did think
In carrying the gold out of that place.
And when this debaucher, with sorry grace, 590
Had with the wine filled the great bottles three,
Back to his fellows once again goes he.
  What need is there to preach about this more?
For just as they had planned his death before, 880
Quickly they slew him, and when it was done, 595
Then right away spoke up the other one:

"Now lat us sitte and drinke, and make us merie,
And afterward we wol his body berie."
And with that word it happed him, par cas,   885
To take the botel ther the poyson was,
And drank, and yaf his felawe drink also,
For which anon they storven bothe two.

      But certes, I suppose that Avicen
Wroot nevere in no canon, ne in no fen,   890
Mo wonder signes of empoisoning
Than hadde thise wrecches two, er hir ending.
Thus ended been thise homicydes two,
And eek the false empoysoner also.

      O cursed sinne of alle cursednesse!   895
O traytours homicyde, O wikkednesse!
O glotonye, luxurie, and hasardrye!
Thou blasphemour of Crist with vileinye
And othes grete, of usage and of pryde!
Allas! mankinde, how may it bityde   900
That to thy Creatour which that thee wroghte,
And with his precious herte-blood thee boghte,
Thou art so fals and so unkinde, allas!

      Now, goode men, God forgeve yow youre trespas,
And ware yow fro the sinne of avaryce.   905
Myn holy pardoun may yow alle waryce—
So that ye offre nobles or sterlinges,
Or elles silver broches, spones, ringes.
Boweth youre heed under this holy bulle!
Cometh up, ye wyves, offreth of youre wolle!   910
Youre names I entre heer in my rolle anon:
Into the blisse of hevene shul ye gon.
I yow assoile, by myn heigh power—
Yow that wol offre—as clene and eek as cleer
As ye were born.—And, lo, sires, thus I preche.   915

"Let us sit and drink and now make merry.
Afterward, we will his body bury."
And with that word, by chance, he did happen
To take up the bottle which held poison,   600
And drank, and gave drink to his fellow, too,
And thus at once they died, both of those two.
      Surely, I suppose that Avicenna[36]
Never wrote, in his treatise or fen,[37] a   890
More wondrous display of poisoning   605
Than these wretches showed before their ending.
Thus ended now are these two homicides,
And also the false poisoner besides.
      O cursed sin of all accursedness!
O homicidal traitors! O wickedness!   610
O gluttony! O gambling and lechery!
You blasphemer of Christ with villainy
And great oaths, through habit and through pride!
Alas, mankind, how may it be denied   900
That to your creator, who has you wrought   615
And with his precious heart's blood has you bought,
Against nature, you're false and unkind, alas?
      Now, good men, God forgive you your trespass.
Beware the sin of avarice so grave!
My holy pardon may you now all save,   620
If you offer coins of gold or sterling,
Or else a silver brooch or spoon or ring.
Bow your head now beneath this holy bull!
Come up, you wives, and offer me your wool!   910
Your names I enter in my roll right so;   625
Into the bliss of heaven shall you go.
I absolve you here through my high power,
To be clean and clear, you who will offer,
As when you were born.—Lo, sires, I thus preach then.

---

36 **Avicenna**: Tenth- to eleventh-century Persian doctor and medical author.
37 **fen**: The name for the sections into which Avicenna divided his medical treatise.

And Jesu Crist, that is our soules leche,
So graunte yow his pardon to receyve,
For that is best; I wol yow nat deceyve.
      But sires, o word forgat I in my tale:
I have relikes and pardon in my male   920
As faire as any man in Engelond,
Whiche were me yeven by the Popes hond.
If any of yow wol of devocioun
Offren and han myn absolucioun,
Cometh forth anon, and kneleth heer adoun,   925
And mekely receyveth my pardoun;
Or elles, taketh pardon as ye wende,
Al newe and fresh, at every myles ende—
So that ye offren alwey newe and newe
Nobles or pens, which that be gode and trewe.   930
It is an honour to everich that is heer
That ye mowe have a suffisant pardoneer
T'assoille yow, in contree as ye ryde,
For aventures whiche that may bityde.
Peraventure ther may falle oon or two   935
Doun of his hors, and breke his nekke atwo.
Look which a seuretee is it to you alle
That I am in youre felaweship y-falle,
That may assoille yow, bothe more and lasse,
Whan that the soule shal fro the body passe.   940
I rede that oure Host heer shal biginne,
For he is most envoluped in sinne.
Com forth, sire Hoste, and offre first anon,
And thou shalt kisse the reliks everichon,
Ye, for a grote: unbokel anon thy purs."   945
      "Nay, nay," quod he, "thanne have I Cristes curs!
Lat be," quod he, "it shal nat be, so theech!

Now Jesus Christ, who is our soul's physician, 630
Grant to you his pardon to receive,
For that is best; I will you not deceive.
    But, sires, one word I forgot in my tale:
My bag holds pardons and relics for sale, 920
As fair as has any man in England, 635
Which were given me by the pope's own hand.
If anyone wants, out of devotion,
To offer and have my absolution,
Come forth now and kneel down here, everyone,
And meekly you can receive my pardon; 640
Or you can take my pardon as you wend,
All new and fresh, as every mile does end,
As long as you give, and always renew,
Nobles[38] or pence, which are both good and true. 930
To each one who's here, it is an honor 645
For you to have a sufficient pardoner
To absolve you in this land as you ride
For whatever happens by the wayside.
Perhaps there may fall one or two of you
Down from his horse and break his neck in two. 650
Look what security it's for you all
That I into your fellowship did fall,
Who may absolve you, the more and the less,
When the soul may from your body pass.[39] 940
I advise that our Host shall here begin 655
Because he is most enveloped in sin.
Come forth, sir Host; to give be the first one,
And you shall kiss the relics every one,
Yes, for a groat! Now unbuckle your purse."
    "No! No!" said he, "then may I have Christ's curse! 660
Leave it," said he, "it shall not be, I swear!

---

38 **Nobles**: Gold coins.

39 **When the soul . . .**: In these lines, the Pardoner is claiming that he can offer sacraments like absolution and the last rites that only the clergy were authorized to administer.

Thou woldest make me kisse thyn olde breech

And swere it were a relik of a seint,

Thogh it were with thy fundement depeint!   950

But by the croys which that Seint Eleyne fond,

I wolde I hadde thy coillons in myn hond

In stede of relikes or of seintuarie.

Lat cutte hem of ! I wol thee helpe hem carie.

Thay shul be shryned in an hogges tord!"   955

      This Pardoner answerde nat a word;

So wrooth he was, no word ne wolde he seye.

      "Now," quod our Host, "I wol no lenger pleye

With thee, ne with noon other angry man."

But right anon the worthy Knight bigan,   960

Whan that he saugh that al the peple lough,

"Namore of this, for it is right ynough!

Sire Pardoner, be glad and mery of chere;

And ye, sire Host, that been to me so dere,

I prey yow that ye kisse the Pardoner.   965

And Pardoner, I prey thee, drawe thee neer,

And, as we diden, lat us laughe and pleye."

Anon they kiste, and riden forth hir weye.

Heere is ended the Pardoners Tale.

You would make me kiss your old underwear,
And swear it was the relic of a saint,
Though on it with your asshole you did paint!   950
Now, by Saint Helen's cross,[40] you understand,   665
I wish I had your balls right in my hand
Instead of relics in their reliquary.
Let them be cut off! Them, I'll help you carry!
They'll be enshrined for good in a hog's turd!"

      This Pardoner answered back not one word;   670
So angry he was, no word would he say.

      "Now," said our Host, "I will no longer play
With you, or with another angry man."
But right away the worthy Knight began,   960
When he saw all of the people laughing,   675
"No more of this, for enough of this thing!
Sir Pardoner, be glad and of good cheer;
And you, sir Host, who are to me so dear,
I pray you the Pardoner to kiss here.
And Pardoner, I pray you, draw you near.   680
As we have done, now let us laugh and play."
At once they kissed and rode forth on their way.

Here is ended the Pardoner's Tale.

---

40 **Saint Helen's cross**: Helen (third to fourth century) was Emperor Constantine's mother. It
was believed she found Christ's cross.

THE PRIORESS'S PROLOGUE

Domine, dominus noster.

     O Lord, oure Lord, thy name how merveillous
Is in this large worlde y-sprad—quod she—
For noght only thy laude precious   455
Parfourned is by men of dignitee,
But by the mouth of children thy bountee
Parfourned is, for on the brest soukinge
Somtyme shewen they thyn heryinge.

Wherfore in laude, as I best can or may,   460
Of thee, and of the whyte lily flour
Which that thee bar, and is a mayde alway,
To telle a storie I wol do my labour;
Not that I may encresen hir honour,
For she hirself is honour, and the rote   465
Of bountee, next hir sone, and soules bote.

THE PRIORESS'S PROLOGUE

Domine, dominus noster.
[*Oh Lord, our Lord.*]

Oh Lord, our Lord, thy name how marvelous
Is all throughout this large world spread—said she—
For not only is thy praising precious
Performed often by men of dignity,
But through the mouths of children thy bounty   5
Performed is, for while on the breast sucking,
Sometime they will also show thy praising.

Wherefore in praise, as I best know or may,   460
Of thee and the same white lily flower
Who bore thee, and remains a maid always,   10
To tell a story, I will do my labor;
Not so that I may increase her honor,
For she herself is honor, and root sure
Of bounty, next her Son, and our soul's cure.

O moder mayde! o mayde moder free!
O bush unbrent, brenninge in Moyses sighte,
That ravysedest doun fro the deitee,
Thurgh thyn humblesse, the goost that in th'alighte,   470
Of whos vertu, whan he thyn herte lighte,
Conceived was the Fadres sapience,
Help me to telle it in thy reverence!

Lady, thy bountee, thy magnificence,
Thy vertu, and thy grete humilitee,   475
Ther may no tonge expresse in no science;
For somtyme, lady, er men praye to thee,
Thou goost biforn of thy benignitee,
And getest us the light, of thy preyere,
To gyden us unto thy Sone so dere.   480

My conning is so wayk, o blisful Quene,
For to declare thy grete worthinesse,
That I ne may the weighte nat sustene;
But as a child of twelf monthe old, or lesse,
That can unnethes any word expresse,   485
Right so fare I, and therfor I yow preye,
Gydeth my song that I shal of yow seye.

Explicit.

Oh mother Maid, and Oh maid Mother free! 15
Oh bush unburned,[1] burning in Moses's sight,
Who ravished here down from the Deity,
Through humbleness, the Ghost who did alight 470
In thee, from whom, when thy heart he did light,
Conceived was then the wisdom of the Father, 20
Help me now to tell it in thy honor!

Lady, thy bounty, thy magnificence,
Thy strength and all thy great humility
No learnèd tongue may tell with eloquence;
Sometimes, Lady, before men pray to thee, 25
Thou go before, from thy benignity,
And get for us the light of thy prayer
To guide us all unto thy dear Son there. 480

My learning is so weak, Oh blissful Queen,
For me to declare thy great worthiness, 30
I can't sustain the weight of what I mean;
But as a child of twelve months old or less,
Who cannot hardly any word express,
Just so fare I, and therefore I you pray,
Guide here my song that I shall of you say. 35

It is done.

---

1 **bush unburned**: Moses's burning bush, which kept burning but was not consumed by fire (Exodus 3:1–5), was taken as an Old Testament symbol of the miraculous physical paradox of Mary and the virgin birth.

THE PRIORESS'S TALE

Heere bigynneth the Prioresses Tale.

Ther was in Asie, in a greet citee,
Amonges Cristen folk, a Jewerye
Sustened by a lord of that contree   490
For foule usure and lucre of vileynye,
Hateful to Crist and to his compaignye;
And thurgh the strete men mighte ryde or wende,
For it was free, and open at either ende.

A litel scole of Cristen folk ther stood   495
Doun at the ferther ende, in which ther were
Children an heep, y-comen of Cristen blood,
That lerned in that scole yeer by yere
Swich manere doctrine as men used there—
This is to seyn, to singen and to rede,   500
As smale children doon in hire childhede.

THE PRIORESS'S TALE

Here begins the Prioress's Tale.

There was in Asia, in a great city,
Among Christian folk, a certain Jewry,[2]
Sustained then by a lord of that country   490
For shameful lucre and foul usury,
Hateful to Christ and to his company;   40
Men through this ghetto's street could ride or wend,
For it was free and open at both ends.

A little school of Christian folk did stand
Down at the farther end, and there were here
Heaps of children from Christian blood at hand,   45
Who in that school were learning, year by year,
The kind of doctrine that men did use here,
This is to say, to sing and to read, too,   500
As in their childhood small children will do.

---

2   **Jewry**: Jewish ghetto.

Among thise children was a widwes sone,
A litel clergeoun, seven yeer of age,
That day by day to scole was his wone,
And eek also, where as he saugh th'ymage   505
Of Cristes moder, hadde he in usage,
As him was taught, to knele adoun and seye
His *Ave Marie*, as he goth by the weye.

Thus hath this widwe hir litel sone y-taught
Our blisful Lady, Cristes moder dere,   510
To worshipe ay; and he forgat it naught,
For sely child wol alday sone lere.
But ay, whan I remembre on this matere,
Seint Nicholas stant evere in my presence,
For he so yong to Crist did reverence.   515

This litel child, his litel book lerninge,
As he sat in the scole at his prymer,
He *Alma redemptoris* herde singe,
As children lerned hire antiphoner,
And, as he dorste, he drough him ner and ner,   520
And herkned ay the wordes and the note,
Til he the firste vers coude al by rote.

Noght wiste he what this Latin was to seye,
For he so yong and tendre was of age;
But on a day his felaw gan he preye   525
T'expounden him this song in his langage,
Or telle him why this song was in usage;
This preyde he him to construe and declare
Ful ofte tyme upon his knowes bare.

Among these children was a widow's son,   50
A little scholar seven years of age;
To go to school each day, he had begun,
And wherever he might see the image
Of Christ's mother, it became his usage,
As he was taught, to kneel right down and say   55
Ave Maria,³ as he makes his way.

Thus has this widow her little son well taught
Our blissful Lady, who is Christ's dear mother,   510
To worship always, and he forgot naught;
The innocent child always learns the sooner.   60
Always, when this matter I remember,
Saint Nicholas⁴ stands ever in my presence,
Who, so young, did to Christ his reverence.

This little child, his little book well learning,
As he sat in school there with his primer,   65
The *Alma redemptoris*⁵ he heard sing,
As children learned antiphons together;
As he dared, he drew himself then closer,   520
And listened always to the words and notes,
Until the first verse he knew all by rote.   70

He knew not what this Latin meant to say,
For he so young and tender was of age.
But on one day, his schoolmate he did pray
To expound this song in his own language,
Or to tell why this song was in usage;   75
He prayed him to construe and to declare,
This to him, kneeling down on his knees bare.

3   *Ave Maria*: Hail Mary, the beginning of the most important prayer to the Virgin.
4   **Saint Nicholas**: Patron saint of school children
5   *Alma redemptoris*: "Gracious Mother of the Redeemer," a hymn to the Virgin Mary.

His felawe, which that elder was than he,   530
Answerde him thus: "This song, I have herd seye,
Was maked of our blisful Lady free,
Hire to salue, and eek hire for to preye
To been oure help and socour whan we dye.
I can no more expounde in this matere: 535
I lerne song, I can but smal grammere."

"And is this song maked in reverence
Of Cristes moder?" seyde this innocent.
"Now certes, I wol do my diligence
To conne it al, er Cristemasse be went.   540
Though that I for my prymer shal be shent,
And shal be beten thryes in an houre,
I wol it conne, oure Lady for to honoure."

His felaw taughte him homward prively,
Fro day to day, til he coude it by rote,   545
And thanne he song it wel and boldely
Fro word to word, acording with the note;
Twyes a day it passed thurgh his throte,
To scoleward and homward whan he wente.
On Cristes moder set was his entente.   550

As I have seyd, thurghout the Jewerye
This litel child, as he cam to and fro,
Ful merily than wolde he singe and crye
O Alma redemptoris everemo.
The swetnesse his herte perced so   555
Of Cristes moder, that, to hire to preye,
He can nat stinte of singing by the weye.

This schoolmate, who was older than he, 530
Answered him thus: "This song, I have heard say,
Was made about our blissful Lady free, 80
Her to salute, and also her to pray
For help and succor on our dying day.
I cannot expound more on this matter.
I learned the song; I know little grammar."

"And is this song then made in reverence 85
Of Christ's dear mother?" said this innocent.
"Now, truly, I will use my diligence
To learn the whole thing before Christmas went. 540
Though skipping lessons gets me punishment,
And being beaten thrice within an hour, 90
I will learn it Our Lady to honor!"

Homeward, his schoolmate taught him privately,
From day to day, till he knew it by rote;
Then he sang it all so well and boldly,
Both word for word and matching all the notes. 95
So twice a day it passed now through his throat,
Both schoolward and back homeward, when he went;
All on Christ's mother set was his intent. 550

As I have said before, through the Jewry
This little child, as he came to and fro, 100
Then he would sing and cry quite merrily
O *Alma redemptoris* as he'd go.
The sweetness throughout his heart did pierce so
Of Christ's dear mother that, to her to pray,
He cannot stop his singing on his way. 105

Oure firste fo, the serpent Sathanas,
That hath in Jewes herte his waspes nest,
Up swal and seide, "O Hebraik peple, allas!   560
Is this to yow a thing that is honest,
That swich a boy shal walken as him lest
In youre despyt, and singe of swich sentence,
Which is agayn oure lawes reverence?"

Fro thennes forth the Jewes han conspyred   565
This innocent out of this world to chace:
An homicyde therto han they hyred,
That in an aley hadde a privee place;
And as the child gan forby for to pace,
This cursed Jew him hente and heeld him faste,   570
And kitte his throte, and in a pit him caste.

I seye that in a wardrobe they him threwe
Where as these Jewes purgen hir entraille.
O cursed folk of Herodes al newe,
What may youre yvel entente yow availle?   575
Mordre wol out, certein, it wol nat faille,
And namely ther th'onour of God shal sprede,
The blood out cryeth on your cursed dede.

O martir souded to virginitee,
Now maystou singen, folwinge evere in oon   580
The Whyte Lamb celestial—quod she—
Of which the grete evangelist Seint John
In Pathmos wroot, which seith that they that goon
Biforn this Lamb and singe a song al newe,
That nevere, fleshly, wommen they ne knewe.   585

Our first foe, that is, the serpent Satan,
Who has within the Jews' hearts his wasps' nest,
Swelled up, and said, "Alas, oh Hebrew men!   560
Is this to you a thing that is honest,
That such a boy will walk as he likes best   110
To spite you, and sing of such a subject,
Which goes against your laws and their respect?"

From that time forward, the Jews have conspired
This innocent out of this world to snare.
And a murderer, therefore, they have hired,   115
Who, in an alley, had a private lair;
And as the child right by that spot passed there,
This cursed Jew him seized, and held him fast,   570
And cut his throat, and in a pit him cast.

I say that in a privy they him threw,   120
There where all these Jews have purged their entrails.
Oh such cursed folk, oh you Herods[6] new,
Your evil intent, what may it avail?
Murder will out, in truth; it will not fail,
And namely, where God's honor spreads indeed;   125
The blood cries out upon your cursed deed.

Oh martyr, soldered to virginity,
Now may thou sing, attending always on   580
The one white Lamb celestial—said she—
Of which the great evangelist, Saint John,[7]   130
On Patmos wrote, who says those who move on
Before this Lamb, they sing a song all new—
For carnally, they never women knew.

6   **Herods new**: King Herod ordered all newborn children to be killed around the time of Christ's birth.
7   **Saint John**: Author on whose vision of the Last Judgment and the end of time the Book of Revelations is based. This is the basis for the idea of the company of the Lamb following Christ in heaven and composed of 144,000 virgins (14:1 ff.).

This povre widwe awaiteth al that night
After hir litel child, but he cam noght;
For which, as sone as it was dayes light,
With face pale of drede and bisy thoght,
She hath at scole and elleswhere him soght,   590
Til finally she gan so fer espye
That he last seyn was in the Jewerye.

With modres pitee in hir brest enclosed,
She gooth, as she were half out of hir minde,
To every place wher she hath supposed   595
By lyklihede hir litel child to finde.
And evere on Cristes moder meke and kinde
She cryde, and atte laste thus she wroghte:
Among the cursed Jewes she him soghte.

She frayneth and she preyeth pitously   600
To every Jew that dwelte in thilke place,
To telle hire if hir child wente oght forby.
They seyde "Nay"; but Jesu, of his grace,
Yaf in hir thought, inwith a litel space,
That in that place after hir sone she cryde   605
Where he was casten in a pit bisyde.

O grete God, that parfournest thy laude
By mouth of innocents, lo heer thy might!
This gemme of chastitee, this emeraude,
And eek of martirdom the ruby bright,   610
Ther he with throte y-corven lay upright,
He *Alma redemptoris* gan to singe
So loude that al the place gan to ringe.

Thus, this poor widow waited all the night
For her little child, but it was for naught;   135
And so, as soon as it should be daylight,
With face all pale from dread and anxious thoughts,
She at the school and elsewhere has him sought,   590
Until finally she began to see
He had last been spied there in the Jewry.   140

With a mother's pity in her breast enclosed,
She goes as though she's half out of her mind,
To every place where she has now supposed
A likelihood her little child to find;
And ever on Christ's mother meek and kind   145
She cried, and finally, she has thus wrought:
Among the cursèd Jews, she has him sought.

She asks there, and piteously she prays   600
To every Jew who dwells within that place,
To tell her if her child went by that way.   150
They told her "No"; but Jesus, by his grace,
Put in her thought within a moment's space
That in the place where to her son she cried,
He had been cast into a pit besides.

Oh great God, who thy praising does herald   155
Through mouths of innocents, lo, hear thy might!
This gem of chastity, this emerald,
And, too, of martyrdom the ruby bright,   610
There where, with throat cut through, he lay upright,
Alma redemptoris began to sing   160
So loudly all the place with it did ring.

The Cristen folk, that thurgh the strete wente,
In coomen for to wondre upon this thing,   615
And hastily they for the provost sente;
He cam anon withouten tarying,
And herieth Crist that is of heven king,
And eek his moder, honour of mankinde,
And after that the Jewes leet he binde.   620

This child with pitous lamentacioun
Up taken was, singing his song alway;
And with honour of greet processioun
They carien him unto the nexte abbay.
His moder swowning by his bere lay.   625
Unnethe might the peple that was there
This newe Rachel bringe fro his bere.

With torment and with shamful deth echon
This provost dooth thise Jewes for to sterve
That of this mordre wiste, and that anon;   630
He nolde no swich cursednesse observe.
"Yvel shal have that yvel wol deserve:"
Therfore with wilde hors he dide hem drawe,
And after that he heng hem by the lawe.

Upon his bere al lyth this innocent   635
Biforn the chief auter, whyl the masse laste,
And after that, the abbot with his covent
Han sped hem for to burien him ful faste;
And whan they holy water on him caste,
Yet spak this child, whan spreynd was holy water,   640
And song O Alma redemptoris mater!

The Christian folk who throughout that street went
Were coming in to wonder on this thing,
And quickly for the magistrate they sent;
He came at once with no more tarrying,   165
And praises Christ who is of heaven king,
And his mother the honor of mankind,
And after gave the call the Jews to bind.   620

This child, with piteous lamentation
Was taken up, singing his song always.   170
With the honor of a great procession,
To a nearby abbey, they take him that day.
His mother, swooning, by his bier did lay;
And hardly might the people who were near
This new Rachel[8] bring away from his bier.   175

With torture and with shameful death besides,
This magistrate has all the Jews well served
Who of this murder knew; he'd not abide   630
And he would not such cursedness observe.
Evil they have who evil will deserve;   180
And thus he did with wild horses them draw,
And then hung them according to the law.

Upon his bier still lies the innocent
In front of the high altar while mass lasts;
Then the abbot and the monks in convent   185
Hurried themselves to bury him quite fast;
And when they holy water on him cast,
He still spoke, sprinkled with holy water,   640
And sung *Alma redemptoris mater*!

---

8   **Rachel:** See Matthew 2:18; Rachel is the biblical archetype of the mother grieving her child's
death.

This abbot, which that was an holy man
As monkes been—or elles oghten be—
This yonge child to conjure he bigan,
And seyde, "O dere child, I halse thee,   645
In vertu of the Holy Trinitee,
Tel me what is thy cause for to singe,
Sith that thy throte is cut, to my seminge?"

"My throte is cut unto my nekke-boon,"
Seyde this child, "and, as by wey of kinde,   650
I sholde have deyed, ye, longe tyme agoon,
But Jesu Crist, as ye in bokes finde,
Wil that his glorie laste and be in minde;
And for the worship of his moder dere
Yet may I singe *O Alma* loude and clere.   655

This welle of mercy, Cristes moder swete,
I lovede alwey as after my conninge;
And whan that I my lyf sholde forlete,
To me she cam, and bad me for to singe
This antem verraily in my deyinge,   660
As ye han herd; and whan that I had songe,
Me thoughte she leyde a greyn upon my tonge.

Wherfore I singe, and singe moot certeyn,
In honour of that blisful mayden free,
Til fro my tonge of taken is the greyn;   665
And afterward thus seyde she to me,
'My litel child, now wol I fecche thee
Whan that the greyn is fro thy tongue y-take;
Be nat agast, I wol thee nat forsake.'"

This abbot, now, who was a holy man,   190
As monks are—or else as they ought to be—
This little child to entreat he began,
And said, "Oh now, dear child, I beg of thee,
By virtue of the Holy Trinity,
Tell me now the reason for your singing,   195
Since your throat is cut, as it is seeming?"

"My throat is cut down down to my neck bone,"
Said this child, "and in way of nature's kind   650
I should have died some time past, as is known.
But Jesus Christ, as you in books may find,   200
Wills that his glory lasts and stays in mind,
And for the worship of his Mother dear
Still may I sing *O Alma* loud and clear.

This well of mercy, Christ's sweet mother dear,
I always loved, according to my learning.   205
When it was time my life I should lose here,
She came to me and bade that I should sing
This anthem truly as I was dying,   660
As you have heard, and when I had it sung,
I thought she laid a grain upon my tongue.

Thus I sing, and sing I must for certain,   211
In honor of that blissful Maiden free
Till from off my tongue the grain is taken;
And after that, thus has she said to me:
'My little child, so now will I fetch thee   215
When that grain from off thy tongue they take.
Don't be afraid; I will not thee forsake.' "

This holy monk, this abbot, him mene I,   670
His tongue out caughte and took awey the greyn,
And he yaf up the goost ful softely.
And whan this abbot had this wonder seyn,
His salte teres trikled doun as reyn,
And gruf he fil al plat upon the grounde,   675
And stille he lay as he had been y-bounde.

The covent eek lay on the pavement,
Weping and herying Cristes moder dere,
And after that they ryse, and forth ben went,
And toke awey this martir fro his bere,   680
And in a tombe of marbulstones clere
Enclosen they his litel body swete.
Ther he is now, God leve us for to mete.

O yonge Hugh of Lincoln, slayn also
With cursed Jewes, as it is notable—   685
For it nis but a litel whyle ago—
Preye eek for us, we sinful folk unstable,
That, of his mercy, God so merciable
On us his grete mercy multiplye,
For reverence of his moder Marye. Amen.   690

Heere is ended the Prioresses Tale.

This holy monk, I mean this abbot, he   670
Stretched out his tongue, and took away the grain,
And he then gave up the ghost quite softly.   220
And when this abbot saw this wonder plain,
His salty tears all trickled down like rain,
And facedown he fell flat upon the ground,
And he lay still as if he had been bound.

The convent too lay upon the pavement⁹   225
Weeping, and praising then Christ's mother dear,
And after that, they rose, and forth they went,
And took away this martyr from his bier;   680
And in a tomb of marble bright and clear
Enclosed they have his little body sweet.   230
There he is now; God grant that we him meet!

Oh young Hugh of Lincoln,¹⁰ slain also
By cursed Jews, as it is notable,
Since it was but a little while ago,
Pray for us, unstable folk so sinful,   235
That of his mercy God so merciful
On us multiply his full great mercy,
For the reverence of his mother Mary. Amen   690

Here is ended the Prioress's Tale.

9   **lay upon the pavement:** All the members of the monastery lie prostrate on the stone floor of
the church, in humility, self-abasement, and awe before the miracle they are witnessing.
10   **Hugh of Lincoln:** Child erroneously believed to have been murdered by Jews in Lincoln in
1255, allegedly for purposes of human sacrifice, or blood libel: that is, using a Christian child's blood
for sacramental purposes. He became a child martyr, although his body was eventually discovered in
a well into which he had fallen.

THE PROLOGUE OF SIR THOPAS

Bihoold the murye wordes of the Hoost to Chaucer.

Whan seyd was al this miracle, every man
As sobre was that wonder was to se,
Til that our Hoste japen tho bigan,
And than at erst he loked upon me
And seyde thus: "What man artow?" quod he.   695
"Thou lokest as thou woldest finde an hare,
For ever upon the ground I see thee stare.

Approche neer and loke up merily.
Now war yow, sirs, and lat this man have place.
He in the waast is shape as wel as I.   700
This were a popet in an arm t'enbrace
For any womman, smal and fair of face.
He semeth elvish by his contenaunce,
For unto no wight dooth he daliaunce.

PROLOGUE TO SIR THOPAS

Behold the merry words of the Host to Chaucer.

When this miracle[1] was all told, every man
So sober was, it wondrous was to see,
Until our Host to jest then he began,
And so at first, he did look straight at me,
And asked me thus: "What man are you?" said he;   5
"You look as though you want to find a hare,
For always on the ground I see you stare.

Approach nearer, and look up merrily.
Now watch out, sirs, and let this man have space!
For in the waist, he's shaped as well as me[2];   10 [700]
He'd be a poppet[3] in arms to embrace
For any woman, small and fair of face.
And he seems elfish by his countenance,
For with no one makes he dalliance.

1 **miracle:** The Miracle of the Virgin story related by the Prioress in her tale, which immediately precedes the tales of Chaucer's eponymous pilgrim-narrator.

2 **shaped as well as me:** Both the Host, Harry Bailley, and Chaucer are well girthed, as Harry notes here.

3 **poppet:** Small doll.

Sey now somwhat, sin other folk han sayd.

Tel us a tale of mirthe, and that anoon."

"Hoste," quod I, "ne beth nat yvel apayd,

For other tale certes can I noon,

But of a ryme I lerned longe agoon."

"Ye, that is good," quod he. "Now shul we here

Som deyntee thing, me thinketh by his chere."

Say something now, since other folks have said;   15
Tell us a tale of mirth, and quickly so."
"Host," said I, "do not be irritated,
For any other tale, I do not know,
Except a rhyme I learned once long ago."
"Yes, that is good," said he; "now shall we hear   20 [710]
Some delightful thing, it seems by his cheer."

THE TALE

Heere bigynneth Chaucers Tale of Thopas.

THE FIRST FIT

Listeth, lordes, in good entent,
And I wol telle verrayment
    Of mirthe and of solas:
Al of a knyght was fair and gent   715
In bataille and in tourneyment;
    His name was sir Thopas.

Y-born he was in fer contree,
In Flaundres al biyonde the see,
    At Popering, in the place.   720
His fader was a man ful free,
And lord he was of that contree,
    As it was Goddes grace.

SIR THOPAS

Here begins Chaucer's Tale of Sir Thopas.[4]

THE FIRST FIT[5]

Listen, lords, with good intent,
And I will tell true as I meant
    About mirth and solace,
All of a knight, fair and elegant   25
In battle and in tournament;
    His name was Sir Thopas.[6]

He was born in a far country,
In Flanders, all beyond the sea,
    At Popering,[7] in that place.   30 [720]
His father was a man noble and free,
And lord he was of that country,
    As it was God's grace.

---

   4   *Tale of Sir Thopas:* Chaucer's tale is a parody of the genre of minstrel romance, a populariza-tion of the romance genre that was current as entertainment outside aristocratic circles in the late Middle Ages. In this parody of a genre that is itself a revision from romance's aristocratic origins, this tale's "hero" is deliberately made inept, as is the rhyme and meter, the plot, the diction: in short, the entire outrageous performance. In giving himself this tale, Chaucer has created an exaggerated parody.

   5   **FIT:** Section of a narrative poem.

   6   **Thopas:** Topaz, the semiprecious stone.

   7   **Popering:** Market town in Flanders.

Sir Thopas wex a doghty swayn.
Whyt was his face as payndemayn,   725
     His lippes rede as rose.
His rode is lyk scarlet in grayn,
And I yow telle in good certayn,
     He hadde a semely nose.

His heer, his berd was lyk saffroun,   730
That to his girdel raughte adoun;
     His shoon of Cordewane.
Of Brugges were his hosen broun,
His robe was of ciclatoun,
     That coste many a jane.   735

He coude hunte at wilde deer,
And ryde an hauking for riveer
     With grey goshauk on honde.
Therto he was a good archeer;
Of wrastling was ther noon his peer,   740
     Ther any ram shal stonde.

Ful many a mayde, bright in bour,
They moorne for him paramour,
     Whan hem were bet to slepe.
But he was chast and no lechour,   745
And sweet as is the bremble-flour
     That bereth the rede hepe.

Sir Thopas waxed a doughty youth in might;
His face like fine wheat bread was white,   35
     His lips red as the rose;
His complexion's like deep-dyed scarlet bright,
And I tell you for certain, as is right,
     He had a seemly nose.

His hair, his beard were like saffron,   40 [730]
That to his girdle fell upon;
     His shoes of Cordovan leather.
From Bruges the brown hose he did don,
His robe with silk and gold was woven on,   44
     Which cost many janes⁸ of silver.

He could hunt for the wild deer,
And ride to hawk for fowl on the river
     With a gray goshawk on hand;
And he was also a good archer;
In wrestling, no one was his peer,   50 [740]
     When as prize a ram⁹ did stand.

So many a maid, bright in bower,
They yearn for him as paramour,
     When they'd be better off asleep;
But he was chaste and not a lecher,   55
Sweet like a wild rose or bramble flower
     That of red hips bears a heap.

---

8   **janes**: Genoese coins.

9   **ram**: Often the prize at a wrestling match, as is evident in the Miller's portrait in *The General Prologue*.

And so bifel upon a day,
For sothe, as I yow telle may,
  Sir Thopas wolde out ryde.   750
He worth upon his stede gray,
And in his honde a launcegay,
  A long swerd by his syde.

He priketh thurgh a fair forest,
Therinne is many a wilde best,   755
  Ye, bothe bukke and hare;
And as he priketh north and est,
I telle it yow, him hadde almest
  Bitid a sory care.

Ther springen herbes grete and smale,   760
The lycorys and cetewale,
  And many a clowe-gilofre;
And notemuge to putte in ale,
Whether it be moyste or stale,
  Or for to leye in cofre.   765

The briddes singe, it is no nay,
The sparhauk and the papeiay,
  That joye it was to here.
The thrustelcok made eek his lay,
The wodedowve upon the spray   770
  She sang ful loude and clere.

Sir Thopas fil in love-longinge
Al whan he herde the thrustel singe,
  And priked as he were wood.
His faire stede in his prikinge   775
So swatte that men mighte him wringe;
  His sydes were al blood.

And so it happened on a day,
Truly, as now I tell you may,
  Sir Thopas wished to ride.   60 [750]
He climbed upon his steed of gray,[10]
And in his hand, a parade lance[11] gay,
  A long sword by his side.

He pricks through a fair forest,
In which many wild beasts rest,   65
  Yes, both buck and hare;
And as he pricks north and west,
I tell it to you, to him almost
  Befell a sorry care.

There spring herbs both great and frail,   70 [760]
Licorice and zedoary in the dale,
  And many a clove all over;
And nutmeg to put in ale,
Whether it's moist and fresh, or stale,
  Or to lay in a coffer.   75

The birds sing, it's no lie I say,
The sparrow hawk and popinjay,
  So a joy it was to hear;
The cock thrush also made their lay,
The wood pigeon upon the spray,   80 [770]
  She sang quite loud and clear.

Sir Thopas fell into a love-longing,
All when he heard the cock thrush sing,
  And pricked like he were mad.
His fair steed, from all his pricking,   85
Sweat so much that men might him out wring,
  His sides so much bled had.

---

10 **steed of gray**: Color associated with a workhorse, not a chivalric warhorse.
11 **parade lance**: Unsuitable for battle, but only for decoration.

Sir Thopas eek so wery was
For prikinge on the softe gras
      (So fiers was his corage)   780
That doun he leyde him in that plas
To make his stede som solas,
      And yaf him good forage.

"O seinte Marie, *benedicite!*
What eyleth this love at me   785
      To binde me so sore?
Me dremed al this night, pardee,
An elf-queen shal my lemman be,
      And slepe under my gore.

An elf-queen wol I love, ywis,   790
For in this world no womman is
      Worthy to be my make
              In toune.
Alle othere wommen I forsake,
And to an elf-queen I me take   795
      By dale and eek by doune."

Into his sadel he clamb anoon
And priketh over style and stoon
      An elf-queen for t'espye,
Til he so longe had riden and goon   800
That he fond, in a privee woon,
      The contree of Fairye
              So wilde.
For in that contree was ther noon
That to him dorste ryde or goon—   805
      Neither wyf ne childe—

Sir Thopas so weary was
From pricking on the soft grass,
  So fierce were his vigor and courage,   90 [780]
That he laid himself down where he was
To give his steed then some solace,
  And he gave him good forage.

"Oh please bless me, Saint Mary!
What is it that love has against me   95
  To bind me so tight?
I dreamed all this night, as God may see,
That an elf-queen shall my mistress be,
  And sleep under my robe at night.

An elf-queen will I love truly,   100 [790]
For in this world no woman may be
  Worthy my mate to make
    In town;
All other women I forsake,
And I to an elf-queen myself take   105
  Over hill and down!"

Into his saddle he climbs a while,
And pricks over stone and stile
  So an elf-queen he can see,
Till he rode so long for many a mile   110 [800]
That he found, as in a private isle,
  The country of Fairy
    So wild;
For in that country was no one for many a mile
Who dared to ride against him in any style,   115
  Neither wife nor child;

Til that ther cam a greet geaunt;
His name was sir Olifaunt,
    A perilous man of dede.
He seyde, "Child, by Termagaunt,   810
But if thou prike out of myn haunt,
    Anon I slee thy stede
        With mace.
Heer is the queen of Fayerye,
With harpe and pype and simphonye   815
    Dwelling in this place."

The child seyde, "Also mote I thee,
Tomorwe wol I mete thee
    Whan I have myn armoure;
And yet I hope, *par ma fay*,   820
That thou shalt with this launcegay
    Abyen it ful soure.
        Thy mawe
Shal I percen, if I may,
Er it be fully pryme of day,   825
    For heer thou shalt be slawe."

Sir Thopas drow abak ful faste;
This geaunt at him stones caste
    Out of a fel staf-slinge.
But faire escapeth child Thopas,   830
And al it was thurgh Goddes gras
    And thurgh his fair beringe.

Until there came a great giant,
His name was Sir Elephant,
    A perilous man in deed.
He said, "Child, by the Saracen idol Termagaunt,[12]   120 [810]
Unless you prick out of my haunt
    At once, I slay your steed
        With a mace.
Here is the queen of Fairy,
With harp and pipe and symphony,   125
    Dwelling in this place."

The Child said, "As I'd prosper, I swear,
Tomorrow will I meet you there,
    When I have my armor;
And yet I hope, *par ma fay*,[13]   130 [820]
That you shall with my parade lance gay
    Pay for it with sorrow more.
        Your maw
Shall I pierce, if I may,
Before it's nine o'clock that day,   135
    You'll be slain here with that draw."

Sir Thopas drew back very fast;
This giant at him stones did cast
    Out of a terrible slingshot.
But fairly escapes Sir Thopas,   140 [830]
And it was all through God's grace,
    And through what his fair bearing got.

12 **Termagaunt**: According to medieval Christian belief and interpretation, the Islamic Saracens were supposed to be polytheistic and worship multiple gods. They therefore worshipped not only Mohammed (Middle English: Mahomet), but also Apollo and Termagaunt, whose identity is not defined.

13 *par ma fay*: By my faith.

The Second Fit

Yet listeth, lordes, to my tale
Merier than the nightingale,
     For now I wol yow roune   835
How sir Thopas, with sydes smale,
Priking over hil and dale,
     Is come agayn to toune.

His merie men comanded he
To make him bothe game and glee,   840
     For nedes moste he fight
With a geaunt with hevedes three,
For paramour and jolitee
     Of oon that shoon ful brighte.

"Do come," he seyde, "my minstrales,   845
And gestours for to tellen tales—
     Anon in myn arminge—
Of romances that been royales,
Of popes and of cardinales,
     And eek of love-lykinge."   850

They fette him first the swete wyn,
And mede eek in a maselyn,
     And royal spicerye
Of gingebreed that was ful fyn,
And lycorys, and eek comyn,   855
     With sugre that is trye.

He dide next his whyte lere
Of clooth of lake fyn and clere
     A breech and eek a sherte;
And next his sherte an aketoun,   860
And over that an habergeoun
     For percinge of his herte;

The Second Fit

Yet listen, lords, to my tale
Which is merrier than the nightingale,
    For I'll tell you as it's come down   145
How, with slender waist and without fail
Sir Thopas, pricking over hill and dale,
    Is come again to town.

His merry men commanded he
To give themselves both game and glee,   150 [840]
    For he needs must fight
With a giant that had heads three,
So he could take his pleasure and his jollity
    From one who shone quite bright.

"Make come," he said, "my minstrels,   155
And jesters to tell tales to all,
    At once for my arming,
About romances that are royal,
About popes and cardinals,
    And also of love's delighting."   160 [850]

They fetched him first some sweet wine,
And meed in a mazer there did shine,
    Royal titbits and condiments,
With gingerbread so he could dine,
And licorice and cumin so fine,   165
    With sugar that is excellent.

Next he put his white flesh near
A linen cloth that was fine and clear,
    Breeches and also a shirt;
And next to his shirt a padded jacket,   170 [860]
And over that, his chain mail yet
    To prevent piercing of his heart;

And over that a fyn hauberk
Was al y-wroght of Jewes werk,
  Ful strong it was of plate;   865
And over that his cote-armour
As whyt as is a lily-flour,
  In which he wol debate.

His sheeld was al of gold so reed,
And therin was a bores heed,
  A charbocle bisyde;   870
And there he swoor on ale and breed
How that the geaunt shal be deed,
  Bityde what bityde.

His jambeux were of quirboilly,   875
His swerdes shethe of yvory,
  His helm of laton bright.
His sadel was of rewel-boon,
His brydel as the sonne shoon,
  Or as the mone light.   880

His spere was of fyn ciprees,
That bodeth werre and nothing pees,
  The heed ful sharpe y-grounde.
His stede was al dappel gray,
It gooth an ambel in the way   885
  Ful softely and rounde
      In londe.
Lo, lordes myne, heer is a fit!
If ye wol any more of it,
  To telle it wol I fonde.   890

And over that fine plate armor,
All wrought from Jews' work,[14] for sure,
    And very strong it was of plate;   175
And his coat of arms over his armor
As white as is the lily flower,
    In which he will fight straight.

His shield was all of gold so red,
And on it was a boar's head,   180 [870]
    With a carbuncle [15] beside;
And there he swore on ale and bread
How the giant shall be dead,
    Come what may on his side!

Of hardened leather were his greaves,   185
Of ivory was his sword's sheath,
    His helmet of latten[16] bright;
His saddle was made of whalebone,
His bridle like the sun shone,
    Or like the moon's light.   190 [880]

His spear was of fine cypress,
That signals war, and nothing less,
    The head sharpened and well ground;
His steed was all of dapple gray,
It ambles as it goes on its way,   195
    All softly and round
      In the land.
Lo, my lords, here is done a fit!
If you want any more of it,
    To tell it I'll try my hand.   200 [890]

14 **Jews' work**: Refers to the Jewish reputation for being expert workers in metal and armor.
15 **carbuncle**: Deep red stone.
16 **latten**: Brass alloy.

THE THIRD FIT

Now hold your mouth, *par charitee*,
Bothe knight and lady free,
  And herkneth to my spelle.
Of bataille and of chivalry,
And of ladyes love-drury   895
  Anon I wol yow telle.

Men speke of romances of prys,
Of Horn child and of Ypotys,
  Of Bevis and sir Gy,
Of sir Libeux and Pleyn-damour.   900
But sir Thopas—he bereth the flour
  Of royal chivalry.

His gode stede al he bistrood,
And forth upon his wey he glood
  As sparkle out of the bronde.   905
Upon his crest he bar a tour,
And therin stiked a lily-flour—
  God shilde his cors fro shonde!

And for he was a knight auntrous,
He nolde slepen in non hous,   910
  But liggen in his hode.
His brighte helm was his wonger,
And by him baiteth his dextrer
  Of herbes fyne and gode.

THE THIRD FIT

Now hold your tongue, *par charitee*,[17]
Both knight and lady free,
    And listen for a spell;
About battle and chivalry,
And of ladies with love courtly   205
    At once my tale I'll tell.

Men speak of fine romances like this,
About the Horn child and about Ypotis,
    About Bevis and Sir Guy, certainly,
About sir Lybeaus and Pleyndamour[18]—   210 [900]
But Sir Thopas, he bears the flower
    Of royal chivalry!

His good steed he did bestride,
And forth on his way he did glide
    Like a sparkle come from a brand;   215
Upon his crest, he had a tower,
And in it, he stuck a lily flower—
    God save his body in this land!

And since he was a knight adventurous,
He would not sleep in any house,   220 [910]
    But lie down in his hood;
His bright helmet was his pillow,
And by him grazes his warhorse so
    On herbs fine and good.

17 *par charitee*: For the sake of charity.
18 **the Horn child . . . Pleyndamour:** Heroes of romance and legend, but Pleyndamour (Full of Love) has not been identified by scholars.

Himself drank water of the wel,   915
As did the knight sir Percivel,
        So worly under wede,
Til on a day—

Heere the Hoost stynteth Chaucer of his Tale of Thopas.

THE PROLOGUE TO
THE TALE OF MELIBEE

    "No more of this, for Goddes dignitee,"
Quod oure Hoste, "for thou makest me   230 [920]
So wery of thy verray lewednesse
That, also wisly God my soule blesse,
Myn eres aken of thy drasty speche;
Now swich a rym the devel I biteche!
This may wel be rym dogerel," quod he.   235
    "Why so?" quod I, "why wiltow lette me
More of my tale than another man,
Syn that it is the beste rym I can?"
    "By God," quod he," for pleynly at a word,
Thy drasty ryming is nat worth a toord;   240 [930]
Thou doost nought elles but despendest tyme,
Sire, at o word, thou shalt no lenger ryme.
Lat see wher thou canst tellen aught in geste,
Or telle in prose somwhat, at the leste,
In which ther be som mirthe or som doctrine."   245
    "Gladly," quod I, "by Goddes sweete pyne,

He himself drank water from the well,   225
Just as did the knight Sir Perceval,[19]
    So worthy in his clothes,
Till on a day—

Here the Host stops Chaucer in his Tale of Sir Thopas.

THE PROLOGUE TO THE TALE OF MELIBEE

    "No more of this, for all God's dignity,"
Said our Host then, "since by now you make me   230 [920]
So tired of your ignorance and crudeness
That, as surely as God my soul may bless,
From your crappy speech, my ears do ache.
Such a rhyme, I say, let the devil take!
This has to be rhyme doggerel," said he,   235
    "Why so?" said I, "why will you now keep me
From more of my tale than another man,
Since this one is the best rhyme that I can?"
    "By God," said he, "for plainly, in one word,
Your crappy rhyming is not worth a turd!   240 [930]
You don't do anything but waste our time.
Sir, in one word, you shall no longer rhyme.
See if you can tell a *chanson de geste*,[20]
Or else something in prose might be the best,
In which some mirth or learning you explain."   245
    "Gladly," said I, "and now by God's sweet pain!

19 **Perceval**: One of the most famous knights of the Round Table and one of the few to complete successfully the quest for the Holy Grail.

20 *chanson de geste*: Medieval literary genre—a story of adventure—the most famous of which, in the Middle Ages, is *Le Chanson de Roland.*

I wol yow telle a litel thing in prose,
That oughte liken yow, as I suppose,
Or elles, certes, ye been to daungerous.
It is a moral tale virtuous,   250 [940]
Al be it told somtyme in sondry wyse
Of sondry folk, as I shal yow devyse.
            As thus: ye woot that every Evaungelist
That telleth us the peyne of Jhesu Crist
Ne saith nat al thing as his felaw dooth,   255
But nathelees, hir sentence is al sooth,
And alle acorden as in hir sentence,
Al be ther in hir telling difference.
For somme of hem seyn more, and somme seyn lesse,
Whan they his pitous passioun expresse—   260 [950]
I mene of Marke, Mathew, Luc, and John—
But doutelees hir sentence is al oon.
Therfore, lordinges alle, I yow biseche,
If that yow thinke I varie as in my speche,
As thus, thogh that I telle somwhat more   265
Of proverbs than ye han herd before,
Comprehended in this litel tretis here,
To enforce with th'effect of my matere,
And though I nat the same wordes seye
As ye han herd, yet to yow alle I preye,   270 [960]
Blameth me nat; for, as in my sentence,
Shul ye nowher fynden difference
Fro the sentence of this tretis lyte
After the which this murye tale I wryte.
And therfor herkneth what I shal seye,   275
And lat me tellen al my tale, I preye."

Explicit

I will tell you a little thing in prose
That should be pleasing to you, I suppose,
Or else, truly, you're too fastidious,
It is a moral tale that's virtuous,   250 [940]
Although it's told sometimes in sundry ways
By sundry folks, as to you I shall say.
   And so: you know each Evangelist thus
Who tells us all the pains of our Christ Jesus
Won't say each thing just as his fellows do;   255
But nonetheless, their meanings are all true,
And all are of one accord in meaning,
Though there is a difference in their telling.
For some of them say more, and some say less,
When they his piteous passion express—   260 [950]
I'm speaking of Mark, John, Luke, and Matthew—
And yet doubtless their meaning is all true.
Therefore, all my lords, I now you beseech,
If you think that I vary in my speech,
As thus, though here I now tell somewhat more   265
Of proverbs than you may have heard before
Included in this little treatise here,
To enforce and make its conclusion clear;
And even though the same words I don't say
As you have heard, yet to you all I pray: 270 [960]
Do not blame me: because in my meaning
You will nowhere find any differing
From the meaning this little treatise recites,
According to which this merry tale I write.
And therefore, hearken now to what I say,   275
And let me tell all of my tale, I pray."

It is finished.

[What follows is the long moral, allegorical prose *Tale of Melibee*, which concerns Melibee, his good wife Prudence, and their daughter Sophie. The tale is liberally embellished and considerably lengthened beyond the original sources with many proverbs.]

THE PROLOGUE OF THE NUN'S PRIEST'S TALE

"Ho!" quod the Knight, "good sir, namore of this:
That ye han seyd is right ynough, ywis,
And mochel more; for litel hevinesse
Is right ynough to mochel folk, I gesse.   2770
I seye for me it is a greet disese,
Where as men han ben in greet welthe and ese,
To heeren of hire sodeyn fal, allas!
And the contrarie is joie and greet solas,
As whan a man hath been in povre estaat,   2775
And clymbeth up, and wexeth fortunat,
And ther abydeth in prosperitee—
Swich thing is gladsom, as it thinketh me,
And of swich thing were goodly for to telle."
"Ye," quod our Hoste, "by Seinte Poules belle,   2780
Ye seye right sooth: this Monk, he clappeth loude.
He spak 'how Fortune covered with a cloude'—
I noot never what. And als of a 'tragedie'
Right now ye herde, and pardee! no remedie
It is for to biwaille ne compleyne   2785
That that is doon, and als it is a peyne,
As ye han seyd, to heere of hevinesse.

THE PROLOGUE OF THE NUN'S PRIEST'S TALE

"Whoa!" said the Knight, "good sire, no more, I pray!
What you have said is just enough today,
And so much more; for a little sadness[1]
Is quite enough for many folks, I guess.   2770
I say, for me, it causes great unease,   5
When men have lived in both great wealth and ease,
To hear about their sudden fall, alas!
The contrary is great joy and solace,
As when a man of a poor rank has been,
And he can climb and wax fortunate then,   10
And rest on high in great prosperity.
Such a thing is pleasing, it seems to me.
Of such a thing it would be good to tell."
"Yes," said our Host, "now by Saint Paul's own bell!   2780
You tell the truth; this Monk, he chatters loud.   15
He said how Fortune covered with a cloud
I know not what; and also tragedy
Right now you heard, and God, no remedy
It is now to lament or to complain
About what's done, and also, it's a pain,   20
As you have said, hearing about sadness.

1   **a little sadness**: The Nun's Priest immediately follows the Monk in the storytelling competition. The Knight interrupts *The Monk's Tale* here because the Monk, depicted as a decidedly hedonistic character in his *General Prologue* portrait, has decided to tell a tale composed of many short tragic stories (from classical sources, the Bible, and medieval literature). The medieval definition of tragedy involved the rapid descent of one raised high on Fortune's wheel who was then sunk into the abyss of misfortune in order to show the precariousness of human life.

Sire Monk, namore of this, so God yow blesse!
Your tale anoyeth al this compaignye.
Swich talking is nat worth a boterflye,   2790
For therinne is ther no desport ne game.
Wherfore sir Monk, or daun Piers by youre name,
I preye yow hertely telle us somwhat elles,
For sikerly, nere clinking of youre belles
That on your brydel hange on every syde,   2795
By hevene king that for us alle dyde,
I sholde er this han fallen doun for slepe,
Althogh the slough had never been so depe.
Than had your tale al be told in vayn;
For certainly, as that thise clerkes seyn,   2800
'Whereas a man may have noon audience,
Noght helpeth it to tellen his sentence.'
      And wel I woot the substance is in me,
If any thing shal wel reported be.
Sir, sey somwhat of hunting, I yow preye."   2805
      "Nay," quod this Monk, "I have no lust to pleye;
Now let another telle, as I have told."
Than spak our Host, with rude speche and bold,
And seyde unto the Nonnes Preest anon,
"Com neer, thou preest, com hider, thou sir John,   2810
Tel us swich thing as may oure hertes glade.
Be blythe, though thou ryde upon a jade!
What though thyn hors be bothe foule and lene?
If he wol serve thee, rekke nat a bene.
Look that thyn herte be mery evermo."   2815
      "Yis, sir," quod he, "yis, Host, so mote I go,
But I be mery, ywis, I wol be blamed."
And right anon his tale he hath attamed,
And thus he seyde unto us everichon,
This sweete preest, this goodly man sir John.   2820

Explicit.

Sir Monk, no more of this, may God you bless!
Your tale's annoying all the company.
Such talking is not worth a butterfly,   2790
For therein is found neither sport nor game.   25
And thus, sir Monk, Don Piers, as is your name,
Something else, heartily I pray, now tell;
If it weren't for the clinking of your bells
That on your bridle hang on every side,
By heaven's king, who for us all has died,   30
I should before have fallen down asleep,
Although the mud had never been so deep;
Then your tale would have been all told in vain.
For certainly, as these clerks do explain,   2800
When there's a man who has no audience,   35
It doesn't help that his tale has substance.
      And well I know, the meaning's clear for me,
When anything shall well reported be.
Sire, tell something of hunting, I you pray."
      "No," said this Monk, "I have no urge to play.   40
Now let another tell, for my tale's told."
Then our Host spoke with his speech rude and bold,
And said right to the Nun's Priest,[2] "Now, come on!
Come near, you priest, come hither, you, sir John!   2810
To cheer our hearts, you should tell us something.   45
Be happy, though on a nag you're riding.
So what if your horse is both foul and lean?
If he serves you, don't count it worth a bean.
See your heart merry while you are alive."
      "Yes, sir," said he, "yes, Host, so may I thrive,   50
Unless I'm merry, I'm a scolded man."
And right away, his tale then he began,
And spoke to each of us as we rode on,
This sweet priest and this goodly man, sir John.   2820

It ends.

---

   2   **Nun's Priest**: The Prioress's chaplain who rides with her group, as we learn in the Prioress's
portrait in *The General Prologue*.

THE NUN'S PRIEST'S TALE

A povre widwe, somdel stape in age,
Was whylom dwelling in a narwe cotage,
Bisyde a grove, stondinge in a dale.
This widwe of which I telle yow my tale,
Sin thilke day that she was last a wyf,   2825
In pacience ladde a ful simple lyf,
For litel was hir catel and hir rente.
By housbondrye of such as God hire sente
She fond hirself and eek hir doghtren two.
Three large sowes hadde she and namo,   2830
Three kyn, and eek a sheep that highte Malle.
Ful sooty was hire bour, and eek hir halle,
In which she eet ful many a sclendre meel.
Of poynaunt sauce hir neded never a deel:
No deyntee morsel passed thurgh hir throte.   2835
Hir diete was accordant to hir cote—
Repleccioun ne made hir never syk.
Attempree diete was al hir phisyk,
And exercyse, and hertes suffisaunce.
The goute lette hire nothing for to daunce,   2840
N'apoplexye shente nat hir heed.
No wyn ne drank she, neither whyt ne reed;
Hir bord was served most with whyt and blak—

THE NUN'S PRIEST'S TALE

Here begins the Nun's Priest's Tale of the Cock and Hen, Chanticleer and Pertelote.

A poor woman, somewhat stooped down with age,   55
Once was dwelling in a narrow cottage,
Beside a grove there, standing in a dale.
This widow, about whom I tell my tale,
Since that day when she was last a wife,
In patience led a very simple life,   60
For small were her income and her chattel.
By husbanding what God has sent her well,
For herself and two daughters she provides.
Three large sows had she, and no more besides,   2830
Three cows, and then also a sheep named Moll.   65
Quite sooty were her bower and her hall,
In which she ate many a slender meal.
With tangy sauce she didn't need to deal.
No dainty morsel through her throat did get,
For her small farm did dictate her diet.   70
Overindulgence never made her sick;
Temperate diet was her only physic,
Exercise, and a heart that was content.
From dancing, the gout did her not prevent,   2840
And apoplexy did not hurt her head.   75
No wine did she drink, neither white nor red;
Her table was served most with white and black—

Milk and broun breed—in which she fond no lak,
Seynd bacoun, and somtyme an ey or tweye,   2845
For she was as it were a maner deye.
      A yerd she hadde, enclosed al aboute
With stikkes, and a drye dich withoute,
In which she hadde a cok hight Chauntecleer:
In al the land of crowing nas his peer.   2850
His voys was merier than the mery orgon
On messe-dayes that in the chirche gon;
Wel sikerer was his crowing in his logge
Than is a clokke or an abbey orlogge.
By nature knew he ech ascencioun   2855
Of the equinoxial in thilke toun:
For whan degrees fiftene were ascended,
Thanne crew he, that it mighte nat ben amended.
His comb was redder than the fyn coral,
And batailed as it were a castel wal.   2860
His bile was blak, and as the jeet it shoon;
Lyk asur were his legges and his toon;
His nayles whytter than the lilie flour,
And lyk the burned gold was his colour.
This gentil cok hadde in his governaunce   2865
Sevene hennes, for to doon al his plesaunce,
Whiche were his sustres and his paramours,
And wonder lyk to him, as of colours;
Of whiche the faireste hewed on hir throte
Was cleped faire damoysele Pertelote.   2870
Curteys she was, discreet, and debonaire,
And compaignable, and bar hirself so faire,
Sin thilke day that she was seven night old,
That trewely she hath the herte in hold
Of Chauntecleer, loken in every lith;   2875
He loved hire so, that wel was him therwith.

Milk and brown bread—in which she found no lack,
Smoked bacon, and sometimes an egg would do,
Because she was a dairywoman, too. 80
          A yard she had, enclosed on every side
With sticks, and a dry ditch on the outside,
In which she had a cock named Chanticleer.
For crowing, in this land, he had no peer, 2850
With his voice merrier than the merry organ 85
Whose notes, on mass-days, in the church began.
When he crowed in his shed, surer was he
Than a clock or timepiece of an abbey.
By nature, he knew each revolution
Of hours as they rose in their ascension, 90
For when fifteen degrees had ascended,[3]
He crowed so it could not be amended.
His comb's redder than the finest coral,
And crenellated like a castle wall; 2860
His bill is black, and just like jet, it glows; 95
Azure like lapus are his legs and toes;
His nails, whiter than the lily flower,
And like burnished gold is all his color.
This gentle cock had in his governing
Full seven hens to do his pleasuring, 100
His sisters, concubines, and paramours,
Wonderfully like him in their colors;
The one whose hue was fairest on her throat
Was called "The Fair Demoiselle Pertelote." 2870
Courteous she was, gracious, debonnaire, 105
Obliging, and she bore herself so fair
Since on the day that she was seven nights old
That truly, she has all the heart to hold
Of Chantecleer, locked up in every limb; 110
He loved her so that all was well with him.

---

3 **fifteen degrees had ascended**: The number of degrees figured to be in a clock hour. Chanticleer knows astronomy so well he can crow on the hour.

But such a joye was it to here hem singe,
Whan that the brighte sonne gan to springe,
In swete acord, "my lief is faren in londe."
For thilke tyme, as I have understonde,   2880
Bestes and briddes coude speke and singe.
            And so bifel that in a daweninge,
As Chauntecleer among his wyves alle
Sat on his perche that was in the halle,
And next him sat this faire Pertelote,   2885
This Chauntecleer gan gronen in his throte
As man that in his dreem is drecched sore.
And whan that Pertelote thus herde him rore,
She was agast, and seyde, "Herte dere,
What eyleth yow to grone in this manere?   2890
Ye been a verray sleper, fy for shame!"
            And he answerde and seyde thus, "Madame,
I pray yow, that ye take it nat agrief:
By God, me mette I was in swich meschief
Right now, that yet myn herte is sore afright.   2895
Now God," quod he, "my swevene recche aright,
And keep my body out of foul prisoun!
Me mette how that I romed up and doun
Withinne our yerde, wher as I saugh a beste,
Was lyk an hound and wolde han maad areste   2990
Upon my body, and wolde han had me deed.
His colour was bitwixe yelow and reed,
And tipped was his tail and bothe his eres
With blak, unlyk the remenant of his heres;
His snowte smal, with glowinge eyen tweye.   2995
Yet of his look for fere almost I deye:
This caused me my groning, doutelees."
            "Avoy!" quod she, "fy on yow, hertelees!
Allas!" quod she, "for, by that God above,
Now han ye lost myn herte and al my love.   2910
I can nat love a coward, by my feith!
For certes, what so any womman seith,

But such a joy it was to hear them sing,
When first the bright sun up began to spring,
In sweet harmony, "My love's left the land!"—
For at that time, as I do understand,   2880
All beasts and birds back then could speak and sing.   115
    So it happened when the day was dawning,
As Chantecleer there among his wives all
Sat on his perch, which was placed in the hall,
And next to him sat his fair Pertelote,
Chantecleer began groaning in his throat,   120
Like a man who, in dreams, has troubles sore.
And when his Pertelote thus heard him roar,
She was aghast and said, "O, my heart dear,
What ails you to groan in this manner here?   2890
You are such a sound sleeper! For shame! Fie!"   125
    "Madame," he said, and thus he answered, "I
Pray to you that from this you take no grief.
By God, I dreamed that I was in such mischief
Right now that my heart still is sore with fright.
Now God," said he, "my dream interpret right,   130
And out of foul prison my body keep!
I roamed around, as I dreamed in my sleep,
Within our yard, when there I saw a beast
Like a hound, who'd have made arrest at least   2900
On my body, or would have had me dead.   135
His color was between yellow and red;
Tipped was his tail and both of his ears there
With black, unlike the rest of all his hairs;
His snout was small; and glowing was his eye.
Yet, from his look, for fear, almost I die.   140
This caused me my groaning, it is doubtless."
    "Shame!" said she, "fie on you, coward spineless!
Alas," said she, "for, by that God above,
Now have you lost my heart and all my love!   2910
By my faith, I cannot love a coward!   145
Surely, as any woman's said or heard,

We alle desiren, if it mighte be,
To han housbondes hardy, wyse, and free,
And secree, and no nigard, ne no fool,   2915
Ne him that is agast of every tool,
Ne noon avauntour. By that God above,
How dorste ye seyn for shame unto your love
That any thing mighte make yow aferd?
Have ye no mannes herte, and han a berd?   2920
Allas! and conne ye been agast of swevenis?
Nothing, God wot, but vanitee in sweven is.
Swevenes engendren of replecciouns,
And ofte of fume, and of complecciouns,
Whan humours been to habundant in a wight.   2925
Certes this dreem, which ye han met tonight,
Cometh of the grete superfluitee
Of youre rede *colera*, pardee,
Which causeth folk to dreden in hir dremes
Of arwes, and of fyr with rede lemes,   2930
Of rede bestes, that they wol hem byte,
Of contek, and of whelpes grete and lyte;
Right as the humour of malencolye
Causeth ful many a man in sleep to crye
For fere of blake beres, or boles blake,   2935
Or elles, blake develes wole hem take.
Of othere humours coude I telle also
That werken many a man in sleep ful wo;
But I wol passe as lightly as I can.
        Lo Catoun, which that was so wys a man,   2940
Seyde he nat thus, 'Ne do no fors of dremes'?
Now, sire," quod she, "whan we flee fro the bemes,
For Goddes love, as tak some laxatyf.

We all desire, if it might ever be,
Husbands bold and wise, generous and free,
Also discreet—and no niggard or fool,
Nor one afraid of each weapon and tool,   150
Nor a boaster, by the good God above!
How dare you say, for shame, right to your love
That there is anything that you have feared?
Have you no man's heart, but still have a beard?   2920
Alas! Aghast of dreams can you now be?   155
God knows, nothing's in dreams but vanity.[4]
Dreams are engendered from satiation,
From gas and bodily disposition,
When your humors abound more than is right.
Surely this dream, which you have had tonight,   160
Comes straight from the great superfluity
Of red choleric humor, as you see,
Which causes folks within their dreams to dread
Both sharp arrows and then fire with flames red,   2930
And red beasts, too, which they fear will them bite,   165
And strife and dogs, both great and small in might;
Just as the humor of melancholy
Makes many men in sleep cry openly
For fear both of black bears and of bulls black,
Or of black devils who might take them back.   170
Of other humors could I tell also
That work so men have sleep that's full of woe;
But I'll pass them by lightly as I can.
     Lo! See Cato, who was so wise a man,   2940
Said he not thus: 'Pay no heed now to dreams'?   175
Sire," said she, "when we fly down from these beams,
For God's love, now, please take some laxative.

---

4 **nothing's in dreams . . .**: Pertelote here initiates the debate with Chanticleer, which will go on
for some lines, about the many ways to interpret dreams. This debate was a lively one throughout the
classical period and into the Middle Ages and involved disputations among many classical, biblical,
and Christian exegetical sources.

Up peril of my soule and of my lyf

I counseille yow the beste, I wol nat lye,   2945

That bothe of colere and of malencolye

Ye purge yow; and for ye shul nat tarie,

Though in this toun is noon apothecarie,

I shal myself to herbes techen yow,

That shul ben for youre hele and for youre prow;   2950

And in oure yerd tho herbes shal I finde

The whiche han of hire propretee by kinde

To purgen yow binethe and eek above.

Forget not this, for Goddes owene love!

Ye been ful colerik of compleccioun.   2955

Ware the sonne in his ascencioun

Ne fynde yow nat repleet of humours hote;

And if it do, I dar wel leye a grote,

That ye shul have a fevere terciane,

Or an agu, that may be youre bane.   2960

A day or two ye shul have digestyves

Of wormes, er ye take your laxatyves,

Of lauriol, centaure, and fumetere,

Or elles of ellebor that groweth there,

Of catapuce, or of gaytres beryis,   2965

Of erbe yve, growing in oure yerd, ther mery is.

Pekke hem up right as they growe, and ete hem in.

Be mery, housbond, for youre fader kin!

Dredeth no dreem: I can say yow namore."

        "Madame," quod he, "*graunt mercy* of youre lore.   2970

But nathelees, as touching daun Catoun,

That hath of wisdom swich a greet renoun,

Though that he bad no dremes for to drede,

By God, men may in olde bokes rede

Of many a man, more of auctoritee   2975

Than ever Catoun was, so mote I thee,

By my soul's peril while here I may live,
I advise for the best—no lies from me—
That both of choler and melancholy   180
You purge yourself; and so you won't tarry,
Though in this town there's no apothecary,
To certain herbs I myself shall you lead
For both your health and benefit, indeed;   2950
And in our yard, those herbs for you I'll find   185
Whose properties, by nature of their kind,
Can purge you both below and then above.
Don't you forget all this, by God's own love!
You're choleric in your disposition;
Watch out that the sun, in its ascension,   190
Won't find you filled up with hot humors yet.
And if it does, a groat I'd dare well bet
You shall have a reoccurring fever,
Or an ague that proves to be a killer.   2960
For a day or two, you'll have digestives   195
Of worms, before you take your laxatives
Made from spurge laurel ⁵and fumitory,
From hellebore growing here and centaury,
From caper spurge, or else then from rhamus,
From ground ivy growing in our yard thus;   200
Peck them right where they grow and eat them in.
Be merry, husband, by your father's kin!
And dread no dream; I can tell you no more."
          "Madame," said he, "all thanks be for your lore.   2970
Nonetheless, regarding good Don Cato,   205
Who, for wisdom, has great renown, I know,
Though he bade us that no dreams should we dread,
By God, in many old books, men have read
From many men of more authority
Than Cato, may I thrive prosperously,   210

---

5 **spurge laurel**, etc.: The herbs in Pertelote's list were used for digestive and purgative purposes
in the Middle Ages, though they would not have been very pleasant tasting.

That al the revers seyn of his sentence,
And han wel founden by experience,
That dremes ben significaciouns
As wel of joye as tribulaciouns   2980
That folk enduren in this lyf present.
Ther nedeth make of this noon argument:
The verray preve sheweth it in dede.
      Oon of the gretteste auctours that men rede
Seith thus, that whylom two felawes wente   2985
On pilgrimage, in a ful good entente;
And happed so thay come into a toun,
Wher as ther was swich congregacioun
Of peple, and eek so streit of herbergage,
That they ne founde as muche as o cotage   2990
In which they bothe mighte y-logged be.
Wherfor thay mosten of necessitee,
As for that night, departen compaignye;
And ech of hem goth to his hostelrye,
And took his logging as it wolde falle.   2995
That oon of hem was logged in a stalle,
Fer in a yerd, with oxen of the plough;
That other man was logged wel ynough,
As was his aventure or his fortune,
That us governeth alle as in commune.   3000
      And so bifel that, longe er it were day,
This man mette in his bed, ther as he lay,
How that his felawe gan upon him calle,
And seyde, 'Allas! for in an oxes stalle
This night I shal be mordred ther I lye.   3005
Now help me, dere brother, or I dye;
In alle haste com to me,' he sayde.
This man out of his sleep for fere abrayde,

Who say the reverse of his evidence,
And who have well found through experience
That dreams become the significations[6]
Both of the joys and the tribulations   2980
That folks here endure in this life present.   215
Of this, we need now make no argument;
The very proof of it shows in the deed.

      Of the greatest authorities men read,
One has said thus: that once two fellows went
On pilgrimage, with quite a good intent.   220
It happened, this was the situation:
In a town with such a congregation
Of people, and with few places to stay,
Not so much as a small cottage found they   2990
In which the two of them might sheltered be.   225
Therefore they must, out of necessity,
For that one night, both part their company;
And each of them goes to his hostelry,
And took his lodging, whereso it might fall.
And one of them was lodged within a stall,   230
Far in a yard, with the plow and oxen;
That other man was lodged well enough then,
As was his fortune or his luck and chance,
That holds the world in common governance.   3000

      So it happened, long before it was day,   235
This man dreamed in his bed, right where he lay,
How his fellow began on him to call,
And said, 'Alas, for in an ox's stall
This night I shall be murdered where I lie!
Now help me, brother dear, or else I'll die,'   240
He said, 'In all haste, now come to me here!'
From his sleep, this man started up in fear;

---

6 **dreams become the significations**: Chanticleer here takes the opposite side from Pertelote
in the medieval debate about dreams. Rather than being purely somatic phenomenon, as Pertelote
argues they are, Chanticleer asserts that dreams are predictive of future events.

But whan that he was wakened of his sleep,
He turned him, and took of this no keep: 3010
Him thoughte his dreem nas but a vanitee.
Thus twyes in his sleping dremed he;
And atte thridde tyme yet his felawe
Cam, as him thoughte, and seide, 'I am now slawe.
Bihold my blody woundes, depe and wyde!   3015
Arys up erly in the morwe tyde,
And at the west gate of the toun,' quod he,
'A carte ful of donge ther shaltow see,
In which my body is hid ful prively:
Do thilke carte aresten boldely.   3020
My gold caused my mordre, sooth to sayn;'
And tolde him every poynt how he was slayn,
With a ful pitous face, pale of hewe.
And truste wel, his dreem he fond ful trewe,
For on the morwe, as sone as it was day,   3025
To his felawes in he took the way;
And whan that he cam to this oxes stalle,
After his felawe he bigan to calle.

      The hostiler answered him anon,
And seyde, 'Sire, your felawe is agon: 3030
As sone as day he wente out of the toun.'

      This man gan fallen in suspecioun,
Remembringe on his dremes that he mette,
And forth he goth, no lenger wolde he lette,
Unto the west gate of the toun, and fond   3035
A dong-carte, wente as it were to donge lond,
That was arrayed in the same wyse
As ye han herd the dede man devyse.
And with an hardy herte he gan to crye,
'Vengeaunce and justice of this felonye!   3040
My felawe mordred is this same night,
And in this carte he lyth gapinge upright.
I crye out on the ministres,' quod he,
'That sholden kepe and reulen this citee,

But when he'd wakened from his sleep indeed,
Over he turned and took of this no heed.   3010
He thought his dream was only vanity.   245
Twice thus while he was sleeping, dream did he;
The third time his friend came, he did explain,
It seemed to him, and said, 'I am now slain.
Behold my wounds bloody and wide and deep!
Tomorrow rise up early from your sleep,   250
And at the west gate of the town,' said he,
'A cart there full of dung then you will see,
In which my body's hidden privately,
And at once have this same cart seized boldly.   3020
My gold has caused my murder, the truth's plain.'   255
In detail he told him how he was slain,
With a piteous face all pale of hue.
And trust it well; his dream he found quite true.
In the morning, as soon as it was day,
Right to his fellow's inn, he took his way;   260
And when he came up to this oxen's stall,
After his fellow, he began to call.
        The innkeeper answered him directly,
And he said, 'sir, your fellow's gone, you see.   3030
As soon as day came, out of town he went.'   265
        The man suspicious got of what he meant,
Remembering what his three dreams did say,
And forth he goes—he'd no longer delay—
To the town's west gate, and he found at hand
A dung cart set up to manure the land,   270
Which was arrayed in the exact same way
As you heard the dead man describe and say.
With an emboldened heart aloud cried he
For a just vengeance on this felony: 3040
'My fellow has been murdered this same night;   275
In this cart, he lies there, gaping upright.
I cry out to the magistrates,' said he,
'Who should both protect and rule this city.

Harrow! allas! heer lyth my felawe slayn!'   3045
What sholde I more unto this tale sayn?
The peple out sterte, and caste the cart to grounde,
And in the middel of the dong they founde
The dede man, that mordred was al newe.
       O blisful God, that art so just and trewe!   3050
Lo, how that thou biwreyest mordre alway!
Mordre wol out, that see we day by day.
Mordre is so wlatsom and abhominable
To God, that is so just and resonable,
That he ne wol nat suffre it heled be.   3055
Though it abyde a yeer, or two, or three,
Mordre wol out, this my conclusioun.
And right anoon, ministres of that toun
Han hent the carter and so sore him pyned,
And eek the hostiler so sore engyned,   3060
That thay biknewe hir wikkednesse anoon,
And were anhanged by the nekke-boon.
       Here may men seen that dremes been to drede.
And certes, in the same book I rede,
Right in the nexte chapitre after this—   3065
I gabbe nat, so have I joye or blis—
Two men that wolde han passed over see,
For certeyn cause, into a fer contree,
If that the wind ne hadde been contrarie:
That made hem in a citee for to tarie   3070
That stood ful mery upon an haven syde.
But on a day, agayn the even-tyde,
The wind gan chaunge, and blew right as hem leste.
Jolif and glad they wente unto hir reste,
And casten hem ful erly for to saille;   3075
But herkneth! To that oo man fil a greet mervaille.
That oon of hem, in sleping as he lay,
Him mette a wonder dreem, agayn the day:
Him thoughte a man stood by his beddes syde,
And him comaunded that he sholde abyde,   3080

Harrow! Alas! Here lies my fellow slain!'

What should I more about this tale explain?   280

Out people ran and cast the cart to ground,

And in the middle of the dung they found

The dead man there, who murdered was all new.

   O blissful God, who is so just and true,   3050

Lo, how you'll reveal a murder always!   285

Murder will out, as we see day by day.

Murder loathsome and abominable

To God, who's so just and reasonable,

That he won't suffer it concealed to be,

Though it should wait a year or two or three.   290

Murder will out; this is my conclusion.

The town's ministers, without hesitation,

Seized the carter and sorely did him torture,

And the innkeep sorely on the rack for sure;   3060

Their wickedness they did confess and own,   295

And both then were hanged right by the neck bone.

   So here may men see that dreams are to dread.

And certainly, in the same book, I read,

Right there in the next chapter after this—

I'm not lying, may I have joy or bliss—   300

Of two men wanting to go out to sea,

For a reason, into a far country,

If the wind had not blown up contrary,

Making them then in a city tarry   3070

That stood there by a harbor pleasantly;   305

But one day, before evening shortly,

The wind did change, and blew as they liked best.

Jolly and glad, they went right to their rest,

And they made plans quite early to set sail.

Hark! One man had a great marvel prevail: 310

For one of them, there sleeping as he lay,

A wondrous dream had early in the day.

It seemed a man was standing at his bedside,

Commanding him that his time he should bide,   3080

And seyde him thus, 'If thou tomorwe wende,
Thou shalt be dreynt: my tale is at an ende.'
He wook, and tolde his felawe what he mette,
And preyde him his viage for to lette;
As for that day, he preyde him to byde.   3085
His felawe, that lay by his beddes syde,
Gan for to laughe, and scorned him ful faste.
'No dreem' quod he, 'may so myn herte agaste
That I wol lette for to do my thinges.
I sette not a straw by thy dreminges,   3090
For swevenes been but vanitees and japes.
Men dreme alday of owles or of apes,
And eke of many a mase therwithal;
Men dreme of thing that nevere was ne shal.
But sith I see that thou wolt heer abyde,   3095
And thus forsleuthen wilfully thy tyde,
God woot it reweth me; and have good day.'
And thus he took his leve, and wente his way.
But er that he hadde halfe his cours y-seyled,
Noot I nat why, ne what mischaunce it eyled,   3100
But casuelly the shippes botme rente,
And ship and man under the water wente
In sighte of othere shippes it byside,
That with hem seyled at the same tyde.
And therfore faire Pertelote so dere,   3105
By swiche ensamples olde maistow lere
That no man sholde been to recchelees
Of dremes, for I sey thee, doutelees,
That many a dreem ful sore is for to drede.
        Lo, in the lyf of Seint Kenelm I rede,   3110
That was Kenulphus sone, the noble king
Of Mercenrike, how Kenelm mette a thing
A lyte er he was mordred on a day.
His mordre in his avisioun he say.
His norice him expouned every del   3115
His sweven, and bad him for to kepe him wel

And told him thus: 'If tomorrow you sail,   315
You shall be drowned; that's the end of my tale.'
He woke and told his friend what he dreamed then,
And prayed him this voyage to abandon;
And for that day, he prayed, his time to bide.
His fellow, who's lying by his bed's side,   320
Began to laugh, and heaped the scorn on fast.
'No dream,' said he, 'makes my heart so aghast
That I will hesitate to do my things.
I don't give a straw for all your dreamings,   3090
For dreams are only vanities and japes.   325
All day men can dream of owls and apes,
And such sources of amazement plenty;
Men dream about things that shall never be.
But, now since you'll wait here, as I see,
And willingly waste your time slothfully,   330
Lord, it makes me sorry. Have a good day!'
And thus he took his leave and went his way.
But before half of his course he had sailed,
I don't know why or what bad luck it ailed,   3100
But, by chance, the ship's bottom was all rent,   335
And ship and man beneath the water went
In sight of other ships there alongside,
Which were sailing with them on the same tide.
Therefore, I say, my dear, fair Pertelote,
That from such old examples, you may note   340
And learn that no man should be so heedless
Of his dreams; for as I tell you, doubtless,
There are many sad dreams that should cause dread.
        Lo, in the life of Saint Kenelm I read—   3110
He who was Kenwulf's son, the noble king   345
Of Mercia—how Kenelm had dreamed a thing.
A bit before he was murdered, one day,
His murder in a vision came his way.
His nurse expounded in every respect
His dream to him, and told him to protect   350

For traisoun; but he nas but seven yeer old,
And therfore litel tale hath he told
Of any dreem, so holy was his herte.
By God, I hadde lever than my sherte   3120
That ye had rad his legende as have I.
      Dame Pertelote, I sey yow trewely,
Macrobeus, that writ the avisioun
In Affrike of the worthy Cipioun,
Affermeth dremes, and seith that they been   3125
Warninge of thinges that men after seen.
And forthermore, I pray yow loketh wel
In the Olde Testament, of Daniel,
If he held dremes any vanitee.
Reed eek of Ioseph, and ther shul ye see   3130
Wher dremes ben somtyme (I sey nat alle)
Warninge of thinges that shul after falle.
Loke of Egipte the king, daun Pharao,
His bakere and his boteler also,
Wher they ne felte noon effect in dremes.   3135
Whoso wol seken actes of sondry remes
May rede of dremes many a wonder thing.
Lo Cresus, which that was of Lyde king,
Mette he nat that he sat upon a tree,
Which signified he sholde anhanged be?   3140
Lo heer Andromacha, Ectores wyf,
That day that Ector sholde lese his lyf,
She dremed on the same night biforn,
How that the lyf of Ector sholde be lorn

Himself from treason; but, seven years old,
Of his dreams, little notice did he hold,
His heart so holy thought dreams could not hurt.
By God! I would for this give up my shirt,   3120
If you had read this legend, just like me.   355
            Dame Pertelote, I say to you so truly,
Macrobius,[7] who wrote the vision so
In Africa of worthy Scipio,
Has affirmed dreams, because they are, says he,
Warnings of things that afterwards men see.   360
And furthermore, I pray you to look well
In the Old Testament, about Daniel,
If he believed that dreams were vanity.
Moreover, read Joseph,[8] and there you'll see   3130
Whether dreams are sometimes—I don't say all—   365
Warnings of things that later should befall.
Look at Egypt's king, at that Don Pharoah,
And his baker and his butler also,
And see if dreams' effects can overwhelm.
Whoso seeks histories of sundry realms   370
Reads about dreams many a wondrous thing.
Lo Croesus, who of Lydia was king,
Dreamed he not he was sitting on a tree,
Which signified that he soon hanged would be?   3140
Lo here Andromache, good Hector's wife,   375
On the same day that Hector lost his life,
She did dream on the very night before
How soon that Hector's life would be no more,

---

7 **Macrobius**: Fifth-century Roman author of a commentary on Cicero's *Somnium Scipionis* (*Dream of Scipio*), originally a part of Cicero's *De Re Publica* (*On the Republic*). In the dream, the great general of the Second Punic War, Scipio Africanus the Elder, comes to his adopted grandson to tell him, from the perspective of the afterlife, about the world, moral conduct, and right living. Medieval writers often mistakenly credited Macrobius with authoring *The Dream of Scipio* (Chaucer makes this mistake here, but not in his *Parliament of Fowls*). Macrobius's commentary became a central source of medieval dream lore.

8 **Daniel; Joseph**: Figures associated with prophetic dream visions in the Bible. See Daniel 7 and Genesis 37 ff.

If thilke day he wente into bataille;   3145
She warned him, but it mighte nat availle;
He wente for to fighte nathelees,
But he was slayn anoon of Achilles.
But thilke tale is al to long to telle,
And eek it is ny day, I may nat dwelle.   3150
Shortly I seye, as for conclusioun,
That I shal han of this avisioun
Adversitee; and I seye forthermore,
That I ne telle of laxatyves no store,
For they ben venimous, I woot it wel;   3155
I hem defye, I love hem never a del.
          Now let us speke of mirthe and stinte al this;
Madame Pertelote, so have I blis,
Of o thing God hath sent me large grace:
For whan I see the beautee of your face—   3160
Ye ben so scarlet reed about your yën—
It maketh al my drede for to dyen.
For, also siker as *In principio*,
Mulier est hominis confusio.
Madame, the sentence of this Latin is   3165
'Womman is mannes joye and al his blis.'
For whan I fele a-night your softe syde,
Al be it that I may nat on you ryde,
For that our perche is maad so narwe, alas!
I am so ful of joye and of solas   3170
That I defye bothe sweven and dreem."
And with that word he fley doun fro the beem,
For it was day, and eek his hennes alle,
And with a chuk he gan hem for to calle,
For he had founde a corn lay in the yerd.   3175
Real he was, he was namore aferd;

For on that day in battle he would fail.
She warned him well, but it was no avail;   380
He went to fight despite all of her pleas.
But at once he was slain by Achilles.
But this same tale is far too long to tell,
And it is almost day; I may not dwell.   3150
Shortly I say, to make my conclusion,   385
That I shall have because of this vision
Adversity; and I say furthermore
That in these laxatives, I set no store;
They are venemous and well I know it;
Them I defy; I love them not one bit!   390
        Now, let us speak of mirth, and stop all this.
Madame Pertelote, so may I have bliss,
In one thing, God has sent to me much grace;
For when I see the beauty of your face—   3160
You are so scarlet red about your eyes—   395
It makes it so that all my dread just dies;
For just as surely as *In principio,*
Mulier est hominis confusio[9]—
Madame, the meaning of the Latin's this,
'Woman is man's joy and all his bliss.'   400
For when I feel at night your soft, warm side—
Although right then on you I cannot ride,
Since our perch is made too narrow, alas—
I am so full of both joy and solace   3170
That I shall defy both vision and dream."   405
        And with that word, he flew down from his beam—
For it was day—and also his hens all,
And with a cluck, then to them he did call,
For he found corn that in the yard had laid.
Regal he was; he was no more afraid.   410

---

9   *In principio, / Mulier est hominis confusio*: In the beginning / Woman is the confusion of
man. Chanticleer goes on to mistranslate the Latin (whether accidentally or on purpose is a matter
for debate) in line 3166.

He fethered Pertelote twenty tyme,
And trad hir eke as ofte, er it was pryme.
He loketh as it were a grim leoun,
And on his toos he rometh up and doun—   3180
Him deyned not to sette his foot to grounde.
He chukketh whan he hath a corn y-founde,
And to him rennen thanne his wyves alle.
Thus royal, as a prince is in his halle,
Leve I this Chauntecleer in his pasture;   3185
And after wol I telle his aventure.
          Whan that the month in which the world bigan,
That highte March, whan God first maked man,
Was complet, and passed were also,
Sin March bigan, thritty dayes and two,   3190
Bifel that Chauntecleer, in al his pryde,
His seven wyves walkinge by his syde,
Caste up his eyen to the brighte sonne,
That in the signe of Taurus hadde y-ronne
Twenty degrees and oon, and somwhat more;   3195
And knew by kynde, and by noon other lore,
That it was pryme, and crew with blisful stevene.
"The sonne," he sayde, "is clomben up on hevene
Fourty degrees and oon, and more, ywis.
Madame Pertelote, my worldes blis,   3200
Herkneth thise blisful briddes how they singe,
And see the fresshe floures how they springe;
Ful is myn herte of revel and solas."
But sodeinly him fil a sorweful cas,
For ever the latter ende of joye is wo.   3205
God woot that worldly joye is sone ago;
And if a rethor coude faire endyte,
He in a cronique saufly mighte it wryte
As for a sovereyn notabilitee.
Now every wys man, lat him herkne me: 3210

Full twenty times he feathered Pertelote,
And before prime tread her as much, you'll note.
He looks like he were the grimmest lion,
As he is roaming, his tiptoes upon;   3180
He didn't deign set his foot on the ground.   415
He clucks whenever some corn he has found,
And to him run his wives then, one and all.
Thus royal, like a prince is in his hall,
This Chantecleer I leave in his pasture,
And after, I'll tell of his adventure.   420
        When the month in which the world began,
Which is called March,[10] when first God had made man,
Was all complete, and then there had passed too,
Since March was over, thirty days and two,   3190
It happened Chantecleer in all his pride—   425
His seven wives were walking by his side—
Cast his eyes upward toward the bright sun,
That in the sign of Taurus then had run
Twenty degrees plus one, and somewhat more,
And knew by instinct, and no other lore,   430
It was nine, and crowed with blissful sound then.
"The sun," he said, "has climbed in the heaven
Forty degrees plus one, and more than this.
Madame Pertelote, of my world, my bliss,   3200
Hark to these blissful birds and how they sing,   435
And see here the fresh flowers, how they spring;
Revelry fills my heart, and contentment!"
But quickly to him came a sad event;
Always the later end of joy is woe.
God knows that soon all worldly joy does go;   440
If a rhetorician could tell fairly,
In a chronicle, he might write safely
This is a sovereign fact quite notable.
Now, each wise man, hark, if he is able;   3210

10 **March:** It was believed in the Middle Ages that God created the world at the vernal equinox.

This storie is also trewe, I undertake,

As is the book of Launcelot de Lake,

That wommen holde in ful gret reverence.

Now wol I torne agayn to my sentence.

     A col-fox, ful of sly iniquitee,   3215

That in the grove hadde woned yeres three,

By heigh imaginacioun forncast,

The same night thurghout the hegges brast

Into the yerd, ther Chauntecleer the faire

Was wont, and eek his wyves, to repaire;   3220

And in a bed of wortes stille he lay,

Til it was passed undren of the day,

Waytinge his tyme on Chauntecleer to falle,

As gladly doon thise homicydes alle,

That in awayt liggen to mordre men.   3225

O false mordrour, lurkinge in thy den!

O newe Scariot, newe Genilon!

False dissimilour, O Greek Sinon,

That broghtest Troye al outrely to sorwe!

O Chauntecleer, acursed be that morwe,   3230

That thou into that yerd flough fro the bemes!

Thou were ful wel y-warned by thy dremes

That thilke day was perilous to thee.

But what that God forwoot mot nedes be,

After the opinioun of certeyn clerkis.   3235

Witnesse on him that any perfit clerk is

That in scole is gret altercacioun

In this matere, and greet disputisoun,

This story is as true, I undertake,   445
As is the book of Lancelot of the Lake,[11]
That women hold in such great reverence.
To tell my meaning, I'll now recommence.
    A black-tipped fox of sly iniquity,
Who, in the grove, had dwelled fully years three,   450
By high imagination as forecast,
Throughout the very hedges that night passed
Into the yard where Chanticleer the fair
With his wives was accustomed to repair;   3220
And in a bed of cabbages, he lay   455
Till it was past midmorning of that day,
Biding his time, on Chanticleer to fall,
As gladly do these homicidals all
Who lie in waiting just to murder men.
O false murderer, lurking in your den!   460
O new Iscariot, new Ganelon,
False dissimulator, O Greek Sinon,[12]
Who brought Troy utterly to sorrowing!
O Chantecleer, accursed be that morning   3230
That you into the yard flew from the beams!
You were full well forewarned then by your dreams   465
This very day would come perilously;
But all that God foreknows, thus it need be[13]—
This opinion of a certain clerk is.
Witness on him who a perfect clerk is,
That in schools is a great altercation   470
In this matter, and great disputation,

11 **Lancelot of the Lake:** The romance of Lancelot and Guinevere, which ends up in disaster, and which, of course, the Nun's Priest suggests, is fiction and thus not true at all.

12 **Iscariot . . . Ganelon . . . Sinon:** Betrayers of Christ, Roland and Charlemagne, and Troy, respectively.

13 **all that God foreknows, thus it need be:** In the lines that follow, the Nun's Priest encapsulates the medieval debate, reaching back to the early Christian Church and Saint Augustine and Boethius, about the relationship between God's foreknowledge, predestination, and humans' free will. As with Pertelote and Chanticleer's debate about the meaning of dreams, the Nun's Priest presents the various aspects of the argument here without ever coming out on one side.

And hath ben of an hundred thousand men.

But I ne can not bulte it to the bren,   3240

As can the holy doctour Augustyn,

Or Boece, or the bishop Bradwardyn,

Whether that Goddes worthy forwiting

Streyneth me nedely for to doon a thing

("Nedely" clepe I simple necessitee);   3245

Or elles, if free choys be graunted me

To do that same thing or do it noght,

Though God forwoot it er that I was wroght;

Or if his witing streyneth never a del

But by necessitee condicionel.   3250

I wol not han to do of swich matere;

My tale is of a cok, as ye may here,

That took his counseil of his wyf, with sorwe,

To walken in the yerd upon that morwe

That he had met the dreem that I yow tolde.   3255

Wommennes counseils been ful ofte colde;

Wommannes counseil broghte us first to wo,

And made Adam fro Paradys to go,

Ther as he was ful mery and wel at ese.

But for I noot to whom it mighte displese,   3260

If I counseil of wommen wolde blame,

Passe over, for I seyde it in my game.

Rede auctours, wher they trete of swich matere,

And has been for a hundred thousand men.
I don't know how to sift it to the bran, then,   3240
As can the holy doctor Augustine,[14]
Boethius,[15] or Bishop Bradwardine,[16]   475
About whether God's worthy foreknowing
Constrains me needfully to do a thing—
"Needfully" I call plain necessity;[17]
Or else, if free choice is granted to me
To do that same thing, or just to do naught,   480
Though God foreknows the deed before it's wrought;
Or if his knowing constrains me not at all
Except by necessity conditional.[18]   3250
I won't deal with such matter, it is clear;
My tale's about a cock, as you may hear,   485
Who took his wife's counsel, to his sorrowing,
To walk in the yard that very morning
When he had dreamed the dream that I've you told.
These women's counsels are fatal and cold;
These women's counsels brought us first to woe   490
And from Paradise, they made Adam go,
Though he'd been merry and well at his ease.
But since I don't know whom it might displease,
If I these women's counsel wished to blame,   3260
Pass over it; I said it in my game.   495
Read authorities who make such matters clear,

14   **Augustine**: Bishop of Hippo (fourth to fifth century) and, as one of the early Church Fathers, one of the most significant voices in the establishment of Christian theology.

15   **Boethius**: Early Christian philosopher from Rome, late fifth through early sixth century, author of *The Consolation of Philosophy*, a work he wrote when he was imprisoned in Pavia and that Chaucer translated; it influenced Chaucer's ideas about free will, fortune, and predestination in its relationship to providence.

16   **Bishop Bradwardine**: A fourteenth-century Archbishop of Canterbury and participant in this debate about free will.

17   **plain necessity**: Cause and effect; God foresees and therefore the deed must come to pass.

18   **necessity conditional**: Conditional or inferential necessity. This is the compromise on this issue that Boethius reached and that characterizes Chaucer's position throughout his writing. With conditional necessity, God has perfect foreknowledge, but that foreknowledge is not causal, leaving humans with free will.

And what thay seyn of wommen ye may here.
Thise been the cokkes wordes, and nat myne;   3265
I can noon harm of no womman divyne.

      Faire in the sond, to bathe hire merily,
Lyth Pertelote, and alle hire sustres by,
Agayn the sonne; and Chauntecleer so free
Song merier than the mermayde in the see—   3270
For Phisiologus seith sikerly
How that they singen wel and merily—
And so bifel that, as he caste his yë
Among the wortes, on a boterflye,
He was war of this fox that lay ful lowe.   3275
Nothing ne liste him thanne for to crowe,
But cryde anon, "Cok cok!" and up he sterte,
As man that was affrayed in his herte.
For naturelly a beest desyreth flee
Fro his contrarie, if he may it see,   3280
Though he never erst had seyn it with his yë.

      This Chauntecleer, whan he gan him espye,
He wolde han fled, but that the fox anon
Seyde, "Gentil sire, allas! wher wol ye gon?
Be ye affrayed of me that am your freend?   3285
Now certes, I were worse than a feend,
If I to yow wolde harm or vileinye.
I am nat come your counseil for t'espye,
But trewely, the cause of my cominge
Was only for to herkne how that ye singe.   3290
For trewely ye have as mery a stevene
As eny aungel hath that is in hevene;
Therwith ye han in musik more feelinge
Than hadde Boece, or any that can singe.

And what they say of women, you may hear.
For these are the cock's words; they are not mine;
In women, I can no harm divine.

      To bathe herself merrily in the sand,   500
Lies Pertelote, with sisters near at hand;
Chanticleer, in the sun, noble and free,
Sang more merrily than mermaids in the sea   3270
(For Physiologus[19] says certainly
How mermaids sing both well and merrily).   505
And so it happened, as he cast his eye
Among cabbages on a butterfly,
He was aware of this fox, lying low.
Nothing at all made him then want to crow;
He cried at once, "Cock! Cock!" and up does start   510
Like men who are quite frightened in their heart.
For naturally, a beast desires to flee
From his enemy, if he can it see,   3280
Even if he'd never seen it with his eye.

      This Chanticleer, when there he did him spy,   515
He would have fled, but to him the fox said,
"Now, gentle sire, alas, where do you head?
Are you afraid of me, who am your friend?
Now, certainly, may I meet a fiend's end,
If to you harm or villainy wished I!   520
I have not come on your secrets to spy,
But, it is true, the cause of my coming
Was only so I could hear how you sing.   3290
In truth, you have a voice as merry then
As an angel who is up in heaven.   525
And thus, you in music have more feeling
Than Boethius[20] or any who can sing.

19 **Physiologus:** Name of an anonymous second-century Greek book or author of a bestiary or group of stories about real and mythological animals that were given Christian allegorical meanings. The mermaids were interpreted as sirens in the Middle Ages.

20 **Boethius:** One of his other writings, along with the *Consolation of Philosophy*, was a textbook on musical theory.

My lord your fader (God his soule blesse!)   3295
And eek your moder, of hire gentilesse,
Han in myn hous y-been, to my gret ese;
And certes, sire, ful fayn wolde I yow plese.
But for men speke of singing, I wol saye,
So mote I brouke wel myn eyen tweye,   3300
Save yow, I herde never man so singe
As dide your fader in the morweninge.
Certes, it was of herte, al that he song.
And for to make his voys the more strong,
He wolde so peyne him that with bothe his yën   3305
He moste winke, so loude he wolde cryen,
And stonden on his tiptoon therwithal,
And strecche forth his nekke long and smal.
And eek he was of swich discrecioun
That ther nas no man in no regioun   3310
That him in song or wisdom mighte passe.
I have wel rad in 'Daun Burnel the Asse,'
Among his vers, how that ther was a cok,
For that a preestes sone yaf him a knok
Upon his leg, whyl he was yong and nyce,   3315
He made him for to lese his benefyce.
But certeyn, ther nis no comparisoun
Bitwix the wisdom and discrecioun
Of youre fader, and of his subtiltee.
Now singeth, sire, for seinte charitee!   3320
Let see, conne ye your fader countrefete?"
      This Chauntecleer his winges gan to bete,
As man that coude his tresoun nat espye,
So was he ravisshed with his flaterye.
      Allas! ye lordes, many a fals flatour   3325

My lord your father—may God his soul bless—
And your mother, out of noble gentleness,
Have both been in my house to my great ease; 530
And, surely, sire, quite gladly I'd you please.
But, since men speak of singing, I will say—
So might I use my two eyes well today— 3300
Except for you, I never heard man sing
Like your father first thing in the morning. 535
True, when he sang, from his heart came his song.
And so that he could make his voice more strong,
He would so pain himself that with both eyes
He then must wink, so loud would be his cries,
And he'd step up upon his tiptoes tall, 540
And stretch forth his neck, which was long and small.
And moreover, he had such discretion
That there was no man in any region 3310
Who him in song or wisdom might surpass.
I have well read in *Don Burnel the Ass*,[21] 545
Among his verses, how there was a cock,
Who, since a priest's son did give him a knock
On the leg when he was young and dumb thus,
He made it so he lost his benefice.
But, surely, here, there's no comparison 550
Between the wisdom and the discretion
Of your father, with all his subtlety.
Now sing, good sire, for holy charity,
Let see: can you your father counterfeit?" 3320

      This Chanticleer was beating his wings yet, 555
Like a man who could not this treason see,
So was he ravished by this flattery.
      Lo, you lords, many a false flatterer

---

21 *Don Burnel the Ass*: Also called *Speculum Stultorum* (*Mirror of Fools*), a satiric work written by the monk Nigel de Longchamps (late twelfth century) containing many stories in which members of the clergy are lampooned as donkeys wandering around trying to find ways to lengthen their tails.

Is in your courtes, and many a losengeour,
That plesen yow wel more, by my feith,
Than he that soothfastnesse unto yow seith.
Redeth Ecclesiaste of flaterye;
Beth war, ye lordes, of hir trecherye.   3330
        This Chauntecleer stood hye upon his toos,
Strecching his nekke, and heeld his eyen cloos,
And gan to crowe loude for the nones;
And daun Russel the fox sterte up at ones
And by the gargat hente Chauntecleer,   3335
And on his bak toward the wode him beer,
For yet ne was ther no man that him sewed.
        O destinee, that mayst nat been eschewed!
Allas, that Chauntecleer fleigh fro the bemes!
Allas, his wyf ne roghte nat of dremes!   3340
And on a Friday fil al this meschaunce.
        O Venus, that art goddesse of plesaunce,
Sin that thy servant was this Chauntecleer,
And in thy service dide al his poweer,
More for delyt than world to multiplye,   3345
Why woldestow suffre him on thy day to dye?
        O Gaufred, dere mayster soverayn,
That whan thy worthy king Richard was slayn
With shot, compleynedest his deth so sore,
Why ne hadde I now thy sentence and thy lore,   3350
The Friday for to chide, as diden ye?
(For on a Friday soothly slayn was he.)
Than wolde I shewe yow how that I coude pleyne

Is in your courts, and many a *losengeour*,²²
Who pleases you much more, as I would guess,   560
Than he who speaks to you with truthfulness.
Read Ecclesiastes on flattery;
Be wary, you lords, of their treachery.   3330
      This Chanticleer stood high upon his toes,
Stretching his neck, and his eyes tight did close,   565
For the occasion, he crowed quite loudly.
Don Russell the fox started up quickly,
And by the throat seized Chanticleer right there,
And on his back, him toward the woods did bear,
For there was no one yet who him pursued.   570
      O destiny that may not be eschewed!
Alas, that Chanticleer flew from those beams!
Alas, his wife cared not a bit for dreams!   3340
On a Friday²³ fell this misadventure.
      Alas, Venus, you goddess of pleasure,   575
Since your own servant was this Chanticleer,
Who in your service did all he might here,
More for delight than the world to multiply,
Why on your own day would you let him die?
      O dear sovereign master, you Sir Geoffrey,²⁴   580
Who, when slain was King Richard so worthy
With an arrow, mourned for his death so sore,
Why have I not your wisdom and your lore,   3350
Like you did to chide Friday, as we see?
For, on a Friday, truly, slain was he.   585
Then I would show you how I could complain

---

22 *losengeour*: Liar or flatterer. In medieval courts, *losengeour* was virtually a technical or profes-
sional term for a whole class of sycophantic hangers-on who flattered those in power and lied about
their competitors in order to advance their own interests.

23 **Friday**: The day dedicated to Venus, but also a day of bad luck in the Judeo-Christian tradi-
tion. Since Friday was Venus's day, and since Venus, as the goddess of love, was notoriously change-
able, Fridays were thought to be as changeable as lovers were under Venus's influence.

24 **Sir Geoffrey**: Geoffrey of Vinsauf, in his thirteenth-century handbook of rhetoric, *Poetria
nova*, provided as a rhetorical example a lament on the death of Richard I.

For Chauntecleres drede, and for his peyne.

    Certes, swich cry ne lamentacioun   3355
Was never of ladies maad when Ilioun
Was wonne, and Pirrus with his streite swerd,
Whan he hadde hent king Priam by the berd,
And slayn him (as saith us *Eneydos*),
As maden alle the hennes in the clos,   3360
Whan they had seyn of Chauntecleer the sighte.
But sovereynly dame Pertelote shrighte
Ful louder than dide Hasdrubales wyf,
Whan that hir housbond hadde lost his lyf,
And that the Romayns hadde brend Cartage: 3365
She was so ful of torment and of rage
That wilfully into the fyr she sterte,
And brende hirselven with a stedfast herte.

    O woful hennes, right so cryden ye
As, whan that Nero brende the citee   3370
Of Rome, cryden senatoures wyves,
For that hir housbondes losten alle hir lyves;
Withouten gilt this Nero hath hem slayn.
Now wol I torne to my tale agayn.

    This sely widwe and eek hir doghtres two   3375
Herden thise hennes crye and maken wo,
And out at dores sterten they anoon,
And syen the fox toward the grove goon,
And bar upon his bak the cok away;
And cryden, "Out! harrow! and weylaway!   3380
Ha, ha, the fox!" and after him they ran,
And eek with staves many another man;
Ran Colle our dogge, and Talbot, and Gerland,
And Malkin, with a distaf in hir hand;

About Chanticleer's dread and for his pain.
    Surely, neither cry nor lamentation
Did ladies ever make when Ilion[25]
Was won, and when, with his sword drawn by him,   590
Pyrrhus,[26] by the beard, had seized king Priam,[27]
And slain him, as it says in the *Aeneid*,
As in the yard there all of those hens did,   3360
When they the sight of Chanticleer did see.
But Dame Pertelote did shriek supremely,   595
Much more loudly than did Hasdrubal's[28] wife,
When her own husband there had lost his life
And the Romans burned Carthage to the ground.
She was so filled by torment's rage profound,
Into the fire willingly she did start   600
And burned herself up with a steadfast heart.
    O woeful hens, you all cried exactly
The way, when Nero had burned the city   3370
Of Rome, then cried all the senators' wives
Because their husbands guiltless lost their lives—   605
Nero slew them all as the city burned.
Now back again to my tale I will turn.
    This widow and her two daughters also,
Unknowing, heard these hens cry and make woe;
Immediately out of doors they drove,   610
And saw the fox then going toward the grove,
Who bore upon his back the cock away,
And they cried, "Out! Harrow and wey-la-way!   3380
Ha! Ha! The fox!" and after him they ran,
And then, with staves, many another man.   615
Colle, our dog ran, and Talbot and Garland,
And Malkyn, with her distaff in her hand;

---

25 **Ilion**: Troy's citadel.
26 **Pyrrhus**: Son of Achilles.
27 **Priam**: King of Troy at the time of the Trojan War.
28 **Hasdrubal**: King of Carthage in 146 B.C.E., at the time the Romans under Scipio destroyed it.

Ran cow and calf, and eek the verray hogges,   3385
So fered for the berking of the dogges
And shouting of the men and wimmen eke,
They ronne so hem thoughte hir herte breke.
They yelleden as feendes doon in helle;
The dokes cryden as men wolde hem quelle;   3390
The gees for fere flowen over the trees;
Out of the hyve cam the swarm of bees;
So hidous was the noyse, a! *benedicite!*
Certes, he Jakke Straw and his meynee
Ne made nevere shoutes half so shrille   3395
Whan that they wolden any Fleming kille,
As thilke day was maad upon the fox.
Of bras thay broghten bemes, and of box,
Of horn, of boon, in whiche they blewe and pouped,
And therwithal thay shryked and they houped: 3400
It seemed as that heven sholde falle.
Now, gode men, I pray yow herkneth alle!
     Lo, how Fortune turneth sodeinly
The hope and pryde eek of hir enemy!
This cok, that lay upon the foxes bak,   3405
In al his drede unto the fox he spak,
And seyde, "Sire, if that I were as ye,
Yet sholde I seyn, as wis God helpe me,
'Turneth agayn, ye proude cherles alle!
A verray pestilence upon yow falle!   3410
Now I am come unto this wodes syde,
Maugree your heed, the cok shal heer abyde;
I wol him ete in feith, and that anon.'"
     The fox answerde, "In feith, it shal be don,"
And as he spak that word, al sodeinly   3415
This cok brak from his mouth delivderly,

Ran cow and calf, and even ran the hogs,
So frightened by the barking of the dogs
And the shouts that the men and women make;   620
They ran so fast they thought their hearts would break.
They yowled just like fiends do down in hell;
The ducks cried like they would be killed as well;   3390
The geese, for fear, flew up over the trees;
Out of the hive there came the swarm of bees.   625
So hideous was the noise—God bless me!—
That surely Jack Straw[29] and his company
Never made shoutings that were half as shrill
When any Flemish they did look to kill,
As that day at the fox all of them would.   630
They brought trumpets made of brass and boxwood,
And horns of bone, in which they puffed and blew,
And with those they shrieked out, and they whooped, too.   3400
It seemed as though right down heaven would fall.
And now, good men, I pray you, listen all: 635
        Lo, see how Fortune does turn suddenly
The hope and pride both of the enemy!
This cock that on the fox's back did lay,
For all his dread, right to the fox did say,
And he spoke thus, "Sire, now, if I were you,   640
I should say, as wise God would help me to,
'Turn back again, you proud churls there, you all!
May a true pestilence upon you fall!   3410
Now right to the woods' side, I have come near;
No matter what you do, the cock stays here.   645
I will eat him, in faith, and quickly, too!'"
        The fox answered, "In faith, that's what I'll do."
And as he spoke that word, all suddenly
This cock broke from his mouth quite agilely,

---

29 **Jack Straw:** This is one of Chaucer's few references to the Peasants' Revolt of 1381. Jack Straw was known as a leader of the revolt, which killed a number of immigrant Flemish cloth workers because they were seen as competition by the English.

And heighe upon a tree he fleigh anon.
And whan the fox saugh that the cok was gon,
"Allas!" quod he, "O Chauntecleer, allas!
I have to yow," quod he, "y-doon trespas,   3420
In as muche as I maked yow aferd
When I yow hente and broghte out of the yerd.
But, sire, I dide it in no wikke entente;
Com doun, and I shal telle yow what I mente.
I shal seye sooth to yow, God help me so."   3425
        "Nay, than," quod he, "I shrewe us bothe two,
And first I shrewe myself, bothe blood and bones,
If thou bigyle me ofter than ones.
Thou shalt namore, thurgh thy flaterye,
Do me to singe and winke with myn yë.   3430
For he that winketh whan he sholde see,
Al wilfully, God lat him never thee!"
        "Nay," quod the fox, "but God yeve him meschaunce,
That is so undiscreet of governaunce
That jangleth whan he sholde holde his pees."   3435
        Lo, swich it is for to be recchelees
And necligent, and truste on flaterye.
        But ye that holden this tale a folye,
As of a fox, or of a cok and hen,
Taketh the moralitee, goode men.   3440
For Seint Paul seith that al that writen is,
To our doctryne it is y-write, ywis.
Taketh the fruyt, and lat the chaf be stille.
        Now, gode God, if that it be thy wille,
As seith my lord, so make us alle good men,   3445
And bringe us to his heighe bliss. Amen.

Heere is ended the Nonnes Preestes Tale.

And up into a tree at once did fly. 650
When the fox saw the cock sit there up high,
"Alas!" said he, "O Chanticleer, alas!
For I have to you done a great trespass. 3420
I made you afraid, catching you off guard,
When I seized you and brought you from the yard. 655
Sire, I did it with no wicked intent.
Come down now, and I'll tell you what I meant;
So God help me, I'll tell the truth to you!"
     "No, then," said he, "I'd curse both of us two.
And first, I'd curse myself, both blood and bone, 660
If you tricked me more than one time alone.
Through flattery, now no more will you try
To make me sing and then wink with closed eye; 3430
For he who winks, when he with eyes should see,
Purposely, nevermore shall prosper he!" 665
     "No," said the fox, "but God give him mischance,
Who's so indiscreet in self-governance
That he jangles when he should be silent."
     Lo, thus it is to be so negligent
And reckless, and to trust in flattery. 670
     But you who think this tale just a folly,
About a fox, or else a cock and hen,
Take from it the morality, good men. 3440
Saint Paul says that all that which is written,
For our teaching is truly written, then; 675
Take the fruit, and let the chaff be still.
     Now, good God, if it should be your will,
As says my Lord, so make us all good men,
And bring us all to his high bliss! Amen.

Here is ended the Nun's Priest's Tale.

THE EPILOGUE

"Sir Nonnes Preest," our Hoste seyde anoon,
"Y-blessed by thy breche and every stoon!
This was a mery tale of Chauntecleer.
But by my trouthe, if thou were seculer,   3450
Thou woldest been a trede-foul aright.
For if thou have corage as thou hast might,
Thee were nede of hennes, as I wene,
Ya, mo than seven tymes seventene.
See, whiche braunes hath this gentil preest,   3455
So greet a nekke, and swich a large breest!
He loketh as a sperhauk with his yën;
Him nedeth nat his colour for to dyen
With brasile, ne with greyn of Portingale.
Now sire, faire falle yow for youre tale!"   3460
And after that he, with ful merie chere
Seide unto another, as ye shuln heere

·   ·   ·

THE EPILOGUE

"Sir Nun's Priest," our Host said to him quickly,   680
"Blessed may both your stones[30] and britches be!
A merry tale of Chanticleer we heard.
But, if you were a layman, by my word,   3450
You would be a good treading-fowl,[31] all right.
If you've got heart and vigor like you might,   685
You'd need some hens, if you know what I mean,
Yea, much more than seven times seventeen.
See now what brawn here has this gentle priest,
So great a neck, such a large breast, at least!
He looks like a sparrow hawk with his eye;   690
No need for him his color now to dye
With red hues made of grains from Portugal.
Sire, for your tale, may good luck you befall!"   3460
And after that he, with quite merry cheer,
Said to another one, as you shall hear.   695

---

30 **stones**: Testicles.
31 **treading-fowl**: A rooster, since treading was the term used for copulating among poultry.

THE PARSON'S PROLOGUE

Heere folweth the Prologe of the Persouns Tale.

By that the Maunciple hadde his tale al ended,
The sonne fro the south lyne was descended
So lowe, that he nas nat, to my sighte,
Degrees nyne and twenty as in highte.
Foure of the clokke it was tho, as I gesse;   5
For elevene foot, or litel more or lesse,
My shadwe was at thilke tyme, as there,
Of swiche feet as my lengthe parted were
In six feet equal of proporcioun.
Therwith the mones exaltacioun,   10
I mene Libra, alwey gan ascende,
As we were entring at a thropes ende;
For which oure Host, as he was wont to gye,
As in this caas, oure joly companye,
Seyde in this wyse: "Lordings everichoon,   15
Now lakketh us no tales mo than oon.
Fulfild is my sentence and my decree;
I trowe that we han herd of ech degree.
Almost fulfild is al myn ordinaunce.

THE PARSON'S PROLOGUE

Here follows the Prologue of the Parson's Tale.

When the Manciple had his tale all ended,
The sun from the south line had descended
Down so low that it was not, to my sight,
More than twenty-nine degrees raised in its height.
Four o'clock it was then, as I would guess,   5
For eleven feet, a little more or less,
My shadow was at that time, as it'd be
If my length were divided evenly
Into six feet equal in proportion.
And with that, the moon's exaltation[1]—   10
I mean in Libra—always there ascended
As we entered where the village ended;
And thus our Host, as wont to guide was he,
As in this case, our jolly company,
Said in this way, "All my lords, everyone,   15
Now we lack no more tales here, except one.
Fulfilled is my order and my decree;[2]
I think from every rank now have heard we;
Almost fulfilled now is my ordinance.

---

1   **exaltation**: Sign of the zodiac in which a planet has its strongest influence.
2   **my decree**: This statement is obviously inconsistent with the Host's plans to have each pilgrim tell two tales going to and two tales coming from Canterbury. It remains a mystery why the plans have changed.

I prey to God, so yeve him right good chaunce,   20
That telleth this tale to us lustily.

     "Sire preest," quod he, "artow a vicary?
Or art a person? Sey sooth, by thy fey!
Be what thou be, ne breke thou nat oure pley;
For every man, save thou, hath told his tale.   25
Unbokele, and shewe us what is in thy male.
For trewely, me thinketh by thy chere,
Thou sholdest knitte up wel a greet matere.
Telle us a fable anon, for cokkes bones!"

     This Persone him answerde, al at ones,   30
"Thou getest fable noon y-told for me;
For Paul, that wryteth unto Timothee,
Repreveth hem that weyven soothfastnesse
And tellen fables and swich wrecchednesse.
Why sholde I sowen draf out of my fest,   35
Whan I may sowen whete, if that me lest?
For which I seye, if that yow list to here
Moralitee and vertuous matere,
And thanne that ye wol yeve me audience,
I wol ful fayn, at Cristes reverence,   40
Do yow pleasaunce leefful, as I can.
But trusteth wel, I am a Southren man:
I can nat geste—rum, ram, ruf—by lettre.
Ne, God wot, rym holde I but litel bettre.
And therfore, if you list, I wol nat glose.   45
I wol yow telle a mery tale in prose
To knitte up al this feeste and make an ende.
And Jesu, for his grace, wit me sende
To shewe yow the wey, in this viage,

I pray to God, may his luck have good chance 20
Who now tells this tale to us lustily.
      Sir priest, are you a vicar now?" said he,
"Or a parson? By your faith, the truth now say!
Whatever you are, don't you break up our play;
Every man has told his tale but you yet. 25
Unbuckle, and show us what's in your wallet;
Sure, it seems to me by your demeanor
You quite well could knit up a great matter.
By cock's bones, tell us a fable quickly!"
      This Parson answered immediately, 30
"You will here get no fable told by me,
For Paul, when he writes unto Timothy,
Reproaches those who will waive truthfulness
And tell fables and such wretchedness.
Why should I now sow chaff out of my fist, 35
When I may sow wheat, if I think it best?
And thus I'll speak, if you should wish to hear
Moral things and virtuous matter here,
And then if you will give me audience,
I will quite gladly, for Christ's reverence, 40
Give you such lawful pleasure, as I can.
But trust me well; I am a Southern man;[3]
I can't tell romances 'rum, ram, ruf,'[4] by letter,
And God knows, I think rhyme but little better;
If you wish—I don't gloss or lie—I chose 45
To tell you here a merry tale in prose
To knit up all this feast and make an end.
May Jesus, by his grace, the wit me send
To show you the way here, in this voyage,

---

    3   **southern man**: The north of England in the fourteenth century was the home of the Alliterative Revival in literature, which reintroduced the alliteration popular in Old English verse as a major structuring principle in the poetic line. Alliteration was not so much in fashion in the south of England in Chaucer's time.

    4   **'rum, ram, ruf'**: These are nonsense words; the Parson is eschewing alliteration, as well as "romances," or secular courtly literature, along with what he considers the fripperies of rhyme.

Of thilke parfit glorious pilgrimage 50
That highte Jerusalem celestial.
And, if ye vouchesauf, anon I shal
Biginne upon my tale, for whiche I preye
Telle youre avys, I can no bettre seye.
       But nathelees, this meditacioun 55
I putte it ay under correccioun
Of clerkes, for I am nat textuel;
I take but the sentence, trusteth wel.
Therfor I make protestacioun
That I wol stonde to correccioun." 60
       Upon this word we han assented sone,
For, as us semed, it was for to done,
To enden in som vertuous sentence,
And for to yeve him space and audience,
And bade oure Host he sholde to him seye 65
That alle we to telle his tale him preye.
       Oure Host hadde the wordes for us alle:
"Sire preest," quod he, "now fayre yow bifalle!
Telleth," quod he, "youre meditacioun.
But hasteth yow, the sonne wol adoun; 70
Beth fructuous, and that in litel space,
And to do wel God sende yow his grace!
Sey what yow list, and we wol gladly here."
And with that word he seyde in this manere:

Of that perfect, glorious pilgrimage 50
Which is called Jerusalem Celestial.
And if you allow me, at once I will
Begin my tale, for which I now you pray
To tell your view; no better can I say.

But nonetheless, this same meditation 55
I submit always to the correction
Of clerks, for I'm no scholar textual;
I take only the meaning, trust it well.
Therefore, I now make this attestation
That I will stand gladly for correction." 60

Upon this word, we all assented soon,
For, as it seemed, it was quite opportune—
To conclude with some virtuous substance,
And to give him both time and audience;
We bid our Host that to him he should say 65
That to tell us his tale we all him pray.

So our Host then spoke to him for us all;
"Sir priest," said he, "now good luck you befall!
Tell us here," said he, "your meditation.
But make haste, for the day is almost done; 70
Be fruitful, but within a little space,
And to do well, now God send you his grace!
Say what you like, and we'll listen gladly."
And with that word, in this manner, spoke he.

CHAUCER'S RETRACTION

Here taketh the makere of this book his leve.

Now preye I to hem alle that herkne this litel tretis or rede, that if ther be any thing in it that lyketh hem, that therof they thanken oure lord Jesu Crist, of whom procedeth al wit and al goodnesse. / And if ther be any thing that displese hem, I preye hem also that they arrette it to the de- faute of myn unconninge and nat to my wil, that wolde ful fayn have seyd bettre if I hadde had conninge. / For oure boke seith, "al that is writen is writen for oure doctrine"; and that is myn entente. / Wherfore I biseke yow mekely, for the mercy of God, that ye preye for me, that Crist have mercy on me and foryeve me my giltes; / and namely of

THE PARSON'S TALE

[The Parson's goes on to deliver a long prose treatise on the Seven Deadly Sins and repentance. It is immediately followed by Chaucer's Retraction.]

THE RETRACTION[5]

Here the maker takes his leave of this book.

Now pray I to them all who hear this little treatise or read it, that if there is anything in it that pleases them, they thank our Lord Jesus Christ for that, from whom proceeds all wisdom and goodness. / And if there is anything that displeases them, I pray to them also that they ascribe it to the fault of my unknowing and not to my will, that would quite gladly have said better if I had had the knowledge. / For our book says, "All that is written is written for our teaching," and that is my intent. / Therefore, I beseech you meekly, for the mercy of God, that you pray for me so that Christ will have mercy on me and forgive me for my sins; / and namely for

5 **Retraction:** Throughout literary history, such retractions of one's writings were not uncommon. A Retraction such as this works coherently not only with the theme of penitence central to *The Parson's Tale* but also with the theme of pilgrimage central to *The Tales* as a whole. Whether we should read this as an autobiographical utterance or as the words of Chaucer's pilgrim-narrator remains, like Chaucer's intention for the retraction, a mystery.

my translacions and endytinges of worldly vanitees, the whiche I revoke in my retracciouns: / as is [1085] the book of Troilus; The book also of Fame; The book of the XXV Ladies; The book of the Duchesse; The book of seint Valentynes day of the Parlement of Briddes; The tales of Caunterbury, thilke that sounen into sinne; / The book of the Leoun; and many another book, if they were in my remembrance; and many a song and many a lecherous lay; that Crist for his grete mercy foryeve me the sinne. / But of the translacion of Boece de Consolacione, and othere bokes of Legendes of seintes, and omelies, and moralitee and devocioun, / that thanke I oure lord Jesu Crist and his blisful moder and alle the seintes of hevene; / bisekinge hem that they from hennes forth, unto my lyves ende, sende me grace to biwayle my giltes, and to studie to the salvacioun of my soule; and graunte me grace of verray penitence, confessioun and satisfaccioun to doon in this present lyf, / thurgh the [1090] benigne grace of him that is king of kinges and preest over alle preestes, that boghte us with the precious blood of his herte; / so that I may been oon of hem at the day of dome that shulle be saved. *Qui cum patre, & c.*

Here is ended the book of the Tales of Caunterbury, compiled by Geffrey Chaucer, of whos soule Jesu Crist have mercy. Amen.

my translations and writings of worldly vanities, which I revoke in my retractions: / as is the book of Troilus [5][1085]; the book also of Fame; the book of the XXV Ladies—the Legend of Good Women; the Book of the Duchess; the book of Saint Valentine's Day of the Parliament of Fowls; the tales of Canterbury, those that are conducive to sin; / the book of the Lion;[6] and many another book, if they were in my memory, and many a song and many a lecherous lay, so that Christ of his great mercy will forgive me the sin. / But of the translation of Boethius of the Consolation, and other books of the legends of saints, and homilies, and morality, and devotion, / for those thank I our Lord Jesus Christ and his blissful Mother, and the saints of heaven, beseeching them that they from henceforward until my life's end send me grace to lament my sins and to study for the salvation of my soul, and grant me the grace of true penitence, confession, and restitution to do in this life, through the benign grace of [10] [1090] him who is king of kings and priest over all priests, who bought us with the precious blood of his heart, / so that I may be one of them at the day of judgment who shall be saved. *Qui cum Patre et Spiritu Sancto vivit and regnat Deus per omnia secula. Amen.* [*Who with the Father and the Holy Spirit lives and reigns, God, through all the ages. Amen.*]

Here is ended the book of the tales of Canterbury, compiled by Geoffrey Chaucer, on whose soul, Jesus Christ have mercy.

Amen.

6   **book of the Lion**: Unknown or lost work.

Suggestions For Further Reading

Editions in Middle English

Benson, Larry D., ed. *The Riverside Chaucer*. Boston: Houghton Mifflin, 1987.

Fisher, John H. and Mark Allen, eds. *The Complete Canterbury Tales of Geoffrey Chaucer*. Boston: Thomson Wadsworth, 2006.

Kolve, V. A. and Glending Olson, eds. *The Canterbury Tales (Norton Critical Edition)*. New York: W. W. Norton & Company, 2005.

General Suggestions

Ackroyd, Peter. *Chaucer*. New York: Doubleday, 2004.

Boitani, Piero and Mann, Jill. *The Cambridge Companion to Chaucer* (second edition). Cambridge: Cambridge University Press, 2003.

Brewer, Derek. *A New Introduction to Chaucer* (second edition). London and New York: Longman, 1998.

_____. *The World of Chaucer*. Cambridge: Boydell & Brewer, 2000.

Brown, Peter, ed. *A Companion to Chaucer*. Oxford: Blackwell, 2000.

Donaldon, E. Talbot. *Speaking of Chaucer*. London: Athlone Press, 2000.

Ellis, Steve, ed. *Chaucer: An Oxford Guide*. Oxford: Oxford University Press, 2005.

Hansen, Elaine Tuttle. *Chaucer and the Fictions of Gender*. Berkeley: University of California Press, 1992.

Howard, Donald R. *Chaucer: His Life, His Works, and His World*. New York: E. P. Dutton, 1987.

_____. *The Idea of The Canterbury Tales*. Berkeley: University of California Press, 1976.

Pearsall, Derek. *The Life of Geoffrey Chaucer: A Critical Biography*. London and New York: Wiley-Blackwell, 1994.

Rudd, Gillian. *The Complete Critical Guide to Geoffrey Chaucer*. London and New York: Routledge, 2001.

Schoeck, Richard and Jerome Taylor, eds. *Chaucer Criticism: Volume I* The Canterbury Tales. Notre Dame: University of Notre Dame Press, 1960.

Some of Chaucer's Central Sources and Influences

Boccaccio, Giovanni. *The Decameron: A New Translation (Norton Critical Editions)*. Trans. and eds., Peter E. Bondanella and Mark Musa. New York: W. W. Norton & Company, 1977.

Boethius. *The Consolation of Philosophy (Norton Critical Editions)*. Ed., Douglas C. Langston. New York: W. W. Norton & Company, 2009.

Dante Alighieri. *The Divine Comedy (in three volumes: Inferno, Purgatorio, Paradiso)*. Trans., Mark Musa. New York: Penguin Classics, 2002.

De Lorris, Guillaume and Jean de Meun. *The Romance of the Rose*. Trans. and ed., Frances Horgan. New York: Oxford University Press, 2009.

Ovid. *The Metamorphoses of Ovid*. Trans., Allen Mandelbaum. New York: Mariner Books, 1995.